29095

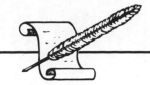

HISTORIC
DOCUMENTS
OF
1994

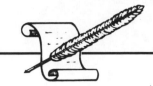

HISTORIC DOCUMENTS OF 1994

Cumulative Index, 1990-1994

✳Congressional Quarterly Inc.

Historic Documents of 1994

Editor: Bruce Maxwell
Production and Assistant Editor: Kerry V. Kern
Contributors: Prudence Crewdson, Hoyt Gimlin, James R. Ingram, Joanne Meil, Susanna Spencer, Margaret C. Thompson
Indexer: Rhonda Holland

Printed in the United States of America

Congressional Quarterly Inc.
1414 22nd St. N.W., Washington, D.C. 20037

The Library of Congress cataloged the first issue of this title as follows:

Historic documents.   1972—
    Washington. Congressional Quarterly Inc.

    1. United States — Politics and government — 1945— — Yearbooks.
2. World politics — 1945— —Yearbooks. I. Congressional Quarterly Inc.

E839.5H57   917.3'03'9205   72-97888

ISBN 0-87187-803-8
ISSN 0892-080X

PREFACE

Earthquakes—both literal and figurative—served as bookends to the year 1994. As the year began, a huge earthquake struck the Los Angeles area, killing sixty-one, injuring thousands, and causing billions of dollars in damage. As it ended, another earthquake—this one of the political variety—rolled through the halls of power in Washington, D.C., as Republicans won control of both houses of Congress for the first time in forty years.

The November election results were not the only bad news President Bill Clinton faced in 1994. His massive plan to reform the nation's health care system, the centerpiece of his domestic agenda, died in Congress without so much as a vote on the proposal. Clinton also had trouble getting and then keeping people for his administration. Bobby Ray Inman publicly withdrew his name from consideration to be secretary of defense, Secretary of Agriculture Mike Espy resigned under an ethical cloud, and Surgeon General Joycelyn Elders was forced to resign after she suggested that schools should consider teaching children about masturbation. As the year ended, Clinton's proposal for a middle-class tax cut appeared dead on arrival on Capitol Hill.

Clinton had far greater success on the economic front. In November he helped persuade Congress to approve expansion of the General Agreement on Tariffs and Trade, which was aimed at knocking down trade barriers among 124 countries. As the year ended he signed an agreement with the leaders of thirty-four Western Hemisphere nations to negotiate a free trade agreement that would make the Western Hemisphere the world's largest free trade zone.

While the trade agreements looked to the future, in 1994 the United States also came to grips with some past events concerning civil rights violence in the South and the Vietnam War that had haunted the nation for decades. In Mississippi a jury convicted Byron De La Beckwith, an unrepentant segregationist, of the 1963 assassination of civil rights leader Medgar Evers.

How to Use This Book

The documents are arranged in chronological order. If you know the approximate date of the report, speech, statement, court decision, or other document you are looking for, glance through the titles for that month in the table of contents.

If the table of contents does not lead you directly to the document you want, turn to the index at the end of the book. There you may find references not only to the particular document you seek but also to other entries on the same or a related subject. The index in this volume is a five-year cumulative index of *Historic Documents* covering the years 1990-1994. There is a separate volume, *Historic Documents Index, 1972-1989*, which may also be useful.

The introduction to each document is printed in italic type. The document itself, printed in roman type, follows the spelling, capitalization, and punctuation of the original or official copy. Where the full text is not given, omissions of material are indicated by the customary ellipsis points.

Beckwith had been tried for the crime twice in the 1960s, but both times all-male, all-white juries had deadlocked. This time, a jury of eight blacks and four whites did not. The same week the jury decided Beckwith's fate, President Clinton lifted the trade embargo imposed on Vietnam in 1964. While administration officials emphasized that the move was just the beginning in the process of improving relations between the United States and Vietnam, many believed it would eventually lead to a normalization of diplomatic relations.

In 1994 the United States said goodbye to four leading figures of the second half of the twentieth century who left the public stage through death, illness, or retirement. Former president Richard Nixon, who opened the door to China and promoted détente with the Soviet Union before resigning in disgrace over the Watergate scandal, died April 22. Ronald Reagan, the president known as the "Great Communicator," announced that he had Alzheimer's disease, a progressive, irreversible neurological disorder. Rep. Dan Rostenkowski, the Democratic power broker from Chicago and chairman of the House Ways and Means Committee, was defeated in the November election after being indicted on seventeen counts of embezzling from his expense accounts. Associate Justice Harry Blackmun, one of the best known justices in the Supreme Court's history because of his authorship of the *Roe v. Wade* decision legalizing abortion, retired from the Court.

Before Blackmun retired, the Court released two critical decisions in the battle over abortion. In January the Court ruled that abortion clinics could use the federal Racketeer Influenced and Corrupt Organizations law to sue protesters who attempted to shut them down. In June the Court upheld the creation of buffer zones around abortion clinics to stop protesters from blocking access to the facilities.

Two new laws approved by state voters in 1994 were nearly as controversial as the abortion decisions. In California voters overwhelmingly approved Proposition 187, which bars illegal aliens from receiving welfare, schooling, and most government-funded health care. The new law was immediately challenged in numerous suits, which were pending as the year ended. In Oregon voters narrowly passed a measure that allows doctors to prescribe lethal drugs for terminally ill patients who request them.

On the foreign front, 1994 saw genocide—the systematic slaughter of people belonging to an ethnic or tribal group—practiced on a scale not seen since World War II. In Rwanda, an estimated half million people were killed in a campaign of genocide carried out by militant members of the dominant Hutu tribe primarily against members of the Tutsi tribe. In Bosnia, Serbs continued their campaign of wholesale murder and brutality aimed at slaughtering or driving from the land all Croat and Muslim inhabitants. The international community provided humanitarian aid in both Rwanda and Bosnia, but could not figure out a way to stop the bloodshed.

Turbulence on a smaller scale struck other countries. Japan's prime minister, Morihiro Hosokawa, was forced to resign after only eight months in office because of financial scandals. In Mexico two of the nation's top political leaders—including the leading candidate for president—were assassinated in separate attacks. Late in the year, after appearing to be on the brink of war, North Korea and the United States signed an agreement under which the communist country agreed to dismantle its nuclear weapons program in exchange for billions of dollars in aid from various countries.

The year also saw many triumphs on the international scene. Only a few years after ending nearly three decades in prison, African National Congress leader Nelson Mandela was sworn in as South Africa's first democratically elected president. In Haiti Father Jean-Bertrand Aristide—backed by thousands of American troops—was restored to power as the nation's president. King Hussein of Jordan and Prime Minister Yitzhak Rabin of Israel signed an accord that formally ended a forty-six-year state of war between their two nations. In Northern Ireland Catholic and Protestant militias declared ceasefires in their decades-old battle over the fate of the British province, leading to the start of negotiations between the British government and Sinn Fein, the political arm of the Irish Republican Army.

These are but some of the topics of national and international interest chosen for *Historic Documents of 1994*. This edition marks the twenty-third year of a Congressional Quarterly project that began with *Historic Documents of 1972*. The purpose of this continuing series is to give students, librarians, journalists, scholars, and others convenient access to important documents on a wide range of world issues.

PREFACE

Each document is preceded by an introduction that provides background information and, when relevant, an account of continuing developments during the year. In our judgment, the official statements, transcripts of press conferences, speeches, reports, and court decisions presented here are of lasting interest and importance.

Bruce Maxwell, Editor
Washington, D.C.
February 1995

CONTENTS

January

February

March

April

May

June

July

August

September

October

November

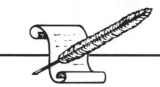

January

CLINTON STATEMENTS
ON LOS ANGELES EARTHQUAKE
January 17 and February 12, 1994

Southern California's most destructive earthquake in twenty-three years struck the Los Angeles area before dawn on January 17, resulting in sixty-one deaths and thousands of injuries. By some estimates, it destroyed 14,000 dwellings and damaged 50,000 others, leaving 25,000 people homeless. Officials said the casualty toll would have been greater had the earthquake not occurred at such an early hour (4:31 a.m. PST) and on a federal holiday (Martin Luther King Jr. Day), when few motorists were on the freeways.

As in other recent major earthquakes in California, some elevated roadways buckled and collapsed or otherwise were so badly damaged that they had to be closed. Among them was the Santa Monica Freeway, the world's busiest. Total damage estimates from the earthquake ran as high as $20 billion.

In the San Fernando Valley suburb of Northridge, directly above the quake's epicenter, violent jolts collapsed an apartment building, killing fourteen people. Powerful shocks, first measured at 6.6 on the Richter scale and later upgraded to 6.7, rolled down the valley into downtown Los Angeles, less than twenty miles away. The earthquake ruptured gas and electrical lines and water mains well beyond Los Angeles and shook buildings as far away as San Diego and Las Vegas, Nevada.

Many persons who were spared death, injury, or home damage nevertheless experienced the loss of electrical power—sometimes for days—and found familiar commuting routes closed. The National Guard and local authorities set up six tent cities to shelter and feed the homeless and those too frightened of aftershocks to return to their standing homes.

Two aftershocks, registering 5.9 and 5.6 on the Richter scale, occurred the same day as the original earthquake. Another aftershock, registering 5.3, struck on March 20, rattling windows and nerves but causing little additional damage.

Clinton Promises Aid

It quickly became evident that an enormous amount of disaster relief was needed. President Bill Clinton held a press conference the afternoon of January 17 to say that he had told Gov. Pete Wilson of California and Mayor Richard Riordan of Los Angeles that the federal government "would do all that we possibly can to be helpful." At the news conference, the president signed an order making the earthquake-stricken areas eligible for federal disaster aid.

At Clinton's urging, on February 11 Congress passed legislation providing $8.6 billion in assistance for the California earthquake victims. It was the biggest peacetime disaster relief package in American history. The package slightly surpassed the combined federal outlays for hurricane damage aid in Florida, Louisiana, and Hawaii in 1991, and greatly exceeded the $4.6 billion that had been spent up to that time to help victims of floods that swept much of the Midwest in 1993.

On February 12 the president signed the measure into law at a White House ceremony, promising that "the benefits will begin flowing tomorrow." The aid package included low-interest loans to replace homes and businesses, cash grants to the needy, housing assistance, emergency jobless funds, and money to rebuild highways, schools, and other public facilities. A state normally is required to kick in 25 percent of the amount the federal government provides for disaster relief, but California's commitment was reduced to 10 percent because the state had suffered other earthquakes in recent years and its economy was in recession.

Quake Was Among California's Largest

The January 17 earthquake was of roughly the same magnitude as another that struck the San Fernando Valley in 1971 and caused sixty-five deaths. Though extensive, the property damage from the earlier earthquake was less because it occurred farther from the populous centers of metropolitan Los Angeles. An even stronger earthquake, of 6.9 magnitude, struck the San Francisco area in 1989, causing sixty-two deaths and $5.9 billion in damage. Tragic as it was, it fell far short of the "Big One" in 1906. That earthquake caused a fire that destroyed much of San Francisco and left more than five hundred people dead or missing.

When the next "big one" will occur is of great concern to California residents. Geologists estimate that there is a fifty-fifty chance that a massive quake will hit southern California within the next two decades. Officials in Washington, D.C., are also concerned about the impact of such disasters on the federal budget. Leon Panetta, director of the Office of Management and Budget, stated shortly after the California quake that the federal government should reexamine how it pays for disaster aid. "Somehow we've got to do a better job of preparing for disasters, either by setting aside some kind of funds . . . or looking to insurance companies to try to deal with those areas that are particularly vulnerable to disasters," Panetta said.

Following are excerpts from President Bill Clinton's news conference on January 17, 1994, where he announced that the southern California area struck by the earthquake was eligible for federal disaster aid, and from his statement at a White House ceremony on February 12, 1994, where he signed legislation providing $8.6 billion in federal assistance to the disaster area:

PRESS CONFERENCE STATEMENT

Good afternoon. As all of you know, this morning at dawn a violent earthquake struck Southern California near Los Angeles. Because it occurred in a densely populated area, it was an unusually destructive one.

We have all seen today on our own televisions the buildings that have collapsed, the freeways turned into rubble. The power has been cut off and gas mains have exploded and, most tragically, many people have been injured and several lives have already been lost.

Due to the damage caused by the earthquake I have, by signing the document that I will sign at the end of this statement, declared these areas of California to be a major disaster, thereby authorizing the expenditures of funds necessary for federal disaster assistance that is requested by Governor Wilson.

This program will include, among other things, low interest loans to replace homes and businesses, cash grants where needed, housing assistance, emergency unemployment assistance, and funds to rebuild the highways, the schools and other infrastructure.

At my direction the director of FEMA [Federal Emergency Management Agency], James Lee Witt, is now on his way to California, along with Secretary of Transportation [Federico] Pena and Secretary of Housing and Urban Development [Henry] Cisneros. In addition, I have directed some senior White House staff to the scene as well.

Our hearts and prayers go out to the people of Southern California. I spoke early this morning with Mayor [Richard] Riordan and then with Governor [Pete] Wilson and wished them well and pledged to them that the United States government would do all that we possibly can to be helpful. They were, obviously, appreciative and were glad that James Lee Witt, as well as our Cabinet secretaries, were on their way to the scene.

The people of Southern California have been through a lot recently with the fires. The economy of the state of California has suffered enormous stresses in the last few years, and I think all of us should be very sensitive to what they are going through now. I know the rest of America will offer them their thoughts and their prayers tonight and will support our common efforts to help them to recover from this tragedy and to get on with the business of rebuilding their lives.

The assistance here will be short-term to help people get through the next few days, but there will also be long-term work to be done and we expect to be involved as full partners in that.

Again, let me say I wish the mayor, the governor, the people of California well. We are looking forward to working with them. I have had the opportunity to speak with both Senator [Barbara] Boxer and Senator [Dianne] Feinstein today, and I am confident that everybody is doing everything they can. . . .

STATEMENT AT BILL SIGNING

I'm glad to be here . . . to sign this bill today.

This was legislation requested by our administration to provide the most comprehensive national response ever to a region experiencing a natural disaster—the earthquake which inflicted such damage in the Los Angeles area on January the 17th. Many people had their lives shaken and transformed by the damage caused by the Northridge quake. They faced the human tragedy of 61 deaths, nearly 10,000 injuries requiring hospitalization and many, many thousands of people who lost their homes, their jobs, or otherwise had their lives turned upside down.

We saw the fierce power of the shifting earth twist and break highways, uproot homes, ignite fires and literally reshape parts of the Los Angeles landscape. More than 150 public schools were damaged, five hospitals suffered destruction requiring as much as $700 million in repair. Much of the damage will take months if not years [to repair]. It is only the latest hardship that the people of that area have experienced.

The first line of defense was the spirit the people of Los Angeles brought to this tragedy. Before the tremors had a chance to subside, we saw all the moving stories of neighbors helping neighbors; police, fire, rescue, and medical people serving without rest; and dedicated public officials who put people above politics.

Although the central highway throughout the region sustained enormous damage, imaginative means were immediately employed to permit a return to some semblance of normal life. Crime was down 21.5 percent in the immediate aftermath of the earthquake. Something good happened amidst all that tragedy as people pulled together, and they stayed together.

The second line of defense against the quake was coordinated by FEMA under the leadership of James Lee Witt. FEMA has already accepted over 300,000 applications for disaster assistance. HUD [Housing and Urban Development] Secretary Henry Cisneros led his department's efforts to provide emergency housing aid. The SBA [Small Business Administration] is processing nearly a quarter of a million applications from home owners and businesses for disaster loans. Transportation Secretary Pena and Highway Administrator Slater are doing work to try to speed the highway repairs, and to try to help provide alternative means of transportation. In each of these agencies, people are serving the way the taxpayers deserve to be treated as customers, neighbors and friends.

Today we put in motion the third line of defense—federal disaster relief for California. It was the largest package of such aid in history, and as Congressman [Harold] Volkmer's presence here reminds us, it also contains some aid for the people who suffered from the 500-year flood in the Middle West.

The bill provides $8.6 billion in housing assistance and home repairs, repairs to public facilities, transit and road reconstruction, school repairs, loans to get businesses back in business, plus funds I'll be able to use to respond to unanticipated needs. Congress considered and adopted this legislation very quickly. Democratic and Republican representatives from California in the affected [area] worked in close cooperation. Senators Boxer and Feinstein, the House delegation, Mayor Riordan, Governor Wilson represented the needs of the city and the state very well. And I want to compliment the legislators throughout the country for recognizing that this is a national problem and making it a national effort.

Ultimately, the reconstruction of Los Angeles will depend upon the resilience and the patience of the people there. Their will has been tested often over the last several years. Their spirit has remained unbroken and I'm confident it will continue to be. Secretary [Ronald] Brown is here to symbolize the ongoing effort we have had to work with the people of California under his coordinated leadership since the beginning of our administration. Just yesterday we had White House officials there working on the long-term repair work to make sure that the people of California did not believe that this was just a short-term effort on our part.

We have to continue to do this. The size of the appropriation and the speed with which Congress adopted it indicates the generosity of the American people when tragedy strikes. What we now have to demonstrate is that we have the consistency of commitment to stay until this matter is put back together. It's the same thing I said to the people in the Middle West who were affected by the floods—we know there's a short-term and a long-term problem. But I must compliment the Congress on this terrific response to the terrible tragedy of January the 17th. And I'm glad to be signing it today and I'm glad that the benefits will begin to flow tomorrow. . . .

INDEPENDENT COUNSEL
ON IRAN-CONTRA AFFAIR
January 18, 1994

Although there was "no credible evidence" that former president Ronald Reagan violated any law, impeachment "certainly should have been considered," said Independent Special Prosecutor Lawrence E. Walsh at a January 18 press conference where he released his long-awaited report on the Iran-contra affair.

The seven-year, $36 million investigation was aimed at determining what happened during a convoluted, murky drama that mired two U.S. administrations in charges of covering up foreign policy actions that had been barred by Congress. The special prosecutor's multivolume report had been completed in August 1993, but its release was delayed by three appellate judges responding to requests by attorneys for Reagan and others who wanted to review the sections of the report about their actions.

Walsh said that Reagan had "set the stage for the illegal activities of others" by encouraging their efforts to free American hostages held in Lebanon through covert arms sales to Iran and then using the profits to fund anticommunist Nicaraguan rebels when Congress had banned such aid. Once those activities were made public, "Reagan administration officials deliberately deceived the Congress and the public about the level and extent of official knowledge of and support for these operations," Walsh said. The administration withheld notes and documents from Congress during its investigation of the Iran-contra affair, Walsh added. In a 126-page response, Reagan called the report "an excessive, hyperbolic, emotional screed that relies on speculation, conjecture, innuendo and opinion instead of proof."

Report Accuses Bush of Lying

The report also sharply criticized Reagan's vice president, George Bush, who later succeeded him as president. "Contrary to his public pronouncements, [Bush] was fully aware of the Iran arms sales . . . and he participated in discussions to obtain third-country support for the contras," the report said. Although the investigators concluded there was no evidence that Bush had violated any law, the report said that Bush had declined to cooperate in the final stages of the independent counsel's investigation. Bush's lawyer, former attorney general Griffin B. Bell, responded that Bush had "fully cooperated" in the investigation.

The report also criticized Bush's decision in December 1992, after he became president, to pardon former defense secretary Caspar W. Weinberger. Weinberger had been indicted in June 1992 on five counts of obstruction of justice, perjury, and making false statements. The report called the pardon "an act of friendship or an act of self-protection."

During his investigation, Walsh, an eighty-two-year-old former federal judge and Republican who had been named special prosecutor in December 1987, prosecuted fourteen people and investigated seventeen others. Two of the central figures in the investigation were National Security Council aide and retired Marine officer Oliver L. North and his supervisor, John M. Poindexter. North was the official most directly involved in selling arms to Iran and diverting proceeds to the contras, and was allowed to operate with "unprecedented latitude," according to Walsh's report. Reagan fired North in November 1985, and Poindexter resigned at the same time. Both were indicted in March 1987. North was convicted of falsifying and destroying documents, accepting an illegal gratuity, and aiding and abetting in the obstruction of Congress by making false statements under oath. He was convicted, but the conviction was eventually dismissed because prosecutors were unable to show that his trial was not tainted by congressional testimony given under a grant of immunity. Poindexter also was charged and convicted, but his conviction was reversed in November 1989.

Impact on North's Election Bid

The special prosecutor's report blasted North, who had announced his Republican candidacy for the Virginia Senate seat held by Democrat Charles Robb. ". . .[N]orth admitted to having assisted the contras during the [congressional] prohibition on U.S. aid," Walsh wrote, "to having shredded and removed from the White House official documents, to having converted traveler's checks for his personal use, to having participated in the creation of false chronologies of the U.S. arms sales, to having lied to Congress and to having accepted a home security system . . . then fabricating letters regarding payment for the system. But North testified, 'I don't believe I ever did anything that was criminal.' "

Some said the report seriously damaged North's political prospects, but North and his supporters dismissed the document. "There are no smoking guns when it comes to me," North said in a statement. "Walsh fired his last shot, and it was a blank. It's over." North went on to win the Republican senatorial nomination, but his candidacy was extremely controversial and sharply split the Republican party in Virginia. Virginia Sen. John W. Warner, a fellow Republican, refused to support North.

The campaign was one of the nastiest, most expensive, and most watched *of 1994. North and Robb ran neck-to-neck until the end. Despite the Republican landslide that swept the country, Robb managed to hold onto his seat. Robb garnered 46 percent of the vote to North's 43 percent. Independent J. Marshall Coleman, a former Republican who left the party to run for the Senate, received 11 percent of the vote. Although North lost the election, most political observers expected he would run again.*

Following are excerpts from the Executive Summary of the Final Report of the Independent Counsel for Iran/Contra Matters, *dated August 4, 1993, and released by Independent Counsel Lawrence E. Walsh on January 18, 1994:*

In October and November 1986, two secret U.S. Government operations were publicly exposed, potentially implicating Reagan Administration officials in illegal activities. These operations were the provision of assistance to the military activities of the Nicaraguan contra rebels during an October 1984 to October 1986 prohibition on such aid, and the sale of U.S. arms to Iran in contravention of stated U.S. policy and in possible violation of arms-export controls. In late November 1986, Reagan Administration officials announced that some of the proceeds from the sale of U.S. arms to Iran had been diverted to the contras.

As a result of the exposure of these operations, Attorney General Edwin Meese III sought the appointment of an independent counsel to investigate and, if necessary, prosecute possible crimes arising from them.

The Special Division of the United States Court of Appeals for the District of Columbia Circuit appointed Lawrence E. Walsh as Independent Counsel on December 19, 1986, and charged him with investigating:

(1) the direct or indirect sale, shipment, or transfer since in or about 1984 down to the present, of military arms, materiel, or funds to the government of Iran, officials of that government, persons, organizations or entities connected with or purporting to represent that government, or persons located in Iran;

(2) the direct or indirect sale, shipment, or transfer of military arms, materiel or funds to any government, entity, or person acting, or purporting to act as an intermediary in any transaction referred to above;

(3) the financing or funding of any direct or indirect sale, shipment or transfer referred to above;

(4) the diversion of proceeds from any transaction described above to or for any person, organization, foreign government, or any faction or body of insurgents in any foreign country, including, but not limited to Nicaragua;

(5) the provision or coordination of support for persons or entities engaged as military insurgents in armed conflict with the government of Nicaragua since 1984.

This is the final report of that investigation.

Overall Conclusions

The investigations and prosecutions have shown that high-ranking Administration officials violated laws and executive orders in the Iran/contra matter. Independent Counsel concluded that:

- the sales of arms to Iran contravened United States Government policy and may have violated the Arms Export Control Act;
- the provision and coordination of support to the contras violated the Boland Amendment ban on aid to military activities in Nicaragua;
- the policies behind both the Iran and contra operations were fully reviewed and developed at the highest levels of the Reagan Administration;
- although there was little evidence of National Security Council level knowledge of most of the actual contra-support operations, there was no evidence that any NSC member dissented from the underlying policy—keeping the contras alive despite congressional limitations on contra support;
- the Iran operations were carried out with the knowledge of, among others, President Ronald Reagan, Vice President George Bush, Secretary of State George P. Shultz, Secretary of Defense Caspar W. Weinberger, Director of Central Intelligence William J. Casey, and national security advisers Robert C. McFarlane and John M. Poindexter; of these officials, only Weinberger and Shultz dissented from the policy decision, and Weinberger eventually acquiesced by ordering the Department of Defense to provide the necessary arms;
- large volumes of highly relevant, contemporaneously created documents were systematically and willfully withheld from investigators by several Reagan Administration officials; and
- following the revelation of these operations in October and November 1986, Reagan Administration officials deliberately deceived the Congress and the public about the level and extent of official knowledge of and support for these operations.

In addition, Independent Counsel concluded that the off-the-books nature of the Iran and contra operations gave line-level personnel the opportunity to commit money crimes.

Prosecutions

In the course of Independent Counsel's investigation, 14 persons were charged with criminal violations. There were two broad classes of crimes charged: Operational crimes, which largely concerned the illegal use of funds generated in the course of the operations, and "cover-up" crimes, which largely concerned false statements and obstructions after the revelation of the operations. Independent Counsel did not charge violations of the Arms Export Control Act or Boland Amendment. Although apparent violations of these statutes provided the impetus for the cover-up, they are not criminal statutes and do not contain any enforcement provisions.

All of the individuals charged were convicted, except for one CIA official whose case was dismissed on national security grounds and two officials who received unprecedented pre-trial pardons by President Bush following his electoral defeat in 1992. Two of the convictions were reversed on appeal on constitutional grounds that in no way cast doubt on the factual guilt of the men convicted. The individuals charged and the disposition of their cases are:

(1) Robert C. McFarlane: pleaded guilty to four counts of withholding information from Congress;

(2) Oliver L. North: convicted of altering and destroying documents, accepting an illegal gratuity, and aiding and abetting in the obstruction of Congress; conviction reversed on appeal;

(3) John M. Poindexter: convicted of conspiracy, false statements, destruction and removal of records, and obstruction of Congress; conviction reversed on appeal;

(4) Richard V. Secord: pleaded guilty to making false statements to Congress;

(5) Albert Hakim: pleaded guilty to supplementing the salary of North;

(6) Thomas G. Clines: convicted of four counts of tax-related offenses for failing to report income from the operations;

(7) Carl R. Channell: pleaded guilty to conspiracy to defraud the United States;

(8) Richard R. Miller: pleaded guilty to conspiracy to defraud the United States;

(9) Clair E. George: convicted of false statements and perjury before Congress;

(10) Duane R. Clarridge: indicted on seven counts of perjury and false statements; pardoned before trial by President Bush;

(11) Alan D. Fiers, Jr.: pleaded guilty to withholding information from Congress;

(12) Joseph F. Fernandez: indicted on four counts of obstruction and false statements; case dismissed when Attorney General Richard L. Thornburgh refused to declassify information needed for his defense;

(13) Elliott Abrams: pleaded guilty to withholding information from Congress;

(14) Caspar W. Weinberger: charged with four counts of false statements and perjury; pardoned before trial by President Bush.

At the time President Bush pardoned Weinberger and Clarridge, he also pardoned George, Fiers, Abrams, and McFarlane.

The Basic Facts of Iran/Contra

The Iran/contra affair concerned two secret Reagan Administration policies whose operations were coordinated by National Security Council staff. The Iran operation involved efforts in 1985 and 1986 to obtain the release of

Americans held hostage in the Middle East through the sale of U.S. weapons to Iran, despite an embargo on such sales. The contra operations from 1984 through most of 1986 involved the secret governmental support of contra military and paramilitary activities in Nicaragua, despite congressional prohibition of this support.

The Iran and contra operations were merged when funds generated from the sale of weapons to Iran were diverted to support the contra effort in Nicaragua. Although this "diversion" may be the most dramatic aspect of Iran/contra, it is important to emphasize that both the Iran and contra operations, separately, violated United States policy and law. The ignorance of the "diversion" asserted by President Reagan and his Cabinet officers on the National Security Council in no way absolves them of responsibility for the underlying Iran and contra operations.

The secrecy concerning the Iran and contra activities was finally pierced by events that took place thousands of miles apart in the fall of 1986. The first occurred on October 5, 1986, when Nicaraguan government soldiers shot down an American cargo plane that was carrying military supplies to contra forces; the one surviving crew member, American Eugene Hasenfus, was taken into captivity and stated that he was employed by the CIA. A month after the Hasenfus shootdown, President Reagan's secret sale of U.S. arms to Iran was reported by a Lebanese publication on November 3. The joining of these two operations was made public on November 25, 1986, when Attorney General Meese announced that Justice Department officials had discovered that some of the proceeds from the Iran arms sales had been diverted to the contras.

When these operations ended, the exposure of the Iran/contra affair generated a new round of illegality. Beginning with the testimony of Elliott Abrams and others in October 1986 and continuing through the public testimony of Caspar W. Weinberger on the last day of the congressional hearings in the summer of 1987, senior Reagan Administration officials engaged in a concerted effort to deceive Congress and the public about their knowledge of and support for the operations.

Independent Counsel has concluded that the President's most senior advisers and the Cabinet members on the National Security Council participated in the strategy to make National Security staff members McFarlane, Poindexter and North the scapegoats whose sacrifice would protect the Reagan Administration in its final two years. In an important sense, this strategy succeeded. Independent Counsel discovered much of the best evidence of the cover-up in the final year of active investigation, too late for most prosecutions. . . .

The Operational Conspiracy

The operational conspiracy was the basis for Count One of the 23-count indictment returned by the Grand Jury March 16, 1988, against Poindexter, North, Secord, and Hakim. It charged the four with conspiracy to defraud the United States by deceitfully:

(1) supporting military operations in Nicaragua in defiance of congressional controls;

(2) using the Iran arms sales to raise funds to be spent at the direction of North, rather than the U.S. Government; and

(3) endangering the Administration's hostage-release effort by overcharging Iran for the arms to generate unauthorized profits to fund the contras and for other purposes.

The charge was upheld as a matter of law by U.S. District Judge Gerhard A. Gesell even though the Justice Department, in a move that Judge Gesell called "unprecedented," filed an amicus brief supporting North's contention that the charge should be dismissed. Although Count One was ultimately dismissed because the Reagan Administration refused to declassify information necessary to North's defense, Judge Gesell's decision established that high Government officials who engage in conspiracy to subvert civil laws and the Constitution have engaged in criminal acts. Trial on Count One would have disclosed the Government-wide activities that supported North's Iran and contra operations.

Within the NSC, McFarlane pleaded guilty in March 1988 to four counts of withholding information from Congress in connection with his denials that North was providing the contras with military advice and assistance. McFarlane, in his plea agreement, promised to cooperate with Independent Counsel by providing truthful testimony in subsequent trials.

Judge Gesell ordered severance of the trials of the four charged in the conspiracy indictment because of the immunized testimony given by Poindexter, North and Hakim to Congress. North was tried and convicted by a jury in May 1989 of altering and destroying documents, accepting an illegal gratuity and aiding and abetting in the obstruction of Congress. His conviction was reversed on appeal in July 1990 and charges against North were subsequently dismissed in September 1991 on the ground that trial witnesses were tainted by North's nationally televised, immunized testimony before Congress. Poindexter in April 1990 was convicted by a jury on five felony counts of conspiracy, false statements, destruction and removal of records and obstruction of Congress. The Court of Appeals reversed his conviction in November 1991 on the immunized testimony issue.

The Flow of Funds

The illegal activities of the private citizens involved with the North and Secord operations are discussed in detail in Part V. The off-the-books conduct of the two highly secret operations circumvented normal Administration accountability and congressional oversight associated with covert ventures and presented fertile ground for financial wrongdoing. There were several funding sources for the contras' weapons purchases from the covert-action Enterprise formed by North, Secord and Hakim:

(1) donations from foreign countries;

(2) contributions from wealthy Americans sympathetic to President

Reagan's contra support policies; and

(3) the diversion of proceeds from the sale of arms to Iran.

Ultimately, all of these funds fell under the control of North, and through him, Secord and Hakim.

North used political fundraisers Carl R. Channell and Richard R. Miller to raise millions of dollars from wealthy Americans, illegally using a tax-exempt organization to do so. These funds, along with the private contributions, were run through a network of corporations and Swiss bank accounts put at North's disposal by Secord and Hakim, through which transactions were concealed and laundered. In late 1985 through 1986 the Enterprise became centrally involved in the arms sales to Iran. As a result of both the Iran and contra operations, more than $47 million flowed through Enterprise accounts.

Professional fundraisers Channell and Miller pleaded guilty in the spring of 1987 to conspiracy to defraud the Government by illegal use of a tax-exempt foundation to raise contributions for the purchase of lethal supplies for the contras. They named North as an unindicted co-conspirator.

Secord pleaded guilty in November 1989 to a felony, admitting that he falsely denied to Congress that North had personally benefited from the Enterprise. Hakim pleaded guilty to the misdemeanor count of supplementing the salary of North. Lake Resources Inc., the company controlled by Hakim to launder the Enterprise's money flow, pleaded guilty to the corporate felony of theft of Government property in diverting the proceeds from the arms sales to the contras and for other unauthorized purposes. Thomas G. Clines was convicted in September 1990 of four unrelated felonies for failing to report all of his income from the Enterprise.

Agency Support of the Operations

Following the convictions of those who were most central to the Iran/contra operations, Independent Counsel's investigation focused on the supporting roles played by Government officials in other agencies and the supervisory roles of the NSC principals. The investigation showed that Administration officials who claimed initially that they had little knowledge about the Iran arms sales or the illegal contra-resupply operation North directed were much better informed than they professed to be. The Office of Independent Counsel obtained evidence that Secretaries Weinberger and Shultz and White House Chief of Staff Donald T. Regan, among others, held back information that would have helped Congress obtain a much clearer view of the scope of the Iran/contra matter. Contemporaneous notes of Regan and Weinberger, and those dictated by Shultz, were withheld until they were obtained by Independent Counsel in 1991 and 1992.

The White House and Office of the Vice President

As the White House section of this report describes in detail, the investigation found no credible evidence that President Reagan violated any criminal statute. The OIC could not prove that Reagan authorized or was aware of the diversion or that he had knowledge of the extent of North's control of the contra-resupply network. Nevertheless, he set the stage for the illegal activities of others by encouraging and, in general terms, ordering support of the contras during the October 1984 to October 1986 period when funds for the contras were cut off by the Boland Amendment, and in authorizing the sale of arms to Iran, in contravention of the U.S. embargo on such sales. The President's disregard for civil laws enacted to limit presidential actions abroad—specifically the Boland Amendment, the Arms Export Control Act and congressional-notification requirements in covert-action laws—created a climate in which some of the Government officers assigned to implement his policies felt emboldened to circumvent such laws.

President Reagan's directive to McFarlane to keep the contras alive "body and soul" during the Boland cut-off period was viewed by North, who was charged by McFarlane to carry out the directive, as an invitation to break the law. Similarly, President Reagan's decision in 1985 to authorize the sale of arms to Iran from Israeli stocks, despite warnings by Weinberger and Shultz that such transfers might violate the law, opened the way for Poindexter's subsequent decision to authorize the diversion. Poindexter told Congress that while he made the decision on his own and did not tell the President, he believed the President would have approved. North testified that he believed the President authorized it.

Independent Counsel's investigation did not develop evidence that proved that Vice President Bush violated any criminal statute. Contrary to his public pronouncements, however, he was fully aware of the Iran arms sales. Bush was regularly briefed, along with the President, on the Iran arms sales, and he participated in discussions to obtain third-country support for the contras. The OIC obtained no evidence that Bush was aware of the diversion. The OIC learned in December 1992 that Bush had failed to produce a diary containing contemporaneous notes relevant to Iran/contra, despite requests made in 1987 and again in early 1992 for the production of such material. Bush refused to be interviewed for a final time in light of evidence developed in the latter stages of OIC's investigation, leaving unresolved a clear picture of his Iran/contra involvement. Bush's pardon of Weinberger on December 24, 1992 preempted a trial in which defense counsel indicated that they intended to call Bush as a witness.

The chapters on White House Chief of Staff Regan and Attorney General Edwin Meese III focus on their actions during the November 1986 period, as the President and his advisers sought to control the damage caused by the disclosure of the Iran arms sales. Regan in 1992 provided Independent Counsel with copies of notes showing that Poindexter and Meese attempted to create a false account of the 1985 arms sales from Israeli stocks, which they believed were illegal, in order to protect the President. Regan and the other senior advisers did not speak up to correct the false version of events. No final legal determination on the matter had been made. Regan said he did not want to be the one who broke the silence among the President's senior advisers, virtually all of whom knew the account was false.

The evidence indicates that Meese's November 1986 inquiry was more of a damage-control exercise than an effort to find the facts. He had private conversations with the President, the Vice President, Poindexter, Weinberger, Casey and Regan without taking notes. Even after learning of the diversion, Meese failed to secure records in NSC staff offices or take other prudent steps to protect potential evidence. And finally, in reporting to the President and his senior advisers, Meese gave a false account of what he had been told by stating that the President did not know about the 1985 HAWK shipments, which Meese said might have been illegal. The statute of limitations had run on November 1986 activities before OIC obtained its evidence. In 1992, Meese denied recollection of the statements attributed to him by the notes of Weinberger and Regan. He was unconvincing, but the passage of time would have been expected to raise a reasonable doubt of the intentional falsity of his denials if he had been prosecuted for his 1992 false statements.

The Role of CIA Officials

Director Casey's unswerving support of President Reagan's contra policies and of the Iran arms sales encouraged some CIA officials to go beyond legal restrictions in both operations. Casey was instrumental in pairing North with Secord as a contra-support team when the Boland Amendment in October 1984 forced the CIA to refrain from direct or indirect aid. He also supported the North-Secord combination in the Iran arms sales, despite deep reservations about Secord within the CIA hierarchy.

Casey's position on the contras prompted the chief of the CIA's Central American Task Force, Alan D. Fiers, Jr., to "dovetail" CIA activities with those of North's contra-resupply network, in violation of Boland restrictions. Casey's support for the NSC to direct the Iran arms sales and to use arms dealer Manucher Ghorbanifar and Secord in the operation, forced the CIA's Directorate of Operations to work with people it distrusted.

Following the Hasenfus shootdown in early October 1986, George and Fiers lied to Congress about U.S. Government involvement in contra resupply, to, as Fiers put it, "keep the spotlight off the White House." When the Iran arms sales became public in November 1986, three of Casey's key officers—George, Clarridge and Fiers—followed Casey's lead in misleading Congress.

Four CIA officials were charged with criminal offenses—George, the deputy director for operations and the third highest-ranking CIA official; Clarridge, chief of the European Division; Fiers; and Fernandez. George was convicted of two felony counts of false statements and perjury before Congress. Fiers pleaded guilty to two misdemeanor counts of withholding information from Congress. The four counts of obstruction and false statements against Fernandez were dismissed when the Bush Administration refused to declassify information needed for his defense. Clarridge was awaiting trial on seven counts of perjury and false statements when he, George and Fiers were pardoned by President Bush.

State Department Officials

In 1990 and 1991, Independent Counsel received new documentary evidence in the form of handwritten notes suggesting that Secretary Shultz's congressional testimony painted a misleading and incorrect picture of his knowledge of the Iran arms sales. The subsequent investigation focused on whether Shultz or other Department officials deliberately misled or withheld information from congressional or OIC investigators.

The key notes, taken by M. Charles Hill, Shultz's executive assistant, were nearly verbatim, contemporaneous accounts of Shultz's meetings within the department and Shultz's reports to Hill on meetings the secretary attended elsewhere. The Hill notes and similarly detailed notes by Nicholas Platt, the State Department's executive secretary, provided the OIC with a detailed account of Shultz's knowledge of the Iran arms sales. The most revealing of these notes were not provided to any Iran/contra investigation until 1990 and 1991. The notes show that—contrary to his early testimony that he was not aware of details of the 1985 arms transfers—Shultz knew that the shipments were planned and that they were delivered. Also in conflict with his congressional testimony was evidence that Shultz was aware of the 1986 shipments.

Independent Counsel concluded that Shultz's early testimony was incorrect, if not false, in significant respects, and misleading, if literally true, in others. When questioned about the discrepancies in 1992, Shultz did not dispute the accuracy of the Hill notes. He told OIC that he believed his testimony was accurate at the time and he insisted that if he had been provided with the notes earlier, he would have testified differently. Independent Counsel declined to prosecute because there was a reasonable doubt that Shultz's testimony was willfully false at the time it was delivered.

Independent Counsel concluded that Hill had willfully withheld relevant notes and prepared false testimony for Shultz in 1987. He declined to prosecute because Hill's claim of authorization to limit the production of his notes and the joint responsibility of Shultz for the resulting misleading testimony, would at trial have raised a reasonable doubt, after Independent Counsel had declined to prosecute Shultz.

Independent Counsel's initial focus on the State Department had centered on Assistant Secretary Elliott Abrams' insistence to Congress and to the OIC that he was not aware of North's direction of the extensive contra-resupply network in 1985 and 1986. As assistant secretary of state for inter-American affairs, Abrams chaired the Restricted Inter-Agency Group, or RIG, which coordinated U.S. policy in Central America. Although the OIC was skeptical about Abrams' testimony, there was insufficient evidence to proceed against him until additional documentary evidence inculpating him was discovered in 1990 and 1991, and until Fiers, who represented the CIA on the RIG, pleaded guilty in July 1991 to withholding information from Congress. Fiers provided evidence to support North's earlier testimony that Abrams was knowledgeable about North's contra-supply network. Abrams pleaded guilty in October 1991 to two counts of withholding information from Congress about secret

Government efforts to support the contras, and about his solicitation of $10 million to aid the contras from the Sultan of Brunei.

Secretary Weinberger and Defense Department Officials

Contrary to their testimony to the presidentially appointed Tower Commission and the Select Iran/contra Committees of Congress, Independent Counsel determined that Secretary Weinberger and his closest aides were consistently informed of proposed and actual arms shipments to Iran during 1985 and 1986. The key evidence was handwritten notes of Weinberger, which he deliberately withheld from Congress and the OIC until they were discovered by Independent Counsel in late 1991. The Weinberger daily diary notes and notes of significant White House and other meetings contained highly relevant, contemporaneous information that resolved many questions left unanswered in early investigations.

The notes demonstrated that Weinberger's early testimony—that he had only vague and generalized information about Iran arms sales in 1985—was false, and that he in fact had detailed information on the proposed arms sales and the actual deliveries. The notes also revealed that Gen. Colin Powell, Weinberger's senior military aide, and Richard L. Armitage, assistant secretary of defense for international security affairs, also had detailed knowledge of the 1985 shipments from Israeli stocks. Armitage and Powell had testified that they did not learn of the November 1985 HAWK missile shipment until 1986.

Weinberger's notes provided detailed accounts of high-level Administration meetings in November 1986 in which the President's senior advisers were provided with false accounts of the Iran arms sales to protect the President and themselves from the consequences of the possibly illegal 1985 shipments from Israeli stocks.

Weinberger's notes provided key evidence supporting the charges against him, including perjury and false statements in connection with his testimony regarding the arms sales, his denial of the existence of notes and his denial of knowledge of Saudi Arabia's multi-million dollar contribution to the contras. He was pardoned less than two weeks before trial by President Bush on December 24, 1992.

There was little evidence that Powell's early testimony regarding the 1985 shipments and Weinberger's notes was willfully false. Powell cooperated with the various Iran/contra investigations and, when his recollection was refreshed by Weinberger's notes, he readily conceded their accuracy. Independent Counsel declined to prosecute Armitage because the OIC's limited resources were focused on the case against Weinberger and because the evidence against Armitage, while substantial, did not reach the threshold of proof beyond a reasonable doubt.

The Reagan, Bush and Casey Segments

The Independent Counsel Act requires a report as to persons not indicted as well as those indicted. Because of the large number of persons investigated, those discussed in individual sections of this report are limited to those as to whom there was a possibility of indictment. In addition there are separate sections on President Reagan and President Bush because, although criminal proceedings against them were always unlikely, they were important subjects of the investigation, and their activities were important to the action taken with respect to others.

CIA Director Casey is a special case. Because Casey was hospitalized with a fatal illness before Independent Counsel was appointed, no formal investigation of Casey was ever undertaken by the OIC. Casey was never able to give his account, and he was unable to respond to allegations of wrongdoing made about him by others, most prominently North, whose veracity is subject to serious question. Equally important, fundamental questions could not be answered regarding Casey's state of mind, the impact, if any, of his fatal illness on his conduct and his intent.

Under normal circumstances, a prosecutor would hesitate to comment on the conduct of an individual whose activities and actions were not subjected to rigorous investigation, which might exculpate that individual. Nevertheless, after serious deliberation, Independent Counsel concluded that it was in the public interest that this report expose as full and complete an account of the Iran/contra matter as possible. This simply could not be done without an account of the role of Director Casey.

Observations and Conclusions

This report concludes with Independent Counsel's observations and conclusions. He observes that the governmental problems presented by Iran/contra are not those of rogue operations, but rather those of Executive Branch efforts to evade congressional oversight. As this report documents, the competing roles of the attorney general—adviser to the President and top law-enforcement officer—come into irreconcilable conflict in the case of high-level Executive Branch wrongdoing. Independent Counsel concludes that congressional oversight alone cannot correct the deficiencies that result when an attorney general abandons the law-enforcement responsibilities of that office and undertakes, instead, to protect the President.

Independent Counsel asks the Congress to review the difficult and delicate problem posed to the investigations and prosecutions by congressional grants of immunity to principals. While recognizing the important responsibility of Congress for investigating such matters thoroughly, Congress must realize that grants of use immunity to principals in such highly exposed matters as the Iran/contra affair will virtually rule out successful prosecution.

Independent Counsel also addresses the problem of implementing the Classified Information Procedures Act (CIPA) in cases steeped in highly classified information, such as many of the Iran/contra prosecutions. Under the Act, the attorney general has unrestricted discretion to decide whether to declassify information necessary for trial, even in cases in which Independent Counsel has been appointed because of the attorney general's conflict of interest. This discretion is inconsistent with the perceived need for independent counsel, particularly in cases in which officers of the intelligence agencies that classify information are under investigation. This discretion gives the attorney general the power to block almost any potentially embarrassing prosecution that requires the declassification of information. Independent Counsel suggests that the attorney general implement standards that would permit independent review of a decision to block a prosecution of an officer within the Executive Branch and legitimate congressional oversight. . . .

INMAN WITHDRAWAL
AS DEFENSE NOMINEE
January 18, 1994

Bobby Ray Inman, a retired admiral and senior intelligence official, told a surprised nation January 18 that he had changed his mind and had informed President Bill Clinton that he did not want to be secretary of defense. The previous month, he had publicly accepted the nomination at a White House ceremony.

At a news conference in his home of Austin, Texas, Inman portrayed himself as the victim of press critics practicing a "new McCarthyism" and as the potential target of a partisan political attack. "I'm simply not prepared to pay the current cost of public service in distortion of my record," he said. In a letter asking Clinton to withdraw his nomination, Inman wrote: "I sense elements in the media and the political leadership of the country who would rather disparage or destroy reputations than work to effectively govern the country."

Inman's remarks surprised Washington officials and media commentators, who generally had applauded his selection and expected swift Senate confirmation. An unnamed person who the Washington Post *said had talked with Inman between the nomination and his withdrawal said Inman "was a guy who knew how to play the game and thought he could play the game. Only he discovered that the game had gotten a lot harder and a lot hotter."*

At his Austin news conference, Inman insisted that no disagreement had arisen with Clinton, even though at the December 16 White House ceremony he had spoken of having to find a "comfort level" with the president. He declared in Austin that there was "no daylight . . . at all" between himself and Clinton. Inman said the president was "disappointed in my decision, but he has supported it." All along, Inman had seemed ambivalent about becoming defense secretary. When his nomination was announced in December, Inman said: "I did not seek the job [and] I did not want the job."

The episode obviously embarrassed Clinton. The president had responded to widespread dissatisfaction with the management style of Secretary of

Defense Les Aspin by accepting his resignation on December 15, 1993. Clinton then set out to find a "big name" successor capable of muting criticism that national security affairs needed better direction. Inman seemed the ideal candidate.

Inman Seen as Washington Insider

Inman had concluded a distinguished naval career in the intelligence service, becoming the Navy's youngest four-star admiral. He won plaudits as deputy director of the Central Intelligence Agency during the Reagan presidency at a time when his boss, William Casey, was often involved in political controversy. Inman later returned to his native Texas to pursue high technology business ventures and teach at the University of Texas.

Unlike Aspin, a former Democratic representative from Wisconsin, Inman was not identified with any political party. In fact, at the White House ceremony in December he volunteered the information that in 1992 he had voted for Clinton's Republican opponent, President George Bush, who he called "a personal friend." Many Washingtonians considered Inman an adroit "insider" who knew how to deal with the press and cultivate friendships among the powerful.

Inman Attacks Columnists, GOP Leader

Inman complained about unfriendly newspaper columnists and contended that Senate Minority Leader Bob Dole (R-Kan.) was planning a partisan attack on his nomination, perhaps in collusion with New York Times *columnist William Safire, a former White House speech writer for Ronald Reagan. Inman said he was fed up with "rush-to-judgment distortions of my record, my character and my reputation." He added: "I've already given 30 years of service to my country, and I don't wish or intend to subject myself to that on a daily basis as the cost of trying to produce change."*

Dole and Safire ridiculed the allegations. Inman later retracted them, although he continued to contend that Safire's criticism was a vendetta against him. Inman said he had incurred Safire's wrath because he limited the information the CIA was sharing with Israel. Safire said he had once angered Inman by asking "why a grown man would call himself Bobby."

Dole denied that he planned a partisan attack on Inman, although he said the Senate Armed Services Committee would have carefully examined Inman's record during confirmation hearings. "He had a failed business; he was going to be asked how it failed," the Senate Republican leader said in a television interview. "He was going to be asked about Social Security [taxes belatedly paid for a housekeeper] . . ." Dole added: "I'm glad he quit. He would have been a big embarrassment to President Clinton."

Perry Named Defense Secretary

Aspin agreed to stay on at the Pentagon until a successor was ready to take office. On January 24 Clinton named Aspin's top deputy, William J. Perry, to succeed him. On a 98-0 vote, the Senate approved Perry's nomina-

tion on February 4. Both Democrats and Republicans praised Perry for his competence in running the Pentagon on a day-to-day basis. He appeared to enjoy the support of military leaders that Aspin had lacked.

> *Following is the text of the letter that Bobby Ray Inman delivered to the White House January 18, 1994, asking President Bill Clinton to withdraw his nomination to be secretary of defense:*

Dear Mr. President,

After much deliberation, I hereby request that you withdraw my nomination to be the Secretary of Defense. I regret letting you down, but I have concluded that it is the right decision for both of us. I have been overwhelmed by the volume of positive public support for the nomination from so many quarters, including former Presidents, and especially from Dick Cheney and Bob Gates, and Senators Sam Nunn, John Warner, John McCain and Kay Hutchison, for which I will be eternally grateful. But the reality is that my family and I have not found it possible to focus on the positive and ignore the negative, but rather have been drawn daily to the rush-to-judgment distortions of my record, my character, and my reputation. I have had many calls from old friends telling me that I simply need thicker skin, but for only the second time in my life (the other was my seventeen months as the Deputy Director of Central Intelligence) I find I wake up in the morning focused on the negatives and not on the opportunities.

The precipitating event for my decision was news first received on December 30th that Senator Dole had directed a partisan response to my nomination. During my years in public service, I did not have an occasion to work with Senator Dole, so he has no personal experience that would have led him to join his fellow Republicans, who have been so supportive. But without solid bipartisan support from the leadership at the outset, I bring no special qualifications to the prospective job. I do not need another title for my resume, and I was willing to leave the private sector only if there was a strong probability for gaining the kind of legislation that would fundamentally change how the Department of Defense spends the taxpayers' dollars. From Austin I sense elements in the media and the political leadership of the country who would rather disparage or destroy reputations than work to effectively govern the country. I do not wish to provide those elements fodder for their daily attacks.

Finally, Mr. President, I want you to know that one of the few positive things I take out of this unhappy experience is a great appreciation for your intellect, for your clear understanding of what has not gone well in the National Security arena in the first year of your Presidency, and of your determination to build on the NAFTA experience to forge new and lasting bipartisan approaches to the intractable problems in front of this Country. I hope you will find a strong candidate for Secretary of Defense who will bring the political skills and toughness that will be required. I am persuaded that you are fully ready and capable of being the Commander in Chief this country must have.

If I had really wanted the job I might have been willing to subject my family to the daily onslaught that awaits those doing highly visible public service. But I have already given more than thirty years of public service to my Country, of which I remain proud, and I have concluded that duty to family must now come before further duty for service to Country.

Very respectfully,

Bobby R. Inman
Admiral, U.S. Navy (Ret.)

SUPREME COURT ON RICO AND ABORTION PROTESTS
January 24, 1994

The Supreme Court gave abortion clinics an important new tool in their fight against antiabortion protesters when it ruled unanimously January 24 that clinics could use the federal Racketeer Influenced and Corrupt Organizations (RICO) law to sue protesters who tried to shut them down.

The ruling reinstated a lawsuit brought by the National Organization for Women (NOW) on behalf of two abortion clinics, the Delaware Women's Health Organization in Wilmington and the Summit Women's Health Organization in Milwaukee. The suit charged that the antiabortion groups Operation Rescue and the Pro-Life Action League, their leaders, and other groups and individuals had engaged in a nationwide conspiracy of violence against abortion clinics, citing incidents of extortion, intimidation, bombings, burglary, criminal damage to clinic property, and other illegal acts.

The Supreme Court did not rule on the merit of those claims. It simply said the eight-year-old suit could proceed in a lower federal court. If NOW ultimately won the suit, it could be a major blow to the antiabortion movement, since the RICO law allows the awarding of triple damages.

Previously, two lower federal courts had dismissed the suit on the grounds that RICO could only be used in cases where the defendants had an economic motive for their actions. The Supreme Court rejected that contention, ruling that the RICO law does not require an economic motive.

In the majority opinion, Chief Justice William Rehnquist wrote that a requirement of economic incentive is "neither expressed nor, we think, fairly implied in the operative sections of the Act." The Court's ruling was yet another broadening of the RICO law, which Congress passed in 1970 to fight organized crime. The law makes it illegal to conduct an "enterprise" that engages in a "pattern of racketeering activity." A pattern is established by committing at least two acts that violate any of a long list of state and federal laws.

Infringement of First Amendment Rights Claimed

The full impact of the Court's decision was not immediately clear. Antiabortion leaders said that permitting RICO suits violated their followers' First Amendment right to engage in peaceful protest. Randall Terry, the founder of Operation Rescue and a defendant in the suit, called the decision "a vulgar betrayal of over 200 years of tolerance towards protest and civil disobedience." Supporters of abortion rights said the decision would have no impact on peaceful protests, because a RICO suit could not be filed without the commission of two criminal acts. "We're not out to stop them from peacefully protesting," said Patricia Ireland, president of NOW.

Many antiabortion leaders said the Court's ruling cleared the way for use of the RICO law against other kinds of groups that engaged in civil disobedience to cause social change. "Under this decision, Martin Luther King Jr. would have been a racketeer," Terry told the New York Times. *"What I'd say to the AIDS activists, the antinuclear groups, the animal-rights people, is get your affairs in order and line up, because you're next."*

In the majority opinion, Rehnquist did not address how the decision affected the First Amendment rights of protesters. But in a separate concurring opinion, Justice David Souter said defendants in RICO cases could raise the First Amendment as a defense. "Conduct . . . may turn out to be fully protected First Amendment activity, entitling the defendant to dismissal on that basis," Souter wrote in the opinion, which was joined by Justice Anthony Kennedy.

Abortion Protests to Continue

While the impact of the ruling was unclear, antiabortion leaders vowed not to be deterred. "We are not racketeers and we are not going to back down from our pro-life activities," said Joseph Scheidler, executive director of the Pro-Life Action League and a defendant in the suit. "If anything, we'll step it up. Social protest is at the heart of what America stands for, and has been since the Boston Tea Party."

Other antiabortion leaders agreed. "For us, this is the same old thing," said Wendy Wright, communications director of Operation Rescue National, in an interview with the New York Times. *"For years, we've faced massive lawsuits and horrendous jail sentences. But we're accountable to God, not to the government, and as long as people believe it's right to save unborn children, they'll be willing to pay the price." Yet some leaders expressed fears that people who were less committed to their cause might be frightened away from protesting in the face of possible RICO action.*

Faced with increasing violence and the frequent inability of local police to cope with massive human blockades of clinics, abortion rights leaders had sought to use various federal laws to keep abortion clinics open. They suffered a defeat in 1993, when the Supreme Court ruled that a federal civil rights law commonly known as the "Ku Klux Klan law" cannot be used to halt blockades of clinics. (Court on Clinic Blockades, Historic Documents of 1993, p. 93)

Debate Over Killing Doctors

The Court's RICO decision came amid a growing debate within the anti-abortion movement over the proper tactics to use to prevent abortions. While many in the movement worked to change laws and engaged in peaceful protests, a loud minority openly advocated killing doctors who performed abortions, claiming that such murders were morally justified by the Bible. Just six months after the Court's ruling, Paul J. Hill, an outspoken advocate of killing doctors, shot to death Dr. John Bayard Britton outside a women's clinic in Pensacola, Florida. Hill also killed James H. Barrett, who was serving as an escort for the doctor, and wounded Barrett's wife, June, who also was an escort. Hill was a former minister in the Presbyterian Church in America and the Orthodox Presbyterian Church. The killing of Barrett was the second murder of an abortion doctor in Pensacola in seventeen months.

While most antiabortion leaders issued statements denouncing the attack on Britton and his escorts, others said such attacks could become more common. "This may be the start of the new civil war everyone has been talking about," said Operation Rescue director Don Treshman in an interview with the New York Times. *"As a result of the Clinton Administration's oppressive efforts to stop even peaceful pro-life activities, I fear there will be more bombings and shootings. Up to now, the killings have been on one side, with 30 million dead babies and hundreds of dead and maimed mothers. On the other side, there are two dead doctors. Maybe the balance is going to start to shift."*

The day after the attack on Britton and his escorts, the Federal Bureau of Investigation opened a preliminary inquiry into allegations that attacks on clinics and doctors were part of a conspiracy among antiabortion militants. The investigation focused on a number of leaders who signed a letter saying it was proper to kill doctors who performed abortions. Abortion rights supporters said such an investigation was long overdue. "We believe there is a nationwide conspiracy," said Kim Gandy, executive vice president of NOW. "The Justice Department and the FBI do not have a handle on it yet. They don't know the extent of the problem."

In June, the Supreme Court handed down a second major abortion decision, ruling 6 to 3 that judges could establish small buffer zones around abortion clinics to keep protesters from blocking access to the clinics. (Supreme Court on Abortion Clinic Protests, p. 311)

> *Following are excerpts from the majority and concurring opinions in the Supreme Court's ruling January 24, 1994, in* National Organization for Women v. Scheidler, *upholding the use of the Racketeer Influenced and Corrupt Organizations (RICO) law in suits to curb antiabortion protests:*

No. 92-780

National Organization for Women,
Inc., etc., et al., Petitioners
v.
Joseph Scheidler et al.

On writ of certiorari to the United
States Court of Appeals for the
Seventh Circuit

[January 24, 1994]

CHIEF JUSTICE REHNQUIST delivered the opinion of the Court.

We are required once again to interpret the provisions of the Racketeer Influenced and Corrupt Organizations (RICO) chapter of the Organized Crime Control Act of 1970. Section 1962(c) prohibits any person associated with an enterprise from conducting its affairs through a pattern of racketeering activity. We granted certiorari to determine whether RICO requires proof that either the racketeering enterprise or the predicate acts of racketeering were motivated by an economic purpose. We hold that RICO requires no such economic motive.

I

Petitioner National Organization for Women, Inc. (NOW) is a national non-profit organization that supports the legal availability of abortion; petitioners Delaware Women's Health Organization, Inc. (DWHO) and Summit Women's Health Organization, Inc. (SWHO) are health care centers that perform abortions and other medical procedures. Respondents are a coalition of antiabortion groups called the Pro-Life Action Network (PLAN), Joseph Scheidler and other individuals and organizations that oppose legal abortion, and a medical laboratory that formerly provided services to the two petitioner health care centers.

Petitioners sued respondents in the United States District Court for the Northern District of Illinois, alleging violations of the Sherman Act and RICO's §§ 1962(a), (c), and (d), as well as several pendent state-law claims stemming from the activities of antiabortion protesters at the clinics. According to respondent Scheidler's congressional testimony, these protesters aim to shut down the clinics and persuade women not to have abortions. Petitioners sought injunctive relief, along with treble damages, costs, and attorneys' fees. They later amended their complaint, and pursuant to local rules, filed a "RICO Case Statement" that further detailed the enterprise, the pattern of racketeering, the victims of the racketeering activity, and the participants involved.

The amended complaint alleged that respondents were members of a nationwide conspiracy to shut down abortion clinics through a pattern of racketeering activity including extortion in violation of the Hobbs Act. Section

29

1951(b)(2) defines extortion as "the obtaining of property from another, with his consent, induced by wrongful use of actual or threatened force, violence, or fear, or under color of official right." Petitioners alleged that respondents conspired to use threatened or actual force, violence or fear to induce clinic employees, doctors, and patients to give up their jobs, give up their economic right to practice medicine, and give up their right to obtain medical services at the clinics. Petitioners claimed that this conspiracy "has injured the business and/or property interests of the [petitioners]." According to the amended complaint, PLAN constitutes the alleged racketeering "enterprise" for purposes of § 1962(c).

The District Court dismissed the case pursuant to Federal Rule of Civil Procedure 12(b)(6). Citing *Eastern Railroad Presidents Conference* v. *Noerr Motor Freight, Inc.* (1961), it held that since the activities alleged "involve[d] political opponents, not commercial competitors, and political objectives, not marketplace goals," the Sherman Act did not apply. It dismissed petitioners' RICO claims under § 1962(a) because the "income" alleged by petitioners consisted of voluntary donations from persons opposed to abortion which "in no way were derived from the pattern of racketeering alleged in the complaint." The District Court then concluded that petitioners failed to state a claim under § 1962(c) since "an economic motive requirement exists to the extent that some profit-generating purpose must be alleged in order to state a RICO claim." Finally, it dismissed petitioners' RICO conspiracy claim under § 1962(d) since petitioners' other RICO claims could not stand.

The Court of Appeals affirmed. As to the RICO counts, it agreed with the District Court that the voluntary contributions received by respondents did not constitute income derived from racketeering activities for purposes of § 1962(a). It adopted the analysis of the Court of Appeals for the Second Circuit in *United States* v. *Ivic*, which found an "economic motive" requirement implicit in the "enterprise" element of the offense. The Court of Appeals determined that "non-economic crimes committed in furtherance of non-economic motives are not within the ambit of RICO." Consequently, petitioners failed to state a claim under § 1962(c). The Court of Appeals also affirmed dismissal of the RICO conspiracy claim under § 1962(d).

We granted certiorari (1993) to resolve a conflict among the courts of appeals on the putative economic motive requirement of 18 U.S.C. § 1962(c) and (d).

II [omitted]

III

. . . Section 1962(c) makes it unlawful "for any person employed by or associated with any enterprise engaged in, or the activities of which affect, interstate or foreign commerce, to conduct or participate, directly or indirectly, in the conduct of such enterprise's affairs through a pattern of racketeering activity or collection of unlawful debt." Section 1961(1) defines "pattern of racketeering activity" to include conduct that is "chargeable" or "indictable" under a host of state and federal laws. RICO broadly defines "enterprise" in § 1961(4) to "includ[e] any individual, partnership, corporation, association, or other legal entity, and any union or group of individuals associated in fact although not a legal entity." Nowhere in either § 1962(c), or in the RICO definitions in § 1961, is there any indication that an economic motive is required.

The phrase "any enterprise engaged in, or the activities of which affect, interstate or foreign commerce" comes the closest of any language in subsection (c) to suggesting a need for an economic motive. Arguably an enterprise engaged in interstate or foreign commerce would have a profit-seeking motive, but the language in § 1962(c) does not stop there; it includes enterprises whose activities "affect" interstate or foreign commerce. Webster's Third New International Dictionary 35 (1969) defines "affect" as "to have a detrimental influence on—used especially in the phrase *affecting commerce*." An enterprise surely can have a detrimental influence on interstate or foreign commerce without having its own profit-seeking motives.

The Court of Appeals thought that the use of the term "enterprise" in §§ 1962(a) and (b), where it is arguably more tied in with economic motivation, should be applied to restrict the breadth of use of that term in § 1962(c). . . .

We do not believe that the usage of the term "enterprise" in subsections (a) and (b) leads to the inference that an economic motive is required in subsection (c). The term "enterprise" in subsections (a) and (b) plays a different role in the structure of those subsections than it does in subsection (c). Section 1962(a) provides that it "shall be unlawful for any person who has received any income derived, directly or indirectly, from a pattern of racketeering activity . . . to use or invest, directly or indirectly, any part of such income, or the proceeds of such income, in acquisition of any interest in, or the establishment or operation of, any enterprise which is engaged in, or the activities of which affect, interstate or foreign commerce." Correspondingly, § 1962(b) states that it "shall be unlawful for any person through a pattern of racketeering activity or through collection of an unlawful debt to acquire or maintain, directly or indirectly, any interest in or control of any enterprise which is engaged in, or the activities of which affect, interstate or foreign commerce." The "enterprise" referred to in subsections (a) and (b) is thus something acquired through the use of illegal activities or by money obtained from illegal activities. The enterprise in these subsections is the victim of unlawful activity and may very well be a "profit-seeking" entity that represents a property interest and may be acquired. But the statutory language in subsections (a) and (b) does not mandate that the enterprise be a "profit-seeking" entity; it simply requires that the enterprise be an entity that was acquired through illegal activity or the money generated from illegal activity.

By contrast, the "enterprise" in subsection (c) connotes generally the vehicle through which the unlawful pattern of racketeering activity is committed, rather than the victim of that activity. Subsection (c) makes it unlawful for "any person employed by or associated with any enterprise . . . to conduct or participate . . . in the conduct of such enterprise's affairs through a pattern of

racketeering activity. . . ." Consequently, since the enterprise in subsection
(c) is not being acquired, it need not have a property interest that can be
acquired nor an economic motive for engaging in illegal activity; it need only
be an association in fact that engages in a pattern of racketeering activity.
Nothing in subsections (a) and (b) directs us to a contrary conclusion.

The Court of Appeals also relied on the reasoning of *United States* v.
Bagaric (1983) to support its conclusion that subsection (c) requires an economic motive. In upholding the dismissal of a RICO claim against a political
terrorist group, the *Bagaric* court relied in part on the congressional statement of findings which prefaces RICO and refers to the activities of groups
that "drain billions of dollars from America's economy by unlawful conduct
and the illegal use of force, fraud, and corruption." The Court of Appeals for
the Second Circuit decided that the sort of activity thus condemned required
an economic motive.

We do not think this is so. Respondents and the two courts of appeals, we
think, overlook the fact that predicate acts, such as the alleged extortion, may
not benefit the protestors financially but still may drain money from the economy by harming businesses such as the clinics which are petitioners in this
case.

We also think that the quoted statement of congressional findings is a
rather thin reed upon which to base a requirement of economic motive neither expressed nor, we think, fairly implied in the operative sections of the
Act. . . .

The Court of Appeals also found persuasive guidelines for RICO prosecutions issued by the Department of Justice in 1981. The guidelines provided
that a RICO indictment should not charge an association as an enterprise,
unless the association exists "for the purpose of maintaining operations directed toward an *economic* goal. . . ." The Second Circuit . . . believed these
guidelines were entitled to deference under administrative law principles.
Whatever may be the appropriate deference afforded to such internal rules,
for our purposes we need note only that the Department of Justice amended
its guidelines in 1984. The amended guidelines provide that an association-in-
fact enterprise must be "directed toward an economic *or other identifiable
goal*" (emphasis added).

Both parties rely on legislative history to support their positions. We believe the statutory language is unambiguous, and find in the parties' submis-
sions respecting legislative history no such "clearly expressed legislative intent to the contrary" that would warrant a different construction.

Respondents finally argue that the result here should be controlled by the
rule of lenity in criminal cases. But the rule of lenity applies only when an
ambiguity is present. . . . We simply do not think there is an ambiguity here
which would suffice to invoke the rule of lenity. . . .

We therefore hold that petitioners may maintain this action if respondents
conducted the enterprise through a pattern of racketeering activity. The questions of whether the respondents committed the requisite predicate acts, and

whether the commission of these acts fell into a pattern, are not before us. We hold only that RICO contains no economic motive requirement.

The judgment of the Court of Appeals is accordingly

Reversed.

JUSTICE SOUTER, with whom JUSTICE KENNEDY joins, concurring.

I join the Court's opinion and write separately to explain why the First Amendment does not require reading an economic-motive requirement into RICO, and to stress that the Court's opinion does not bar First Amendment challenges to RICO's application in particular cases.

Several respondents and *amici* argue that we should avoid the First Amendment issues that could arise from allowing RICO to be applied to protest organizations by construing the statute to require economic motivation, just as we have previously interpreted other generally applicable statutes so as to avoid First Amendment problems. The argument is meritless in this case . . . for this principle of statutory construction applies only when the meaning of a statute is in doubt and here "the statutory language is unambiguous."

Even if the meaning of RICO were open to debate, however, it would not follow that the statute ought to be read to include an economic-motive requirement, since such a requirement would correspond only poorly to free-speech concerns. Respondents and *amici* complain that, unless so limited, the statute permits an ideological organization's opponents to label its vigorous expression as RICO predicate acts, thereby availing themselves of powerful remedial provisions that could destroy the organization. But an economic-motive requirement would protect too much with respect to First Amendment interests, since it would keep RICO from reaching ideological entities whose members commit acts of violence we need not fear chilling. An economic-motive requirement might also prove to be underprotective, in that entities engaging in vigorous but fully protected expression might fail the proposed economic-motive test . . . and so be left exposed to harassing RICO suits.

An economic-motive requirement is, finally, unnecessary, because legitimate free-speech claims may be raised and addressed in individual RICO cases as they arise. . . . [N]othing in the Court's opinion precludes a RICO defendant from raising the First Amendment in its defense in a particular case.Conduct alleged to amount to Hobbs Act extortion, for example, or one of the other, somewhat elastic RICO predicate acts may turn out to be fully protected First Amendment activity, entitling the defendant to dismissal on that basis. And even in a case where a RICO violation has been validly established, the First Amendment may limit the relief that can be granted against an organization otherwise engaging in protected expression.

This is not the place to catalog the speech issues that could arise in a RICO action against a protest group, and I express no view on the possibility of a First Amendment claim by the respondents in this case. . . . But I think it prudent to notice that RICO actions could deter protected advocacy and to caution courts applying RICO to bear in mind the First Amendment interests that could be at stake.

STATE OF THE UNION ADDRESS AND REPUBLICAN RESPONSE

January 25, 1994

President Bill Clinton used his State of the Union speech to a joint session of Congress to urge passage of legislation that would provide health insurance for all Americans. In the speech's most dramatic moment, Clinton raised a pen and threatened to use it to veto any health care bill that did not include universal coverage. However, he also made it clear he was willing to negotiate on all other aspects of a health care plan.

Clinton said that Americans paid "more and more money for less and less care. Every year fewer and fewer Americans even get to choose their doctors. Every year doctors and nurses spend more time on paperwork and less time with patients because of the absolute bureaucratic nightmare the present system has become. This system is riddled with inefficiency, with abuse, with fraud, and everybody knows it."

The president had especially harsh words for insurance companies, which he said "call the shots. They pick whom they cover and how they cover them. They can cut off your benefits when you need your coverage the most. They are in charge."

Clinton also attacked those people, primarily Republicans, who contended that the nation did not have a health care crisis. He spoke of 58 million Americans who had no health insurance at all for at least part of each year, 81 million Americans whose preexisting conditions made it impossible or expensive for them to get insurance, and small businesses harmed by skyrocketing insurance costs. "So if any of you believe there's no crisis, you tell it to those people—because I can't," he said. Clinton also noted that it was a Republican president, Richard Nixon, who twenty years earlier first proposed employer-based private insurance for every American.

In a prod to the assembled members of Congress, Clinton pointed out that they enjoyed excellent health insurance provided by the American people. Those constituents deserve the same high-quality coverage, the president said.

What Clinton did not spell out in his speech was the timetable for providing universal health care coverage. Previously, White House aides had indicated that because of budget constraints, they would not object to phasing in the health care plan over a decade or even longer.

Clinton's emphasis on health care in the State of the Union speech was an attempt to get his health care plan back on track. After releasing the plan in September 1993, the administration did little to sell it.

Opponents were not so reticent. Led by the Health Insurance Association of America, a lobbying group for insurance companies, they unleashed a multimillion-dollar attack that included highly effective television ads claiming the plan would result in a huge governmental bureaucracy and less choice for Americans. Administration officials admitted that the ads confused and scared many people.

In his speech, Clinton also stressed the need for welfare reform. He admitted that passing both welfare and health care reform in the same year would be difficult, but said the two issues were intertwined. An estimated one million people were on welfare, Clinton said, because it was the only way they could get health care coverage for their children. "We have got solve the health care problem to have real welfare reform," the president said.

Crime, which polls showed was Americans' top concern, also was a major issue in Clinton's speech. The president endorsed legislation that would impose life prison sentences on people convicted of three violent crimes. However, the federal bill would have a limited impact because most violent crimes fall under the jurisdiction of the states. Clinton also called for putting more police officers on the streets.

Clinton used this State of the Union speech to touch on numerous other issues on his agenda, including education reform, improvements in the job training system, creation of the information superhighway, and campaign finance reform.

Republican Response

In the official Republican response, which was televised immediately after Clinton's speech, Senate Minority Leader Robert J. Dole of Kansas disputed the president's contention that the nation faced a health care crisis. "Our country has health care problems, but no health care crisis," he said. "But we will have a crisis if we take the president's medicine—a massive overdose of government control."

Dole, like most other Republicans, said that comprehensive reform was unnecessary. "We can fix our most pressing problems without performing a triple bypass operation on our health care system," he said.

Dole said the president's 1,342-page health care bill would create a huge bureaucracy. He held up a chart that he said showed what the health care bureaucracy would look like under Clinton's plan. "It's a big chart, containing 207 boxes," Dole said. "It would take a long time to explain—if I fully understood it myself."

Other Reaction

Others generally gave Clinton's speech positive reviews, although there was some concern on Capitol Hill about Clinton's pledge to veto any health care bill that did not include universal coverage. Some said the threat would hurt efforts to work out a compromise with Republicans in the Senate.

In an editorial, the Washington Post *praised Clinton for giving "a strong speech." The paper's TV critic, Tom Shales, was not so kind. "Clinton was hopscotching through a wish list and apparently trying to touch on every major and minor issue of our time," Shales wrote. "It was too much and not enough, a drib here and a drab there, and at times so oddly disorganized as to suggest he shuffled his index cards a few too many times." Shales called Clinton's effort "a State of the Union speech that seemed doomed to be forgotten within 24 hours, but perhaps most of them are."*

Clinton's First Year in Office

The State of the Union speech came at the end of Clinton's first full year in office, a year marked by both accomplishments and disappointments. The largest accomplishments included passage by Congress of the North American Free Trade Agreement; passage of the Brady Bill, which required a five-day waiting period before a person could buy a gun; passage of the Family and Medical Leave Act, which gave workers time off for the birth or adoption of a child or for family emergencies; approval of higher taxes on the richest Americans and a boost in the gasoline tax; approval of a national service program; and the overturning of bans on fetal tissue research and abortion counseling at clinics that received federal funds.

The major disappointments of his first full year in office included problems in nominating an attorney general, which took three tries; the resignation of Defense Secretary Les Aspin after less than a year on the job; confusion over how to push forward the health care plan; problems in quickly filling administrative jobs; and controversy over a compromise that allowed homosexuals to serve in the military as long as they did not tell anyone they were homosexual.

After one year in office Clinton and his wife, Hillary, also found themselves under increasing scrutiny for their alleged roles in a complex affair dubbed "Whitewater," which involved a failed savings and loan and land deals made while Clinton was governor of Arkansas. Clinton steadfastly maintained that he and his wife had done nothing wrong, but the growing clamor over Whitewater threatened to sidetrack the president's legislative agenda.

Following are the White House text of President Bill Clinton's State of the Union address, as delivered to a joint session of Congress on January 25, 1994, and the text of the televised Republican response by Senate Minority Leader Robert J. Dole of Kansas:

STATE OF THE UNION ADDRESS

Thank you very much. Mr. Speaker, Mr. President, members of the 103rd Congress, my fellow Americans:

I'm not at all sure what speech is in the TelePrompter tonight—but I hope we can talk about the state of the Union.

I ask you to begin by recalling the memory of the giant who presided over this Chamber with such force and grace. Tip O'Neill liked to call himself "a man of the House." And he surely was that. But, even more, he was a man of the people, a bricklayer's son who helped to build the great American middle class. Tip O'Neill never forgot who he was, where he came from, or who sent him here. Tonight he's smiling down on us for the first time from the Lord's Gallery. But in his honor, may we, too, always remember who we are, where we come from, and who sent us here.

If we do that we will return over and over again to the principle that if we simply give ordinary people equal opportunity, quality education, and a fair shot at the American Dream, they will do extraordinary things.

We gather tonight in a world of changes so profound and rapid that all nations are tested. Our American heritage has always been to master such change, to use it to expand opportunity at home and our leadership abroad. But for too long, and in too many ways, that heritage was abandoned, and our country drifted.

For 30 years, family life in America has been breaking down. For 20 years, the wages of working people have been stagnant or declining. For the 12 years of trickle-down economics, we built a false prosperity on a hollow base as our national debt quadrupled. From 1989 to 1992, we experienced the slowest growth in a half century. For too many families, even when both parents were working, the American Dream has been slipping away.

In 1992, the American people demanded that we change. A year ago I asked all of you to join me in accepting responsibility for the future of our country. Well, we did. We replaced drift and deadlock with renewal and reform. And I want to thank every one of you here who heard the American people, who broke gridlock, who gave them the most successful teamwork between a President and a Congress in 30 years.

This Congress produced a budget that cut the deficit by half a trillion dollars, cut spending and raised income taxes on only the wealthiest Americans. This Congress produced tax relief for millions of low income workers to reward work over welfare. It produced NAFTA. It produced the Brady bill, now the Brady law. And thank you, Jim Brady, for being here, and God bless you, sir.

This Congress produced tax cuts to reduce the taxes of nine out of 10 small businesses who use the money to invest more and create jobs.

It produced more research and treatment for AIDS, more childhood immunizations, more support for women's health research, more affordable college loans for the middle class; a new national service program for those who want to give something back to their country and their communities for higher education; a dramatic increase in high-tech investments to move us from a defense to a domestic high-tech economy. This Congress produced a new law, the Motor Voter bill, to help millions of people register to vote. It produced Family and Medical Leave.

All passed. All signed into law with not one single veto. These accomplishments were all commitments I made when I sought this office. And, in fairness, they all had to be passed by you in this Congress. But I am persuaded that the real credit belongs to the people who sent us here, who pay our salaries, who hold our feet to the fire.

But what we do here is really beginning to change lives. Let me just give you one example. I will never forget what the Family and Medical Leave law meant to just one father I met early one Sunday morning in the White House.

It was unusual to see a family there touring early Sunday morning, but he had his wife and his three children there, one of them in a wheelchair. I came up, and after we had our picture taken and had a little visit, I was walking off and that man grabbed me by the arm and he said, "Mr. President, let me tell you something. My little girl here is desperately ill. She's probably not going to make it. But because of the Family Leave law, I was able to take time off to spend with her—the most important time I ever spent in my life—without losing my job and hurting the rest of my family. It means more to me than I will ever be able to say. Don't you people up here ever think what you do doesn't make a difference. It does."

Though we are making a difference, our work has just begun. Many Americans still haven't felt the impact of what we've done. The recovery still hasn't touched every community or created enough jobs. Incomes are still stagnant; there's still too much violence and not enough hope in too many places. Abroad, the young democracies we are strongly supporting still face very difficult times and look to us for leadership. And so tonight, let us resolve to continue the journey of renewal; to create more and better jobs; to guarantee health security for all; to reward work over welfare; to promote democracy abroad; and to begin to reclaim our streets from violent crime and drugs and gangs; to renew our own American community.

Last year we began to put our house in order by tackling the budget deficit that was driving us toward bankruptcy. We cut $255 billion in spending, including entitlements, and over 340 separate budget items. We froze domestic spending and used honest budget numbers.

Led by the Vice President, we launched a campaign to reinvent government. We cut staff, cut perks, even trimmed the fleet of federal limousines. After years of leaders whose rhetoric attacked bureaucracy but whose actions expanded it, we will actually reduce it by 252,000 people over the next five years. By the time we have finished, the federal bureaucracy will be at its lowest point in 30 years.

Because the deficit was so large and because they benefited from tax cuts in the 1980s, we did ask the wealthiest Americans to pay more to reduce the deficit. So on April 15th, the American people will discover the truth about what we did last year on taxes. Only the top 1—yes, listen—the top 1.2 percent of Americans, as I said all along, will pay higher income tax rates. Let me repeat—only the wealthiest 1.2 percent of Americans will face higher income tax rates and no one else will. And that is the truth.

Of course, there were, as there always are in politics, naysayers who said this plan wouldn't work. But they were wrong. When I became President the experts predicted that next year's deficit would be $300 billion. But because we acted, those same people now say the deficit is going to be under $180 billion—40 percent lower then was previously predicted.

Our economic program has helped to produce the lowest core inflation rate and the lowest interest rates in 20 years. And because those interest rates are down, business investment and equipment is growing at seven times the rate of the previous four years; auto sales are way up; home sales are at a record high. Millions of Americans have refinanced their homes, and our economy has produced 1.6 million private sector jobs in 1993—more than were created in the previous four years combined.

The people who supported this economic plan should be proud of its early results. Proud. But everyone in this chamber should know and acknowledge that there is more to do.

Next month I will send you one of the toughest budgets ever presented to Congress. It will cut spending in more than 300 programs, eliminate 100 domestic programs, and reform the ways in which governments buy goods and services. This year we must again make the hard choices to live within the hard spending ceilings we have set. We must do it. We have proved we can bring the deficit down without choking off recovery, without punishing seniors or the middle class, and without putting our national security at risk. If you will stick with this plan, we will post three consecutive years of declining deficits for the first time since Harry Truman lived in the White House. And once again, the buck stops here.

Our economic plan also bolsters our strength and our credibility around the world. Once we reduced the deficit and put the steel back into our competitive edge, the world echoed with the sound of falling trade barriers. In one year, with NAFTA, with GATT, with our efforts in Asia and the National Export Strategy, we did more to open world markets to American products than at any time in the last two generations.

That means more jobs and rising living standards for the American people; low deficits; low inflation; low interest rates; low trade barriers and high investments. These are the building blocks of our recovery. But if we want to take full advantage of the opportunities before us in the global economy, you all know we must do more.

As we reduce defense spending, I ask Congress to invest more in the technologies of tomorrow. Defense conversion will keep us strong militarily and create jobs for our people here at home.

As we protect our environment, we must invest in the environmental technologies of the future which will create jobs. This year we will fight for a revitalized Clean Water Act and a Safe Drinking Water Act and a reformed

Superfund program. And the Vice President is right—we must also work with the private sector to connect every classroom, every clinic, every library, every hospital in America into a national information superhighway by the year 2000.

Think of it—instant access to information will increase productivity, will help to educate our children. It will provide better medical care. It will create jobs. And I call on the Congress to pass legislation to establish that information superhighway this year.

As we expand opportunity and create jobs, no one can be left out. We must continue to enforce fair lending and fair housing and all civil rights laws, because America will never be complete in its renewal until everyone shares in its bounty.

But we all know, too, we can do all these things—put our economic house in order, expand world trade, target the jobs of the future, guarantee equal opportunity—but if we're honest, we'll all admit that this strategy still cannot work unless we also give our people the education, training and skills they need to seize the opportunities of tomorrow.

We must set tough, world-class academic and occupational standards for all our children and give our teachers and students the tools they need to meet them. Our Goals 2000 proposal will empower individual school districts to experiment with ideas like chartering their schools to be run by private corporations, or having more public school choice—to do whatever they wish to do as long as we measure every school by one high standard: Are our children learning what they need to know to compete and win in the global economy?

Goals 2000 links world-class standards to grass-roots reforms. And I hope Congress will pass it without delay.

Our School to Work Initiative will for the first time link school to the world of work, providing at least one year of apprenticeship beyond high school. After all, most of the people we're counting on to build our economic future won't graduate from college. It's time to stop ignoring them and start empowering them.

We must literally transform our out-dated unemployment system into a new reemployment system. The old unemployment system just sort of kept you going while you waited for your old job to come back. We've got to have a new system to move people into new and better jobs because most of those old jobs just don't come back. And we know that the only way to have real job security in the future, to get a good job with a growing income, is to have real skills and the ability to learn new ones. So we've got to streamline today's patchwork of training programs and make them a source of new skills for our people who lose their jobs.

Reemployment, not unemployment, must become the centerpiece of our economic renewal. I urge you to pass it in this session of Congress.

And just as we must transform our unemployment system, so must we also revolutionize our welfare system. It doesn't work. It defies our values as a nation. If we value work, we can't justify a system that makes welfare more attractive than work if people are worried about losing their health care. If we value responsibility, we can't ignore the $34 billion in child support absent parents ought to be paying to millions of parents who are taking care of their children. If we value strong families, we can't perpetuate a system that actually penalizes those who stay together.

Can you believe that a child who has a child gets more money from the government for leaving home than for staying home with a parent or a grandparent? That's not just bad policy, it's wrong. And we ought to change it.

I worked on this problem for years before I became President, with other governors and with members of Congress of both parties and with the previous administration of another party. I worked on it with people who were on welfare—lots of them. And I want to say something to everybody here who cares about this issue. The people who most want to change this system are the people who are dependent on it. They want to get off welfare. They want to go back to work. They want to do right by their kids.

I once had a hearing when I was a governor and I brought in people on welfare from all over America who had found their way to work. The woman from my state who testified was asked this question: What's the best thing about being off welfare and in a job? And, without blinking an eye, she looked at 40 governors and she said, "When my boy goes to school and they say what does your mother do for a living, he can give an answer." These people want a better system and we ought to give it to them.

Last year we began this. We gave the states more power to innovate because we know that a lot of great ideas come from outside Washington, and many states are already using it. Then this Congress took a dramatic step. Instead of taxing people with modest incomes into poverty, we helped them to work their way out of poverty by dramatically increasing the earned income tax credit. It will lift 15 million working families out of poverty, rewarding work over welfare, making it possible for people to be successful workers and successful parents. Now that's real welfare reform.

But there is more to be done. This spring I will send you a comprehensive welfare reform bill that builds on the Family Support Act of 1988 and restores the basic values of responsibility. We'll say to teenagers, if you have a child out of wedlock, we will no longer give you a check to set up a separate household. We want families to stay together. Say to absent parents who aren't paying their child support, if you're not providing for your children, we'll garnish your wages, suspend your license, track you across state lines, and if necessary, make some of you work off what you owe.

People who bring children into this world cannot and must not walk away from them. But to all those who depend on welfare, we should offer ultimately a simple compact. We'll provide the support, the job training, the child care you need for up to two years. But after that, anyone who can work must—in the private sector, wherever possible; in community services, if necessary. That's the only way we'll ever make welfare what it ought to be—a second chance, not a way of life.

I know it will be difficult to tackle welfare reform in 1994 at the same time we tackle health care. But let me point out, I think it is inevitable and imperative. It is estimated that one million people are on welfare today because it's the only way they can get health care coverage for their children. Those who choose to leave welfare for jobs without health benefits—and many entry level jobs don't have health benefits—find themselves in the incredible position of paying taxes that help to pay for health care coverage for those who made the other choice to stay on welfare. No wonder people leave work and go back to welfare to get health care coverage. We have got to solve the health care problem to have real welfare reform.

So this year, we will make history by reforming the health care system. And I would say to you, all of you, my fellow public servants, this is another issue where the people are way ahead of the politicians. That may not be popular with either party, but it happens to be the truth.

You know, the First Lady has received now almost a million letters from people all across America and from all walks of life. I'd like to share just one of them with you.

Richard Anderson of Reno, Nevada, lost his job and, with it, his health insurance. Two weeks later, his wife, Judy, suffered a cerebral aneurysm. He rushed her to the hospital, where she stayed in intensive care for 21 days.

The Andersons' bills were over $120,000. Although Judy recovered and Richard went back to work, at $8 an hour, the bills were too much for them and they were literally forced into bankruptcy.

"Mrs. Clinton," he wrote to Hillary, "no one in the United States of America should have to lose everything they've worked for all their lives because they were unfortunate enough to become ill."

It was to help the Richard and Judy Andersons of America that the First Lady and so many others have worked so hard and so long on this health care reform issue. We owe them our thanks and our action.

I know there are people here who say there's no health care crisis. Tell it to Richard and Judy Anderson. Tell it to the 58 million Americans who have no coverage at all for some time each year. Tell it to the 81 million Americans with those preexisting conditions—those folks are paying more or they can't get insurance at all, or they can't ever change their jobs because they or someone in their family has one of those preexisting conditions. Tell it to the small businesses burdened by the skyrocketing cost of insurance. Most small businesses cover their employees, and they pay on average 35 percent more in premiums than big businesses or government. Or tell it to the 76 percent of insured Americans, three out of four whose policies have lifetime limits. And that means they can find themselves without any coverage at all just when they need it the most.

So if any of you believe there's no crisis, you tell it to those people—because I can't.

There are some people who literally do not understand the impact of this problem on people's lives. And all you have to do is go out and listen to them. Just go talk to them anywhere in any congressional district in this country. They're Republicans and Democrats and independents—it doesn't have a lick to do with party.

They think we don't get it. And it's time we show them that we do get it.

From the day we began, our health care initiative has been designed to strengthen what is good about our health care system: the world's best health care professionals, cutting edge research and wonderful research institutions, Medicare for older Americans. None of this—none of it should be put at risk.

But we're paying more and more money for less and less care. Every year fewer and fewer Americans even get to choose their doctors. Every year doctors and nurses spend more time on paperwork and less time with patients because of the absolute bureaucratic nightmare the present system has become. This system is riddled with inefficiency, with abuse, with fraud, and everybody knows it.

In today's health care system, insurance companies call the shots. They pick whom they cover and how they cover them. They can cut off your benefits when you need your coverage the most. They are in charge.

What does it mean? It means every night millions of well-insured Americans go to bed just an illness, an accident or a pink slip away from having no coverage or financial ruin. It means every morning millions of Americans go to work without any health insurance at all—something the workers in no other advanced country in the world do. It means that every year, more and more hard-working people are told to pick a new doctor because their boss has had to pick a new plan. And countless others turn down better jobs because they know if they take the better job, they will lose their health insurance.

If we just let the health care system continue to drift, our country will have people with less care, fewer choices and higher bills.

Now, our approach protects the quality of care and people's choices. It builds on what works today in the private sector—to expand employer-based coverage, to guarantee private insurance for every American. And I might say, employer-based private insurance for every American was proposed 20 years ago by President Richard Nixon to the United States Congress. It was a good idea then, and it's a better idea today.

Why do we want guaranteed private insurance? Because right now nine out of 10 people who have insurance get it through their employers. And that should continue. And if your employer is providing good benefits at reasonable prices, that should continue, too. That ought to make the Congress and the President feel better.

Our goal is health insurance everybody can depend on—comprehensive benefits that cover preventive care and prescription drugs; health premiums that don't just explode when you get sick or you get older; the power no matter how small your business is to choose dependable insurance at the same competitive rates governments and big business get today; one simple form for people who are sick; and, most of all, the freedom to choose a plan and the right to choose your own doctor.

Our approach protects older Americans. Every plan before the Congress proposes to slow the growth of Medicare. The difference is this: We believe those savings should be used to improve health care for senior citizens. Medicare must be protected, and it should cover prescription drugs, and we

43

should take the first steps in covering long-term care.

To those who would cut Medicare without protecting seniors, I say the solution to today's squeeze on middle-class working people's health care is not to put the squeeze on middle-class retired people's health care. We can do better than that.

When it's all said and done, it's pretty simple to me. Insurance ought to mean what it used to mean—you pay a fair price for security, and when you get sick, health care's always there, no matter what.

Along with the guarantee of health security, we all have to admit, too, there must be more responsibility on the part of all of us in how we use this system. People have to take their kids to get immunized. We should all take advantage of preventive care. We must all work together to stop the violence that explodes our emergency rooms. We have to practice better health habits, and we can't abuse the system. And those who don't have insurance under our approach will get coverage, but they'll have to pay something for it, too. The minority of businesses that provide no insurance at all, and in so doing, shift the cost of the care of their employees to others, should contribute something. People who smoke should pay more for a pack of cigarettes. Everybody can contribute something if we want to solve the health care crisis. There can't be any more something for nothing. It will not be easy but it can be done.

Now, in the coming months I hope very much to work with both Democrats and Republicans to reform a health care system by using the market to bring down costs and to achieve lasting health security. But if you look at history we see that for 60 years this country has tried to reform health care. President Roosevelt tried. President Truman tried. President Nixon tried. President Carter tried. Every time the special interests were powerful enough to defeat them. But not this time.

I know that facing up to these interests will require courage. It will raise critical questions about the way we finance our campaigns and how lobbyists yield their influence. The work of change, frankly, will never get any easier until we limit the influence of well-financed interests who profit from this current system. So I also must now call on you to finish the job both Houses began last year by passing tough and meaningful campaign finance reform and lobby reform legislation this year.

You know, my fellow Americans, this is really a test for all of us. The American people provide those of us in government service with terrific health care benefits at reasonable costs. We have health care that's always there. I think we need to give every hard-working, tax-paying American the same health care security they have already given to us.

I want to make this very clear. I am open, as I have said repeatedly, to the best ideas of concerned members of both parties. I have no special brief for any specific approach, even in our own bill, except this: If you send me legislation that does not guarantee every American private health insurance that can never be taken away, you will force me to take this pen, veto the legislation, and we'll come right back here and start all over again.

But I don't think that's going to happen. I think we're ready to act now. I believe that you're ready to act now. And if you're ready to guarantee every American the same health care that you have, health care that can never be taken away, now—not next year or the year after—now is the time to stand with the people who sent us here. Now.

As we take these steps together to renew our strength at home, we cannot turn away from our obligation to renew our leadership abroad. This is a promising moment. Because of the agreements we have reached this year, last year, Russia's strategic nuclear missiles soon will no longer be pointed at the United States, nor will we point ours at them. Instead of building weapons in space, Russian scientists will help us to build the international space station.

Of course, there are still dangers in the world—rampant arms proliferation, bitter regional conflicts, ethnic and nationalist tensions in many new democracies, severe environmental degradation the world over, and fanatics who seek to cripple the world's cities with terror. As the world's greatest power, we must, therefore, maintain our defenses and our responsibilities.

This year, we secured indictments against terrorists and sanctions against those who harbor them. We worked to promote environmentally sustainable economic growth. We achieved agreements with Ukraine, with Belarus, with Kazahkstan to eliminate completely their nuclear arsenal. We are working to achieve a Korean Peninsula free of nuclear weapons. We will seek early ratification of a treaty to ban chemical weapons worldwide. And earlier today, we joined with over 30 nations to begin negotiations on a comprehensive ban to stop all nuclear testing.

But nothing, nothing is more important to our security than our nation's armed forces. We honor their contributions, including those who are carrying out the longest humanitarian air lift in history in Bosnia; those who will complete their mission in Somalia this year and their brave comrades who gave their lives there.

Our forces are the finest military our nation has ever had. And I have pledged that as long as I am President, they will remain the best equipped, the best trained and the best prepared fighting force on the face of the Earth.

Last year I proposed a defense plan that maintains our post-Cold War security at a lower cost. This year many people urged me to cut our defense spending further to pay for other government programs. I said no. The budget I send to Congress draws the line against further defense cuts. It protects the readiness and quality of our forces.

Ultimately, the best strategy is to do that. We must not cut defense further. I hope the Congress without regard to party will support that position.

Ultimately, the best strategy to ensure our security and to build a durable peace is to support the advance of democracy elsewhere. Democracies don't attack each other, they make better trading partners and partners in diplomacy. That is why we have supported, you and I, the democratic reformers in Russia and in the other states of the former Soviet bloc. I applaud the bipartisan support this Congress provided last year for our initiatives to help Russia, Ukraine, and the other states through their epic transformations.

Our support of reform must combine patience for the enormity of the task and vigilance for our fundamental interest and values. We will continue to urge Russia and the other states to press ahead with economic reforms. And we will seek to cooperate with Russia to solve regional problems, while insisting that if Russian troops operate in neighboring states, they do so only when those states agree to their presence and in strict accord with international standards.

But we must also remember as these nations chart their own futures—and they must chart their own futures—how much more secure and more prosperous our own people will be if democratic and market reform succeed all across the former communist bloc. Our policy has been to support that move and that has been the policy of the Congress. We should continue it.

That is why I went to Europe earlier this month—to work with our European partners, to help to integrate all the former communist countries into a Europe that has a possibility of becoming unified for the first time in its entire history—its entire history—based on the simple commitments of all nations in Europe to democracy, to free markets and to respect for existing borders.

With our allies we have created a Partnership For Peace that invites states from the former Soviet bloc and other non-NATO members to work with NATO in military cooperation. When I met with Central Europe's leaders, including Lech Walesa and Vaclav Havel, men who put their lives on the line for freedom, I told them that the security of their region is important to our country's security.

This year we must also do more to support democratic renewal and human rights and sustainable development all around the world. We will ask Congress to ratify the new GATT accord. We will continue standing by South Africa as it works its way through its bold and hopeful and difficult transition to democracy. We will convene a summit of the Western Hemisphere's leaders from Canada to the tip of South America. And we will continue to press for the restoration of true democracy in Haiti.

And as we build a more constructive relationship with China, we must continue to insist on clear signs of improvement in that nation's human rights record.

We will also work for new progress toward the Middle East peace. Last year the world watched Yitzhak Rabin and Yassir Arafat at the White House when they had their historic handshake of reconciliation. But there is a long, hard road ahead. And on that road I am determined that I and our administration will do all we can to achieve a comprehensive and lasting peace for all the peoples of the region.

Now, there are some in our country who argue that with the Cold War over, America should turn its back on the rest of the world. Many around the world were afraid we would do just that. But I took this office on a pledge that had no partisan tinge to keep our nation secure by remaining engaged in the rest of the world. And this year, because of our work together—enacting NAFTA, keeping our military strong and prepared, supporting democracy abroad—we have reaffirmed America's leadership, America's engagement. And as a result, the American people are more secure than they were before.

But while Americans are more secure from threats abroad, I think we all know that in many ways we are less secure from threats here at home. Every day the national peace is shattered by crime. In Petaluma, California, an innocent slumber party gives way to agonizing tragedy for the family of Polly Klaas. An ordinary train ride on Long Island ends in a hail of 9-millimeter rounds. A tourist in Florida is nearly burned alive by bigots simply because he is black. Right here in our Nation's Capital, a brave young man named Jason White, a policeman, the son and grandson of policemen, is ruthlessly gunned down. Violent crime and the fear it provokes are crippling our society, limiting personal freedom and fraying the ties that bind us.

The crime bill before Congress gives you a chance to do something about it—a chance to be tough and smart. What does that mean? Let me begin by saying, I care a lot about this issue. Many years ago, when I started out in public life, I was the attorney general of my state. I served as a governor for a dozen years; I know what it's like to sign laws increasing penalties, to build more prison cells, to carry out the death penalty. I understand this issue. And it is not a simple thing.

First, we must recognize that most violent crimes are committed by a small percentage of criminals who too often break the laws even when they are on parole. Now those who commit crimes should be punished. And those who commit repeated, violent crimes should be told, when you commit a third violent crime, you will be put away, and put away for good. Three strikes, and you are out.

Second, we must take serious steps to reduce violence and prevent crime, beginning with more police officers and more community policing. We know right now that police who work the streets, know the folks, have the respect of the neighborhood kids, focus on high crime areas—we know that they are more likely to prevent crime as well as catch criminals. Look at the experience of Houston, where the crime rate dropped 17 percent in one year when that approach was taken.

Here tonight is one of those community policemen—a brave, young detective, Kevin Jett, whose beat is eight square blocks in one of the toughest neighborhoods in New York. Every day he restores some sanity and safety and a sense of values and connections to the people whose lives he protects. I'd like to ask him to stand up and be recognized tonight. Thank you, sir.

You will be given a chance to give the children of this country, the law-abiding working people of this country—and don't forget, in the toughest neighborhoods in this country, in the highest crime neighborhoods in this country, the vast majority of people get up every day and obey the law, pay their taxes, do their best to raise their kids. They deserve people like Kevin Jett. And you're going to be given a chance to give the American people another 100,000 of them well trained. And I urge you to do it.

You have before you crime legislation which also establishes a police corps to encourage young people to get an education and pay it off by serving as police officers; which encourages retiring military personnel to move into police forces, an inordinate resource for our country—one which has a safe schools provision which will give our young people the chance to walk to school in safety and to be in school in safety instead of dodging bullets. These are important things.

The third thing we have to do is to build on the Brady Bill—the Brady Law. To take further steps to keep guns out of the hands of criminals.

I want to say something about this issue. Hunters must always be free to hunt. Law-abiding adults should always be free to own guns to protect their homes. I respect that part of our culture, I grew up in it. But I want to ask the sportsmen and others who lawfully own guns to join us in this campaign to reduce gun violence. I say to you, I know you didn't create this problem, but we need your help to solve it. There is no sporting purpose on Earth that should stop the United States Congress from banishing assault weapons that out-gun police and cut down children.

Fourth, we must remember that drugs are a factor in an enormous percentage of crimes. Recent studies indicate, sadly, that drug use is on the rise again among our young people. The crime bill contains—all the crime bills contain—more money for drug treatment for criminal addicts, and boot camps for youthful offenders that include incentives to get off drugs and to stay off drugs.

Our administration's budget with all its cuts can paint a large increase in funding for drug treatment and drug education. You must pass them both. We need them desperately.

My fellow Americans, the problem of violence is an American problem. It has no partisan or philosophical element. Therefore, I urge you to find ways as quickly as possible to set aside partisan differences and pass a strong, smart, tough crime bill. But further, I urge you to consider this: As you demand tougher penalties for those who choose violence, let us also remember how we came to this sad point.

In our toughest neighborhoods, on our meanest streets, in our poorest rural areas, we have seen a stunning and simultaneous breakdown of community, family and work—the heart and soul of civilized society. This has created a vast vacuum which has been filled by violence and drugs and gangs. So I ask you to remember that even as we say no to crime, we must give people—especially our young people—something to say yes to.

Many of our initiatives—from job training to welfare reform to health care to national service—will help to rebuild distressed communities, to strengthen families, to provide work. But more needs to be done. That's what our community empowerment agenda is all about—challenging businesses to provide more investment through empowerment zones; ensuring banks will make loans in the same communities their deposits come from; passing legislation to unleash the power of capital through community development banks to create jobs—opportunity and hope where they're needed most.

I think you know that to really solve this problem we'll all have to put our heads together, leave our ideological armor aside and find some new ideas to do even more. And let's be honest; we all know something else too: Our problems go way beyond the reach of government. They're rooted in the loss of values, in the disappearance of work and the breakdown of our families and our communities.

My fellow Americans, we can cut the deficit, create jobs, promote democracy around the world, pass welfare reform and health care, pass the toughest crime bill in history, but still leave too many of our people behind.

The American people have got to want to change from within if we're going to bring back work and family and community. We cannot renew our country when within a decade more than half of the children will be born into families where there has been no marriage. We cannot renew this country when 13-year-old boys get semi-automatic weapons to shoot 9-year-olds for kicks. We can't renew our country when children are having children and the fathers walk away as if the kids don't amount to anything. We can't renew the country when our businesses eagerly look for new investments and new customers abroad, but ignore those people right here at home who would give anything to have their jobs and would gladly buy their products if they had the money to do it.

We can't renew our country unless more of us—I mean all of us—are willing to join the churches and the other good citizens—people like the black ministers I've worked with over the years, or the priests and the nuns I met at Our Lady of Help in East Los Angeles, or my good friend, Tony Campollo in Philadelphia—unless we're willing to work with people like that, people who are saving kids, adopting schools, making streets safer—all of us can do that. We can't renew our country until we realize that governments don't raise children, parents do.

Parents who know their children's teachers and turn off the television and help with the homework and teach their kids right from wrong—those kinds of parents can make all the difference. I know, I had one.

I'm telling you, we have got to stop pointing our fingers at these kids who have no future, and reach our hands out to them. Our country needs it, we need it, and they deserve it.

So I say to you tonight, let's give our children a future. Let us take away their guns and give them books. Let us overcome their despair and replace it with hope. Let us, by our example, teach them to obey the law, respect our neighbors, and cherish our values. Let us weave these sturdy threads into a new American community that can once more stand strong against the forces of despair and evil because everybody has a chance to walk into a better tomorrow.

Oh, there will be naysayers who fear that we won't be equal to the challenges of this time. But they misread our history, our heritage, even today's headlines. All those things tell us we can and we will overcome any challenge.

When the earth shook and fires raged in California, when I saw the Mississippi deluge the farmlands of the Midwest in a 500-year flood, when the century's bitterest cold swept from North Dakota to Newport News, it seemed as though the world itself was coming apart at the seams.

But the American people—they just came together. They rose to the occasion, neighbor helping neighbor, strangers risking life and limb to save total strangers—showing the better angels of our nature.

Let us not reserve the better angels only for natural disasters, leaving our deepest and most profound problems to petty political fighting. Let us instead be true to our spirit—facing facts, coming together, bringing hope and moving forward.

Tonight, my fellow Americans, we are summoned to answer a question as old as the republic itself: What is the state of our union? It is growing stronger, but it must be stronger still. With your help, and God's help, it will be.

Thank you and God bless America.

DOLE'S REPUBLICAN RESPONSE

Good evening. I'm Bob Dole, the Senate Republican leader. Tonight, I'm speaking for congressional Republicans, for Republican governors, state legislators, mayors and other elected officials, and I hope for you, if you believe as we do, that America's taxes should be lower, that the government should spend less, that the people—not the government—should control more, and that our armed forces must be strong.

Now, here in Congress we're the minority party. The Democrats have many more votes than we do in both the House and the Senate. So, when the president spoke tonight, and he did a good job, he knew that whatever he really wants he stands a good chance of getting because most Democrats will vote with him. And when Republicans believe President Clinton is moving America in the right direction, as he did with the North American Free Trade Agreement, then he can count on our votes and our cooperation, too.

But far more often than not, the president and his Democrat majority have taken what we believe is the wrong fork in the road, not just on one or two matters of policy, but on their entire approach to government. And health care is a good example.

The president and Mrs. Clinton deserve credit for starting the debate. It has been very helpful. Now, nearly a year later, we really better understand this most important issue. We know that America has the best health-care system in the world, that people from every corner of the globe come here when they need the very best treatment, and that our goal should be to ensure that every American has access to this system.

Of course, there are many Americans with a sick child or sick parent in real need, both in rural and urban America. Our country has health-care problems, but not a health-care crisis. But we will have a crisis if we take the president's medicine—a massive overdose of government control.

How massive? My colleague, Sen. Arlen Specter [R] of Pennsylvania, has prepared a chart of what the health-care bureaucracy would look like under the president's plan, and I'd like to show you this chart. It's a great big chart. It contains 207 boxes. It would take a long time to fully explain it, and frankly, I have difficulty understanding it myself.

Let me point out some of the new bureaucracies that the president's plan will create. Way up here is the National Health Board. Over here is the Advisory Commission on Regional Variations of Health Expenditures. And here's the National Institute for Health Care Workforce Development.

Now, you and I are way down here, way at the bottom. I don't know why we're not at the top, but we're at the bottom.

Now, the president's idea is to put a mountain of bureaucrats between you and your doctor. For example, if you or a family member want to receive care from a specialist or a clinic outside your own state—let's say you live in Kansas and you want to go to Minnesota—then you probably can't do it without asking for approval. And under his plan, information about your health and your treatment can be sent to a national data bank without your approval. And that's a compromise of privacy none of us should accept.

Now, these just are two examples, but there are many, many more. Clearly, the president is asking you to trust the government more than you trust your doctor and yourselves with your lives and the lives of your loved ones. More cost. Less choice. More taxes. Less quality. More government control. Less control for you and your family. That's what the president's government-run plan is likely to give you.

Now, we can fix our most pressing problems without performing a triple bypass operation on our health-care system. We can do it without the estimated $1 trillion gap—yes, $1 trillion gap—between the administration's own projections, their projections, of spending under the plan and the funds available to pay for it, and we can do it now. Republicans, and I believe many, many Democrats, are ready to vote for legislation containing some common-sense solutions—solutions like guaranteeing uninterrupted coverage to everyone who is insured, even if you leave or lose your job, and guaranteeing that your coverage cannot be denied because of a serious illness or pre-existing condition; giving relief to small businesses by allowing them to join together to buy insurance—that lowers the rates, that saves them money; giving individuals like yourselves who buy their own insurance a 100 percent tax deduction; changing the law to allow you to open your own medical savings account or to buy what we refer to or call medical IRAs; and helping uninsured low-income Americans pay for coverage through tax credits or vouchers; and, finally, cutting government red tape and reforming medical malpractice laws that make our health-care system so expensive.

Debate on the president's massive and complex program will continue for most of the year, but the changes I just mentioned can be made now, so why wait? Why not act to put you and your family in control of your health care right now?

This evening the president also spoke at length about crime, and he's right. We all must take responsibility as individuals. And after years of debate, many Democrats are now joining Republicans behind this view.

Criminals are not the victims of society; society is the victim of criminals. And the best way to make America's streets and schools and homes safer is to put violent criminals in jail and to keep them there. And most provisions of this bill do just that. It passed the Senate last November by a vote of 94-4.

Now let me give you just a few examples. Life imprisonment for those convicted of three violent felonies, call it three strikes and you're in, you're in for life; tough mandatory sentences for those who use a gun in the commission of a crime; violent juveniles will be treated as adults when they use a gun in a crime.

But as you know very well, just putting criminals behind bars is not enough. There is a big, big second step, and that's padlocking the revolving door, keeping violent criminals in jail for their entire sentence. A 20-year sentence should mean just that, 20 years or darned close to it. Not five, not 10, not even 15.

So this bill would authorize ten new regional prisons, federal prisons. But before states can send their violent criminals to those prisons, they must adopt truth-in-sentencing laws. In other words, if you do the crime, you are really going to do the time.

Now, the Senate has passed tough crime bills before, but every time we do, liberal congressional Democrats remove the toughest provisions, and that must not happen again. Republicans want President Clinton to sign the toughest bill possible, and I've got the toughest bill around this town in my hands right now. Here it is, here it is. We hope the House passes it; we hope the Senate . . . the president will sign it.

Now, the president used some tough, tough language tonight, and that's good, but will he follow through, and will he act on it? Will he insist on the tough provisions, like ten new regional federal prisons, like truth-in-sentencing laws, like [a] tough, mandatory sentence for using a gun, and the death penalty for drug kingpins?

Unfortunately, the administration has damaged its credibility on the crime issue by cutting the federal prison construction budget by 20 percent, and by the 94 percent cut in the drug czar's office. And yes, the talk in the administration of legalizing drugs doesn't help much, either.

Now, many people are confused when the president's actions appear different than his words. For example, the president talks about education, but he opposes school choice, which could give parents more control over the education of their children. He promised to "end welfare as we know it," yet everyone waits for his proposal.

In the meantime, Republicans here in Congress and Republican governors across the nation are fighting for changes that make work, self-sufficiency, and reducing illegitimacy top priorities.

The president promised a middle-class tax cut, yet he and his party imposed the largest tax increase in American history. This $255 billion tax increase was opposed by every Republican in the House and in the Senate. We hope his higher taxes will not cut short the economic recovery and declining interest rates that he inherited.

The two-year mark, coming at the end of this year, is when the economy usually starts to feel the results of a new administration's policies. Now instead of stifling growth and expansion through higher taxes and increased government regulations, Republicans would take America in a different direction, and we can do that through alternatives that reward risk-taking and the creation of new jobs, and that give our small-businessmen and women relief from the heavy hand of government.

Now, the president told you tonight that the deficit is projected to decrease next year, and that's true. After all, the largest tax increase in American history would decrease any deficit—temporarily. But in the words of [radio commentator] Paul Harvey, I want to tell you "the rest of the story." Under [Clinton's] budget, government spending will increase by at least $343 billion in the next five years, and in the same time period, the nonpartisan—let me repeat—the nonpartisan Congressional Budget Office projects that $1 trillion will be added to our national debt.

Now, the one place the president has cut drastically is precisely the wrong place—national security. Slashed to the lowest level since before Pearl Harbor. History tells us, and many of us know firsthand, that America cannot afford to have a hollow military, nor can we afford to let the United Nations dictate what is in America's national interest.

But I want to close tonight by talking about America, the greatest country on the face of the earth. I believe America has an enduring mission, a mission of leadership. Fifty years ago, when Hitler's tyranny was on the march, it was only because of strong American leadership that freedom was preserved. In the Cold War, for millions behind the Iron Curtain and in the many nations that depended on us to protect them, it was again only because of strong American leadership that freedom prevailed. And now, as countries that were tyrannies learn democracy, as people learn about free markets where a short time ago buying and selling without the state's permission was illegal, the world again waits and wants strong—and needs strong—American leadership so that freedom will endure.

You know, many times over the past few years, right here in this office in the Capitol, I've met with representatives from the new emerging democracies. Some were leaders of their countries. Some were ordinary citizens. Some had been in jail for many years for just speaking out in public. And they all told me about the same thing—some with tears in their eyes, some could hardly speak—and they all said, "We want to be like America." That's what they said. "We want to be like America."

In this great, good, and generous nation, the American mission endures here at home and around the world. We are its stewards, and it's up to us to ensure that, wherever the road divides, that America takes the right path, remains true to our mission of leadership, and remains the light and the hope of humanity.

Thank you. And to the people of Southern California, please know that all of us in Washington will be working with [Republican] Gov. [Pete] Wilson and your congressional delegation to provide the help you need.

And if you'd like a copy of this chart, just write Sen. Arlen Specter, care of the Capitol, Washington, D.C.

Thank you and good night.

SECRETARY OF ENERGY ON HUMAN RADIATION EXPERIMENTS
January 25, 1994

Promising a new openness in government, Secretary of Energy Hazel R. O'Leary on January 25 outlined steps that were being taken to review radiation experiments that government scientists conducted with human subjects during the Cold War. She made the comments in testimony before the Senate Committee on Governmental Affairs.

The experiments, conducted from the 1940s through the early 1970s, were aimed at finding out how radiation exposure would affect civilians and soldiers and how radioactive particles would spread through the environment. Some of the experiments involved releasing massive amounts of radioactive materials from nuclear weapons plants, injecting people with radioactive substances, requiring military planes to fly through radioactive clouds and then measuring the exposure received by the flight crews, and having soldiers watch atomic explosions from only a few thousand yards away and then marching them to the site of the blast shortly after the bomb detonated. In many cases, the human subjects did not know they were being used in experiments. Even when they consented to the experiments, they frequently were not told the exact nature and potential effects of the tests.

In her testimony, O'Leary said she was frequently asked why the experiments were allowed to occur. While not providing an answer, she said some people "have expressed the view that they were motivated by concern about a need to counter Soviet threats of nuclear war and [were conducted in] the atmosphere of secrecy that surrounded research in nuclear energy and ionizing radiation since the Manhattan Project." The Manhattan Project was the United States's effort to develop a nuclear bomb during World War II.

Experiments First Made Public in 1986

A veil of secrecy surrounded the tests until a 1986 congressional hearing uncovered evidence about some experiments. However, the real impetus for a new openness was a series of articles appearing in the Albuquerque Tribune *in 1993 that revealed that during the 1940s eighteen people had been injected with plutonium so that doctors could see how it moved through their bodies. Shortly after the articles appeared, agencies throughout the federal government started digging through their files in an effort to determine what tests had been conducted, whether the tests were conducted ethically, and whether participants should be compensated for any injuries they suffered.* (Radiation Tests, Historic Documents of 1993, p. 987)

In January 1994, President Bill Clinton created an Advisory Committee on Human Radiation Experiments to coordinate the government's investigation into past practices. In October, the committee issued a preliminary report on its investigation. The panel said it believed that thousands of tests had been conducted, a number many times higher than previous estimates. Dr. Ruth Faden, the committee chairman, told the New York Times *that the panel believed radiation had been deliberately released into the environment hundreds of times during dozens of experiments. Previously, scientists had only been aware of thirteen such experiments.*

Faden said that the panel had run into resistance during its investigation. The Department of Energy (DOE) and Defense Department allowed panel members to review documents about intentional releases of radiation but refused to declassify the documents. The panel sought broad declassification of documents to reassure the public that the government was not hiding anything. "We would like to make everything public," Faden said.

With the early phase of its study complete, in late 1994 the committee started examining the ethics of the experiments to see whether they met current standards. The panel was expected to release a final report in 1995.

Participants Seek Compensation

For people exposed to radiation during the experiments, two pressing questions remained: Would the government tell them about any current dangers they faced resulting from the past experiments, and would the government compensate them for any harm they suffered? On the first issue, O'Leary pledged in her testimony that human subjects and their families would receive information "as soon as it becomes available" and that they— or their descendants—would be notified if they were in danger of any health risks or in need of medical follow-up.

The issue of compensation was tougher, at least partially because it was difficult if not impossible to prove a cause-and-effect relationship between the experiments and health problems that may have developed years or decades later. "The range of federal responses under consideration include potential monetary compensation, medical follow-up, disclosure of detailed information, formal apologies or other recognition, and ongoing research, education and information programs," O'Leary said.

In response to press reports, O'Leary also revealed that the DOE and its contractors were currently conducting more than 200 tests involving human subjects. Other DOE officials told reporters that about 40 percent of those tests involved exposing people to radiation, generally at very low lev-

els. "As far as we have been able to ascertain, the Department is not conducting any experiments that violate medical [standards], ethical standards, or
the Nuremburg code," O'Leary told the committee. She said that full details
of the experiments would be made available in a public database by March.

*Following is the text of Energy Secretary Hazel R. O'Leary's
testimony January 25, 1994, to the Senate Committee on Governmental Affairs concerning human radiation experiments:*

I am pleased to have the opportunity to appear before the Committee this
morning. At the outset I want to recognize the long-standing and active interest of this Committee in the well-being of workers and members of the public
who are at risk due to radiation and other toxic exposures resulting from
nuclear weapons production. This Committee has done the public and the
Department of Energy a great service over the past several years through its
efforts to shed light on the range and complexity of occupational hazards and
environmental problems confronting the Department. I am therefore particularly pleased to come before you to speak about recent reports of potentially
unethical conduct involving experiments using radiation on human subjects
during the Cold War. As you know, this subject has generated intense public
and media attention over the past several weeks. During this time, I have spoken with many Americans around the country, some of whom were experimental subjects or the relatives of subjects. They have been deeply troubled,
as I was, by these reports.

I have been asked frequently why these activities were allowed to take
place. Some have expressed the view that they were motivated by concern
about a need to counter Soviet threats of nuclear war and the atmosphere of
secrecy that surrounded research in nuclear energy and ionizing radiation
since the Manhattan Project. With the end of the Cold War and President Clinton's strong commitment to openness in government these conditions have
changed dramatically.

This change has brought about a unique opportunity for the nation to debate important questions raised by some of the human radiation experiments—questions about the role of secrecy in a democratic society, and the
need for proper safeguards to ensure the rights of individuals to determine
their own fates. We must take the necessary steps to ensure all Americans—
whether they are uneducated or poor or mentally retarded or incarcerated—
that they are not being used unwittingly in federally-sponsored research.

The Clinton Administration is determined to disclose all records on experiments involving ionizing radiation on humans. In a moment, I will discuss the
steps we are taking to release information as quickly as possible, to ensure
that we have a serious, thoughtful debate about the lessons these experiments
teach us, and to make sure that the highest standards of ethical and scientific
conduct are followed in all research involving human beings.

As we examine this dark and narrow corner of scientific experimentation, we must keep in mind several points. As unsettling as some of these experiments were, and as feared as radiation may be to many people, it is important to remember that many lives have been saved using radiation in the diagnosis and treatment of disease. During the same Cold War period that some scientists were conducting these controversial experiments, other scientists were inventing vaccines against polio, new and effective treatments for cancer, and new ways of visualizing the human body with CAT and cardiac scans. Science itself is not at issue here. What is at issue is the secrecy with which some scientists may have practiced their craft.

I also want to caution the American public against inordinate fear of current research practices. Institutional Review Boards enforce strict requirements for informed consent of any human subjects involved in scientific experiments. It is difficult to conceive of the ethical abuses about which we've been hearing occurring today in the United States.

As I will describe, we are committed to a serious review of all experiments sponsored or carried out by government agencies that involved intentional human exposure to ionizing radiation. We will use the results of this review to try and repair any wrongs that might have been done, and will, if necessary, take action to make today's standards even more stringent.

The Department of Energy's Approach to Declassification

The important expanding involvement of members of the public, workers, scientists, and others in the activities of the Department of Energy has resulted in a significant increase in requests over the past few years for Departmental records, many of which are classified or contain restricted data. Nuclear proliferation remains, of course, a national security concern. However, dramatic changes over the past few years in the international arena have significantly reduced the classification requirements for much information and, after proper review, such information will be released to the public.

A significant number of Department of Energy records requiring systematic review are currently held by the National Archives and Records Administration. The Department of Energy has agreed to transfer additional Atomic Energy Commission records to the Archives. In order to deal with this large volume of classified records, the Department is providing the Archives with authorized reviewers to work in a systematic declassification program. We are also working closely with the Department of Defense to review appropriate information for declassification.

The benefits of our declassification initiative include an enhanced ability to fill in the blanks of Cold War history—including the public disclosure of documents relevant to radiation experiments; improved studies of the health and safety of Department workers and the public; and increased trust in government. Also, through this initiative, the United States sets an example for other nuclear nations to follow. We recognize, however, that there is a continued need to balance our declassification needs with our nonproliferation objectives.

State of Present Knowledge on Radiation Experiments

We do not yet know if the radiation experiments noted in the 1986 Congressional report by the House Energy, Conservation and Power Subcommittee and the experiments involving deliberate environmental releases discussed in the General Accounting Office report prepared for this Committee in December of last year comprise the bulk of experiments that might be subject to questions of scientific and ethical propriety. We also do not yet know the full extent of the records pertaining to Department of Energy-sponsored experiments that need to be examined.

I am taking action to assure that the records search being conducted by the Department of Energy and its contractors will be thorough and comprehensive as we endeavor to tell the full story. At the Department of Energy, we have developed an action plan to expedite the identification, retrieval, management, declassification, and dissemination of information regarding human radiation experiments. Department of Energy personnel have been directed to cease routine and non-routine destruction of documents and to identify all pertinent records and information in the Department's possession and in the possession of our laboratories and contractors.

I have established a multi-disciplinary committee under the authority of the Assistant Secretary for Environment, Safety and Health. The Committee is issuing detailed guidance to the field. The committee includes specialists in health, environment, and legal issues among other disciplines. The Department, both at Headquarters and in the field, has already undertaken activities to begin to collect and review the pertinent documents. For example, over 130 cubic feet of files have been collected and are being reviewed at Headquarters.

Allow me to stress that our goal is to get all the facts out. We will also do our best to provide information as we learn it. All pertinent information that is found regarding human experimentation will be declassified as necessary on an expedited basis and permanently preserved for public review in an appropriate public archive. At the same time, we are taking appropriate steps to protect the privacy of people who were the subjects of experiments as well as their families.

From what we know thus far, human experiments involving ionizing radiation conducted or sponsored by the Department of Energy or its predecessor agencies fall into one of four categories:

1. Experiments designed to investigate the effects of radiation on humans or the way the human body metabolizes radioactive substances;
2. Experiments using radioisotopes as tools to study the biochemistry of normal metabolic processes;
3. Experiments designed to investigate the therapeutic uses of radiation in the treatment of diseases such as cancer; and
4. Experiments involving intentional releases of radiation to the environment for purposes of assessing the behavior of such releases.

Some of the More Troubling Aspects of the Experiments

The radiation experiments that have come to light are disturbing for several reasons. It is not clear that all subjects were properly informed of the purposes or risks associated with the experiments in which they were participants.

Some of the experiments also raise questions about how the experimental subjects were selected. There is, at least on first inspection, the appearance of a pattern of choosing subjects from relatively vulnerable populations such as persons of color, poor people, prisoners, and retarded children. This appearance of treating some citizens as "expendable," to use Congressman Markey's phrase, is especially repugnant in a country that prides itself on its diversity, and that has, as its goal, providing equal opportunity for all its citizens.

Current Experiments Involving Human Subjects

Regarding press reports on the Department's current projects, we are funding approximately 120 experiments, and providing facilities for another 100 experiments involving human subjects. Not all of those experiments involve radiation, and the majority of those that do relate to nuclear medicine involve the use of low tracer doses.

To illustrate, there are 24 studies at Los Alamos National Laboratory under the purview of their Institutional Review Board. In no case is there any exposure of living human subjects to radioactive or chemical agents. In addition, none of these projects is classified.

The Office of Energy Research is preparing a list of all Department of Energy experiments identified by institution, title, principal investigator, and funding source. We estimate that the total funding of these projects is approximately $50 million.

The complete details of all human subject experiments conducted by the Department, or at Departmental facilities (including funding, location, number of volunteers, procedures, and other agency contributors) will be available on a computer retrievable data base by March 15, 1994.

The data base will serve the Department of Energy clearinghouse for all current and future experiments involving human subjects.

As far as we have been able to ascertain, the Department is not conducting any experiments that violate medical, ethical standards, or the Nuremburg code. All Department of Energy experiments are, we believe, in compliance with the Federal Policy on Protection of Human Subjects. The Department of Energy assisted in drafting this Federal Policy during the 1980s and adopted it along with 16 other Federal agencies (including the Department of Health and Human Services) in July 1991, when the rulemaking process was complete.

Human Radiation Interagency Working Group

On January 3, 1994, the White House convened a meeting of senior staff from government agencies with potential involvement in human radiation experiments. The White House has established a Human Radiation Interagency

Working Group consisting of myself and the Secretaries of Defense, Health and Human Services, and Veterans Affairs. The Directors of the Central Intelligence Agency and the Office of Management and Budget, the Attorney General, and the Administrator of the National Aeronautics and Space Administration are also on the Working Group. Five subcommittees have been formed under the Working Group to address the following specific issues: 1) Public Information and Communications; 2) Retrieval and Review of Records; 3) Ethical and Scientific Standards; 4) Congressional Relations; and 5) Legal Issues. These subcommittees are composed of staff from all relevant Federal agencies.

The President's Executive Order, signed on January 15, 1994, established the Advisory Committee on Human Radiation Experiments, consisting of nongovernmental experts in the fields of ethics, science, medicine, and law. The Advisory Committee on Human Radiation Experiments will review records of experiments on ionizing radiation on humans and will advise the Interagency Working Group on whether any lapses of scientific or ethical standards occurred.

The Human Experimentation
Helpline and Correspondence

The Department of Energy has established a toll-free telephone Helpline. The purpose of the Helpline is to aid us in identifying those persons who may have been affected by the activities in question. The number of calls to the Helpline has been overwhelming. We have received more than 15,000 telephone calls since December 24, 1993.

The majority of callers appear not to have been subjects of human radiation experiments. The calls do reflect the concerns of people in every state and of all different backgrounds. The Department is requesting that callers provide additional written information that can be used to identify and locate documents related to these experiments.

In addition, we have received over 1,000 letters in the last two weeks. Approximately one-third of the letters are from individuals or their relatives who believe that they may have been subjects of human experimentation and another third of the letters are from individuals who believe that they have been exposed to radiation while serving in the military or while living next to a government facility. The remaining third of the letters express support, offer assistance, or request information on the nature of the Department's efforts.

Administration Position on Compensation
Related to Human Radiation Experiments

If our review determines that American citizens were treated wrongfully by their government, we believe this Administration owes the American people a full accounting and, where justified, an attempt to right any wrong done to individuals.

The Administration is planning to take the following actions in response to individuals affected by the human radiation experiments:

1. Information will be provided to subjects and their families as soon as it becomes available.
2. When required to protect the health of individuals who were subjects of human radiation experiments, or their descendants, the government will notify these subjects, or their descendants, of any potential health risk or the need for medical follow-up.
3. The Legal Issues Subcommittee is currently examining various models for appropriate federal responses, including those incorporated into other federal programs such as those used to respond to "down-winders," veterans exposed to radiation, and the Japanese-Americans interned in the United States during World War II. The range of federal responses under consideration include potential monetary compensation, medical follow-up, disclosure of detailed information, formal apologies or other recognition, and ongoing research, education and information programs.
4. We are also developing specific recommendations for legislative and other action that may be appropriate once the Working Group and Advisory Committee have at least completed their first phase of work. This will be in six months, when the Advisory Committee's interim report is issued to the Administration's Human Radiation Interagency Working Group.

Throughout all of this activity, the Administration will continue to work closely with the Congress.

Conclusion

We are committed to do right by the subjects of the experiments and their families. If the government made mistakes or committed wrongs, we, as government officials, must admit them. We want to give the American people reason to have greater trust in their government. A serious, thoughtful debate must occur regarding the scientific and ethical propriety of these experiments. If necessary, current federal rules must be further strengthened to protect individuals from future scientific aberrations.

Only by "coming clean" on the details of these experiments and separating Cold War habits of secrecy from proper ethics in scientific and medical research will we eventually reduce the bitterness and suspicion which has surrounded the debate on the health effects of radiation. And only through a careful and balanced review will we be able to emphasize the critical role radiation has played in modern medicine's ability to diagnose and treat disease.

Finally, let me reiterate to you and the American people our commitment to opening up the Department of Energy. We have a tremendous amount of work to do in this area, but I believe we have made a good start.

JUSTICE DEPARTMENT REPORT ON VIOLENCE AGAINST WOMEN
January 30, 1994

In a year when the criminal cases of Lorena Bobbitt and O. J. Simpson focused public attention on the issue of domestic violence, a Justice Department report issued January 30 concluded that women were far more likely to be victimized by someone they knew than by strangers. "Nearly two in three female victims of violence were related to or knew their attacker," said the report, which added that the rate of violence committed by intimates such as spouses, ex-spouses, and boyfriends was nearly ten times greater for females than for males.

The report, "Violence Against Women," was the most comprehensive study to date on the extent of violence against women in the United States. It was based on data compiled from 400,000 interviews. While the report focused on violence against women, it noted that more men than women were victims of violence, with 3.9 million male victims and 2.6 million female victims annually.

Among women, the poorest were most vulnerable to all forms of violent crime, and women living in central cities were more likely to be victimized than those who lived in suburban and rural areas. Black women were more likely to be raped, robbed, and physically assaulted than white women. Among various age groups, women ages twenty to twenty-four—whether black or white—were most vulnerable to all types of violent crime.

Bobbitts Become Domestic Violence Symbols

The January trial of Lorena Bobbitt, the Virginia woman who cut off her husband's penis with a knife while he slept, drew renewed attention to the pervasive problem of violence against women. Two months before her trial, Lorena's husband, John, an ex-marine, was acquitted of raping Lorena at a trial where evidence about his repeated abuse of her was not admitted.

At her trial, Lorena was allowed to testify that her husband had repeatedly physically assaulted her. She said that he raped her the night of June 23,

1993, and she cut off his penis in a fit of temporary insanity after he fell asleep. The jury acquitted her by reason of insanity, and the judge sent her to a state hospital for psychiatric treatment. She was released after a month's stay. As for her husband, whom she divorced, he later got in trouble with the law after allegedly assaulting his new fiancee. He also appeared in a pornographic movie to document the success of the surgery that reattached his penis.

Lorena's trial was carried live by CNN and Court TV, and a poll by Newsweek *found that 60 percent of people were following the trial. "The avenging wife has become a new media model," said Debra Haffner, executive director of the U.S. Sex Information and Education Council. "She's part of this idea of women standing up for themselves and getting even. . . ."*

Most Crimes Go Unreported

In contrast to the example of Lorena Bobbitt, the Justice Department report noted that only 30 percent of women victims defended themselves physically and just over half reported the attack to the police. "Female victims who knew their assailants most often did not report because they believed the incident was a private or personal matter," the report said. Women victimized by strangers did not report the incident usually because "they felt the incident was minor and might not have been classified as a crime," according to the report.

Upon his election as president of the American Medical Association (AMA) in June, Dr. Robert A. McAfee said that domestic violence was so frequent that any doctor who treated adult patients had almost surely seen "at least one victim of family violence in the past two weeks." According to studies cited by the AMA, battered women accounted for 19 percent to 30 percent of visits by injured women to hospital emergency rooms, 25 percent of female suicides, and 25 percent of women seeking emergency psychiatric help. In 1992 the AMA Council on Judicial and Ethical Affairs had declared that doctors should "routinely inquire about abuse as part of the [patient's] medical history," that medical students should receive training about domestic violence, and that hospitals should adopt protocols for treatment. However, a survey of doctors in Seattle revealed that they were reluctant to broach the subject with patients.

An August report issued by the American Bar Association, titled "The Impact of Domestic Violence on Children," noted that children who witness domestic violence in their homes were victims as well, suffering "traumatic effects." ABA President R. William Ide III said that "too often public attention has only focused on family violence when it has surrounded a case involving a celebrity." He added that "such cases furnish vivid reminders that the legal system commonly fails to protect the victims in family violence."

The case Ide referred to involved O. J. Simpson, the former sports broadcaster and football star who was arrested June 17 and charged with murdering his ex-wife, Nicole Brown Simpson, and her friend, Ronald Goldman, on June 12. The two were stabbed to death outside her Los Angeles home while

*the Simpsons' two young children slept inside. Although jury selection in
Simpson's trial took place in the fall of 1994, the trial was expected to run
well into 1995.*

*According to police records, O. J. Simpson had a history of abusing his
wife. In 1989, he pleaded no contest to charges that he had beaten her and
was fined $700 and sentenced to two years' probation. Police records also
showed that Nicole Simpson had frequently made emergency calls to police
to report that her husband was beating her.*

*Violence against women was not limited to the United States, the State
Department said in its annual report on global human rights in January.
Based on observations of American diplomats, the report detailed widespread violence against women, including genital mutilation of girls in
some African countries, rape of female prisoners in Pakistan, physical and
sexual abuse of women servants in the Persian Gulf states, wife murders in
India, and the forced prostitution of women and girls on several continents.
Violence was not the only problem women faced in many foreign countries,
the report said. "All too often," it said, "women and girls find that their
access to education, employment, health care, and even food is limited because of their gender."*

> *Following is an excerpt from a Justice Department report
> titled "Violence Against Women," which was released January
> 30, 1994:*

Introduction

This report uses data from the National Crime Victimization Survey (NCVS)
of the Bureau of Justice Statistics (BJS) to provide a detailed accounting of
violent crime victimization against women and how this victimization differs
from victimization against men. Several types of violent crime were investigated, including rape, robbery, and assault. In addition, a special section examined the incidence rates and contextual characteristics of personal larceny
victimizations which involved contact, such as purse snatching and pocket
picking.

Another section of the analysis presents the characteristics of violent victimizations by victim-offender relationship:

- *intimate* (for example, boyfriend, girlfriend, spouse, ex-spouse),
- *other relative* (for example, parent, sibling, grandparent, in-law, cousin),
- *acquaintance* (for example, friend, someone known by face only), and
- *stranger.*

Major findings from the NCVS data include:

- Although women were significantly less likely to become victims of violent crime, they were more vulnerable to particular types of perpetrators.
  Whereas men were more likely to be victimized by acquaintances or

strangers, women were just as likely to be victimized by intimates, such as husbands or boyfriends, as they were to be victimized by acquaintances or strangers. The rate of violence committed by intimates was nearly 10 times greater for females than for males.

- Over two-thirds of violent victimizations against women were committed by someone known to them: 31% of female victims reported that the offender was a stranger. Approximately 28% were intimates such as husbands or boyfriends, 35% were acquaintances, and the remaining 5% were other relatives. In contrast, victimizations by intimates and other relatives accounted for only 5% of all violent victimizations against men. Men were significantly more likely to have been victimized by acquaintances (50%) or strangers (44%) than by intimates or other relatives.
- Women who were the most vulnerable to becoming the victims of violent crime were black, Hispanic, in younger age groups, never married, with lower family income and lower education levels, and in central cities.
- Among women who experienced a violent victimization, injuries occurred almost twice as frequently when the offender was an intimate (59%) than when a stranger (27%). Injured women were also more likely to require medical care if the attacker was an intimate, (27%) rather than a stranger (14%).

For rape victims, however, the outcome was different: Women who were raped by a stranger sustained more serious injuries than women raped by someone they knew.

- Almost 6 times as many women victimized by intimates (18%) as those victimized by strangers (3%) did not report their violent victimization to police because they feared reprisal from the offender.
- Rape was more likely to be committed against women by someone known to them (55%) than by a stranger (44%).
- Rape victimizations involving known offenders were almost twice as likely to occur at or near the victim's home (52%) compared to rapes by strangers, which were more likely to occur in an open area or public place (43%). However, almost a quarter of rapes by strangers did occur at or near the victim's home.

Incidence Rates and Characteristics of
Criminal Victimization for Males and Females

- The violent crime rate for males has decreased since 1973; however, the rate of violent crime for females has not. Rates of violent victimization against females remained relatively consistent from 1973 to 1991. The 1991 female rate of 22.9 translates as approximately 2,500,000 women in the United States experiencing a violent crime in that year.
- Theft victimization rates for both females and males were generally declining during the 1973-91 period. The decline for males, however, was much faster than the decline for females.
- Except for rape, females were significantly less likely than males to experience all forms of violent crime during 1987-91.

- Although overall theft victimization rates were higher for males than females, no significant differences between the sexes existed in the rates of personal larceny with contact (purse snatching and pocket picking). . . .
- Black and Hispanic females had a higher risk of experiencing a crime of violence than white and non-Hispanic females.
- Both non-Hispanic males and females experienced higher rates of crimes of theft than their Hispanic counterparts.
- While white females experienced higher theft victimization rates than black females, the converse was true for males. Black males had higher theft victimization rates than white males.
- Younger females and males were more likely than all older persons to experience both violent and theft victimizations. Females over age 35 were victimized by personal theft at about the same rate as males over age 35.
- Both females and males with higher family incomes experienced fewer crimes of violence than those in the lower income categories. Females in families making less than $9,999 had a higher violent victimization rate than males in the highest income category of $50,000 or more.
- The risk of experiencing a crime of theft was greater for females in the higher income categories, compared to those with lower family incomes. There was no consistent relationship, however, between rates of theft and family income for males.
- Females with either some college or a college degree had higher theft victimization rates and lower violent victimization rates than females with less education.
- Males who had never married were the most likely to experience a violent crime, followed by females who were divorced or separated. For both women and men, those who were widowed were the least likely to be victims of a violent crime.
- For crimes of theft, both females and males who had never married were more likely to be victimized, followed by divorced or separated individuals, those who were married, and widowers, respectively.
- Both females and males residing in central cities experienced the highest rates of both violent and theft crime victimizations, compared to their suburban or rural counterparts. Rural female and male residents had the lowest rates of victimization.

Demographic Characteristics of Female
Victims of Rape, Robbery, and Assault

- Black females were more than twice as likely to experience a robbery as white females. No significant differences separated females of different races for the rates of rape and of aggravated or simple assault.
- Hispanic females were more likely to experience a robbery than non-Hispanic females, but Hispanic and non-Hispanic females were equally likely to experience other violent crimes.
- Women age 20-24 were the most likely to experience all types of violent

crime. While the risk of becoming a victim of rape or assault decreased after age 34, women over age 65 were just as likely to become robbery victims as those between ages 35 and 64.

- Women with less education generally experienced higher rates of aggravated and simple assault than women with more education. For the rates of rape or robbery, however, no significant differences occurred between women in diverse educational categories.
- Those in the lowest family income category of $9,999 or less experienced the highest rates of all forms of violent crime. Rates of violent victimization decreased as income levels increased.
- For all forms of violent crime, females who either had never married or were divorced or separated experienced a greater risk of victimization than other females. Widows were generally the least likely of all categories to become victims of violence.
- Females residing in central cities were more vulnerable to all types of violent crime. They were twice as likely to experience a rape as suburban or rural females. Central city females were also over twice as likely to experience a robbery as their suburban counterparts and almost 4 times as likely to be robbed as females living in rural areas.
- Females living in suburban and rural residences experienced similar rates of rape, robbery, and assault.

Purse Snatching and Other Personal Larceny Involving Contact

Because females, particularly elderly women, were found to be just as vulnerable as males to personal larceny involving contact (purse snatching and pocket picking), the characteristics of these victimizations against women warrant a more detailed description.

- White females were less likely to experience a personal larceny involving contact than were black females or females from another racial group. Hispanic females were also more likely to experience this type of victimization than non-Hispanic females.
- Females in all age groups had equivalent rates of personal larceny involving contact. This pattern is quite different from the pattern observed for violent crime in which the risk of victimization decreased with age.
- Widowed females were as likely to experience personal larceny with contact as were those who had never married or who had divorced or separated.
- Females in central cities were over 3 times more likely to experience a personal larceny that involved contact than those in suburban areas and over 6 times more likely than females residing in rural locations.

Characteristics of personal larceny which involved contact differed between those females under age 65 and those who were age 65 or older.

- Regardless of age, most female victims of personal larceny involving contact were victimized in an open area or public place. However, almost twice as many victims over age 65 as younger victims were victimized at or near their home.

- Female victims in all age categories who experienced personal larceny with contact were more likely to be victimized between noon and 6 p.m., compared to any other period.
- Female victims of personal larceny age 65 or older were less likely to take self-protective action and more likely to report their victimization to police than their younger counterparts.

Characteristics of Offenders Who
Committed Violent Crimes Against Women

In general, most female victims of violence were attacked by lone offenders. Robbery was the violent crime most likely to involve more than one offender. Rape was the violent victimization least likely to involve more than one offender. Less than 10% of all rape victimizations involved more than one offender.

Because multiple-offender victimizations represent very different experiences for female victims compared to single offender victimizations, the remainder of this report will examine these types of victimizations separately. Unless otherwise noted, analyses which follow focus exclusively on one-on-one incidents of violence. This specification was also necessary to determine the exact relationship (intimate, acquaintance, or stranger) between the victim and the offender.

- Female victims of all types of violent crime were more likely to be victimized by male offenders than female offenders. Females, however, committed about a quarter of all assaults against females.
- Most violent offenders who victimized females were perceived by the victim to be over age 21.
- Female victims of rape and aggravated assault were significantly more likely to perceive their attackers to be under the influence of drugs or alcohol than females who experienced a robbery or simple assault.
- When offenders were perceived by female victims to be under the influence of alcohol or drugs, a higher percentage of rape and assault offenders were reported to have been using alcohol rather than other drugs. For robbers perceived to be under the influence, a higher percentage were reported to have been under the influence of drugs rather than alcohol.
- In general, violent crime against women was primarily intra-racial. Eight out of ten violent crimes against white women were perpetrated by white offenders. Similarly, almost 9 out of 10 violent victimizations sustained by black women were committed by black offenders.
- Robberies of white females were the victimizations most often inter-racial. A white female robbery victim was as likely to have been victimized by a black offender as a white offender. Robberies experienced by black females were primarily intra-racial.

Family Violence

Family violence is difficult to measure because it most often occurs in private, and victims may be reluctant to report it because of shame or fear of reprisal by the offender. As do all NCVS data, estimates of family violence rely on victims being willing and able to report incidents to survey interviewers. These estimates include any rape, robbery or assault that was committed by intimates, including spouses, ex-spouses, boyfriends, girlfriends, parents, children, or other relatives. . . .

- Annually, compared to males, females experienced over 10 times as many incidents of violence by an intimate. On average each year, women experienced 572,032 violent victimizations at the hands of an intimate, compared to 48,983 incidents committed against men.
- Women were just as likely to experience a violent victimization by an intimate or relative (33%) as they were to be victimized by an acquaintance (35%) or a stranger (31%). Family-related violence, however, accounted for only 5% of all violent victimizations against men. Men were far more likely to be victimized by an acquaintance (50% of all male victimizations) or a stranger (44% of all male victimizations) than by an intimate or family member.
- White and black women experienced equivalent rates of violence committed by intimates and other relatives. However, black women were significantly more likely than white women to experience incidents of violence by acquaintances or strangers.
- Women with lower education and family income levels were more likely to be victimized by intimates than women who had graduated from college and who had higher family incomes. Women with family incomes less than $9,999 were more than 5 times as likely to experience a violent victimization by an intimate and more than twice as likely to be victimized by an acquaintance than those with family incomes over $30,000.
- Living in suburban or rural areas did not decrease a woman's risk of experiencing an act of violence by an intimate. Women living in central cities, suburban areas and rural locations experienced similar rates of violence committed by intimates.
- Violence by strangers was more likely to occur in central cities than in the suburbs or rural areas. Females living in central cities were 4 times more likely to be victimized by a stranger than rural females and almost 2 times more likely than suburban females.
- Robbery was the only crime in which women were more likely to be victimized by strangers rather than intimates, other family members, or acquaintances. Female victims of simple assault were more likely to be victimized by an intimate or an acquaintance rather than a stranger or a relative who was not an intimate.

Characteristics of Violence by
Family, Acquaintance, and Stranger

- Women who were victimized by strangers were more likely to face an armed offender (33%) compared to those victimized by offenders who were intimates (18%), other relatives (22%), or acquaintances (21%).
- When weapons were present during a violent victimization, strangers, compared to other types of offenders, were more likely to be armed with guns. Intimates and other relatives were more likely to be armed with knives or other sharp instruments.
- Women suffering violent victimizations were almost twice as likely to be injured if the offender was an intimate (59%) compared to offenders who were strangers (27%). Women were also more likely to receive injuries requiring medical care if the attacker was an intimate (27%) compared to a stranger (14%). For rape victims, however, the outcome was different: Women who were raped by a stranger were injured more often than women raped by someone whom they knew. . . .
- Although the percentage of female victims of violence who reported their victimization to police did not vary by victim-offender relationship, the reasons given by victims for not reporting an incident did. Female victims who knew their assailants most often did not report because they believed the incident was a private or personal matter. The most important reason for not reporting given by females victimized by strangers was that they felt the incident was minor and might not have been classified as a crime.
- Almost 6 times as many women victimized by intimates (18%) as those victimized by strangers (3%) did not report their violent victimization to police because they feared reprisal from the offender.
- The most common reason given for reporting a victimization to police, regardless of the relationship the victim had to the offender, was to punish the offender.
- Police responded to over three-quarters of all reports by females victimized by intimates, acquaintances, other relatives, or strangers by coming to the crime scene.
- Police were more likely to respond within 5 minutes if the offender was a stranger than if an offender was known to the female victim.
- Police took a report in over two-thirds of all incidents of violence reported, regardless of the relationship between the victim and offender. However, the police were more likely to take a formal report if the offender was a stranger (77%) rather than an intimate (69%), other relative (67%), or acquaintance (70%).
- The police questioned witnesses in about the same proportion of violent victimizations of females, regardless of the victim-offender relationship. Searching the scene for evidence occurred more often when a stranger, rather than other types of offenders, had committed the crime.
- Although a similar proportion of females victimized by either known or

unknown offenders used self-protective behavior, the type of self-protection varied by the victim-offender relationship. Women victimized by an intimate or another family member were almost 2 times more likely to use physical self-protection such as fighting back, compared to women victimized by a stranger. Women were most likely to argue, reason, or cooperate when offenders were strangers.

- Over half of women who tried to protect themselves against offenders who were intimates believed their self-protective behavior helped the situation. Almost a quarter of the women, however, believed their actions actually made the situation worse.
- Women who tried to protect themselves against strangers were significantly more likely to believe their actions helped the situation than to believe they made the situation worse.

Rape Victimization

Rape, as defined by the NCVS for the time period studied in this report, was self-classified by all respondents. Each respondent was asked if she had been attacked during the previous 6 months; if she reported that she had been raped, the incident was classified as a completed rape. If the victim reported that the offender(s) had tried to rape her, the incident was classified as an attempted rape. . . .

- Data from 1987 to 1991 indicated that every year nearly 133,000 women age 12 or older were victims of rape or attempted rape. More of these rapes were committed by someone known to the victim (55%) than by a stranger (44%).
- Rapes committed by nonstrangers were more likely to occur at or near the victim's home (52%), while rapes by strangers were more likely to occur in an open area or another public place (43%). About a fourth of the rapes by strangers took place at or near the victim's home.
- Rapes were more likely to take place after dark between 6 p.m. and midnight regardless of the victim-offender relationship.
- Nonstranger rapists were almost 70% more likely to have been under the influence of drugs or alcohol at the time of the victimization compared to rapists who were strangers.
- Victims of rape by a stranger or non-stranger reported their victimization to police to about the same extent. Just over half of all rape victimizations were reported.
- Most females reported their victimization because they wanted to punish the offender regardless of the relationship they had with them. More females raped by men whom they knew, compared to females raped by strangers, did not report the victimization to police because they believed it to be a private or personal matter.
- A rape victim was more likely to report her victimization to police if the offender used a weapon, if she sustained an additional injury as the result of her victimization, and if she required medical care.

- A higher proportion of rapists who were strangers (29%) than those whom the victim knew (17%) were armed with a weapon. Of those armed, strangers were just as likely to use handguns (42%) as knives (44%), while rapists known to the victim were more likely to use knives or other sharp instruments (51%) in the attack.
- A larger percentage of victims of rape by strangers (60%) than other rape victims (43%) were injured. As reported earlier, this relationship was reversed for crimes of violence in general in which females were more likely to sustain an injury if the offender was known. . . .

STATE DEPARTMENT REPORT ON HUMAN RIGHTS IN CHINA
January 31, 1994

The Chinese government's "overall human rights record in 1993 fell far short of internationally accepted norms," the State Department announced January 31 in its annual report examining human rights practices in every country in the world. The department said Chinese government security forces were "responsible for well-documented human rights abuses, including torture, forced confessions, and arbitrary detentions."

At a press conference where the report was released, John F. Shattuck, assistant secretary of state for human rights, said the document showed "that during 1993, China had a continued climate of repression, a pattern of abuse in its prisons, difficulties for dissenters, and particular repression in Tibet," a neighboring state that China had forcibly annexed.

Human rights groups cited the report as evidence that the United States should revoke China's most favored nation trade status, which allowed the nation to export goods to the United States at low tariffs. Nevertheless, President Bill Clinton renewed China's favored status for another year at a White House news conference May 26, despite acknowledging China's lack of progress toward eliminating human rights abuses. A year earlier, he had set the end of such abuses as a condition for renewing China's most favored status. Clinton said he renewed the status to avoid "isolating China" and to permit the United States to make further cultural, educational, and economic contacts with the country. That approach would "make it more likely that China will play a responsible role, both at home and abroad," the president said.

Clinton began his news conference by noting that China "is a major factor in Asian and global security" and is "the world's fastest growing economy." He said U.S. exports to China in 1993 amounted to $8 billion and supported 150,000 American jobs. This emphasis on the importance of economic ties with China reflected a change of attitude within the administration and the apparent pressure of business interests eager for increased access to China's huge markets.

Clinton said the question had become not whether to continue to support human rights in China but how to support them "and advance our other very significant interests." Anthony Lake, the president's national security adviser, contended that it was Clinton's position during the campaign and in 1993 that "allowed us to achieve" some progress. Clinton said that progress included some action toward allowing emigration of dissidents' families and development of a plan to prevent the American import of goods made by Chinese prison labor.

Separating Trade from Human Rights

The link between trade policy and human rights had arisen following the Chinese government's violent suppression of a student-led demonstration for democracy in Beijing's Tiananmen Square in June 1989. The brutal crackdown prompted liberal Democrats, led by Senate Majority Leader George Mitchell, to demand retaliation in the form of trade sanctions against China. (Repression in China, Historic Documents of 1989, p. 275)

Retaliation was opposed by President George Bush, who drew support from other members of Congress and the business community. They argued that despite China's terrible record on human rights, America's long-term interests lay in cooperation on arms control, economic matters, and environmental problems.

During the 1992 presidential election campaign, Clinton accused Bush of "coddling tyrants." After taking office, Clinton issued an executive order linking China's trade status to its treatment of dissidents and political prisoners.

The Clinton administration initiated a series of high-level meetings with Chinese officials in an effort to bring about changes in the nation's human rights practices. These meetings culminated in a visit to China in March 1994 by Secretary of State Warren Christopher. The visit was frequently marked by heated exchanges. Chinese Prime Minister Li Peng declared that his country would never accept the U.S. concept of human rights. In the end, both sides retreated from outright confrontation. Christopher's proposal to treat human rights as "a generic condition rather than one that's filled with specific conditions" was met with only minor concessions by the Chinese government.

Security Reasons for China Ties

Besides the opposition of big American businesses to breaking trade ties with China, the administration was told there were security reasons for maintaining them. Sen. Sam Nunn (D-Ga.), chairman of the Senate Armed Services Committee, said early in the year that as long as North Korea remained a nuclear threat, China's cooperation in regional security had to take precedence over concerns about human rights.

During a week-long trip to China in August, Secretary of Commerce Ron Brown signed an agreement to revive a joint U.S.-China commission on trade that had been suspended in 1989. He also attended signing ceremonies *for almost $5 billion worth of contracts with U.S.-based companies. Brown was criticized for only raising human rights issues in private conversations.*

Following is an excerpt from the section of the State Department's "Human Rights Country Reports" dealing with China, released January 31, 1994:

The People's Republic of China (PRC) remains a one-party state ruled by the Chinese Communist Party through a 21-member Politburo and a small circle of officially retired but still powerful senior leaders. Almost all top civilian, police, and military positions at the national and regional levels are held by party members. Despite official adherence to Marxism-Leninism, in recent years economic decisionmaking has become less ideological, more decentralized, and increasingly market oriented. Fundamental human rights provided for in the Constitution are frequently ignored in practice, and challenges to the Communist Party's political authority are often dealt with harshly and arbitrarily.

Security forces, comprised of a nationwide network which includes the People's Liberation Army, the Ministry of State Security, the Ministry of Public Security, the People's Armed Police, and the state judicial, procuratorial, and penal systems, are poorly monitored due to the absence of adequate legal safeguards or adequate enforcement of existing safeguards for those detained, accused, or imprisoned. They are responsible for widespread and well-documented human rights abuses, including torture, forced confessions, and arbitrary detentions.

A decade of rapid economic growth, spurred by market incentives and foreign investment, has reduced party and government control over the economy and permitted ever larger numbers of Chinese to have more control over their lives and livelihood. Despite significant income disparities between coastal regions and the interior, there is now a growing "middle class" in the cities and rural areas as well as a sharp decline in the number of Chinese at the subsistence level. These economic changes have led to a de facto end to the role of ideology in the economy and an increase in cultural diversity. An example of this is the media, which remains tightly controlled with regard to political questions, although it now is free to report on a wider variety of other issues.

The Government took some positive steps on human rights issues during 1993. It released some prominent political prisoners early or on medical parole; many had served long terms in prison. The Government still has not provided a full or public accounting of the thousands of persons detained during the suppression of the 1989 democracy movement, when millions of students, workers, and intellectuals defied the Government and participated in public demonstrations. Most of these detainees appear to have been released, however, some after serving periods of detention without charges having been brought and some after having completed their prison sentences. The Government says it has released the remaining imprisoned or detained Vatican loyalists among the Catholic clergy. Although it continues to restrict the movements and activities of some elderly priests and bishops, the Government announced in November that two priests, whose movements had been restricted, were free to return to their homes. The authorities also allowed a number of prominent political dissidents to leave China in 1993. In November the Government announced it would give positive consideration to a request from the International Committee of the Red Cross (ICRC) to visit China.

Nevertheless, the Government's overall human rights record in 1993 fell far short of internationally accepted norms as it continued to repress domestic critics and failed to control abuses by its own security forces. The Government detained, sentenced to prison, or sent to labor camps, and in a few cases expelled from the country, persons who sought to exercise their rights of freedom of assembly and speech. The number of persons in Chinese penal institutions considered political prisoners by international standards is impossible to estimate accurately. In 1993 hundreds, perhaps thousands, of political prisoners remained under detention or in prison. Physical abuse, including torture by police and prison officials, persisted, especially in politically restive regions with minority populations like Tibet. Criminal defendants continue to be denied legal safeguards such as due process or adequate defense. In many localities, government authorities continued to harass and occasionally detain Christians who practiced their religion outside the officially sponsored religious organizations.

Respect for Human Rights

Section 1   Respect for the Integrity of the Person, Including Freedom from:

a. Political and Other Extrajudicial Killing

There were accounts of extrajudicial killings by government officials in 1993. A few cases resulted in severe punishment for the officials involved and were widely publicized as admonitory examples. Local officials beat to death an Anhui farmer in February after he protested the level of taxes and fees. Those found directly responsible for the beating, including a local public security official, received long prison terms and, in one case, a death sentence. Other officials were dismissed or disciplined. Also, in another well-publicized case, the powerful local Communist party secretary of a village near Tianjin was sentenced in August to 20 years in prison for obstruction of justice and other offenses related to a December 1992 beating death. Those who actually took part in the beating also received long prison terms.

The official responses to other cases served to cover up abuses, however. Credible reports indicated that a Shaanxi man beaten by public security officials in March, during a raid on an unauthorized Protestant gathering, died as a result of his injuries and the lack of timely medical care while in police custody. An official autopsy ascribed the death to an unrelated illness.

Because the Government often restricts access to such information, it is impossible to determine the total number of such killings. However, according to a credible report issued in 1993 by a human rights group, at least 12 persons died in 1992 as a result of torture while in police custody.

b. Disappearance

There were no reported cases in 1993 in which persons who disappeared were suspected to have been killed by officials; however, the Government has still not provided a comprehensive, credible public accounting of all those missing or detained in connection with the suppression of the 1989 demonstrations.

c. Torture and Other Cruel, Inhuman, or Degrading Treatment or Punishment

Cases of torture and degrading treatment of detained and imprisoned persons persisted. Both official Chinese sources and international human rights groups reported many instances of torture. Persons detained pending trial were particularly at risk as a result of weaknesses in the legal system, including the emphasis on obtaining confessions as a basis for convictions and the lack of access to prisoners, even by family members, until after formal charges are brought, a step that can be delayed for months. Former detainees have credibly reported the use of cattle prods and electrodes, prolonged periods of solitary confinement and incommunicado detention, beatings, shackles, and other forms of abuse against detained women and men.

While generally refusing to allow impartial observers to visit prisoners, officials stated that internal monitoring and laws to prevent and punish abuses continue to be strengthened. Procurator General Liu Fuzhi said in March that 2,800 procuratorate offices had been set up in jails and detention centers to safeguard the welfare of detainees. In response to a call by the Chairman of the National People's Congress (NPC), a national-level procuratorial conference held in Shanghai in early April focused on measures to improve the Procuratorate's supervision of law enforcement personnel and government officials who violate the civil rights of citizens. In August the Guangdong provincial public security bureau issued a regulation forbidding police torture during interrogations. In April China told the U.N. Committee Against Torture that 339 cases of torture to extract confessions were investigated during 1992, 209 cases were reported to the Procuratorate with a view to prosecution, and 180 prosecutions were brought. No information on convictions or punishments was provided. While Chinese officials said in December that 23 prison officials had been punished in serious cases of mistreatment of prisoners, the number of actual incidents of torture and ill-treatment by government officials is almost certainly far greater than this number.

Conditions of imprisonment for political prisoners vary widely. Some prisoners, including the student leader Wang Dan, who was released in February, have stated they were treated reasonably well. Credible reports indicate others have been abused. Political prisoners are often intermingled with common criminals. Credible reports persisted in 1993 that Liu Gang, a political prisoner held at a Liaoning labor camp, suffers ill health as a result of beatings and other mistreatment, and that prison officials instigated some beatings by cellmates. Officials strongly denied these allegations and arranged for an interview with Liu and his jailers, which was published in August by a Chinese English-language journal. They declined repeated requests by foreign groups to allow access to the jailed dissident by independent observers.

There was limited evidence that, at least in a few cases, detained dissidents have been incarcerated in psychiatric institutions and treated with drugs. The lack of independent outside access to such persons made it impossible to verify the reports. Shanghai dissident Wang Miaogen was detained by public security officials in May and committed to a mental institution after he attempted to protest the holding of the East Asia games. Wang had earlier chopped off four of his fingers in a protest over alleged persecution. Wang Wanxing, detained in 1992 while attempting to stage a one-man protest on Tiananmen Square, continued to be held in a Beijing-area mental hospital.

Conditions in Chinese penal institutions are generally harsh and frequently degrading, and nutritional and health conditions are sometimes grim. Medical care for prisoners has been a problem area, despite official assurances that prisoners have the right to maintain good health and receive prompt medical treatment if they become ill. In 1993 political prisoners who reportedly had difficulties in obtaining timely and adequate medical care included Wang Juntao, Chen Ziming, and Ren Wanding. Medical paroles may be granted to ailing prisoners, and 1989 detainee Li Guiren was released in January to obtain medical treatment. Working conditions for prisoners in many facilities are similar to those in ordinary factories, but some prisoners working in penal coal mines and at other sites must endure dangerous conditions.

Political prisoner Qi Dafeng continued to serve a 2-year sentence in a coal mine in Anhui, where he had been sent under the nonjudicial "reeducation through labor" program in late 1992.

d. Arbitrary Arrest, Detention, or Exile

China's Criminal Procedure Law proscribes arbitrary arrest or detention, limits the time a person may be held in custody without being charged, and requires officials to notify the detainee's family and work unit of the detention within 24 hours. These provisions are subject to several important exceptions, including the sweeping provision that notification may be withheld if it would "hinder the investigation" of a case. Senior judicial officials acknowledged in 1993 that limits on detention are frequently ignored in practice or circumvented by various informal mechanisms. In numerous cases, the precise legal status or location of detainees is unclear. Public security authorities often detain people for long periods of time under mechanisms not covered by the Criminal Procedure Law. These include unpublished regulations on "taking in for shelter and investigation" and "supervised residence" as well as other methods not requiring procuratorial approval. According to the Chinese media, close to 1 million detentions under "shelter for investigation" have been carried out annually in recent years. No statistics were available to indicate the usual length of these detentions, but at least some lasted several months. Links between local officials and business leaders have resulted in scattered detentions as a means of exerting pressure in economic disputes. The legality of detentions may be judicially challenged under the Administrative Procedures Law, but such challenges are rare and there is little evidence that this is an adequate or timely remedy for improper actions. There is no judicially supervised system of bail, but at the discretion of public security officials some detainees are released pending further investigation.

Political dissidents are often detained or charged for having committed "crimes of counterrevolution" under Articles 90 through 104 of the Criminal Law. Counterrevolutionary offenses range from treason and espionage to spreading counterrevolutionary propaganda. These articles have also been used to punish persons who organized demonstrations, disrupted traffic, disclosed official information to foreigners, or formed associations outside state control. Detention and trial of dissidents on other charges is also possible. People participating in unauthorized religious organizations may be charged with criminal offenses such as receiving funds from abroad without authorization or changing such funds on the black market. Legal provisions requiring family notification and limiting length of detention are often ignored in political cases. Liao Jia'an, a university student in Beijing detained in 1992 for peaceful expression of his political views, was held for a year before being formally arrested in mid-1993 for counterrevolutionary crimes.

· A well-documented estimate of the total number of those subjected to new or continued arbitrary arrest or detention for political reasons is not possible due to the Government's tight control of information. Individuals reported detained are sometimes released without charge after several days or weeks of interrogation. There were several reported lengthier detentions of dissidents, including Sun Lin, Wang Miaogen, and Zhang Xianliang, in Shanghai during 1993. Sun was released in August after 5 months in detention. Democracy activists Qin Yongmin, Yang Zhou, and Zheng Xuguang were detained in November in connection with the formation of a group called the "Peace Charter." Yang Zhou was released from detention on December 31, but the authorities had not provided information on the status or location of the other peace charter detainees. Several dozen Tibetans were also reported to have been detained after participation in proindependence demonstrations or activities. Gendun Rinchen, a Tibetan tour guide who had been detained in May 1993, was released on January 14, 1994.

e. Denial of Fair Public Trial

Officials insist that China's judiciary is independent but acknowledge that it is subject to the Communist Party's policy guidance. In actuality, party and government leaders almost certainly predetermine verdicts and sentences in some sensitive cases. According to the Constitution, the court system is equal in authority to the State Council and the Central Military Commission, the two most important government institutions. All three organs are nominally under the supervision of the National People's Congress. The Supreme People's Court stands at the apex of the court system, followed in descending order by the higher, intermediate, and basic people's courts.

Due process rights are provided for in the Constitution but are often ignored in practice. Both before and after trial, prisoners are subject to severe psychological pressure to confess their "errors." Defendants who fail to "show the right attitude" by confessing their crimes are typically sentenced more harshly. Despite official media and other reports that indicate coerced confessions have led to erroneous convictions, a coerced confession is not automatically excluded as evidence. According to judicial officials, however, confessions without corroborating evidence are an insufficient basis for conviction.

Accused persons are given virtually no opportunity to prepare a defense in the pretrial process, during which the question of guilt or innocence is essentially decided administratively. Defense lawyers may be retained only 7 days before the trial. In some cases even this brief period has been shortened under regulations issued in 1983 to accelerate the adjudication of certain serious criminal cases. Persons appearing before a court are not presumed innocent; despite official denials, trials are essentially sentencing hearings. Conviction rates average over 99 percent. There is an appeal process, but initial decisions are rarely overturned, and appeals generally do not provide meaningful protection against arbitrary or erroneous verdicts. Like the initial court verdict, the judgment of the Appeals Court is subject to Communist Party "guidance."

Under the Criminal Procedure Law, persons "exempted from prosecution" by procurators are deemed to have a criminal record, despite the lack of a judicial determination of guilt. Such provisions can be applied in "counter-revolutionary crimes" as well as for ordinary criminal offenses. In August Shanghai activists Sun Lin, Yao Tiansheng, and Han Lifa were "exempted from prosecution" for counterrevolutionary offenses and released.

Some officials have acknowledged that trials in China are conducted too rapidly. These officials state that China's 70,000 lawyers, most of whom are engaged in commercial law, are insufficient to meet the country's expanding legal needs and point to the Government's intention to increase this number to at least 150,000. Knowledgeable observers report that defense attorneys appear in only a small number of criminal trials. Under Chinese law, there is no requirement that the court appoint a defense attorney for the defendant unless the defendant is deaf, dumb, or a minor. When attorneys do appear, they have little time to prepare a defense and rarely contest guilt; their function is generally confined to requesting clemency. Defense lawyers, like other Chinese, generally depend on an official work unit for employment, housing, and many other aspects of their lives. They are therefore often reluctant to be viewed as overzealous in defending persons accused of political offenses.

The need for adequate, independent legal aid is increasingly understood in legal circles and within the Government. In many cities, law firms are being organized outside the framework of established government legal offices.

These firms are self-regulating and do not have their personnel or budgets determined directly by the State. The Minister of Justice announced in October that China would gradually increase the number of autonomous law firms from the current total of 410.

The Criminal Procedure Law requires that all trials be held in public, except those involving state secrets, juveniles, or "personal secrets." Details of cases involving "counterrevolutionary" charges, however, have frequently been kept secret, even from defendants' relatives, under this provision. The 1988 Law on State Secrets affords a ready basis for denying a public trial in cases involving "counterrevolution."

Lack of due process is particularly egregious when defendants receive the death sentence. Chinese officials refuse to provide comprehensive statistics on death sentences or executions, but hundreds of executions are officially reported annually. The actual numbers may be much higher. All death sentences are nominally reviewed by a higher court. Reviews are usually completed within a few days after sentencing and consistently result in a perfunctory confirmation of sentence. However, no executions for political offenses are known to have occurred in 1993.

In addition to the formal judicial system, government authorities can assign persons accused of "minor" public order and "counterrevolutionary" offenses to "reeducation through labor" camps in an extrajudicial process. In 1990 Chinese officials stated that 869,934 Chinese citizens had been assigned to these camps since 1980, with about 80,000 assigned each year. Chinese officials reported 120,000 prisoners were undergoing "reeducation through labor" at the end of 1993. Other estimates of the number of inmates are considerably higher. Terms of detention run from a normal minimum of 1 year to a maximum of 3 years. The "labor reeducation" committee which determines the term of detention may extend an inmate's sentence for an additional year. Under a State Council regulation issued in early 1991, those sentenced to "reeducation through labor" may ask the committee to reconsider their decision. Since 1990, "reeducation through labor" sentences may also be judicially challenged under the Administrative Procedures Law. While some persons have gained reduction or withdrawal of their sentence after reconsideration or appeal, in practice these procedures are rarely used, and short appeal times, lack of access to lawyers, and other problems weaken their potential assistance in preventing or reversing arbitrary decisions.

The system of "reeducation through labor" sometimes is used by security authorities to deal with political and other offenders without reference to even the nominal procedures and protections the formal criminal process offers. In Shanghai, Fu Shenqi and Zhang Xianliang were given 3-year "reeducation through labor" sentences in July for "provoking incidents" and "inciting trouble" which disturbed public order.

Government officials deny that China has any political prisoners, asserting that persons are detained not for the political views they hold, but because they have taken some action which violates the Criminal Law. The number of persons in Chinese penal institutions considered political prisoners by international standards is impossible to estimate accurately. Hundreds, perhaps thousands, of political prisoners remained imprisoned or detained. Estimates by some foreign researchers of the number of political prisoners are much higher. Many if not most people held for political offenses are charged as counterrevolutionaries. Chinese officials said in December there were 3,172 persons serving sentences for counterrevolutionary crimes, down from a figure of 3,317 given to an American human rights monitor in October. As part of the October figure, officials also indicated that 560 persons convicted of counterrevolutionary crimes had been paroled. Those convicted of counterrevolutionary crimes make up 0.2 percent of the total prisoner population of 1.22 million, but they are about 5 percent of total parolees. As recently as November 1992, an Australian delegation was told there were 4,000 in prison for counterrevolutionary crimes. All these estimates almost certainly include a substantial number of persons convicted of espionage or other internationally recognized criminal offenses. At the same time, the figures exclude many political prisoners detained but not charged, persons held in labor reeducation camps and an undetermined number of persons sentenced for criminal offenses due solely to their nonviolent political or religious activities.

Many prominent activists, including Chen Ziming, Wang Juntao, and Liu Gang (all three held since 1989), remained imprisoned in 1993. Some persons detained for political reasons were released on parole before the end of their sentences. Those released early included longtime political prisoners Wei Jingsheng, Wang Xizhe, and Xu Wenli, and Tiananmen-related detainees Wang Dan, Gao Shan, Zhai Weimin, Wu Xuecan, and Guo Haifeng. Shanghai activist Fu Shenqi was released in March but reimprisoned on other charges in June. Even after release, such persons have a criminal record, and their status in society, ability to be employed, freedom to travel, and numerous other aspects of their lives are often severely restricted. Economic reform and social change have somewhat diminished these problems, but some people continue to experience serious hardships. For example, the families of political prisoners sometimes encounter difficulty in obtaining or keeping employment and housing. Zhang Fengying, wife of imprisoned activist Ren Wanding, remained in poor housing conditions in 1993. Zhang and her teenage daughter were evicted from their apartment in 1992. Ren's work unit owns the apartment. While the work unit asserted it wanted to reassign the housing to another worker, the apartment reportedly has remained vacant.

f. Arbitrary Interference with Privacy, Family, Home, or Correspondence

The authorities extensively monitor and regulate personal and family life, particularly in China's cities. Most persons in urban areas still depend on their government-linked work unit for housing, permission to marry or have a child, approval to apply for a passport, and other aspects of ordinary life. The work unit, along with the neighborhood watch committee, is charged with monitoring activities and attitudes. However, changes in the economic structure, including the growing diversity of employment opportunities and the increasing market orientation of many work units, are undermining the effectiveness of this system. Search warrants are required by law before security forces can search premises, but this provision is often ignored. In addition, both the Public Security Bureau and procuracy apparently can issue search warrants on their own authority.

The 1982 Constitution states that "freedom and privacy of correspondence of citizens . . . are protected by law," but, according to a Western expert on Chinese law, legislation for this purpose does not exist. In practice, some telephone conversations are recorded, and mail is frequently opened and censored. The Government often monitors and sometimes restricts contact between foreigners and Chinese citizens, particularly dissidents.

The Government has continued its effort to control citizens' access to outside sources of information, selectively jamming Chinese language broadcasts of the Voice of America (VOA) and the British Broadcasting Corporation. Despite the effort made to jam VOA, the effectiveness of the jamming varies considerably by region, with audible signals reaching most parts of China. A small but rapidly growing segment of the population has access to satellite television broadcasts. Authorities issued new regulations on the installation and operation of satellite dishes in October, requiring permits for operation and banning private ownership and operation except under limited circumstances. However, China has not been very successful in implementing past regulations restricting the use of satellite dishes. Satellite television dishes are widely available for sale, and a licensing scheme which nominally controls purchase of the equipment is loosely enforced.

China's population has roughly doubled in the past 40 years to nearly 1.2 billion people, over a fifth of all humanity. In the 1970's and 1980's China adopted a comprehensive and highly intrusive family planning policy. This policy most heavily affects Han Chinese in urban areas. For urban couples, obtaining permission, usually issued by their work units, to have a second child is very difficult. Numerous exceptions are allowed for the 70 percent of Han who live in rural areas. Ethnic minorities are subject to less stringent population controls. Enforcement of the family planning policy is inconsistent, varying widely from place to place and year to year.

The population control policy relies on education, propaganda, and economic incentives, as well as more coercive measures, including psychological pressure and economic penalties. Rewards for couples who adhere to the policy include monthly stipends and preferential medical and educational benefits.

Disciplinary measures against those who violate the policy include stiff fines, withholding of social services, demotion, and other administrative punishments, including, in some instances, loss of employment. Unpaid fines have sometimes resulted in confiscation or destruction of personal property. Because penalties for excess births may be levied against local officials and the mothers' work units, many persons are affected, providing multiple sources of pressure.

Physical compulsion to submit to abortion or sterilization is not authorized, but Chinese officials acknowledge privately that there are still instances of forced abortions and sterilizations in remote, rural areas. Officials maintain that, when discovered, abuses by local officials result in discipline or retraining. They admit, however, that stronger punishment is rare and have not documented any cases where punishment has occurred. A sharp reported drop in fertility rates in 1991-92 sparked concern about a possible upturn in incidents of coercion. One cause for worry about such increased pressures was a policy change in early 1991 making local political officials more directly responsible for success in meeting family quotas. There was strong evidence, however, that the magnitude of the reported fertility drop was sharply exaggerated, in part because the policy change intensified strong existing incentives for officials and families to underreport births.

At least five provincial governments have implemented regulations with eugenics provisions, beginning with Gansu in 1988. These regulations seek to prevent people with severe mental handicaps from having children. National family planning officials say they oppose such legislation, but the Government has taken no action to overturn these local laws.

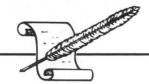

February

GAO REPORT ON DRUG PRICES
February 2, 1994

Drug makers charged an average of 60 percent more in the United States than the United Kingdom for identical, best-selling drugs, according to a study by the General Accounting Office (GAO), the investigative arm of Congress. The GAO reported the results of its study January 12 to Rep. Henry A. Waxman (D-Calif.), chairman of the House Subcommittee on Health and Environment and a critic of high health care costs, and released the report publicly February 2.

Several members of Congress said the study's findings supported President Bill Clinton's proposal that the government impose restraints on drug prices to bring down health care costs. Between 1980 and 1991, U.S. pharmaceutical prices rose an average of 3.4 percent per year above the general rate of inflation, while in the United Kingdom they declined by 1.3 percent a year after adjusting for inflation, according to the report. A similar GAO study released in 1992 comparing drug prices in the United States and Canada found that, on average, the wholesale price of drugs widely dispensed in the United States was 32 percent higher than for the same drugs in Canada.

The new report acknowledged that the rate of increases in U.S. drug prices had slowed since 1990, reflecting voluntary price restraints imposed by drug manufacturers. Nonetheless, both consumers and policy makers remained unhappy about the high cost of drugs in the United States, largely because of perceptions that the same drugs were sold elsewhere more cheaply, the report said.

The GAO study examined wholesale prices as of May 1, 1992. Generally, those prices were two-thirds of what retailers charged consumers at local drug stores. Starting with a list of the two hundred drugs most frequently dispensed in the United States in 1991, the GAO compared the prices of seventy-seven drugs that were sold in the same form and dosage in the United Kingdom.

The GAO found that Amoxil, the most commonly dispensed drug in the United States, actually cost 40 percent less in the United States than in the United Kingdom. However, the next four most commonly dispensed drugs in the United States—Premarin, Zantac, Lanoxin, and Xanax—cost 197, 58, 169, and 278 percent more, respectively, in the United States than in the United Kingdom. Of the seventy-seven drugs reviewed, prices for forty-seven were at least twice as high in the United States as in the United Kingdom.

Manufacturers Cite Research Costs

The Pharmaceutical Manufacturers Association criticized the new GAO report, as it had the earlier Canadian study, saying that those studies did not account for the cost of extensive research that American pharmaceutical companies undertake. The study of drug prices in the United States and the United Kingdom, the association said, "compares prices in the best health care system in the world with prices in one of the worst systems among major industrialized countries."

The GAO report noted that Canada did not have a big drug industry involved in research. In contrast, it said, drug manufacturing in Great Britain was large-scale and active in research and development. However, it portrayed the market as being dominated by the National Health Service, which reimbursed nearly all prescription drug purchases and regulated drug company profits. The United States market, by contrast, was characterized by many buyers and unregulated prices.

The Pharmaceutical Manufacturers Association reported in May 1992 that drug manufacturers spent an average of $231 million over twelve years of development and testing to bring a new drug to market. At Waxman's request, in 1993 the congressional Office of Technology Assessment (OTA) looked into the drug industry's assertion that high research costs justified the prices manufacturers set for drugs. OTA researchers reported that most of the drugs introduced in the United States between 1975 and 1989 "offered little therapeutic advantage over preexisting competitors." Waxman said the report found that "58 percent of industry research was invested in so-called me-too drugs, drugs that are designed to make a profit but which add nothing in terms of therapeutic benefits to patients." (OTA Report on Prescription Drug Prices, Historic Documents of 1993, p. 197)

Other Drug Price Inquiries

The GAO and OTA reports were far from the first to challenge drug prices. In 1959 a Senate panel headed by Sen. Estes Kefauver, D-Tenn., began hearings into the drug industry's pricing, patent, and business policies. Senate investigators concluded that drug prices were "unreasonable," but price regulations were dropped from the resulting legislation.

In 1984 Congress again addressed the price question by making it easier to market generic copies of drugs whose patents had expired. Generic drugs were invariably cheaper than the original versions. In 1991 the Senate Special Committee on Aging issued a staff report saying high drug prices had

produced "excessive and unconscionable profits" for pharmaceutical com-
panies.

Another challenge to the drug manufacturers came in October 1994 from
retailers. More than 1,300 pharmacies in fifteen states joined in a broad
legal challenge to the manufacturers' practice of charging retailers higher
prices for prescription drugs than they charged certain health plans, hospi-
tals, and mail-order prescription services. The retailers contended that the
manufacturers' pricing methods were helping to force many retail pharma-
cies out of business. The lawsuits were consolidated in U.S. District Court
in Chicago for a trial that was expected to begin in early 1996.

Following is an excerpt from the General Accounting Office
report, "Prescription Drugs: Companies Typically Charge
More in the United States Than in the United Kingdom," dated
January 12, 1994, and publicly released on February 2, 1994:

Background

Both the differences and the similarities between the United States and the
United Kingdom make a comparison between the two countries' pharmaceutical sectors illuminating. While pharmaceutical companies in the two
countries are similar in several respects, U.S. and U.K. firms face very different market conditions.

The United Kingdom, like the United States but unlike Canada, is home to a
strong, research-oriented pharmaceutical industry. The U.K. pharmaceutical
industry, which consists of privately owned and operated companies, remains
with the United States as one of the world's leaders in pharmaceutical research and development. The United Kingdom ranks third in the world—
behind only the United States and Japan—in the number of major global
drugs introduced between January 1970 and May 1992. As of 1991, three of the
world's 20 top-selling pharmaceutical firms were based in the United Kingdom, including the world leader, Glaxo.

Despite the similarity between the two industries, firms in the United Kingdom operate in a very different market environment compared with companies in the United States. The United Kingdom has a much smaller market,
with a population about one-fifth the size of the United States. Furthermore,
in the United Kingdom, the prescription drug market is dominated by the government, which reimburses nearly all prescription drug purchases and regulates drug company profits. By contrast, the U.S. market is dominated by private payers, including many consumers who lack insurance coverage to pay
for prescription drugs and who pay prices for pharmaceuticals that are not
subject to regulation. While the U.K. government is tantamount to the single
purchaser of prescription drugs in that country, the U.S. pharmaceutical market is characterized by many buyers. As a result, U.S. drug manufacturers can
offer lower prices to certain buyers, like mail order pharmacies and some

managed care organizations, while charging relatively higher prices to other buyers, such as wholesalers who serve typical retail pharmacies.

Since 1980, the United States has experienced greater drug price increases than has the United Kingdom. Between 1980 and 1991, U.K. pharmaceutical prices declined an average of 1.3 percent per year after adjusting for overall inflation. By contrast, U.S. pharmaceutical prices increased by an average of 3.4 percent per year, after adjusting for overall inflation. (However, since 1990, consistent with drug manufacturers' public pledges of self-restraint in pricing, the growth in U.S. drug prices has declined.)

Scope and Methodology

The results of our analysis are restricted to the May 1, 1992, prices of the drugs that we analyzed and cannot be projected beyond the scope of our study. In addition, our study is based on the prices for which drug manufacturers sell their products to wholesalers; it does not measure retail prices paid by consumers for drugs at pharmacies in the United States or the United Kingdom. As agreed . . . we defined the scope of our study as follows.

First, for the identical drugs sold in the United States and the United Kingdom, we compared manufacturers' factory prices. We focused on these prices because—unlike wholesale or retail prices—factory prices allow us to determine whether drug manufacturers are charging higher prices in the United States for drugs sold in both countries. Further, manufacturers' charges are a significant component of final consumer costs as they account for roughly two-thirds of the final or retail average prescription charge in the United States.

Second, we studied the prices of brand-name drugs. In focusing on the manufacturer's role in pricing, we compared the factory prices of the identical drugs sold in the United States and the United Kingdom by the same manufacturers (or their foreign affiliates). This same manufacturer criterion led us to exclude generic drugs from our sample because generic drugs are usually manufactured and sold in the United States and other countries by different, unaffiliated companies.

Third, we concentrated our analysis on that segment of the drug market populated by the typical consumer who, in both the United States and the United Kingdom, buys prescription drugs at retail pharmacies. We focused our study on this market segment because in the United States these consumers are relatively vulnerable to high drug prices. Although these consumers account for at least 55 percent of all outpatient prescriptions in 1992, they generally do not benefit from discounts that certain purchasers, such as hospitals, mail order pharmacies, and certain health maintenance organizations (HMOs), may obtain from manufacturers.

We summarized the spectrum of differences in drug prices between the United States and the United Kingdom by constructing a price index that accounts for differences in the quantities of each drug sold in the United States. To identify the likely causes of drug price differences across countries, we interviewed U.K. government officials, as well as industry representatives and academic experts in both countries.

To provide perspective on our central findings, we conducted additional price comparisons. First, to permit us to contrast the typical consumer's perspective on factory prices of drugs with the manufacturer's perspective, we also estimated U.S.-U.K. price differentials using an average U.S. price measure that includes discounts and rebates provided to certain nonfederal institutional buyers. The average U.S. price does not address our central question—how factory prices differ between the market segments frequented by typical consumers in the United States and the United Kingdom. Nonetheless, the average U.S. price does help shed light on a related question that is vital to manufacturers—how the amount of revenue per package received by the manufacturers differs between the United States and the United Kingdom. Second, because lower priced generic drugs are available as alternatives to some higher priced brand-name drugs, we also estimated the price differential that would occur if American consumers always substituted generic drugs, if available, for the brand-name drugs in our sample. . . .

Principal Findings

Manufacturers Typically Charge More for Prescription Drugs in the United States Than in the United Kingdom

We found significant differences in the prices that manufacturers charge wholesalers for identical, frequently dispensed prescription drugs sold in retail pharmacies in the United States and the United Kingdom. A market basket of 77 frequently dispensed drugs that we analyzed would cost wholesalers 60 percent more in the United States than in the United Kingdom. A total of 66 drugs (86 percent) were priced higher in the United States than in the United Kingdom, and 47 (61 percent) were priced more than twice as high in the United States as in the United Kingdom. U.S.-U.K. drug price differentials varied substantially among individual products. U.S. prices ranged from 62 percent lower to 1,712 percent higher than the U.K. prices.

Price Differentials Smaller for Newer Medicines and Single-Source Drugs

Price differentials tended to be dramatically smaller for more recently introduced drugs in our sample than for older products. In our sample, the market basket of drugs introduced before 1980 cost 120 percent more in the United States than in the United Kingdom, while the market basket of drugs first introduced between 1980 and 1985 cost 60 percent more in the United States, and the market basket of drugs introduced between 1986 and 1992 cost 17 percent more in the United States. This pattern is consistent with both the effect of U.K. restrictions on price increases and with reports that manufacturers have narrowed country-by-country differences in the introductory prices of new drugs in recent years.

In addition, price differentials tended to be smaller for single-source brand-name drugs in our sample than for brand-name drugs that have generic substitutes. For example, the market basket of drugs that were multiple source in both countries cost 125 percent more in the United States than in the United Kingdom, while for single-source drugs the corresponding difference was 45 percent. Because drugs with generic substitutes have usually been on the market longer, this finding is consistent with our result that older drugs have wider price differentials. In addition, this result is consistent with findings from other studies that suggest that, in the U.S. market, manufacturers respond to competition from lower priced generic drugs by increasing—rather than decreasing—the prices of brand-name products.

Methodological Choices Do Not Significantly Alter Qualitative Results

In conducting international comparisons of drug prices, the precise size of drug price differentials depends on the methodological choices made. Other researchers might make different decisions than we did and, consequently, report price differentials that are smaller or larger than what we found. Nonetheless, our qualitative result—that prescription drug prices are significantly higher in the United States than in the United Kingdom—is largely unaffected by the methodological decisions we made.

Some of these methodological choices depend on the particular question being asked. Consider the following examples:

- Other researchers might be concerned with how manufacturers' factory prices charged in the United Kingdom compare to the average factory prices paid by all market segments in the United States (including those who have access to manufacturers' discounts), rather than to the segment consisting of the typical U.S. consumer. We found, however, that whether one looks at the typical consumer market segment or the entire market had a modest impact on the overall price differential.
- Others may also want to calculate how price differentials vary when accounting for the possibility that consumers can sometimes buy less expensive generic substitutes. We found that, for the brand-name drugs in our sample, if U.S. consumers purchased lower priced generic substitutes when available, and U.K. consumers did not, U.S. consumers would still pay substantially more for our market basket of drugs.

Other choices relate to the more technical issues of performing an international drug price comparison, such as how to convert U.K. prices into U.S. dollars. For example, we still found substantial drug price differentials by using the 1992 purchasing power parity (rather than the May 1, 1992, exchange rate) to express U.K. drug prices in U.S. dollars. There was also little change in the results when we used either the second quarter 1992 exchange rate or the 1992 average exchange rate to convert pounds sterling to dollars. These rates were similar to the May 1, 1992, exchange rates.

Primary Factors Contributing to U.S.-U.K. Price Differentials

Most of the differences in prescription drug prices between countries cannot be attributed to differences in manufacturers' costs. This conclusion holds for differences in costs whether they are associated with research and development, marketing, production, or distribution. Pharmaceutical manufacturers' officials and industry experts agree that cost differences are not a major factor in determining prices for individual drug products.

Instead, we found that U.S.-U.K. drug price differences are primarily due to the regulatory constraints that manufacturers face in pricing their drugs on the U.K. market and to the lack of similar constraints in the United States. In the United Kingdom, the government, operating within a health system that is publicly financed and run, is tantamount to the sole payer for prescription drugs. The U.K. government exercises its concentrated buying power through an agreement with drug manufacturers; this agreement limits the profits that drug manufacturers earn on sales in the United Kingdom. Although manufacturers are generally free to set the introductory prices of newly released drugs in the United Kingdom, each manufacturer's profits must not exceed the maximum level established by the government. Furthermore, once introductory prices are set, the government restricts manufacturers from increasing prices on existing products.

Qualitative evidence suggests that other competitive factors in the U.K. market may work together to lower average brand-name drug prices:

- Pharmaceutical information is more widely available in the United Kingdom than in the United States, perhaps enhancing price competition among drug manufacturers in the United Kingdom. U.K. physicians receive information on their own prescribing patterns and on the comparative prices and efficacy of drugs. In addition, physicians in the United Kingdom are given prescribing benchmarks, referred to as indicative amounts, that encourage them to be aware of the prices of the drugs they prescribe and how their prescribing patterns compare to national averages.
- The government can remove drugs in certain therapeutic categories from its list of reimbursable products if the manufacturers' prices for those drugs are considered excessive.
- Wholesalers and retailers can import brand-name drug products into the United Kingdom from other European countries where drugs are available at lower prices (known as parallel importing). Parallel importing may exert downward pressure on prices of some brand-name drugs, thereby contributing to lower average U.K. drug prices.

Implications of U.K.-Style Government Intervention in the U.S. Market Remain Unclear

Although government regulation has restrained drug prices in the United Kingdom, the implications of similar intervention in the U.S. pharmaceutical market are unclear. Little agreement exists on the appropriate level of U.S. drug prices, and no consensus has emerged on what, if any, mechanism should be used to achieve this price level. Regulatory approaches used in the United Kingdom, while apparently effective at restraining drug prices in that country, may not be easily transferrable to the United States because of the many institutional differences between the two countries. In addition, the debate over the potential effects of drug price regulation—particularly the contention that higher drug prices encourage pharmaceutical research and development—cannot be resolved solely by referring to U.K. drug prices. This larger issue is beyond the scope of our study. . . .

LIFTING OF TRADE EMBARGO AGAINST VIETNAM
February 3, 1994

Nineteen years after the end of the Vietnam War in 1975, when U.S.-backed South Vietnam fell to communist North Vietnam, President Bill Clinton announced February 3 that he was lifting the U.S. trade embargo against Vietnam. The embargo had been imposed upon North Vietnam in 1964 and was extended to the rest of the country in 1975. In lifting the embargo, the president said he was "absolutely convinced" that the decision "offers the best way to resolve the fate of those [Americans] who remain missing and about whom we are not sure." When Clinton made his announcement, more than 2,200 Americans were still officially listed as missing in Indochina.

In a briefing shortly before the announcement, a senior administration official emphasized that lifting the embargo was "just the beginning" in the process of improving relations between the two nations. "This is not normalization of diplomatic relations," he said.

The day after Clinton's announcement, Vietnam's foreign ministry issued a statement hailing the move and pledging to "continue to cooperate fully" in resolving the issue of missing Americans. Hanoi also agreed to the establishment of liaison offices between the two countries as a step toward full diplomatic relations. At the same time, Deputy Foreign Minister Le Mai rejected Clinton's remark that lifting the embargo was not "irreversible," and that it could be reimposed if Hanoi backtracked on its cooperation in accounting for missing Americans. "No nation in the world has the right to impose a trade embargo on another nation or to threaten to reimpose an embargo," he said.

Impact on Vietnam Economy, U.S. Investment

Lifting the embargo was expected to have a positive economic impact on Vietnam, where the average annual income of the 69 million citizens was only about $200 a year. Beginning in 1986, when the Soviet Union reduced *its aid, Hanoi started emphasizing the creation of a market economy, legalized private production, and encouraged foreign investment and diplomatic contacts. The result was that gross domestic product in 1993 grew by 7 percent, and foreign investment by thirty-four countries climbed to $7.5 billion in January 1994.*

Speculation about the impact of U.S. investment focused on the fact that Vietnam, one of the poorest nations in the world, was unlikely to provide much of a market in the immediate future for U.S. goods. However, the country was seen as a potentially lucrative site for investment. Yet some $230 million in U.S. private claims against Vietnam remained unresolved, most of them involving American business investments in South Vietnam seized by the government when the war ended.

The POW/MIA Issue

Clinton's announcement followed stepped-up administration efforts to account for prisoners of war (POWs) and those missing in action (MIAs). In announcing the embargo action, the president emphasized that the embargo could be reimposed if Vietnam's cooperation on the POW/MIA issue ceased. Shortly before he made his remarks, the president met with veterans groups to assure them that lifting the embargo could serve as a spur to progress in accounting for missing Americans by further improving relations between the two countries. In 1993, sixty-seven remains had been recovered, more than double the number recovered the previous year. In 1992, the Vietnamese government had started encouraging citizens to turn over any remains they might be holding and also established an office to increase efforts to recover remains.

In the United States, by 1994 virtually all the Vietnam War POW/MIA documents had been declassified, with more than 1.5 million pages available for review at the Library of Congress. U.S. investigators had determined the fate of all but seventy-three of the missing Americans. Nonetheless, veterans groups and MIA family organizations firmly opposed lifting the embargo, arguing that Vietnam was still withholding information about missing Americans. The American Legion called on its 3.1 million members to wage a "no holds barred" campaign to maintain the embargo.

Strong Support for Lifting the Embargo

In contrast to the concern expressed by veterans groups, political support for lifting the embargo had grown steadily. It had been helped by the release in January 1993 of a 1,223-page report by the Senate Select Committee on POW/MIA Affairs that concluded there was "no compelling evidence" that American servicemen listed as missing were still alive and being held as POWs. (Senate Report on Vietnam POWs, Historic Documents of 1993, p. 113)

Returning from a visit to Vietnam in mid-January 1994, Sen. John F. Kerry (D-Mass.), chairman of the Senate Subcommittee on East Asian and Pacific Affairs and a highly decorated Vietnam War veteran, said the em-

bargo no longer served any useful purpose and was only hurting U.S. businesses by denying them access to markets. On January 27, a bipartisan group of senators approved by a 62-38 vote a nonbinding resolution urging Clinton to lift the embargo. The resolution was sponsored by Kerry and Sen. John McCain (R-Ariz.), who had spent nearly seven years as a POW in Vietnam.

The Washington Post *also cautiously endorsed ending the embargo. In an editorial published shortly before Clinton's announcement, the newspaper said that "progress had to be dragged out of the Vietnamese practically one name and one soldier's remains at a time. . . . Vietnam remains a totalitarian state, and this poses severe restrictions on what information Americans can expect to gain even in a context of improving official relations. But it is time to cross over and try the new path."*

Less than two weeks after Clinton's action on the embargo, United Nations High Commissioner for Refugees Sadako Ogata announced that Vietnamese refugees would no longer be automatically eligible for asylum as political refugees. "A chapter is coming to an end in Indochina and Southeast Area," said Ogata. Between 1975 and the early 1980s, hundreds of thousands of "boat people" fled Vietnam, most of them traveling to the United States. In 1979, Vietnam agreed to the "Orderly Departure Program," which allowed legal immigration. Under that program, nearly 500,000 Vietnamese citizens emigrated, more than 350,000 of them to the United States.

Following are President Bill Clinton's February 3, 1994, remarks announcing the lifting of the U.S. trade embargo against Vietnam:

From the beginning of my administration, I have said that any decisions about our relationships with Vietnam should be guided by one factor and one factor only: gaining the fullest-possible accounting for our prisoners of war and our missing in action. We owe that to all who served in Vietnam and to the families of those whose fate remains unknown.

Today I am lifting the trade embargo against Vietnam because I am absolutely convinced it offers the best way to resolve the fate of those who remain missing and about whom we are not sure. We've worked hard over the last year to achieve progress. On Memorial Day I pledged to declassify and make available virtually all government documents related to our POWs and MIA. On Veterans Day I announced that we had fulfilled that pledge. Last April, and again in July, I sent two presidential delegations to Vietnam to expand our search for remains and documents.

We intensified our diplomatic efforts. We have devoted more resources to this effort than any previous administration. Today, more than 500 dedicated military and civilian personnel are involved in this effort under the leadership of General Shalikashvili, Secretary Aspin and our Commander in the Pacific, Admiral Larson.

Many work daily in the fields, the jungles, the mountains of Vietnam, Cambodia and Laos, often braving very dangerous conditions, trying to find the truth about those about whom we are not sure. Last July I said any improvement in our relations with Vietnam would depend on tangible progress in four specific areas:

First, the recovery and return of remains of our POWs and MIA. Second, the continued resolution of discrepancy cases—cases in which there is reason to believe individuals could have survived the incident in which they were lost. Third, further assistance from Vietnam and Laos on investigations along their common border, an area where many U.S. servicemen were lost and pilots downed. And, fourth, accelerated efforts to provide all relevant POW/MIA-related documents.

Today, I can report that significant, tangible progress has been made in all these four areas. Let me describe it. First, on remains. Since the beginning of this administration, we have recovered the remains of 67 American servicemen. In the seven months since July, we've recovered 39 sets of remains, more than during all of 1992.

Second, on the discrepancy cases. Since the beginning of the administration, we've reduced the number of these cases from 135 to 73. Since last July, we've confirmed the deaths of 19 servicemen who were on the list. A special United States team in Vietnam continues to investigate the remaining cases.

Third, on cooperation with Laos. As a direct result of the conditions set out in July, the governments of Vietnam and Laos agreed to work with us to investigate their common border. The first such investigation took place in December and located new remains as well as crash sites that will soon be excavated.

Fourth, on the documents. Since July, we have received important wartime documents from Vietnam's military archives that provide leads on unresolved POW/MIA cases. The progress achieved on unresolved questions is encouraging, but it must not end here. I remain personally committed to continuing the search for the answers and the peace of mind that families of the missing deserve.

There's been a substantial increase in Vietnamese cooperation on these matters over the past year. Everyone involved in the issue has affirmed that. I have carefully considered the question of how best to sustain that cooperation in securing the fullest possible accounting. I've consulted with my national security and veterans affairs advisers, with several outside experts, such as General John Vessey, the former Chairman of the Joint Chiefs of Staff, who has been an emissary to Vietnam for three presidents now. It was their view that the key to continued progress lies in expanding our contacts with Vietnam.

This was also the view of many distinguished Vietnam veterans and former POWs who now serve in the Congress, such as Senator Bob Kerrey and Congressman Pete Peterson, who are here. And I want to say a special word of thanks to Senator John Kerry—is he here? There he is. He just came in. And Senator John McCain, who had to go home on a family matter and could not be here. But I thank the two of you so much for your leadership and your steadfastness. And all the rest of you—Senator Robb and so many others, especially those who served in Vietnam, for being counted on this issue and for taking all the care you have for such a long time.

I have made the judgment that the best way to ensure cooperation from Vietnam and to continue getting the information Americans want on POWs and MIAs is to end the trade embargo. I've also decided to establish a liaison office in Vietnam to provide services for Americans there and help us to pursue a human rights dialogue with the Vietnamese government.

I want to be clear: These actions do not constitute a normalization of our relationships. Before that happens, we must have more progress, more cooperation and more answers. Toward that end, this spring I will send another high-level U.S. delegation to Vietnam to continue the search for remains and for documents.

Earlier today, I met with the leaders of our nation's veterans organizations. I deeply respect their views. Many of the families they represent have endured enormous suffering and uncertainty. And their opinions also deserve special consideration. I talked with them about my decision. I explained the reasons for that decision. Some of them, in all candor, do not agree with the action I am taking today.

But I believe we all agree on the ultimate goal—to secure the fullest possible accounting of those who remain missing. And I was pleased that they committed to continue working with us toward that goal.

Whatever the Vietnam war may have done in dividing our country in the past, today our nation is one in honoring those who served and pressing for answers about all those who did not return. This decision today, I believe, renews that commitment and our constant, constant effort never to forget those until our job is done. Those who have sacrificed deserve a full and final accounting. I am absolutely convinced, as are so many in the Congress who served there and so many Americans who have studied this issue, that this decision today will help to ensure that fullest possible accounting.

DE LA BECKWITH'S RETRIAL FOR EVERS ASSASSINATION
February 4, 1994

When Hinds County assistant district attorney Bobby DeLaughter began his closing argument February 4 in the murder trial of Byron De La Beckwith, an unrepentant segregationist, in the assassination of civil rights leader Medgar Evers, he faced a jury that included members who were not even born in 1963, the year Beckwith allegedly committed his crime.

The path from the night of June 12, 1963, when an assassin shot Evers in the back with a 1917 Enfield 30.06 rifle as Evers returned to his home in Jackson, Mississippi, to this day nearly thirty-one years later had been a long and tortuous one. Evers had been the first Mississippi field secretary for the National Association for the Advancement of Colored People (NAACP), a job that in the late 1950s and early 1960s involved extreme danger. Evers organized voter registration drives for blacks, arranged economic boycotts of businesses that discriminated against blacks, and investigated violence and discrimination against blacks for NAACP headquarters. According to his wife, Evers knew that sooner or later he would be killed, as were so many other civil rights workers. Only days before the assassination, Evers's home had been bombed.

The night of June 12, Evers had attended a meeting, while his wife and three children sat at home watching President John F. Kennedy make a groundbreaking speech on television about civil rights. "We face . . . a moral crisis as a country and a people," Kennedy said. "A great change is at hand and our task, our obligation, is to make that revolution, that change, peaceful and constructive for all."

As Evers stepped from his car in his driveway, a single, fatal shot rang out. In nearby bushes, police found a rifle that belonged to Beckwith and had his fingerprint. Beckwith was a well-known racist in a state where a black person who attempted to register to vote might be pistol whipped or worse. In 1957, he wrote to the Jackson Daily News: *"I do believe in segregation like I believe in God. I shall make every effort to rid the U.S. of integrationists."*

Beckwith was charged with murdering Evers. During jury selection for Beckwith's first trial in 1964, the tone was set by a question from the prosecutor: "Do you believe it is a crime to kill a nigger in Mississippi?" Any person who hesitated in answering the question was immediately excluded from the jury. Later in the trial, the prosecutor called Evers's work for the NAACP "repugnant, repulsive, obnoxious." Beckwith's defense rested primarily on the testimony of three police officers who said they had seen him ninety miles from the crime scene at about the time Evers was murdered. Beckwith also claimed that his gun had been stolen before the murder. As the jury started deliberating, Gov. Ross Barnett strode into the courtroom to shake Beckwith's hand, a gesture that made it clear where the white establishment stood in the case. The all-male, all-white jury deadlocked, as did a similar panel at a second trial, and Beckwith walked away a free man.

Newspaper's Investigation Reopens Case

That is where the case stood until 1989, when the Clarion Ledger *newspaper in Jackson published an article stating that a former state agency known as the State Sovereignty Commission had helped the defense screen jurors in Beckwith's two trials. Prodded by the newspaper article, Hinds County District Attorney Ed Peters reopened the case. Although the investigation did not find any jury tampering, it did find new witnesses who said that Beckwith had bragged to them about murdering Evers or that they had seen Beckwith's car near Evers's home around the time of the murder. Based on the new witnesses, Beckwith was indicted again in 1990.*

By the time the new trial opened in early 1994, Beckwith was seventy-three, many of the witnesses from the earlier trials had died, and some of the evidence—including the bullet that killed Evers—was missing. The new jury was far different from the previous panels, consisting of eight blacks and four whites. It seemed the only thing that had not changed was Beckwith, who was still as violently racist as ever. "I'm proud of my enemies," said the man who wore a Confederate flag pin in his lapel each day of the trial. "They're every color but white, every creed but Christian."

During the new trial, six people testified that Beckwith had told them, either directly or indirectly, that he had killed Evers. Perhaps the most damaging witness was Mark Reiley, a former guard in the prison ward of a Louisiana hospital whom Beckwith befriended after being arrested for bomb possession. Reiley testified that a black nurse had taken offense when Beckwith had called her a "nigger," and that a loud fight ensued. "He was screaming back at her, 'If I could get rid of an uppity nigger like Medgar Evers, I would have no problem with a no-account nigger like you,' " Reiley testified. Other witnesses testified that they had seen Beckwith's distinctive car near Evers's home the night of the murder.

Ghost Witnesses Testify at Trial

Some of the testimony came from the grave, with the judge allowing lawyers to introduce testimony given at Evers's first two trials by people who had since died. The ghost witnesses included two FBI agents, a Hinds County sheriff, Jackson City police detectives, a cab driver, and a gun shop owner. Defense attorneys objected, saying that introducing the testimony was unfair because they could not cross-examine the witnesses.

The chief defense witness was one of the police officers who had testified thirty years earlier that he had seen Beckwith ninety miles away at the time of the crime. He stuck to his story, despite harsh cross-examination. One of the other officers had since died, and the third was too ill to testify. The judge allowed their testimony from Beckwith's earlier trials to be read to the jury.

It took the jury only six hours to convict Beckwith of murder, and the judge immediately sentenced him to life in prison. It was unclear, however, whether Beckwith would actually serve any time in jail, since it could take years for his appeals to proceed through the courts. Some legal observers said Beckwith had a strong appeal, based on claims that his constitutional rights to a speedy trial and to due process had been violated by the new trial. Meanwhile, some activists hoped that Beckwith's case would lead to the reopening of other decades-old civil rights cases.

> *Following are excerpts from the closing argument of Hinds County assistant district attorney Bobby DeLaughter on February 4, 1994, in the Circuit Court of the First Judicial District of Hinds County, Mississippi, trial of Byron De La Beckwith, who was charged with murdering Medgar Evers in 1963:*

When we started the testimony a little over a week ago now, I stood before you and I told you what the evidence would show in this case. I told you then that when all the evidence was in, you would see what this case was about; you would see what this case was not about; and now that you have all the evidence before you; now that the judge has instructed you on the law, then you know what this case is about. And you know that what it is about is about an unarmed man, arriving home the late hours of the night, having been working, coming home to his family, his wife, three small children that were staying up, waiting on him to get home inside the home there, getting out of his automobile with his back turned, and being shot down by a bushwacker from ambush. And that he dropped T-shirts in his arms, and he crawled from that automobile where he was gunned down, down the side of that carport, into the carport, trying to make it to his door, in this puddle of blood, with his keys in his hand, and his wife and children coming out when they hear the shot, and his three children stating over and over, "Daddy, daddy, please get up." And that's what the case is about. This man being gunned down and shot down in the back in the dark from ambush, not able to face his self-appointed accuser, his judge, and his executioner.

And the Court has given you several instructions. And this instruction here tells you what the case is about legally. Legally, it's about whether or not this defendant killed and murdered Medgar Evers on June the 12th, 1963. And you've taken an oath to make that determination, not on speculation, not on conjecture, and not on guesswork, and not what if and not what maybe, but on the evidence. And this doesn't say unless the defendant is of a certain age, because no man, ladies and gentlemen, is above the law. And if we start making decisions like that doesn't have anything to do with the law, eventually, where do we draw the line. Do we say in this case, "We're gonna draw the line when the person is 70-something," and in another case if they're 65. No man, regardless of his age, is above the law. And it doesn't say, "Unless you find that this offense was committed 30 years ago." It says, "If you believe from the evidence that he did it on June 12th of 1963, he's guilty, and it's your duty to find him guilty."

Because you see, ladies and gentlemen, what we're talking about here, this type of offense, this type of murder, this assassination by a sniper from ambush is something that's timeless. This is something that spans the races. It is something that every decent human being should absolutely be sickened by, whether you be black, white, Hispanic; it doesn't matter. Murder by ambush is the most vile, savage, reprehensible type of murder that one can imagine. And that's what you've got here.

This isn't about black versus white or white versus black. This is about something that is reprehensible to decent minds. This is about society, civilized society, versus the vile, society versus the reprehensible, society versus the shocking. This, ladies and gentlemen, is about the State of Mississippi versus this defendant, Byron De La Beckwith. . . .

And so we know from the evidence that on Saturday before Medgar Evers was gunned down, this defendant was in Jackson, Mississippi; couldn't find his prey's residence. Why? Because Medgar Evers, by that time, had to get an unlisted phone number. He couldn't just go to a phone book and look up his number and his address. And so he was down there at the Continental Trailways bus station trying to find out where he lived. And we know from the evidence that he went up to some cab drivers trying to find out. And then, we know after that his car was seen parked on the north side of Pittman's Grocery, right there in the area. And so we know he was here on Saturday trying to find where Medgar Evers lived; was able to find where Medgar Evers lived; drove to the location; walked into that vacant lot, getting things ready and set up. And then we know he went back to Greenwood; got this rifle; got the scope that was on there that he had just bought from John Goza a month before this; went out; target practiced, getting those cross hairs, those sights set in for his target; got that scar over his right eye when the recoil of that rifle, when that scope jammed his eyeball there; went to work on Monday; worked all day; but what was on his mind? What did John Book tell you? All he wanted to do was talk about integration and guns. Couldn't even keep his mind on his business that day.

And so the next day was the day. The next day was the day, and his car is seen by those then-teenage boys in that area again. His car is seen by Barbara Holder who worked at times at Joe's Drive-In. This car, his car, is seen parked in that corner with the rear end backed into it, where all he's got to do is get out of that car right here in the corner where it was parked; walk down that path as shown in the pictures; get to this clump of trees; and wait. And he waited, and while he's waiting, he takes his hand and he breaks off this branch here, and what does he have? He has a hole. And what do you see in that hole? His perfect view of the driveway of Medgar Evers, and he waits.

And after midnight that night, Medgar Evers, unsuspecting, gets out; gets his T-shirts out of the car; and this rifle was propped up against this sweet gum tree that we know from the testimony of Officer Luke and the other detectives that were in the area that described the scratch mark in the bark there. And so he takes this rifle, and he braces it up against a tree, and he finds Medgar Evers, his prey in this scope, and he pulls the trigger, and ends his life in one fatal shot, leaving six live cartridges in the weapon.

He gets in his car. On the way out, he cannot be found holding that weapon in his car. No matter what his planning, no matter his effort—remember what Barbara Holder told you of when he pulled in to this area, instead of driving up in here, instead of coming around the front, the car came from around the back. And so after he does his dirty work and he's on the way back to his car, per chance if he's seen or stopped, he can't afford to have this rifle with him in that automobile. And so he takes it, and he sticks it in the honeysuckle vines right here behind this hedge row. Gets in his car, and leaves directly, and he's heading north on Delta Drive, Highway 49, back to his home in Greenwood.

And so the gun is found in the search the next day. His gun. The same gun that he had traded, had obtained from Ennis Thorn McIntyre. We know that how? Several ways. The serial number on this gun matches the serial number on the invoice where Mr. McIntyre first purchased it from International Firearms. We also know from the testimony of that FBI agent at the crime lab, Richard Poppleton. Remember when he told you that he compared the cartridges that had been removed from this weapon with cartridges that McIntyre had provided to the FBI, and from comparing the individual microscopic characteristics that would be caused by that firing pin, and that breech face, and that firing pin and that breech face alone matched. Those cartridges came from one and the same gun, and you're looking at it. This defendant's gun. This defendant's scope. His gun. His fingerprint. His car.

We're not just talking about some 1960s model white Valiant. We're talking about a 1962 white Valiant that witnesses say what? It also had a long aerial on it. And we're not even just talking about a car that witnesses say was a 1960s white Valiant with a long aerial. What did they say? What did they say, not only in this courtroom, but in the courtroom 30 years ago and to the police, it was a white Valiant—Ronald Pittman said it was a white Valiant, a 1962 white Valiant, long antenna on it, long aerial, and what else? "The thing I remember most about it, when we got up close was that emblem on the rear view mirror."

And so what did the police do? What did we have the police do? What did we have the FBI do in recent years? To go back and get this photograph, the negative from this photograph, enlarge this area here, and let's see if it has any type of emblem hanging from it. And so, lo and behold, there she is. Now, a person's words may be one thing, but a picture speaks a thousand words.

His gun. His scope. His fingerprint. His car. And lastly, but certainly not least, his mouth. When he thought he had beat the system 30 years ago, he couldn't keep his mouth shut with people that he thought were gonna be impressed by him, and that he thought were his buddies and comrades, two of them from the Klan, one in Florida, one from Mississippi testified. At least six people have given you sworn testimony that at various times in different locations, none of whom knew each other or came across each other at any time, told you what he has said about this. He wants to take credit for what he has claimed should be done, but he just don't want to pay the price for it. And so he hasn't been able to keep his mouth shut.

And so not only do we have his car, his gun, his scope, his fingerprint, his mouth, we've got his own venom. His venom has come back to poison him just as effectively as anything else.

And why did this happen? Why did any of this happen? For what reason was Medgar Evers assassinated? For what he believed. Not in necessary self-defense was this done. Medgar Evers didn't do anything of a violent nature to this defendant. What he did was to have the people gall, the uppitiness (sic) to want for his people. Things like what? To be called by name, instead of boy, girl. . . . To go in a restaurant, to go in a department store, to vote, and for your children to get a decent education in a decent school. For wanting some degree of equality for himself, his family, and his fellow man, and for them to be accepted as human beings with some dignity. This kind of murder, ladies and gentlemen, no matter who the victim, no matter what his race; this kind of murder, when you're talking about somebody that's assassinated, shot down in the back for what they believe, for such meager things as wanting some dignity, when that kind of murder happens, there is just a gaping wound laid on society as a whole. And even where justice is fulfilled, that kind of murder, that kind of wound will always leave a scar that won't ever go away. We have to learn from the past, folks, and where justice is never fulfilled—justice has sometimes been referred to as that soothing balm to be applied on the wounds inflicted on society—where justice is never fulfilled and that wound can never be cleansed, all it does is just fester and fester and fester over the years.

And so it is up to the system; it's up to the law-abiding citizens, and the law of the State of Mississippi that the perpetrator of such an assassination be brought to justice. This defendant. So that the decent law-abiding people of this state will maintain a new respect for the value of human life, and that our state will truly be one that is of the people, for the people, and by the people, no matter what your race, color or creed is.

One of the defense attorneys early on in the jury selection process asked whether or not any of you had heard something to the effect of the eyes being on Mississippi or Mississippi on trial. Mississippi is not on trial. And I'm not sure what eyes are on Mississippi, but this I do know. Justice in this case, in whatever case, is what the jury says it is. Justice in this case is what you twelve ladies and gentlemen say it is. So in this case, in effect, you are Mississippi. So what is Mississippi justice in this case, ladies and gentlemen? What is Mississippi justice for this defendant's hate-inspired assassination; assassination of a man that just desired to be free and equal?

If you analyze the evidence, use your common sense that God gave you, examine your heart, your consciences, and base your verdict on the evidence and the law, then you will have done the right thing. If you base it on the law and the evidence, and in the spirit of human dignity, there's no question in my mind that whatever you come out with, it'll be the right thing, because I have faith that it will be to hold him accountable. And the only way to do that is to find him guilty.

Remember the words of the Psalms—psalmist, as I have over the past four years. "Commit your way to the Lord, trust in Him, and He will act. He will make your vindication shine like the light, and the justice of your cause as the noon day." From the evidence in this case, the law that you've sworn to apply, it can't be but one way if justice is truly going to be done.

And so on behalf of the State of Mississippi, I'm gonna do what I told you I was gonna do in the very beginning. I'm gonna ask you to hold this defendant accountable. You have no part in sentencing. That's something that the law will take care of. It's up to the Court. But to hold him accountable, find him guilty, simply because it's right, it's just, and Lord knows, it's just time. He has danced to the music for 30 years. Isn't it time that he pay the piper? Is it ever too late to do the right thing? For the sake of justice and the hope of us as a civilized society, I sincerely hope and pray that it's not.

DECISION IN TAILHOOK
COURT-MARTIALS
February 8, 1994

In a court-martial proceeding arising from the 1991 Tailhook scandal, a military judge dismissed charges against three Navy officers on the grounds that misconduct by Adm. Frank B. Kelso II, the chief of naval operations, tainted the case.

Tailhook was a convention in Las Vegas attended by thousands of Navy and Marine Corps fliers. An investigation by the Pentagon inspector general found that eighty-three women—many of them military officers—had been fondled or sexually assaulted at Tailhook. Many of the assaults occurred in a "gauntlet" formed by drunken aviators on the convention hotel's third floor. The men grabbed the breasts and buttocks of women who walked by to get to hospitality suites. In some cases, the women's clothes were ripped off.

Two of the three Navy officers charged in the court-martial were accused of failing to stop junior officers from assaulting women. The third was accused of assaulting a woman himself. Their defense rested largely on a contention that Kelso, the Navy's top officer, witnessed improper activities, did nothing to stop them, and then covered up his role in the affair.

In a 111-page decision, Circuit Military Judge William T. Vest Jr. said the evidence supported the defense's claim and he dismissed the case. More than a dozen witnesses placed Kelso in the area where sexual misconduct occurred, and Kelso actually witnessed public nudity and "leg shaving" of women, Vest wrote. The judge also said it was improper for Kelso to appoint the officer who supervised punishment of those implicated in Tailhook when he faced the possibility of charges himself.

In addition, Vest blasted Kelso and other senior Navy officials for knowing about problems at past Tailhook conventions but taking no action. "As events have proven, this embarrassing failure of leadership and 'head in the sand' attitude, which conveyed a signal of condonation, contributed to the sexually offensive conduct which later escalated to the actual sexual assaults on female attendees," he wrote.

Vest's criticism of the Navy's leadership echoed a report issued in April 1993 by the Pentagon inspector general. Many fliers considered the annual conference a "free fire zone" where drunkenness and sexual misconduct were officially condoned, the 1993 report said. For years, senior Navy officers knew Tailhook included heavy drinking, strippers, sexual assaults, indecent exposure, and other improper behavior, but did nothing. Instead, they continued to spend thousands of dollars annually to send aviators to the conference, which was sponsored by a private organization for Navy and Marine Corps aviators. Once the scandal became public in the fall of 1991, the Navy severed its official relationship with the Tailhook Association. (Defense Department Report on Tailhook, Historic Documents of 1993, p. 315)

Kelso Denies Charges

Kelso angrily defended himself after the court-martial decision was released. As he had during the trial of the three officers, Kelso asserted that he had not witnessed anything improper at Tailhook and denied being in the areas where sexual activities occurred.

Kelso also said he had done nothing to cover up his activities at the convention and released documents supporting his version of events. One was a memorandum to Defense Secretary William J. Perry from the Pentagon's deputy inspector general, who conducted an extensive investigation into Tailhook. "During our investigation, we were unable to find any credible evidence that Admiral Kelso had specific knowledge of the improper incidents and events that took place," wrote Deputy Inspector General Derek J. Vander Schaaf.

Despite Kelso's pledge that he would not resign, within a week after the court-martial ended he announced his early retirement. It came as part of a deal in which Perry and Navy Secretary John Dalton issued statements praising Kelso's integrity and honesty. Kelso reportedly sought the statements to rebut the damage to his reputation caused by the judge's decision. Kelso's early retirement was largely symbolic, however, since it came only two months before he was scheduled to retire anyway and he received his full pension.

Kelso had nearly lost his job in late 1993, when Dalton tried to fire him for his lack of leadership on Tailhook. Dalton ultimately was overruled by Defense Secretary Les Aspin.

The day after the court-martial decision was released, the last case stemming from Tailhook was dismissed because of insufficient evidence. It involved a Marine Corps lieutenant colonel who was charged with lying and obstructing justice during the Tailhook investigation, assaulting a Tailhook investigator, and spending a night during the convention with a woman who was not his wife.

Thus ended efforts to discipline 140 Navy and Marine officers accused by the Pentagon inspector general of improper activities at Tailhook. Most of the cases were dismissed, although approximately 50 officers received ad-

ministrative discipline of varying degrees. In some cases, the disciplinary action effectively blocked further promotion.

The investigations into officers' conduct at Tailhook were severely hampered by a lack of cooperation by witnesses, many of whom were fellow officers. In an editorial, the Washington Post *said: "No one was convicted because scores of commissioned officers lied about what they had witnessed."*

Coughlin Resigns

The day after the last Tailhook case was dismissed, the woman who filed the first complaint about being assaulted at Tailhook resigned from the Navy. Lt. Paula Coughlin, a helicopter pilot, said in her letter of resignation that the attack at Tailhook "and the covert attacks on me that followed have stripped me of my ability to serve." Coughlin had accused a Marine captain of assaulting her, but prosecutors dropped the case after deciding she was mistaken about the identity of her attacker.

Less than a month after the last Tailhook case was dismissed and Kelso resigned, four women who served in the military told a House committee that despite reforms that allegedly occurred after Tailhook, the military still handled sexual complaints improperly. The women, who represented each of the armed services, said they—not their attackers—were punished when they filed complaints about improper sexual advances or assaults.

Lt. Darlene Simmons, a lawyer in the Navy Reserves, said she was forced to undergo a psychiatric examination after she reported that her commander was sexually harassing her. Superiors to whom she reported the harassment told her to keep the matter quiet. The examination found that Simmons was fit to serve, and the commander who harassed her eventually retired. Simmons said that before reporting the harassment, she "was a successful attorney with an impeccable reputation, and now I am regarded as a trouble maker with no future in the Navy."

As the women testified on Capitol Hill, the first of about 500 women were receiving orders assigning them to serve on the USS Eisenhower, an aircraft carrier. They became the first women to serve as full-time crew members on combat ships, although women had been allowed to serve on Navy support ships since 1978. In the 1993 defense authorization bill, Congress cleared the way for women to serve on combat ships.

Some believed that allowing men and women to serve together would reduce the incidence of sexual abuse. Ironically, one who took that view was Kelso, who in 1992 admitted that excluding women from combat may have contributed to the Tailhook incident.

> *Following is an excerpt from the decision of Circuit Military Judge William T. Vest Jr., issued February 8, 1994, in the cases of* United States v. Thomas R. Miller, CDR USN; United States v. Gregory E. Tritt, CDR USN; and United States v. David Samples, LT USN, *a general court-martial related to events at the Tailhook convention:*

I. Nature of Motion

On motion through defense counsel, CDR Miller, CDR Tritt, and LT Samples move this court to dismiss the charges brought against them for the following two separate but related reasons.

First, that ADM Frank B. Kelso II, Chief of Naval Operations (CNO) is an "accuser" within the meaning of Article 1(9), Uniform Code of Military Justice (UCMJ). Further, that he was an "accuser" at the time he appointed VADM Paul Reason, Commander Naval Surface Force, U.S. Atlantic Fleet, to act as the convening authority in their respective cases. The defense then argues that pursuant to Rule for Courts-Martial (R.C.M.) 504, ADM Kelso's status as an "accuser" must result in the disqualification of VADM Reason from acting as the convening authority. This would be true if ADM Kelso is an "accuser," as R.C.M. 504 requires the disqualification of any convening authority junior in rank or command.

Second, the defense contends that since ADM Kelso may have been guilty of the same or similar crimes of omission as those alleged against CDRs Miller and Tritt, his appointment of a subordinate officer to act as convening authority effectively shielded him from prosecution and thus amounted to unlawful command influence within the meaning of Article 37, UCMJ.

In support of these two broad contentions, CDR Miller, CDR Tritt and LT Samples more specifically contend the following chain of events:

(1) CDR Miller and CDR Tritt are charged, *inter alia*, with being present and then failing to take action to stop subordinate officers, including several officers assigned to their command, from assaulting certain unidentified females by touching them on the buttocks with their hands during the 1991 Tailhook Symposium (hereinafter "Tailhook 91").

(2) The alleged failure to act as well as the alleged assaults on the unidentified females by the subordinate Navy officers took place on the third floor pool patio of the Las Vegas Hilton (hereinafter "patio") during the evening hours of Saturday, 07 September 1991.

(3) ADM Frank B. Kelso II, CNO, was also present on the patio on 07 September 1991 at or about the time these alleged crimes took place.

(4) ADM Kelso later denied being present on the patio at any time during the evening hours of Saturday, 07 September 1991. He likewise denied being in the third floor hallway or in any of the various squadron hospitality suites at any time.

(5) Subsequent to this interview, the Defense Criminal Investigative Service (DCIS) obtained the statements of a substantial number of eyewitnesses who recalled seeing, and in some cases speaking with, ADM Kelso on the patio during the evening hours of Saturday, 07 September 1991.

(6) Based on these eyewitness statements, ADM Kelso was reinterviewed by DCIS on 15 April 1993. At this interview ADM Kelso was advised of his rights under Article 31(b), UCMJ, as a suspect. He was advised that he was under suspicion of violating Articles 107 and 134, UCMJ (Mak-

ing a False Official Statement and False Swearing, respectively), both suspected crimes stemming from his 23 July 1992 statement wherein he denied being on the patio Saturday evening, 07 September 1991.

(7) That likewise on the prior evening, Friday, 06 September 1991, ADM Kelso was present on the patio, which he acknowledges, and also in the third floor hallway and made personal visits to the various squadron hospitality suites, which ADM Kelso denies.

(8) That during this earlier Friday visit, ADM Kelso witnessed inappropriate conduct occurring on the patio and in the hospitality suites, including female "leg shaving." This personal knowledge of inappropriate behavior by subordinate officers, combined with his failure as the senior Navy officer present to stop the behavior, is sufficient to make ADM Kelso a suspect in the commission of the same type of crimes (failure to act) alleged against CDR Miller and CDR Tritt. At the very least he would be considered a material witness to these events. That, furthermore, ADM Kelso's personal knowledge and involvement with the misconduct at Tailhook 91, and the subsequent publicity surrounding the allegations of assault and failure of Navy leadership, have so closely connected him with these events that he would reasonably be perceived to have a personal interest in the courts-martial of CDRs Miller and Tritt and LT Samples.

(9) On 01 February 1993, ADM Kelso personally appointed VADM Reason to act as the Consolidated Disposition Authority (CDA) to take administrative and disciplinary action for all Navy personnel found to have committed misconduct at Tailhook 91. ADM Kelso further directed that all related matters requiring review would be forwarded to his office for action.

The defense contends these events taken together lead to the disqualification of the convening authority. In short, they reason as follows: ADM Kelso's presence on the patio during the evening hours of 06 and 07 September 1991, at which times he either observed or knew of the inappropriate behavior of his subordinates and failed to act to stop such behavior; ADM Kelso's subsequent status as a criminal suspect and as a potential material witness; and, the current controversy regarding ADM Kelso's denial that he was ever physically present on the patio during the evening hours of 07 September 1991—viewed either separately or collectively—give him an interest "other than official" in the outcome of the prosecution of courts-martial stemming from Tailhook 91.

If ADM Kelso has an "other than official interest" in this litigation generally or these three accused's cases specifically, he is an "accuser" within the meaning of Article 1(9), UCMJ. As an "accuser," ADM Kelso was disqualified from appointing any subordinate in rank or command to convene a court-martial stemming from Tailhook 91, and as a subordinate in rank and command to ADM Kelso, VADM Reason became a "junior accuser" and was disqualified from acting as the convening authority in these cases pursuant to R.C.M. 504(c)(2).

Finally, that ADM Kelso's action in appointing a subordinate, VADM Reason, to act as the CDA when ADM Kelso knew himself to be a possible suspect for his own actions related to Tailhook 91, which appointment effectively shielded himself and possibly other officers senior to VADM Reason from courts-martial, amounted to unlawful command influence within the meaning of Article 37, UCMJ.

Briefly, the government generally denies the above contentions and responds that ADM Kelso never visited the third floor hallway or the hospitality suites during his stay at Tailhook 91 and, although he did visit the patio on Friday, he never went to the third floor at all on Saturday evening, 07 September 1991. Further, since ADM Kelso never personally witnessed any inappropriate conduct, he would not be a material witness. That throughout this court-martial process, ADM Kelso has had only an official interest in the litigation and has taken no action that would in any way influence these proceedings. Finally, the government responds that the evidence fails to establish that ADM Kelso has been so closely connected to these events that a reasonable person would conclude that he had more than simply an official interest in the cases of CDRs Miller and Tritt and LT Samples.

II. Background to Tailhook 91

The defense claims that the nexus linking ADM Kelso's personal involvement in Tailhook 91 to the charges before this court does not arise from any single event. The defense argues that ADM Kelso's personal involvement derives from all of his connections with the events of these courts-martial beginning with his knowledge of reported incidents of inappropriate behavior at Tailhook Symposiums prior to 1991, and continuing up to his appearance as a witness before this court. In order to assess the merit of this claim by the defense, and to bring Tailhook 91 events germane to the defense issues into proper perspective, the court will begin with an analysis of the evidence relating to the Navy's past sponsorship of the Tailhook Association. This includes reports of inappropriate behavior occurring at past Tailhook Symposiums and the Navy's response to these reports.

This court finds that:

1. Tailhook 91 was held at the Las Vegas Hilton Hotel, Las Vegas, Nevada, from 05 through 08 September 1991. It was attended by hundreds of aviators, male and female, including active duty, reserve, and retired officers from both the Navy and Marine Corps aviation communities. Also in attendance were many high ranking uniformed Navy and Marine Corps officers and civilian Department of the Navy (DON) personnel, including ADM Kelso and then Secretary of the Navy (SECNAV), H. Lawrence Garrett III.

2. The Tailhook Symposium was an annual event sponsored by the Tailhook Association. At the time of Tailhook 91, the Association was officially sanctioned by the Department of the Navy. However, following reports of alleged assaults on female attendees and other inappropriate conduct at Tailhook 91, the Navy withdrew its support of the Association.

The stated purpose of the annual symposium was to provide a single forum within the Navy and Marine Corps aviation communities to address a broad range of matters affecting the state and future of naval aviation. Tailhook 91 was to be particularly significant since it provided an opportunity to address the recent combat successes of "Operation Desert Storm," and a future aviation plan then under consideration by the Congress. The future role of female aviators would also be a major topic of discussion, which was one of the primary reasons that ADM Kelso attended.

3. Despite the worthy official purpose, the evidence is replete with references to the annual symposium's long-standing and widely-known reputation for wild partying, heavy drinking, and lewd behavior by some attendees, particularly junior aviators. Reports of such activities at past Tailhook Symposiums had sparked concerns at the highest levels of the Navy.

In 1986, VADM Martin, then serving as the Assistant Chief of Naval Operations for Air Warfare (OP-05), formally expressed his concerns in writing regarding inappropriate behavior at the 1985 Symposium. This led to a routine practice by Tailhook Association Presidents of sending a letter to aviation squadron commanders prior to each annual symposium urging moderation regarding social activities. CAPT Ludwig, then President of the Tailhook Association, sent such a letter to squadron commanders some weeks prior to Tailhook 91. In his correspondence, CAPT Ludwig, being concerned with past incidents of misbehavior among some symposium attendees, urged squadron commanders to guard against what he termed "late night gang mentality."

Col. Wayne Bishop, USMC, former Special Assistant and Marine Corps Aide to SECNAV, and who attended Tailhook 91 with Secretary Garrett, harbored serious reservations concerning both Secretary Garrett's and his own attendance at Tailhook 91. Col. Bishop's concerns stemmed from reports he had received of inappropriate behavior occurring at past Tailhook Symposiums. This included what he described as:

> stories concerning pornographic movies, strippers and prostitutes . . . lots of drinking, junior officers and senior officers, flag officers, removing themselves from their office for the purpose of discussing contentious issues in the aviation community one-on-one.

VADM Dunleavy, who was serving as the Assistant Chief of Naval Operations for Air Warfare (OP-05) at the time of Tailhook 91, was also keenly aware of the social climate at past Tailhook Symposiums. In his sworn statement to Mr. Suessman, DCIS, of 28 July 1992, VADM Dunleavy acknowledged his attendance at the 1990 Tailhook Symposium. In discussing his knowledge of reported incidents of inappropriate behavior at that Symposium, VADM Dunleavy stated,

> I've seen some wild stuff over the years . . . broken furniture and spilled drinks. . . . I heard of the '90 Gauntlet from my son . . . he says it is a bunch of drunks running around chasing girls. . . . It's a grab ass of JOs [junior officers] . . . everyone just lines up in the passageway and every good looking girl that goes through they grab at some of that.

In commenting on the term "late night gang mentality" used by CAPT Ludwig in his letter to squadron commanders prior to Tailhook 91, VADM Dunleavy stated, "[t]he kids just getting out of hand in the sense of dancing and, you know, mooning people. . . ."

Secretary Garrett was also aware of the potential for inappropriate activities at Tailhook 91. He attended the 1990 Tailhook Symposium, at which time he acknowledged witnessing "female leg shaving" activities. The potential for inappropriate behavior at Tailhook 91 was also anticipated by members of Secretary Garrett's personal staff. He was warned by at least one highly vocal member of his staff not to attend Tailhook 91 because of the well-known reputation for lewd and inappropriate behavior.

4. This court finds that this quantum of information concerning the symposium's notorious social reputation prior to Tailhook 91, and in particular the warnings given by VADM Martin and CAPT Ludwig, could not have escaped ADM Kelso's attention. It served to place him and other high ranking officers on notice as to the social climate at past Tailhook Symposiums, and the kind of social environment to expect at Tailhook 91.

The failure by those responsible to take strong corrective action regarding inappropriate behavior that obviously occurred at past Tailhook Symposiums is incomprehensible. As events have proven, this embarrassing failure of leadership and "head in the sand" attitude, which conveyed a signal of condonation, contributed to the sexually offensive conduct which later escalated to the actual sexual assaults on female attendees. This excusing attitude was underscored by Secretary Garrett's in-court testimony that he did not find the female leg shaving exhibition to be offensive. He further stated that he viewed the female leg shaving to be permissible as "conduct between consenting adults."

Excessive drinking, "pornographic movies, strippers, and prostitutes," all of which had been a well known part of past Tailhook conferences, were repeated again at Tailhook 91 as part of the planned activities in the hospitality suites. Finally, the infamous gauntlet, in which male Navy officers felt it was permissible to grab at any woman who walked past—and which was at the heart of the complaints by female attendees—was likewise a tradition of past Tailhook conferences. It should go without saying that this behavior should have never been permitted to start, having started should have been swiftly ended, and that over the years of permissive leadership had gotten completely out of hand. This common knowledge of inappropriate and offensive behavior at past symposiums and failure by senior Navy leadership to take corrective action is an inseparable part of the motion before this court.

5. Within days following Tailhook 91, LT Paula Coughlin, a female aviator, was the first to formally complain to the Naval Investigative Service (NIS) that she had been the victim of an assault in the gauntlet on the third floor. In the weeks that followed, other female attendees also came forward to complain of being assaulted. The growing reports of sexual assault quickly generated public outrage and a demand by the Congress for an investigation to both identify the assailants and secure individual accountability under the UCMJ. It is the actions of ADM Kelso in carrying out his codal rule in the ensuing mili-

tary justice process, and the extent to which his own accountability and personal involvement at Tailhook 91 may have affected the lawfulness of this process, that have been called into question by the defense.

[III and IV omitted]

V. Legal Analysis

. . . IT IS HEREBY ORDERED, based upon the findings of this court (1) that ADM Kelso is an "accuser" within the meaning of Article 1(9), UCMJ, with regard to each accused and (2) that there has been both actual and apparent unlawful command influence in each case, the charges against CDR Thomas R. Miller, U.S. Navy, CDR Gregory E. Tritt, U.S. Navy, and LT David Samples, U.S. Navy are hereby DISMISSED WITHOUT PREJUDICE to the government's right to reinstate court-martial proceedings against the accused for the same offenses at a later date. . . .

GAO TESTIMONY ON CHILD CARE QUALITY
February 11, 1994

The need for daytime child care was growing at the same time that the ability of state regulators to monitor and assure the quality of that care was declining, according to testimony by Joseph F. Delfico, director of income security issues at the U.S. General Accounting Office (GAO), during a February 11 hearing by the House Subcommittee on Regulation, Business Opportunities, and Technology. The GAO is the investigative arm of Congress.

The lack of inspections often resulted in unsafe conditions for children, said June Gibbs Brown, inspector general of the Department of Health and Human Services, at the same hearing. Brown told the panel that unannounced federal inspections of day care centers in North Carolina, South Carolina, Nevada, and Wisconsin had found toilets that did not work or had not been flushed, raw sewage in areas where children played, infestations by roaches, fire exits that were locked or blocked, and broken glass, sharp knives, and toxic substances within easy reach of children. Even after the deficiencies were identified, some went uncorrected, she said.

In his testimony, Delfico said many states also did not check the backgrounds of child care workers. For example, seventeen states did not conduct criminal background checks on workers, and nineteen did not check whether the workers' names appeared on child abuse registries. Brown agreed that the lack of background checks was a major problem. In North Carolina, she said, federal investigators found child care workers who had been arrested for prostitution, theft, and possession of illegal drugs.

States were responsible for enforcing day care standards. In 1990, when Congress created a program that awarded grants to child care centers, there was debate about whether the federal government should set standards for day care. Proponents of federal action lost the debate, leaving states to set and enforce their own standards. In that same year, nearly 12 million children were in day care.

Delfico said that while the demand for day care was surging because the number of women entering the labor force was skyrocketing, state budget problems were reducing oversight of day care centers. Most state licensing directors said on-site monitoring was critical in ensuring that centers met state standards, yet eighteen states had recently reduced the frequency of their on-site inspections, Delfico reported. Inspectors in thirty-eight states checked each center less than twice each year.

Inspections of home-based day care facilities were even less frequent, Delfico said. Six states did not inspect these facilities at all. Twenty-nine states averaged one or fewer visits each year for each facility, with some of them visiting only a sample of the facilities. He also cited a 1990 study by the Department of Education that estimated that 82 percent to 90 percent of home-based day care facilities were exempt from all standards.

The frequency of inspections was decreasing because many states had been forced to cut funding and staff, Delfico said. Thirty-two states had been forced to make cutbacks in 1991 alone, he said, at the same time that caseloads were rapidly increasing. State officials predicted that caseloads would continue to rise.

The hearing was especially significant because welfare reform plans being considered by Congress would provide education and training for welfare recipients—especially single mothers—to enable them to hold jobs and become economically self-sufficient. Adoption of such a plan would further boost the demand for day care and put an even greater strain on state enforcement efforts.

Another report issued two months later also painted a bleak picture of the day care situation. On April 7, the Families and Work Institute, a private research group in New York, released a report that found that only 9 percent of home-based facilities provided high-quality care. The report, titled "The Study of Children in Family Child Care and Relative Care," examined family day care in Los Angeles, Dallas, and Charlotte. The report rated more than half the homes only adequate or "custodial," meaning they neither harmed nor helped a child's development. Another third of the homes were considered potentially harmful. It also found that 81 percent of the facilities were unregulated, in violation of state law.

In an interview with the New York Times, *Jay Belsky, a child care researcher at Pennsylvania State University who was not associated with any of the studies, said the poor quality of child care in America was "one of our best-kept secrets. The moral of the story here is not that day care is inevitably bad for children, but that the care that America dispenses to its children leaves a lot to be desired. The crime is that we know how to make it better. It's an issue of will and money."*

Some good news was reported in May in a study by the National Center for Children in Poverty titled "In the Neighborhood: Programs That Strengthen Family Day Care for Low-Income Families." It found that home-based day care in low-income neighborhoods could be of excellent quality if a network of support services existed for the providers. The report examined ten pro-

grams around the country and found that the successful efforts carefully chose providers, trained them, monitored children in the homes, and provided networking opportunities for the providers.

Following is the text of a statement titled "Child Care Quality: States' Difficulties Enforcing Standards Confront Welfare Reform Plans," delivered February 11, 1994, before the House Subcommittee on Regulation, Business Opportunities, and Technology, by Joseph F. Delfico, director of income security issues for the U.S. General Accounting Office:

During the past two decades the number of women in the labor force has soared. This has led to a surge in the demand for child care—a surge expected to continue. As of 1990, 7.6 million children under the age of 13 were enrolled in centers and 4 million were in family day care homes. Responsibility for the quality of that care, through the setting of quality standards and enforcement, rests almost exclusively with state and local governments. We conducted a survey of the states to get a nationwide picture of how well states are enforcing their child care standards. We found some erosion in the use of their most effective enforcement practices, as well as innovations designed to compensate for that erosion. As demand for child care continues climbing throughout this decade, states will be further challenged to ensure the health and safety of children in care.

Welfare reform may pose an additional test to states' ability to protect children. Currently, more than 9 million children are on welfare, and the present welfare system requires only a small fraction of their parents to be in school or training. However, new proposals discuss requiring more welfare clients to participate in education or training, as well as requiring them to find work after 2 years. Should this happen, more welfare parents will enter the child care market, possibly straining state enforcement resources further.

In my statement today, I would like to discuss four topics: (1) a brief description of the growth in demand and supply of child care, (2) what is quality child care and why it is important, (3) what states do to protect children in care and why this has become difficult, and (4) further complications for states under welfare reform.

During the last 20 years, the demand for child care has steadily increased. In that time, the number of working women with children under age 6 has doubled—from 30 percent in 1970 to 60 percent in 1991. Similarly, in the last 20 years, the supply of child care has increased. For example, since the mid-1970s, the number of child care centers has tripled, going from more than 18,000 in 1976-77 to almost 56,000 in 1990. The number of children cared for full-time in centers quadrupled, going from approximately 900,000 in 1976-77 to 3.8 million in 1990.

Given these trends, the number of new providers is likely to continue to grow, renewing interest in the quality of the care being provided.

The question of quality arose recently during the passage of the Child Care and Development Block Grant. The purpose of the block grant, which was passed in 1990, is to assist states in purchasing child care for low-income parents, as well as to increase the availability and quality of child care for all families. The block grant is one of very few programs that requires states to spend some of their block grant money on improving the quality of child care. During its passage, a protracted debate occurred over whether the block grant should impose federal child care quality standards on states. Although those arguing for federal standards lost, concerns remain about the states' role in ensuring quality services for all families.

What is quality child care, and why is it important?

Simply put, quality care is care that nurtures children in a stimulating environment, safe from harm. Quality care has two critical elements. First, at its most basic level, it must provide care that protects children's safety and health. This means that child care facilities have working smoke detectors, covered electrical outlets, properly stored food, and no dangerous chemicals within reach of children. To this end, states have a significant role to play. Second, quality care must be enriching and developmentally appropriate. This means it must have adequately trained staff, low staff-to-child ratios, low staff turnover, and age-appropriate materials and space.

Why is it important? Children start learning from the time they are born, according to the latest research. And the quality of care they receive, whether from a parent or someone outside the home, can either nurture their learning or inhibit it. A child's success later in life, particularly in school, will depend on this early support. With about 12 million children in full- or part-time child care today, it is easy to see that the quality of this care has enormous implications not only for the well-being of our children but also our society.

With almost 12 million children in child care as of 1990, states' responsibility for protecting these children is a formidable task. How do states ensure that child care meets accepted safety and health standards? In all states, the key activities for doing this are setting standards, screening prospective providers, conducting on-site monitoring, and imposing sanctions.

First, through their legislatures, states set their own standards that child care providers must meet. As a result, child care standards vary considerably among states. If a provider does not meet these standards, it cannot operate—at least, not legally. While these standards cover a broad range of areas, such as the number of caregivers required per child to the amount of square footage needed, many focus on safety and health aspects. For example, state standards might stipulate the number of fire extinguishers needed by a provider or whether a child must be immunized before entering care.

Standards not only specify the level of care that providers must meet; they also determine which providers must meet them. In fact, states exempt a significant number of providers from state standards. For example, a 1990 national study funded by the Department of Education estimates that approximately 82 to 90 percent of family day care providers—those who care for children in their homes—are exempt. Examples of other types of child care that states may exempt are those sponsored by religious organizations, in government entities like schools, or those operating for part of the day.

Finally, for those providers who are regulated, different standards apply to different types of providers. Centers generally must meet more rigorous standards; family day care providers usually must meet fewer and less stringent ones.

Second, states screen prospective providers to determine suitability by eliminating individuals who do not meet the standards, such as for age (e.g., too young), criminal background, and others. Several licensing directors believe that comprehensive screening up front helps prevent enforcement problems later. To this end, screening is seen as a cost-efficient prevention tool: it helps eliminate people who see child care as an easy business to start, but who may be unqualified to care for children.

Regarding the issue of screening providers, federal legislation passed in November 1993 requires states to submit their child abuse crime information to the Federal Bureau of Investigation's criminal history background check system. The purpose of this law is to give states access to these records in order to conduct criminal background checks on child care providers. At the time of our report, we found that 17 states did not conduct criminal background checks on center providers, and 21 states did not do this for family day care providers. We also found that 19 states did not conduct child abuse registry checks for centers, and 17 did not do this for family day care providers.

Through on-site monitoring, licensing officials periodically visit providers to determine whether state standards are being met. These visits can be either announced or unannounced. An on-site visit is believed to help deter noncompliance, as well as present opportunities to educate and help providers comply with state standards. In these ways, states use on-site monitoring as an oversight and a prevention tool for ensuring that a basic level of care is provided.

As with standards, states differ in the frequency with which they monitor providers and in the type of provider monitored. From our work, we found that 38 states monitor centers, on average, less than twice each year. Regarding monitoring family day care providers, 6 states do not visit this type of provider at all; 29 states average one or fewer visits and 10 of these visit only a sample of these providers.

Sanctions are penalties imposed by a state when a provider does not meet state standards. As such, a state's ability to sanction is closely linked to its monitoring capacity. Sanctions range from requiring corrective action plans to closing a facility.

In our survey, more than two-thirds of state licensing directors ranked on-site monitoring as their most effective tool for assuring that standards are met. Yet some states' capacity to do this has been eroding. In 1989, several states began conducting monitoring less often than in the past or less often than their policy required. At the time of our survey, for example, 18 states have reduced the frequency of their visits, averaging 1.7 visits a year per center. Thirteen states conducted visits less often than state policy required; most visited centers about once a year while their policy required two visits.

Further, we compared state monitoring practices with monitoring standards set by the National Association for the Education of Young Children (NAEYC). NAEYC is the nation's largest association of early childhood professionals whose main purpose is to improve professional practice in early childhood care. It sets a minimum standard of at least one *unannounced* visit per year. We found that 20 states do not meet this standard. NAEYC recommends a higher standard of at least two visits per year—one, unannounced. Our survey found that 39 states do not meet this standard.

The primary reason for monitoring cutbacks was budget cuts resulting in shortages. For example, 32 states had to cut funding and staff for programs in 1991. Budget-reduction strategies included hiring freezes, across-the-board cuts, and layoffs. This was coupled with increased caseloads, that is, the number of providers they had to visit increased. More than two-thirds of the states reported to us larger caseloads of centers and family day care homes. Furthermore, almost as many states predicted increased caseloads in the next 2 years.

Because of tight budget conditions, states have tried to "work smarter," especially in regard to on-site monitoring. Examples of this included prioritizing inspections to focus on providers with a poor compliance history, reducing the amount of time for visits by monitoring only key standards, and automating data collection tasks to process paperwork quickly.

Further evidence of states' adjusting to their fiscal constraints was their pursuit of other activities to supplement screening, monitoring, and sanctioning efforts. Many focused on preventive strategies, such as provider training and educating parents to protect children and improve quality with fewer resources.

Most states regulate only a small portion of the providers in their states, and they are struggling to do even that. Given this, an important question still remains: Will the quantity of child care providers overwhelm the states' capacity to ensure safety?

This question is important in light of current welfare reform proposals. The proposals before the Congress and many already initiated by states expand work and training requirements for welfare clients, which means that an expanded use of child care will occur simultaneously. We believe this will add to burgeoning state licensing and monitoring caseloads and exacerbate the states' difficulties by drawing more providers into the market.

However, another complication may arise. If child care supply grows to meet a new demand spawned by welfare reform, it may be in that part of the market that states already exempt from standards. For example, some low-income families, in particular, working-poor, single mothers, rely heavily on relative and family day care. More than 50 percent of low-income children in these families had such arrangements in 1990. But, as mentioned earlier, family day care is mostly unregulated, as is care provided by relatives. Given that states cannot regulate all providers nor is regulation appropriate for some types of providers, states pursue other methods to help build safe, quality care in their states. Examples of these activities include educating parents on how to choose safe care and training providers about state standards and good practices. But, these activities take resources, too. Given this, GAO believes that assessing state efforts to protect children in child care in the face of expanding child care services is critical. The new welfare reform initiatives only underscore the urgency of this task. . . .

As a postscript, while there is cause for concern about states' ability to protect children while in care, there is also cause for hope. In the most recent *Fiscal Survey of the States*, published in October 1993, 38 states reported that revenues matched or exceeded projected revenues. This contrasts with several prior years in which many states' revenues fell so short of projections that states were forced to reduce, mid-year, their enacted budgets. The National Association of State Budget Officers believes that its fiscal survey, to be released in April 1994, will show even more improvement. Should that prove true, more state resources may be available to help state licensing offices with their critical task of ensuring safe and healthy child care.

PRESIDENT'S ECONOMIC REPORT, ECONOMIC ADVISERS' REPORT

February 14, 1994

President Bill Clinton and his Council of Economic Advisers (CEA) painted a generally optimistic picture of the American economy in their economic reports to Congress on February 14. The reports built on Clinton's five-year, $5 billion deficit reduction plan, which he presented to a joint session of Congress on February 17, 1993, slightly less than a month after he was sworn in as the nation's forty-second president. (Clinton's Five-Year Economic Plan, Historic Documents of 1993, p. 181)

In his report, Clinton said that "for too long and in too many ways, our Nation has been drifting," which he attributed to "a false prosperity on a mountain of Federal debt." The president said that his administration had replaced "drift and deadlock with renewal and reform. . . . As a result of our efforts, the economy is now on a path of rising output, increasing employment, and falling deficits." The president attributed his success to congressional approval of increased taxes and cuts in federal spending.

Although predicting continued growth in the U.S. economy, Clinton's report cautioned that problems could lie ahead if long-term interest rates rose, consumer spending took a downturn, and growth in the European and Japanese economies continued to be sluggish.

Clinton's philosophy represented a departure from that of his Republican predecessors, who had called for less government interference in the economy and lower tax rates. Clinton's report depicted an active government role in investing more heavily in education, job training, and research. (President's Economic Report; Economic Advisers' Report, Historic Documents of 1992, p. 97)

Deficit Reduction Boosts Growth

The report by the CEA took up the same theme in a section that called on the government to assume a more active role in manufacturing research and policing monopolies and private sector pollution. "I think there is some-

thing different about the whole tone of this [report]," said CEA Chair Laura D'Andrea Tyson at a press conference where the document was released. "There is a lot here implicitly about the role for the government to do something that would be beneficial to the future performers of the economy, not harmful."

The CEA forecast strong economic growth due in large part to successful efforts to reduce the deficit. The council forecast that the economy would grow by 3 percent in 1994, creating 8 million jobs in the next four years. It predicted that consumer and investor spending would continue to be strong because of gains in employment and output, low long-term interest rates, and continued growth in demand. The report also forecast a shrinking trade deficit.

Among the principal indicators of a healthy economy, the report cited the following:

- *In 1993, 162,000 new jobs were created each month—twice the rate of 1992.*
- *From December 1992 to December 1993, the unemployment rate fell from 7.3 percent to 6.4 percent—the largest annual decline since 1987.*
- *During 1993, business investment in durable equipment expanded at the fastest rate since 1972.*
- *By December 1993, housing starts had risen 25 percent from the July rate.*
- *The inflation rate, as measured by the consumer price index, increased at 2.7 percent during 1993—the smallest increase since 1986.*

Tyson noted, however, that there were long-term problems involving a "disappointing growth in per capita real incomes" and "absolute declines in family incomes.... [T]he fundamental challenge is restoring brisker growth to the compensation Americans earn...."

Who Gained from the Upswing?

Many economic analysts agreed with the administration's forecasts. More good economic news came in a Congressional Budget Office (CBO) report, which was released shortly before the CEA report. The CBO calculated that the proportion of the deficit to the overall economy would be smaller in fiscal 1995 than at any time since 1979. Federal Reserve Board Chairman Alan Greenspan also said that the outlook for continued growth was "increasingly well-entrenched."

While the economic news was generally good, it remained unclear exactly who was benefiting from the upswing. On March 8, the Labor Department reported that although productivity gains were high, investors rather than workers were enjoying most of the benefits. The Labor Department said that worker wages and benefits increased only 0.6 percent in 1993, compared with a productivity increase of 1.7 percent. "Wealth is being generated by the recovery, but it is not being distributed very equitably," said Jeff Faux, president of the Economic Policy Institute, a liberal think tank in Washington, D.C.

In addition, some Republicans said administration policies should not take all the credit for improvements in the economy. Some said that actions by agencies such as the Federal Reserve deserved far more credit than the administration. "In considering President Clinton's gusher of praise for his economic record today, we should remember that no modern president's economic program has required less than eighteen months to have an impact on the economy," said Sen. Phil Gramm (R-Texas), a potential contender for his party's presidential nomination in 1996.

Following is the text of the Economic Report of the President and excerpts of chapter 1, "A Strategy for Growth and Change," from the Annual Report of the Council of Economic Advisers, both issued by the White House February 14, 1994:

ECONOMIC REPORT OF THE PRESIDENT

To the Speaker of the House of Representatives and the President of the Senate:

America has always thrived on change. We have used the opportunities it creates to renew ourselves and build our prosperity. But for too long and in too many ways, our Nation has been drifting.

For the last 30 years, family life in America has been breaking down. For the last 20 years, the real compensation of working Americans has grown at a disappointing rate. For 12 years a policy of trickle-down economics built a false prosperity on a mountain of Federal debt. As a result of our national drift, far too many American families, even those with two working parents, no longer dream the American dream of a better life for their children.

In 1992, the American people demanded change. A year ago, I sought your support for a comprehensive short-term and long-term strategy to restore the promise of our country's economic future. You responded, and together we replaced drift and gridlock with renewal and reform. Together we have taken the first necessary steps to restore growth in the living standards of all Americans. We have created a sound macroeconomic environment and strengthened the foundations of future economic growth. As a result of our efforts, the economy is now on a path of rising output, increasing employment, and falling deficits.

Establishing the Fiscal Conditions
for Sustained Growth

For more than a decade, the Federal Government has been living well beyond its means—spending much more than it has taken in, and borrowing the difference. The resulting deficits have been huge, both in sheer magnitude and as a percentage of the Nation's output. Since 1981 the Federal debt has been growing faster than the economy, reversing the trend of the previous three decades. As a consequence of this binge of deficit financing, Federal budget deficits have been gobbling up an inordinate share of the Nation's savings, driving up real long-term interest rates, discouraging private investment, and impeding long-run private sector growth.

On August 10, 1993, I signed the historic budget plan that you passed several days earlier. It will reduce Federal deficits by more than $500 billion. The plan is a balanced package of cuts in spending and increases in revenues. The spending cuts are specific, far-reaching, and genuine. They will reduce discretionary spending by over 12 percent in real terms in 5 years. The plan increases income tax rates for only the top 1.2 percent of taxpayers, the group of Americans who gained the most during the 1980s and are most able to pay higher taxes to help reduce the deficit. At the same time, a broad expansion of the earned income tax credit will help make work pay for up to 15 million American families. Nine out of ten small businesses will benefit from more-generous tax breaks that will help them invest and grow. And new, targeted capital gains tax relief will encourage investment in new small businesses.

Our deficit reduction plan has been the principal factor in the dramatic decline in long-term interest rates since my election in November 1992. Lower interest rates, in turn, have sparked an investment-driven economic expansion that has created more private sector jobs during the last year than were created during the previous four. The fact that investment is leading the recovery is good news for living standards, because investment is the key to productivity growth and hence to growth in real incomes for all Americans.

Investing in Our Nation's Future

Laying the macroeconomic groundwork for sustained growth is the government's first responsibility, but not its only responsibility. Government also has a vital role to play in providing some of the critical raw materials for economic growth: science and technology, an educated and well-trained work force, and public infrastructure. For much too long we have underinvested in these areas, in comparison both with our global competitors and with our own economic history. Our overall budget deficit has masked another, equally disturbing deficit—a deficit in the kinds of public investments that lay the foundations for private sector prosperity.

Like private investments, well-chosen public investments raise future living standards. As a consequence, deficit reduction at the expense of public investment has been and will continue to be self-defeating. That is why our budget package increases much-needed public investment even as it takes steps to reduce the budget deficit. One without the other will not work.

With the help of the Congress, our public investment initiatives in the areas of technology, infrastructure, the environment, and education and training received about 70 percent of the funding we requested in fiscal year 1994. We increased funding for such proven successes as Head Start and the WIC program in the human resources area, and the Advanced Technology Program of the National Institute of Standards and Technology in the area of technological research. We also launched a number of new initiatives, including the National Service program, a new program of empowerment zones and enterprise communities for urban and rural development, and several new technology programs, including the Technology Reinvestment Project, designed to help defense contractors retool to serve civilian markets. We increased funding for research into new environmental technologies. In addition, we developed a comprehensive, cost-effective Climate Change Action Plan, comprising nearly 50 initiatives to reduce U.S. greenhouse gas emissions to 1990 levels by the year 2000.

As these examples bear witness, we have made significant progress on our investment agenda, but much more remains to be done. We will have to work together to find room to fund essential new investments even as we reduce real government outlays to meet tight annual caps on discretionary spending. This will not be easy. But it is essential, for we face a dual challenge—we must fundamentally change the composition of discretionary spending even as we reduce it in real terms.

This year my Administration is requesting funding for several new investment initiatives. Our Goals 2000 proposal will encourage local innovation in and accelerate the pace of school reform. It will link world-class academic and occupational standards to grassroots education reforms all across America. Our School-to-Work initiative will provide opportunities for post-secondary training for those not going on to college. Our reemployment and training program will streamline today's patchwork of training programs and make them a source of new skills for people who lose their jobs. Finally, our proposed welfare reform will provide the support, job training, and child care necessary to move people off welfare after 2 years. That is the only way we will make welfare what it ought to be: a second chance, not a way of life.

Reforming Our Health Care System

This year we will also make history by reforming the Nation's health care system. We face a health care crisis that demands a solution, both for the health of our citizens and for the health of our economy over the long run. The United States today spends more on health care relative to the size of its economy than any other advanced industrial country. Yet we insure a smaller fraction of our population, and we rank poorly on important overall health indicators such as life expectancy and infant mortality. Over 15 percent of Americans—nearly 39 million people—were uninsured throughout 1992. And tens of millions more have inadequate insurance or risk becoming uninsured should they lose their jobs. Meanwhile health care costs continue to climb, increasing premiums and medical bills for American families and aggravating budget crises at all levels of government. Both the Office of Management and Budget and the Congressional Budget Office have concluded that unless the system is reformed, rising health care costs will begin pushing the Federal budget deficit back upward as this century comes to a close.

Piecemeal approaches to solving our health care crisis will not work. If we simply squeeze harder on Federal health spending, without attempting system-wide reform, more of the costs of covering health services guaranteed by the government will be shifted to the private sector, and medical care for the elderly, the disadvantaged, and the disabled will be put at risk. Similarly, if we attempt to provide universal coverage without complementary measures to improve competition and sharpen incentives for cost-conscious decisions, costs will continue to escalate.

Our health care reform proposal, while bold and comprehensive, builds on the strengths of our current, market-based system. Our approach preserves consumer choice and our largely employer-based private insurance arrangements. It relies on market competition and private incentives, not price controls and bureaucracy, to provide health security for all Americans, to rein in health care costs, and to solve our long-run budget deficit problem.

Opening Foreign Markets

Raising the living standards of all Americans is the fundamental economic goal of my Administration. That is why all of our initiatives in international trade share a common purpose: to open markets and promote American exports. This emphasis on exports is driven by two simple facts. First, America is part of an increasingly integrated world economy and must adapt to this new reality if we are to stay on top. There is simply no way to close our borders and return to the insular days of the 1950s. To try to do so would be an exercise in futility, doomed not only to fail but to lower living standards in the process. Second, export industries offer the kind of high-wage, high-skill jobs the country needs. By shifting production toward more exports, we will shift the composition of employment toward better jobs. In short, to realize our goal of higher living standards for all Americans, we must compete, not retreat.

The year just past will go down in the history books as a watershed for trade liberalization. With your help, we enacted the North American Free Trade Agreement, which links the United States, Canada, and Mexico together in the world's largest marketplace. We also successfully completed the Uruguay Round of the General Agreement on Tariffs and Trade, which promises to add as much as $100 billion to $200 billion to the Nation's output by the end of a decade. And we are now on a course of increasing trade and investment liberalization with the rapidly growing economies of East Asia and the Pacific, which will be a major source of new export opportunities for American products in the coming years. At home we have eliminated much of our export control system and have rationalized our export promotion activities to help our producers, workers, and farmers increase their sales around the world.

Improving the Efficiency of Government

My Administration is committed to improving the Federal government's efficiency across the board. The National Performance Review (NPR), completed under the bold leadership of Vice President Gore, provides a road map for what must be done. The NPR's report shows how substantial budgetary savings can be realized by making existing programs more efficient and cutting those that are no longer necessary. As a result of our efforts to reinvent how the government performs, we will reduce the Federal bureaucracy by 252,000 positions, bringing it down to the lowest level in decades.

My Administration is also committed to reducing the burden of government regulations by improving the regulatory review process. My Executive Order on Regulatory Planning and Review requires that all new regulations carefully balance costs and benefits, that only those regulations whose benefits exceed their costs be adopted, and that in each case the most cost-effective regulations be chosen.

This year we will also work with the Congress to develop the new regulatory framework required to encourage the development of the national information superhighway. We must cooperate with the private sector to connect every classroom, every library, and every hospital in America to this highway by the year 2000. Rapid access to the most advanced information available will increase productivity and living standards, help to educate our children, and help health providers improve medical care for our citizens.

The Economic Outlook

An economic strategy built on long-run investments will not bear fruit overnight. But there are already signs that our policy initiatives are beginning to pay off. Prospects for sustained economic expansion look far brighter now than they did a year ago, when my Administration first asked for your support. Growth of real gross domestic product increased steadily over the course of 1993, and the economic expansion has continued into 1994. Consumer spending should remain healthy because of continued gains in employment and output, and investment spending should remain strong because of low long-term interest rates and increasing levels of demand. Low interest rates will also continue to support the recent expansion in residential construction. The Administration forecasts that the economy will grow at 3 percent in 1994 and will remain on track to create 8 million jobs over 4 years.

As 1994 begins, our economy is strong and growing stronger. With continued deficit reduction, more public investment, a reformed health care system, increased exports, and a reinvented government, we can create the foundations for an even more prosperous America.

THE ANNUAL REPORT OF THE COUNCIL OF ECONOMIC ADVISERS

A Strategy for Growth and Change

On Election Day 1992, the American economy faced a number of daunting challenges—both short term and long term. The principal short-term problem was that recovery from the 1990-91 recession had been disappointing in almost all respects. Real gross domestic product (GDP) had grown at only a 2.2-percent annual rate from the first quarter of 1991 through the third quarter of

1992, less than half the pace of a typical recovery. Payroll employment had actually fallen during the first year of recovery and had risen a scant 0.4 percent from March 1991 to October 1992. Furthermore, the seesaw pattern that had plagued the recovery raised fears that the weak economy might relapse into recession.

But America's long-run problems ran deeper and their causes were less well understood. While U.S. workers and firms remained the world's most productive, our productivity *growth* had been sluggish for almost two decades. In consequence, real hourly compensation and GDP per capita had advanced extremely slowly, and real median family income had barely increased at all. In addition, inequality had been rising for more than a decade, leaving the American economy with the most unequal distribution of income in its postwar history. The combination of stagnant average incomes and widening dispersion meant that many middle-class and low-income families had actually suffered declines in their real incomes.

Finally, the Federal budget deficit was large and rising, the national debt had been growing faster than GDP for about a decade, and huge amounts of foreign borrowing had transformed the United States from the world's biggest creditor nation into its biggest debtor.

National economic policy was the major cause of some of our economic difficulties, such as the Federal budget deficit, but only a contributing factor to others, such as growing income inequality. Although the economic policy agenda of the new Administration cannot cure all of these problems overnight, steps we have taken have already contributed to noticeable progress on several fronts. The recovery has solidified. Job growth has resumed. Fiscal policies that will reduce the Federal deficit substantially have been put in place. Although much more needs to be done, taxes have been made more progressive and starts have been made on education and labor market policies that will address the inequality problem. And, perhaps most fundamentally of all, the Administration has embarked on a comprehensive investment agenda designed to raise productivity, which is the wellspring of higher living standards in the long run. . . .

The Legacy of the Recent Past

The policies of any new Administration are dictated in part by the challenges it faces and the problems it inherits from the past. Because America's current problems are both short run and long run in nature, the solutions must be, too.

Inadequate Recovery from Recession

Short-run cyclical problems are, almost by definition, transitory. But when the American macroeconomy performs poorly, that one fact seems to overwhelm all others and crowd out consideration of longer run problems. In fact, the U.S. economy has been operating well below its productive capacity for years now. From 1989 through 1992, real GDP grew only 1.5 percent per year, and the civilian unemployment rate . . . has remained above 6 percent since

November 1990. Under such circumstances, public concerns with economic policy tend to be summarized in a single word: jobs.

... [T]he recovery that began in the second quarter of 1991 has been exceptionally slow by historical standards—so slow, in fact, that the unemployment rate was still rising more than a year into the "recovery." Only in mid-1993 did unemployment fall back to its rate at the recession trough. Growth has been not only slow but extremely uneven, proceeding in fits and starts which have left consumers and business people wondering how long the recovery would last.

Thus the Administration's first task was to put the recovery on a sound footing—not to produce a short-run burst of activity, but to lay the groundwork for a sustained expansion that would restore confidence and encourage firms to resume hiring. In large measure this task was accomplished in 1993. ... Sluggish economic growth in the first half of the year gave way to solid growth in the second half. More important, job growth began in earnest: Employers added about 2 million jobs to nonfarm payrolls between December 1992 and December 1993. As 1994 began, the outlook for sustained expansion looked brighter than it had in a long time.

Inadequate Productivity Growth

The economy's longer run problems will not be dealt with so quickly. They require sustained attention over a long period of time. Primary among them is the troubling fact that growth in productivity has been anemic for about two decades. ...

Labor productivity—output per hour of work—may seem an abstract concept, of more interest to analysts than to working men and women. But without productivity growth, higher real wages would lead directly to lower employment as profit-oriented firms reacted to higher labor costs by trimming their work forces. It is only steady productivity gains that enable the economy to generate more jobs and rising real wages at the same time. ... [G]rowth in both real compensation per hour and real median family income slowed markedly at just about the time that productivity growth slowed. This coincidence in time is, of course, no coincidence at all. Productivity growth is the ultimate source of growing real wages and family incomes.

Nothing is more important to the long-run well-being of the U.S. economy than accelerating productivity growth. Most of the Administration's economic strategy is therefore devoted to that end.

Worsening Income Inequality

Starting some time in the late 1970s, income inequalities widened alarmingly in America. ... [T]he share of the Nation's income received by the richest 5 percent of American families rose from 18.6 percent in 1977 to 24.5 percent in 1990, while the share of the poorest 20 percent fell from 5.7 percent to 4.3 percent. Part of this change was due to the cuts in taxes and social spending of the early 1980s, the net benefits of which were heavily skewed toward the rich. But there was a much more powerful force at work, one not attributable to fiscal policy: The distribution of *wage rates* grew substantially more unequal. In real terms, wages at the bottom of the distribution fell while wages at the top rose.

The forces underlying this widening of the wage distribution are not well understood. . . . But the facts are stark. Between 1979 and 1990, the real median income of males with 4 years of college fell about 1 percent, but that of males with only 4 years of high school fell a stunning 21 percent, and high school dropouts fared even worse. A similar pattern emerges almost any way one slices the data: Wages near the top of the distribution rose faster than wages near the bottom. Salaries of chief executive officers rose rapidly while the minimum wage fell in real terms. Wages of skilled workers rose faster than those of the unskilled. Wages of experienced workers grew faster than entry-level wages.

The widening dispersion of wages accounts for most of the squeeze on the middle class, because the middle 60 percent of the income distribution derives about three-quarters of its income from wages and salaries. And these people do not bring home the highest wages, but those nearer the middle. When middle-class wages stagnate, middle-class family incomes do, too. That is precisely what happened in the 1980s.

In sum, for whatever reasons, in the late 1970s our market economy began to dish out more-handsome rewards to the well-off and stingier ones to the middle class. Government policies compounded the problem by weakening the social safety net, lowering the tax burdens of the wealthy, and driving up real interest rates. In concert, the market and the government produced the greatest disequalization of incomes since at least before World War II.

This Administration sees the combination of stagnating average incomes and rising inequality as a threat to the social fabric that has long bound Americans together and made ours a society with minimal class distinctions. Although the underlying forces of the market are vastly more powerful than anything the government can do, the right kinds of policies can make a difference. For example, changes in Federal tax policy have already shifted the burden of taxation away from the working poor and toward the well-to-do. And several initiatives in the human investment arena . . . should help mitigate rising wage inequality.

Large Deficits, Mounting Debt

Of all the Nation's economic problems, the one most directly traceable to government policy is the large Federal budget deficit. Although the Federal budget has been in deficit almost every year of the postwar period, until the 1980s these deficits were small enough that the ratio of public debt to GDP was stable or falling. In fact, the structural budget (that is, the one that would result if the economy were at a high level of employment) after adjustment for inflation was on average roughly balanced for decades. . . . This approximate balance was not achieved by any formal, legal requirement, but rather through an informal, unstated political consensus.

The budget picture changed dramatically with the tax cuts of the early

1980s, and the structural, inflation-adjusted budget began to display chronic, large deficits for the first time. The deficit in fiscal 1992, the last year before the election of President Clinton, was a whopping $290 billion in the unified budget and $131 billion on a structural, inflation-adjusted basis. Worse yet, both the deficit and the debt-GDP ratio were expected to rise further. . . .

Deficits of this magnitude—around 5 percent of GDP—would have been far less worrisome if American households were saving enough to cover both the government budget deficit and the needs of business to finance investment. But, in fact, American household saving rates not only are among the lowest in the world, but actually fell in the 1980s. So for both of these reasons—declining household saving and rising budget deficits—*national* saving as a share of GDP dropped sharply in the 1980s.

Casual discussions often equate national saving with domestic investment, but the two can differ in an open economy. . . . And in the United States of the 1980s, they differed dramatically. While national saving was falling as a share of GDP, the share of domestic investment, although low by international standards, was roughly constant. To plug the gap between saving and investment, the United States had to import massive amounts of foreign capital. In consequence, our current account balance went from a small surplus to a large deficit in the 1980s.

All this foreign capital had its positive side: By limiting the rise of real U.S. interest rates, it partly shielded investment from the consequences of huge Federal deficits. But it left the United States the greatest debtor nation in the world. Even more disturbing, all this borrowing from abroad went to *maintaining* the Nation's comparatively meager investment rate, not to increasing it.

The legacy of foreign debt was not the only cost of our addiction to foreign borrowing. To attract the needed capital to American shores, the United States had to offer interest rates higher than those prevailing in the other leading industrialized countries. This gap between U.S. and foreign interest rates, in turn, led to a sharp appreciation of the dollar, as foreign investors demanded more dollar-denominated assets. The sky-high dollar made life exceedingly pleasant for American tourists in Europe in the mid-1980s. But it handicapped portions of American industry by making many U.S. manufactured goods uncompetitive on world markets. It has taken years for our manufacturing sector to recover from this shock.

Inadequate Public Investment

The budget deficit and the trade deficit were major national concerns in the 1980s and on into the 1990s. But there was also a third deficit: a shortage of funds for public investment in critical national needs like education and training, transportation facilities, and environmental infrastructure.

The share of Federal civilian fixed investment in GDP is only about half what it was in the 1960s. Furthermore, the share of the Federal budget devoted to *all* types of public investment—including education and research and development, as well as civilian and military fixed investment—fell from

35 percent in 1963 to 17 percent in 1992. As the 1990s started, more and more Americans were becoming painfully aware that our public investment was not what it should be.

Prosperity and Growth: The Benefits of Economic Change

The economic strategy of this Administration follows logically from this legacy. We must secure the expansion and spur long-term economic growth. We must reverse the trend toward rising inequality. We must reduce Federal borrowing and shrink the trade deficit. We must invest more in both private and public capital. And we must bolster our human resources.

While the Administration's economic policy agenda is broad and varied, it can be summarized in a single word: *investment*—investment in private capital, investment in people, investment in public infrastructure, investment in technology, and investment in environmental preservation. Six major themes stand out and define the essence of the Administration's economic strategy: deficit reduction; investments in human capital; investments in public infrastructure; investments in technology; expanding international trade; and health care reform.

Reducing the Deficit to Promote Capital Formation

The legacy of large and growing Federal budget deficits required that first attention be devoted to their reduction, so as to free up resources for expansion of private physical capital—the machines, factories, and offices that make American labor more productive. For too long, Federal budget deficits have been gobbling up an inordinate share of the Nation's saving, thereby keeping real interest rates too high and leaving the Nation with a Hobson's choice between lower domestic investment and higher foreign borrowing. Reducing the budget deficit was a necessary part of clearing away the financial underbrush that had grown up around us in the 1980s—so that economic growth could be put on a sounder and more sustained footing.

Deficit reduction is difficult and painful. But the President concluded that the Nation could not remain on the path bequeathed us by the previous Administration—a path on which the national debt was growing faster than GDP and deficits were threatening to explode. So he gave first priority to putting the Nation's fiscal house back in order.

Policy changes in the President's deficit reduction package will gradually reduce the Federal deficit after 5 years by 1 3/4 percent of GDP. By fiscal 1998, the last year of the program, the deficit is expected to be $146 billion below what it otherwise would have been: falling from $333 billion to $187 billion. The ratio of debt to GDP at the end of fiscal 1998 falls from a projected 51 percent without the deficit reduction program to 46 percent with it.

The Omnibus Budget Reconciliation Act of 1993

Because the President did not want to delay deficit reduction for another year, the fiscal 1994 budget had to be prepared on a compressed schedule.

The President introduced a detailed budget plan to a joint session of the Congress in February 1993, just 4 weeks after taking office. The House and Senate passed the final version of the budget resolution on April 1—the earliest date in the history of the modern congressional budget process. A spirited congressional debate followed, leading to enactment of the Omnibus Budget Reconciliation Act of 1993 (OBRA93) in August.

Several principles guided the design of OBRA93. First and foremost, the deficit reduction had to be large, genuine, and credible. To this end, the Administration proposed hundreds of specific spending cuts and increases in revenue. Second, the package had to be balanced between expenditure cuts and tax increases. Specifically, the $146 billion of deficit reduction in fiscal 1998 consists of $87 billion in net spending cuts—including $25 billion in lower debt service—and $59 billion in additional net revenue. Third, the tax increases were highly progressive—heavily skewed toward the people who are most able to pay and who benefited most from the large tax cuts of the early 1980s. Income tax rates were raised for only about the top 1.2 percent of taxpayers. Some 90 percent of the new taxes in OBRA93 will be borne by the upper 6.5 percent of the income distribution. Fourth, even while cutting the deficit, room had to be found in the budget for a variety of critical public investments (more on this below).

The spending cuts touched virtually every part of the budget. On the discretionary side, the Congress imposed what amounts to a 5-year freeze on nominal spending, capping fiscal 1998 spending at $548 billion, or about $2.5 billion below the fiscal 1993 level. With inflation (as measured by the implicit deflator for GDP) projected to average about 2.8 percent per year over the period, the implied cut in *real* discretionary spending is about 13 percent. Furthermore, if inflation comes in lower than the forecast, the caps will be lowered commensurately. The budget cuts in OBRA93 include a reduction in the Federal work force by 100,000 positions (since raised to 252,000 positions), delay of the 1994 cost-of-living adjustment for Federal employees, defense cutbacks beyond those projected by the previous Administration, and a host of smaller cuts in discretionary programs.

On the mandatory side of the budget, the largest cuts were in the Medicare program (about $18 billion by fiscal 1998). But there were also reductions in agricultural and veterans' programs, savings in the student loan program, new receipts from auctioning portions of the radio spectrum . . . , and savings from shortening the maturity structure of the national debt. Total cuts in mandatory spending other than debt service are expected to reach $25.6 billion by fiscal 1998.

OBRA93 also increased taxes. Higher income tax rates on the top 1.2 percent of households constitute the biggest source of new revenue by far: $27.2 billion by fiscal 1998. . . . In addition, the 2.9-percent payroll tax for medicare, which formerly applied only to the first $135,000 of earnings, now applies to all earnings (raising $7.2 billion by fiscal 1998), the taxable portion of Social Security benefits was raised for the top 13 percent of recipients ($4.5 billion), and the motor fuels tax went up by 4.3 cents per gallon in October 1993

($5 billion). Finally, OBRA93 increased the top corporate tax rate and closed a variety of business tax loopholes, but also enhanced or created several tax incentives for investment. The net effect of these increases and decreases in business taxes should yield about $8 billion in revenue by fiscal 1998.

OBRA93, Interest Rates, and Investment

As critical elements of the President's deficit reduction package started to become known, long-term interest rates began to fall—indicating that the financial markets viewed the proposals as substantial, genuine, and credible. . . . Rates fell dramatically between January and October 1993 before backing off a bit late in the year.

As documented more completely in Chapter 2, the medicine of low interest rates now seems to be taking hold. Business investment has been leading the economy's expansion, with consumer durables and housing important sources of strength. If we divide GDP into its interest-sensitive components (business fixed investment, housing, and consumer durables) and everything else, the data tell a fascinating story. While the three interest-sensitive pieces typically account for about 30 percent of GDP growth, in 1993 they accounted for virtually all of GDP growth. The rest of GDP barely increased over the year. . . .

It is important to understand *why* this Administration made deficit reduction a top priority and worked so hard to see it through the Congress. One important reason was the concern being expressed in many quarters that deficits were growing out of control and might threaten financial stability—and thereby macroeconomic stability. . . .

But the central objective of deficit reduction was and remains *expenditure switching*—away from consumption and government purchases toward investment. The lower interest rates brought about by deficit reduction are the way the market accomplishes this expenditure switching.

The reasons for wanting to raise the investment share of GDP are straightforward: Workers are more productive when they are equipped with more and better capital, more-productive workers earn higher real wages, and higher real wages are the mainspring of higher living standards. Few economic propositions are better supported than these—or more important. . . . [I]nvestment rates and productivity growth rates correlate well across countries. Lower budget deficits that raise private investment are therefore critical to raising the economy's long-run growth rate.

However, some people worry that deficit reduction might retard growth in the short run by siphoning off aggregate demand. Such a concern is justified. Deficit reduction *by itself* certainly does tend to contract the economy. After all, raising taxes and cutting government spending reduce the demand for goods and services. But deficit reduction *accompanied by sufficient declines in long-term interest rates* need not be contractionary. It is, of course, the latter, not the former, that we experienced in 1993.

Economists judge the impact of fiscal policy on aggregate demand by looking at changes in the structural deficit. . . . OBRA93 will reduce the structural deficit by about $65 billion from fiscal 1993 to fiscal 1995, after which it is expected to rise slightly. The large deficit reductions after fiscal 1995 serve to limit what would otherwise have been even larger increases in the structural deficit—mainly due to rising expenditures on health care. Analysis by the Council of Economic Advisers suggests that the declines in long-term interest rates that have occurred since the 1992 election, even after the backup late in 1993, are more than enough to offset the contractionary effects of this decrease in the structural deficit. Hence the economy should be able to grow right through the deficit reduction period. . . .

There are limits, however, to the amount of deficit reduction an economy can be expected to withstand within a short period without endangering economic growth. The Administration's judgment is that cutting the annual deficit by about $140 billion to $150 billion over a period of 5 years is roughly the right amount, given the current strength of our economy. Some critics dispute this judgment and call for much deeper cuts in spending than those provided in OBRA93, or for substantial increases in taxes. The Administration views this strategy of more aggressive deficit cutting in the near term as risky.

A *small* amount of additional deficit reduction would, of course, have only small effects on the economy. But further large spending cuts or tax increases at this time would require additional *large* declines in long-term interest rates to replace the lost aggregate demand. Should interest rates decline by less than the required amount, economic growth would slow and jobs would be lost. For example, a deficit reduction package substantially larger than OBRA93 would be needed to comply with the proposed balanced budget amendment to the Constitution. The Council estimates that it would take a decline in long-term interest rates of roughly 3 percentage points to offset the contractionary effect of such a large fiscal package. Since a 3-percent long-term interest rate seems quite unlikely, complying with a balanced budget amendment seems likely to harm the economy—perhaps severely.

Deficit Reduction and Public Investment

Once it is understood that deficit reduction is not an end in itself, but a means to an end—the end of greater investment—two important principles become evident.

First, it is clear that deficit reduction is only a first step. We must start to build—to invest in our future. That is why the President's economic plan contains more than just deficit reduction; it also includes new proposals to encourage private investment and needed public investments in education and training, public infrastructure, and technology. We must worry about the debt we bequeath to our children, but we must also worry about the quality and quantity of capital—broadly conceived—that they will inherit.

Second, it is clear that squeezing worthwhile public investments out of the budget is the wrong way to reduce the deficit. After all, the main purpose of deficit reduction is to pave the way for more private investment. Cutting *public* investment to make room for more *private* investment is like running on a treadmill. America needs more of both, not a swap of one for the other.

Shifting Federal spending priorities from consumption to investment is one of the hallmarks of this Administration's approach to economic policy. We seek not only to constrain total government spending, but also to reorient it toward more productive uses. Doing so will take time and requires use of the surgical scalpel, not the meat-ax, in cutting the budget. As the Administration and the Congress struggle together over tight Federal budgets in fiscal 1995 and beyond, it is essential that we not allow fiscal myopia to lead to underinvestment in America's future.

Investing in People

The American work force remains the most productive in the world. Our aim should be simple: to keep it that way. But the rest of the world is not standing still; it is gaining on us, becoming ever more productive. And that is what compels change.

America has never competed on the basis of low wages, and we must not start doing so now. It is widely believed that modern industrial processes demand workers with higher levels of education and training; and evidence on the relative wages of, say, college-educated versus high school-educated labor . . . seems to bear this out. In 1981, workers with college degrees earned about 45 percent more than workers with only high school degrees; by 1992, this gap had reached almost 65 percent.

Some observers claim that average work force quality may actually have deteriorated in the United States in recent decades. Whether or not this is true, few dispute that the supply of work force skills has failed to keep pace with the growing demand. Although Americans are, if measured by average years of schooling, among the most educated people on earth, the rate of illiteracy in our country has long been high. Tens of millions of adult Americans are either functionally illiterate or barely literate. International test scores suggest that our primary and secondary students are learning less science and mathematics than their counterparts in other countries.

This educational record is not good enough in a world economy that grows ever more competitive and ever more skill-intensive. American workers must build the additional human capital they need as a bridgehead to higher wages and living standards. Lifelong learning must cease being a slogan and become a reality.

In a fundamental sense, each American must be responsible for his or her own education and training. This Administration is committed to creating the requisite opportunities through a comprehensive agenda of education and training that starts before formal schooling and extends into the workplace. For example:

- Head Start will be expanded so that disadvantaged children have a chance to get ahead. Head Start has been proved effective in preparing these children for primary school, and has been estimated to save about six dollars in future government spending for every dollar invested today.
- Goals 2000 is a comprehensive legislative package that will set higher

performance standards for American teachers and students.

- The Departments of Labor and Education are collaborating on a new School-to-Work transition program that will help students get hands-on, work-related training while still in high school. This is an area of our educational system that has been neglected for too long.
- The new National Service program will not only provide opportunities for community service and the acquisition of job-related skills, but also help send more Americans to college.
- The reformed student loan program will also help more of America's youth attend college by reducing borrowing costs and offering, for the first time on a national scale, loans whose repayment schedules depend on future earnings.
- The new program for dislocated workers will have an important retraining component, which will make opportunities available to displaced American workers. Some income support will be provided so that displaced workers can afford to take advantage of the training.

Each of these programs will help augment the Nation's stock of human resources, thereby raising the American standard of living.

Investing in Public Infrastructure

The most obvious kind of public investment is building new public infrastructure—the Nation's highways, bridges, airports, and water and sewage systems. The Administration believes the United States has underinvested in its public infrastructure. For example, the Department of Transportation estimates that almost 20 percent of our Nation's highways have poor or mediocre pavement and about 20 percent of our bridges are structurally deficient.

A variety of evidence indicates that there has been underinvestment. First, while the statistical evidence is not unequivocal, the weight of it points to handsome rates of return on well-planned investments in public infrastructure. Second, estimated benefit-cost ratios on specific infrastructure projects are often quite high. Third, the ratio of public to private capital has fallen markedly since the 1960s. Unless the data are grossly misleading, the principle of diminishing marginal returns leaves only two possible conclusions: Either America was overinvested in public capital in the early 1970s, or it is underinvested today.

Finally, there is the evidence of the senses: America's roads and bridges are badly in need of repair, a number of our airports are overcrowded, and our sewage treatment facilities are overburdened. To many thoughtful observers, America's public infrastructure is simply not commensurate with our bounteous private wealth.

Investing in Technology

But physical capital is not the only determinant of productivity, nor even the most important. Over long periods of time, rising productivity and hence advances in living standards depend on the upward march of technology. Indeed, studies of long-term economic growth attribute a large share of growth to improvements in know-how. The history of progress in the industrial world is working smarter, not working harder.

Technological change does not come for free. Technology advances because scientists and engineers working in laboratories and on shop floors make new discoveries. And research is expensive.

Since the dawn of the industrial revolution, alarmists have argued that technology and automation threaten jobs. Such claims are still heard today. But history shows that they have never been right in the past and suggests that they are wrong again. Time after time, in epoch after epoch and country after country, technological advance has produced higher wages and living standards, not mass unemployment. That is exactly what we expect to happen again in the 21st century. And the government should be helping this process along—facilitating growth and change, not impeding it.

While the bulk of research and development (R&D) must and should be done by private industry, support for basic and generic research has long been recognized as a legitimate function of government because of informational externalities. New technology is expensive to *discover* but cheap to *disseminate.* So what one company learns passes quickly to others, making it impossible for the innovator to capture all the returns from its discovery. In fact, estimates find that innovating businesses capture less than half of the social returns to their R&D. Furthermore, estimated social rates of return on R&D range as high as 50 to 100 percent, suggesting that there is systematic underinvestment.

For this reason, the Administration asked the Congress to extend the research and experimentation tax credit, which was done in OBRA93. For the same reason, the Administration is increasing funding for research partnerships with industry, such as the Advanced Technology Program, and adding dozens of new manufacturing extension centers. Each of these initiatives and others are designed to speed the pace at which precompetitive technologies are invented and disseminated. Once that stage is passed, the market mechanism should and will take over. . . .

The development and deployment of new technology have long been of interest to the government. But technology policy is especially critical in a period of large-scale defense cutbacks, because more than half of total Federal support for R&D has traditionally been related to national defense. With less need for research on weaponry, the Federal Government must now make a choice. Will we reduce total research support, or will we shift the research dollars into civilian technologies? The President believes that the latter is the wiser course, which is why the Administration is reorienting the research capabilities of the Defense Department and the national laboratories toward R&D partnerships with industry.

Technology surely creates the wave of the future. America must be on the crest of that wave—with the technology, capital, and skilled work force needed to take advantage of tomorrow's economy.

Trade Policy and Living Standards

This Administration's policies toward private physical capital, human capital, public infrastructure, and technology all share a common objective: to raise the living standards of American families. Trade policy is yet another means toward that same end. This Administration vigorously supported the North American Free Trade Agreement (NAFTA), worked hard to complete the Uruguay Round of the General Agreement on Tariffs and Trade (GATT), streamlined the Nation's export promotion programs and eased restrictions on exports, and is striving to open the Japanese market through bilateral negotiations, all for the same reason—to open markets and boost American exports. . . . The emphasis on trade expansion is, in turn, driven by two simple facts.

First, Americans now live in an increasingly integrated world economy and must therefore become increasingly outward-looking to stay on top. There is simply no way to close America's borders and return to the insular days of the 1950s and 1960s. Trying to do so would be an exercise in futility, doomed not only to fail but to lower living standards in the process. International competition through trade has long been a powerful engine of change and progress—for America and for the world. We must not let that engine idle. Instead, we must use it to power America up the technology ladder—by moving our workers into the jobs of the future, not keeping them mired in the jobs of the past. In the President's words, we must "compete, not retreat."

Second, jobs in export industries pay wages that are about 22 percent above the economy-wide average, according to the Council's latest estimates. The implication is that, if the Administration succeeds in shifting the composition of GDP toward more exports, we will automatically shift the composition of American employment toward better paying jobs. No government program or central direction is needed to accomplish this. The market will do the work for us.

Trade expansion is sometimes inaccurately characterized as "exporting jobs." Nothing could be further from the truth. A more accurate description is that international trade and investment lead low-skill, low-paid jobs that would inevitably migrate to poorer countries to go there in exchange for high-skill, better-paying jobs in the United States. American companies that compete successfully both at home and in foreign markets offer the best job opportunities for their workers. The history of capitalism throughout the world shows that companies and industries sheltered from the winds of competition tend to stagnate.

This Administration's focus on exports does not signal a revival of mercantilism. Rather, it reflects a belief that America's export promotion efforts have lagged behind those of other countries and that our markets are already among the most open in the world. The Administration fully expects trade liberalization—such as through NAFTA and the Uruguay Round of GATT—to raise *both* U.S. exports *and* U.S. imports. And we welcome both.

The North American Free Trade Agreement

Indeed, the recently ratified NAFTA illustrates the basic goals of Administration trade policy extremely well. NAFTA should boost trade with Mexico in both directions. In consequence, economic resources will be allocated more efficiently on both sides of the border. Inevitably, some American industries will therefore contract while others expand. Supported by the overwhelming preponderance of scholarly evidence, the Administration believes that NAFTA will lead to *net* job creation in the United States.

Equally important is the composition of those jobs, however. The new jobs that will arise in the United States will, on average, pay higher wages than the jobs that migrate south. It would be surprising indeed if anything else happened when a low-wage country and a high-wage country reduced trade barriers. In addition, the lower tariffs and reduced trade barriers from NAFTA will reduce prices for a variety of goods that American families buy. Together, the shift in the composition of employment toward higher paid jobs and the reduction in prices lead to a clear conclusion: NAFTA will raise the standard of living of the average American family—and the average Mexican family as well.

The Uruguay Round of GATT

The recently completed Uruguay Round of GATT was a landmark achievement for the entire world trading system. It literally rewrites the rules of trade for the start of the next century.

Earlier rounds of GATT talks had focused almost exclusively on tariff reductions. The market access component of the Uruguay Round continues this tradition by reducing tariffs on literally thousands of manufactured goods by more than one-third on average. Such tariff reductions should be a tonic for world trade and growth, just as they have been in the past, and should increase specialization and economic efficiency around the globe. As usual, producers will gain from bigger markets and consumers will gain from lower prices.

But the most remarkable achievements of the Uruguay Round are to be found elsewhere. For the first time, trade in agricultural commodities has been brought under GATT—a goal that had eluded trade negotiators for decades. When fully effective, the agreement will reduce agricultural export subsidies by 21 percent in volume and 36 percent in value, saving taxpayers and consumers in many countries billions of dollars. Trade in agricultural goods will also be liberalized by reducing tariffs on certain commodities (like beef and fruits and vegetables), partially opening markets that were previously closed (like rice in Japan and the Republic of Korea), and prohibiting certain food "safety" measures that were really disguised trade barriers. America's farmers, consumers, and taxpayers all stand to gain handsomely from this agreement.

In addition, for the first time GATT disciplines have been extended to a variety of service industries. This achievement of the Uruguay Round is a vitally important precedent for the United States for two reasons. One is that production patterns both here and elsewhere have been shifting and will continue to shift toward services. The other is that the United States seems to have a strong comparative advantage in many service industries; in fact, our trade surplus in services is already three times larger than our trade surplus in agriculture.

The United States did not succeed in bringing all services into the agreement, and will continue to press for trade liberalization in sectors that were left out of the Uruguay Round. But the gains were still significant: Trade rules in such important industries as accounting, consulting, construction, and telecommunications will now require that foreign countries grant the same treatment to American firms operating abroad as they do to their own companies.

Finally, the path-breaking agreement will provide much stronger protection for a range of intellectual property rights including patents, copyrights, trademarks, and trade secrets. Since the United States is the home of so much commercial innovation, we will reap large gains from the agreement. Among the biggest industrial winners are software, pharmaceuticals, and biotechnology.

In sum, the Council estimates that the various provisions of the Uruguay Round, once fully phased in after a decade, will increase U.S. GDP by at least 1 1/2 percent by raising real wages, lowering consumer prices, and protecting our national property rights.

Health Care Reform

Successful health care reform will accomplish many things. Perhaps primary among them is health security for all Americans—a precious commodity that too many of our citizens have been denied for too long. In today's United States, workers who lose their jobs often lose their health insurance, too. Other people and businesses lose their coverage because a family member or employee becomes ill and incurs large medical bills. Still other people are afraid to take jobs that would lift them out of welfare because they cannot risk losing Medicaid coverage. In total, nearly 39 million Americans lack health insurance, millions more are inadequately covered, and tens of millions live in fear of losing the coverage they have. Few people in other industrialized countries face such insecurity.

Under the President's health care reform proposal, which is described in detail in Chapter 4, none of this would ever happen again. Americans would know that their health insurance would never lapse, whether they changed jobs, moved, quit to start a new business, or had the misfortune of serious illness in the family. When effective health care reform is enacted, one of the major sources of economic insecurity facing Americans today will have been removed.

Health care reform is also fundamental to long-run budget control. It is often said that the fastest growing part of the budget is "entitlements." But the fastest growing part of the entitlement budget by far is health care spending. As the President has repeatedly emphasized, controlling the costs of medical care is the key to controlling entitlements, and therefore to long-run deficit reduction.

But health care reform will accomplish more than just budget control and security. The Administration also sees it as a route to higher standards of living.

For years, the rising cost of health care has forced a shift in the composition of the typical pay packet away from wages and salaries toward fringe benefits, especially health insurance. . . . [T]he share of health benefits in total labor compensation rose from 1.8 percent in 1960 to 8.5 percent in 1992. Correspondingly, the share of cash wages fell. In absolute terms, in fact, real wages and salaries have barely increased in 20 years. Almost all the gains in compensation have been taken as fringe benefits. This means that working men and women have, for the most part, paid for their escalating health costs by taking home lower wages than they would have otherwise.

We can arrest this process only by containing medical costs. The President's health care reform is designed to do precisely that by making the market more competitive and making both consumers and providers more cost conscious. On the assumption that the future will look like the past, the Administration expects most of the benefits from effective health care cost containment to redound to working Americans in the form of higher take-home pay.

Summary: Prosperity and Change

All of the policy initiatives described here—from deficit reduction, to public investments (both human and physical), to trade expansion, to health care—share a common goal: raising the standard of living of average American families. But all of them also require change, sometimes wrenching change. Deficit reduction required a host of painful changes in government programs and some increased taxes. Lifelong learning requires changes in the way we view education. Freer trade and export expansion mean that some jobs will disappear so that more and better jobs can be created. And health care reform requires nothing less than a major overhaul of one-seventh of our economy.

None of this will be quick or easy. Real change rarely is. But, in truth, we have no choice, for standing still is not an option that history allows. The secret to economic success is making change our friend, not our enemy—coming to view change as the opportunity for advancement that it is, not as the threat that it sometimes appears to be.

Creating Opportunity

Our focus on raising the standard of living of middle-class Americans must not blind us to the fact that some of our fellow citizens have not managed to attain a middle-class living standard. And change is especially threatening to those at the bottom of the economic ladder.

When money incomes are corrected for purchasing power, America is the richest of the world's major nations in terms of per capita income. But a nagging poverty problem remains in this land of plenty. Millions of Americans have little or no earning power and are therefore on the public dole. Millions more work but do not earn enough to support their families. Two key policy initiatives enacted in 1993, the expansion of the earned income tax credit and the introduction of empowerment zones, were designed to help low-income workers by making work pay.

The earned income tax credit (EITC) provides needy families with both income support and greater rewards for working. In part, the credit offsets income taxes that low-income working families would otherwise have to pay. But the credit is also *refundable*, meaning that if a family's credit exceeds its tax liability, the Internal Revenue Service sends a check for the difference. As part of OBRA93, the EITC was increased substantially, both by making payments more generous and by extending the credit to more families.

As a first step toward welfare reform, the EITC has many virtues. It will lift many families with children out of poverty. It provides positive work incentives for many of the lowest-paid employees in our society. It is better targeted on the low-income population than is, say, an increase in the minimum wage, because minimum-wage workers are found in all family-income brackets. It is simple to administer, requiring no special bureaucracy. And, finally, it apparently reaches a larger fraction of the eligible recipients than is typical of other income-support programs, perhaps because it is easy to claim and carries no stigma.

The goal of the innovative empowerment zone program is to strengthen business activity in certain geographic areas that are extremely depressed, so that synergies from concentrated economic activity can help revive these areas. The program's main tax incentive is a 20-percent tax credit for wages up to $15,000 per year paid by a zone business to a zone resident. This should be a powerful incentive to create jobs in the zones. In addition, a variety of regulatory waivers may be granted to give communities greater flexibility, and several Federal agencies will direct spending toward the zones.

Beginning this year, nine empowerment zones, six urban and three rural, will be selected by a competitive process that should encourage both imaginative thinking and private-public partnerships. In addition, 95 other neighborhoods will be designated enterprise communities and be granted smaller benefits than the zones while sharing the relaxed regulatory environment. The program will be carefully monitored and evaluated over a 10-year period, during which time we should learn a great deal about what works and what does not.

No American should think that programs like empowerment zones, the EITC, and welfare reform serve *only* the poor. Every citizen benefits when the welfare rolls are reduced, when low-income families earn more, when blighted neighborhoods come to life, and when city streets once again become safe. We are, after all, one Nation.

Summary

An economic strategy based on long-run investments, as ours is, will not bear fruit overnight. It takes time to see tangible results and patience to wait for them. The important thing is to get started down the right path—and soon. The Administration believes that 1993 marked a turning point in that regard. Recovery firmly took hold in 1993, and prospects for sustained economic expansion look far brighter now than they did a year ago. The long-run deficit problem, while not completely solved, looks far less threatening than it did then. The Congress has begun to fund the President's ambitious investment agenda—including infrastructure, human capital, technology, and environmental preservation. Two historic trade agreements whose negotiations began years ago—NAFTA and the Uruguay Round of GATT—were brought to a successful conclusion. And the stage has been set for a much-needed national debate on health care reform in 1994. All of these accomplishments set in place the foundation for a more prosperous America.

REPORTS ON GREAT LAKES, MISSISSIPPI RIVER

February 20 and 28, 1994

Two of the nation's most treasured environmental resources—the Great Lakes and the Mississippi River—face critical dangers, according to two reports released in late February. The reports pointed out that the dangers facing the waterways also confronted the people, wildlife, and fish that were dependent on them. The two reports were the "Seventh Biennial Report on Great Lakes Water Quality," issued by the International Joint Commission (IJC), and "Restoring the Big River: A Clean Water Act Blueprint for the Mississippi," prepared jointly by the Izaak Walton League of America and the Natural Resources Defense Council.

Both reports emphasized the dangers posed by the toxic substances that have been found in the vast waterways. For example, the Mississippi River analysis said that the river was being "degraded" by pollution from cities, industries, and farms. It added that toxic materials posed "serious water quality problems both from a human health and an ecosystem perspective." Toxic pollutants in the river included toxic metals, organic chemicals such as polychlorinated biphenyl (PCB), dioxin, and pesticides, and "a few other substances that are hard to classify, but are sometimes considered 'toxic' because of their impacts, such as un-ionized ammonia," the report noted.

Toxic Substances Threaten Great Lakes

Similar problems faced the Great Lakes, according to the IJC. In its report, the commission said that the "integrity of the Great Lakes and life forms that depend on them remain at an unacceptable level of risk from persistent toxic substances." It added that "persistent" chemicals such as PCBs, dioxin, strazine, and hexachlorobenzene posed the greatest danger, and stressed that an action plan must be adopted "to virtually eliminate persistent toxic substances that are threatening human health and the future of the . . . ecosystem."

The IJC particularly attacked the use of chlorine in manufacturing and urged the United States and Canadian governments to work with the chemical industry to develop a total ban on the practice. The Associated Press quoted Gordon K. Durnil, the IJC's American co-chairman, as saying, ". . . [T]he weight of evidence says there is a danger from organochlorides. You've got some really major problems going on, increases in breast cancer, prostate cancer, endometriosis. You can in many cases trace it to an organochloride."

While a number of environmental groups praised the IJC's report, the chlorine industry attacked it. A spokesman for the Chlorine Chemical Council said the report was not a "sound-science approach to decision making." The chlorine industry contended that any consideration of a ban on the chemical should take into account the negatives of not having the chemical available for manufacturing.

Reports Admit Some Progress Had Occurred

While the reports painted generally bleak pictures, both said that progress had been made in the struggle to improve water quality. The Mississippi River report said the Clean Water Act of 1972 had "had a positive impact on the Mississippi." The Great Lakes report acknowledged that since the United States and Canada signed the Great Lakes Water Quality Agreement in 1972, "[d]ischarges of contaminants in the Great Lakes and their levels in the environment have been reduced, the water quality has visibly improved, and some biological communities have been restored to viability."

Optimistic news about the Great Lakes basin also emerged from a scientific conference in Detroit in May. At the conference, Canadian scientists reported that a U.S. ban on the insecticide DDT had led to sharply lower levels of the chemical in the milk of nursing mothers. Since 1972, the year of the ban, levels of DDT in the milk had dropped nearly 90 percent, the researchers said. American researchers reported that levels of PCBs, a chemical used in electrical equipment until it was banned in 1978, had dropped nearly 90 percent in Great Lakes trout since 1973.

While some scientists at the conference called the Great Lakes cleanup a tremendous success story, others were more cautious. They noted that levels of some toxic chemicals had stopped dropping in the Great Lakes, and that the incineration of hazardous waste in the United States was causing mercury levels in the region to rise. They added that although the levels of toxic chemicals in humans had dropped, the levels still might be high enough to cause such health problems as cancer and infertility.

> *Following are excerpts from the "Seventh Biennial Report on Great Lakes Water Quality," released February 20, 1994, by the International Joint Commission, and from "Restoring the Big River: A Clean Water Act Blueprint for the Mississippi," released February 28, 1994, by the Izaak Walton League and the Natural Resources Defense Council:*

GREAT LAKES REPORT

Despite progress in cleaning up industrial and municipal pollution over the past 20 years, the integrity of the Great Lakes and life forms that depend on them remain at an unacceptable level of risk from persistent toxic substances. Effective solutions must be found and will require a new approach to environmental management.

Since the Great Lakes Water Quality Agreement was first signed in 1972, various forms of Great Lakes pollution have been identified and reduced. Technology, governmental regulation, and public and private funds have been directed at limiting inputs of phosphorus and other specific chemicals. It is more difficult for polluters to put wastes into the water, air and the ground. Discharges of contaminants to the Great Lakes and their levels in the environment have been reduced, the water quality has visibly improved, and some biological communities have been restored to viability.

In addition, much has been learned about the Great Lakes ecosystem, and a strong binational research community has been fostered by Agreement-related work. New networks and structures to manage and coordinate efforts among the various jurisdictions, primarily under the institutional umbrella of the International Joint Commission, have been created. Since the 1987 Protocol, however, these activities have come under bilateral rather than Commission auspices and have somewhat diminished in intensity.

At the same time progress on "conventional" pollutants was being made, scientists began to identify and understand more complicated issues concerning the use and discharge of toxic and persistent toxic substances. Many persistent chemicals stay in the environment and food chain for very long periods, accumulate in organisms, and injure the functioning of aquatic and other life. We have learned and continue to learn about the harmful impacts of persistent toxic substances on biota, including humans.

While earlier programs reduced some of these substances in the environment, inputs continue to exceed even interim objectives. Many still enter the Great Lakes environment from a wide variety of sources.

Health Effects of Persistent Toxic Substances

Over the past four years, the Commission's major focus has been the linkages between persistent toxic substances, environmental conditions and human health. These linkages have also been a matter of strong and widespread public concern. There are many examples at various scales, from the local issue to lakewide, continental and even global dimensions.

In April 1990, the Commission reported its concerns about the exposure of humans—particularly children—to persistent toxic substances, a subject that until then had not received extensive policy discussion. The 1990 and 1992 Biennial Reports contained summaries of pertinent research findings that document injury to humans and a range of fish and wildlife species.

The Commission warned that humans do hold persistent toxic substances in varying levels in their bodies, including their reproductive systems, as do many species of fish, birds, mammals and other biota. The Commission's declaration was and remains: *"What we do to the Great Lakes, we do to ourselves and to our children."*

Little evidence has been presented, in the Commission's view, to seriously challenge these earlier findings or the urgent need to address them. Most of the subsequent debate has centred on methodology, on whether the Commission's science is "good" (an issue discussed elsewhere in this report), and on the economic significance of production and use of these chemicals.

And yet, mounting evidence continues to reinforce concerns about the effects of persistent toxic substances. Long-term exposure of fish, wildlife and humans to these substances has been linked to reproductive, metabolical, neurological and behavioural abnormalities; to immunity suppression leading to susceptibility to infections and other life-threatening problems; and to increasing levels of breast and other cancers. Available evidence also points to long-term reproductive and intergenerational effects.

One growing concern is effects on endocrine systems. Research has shown persistent chemicals such as PCBs, dioxins, atrazine, hexachlorobenzene, as well as other organochlorines and polycyclic aromatic hydrocarbons (PAHs), to be strongly implicated in the disruption of endocrine systems, including estrogenic effects, in laboratory animals and in wildlife. The substances appear to act as artificial, external hormones that disrupt the normal balance of hormonal activity in animals.

Studies have also shown similar effects in humans. Levels of these chemicals have been found in humans within the same range, or in some cases at even higher levels, as those found in adversely affected animals. The biological reactions are known to be similar. Furthermore, many of these hormonally active chemicals are found in fish, wildlife and human tissues in the Great Lakes ecosystem.

Biological impacts on organisms need not depend on long-term exposure. A number of studies have indicated that even single doses of some substances at a critical time can affect the offspring of a pregnant animal. Evidence of this phenomenon was given at a workshop held by the Commission's Great Lakes Water Quality Board in 1992 and in a recent review of dioxin by the United States Environmental Protection Agency.

Nor are the effects of persistent toxic substances found only in females. Various studies have indicated increased infertility as well as cancers and other abnormalities in male reproductive systems. Human sperm counts have been reported to have declined by 50 percent over the past 50 years. Sperm samples tested in one recent Canadian study indicated the presence of several persistent organochlorine substances.

We do not know what *all* of the effects of human exposure will be over many years. Future research will clarify whether low-level and long-term exposures, repeated exposures, or isolated short-term exposures at sensitive stages of fetal development are most critical. For the Commission, however, there is sufficient evidence *now* to infer a real risk of serious impacts in humans. Increasingly, human data support this conclusion.

Implications of Inaction

The questions then become: what—if any—risks of injury are we as individuals and as a society willing to accept? How long can we afford to wait before we act? Why take any risk of having such potentially devastating results? In this vein, the Commission poses a number of other specific but very fundamental questions:

- What if, as current research suggests, the startling decrease in sperm count and the alarming increase in the incidence of male genital tract disorders are in fact caused in part as a result of *in utero* exposure to elevated levels of environmental estrogens?
- What if, as current research suggests, the epidemic in breast cancer is a result in part of the great numbers and quantities of estrogen-like compounds that have been and are being released into the environment?
- What if the documented declining learning performance and increasing incidence of problem behaviour in school children are not functions of the educational system? What if they are the result of exposure to developmental toxicants that have been and are being released into the children's and parents' environment, or to which they have been exposed *in utero?*

The implications of *any* of the above questions being answered in the affirmative are overwhelming. The implications of *all* of the above questions being answered in the affirmative are catastrophic, in terms of human suffering and the potential liability for that suffering and attendant health costs. Mounting evidence points to the latter possibility. Surely, there can be no more compelling self interest to force us to come to grips with this problem than the spectre of damaging the integrity of our own species and its entire environment.

It is the conviction of the International Joint Commission that the risk of such damage exists, and that virtually any level of risk of this type should be considered too high to accept. Our society cannot afford to take this risk and should reduce it. Yet, Great Lakes basin inhabitants continue to be the recipients of persistent toxic substances produced and justified as the basis for jobs and our way of life.

The Commission strongly affirms that the danger posed to living organisms from exposure to persistent toxic substances is the most significant problem to be confronted in the Great Lakes Basin Ecosystem. In terms of the Agreement and the human condition generally, policy makers must take this situation seriously and act accordingly.

Particular concern should be acknowledged for impacts on the development and functioning of the endocrine, nervous and immune systems in offspring of exposed individuals. This "hidden" effect injects additional urgency and importance to a precautionary approach. Additional research is needed but it must not be the reason to delay action. We also need a broad consensus-based strategy for changes as to how decisions are made with respect to producing, marketing and releasing persistent toxic substances to the Great Lakes and wider ecosystems.

MISSISSIPPI RIVER REPORT

The Mississippi River is being degraded by pollution from cities, industries and farms, development along the river and in the watershed, destruction of filtering wetlands that control flooding and provide important habitat for wildlife and fisheries, operation and maintenance of the navigation system, and movement of recreational craft. Some of these problems are unique to the Mississippi. Many are not.

The nation's Clean Water Act seeks to restore and maintain the "chemical, physical and biological integrity" of our waters—including the Mississippi River and its tributaries, and to make all waters "swimmable and fishable."

The Clean Water Act has had a positive impact on the Mississippi. Dumping of raw sewage is less common today, and in some respects the general quality of the water has improved over the last 20 years. Even so, many problems continue, and some are thought to have worsened. For example, exceedances of water quality standards for mercury and phosphorus, common in the River in the 1970s, seldom occurred in the 80s, according to a report by the Upper Mississippi River Basin Association. The report cautions, however, that apparent improvements may be due primarily to differences in standards over time that do not allow for accurate comparisons.

Fish Kills and Advisories

One of the most important indicators of water quality is how well fisheries are supported in a water body. Nationally, the number of reported fish kills caused by pollution appear to be unabated (although the severity of the average incident has declined). While reporting may have improved, this nevertheless shows a lack of progress in reaching the Clean Water Act's goals. Trends in numbers of reported fish kill incidents, adjusted to reflect variations in the number of states reporting, suggest an increase from roughly 750 incidents per year in the early 1970s to between 800-1,000 incidents per year in the late 1970s and 1980s. From 1986-1988, an estimated 700 fish kills took place in the seven Mississippi River states reporting to the EPA.

Fish can accumulate contaminants from the sediment, the water column, or through the food chain. According to a strict interpretation of the 1987 EPA guidelines, a river reach is defined as not supporting the fishable use if there are fish advisories for that section of the river. However, since states interpret this guidance differently or devise their own guidelines, not all waters with fish advisories are considered by states as not supporting the fishable use. On the Upper Mississippi, 519 miles had fish advisories in 1989. Advisories were caused by the presence of compounds including polychlorinated biphenyls (PCBs), chlordane, dioxin and mercury.

The Mississippi's Water Quality

Water quality problems occur throughout the length of the Mississippi, though the type of problems and their seriousness vary greatly. The most severe and immediate water quality problems tend to occur adjacent to and downstream from major metropolitan areas, the result of point-source pollution from industry, power plants and wastewater treatment plants, as well as polluted runoff from city streets, parking lots and construction sites.

Point-source pollution is a particularly serious problem in the lower River where the states from Arkansas to Louisiana are home to some of the country's most polluting industries. In 1989, Fremling et al. reported 130 industrial and 29 municipal discharges greater than 50,000 gallons per day along the lower 264 miles of the Mississippi. On the Upper Mississippi River, the impacts of point discharges also are significant, but more localized. Here, polluted runoff from urban areas and agricultural land probably is a more significant source of pollution.

The most severe water quality problems attributed to nonpoint polluted runoff in the Upper Mississippi are excessive loadings of suspended solids, nutrients and sediment, and contamination from toxic materials including pesticides and heavy metals. These problems are associated with the rapid accumulation of silt and sediment in the backwaters of the River, increased rates of eutrophication from elevated nutrient levels, and increased levels of ammonia and pathogens from animal wastes.

Drinking Water

Ironically, it is easier to find information on the impacts of pollution to fisheries and aquatic habitat than about threats to drinking water and its safety—a major water use that directly affects human beings. One of the most useful sources of information is the Environmental Protection Agency's database on drinking water standards violations around the country. The EPA records indicate 25,000 violations from 1991-1992 of the health-based standards for drinking water (Maximum Contaminant Levels or MCLs), affecting 28 million people nationally. About half of the states failed to submit data to EPA on monitoring and reporting violations for chemical and radiological contaminants in those years. According to data from the EPA, those states included Arkansas, Louisiana, Minnesota, Mississippi and Missouri.

State water quality assessments, required to be submitted every two years to the EPA, vary widely in terms of emphasis and thoroughness, and generally provide limited information on drinking water supplies. The most recent state water quality reports indicate that several states along the Mississippi had to temporarily close down drinking water supplies or issue advisories because of impairments. A sampling of water quality information from the mainstem Mississippi River states provides some clues of regional drinking water concerns. In Iowa, aside from flood-related interruption of water supplies in Des

153

Moines in 1993, no surface drinking water supplies were closed. However, high levels of nitrate in the Iowa, Des Moines and Raccoon rivers led to drinking water advisories in Iowa City, Des Moines and some smaller towns. In Illinois, on the limited amount of stream miles that provide public water supplies in the Mississippi basin, 14% of stream miles were rated as having minor impairment for drinking water use. In Missouri, only 3,160 out of 21,015 classified stream miles identified as "protected" for drinking water supply were reported to be "fully supporting" this use. The rest were rated as "not attainable," noting that the availability of high-quality groundwater in many areas of the state makes it the preferred alternative. All surface drinking water supplies in Louisiana were reported in compliance with national standards, though in "some cases, the treatment process (chlorination) has caused noncompliance due to levels of trihalomethanes." However, other sources show that Louisiana had 529 MCL violations by community systems and 142 MCL violations by noncommunity systems during 1991-1992, with more than one million people affected.

Toxic Contamination

Toxic materials pose serious water quality problems both from a human health and an ecosystem perspective. For residents of most urban areas and small towns, drinking water is treated prior to human consumption, but the costs of such treatment are substantial, and treatment may not remove some toxic compounds. Human health is also at risk from consumption of contaminated fish. Toxic pollutants of concern in the Mississippi include organic chemicals (such as PCBs, dioxin and pesticides), toxic metals and a few other substances that are hard to classify, but are sometimes considered "toxic" because of their impacts, such as un-ionized ammonia.

In the Upper Mississippi River System, unacceptable levels of polychlorinated biphenyls (PCBs) have been found in a number of areas, including the Minneapolis-St. Paul corridor and Lake Pepin in Minnesota; Pool 15 near Davenport, Iowa; St. Louis, Missouri; and stretches of the Illinois River. The Minneapolis, St. Paul area is known to have elevated levels of PCBs below the discharge of the Metro Wastewater Treatment Plant, one of the largest facilities of its kind in the United States. The PCB levels in fish in Lake Pepin, Wisconsin often exceed EPA's established health standards by many times, and Lake Pepin is also polluted with mercury, cadmium and lead. High levels of PCBs are found adjacent to the Quad Cities of Illinois and Iowa, traced primarily to an industrial waste oil disposal lagoon on the Iowa shore. The St. Louis region has problems with PCBs, toxic metals, suspended solids, ammonia and low dissolved oxygen (DO).

Toxic pollutants on the lower Mississippi include PCBs, pesticides, volatile organic chemicals (VOCs), oils, heavy metals and dioxins. Areas known to be dangerously contaminated include stretches adjacent to Memphis, Tennessee, polluted with unsafe levels of the pesticides chlordane, dieldrin and endrin, PCBs and dioxin, and north of Baton Rouge, Louisiana, polluted with

VOCs as well as the 150-mile "Chemical Corridor" from Baton Rouge to New Orleans.

Other toxic "hot spots" on the Mississippi include Sauget, Illinois; Calvert City, Kentucky; Osceola and West Helena in Arkansas; and Vicksburg, Mississippi.

In addition to human health impacts, there are the often subtle, chronic impacts of toxic contamination to fish and wildlife. These are difficult to detect, but over time, may be devastating. Recent studies suggest that toxic pollution is at least partially to blame for a variety of substantial declines in the animal communities of the Upper Mississippi, including mink populations and bottom-dwelling aquatic invertebrates, particularly fingernail clams and unionid mussels. Backwaters along the Upper Mississippi are especially susceptible to contaminants, since the fine-grained sediments that are most contaminated tend to accumulate there.

Many contaminants accumulate over time in the sediments of the River, and can be resuspended or released, reintroducing them into the water column again and again. Contaminants can also be transferred from sediments to higher animal forms through the food chain. For example, catfish in the River contain significant levels of the insecticide DDT and its metabolites in their fatty tissue. Even though use of DDT has been banned in the U.S. since 1972, enough DDT remains stored in sediments to continue contaminating bottom-feeding catfish.

Goals for the reduction of toxic pollutants already exist in the form of standards established by the EPA and state governments. However, ecosystem and human health problems continue despite the fact that there are generally not widespread persistent exceedances of current water quality standards in the River. This disparity strongly suggests that existing water quality standards are not offering sufficient protection, nor are they adequately expressing the goals necessary to protect the Mississippi. It also may reflect inadequate monitoring and enforcement.

Toxics from Point Sources

Nationally, industrial pollution controls implemented in 22 industries since 1972 have reduced releases of selected "priority" toxic organic pollutants by 99 percent from those industries. Unfortunately, the picture looks different if one considers how much pollution continues to be released by industries. According to EPA's most recent Toxic Release Inventory (TRI), U.S. industries released almost 200 million pounds of selected toxics into surface waters in 1990. Almost another 450 million pounds a year are released into public sewers. However, many chemicals and facilities are not covered by this reporting system.

Included in the TRI for 1990 is a listing by each state of its top 10 facilities for toxic releases. An evaluation of this list for Mississippi River states shows that many of these facilities are located in cities along the Mississippi River, where the releases have a high likelihood of directly or indirectly impacting the River.

Point sources of toxics along the Mississippi are abundant. One review of toxics information estimates that there are at least 150 major chemical manufacturing facilities along the Mississippi River alone, not including contributions from the tributaries. Forty-seven of these facilities discharge more than 1 billion pounds of toxic chemicals into the environment each year, including 296 million pounds directly into the Mississippi or to sewage treatment plants that discharge into the River. This does not include at least 591 other industries that discharge contaminated wastewater to the river, 26 federal facilities along the river with hazardous waste problems, 621 municipal wastewater treatment facilities that discharge more than one billion gallons per day of wastewater directly into the river, and numerous other point sources of toxics, such as landfills.

In 1991 five Mississippi River states ranked in the top 15 states releasing toxic discharges into surface waters. They included Louisiana, which was number one nationally, and Illinois (number 3), Tennessee (10), Arkansas (13), and Mississippi (15). Three of the top five facilities nationally discharging to surface waters were located in Louisiana.

That same year, five mainstem states also ranked among the national top 15 toxic dischargers to publicly owned sewage treatment works (POTW) facilities, including Illinois, which ranked highest nationally, and Missouri (number 6), Tennessee (8), Iowa (14) and Wisconsin (15). Two of the top five facilities in the country discharging toxics to sewage treatment works in 1991 were located in Illinois, and one was in Missouri.

On the lower river, industrial and municipal discharges have increased since the 1960s. In Louisiana, approximately 98 percent of the toxic releases into water in 1990 occurred in the Mississippi River corridor, south of St. Francisville. In this stretch, more than 350 industrial and municipal facilities are located adjacent to the River, about half of which discharge wastewater to the River. This same area, which includes nine parishes that straddle the River, is home to 36 percent of the state's population.

In many areas, especially along the upper river, point source problems are reportedly showing initial signs of improvement, though total discharges remain alarmingly high. For example, the Twin Cities wastewater treatment plant, which receives effluent from 500-700 industrial facilities, has reduced its loadings of heavy metals by 50-85 percent in recent years. The 3M Corporation (Minnesota and Illinois), Monsanto (in Iowa, Missouri, Illinois and Louisiana), Dow Chemical (in Louisiana) and other companies have embarked on campaigns to reduce discharges of pollutants to air and water, due to factors that include public demand for change, the growing costs of disposal and liability. Another important factor likely has been the reporting standards through the toxics release inventory provisions of the Superfund Amendments and Reauthorization Act (SARA) that, since 1988, require facilities discharging any of 307 hazardous chemicals to submit annual estimates of discharges both on- and off-site to the EPA. This opportunity for public access to information has helped pressure companies to take action to reduce pollution.

Toxics from Polluted Runoff Sources

Toxic polluted runoff from urban areas and farms is also a serious problem in the Mississippi's watershed. Persistent problems of polluted runoff are impeding progress in meeting water quality goals. A wide range of compounds that can be traced to runoff, including dioxins and heavy metals, PCBs and insecticides such as chlordane (once routinely used as a household and lawn care product) and endrin, are showing up in the tissues of fish, prompting fish advisories along the Mississippi. Many of the problem compounds now have been banned for most or all uses in the United States, but still persist in the environment and continue to accumulate in fish and other river creatures.

Farm chemicals also pose serious toxics problems for the Mississippi and other waterways. Agricultural activities, including use of pesticides and animal feedlot/waste operations, are two categories of problems often cited as the most prevalent causes of fish kills. Insecticides that have been identified as problems range from the old organochlorines, such as DDT, mirex, dieldrin and dicofol, most of which have been banned but are still showing up in the Mississippi, to newer organophosphates and caroamates that do not tend to bioaccumulate, but often are still very toxic—especially to aquatic invertebrates and fish.

Pesticides pollute both surface and groundwater (considered to be the source of approximately 30 percent of streamflow nationally). According to EPA's compilation of the States' 1988/89 305(b) reports, pesticides impaired 11.2 percent of all assessed river miles. Those of highest concern include the herbicides atrazine and alachlor, both of which are relatively longlasting and quite soluble in water, thus easily transported during spring snowmelt and periods of high rainfall. Both chemicals can leach into groundwater that later emerges in seeps and springs, mixing with surface water.

In the Midwest, where agriculture is a predominant land use, millions of pounds of herbicides are applied annually to cropland and pastureland. Recent studies by the U.S. Geological Survey (USGS) in the Mississippi River basin show that significant quantities of these herbicides are "flushed" into streams each year during late spring and summer, eventually moving into the Mississippi and the Gulf. For example, the USGS found one or more herbicides in each of 146 samples collected from eight sites on the Mississippi River and its major tributaries in April, May and June 1991. Atrazine concentrations exceeded the EPA's health-based limits for drinking water in 27 percent of the samples, and alachlor exceeded the limits in 4 percent of the samples. In some cases, the concentrations were elevated for several weeks in the spring, even in rivers as large as the Missouri and Mississippi. More than three-fourths of these samples also contained the herbicides cyanazine and metolachlor.

After major flooding in the Midwest in 1993, researchers expected farm chemical levels in the Mississippi to be reduced due to dilution. Instead, concentrations of atrazine, alachlor, cyanazine and metolachlor were similar to or higher than the maximum concentrations measured previously. The total atrazine load transported to the Gulf of Mexico from April through August 1993 (539,000 kilograms) was about 80 percent higher than for the same period in 1991 and 235 percent higher than for the same period in 1992. In some samples, atrazine and cyanazine exceeded health-based limits for drinking water.

Sedimentation

Sedimentation is also a significant problem in the Mississippi, and is sometimes considered the Upper Mississippi's number one problem. Annual sediment inputs to the Upper Mississippi River basin range from minimal in the largely forested reaches of the northernmost watersheds to about 210,000 kg/hectare in critical sediment producing areas of the Midwest. The Missouri River historically has been the principal supplier of sediment to the lower Mississippi River.

Sedimentation into the Upper Mississippi is a major cause of habitat degradation in the Upper Mississippi River. For example, sediment has been implicated in the decline of largemouth bass, a valuable sport-fishing species highly preferred by anglers. If recent levels of erosion continue, it is estimated that many of the large, open water marshes and backwater lakes will fill in within the next century, creating shrub swamps and eventually bottomland hardwood forests.

A number of waterfowl species, including canvasback ducks and tundra swans, prefer food sources such as wild celery and arrowhead that have both declined rapidly in recent years. Factors contributing to the decline are thought to include lack of light from excess turbidity due to suspended sediment. The problem of declining food availability is a growing concern among biologists.

The main source of fine sediment coming into the River is upland erosion from farmlands. Other major sources of sediment and related pollutants include mining, which also causes drainage of acids and heavy metals, and forestry activities. Mississippi River states that report mining as a significant source of water impairment include Arkansas, Illinois, Kentucky, Louisiana, Minnesota, Mississippi, Missouri and Tennessee. States that report major impairments to streams from forestry include Arkansas, Illinois, Kentucky, Louisiana, Minnesota and Mississippi. The operation and maintenance of the navigation system, and bank erosion from increasing numbers of large horsepower recreation and commercial craft, also play a role in the River's sedimentation problems.

A significant amount of sediments from past erosion events are "stored" in the hill slopes and floodplain of the River system, where they can be resuspended during high rainfall or flood events. When storms sweep through the Midwest in spring and summer, accelerated runoff carries huge quantities of topsoil into the River from its network of tributary streams. Once the topsoil reaches the River, many of the heavier constituents settle out in slower moving water behind the dams and in the shallow backwaters.

Although sediments are being continually introduced to the River, the contribution of sources already "in place" in the system are also believed to be significant. The presence of toxic contaminants in suspended and "bed" sediments already deposited on the riverbottom is a special concern.

Ironically, though erosion levels on the Upper River are a serious pollution problem, changes in the watershed that have drastically reduced the sediment load to the Lower Mississippi also are causing problems. The Missouri River's sediment load has greatly decreased since the early 1960s, due to construction of several dams above Yankton, South Dakota. Current discharges of sediment to the Gulf of Mexico by the Mississippi averages about 210 million tons per year, less than one-half of what they were before 1953. This decrease is contributing to a rapid recession of shorelines in the subsiding Mississippi delta.

Nutrients

The nutrients phosphorus and nitrogen from manure and artificial fertilizer applications are major water pollutants. At high levels, phosphorus is acutely toxic to fish; at lower levels phosphorus and nitrogen over-enrich water bodies, causing them to fill up with algae (a process called "eutrophication"). Nitrogen, especially in the form of nitrate, is a concern for human and livestock health. In the form of ammonia, nitrogen also is acutely toxic to fish. Nutrient enrichment from the Mississippi River is a devastating problem for the Gulf of Mexico and its fisheries.

Per-acre use of fertilizers doubled between 1964 and 1984, while use of nitrogen fertilizers in the U.S. increased by more than a factor of four between 1960 and 1981, to a total of 11.9 million tons per year. Since then, nitrogen fertilizer use has declined somewhat nationally, with use fluctuating between 10.7 and 11.2 million tons since 1988.

Livestock confinement facilities and feedlots, although a potent form of water contamination from nutrients and bacteria, are largely exempt from Clean Water Act mandates, which only require permits for the largest feedlots with more than 1,000 animal units. Several Mississippi River states have specifically identified agricultural runoff from animal wastes as a major impairment of streams, including Arkansas, Iowa, Mississippi, Missouri and Wisconsin.

Nutrient runoff and infiltration into surface and ground waters of fertilizers from farm fields, lawns and golf courses, and animal manures, is a major cause of elevated nutrient levels in the Mississippi River and its tributaries. More clearly than many other problems, nutrient overenrichment links the upper and lower sections of the Mississippi's complex system.

The Mississippi River currently contributes to unnaturally high levels of nutrients to the warm Gulf waters. These nutrients are considered largely to blame for development of large oxygen-depleted, "anoxic" areas, also known as "dead zones" in the Gulf of Mexico. These dead zones, responsible for massive fish kills, now cover extensive areas of the continental shelf south of Louisiana at certain times of the year. Related problems of nutrient enrichment and eutrophication include noxious algal blooms that may have toxic effects on marine life or humans consuming tainted seafood. Indirect effects include changing the makeup of microscopic life that forms the basis of the food web for the Gulf's $780 million fishery that represents almost 20 percent of the national total annual domestic harvest of commercial fish.

For an average day in 1989, it is estimated that more than 379,000 pounds of phosphorus and more than 1,872,600 pounds of nitrogen (measured as total Kjeldahl nitrogen) were discharged into the Gulf of Mexico from the surface waters of the United States. More than 90 percent of each nutrient came from the Mississippi River system, much of it originating far from the Gulf region. Indeed the Upper Mississippi and Ohio River basins are the major source of both nutrients during much of the year. In both cases, agricultural sources provide by far the largest contribution of nutrient pollution.

BLACKMUN RENUNCIATION OF THE DEATH PENALTY
February 22, 1994

Perhaps with an eye toward his place in the history books, Supreme Court Justice Harry A. Blackmun on February 22 changed his position after more than two decades on the Court and declared that the death penalty is unconstitutional.

"From this day forward, I no longer shall tinker with the machinery of death . . .," Blackmun wrote. "Rather than continue to coddle the Court's delusion that the desired level of fairness has been achieved and the need for regulation eviscerated, I feel morally and intellectually obligated simply to concede that the death penalty experiment has failed."

Blackmun's change of heart had no practical impact, since it came as a dissent to a majority decision not to review the case of a Texas man who was sentenced to die. Less than two months after writing the opinion, the eighty-five-year-old justice retired from the Court. Some saw the opinion as an attempt by Blackmun to affect how historians would view his tenure.

Since his appointment to the Court in 1970 by President Richard Nixon, Blackmun had consistently voted to uphold death sentences. Yet there had been signs almost from the beginning that he might harbor misgivings about the death penalty. In a 1972 opinion, he wrote: "I yield to no one in the depth of my distaste, antipathy, and indeed, abhorrence, for the death penalty."

In the new opinion, Blackmun wrote that it was impossible to reconcile two competing objectives: treating defendants uniformly while also taking into consideration the individual circumstances of their cases. In previous cases, the Court had said that juries had to follow narrow rules in choosing the death penalty so that it would be applied uniformly. In other cases, the Court had said that juries needed to take into account mitigating circumstances, such as a defendant's rough upbringing, when considering death sentences.

Blackmun wrote that states and courts had struggled to devise procedural rules aimed at satisfying both objectives, but that doing so was impossible.

The result was that the death penalty "remains fraught with arbitrariness, discrimination, caprice, and mistake," Blackmun said. Despite his claim that some innocent people had been mistakenly executed, Blackmun cited no cases where he thought this had occurred.

The Court majority issued no opinion in the case, but Justice Antonin Scalia wrote a sharply worded opinion agreeing with the majority's decision not to review it. Scalia wrote that the Constitution clearly allowed capital punishment, and the fact that the Court had issued two competing commands to juries in capital cases meant it had been wrong at least once. "Convictions in opposition to the death penalty are often passionate and deeply held," Scalia wrote. "That would be no excuse for reading them into a Constitution that does not contain them, even if they represented the convictions of a majority of Americans."

Defendants Win Two Victories

Ironically, in the weeks between Blackmun's dissent and his departure from the Court, the justices gave death row inmates victories in two separate cases. In the first case, Simmons v. South Carolina, *the justices held that juries choosing between sentences of life in prison and death must be told if state law forbids parole for those sentenced to life. In the second case,* McFarland v. Scott, *the Court ruled that federal judges can halt executions to give an inmate time to find a lawyer to file a "habeas corpus" petition challenging the death sentence. In the latter case, Blackmun wrote the majority opinion for a 5-4 Court.*

In 1972, only two years after Blackmun joined the Court, executions stopped when the justices effectively overturned state capital punishment laws because they did not have consistent standards. In 1976, executions resumed when the justices said the death penalty could be reinstated if procedural safeguards were followed. Between 1976 and early 1994, 228 defendants were executed, according to figures compiled by the NAACP Legal Defense and Educational Fund. In the 1990s, as the public increasingly focused on crime and demanded tougher sentencing, the pace of executions quickened. In 1991, 14 prisoners were executed. That number rose to 31 in 1992 and 38 in 1993. At the time of Blackmun's opinion, more than 2,800 prisoners sat on death rows across the country.

When Blackmun wrote his opinion, a solid majority of the justices supported the death penalty. Previously, Justices Thurgood Marshall and William J. Brennan Jr. had consistently opposed the death penalty, with both justices believing that it constituted cruel and unusual punishment in violation of the Constitution. With Brennan's retirement in 1990 and Marshall's in 1991, the Court was left without a strong voice against the death penalty.

Blackmun Vilified for Roe v. Wade

Blackmun was best known as the author of the majority opinion in Roe v. Wade, *the Court's 1973 ruling that legalized abortion. In the opinion, Black-*

mun wrote that the constitutional right of privacy "is broad enough to encompass a woman's decision whether or not to terminate her pregnancy." The decision made Blackmun the most hated man in the Supreme Court's history.

Nixon appointed Blackmun to the Court in 1970 on the recommendation of Chief Justice Warren E. Burger, who was a grade school friend of Blackmun's. Blackmun was Nixon's third choice for the job. Blackmun only got it after the Senate refused to confirm Clement F. Haynsworth Jr. and G. Harrold Carswell, Nixon's first two choices. Initially, Blackmun voted with the conservative chief justice in nearly all cases. Within a few years, however, Blackmun started taking positions that were more liberal. With the resignations of Marshall and Brennan, Blackmun became the Court's leading liberal voice.

Blackmun denied that he had changed while on the Court, contending instead that it was the Court itself that had changed. In a 1991 interview, he said: "Republicans think I am a traitor and Democrats don't trust me. So I twist in the wind, owing allegiance to no one, which is precisely where I want to be."

President Bill Clinton's first choice to succeed Blackmun, Senate Majority Leader George J. Mitchell of Maine, turned down the job. Mitchell said he did so because he wanted to help push Clinton's health care plan through Congress, but some believed that Mitchell really wanted to be named commissioner of Major League Baseball. Clinton then chose Stephen G. Breyer, chief judge of the First U.S. Circuit Court of Appeals in Boston. In July, the Senate confirmed Breyer by an 87-9 vote. Breyer told the Washington Post *that his role on the Court would be "to make the average person's ordinary life better."*

Following are excerpts from the concurring opinion of Justice Antonin Scalia and from the dissenting opinion of Justice Harry A. Blackmun in the case of Callins v. Collins, *decided February 22, 1994:*

No. 93-7054

Bruce Edwin Callins, Petitioner *v.* James A. Collins, Director, Texas Department of Criminal Justice	On writ of certiorari to the United States Court of Appeals for the Fifth Circuit

[February 22, 1994]

The petition for a writ of certiorari is denied.
JUSTICE SCALIA, concurring.

JUSTICE BLACKMUN dissents from the denial of certiorari in this case with a statement explaining why the death penalty "as currently administered," is contrary to the Constitution of the United States. That explanation often refers to "intellectual, moral and personal" perceptions, but never to the text and tradition of the Constitution. It is the latter rather than the former that ought to control. The Fifth Amendment provides that "[n]o person shall be held to answer for a capital . . . crime, unless on a presentment or indictment of a Grand Jury, . . . nor be deprived of life . . . without due process of law." This clearly permits the death penalty to be imposed, and establishes beyond doubt that the death penalty is not one of the "cruel and unusual punishments" prohibited by the Eighth Amendment.

As JUSTICE BLACKMUN describes, however, over the years since 1972 this Court has attached to the imposition of the death penalty two quite incompatible sets of commands: the sentencer's discretion to impose death must be closely confined, see *Furman v. Georgia,* but the sentencer's discretion not to impose death (to extend mercy) must be unlimited, see *Eddings v. Oklahoma* (1982); *Lockett v. Ohio* (1978). These commands were invented without benefit of any textual or historical support; they are the product of just such "intellectual, moral, and personal" perceptions as JUSTICE BLACKMUN expresses today, some of which (viz., those that have been "perceived" simultaneously by five members of the Court) have been made part of what is called "the Court's Eighth Amendment jurisprudence."

Though JUSTICE BLACKMUN joins those of us who have acknowledged the incompatibility of the Court's *Furman* and *Lockett-Eddings* lines of jurisprudence, he unfortunately draws the wrong conclusion from the acknowledgment. He says:

"[T]he proper course when faced with irreconcilable constitutional commands is not to ignore one or the other, nor to pretend that the dilemma does not exist, but to admit the futility of the effort to harmonize them. This means accepting the fact that the death penalty cannot be administered in accord with our Constitution."

Surely a different conclusion commends itself—to wit, that at least one of these judicially announced irreconcilable commands which cause the Constitution to prohibit what its text explicitly permits must be wrong.

Convictions in opposition to the death penalty are often passionate and deeply held. That would be no excuse for reading them into a Constitution that does not contain them, even if they represented the convictions of a majority of Americans. Much less is there any excuse for using that course to thrust a minority's views upon the people. JUSTICE BLACKMUN begins his statement by describing with poignancy the death of a convicted murderer by lethal injection. He chooses, as the case in which to make that statement, one of the less brutal of the murders that regularly come before us—the murder of a man ripped by a bullet suddenly and unexpectedly, with no opportunity to prepare himself and his affairs, and left to bleed to death on the floor of a tavern. The death-by-injection which JUSTICE BLACKMUN describes looks pretty desirable next to that. It looks even better next to some of the other cases currently before us which JUSTICE BLACKMUN did not select as the vehicle for his announcement that the death penalty is always unconstitutional—for example, the case of the 11-year-old girl raped by four men and then killed by stuffing her panties down her throat. How enviable a quiet death by lethal injection compared with that! If the people conclude that such more brutal deaths may be deterred by capital punishment; indeed, if they merely conclude that justice requires such brutal deaths to be avenged by capital punishment; the creation of false, untextual and unhistorical contradictions within "the Court's Eighth Amendment jurisprudence" should not prevent them.

JUSTICE BLACKMUN, dissenting.

On February 23, 1994, at approximately 1:00 a.m., Bruce Edwin Callins will be executed by the State of Texas. Intravenous tubes attached to his arms will carry the instrument of death, a toxic fluid designed specifically for the purpose of killing human beings. The witnesses, standing a few feet away, will behold Callins, no longer a defendant, an appellant, or a petitioner, but a man, strapped to a gurney, and seconds away from extinction.

Within days, or perhaps hours, the memory of Callins will begin to fade. The wheels of justice will churn again, and somewhere, another jury or another judge will have the unenviable task of determining whether some human being is to live or die. We hope, of course, that the defendant whose life is at risk will be represented by competent counsel—someone who is inspired by the awareness that a less-than-vigorous defense truly could have fatal consequences for the defendant. We hope that the attorney will investigate all aspects of the case, follow all evidentiary and procedural rules, and appear before a judge who is still committed to the protection of defendants' rights—even now, as the prospect of meaningful judicial oversight has diminished. In the same vein, we hope that the prosecution, in urging the penalty of death, will have exercised its discretion wisely, free from bias, prejudice, or political motive, and will be humbled, rather than emboldened, by the awesome authority conferred by the State.

But even if we can feel confident that these actors will fulfill their roles to the best of their human ability, our collective conscience will remain uneasy. Twenty years have passed since this Court declared that the death penalty must be imposed fairly, and with reasonable consistency, or not at all, and, despite the effort of the States and courts to devise legal formulas and procedural rules to meet this daunting challenge, the death penalty remains fraught with arbitrariness, discrimination, caprice, and mistake. This is not to say that the problems with the death penalty today are identical to those that were present 20 years ago. Rather, the problems that were pursued down one hole with procedural rules and verbal formulas have come to the surface somewhere else, just as virulent and pernicious as they were in their original form. Experience has taught us that the constitutional goal of eliminating arbitrariness and discrimination from the administration of death can never be achieved without compromising an equally essential component of fundamental fairness—individualized sentencing.

It is tempting, when faced with conflicting constitutional commands, to sacrifice one for the other or to assume that an acceptable balance between them already has been struck. In the context of the death penalty, however, such jurisprudential maneuvers are wholly inappropriate. The death penalty must be imposed "fairly, and with reasonable consistency, or not at all."

To be fair, a capital sentencing scheme must treat each person convicted of a capital offense with that "degree of respect due the uniqueness of the individual." That means affording the sentencer the power and discretion to grant mercy in a particular case, and providing avenues for the consideration of any and all relevant mitigating evidence that would justify a sentence less than death. Reasonable consistency, on the other hand, requires that the death penalty be inflicted evenhandedly, in accordance with reason and objective standards, rather than by whim, caprice, or prejudice. Finally, because human error is inevitable, and because our criminal justice system is less than perfect, searching appellate review of death sentences and their underlying convictions is a prerequisite to a constitutional death penalty scheme.

On their face, these goals of individual fairness, reasonable consistency, and absence of error appear to be attainable: Courts are in the very business of erecting procedural devices from which fair, equitable, and reliable outcomes are presumed to flow. Yet, in the death penalty area, this Court, in my view, has engaged in a futile effort to balance these constitutional demands, and now is retreating not only from the *Furman* promise of consistency and rationality, but from the requirement of individualized sentencing as well. Having virtually conceded that both fairness and rationality cannot be achieved in the administration of the death penalty the Court has chosen to deregulate the entire enterprise, replacing, it would seem, substantive constitutional requirements with mere aesthetics, and abdicating its statutorily and constitutionally imposed duty to provide meaningful judicial oversight to the administration of death by the States.

From this day forward, I no longer shall tinker with the machinery of death. For more than 20 years I have endeavored—indeed, I have struggled—along with a majority of this Court, to develop procedural and substantive rules that would lend more than the mere appearance of fairness to the death penalty endeavor. Rather than continue to coddle the Court's delusion that the desired level of fairness has been achieved and the need for regulation eviscerated, I feel morally and intellectually obligated simply to concede that the death penalty experiment has failed. It is virtually self-evident to me now that no combination of procedural rules or substantive regulations ever can save the death penalty from its inherent constitutional deficiencies. The basic question—does the system accurately and consistently determine which defendants "deserve" to die?—cannot be answered in the affirmative. It is not simply that this Court has allowed vague aggravating circumstances to be employed, relevant mitigating evidence to be disregarded, and vital justice to be blocked. The problem is that the inevitability of factual, legal, and moral error gives us a system that we know must wrongly kill some defendants, a system that fails to deliver the fair, consistent, and reliable sentences of death required by the Constitution.

A

There is little doubt now that *Furman*'s essential holding was correct. Although most of the public seems to desire, and the Constitution appears to permit, the penalty of death, it surely is beyond dispute that if the death penalty cannot be administered consistently and rationally, it may not be administered at all. . . . I faithfully have adhered to the *Furman* holding and have come to believe that it is indispensable to the Court's Eighth Amendment jurisprudence.

Delivering on the *Furman* promise, however, has proved to be another matter. *Furman* aspired to eliminate the vestiges of racism and the effects of poverty in capital sentencing; it deplored the "wanton" and "random" infliction of death by a government with constitutionally limited power. *Furman* demanded that the sentencer's discretion be directed and limited by procedural rules and objective standards in order to minimize the risk of arbitrary and capricious sentences of death.

In the years following *Furman*, serious efforts were made to comply with its mandate. State legislatures and appellate courts struggled to provide judges and juries with sensible and objective guidelines for determining who should live and who should die. Some States attempted to define who is "deserving" of the death penalty through the use of carefully chosen adjectives, reserving the death penalty for those who commit crimes that are "especially heinous, atrocious, or cruel," or "wantonly vile, horrible or inhuman." Other States enacted mandatory death penalty statutes, reading *Furman* as an invitation to eliminate sentencer discretion altogether. Still other States specified aggravating and mitigating factors that were to be considered by the sentencer and weighed against one another in a calculated and rational manner.

Unfortunately, all this experimentation and ingenuity yielded little of what *Furman* demanded. It soon became apparent that discretion could not be eliminated from capital sentencing without threatening the fundamental fairness due a defendant when life is at stake. Just as contemporary society was no longer tolerant of the random or discriminatory infliction of the penalty of death, evolving standards of decency required due consideration of the uniqueness of each individual defendant when imposing society's ultimate penalty.

This development in the American conscience would have presented no constitutional dilemma if fairness to the individual could be achieved without sacrificing the consistency and rationality promised in *Furman*. But over the past two decades, efforts to balance these competing constitutional commands have been to no avail. Experience has shown that the consistency and rationality promised in *Furman* are inversely related to the fairness owed the individual when considering a sentence of death. A step toward consistency is a step away from fairness.

B

There is a heightened need for fairness in the administration of death. This unique level of fairness is born of the appreciation that death truly is different from all other punishments a society inflicts upon its citizens. "Death, in its finality, differs more from life imprisonment than a 100-year prison term differs from one of only a year or two." Because of the qualitative difference of the death penalty, "there is a corresponding difference in the need for reliability in the determination that death is the appropriate punishment in a specific case." In *Woodson*, a decision striking down mandatory death penalty statutes as unconstitutional, a plurality of the Court explained: "A process that accords no significance to relevant facets of the character and record of the individual offender or the circumstances of the particular offense excludes from consideration in fixing the ultimate punishment of death the possibility of compassionate or mitigating factors stemming from the diverse frailties of humankind."

While the risk of mistake in the determination of the appropriate penalty may be tolerated in other areas of the criminal law, "in capital cases the fundamental respect for humanity underlying the Eighth Amendment . . . requires consideration of the character and record of the individual offender and the circumstances of the particular offense as a constitutionally indispensable part of the process of inflicting the penalty of death." Thus, although individualized sentencing in capital cases was not considered essential at the time the Constitution was adopted, *Woodson* recognized that American standards of decency could no longer tolerate a capital sentencing process that failed to afford a defendant individualized consideration in the determination whether he or she should live or die.

The Court elaborated on the principle of individualized sentencing in *Lockett v. Ohio*. In that case, a plurality acknowledged that strict restraints on sentencer discretion are necessary to achieve the consistency and rationality promised in *Furman*, but held that, in the end, the sentencer must retain unbridled discretion to afford mercy. Any process or procedure that prevents the sentencer from considering "as a mitigating factor, any aspect of a defendant's character or record and any circumstances of the offense that the defendant proffers as a basis for a sentence less than death," creates the constitutionally intolerable risk that "the death penalty will be imposed in spite of factors which may call for a less severe penalty." The Court's duty under the Constitution therefore is to "develop a system of capital punishment at once consistent and principled but also humane and sensible to the uniqueness of the individual."

C

I believe the *Woodson-Lockett* line of cases to be fundamentally sound and rooted in American standards of decency that have evolved over time. The notion of prohibiting a sentencer from exercising its discretion "to dispense mercy on the basis of factors too intangible to write into a statute," is offensive to our sense of fundamental fairness and respect for the uniqueness of the individual. . . .

Yet, as several Members of the Court have recognized, there is real "tension" between the need for fairness to the individual and the consistency promised in *Furman*. On the one hand, discretion in capital sentencing must be "controlled by clear and objective standards so as to produce non-discriminatory [and reasoned] application." On the other hand, the Constitution also requires that the sentencer be able to consider "any relevant mitigating evidence regarding the defendant's character or background, and the circumstances of the particular offense." The power to consider mitigating evidence that would warrant a sentence less than death is meaningless unless the sentencer has the discretion and authority to dispense mercy based on that evidence. Thus, the Constitution, by requiring a heightened degree of fairness to the individual, and also a greater degree of equality and rationality in the administration of death, demands sentencer discretion that is at once generously expanded and severely restricted. . . .

[D Omitted]

E

The arbitrariness inherent in the sentencer's discretion to afford mercy is exacerbated by the problem of race. Even under the most sophisticated death penalty statutes, race continues to play a major role in determining who shall live and who shall die. Perhaps it should not be surprising that the biases and prejudices that infect society generally would influence the determination of who is sentenced to death, even within the narrower pool of death-eligible defendants selected according to objective standards. No matter how narrowly the pool of death-eligible defendants is drawn according to objective standards, *Furman*'s promise still will go unfulfilled so long as the sentencer is free to exercise unbridled discretion within the smaller group and thereby to discriminate. " 'The power to be lenient is the power to discriminate.' ". . .

The fact that we may not be capable of devising procedural or substantive rules to prevent the more subtle and often unconscious forms of racism from creeping into the system does not justify the wholesale abandonment of the *Furman* promise. To the contrary, where a morally irrelevant—indeed, a repugnant—consideration plays a major role in the determination of who shall live and who shall die, it suggests that the continued enforcement of the death penalty in light of its clear and admitted defects is deserving of a "sober second thought.". . .

F

In the years since *McCleskey*, I have come to wonder whether there was truth in the majority's suggestion that discrimination and arbitrariness could not be purged from the administration of capital punishment without sacrificing the equally essential component of fairness—individualized sentencing. Viewed in this way, the consistency promised in *Furman* and the fairness to the individual demanded in *Lockett* are not only inversely related, but irreconcilable in the context of capital punishment. Any statute or procedure that could effectively eliminate arbitrariness from the administration of death would also restrict the sentencer's discretion to such an extent that the sentencer would be unable to give full consideration to the unique characteristics of each defendant and the circumstances of the offense. By the same token, any statute or procedure that would provide the sentencer with sufficient discretion to consider fully and act upon the unique circumstances of each defendant would "thro[w] open the back door to arbitrary and irrational sentencing." *Graham v. Collins*. All efforts to strike an appropriate balance between these conflicting constitutional commands are futile because there is a heightened need for both in the administration of death. But even if the constitutional requirements of consistency and fairness are theoretically reconcilable in the context of capital punishment, it is clear that this Court is not prepared to meet the challenge. In apparent frustration over its inability to strike an appropriate balance between the Furman promise of consistency and the *Lockett* requirement of individualized sentencing, the Court has retreated from the field, allowing relevant mitigating evidence to be discarded, vague aggravating circumstances to be employed, and providing no indication that the problem of race in the administration of death will ever be addressed. In fact some members of the Court openly have acknowledged a willingness simply to pick one of the competing constitutional commands and sacrifice the other. These developments are troubling, as they ensure that death will continue to be meted out in this country arbitrarily and discriminatorily, and without that "degree of respect due the uniqueness of the individual." In my view, the proper course when faced with irreconcilable constitutional commands is not to ignore one or the other, nor to pretend that the dilemma does not exist, but to admit the futility of the effort to harmonize them. This means accepting the fact that the death penalty cannot be administered in accord with our Constitution.

II

My belief that this Court would not enforce the death penalty (even if it could) in accordance with the Constitution is buttressed by the Court's "obvious eagerness to do away with any restriction on the States' power to execute whomever and however they please." I have explained at length on numerous occasions that my willingness to enforce the capital punishment statutes enacted by the States and the Federal Government, "notwithstanding my own deep moral reservations . . . has always rested on an understanding that certain procedural safeguards, chief among them the federal judiciary's power to reach and correct claims of constitutional error on federal habeas review, would ensure that death sentences are fairly imposed." In recent years, I have grown increasingly skeptical that "the death penalty really can be imposed fairly and in accordance with the requirements of the Eighth Amendment," given the now limited ability of the federal courts to remedy constitutional errors.

Federal courts are required by statute to entertain petitions from state prisoners who allege that they are held "in violation of the Constitution or the treaties of the United States." Serious review of these claims helps to ensure that government does not secure the penalty of death by depriving a defendant of his or her constitutional rights. At the time I voted with the majority to uphold the constitutionality of the death penalty in *Gregg v. Georgia* (1976), federal courts possessed much broader authority than they do today to address claims of constitutional error on habeas review. In 1976, there were few procedural barriers to the federal judiciary's review of a State's capital sentencing scheme, or the fairness and reliability of a State's decision to impose death in a particular case. Since then, however, the Court has "erected unprecedented and unwarranted barriers" to the federal judiciary's review of the constitutional claims of capital defendants.

The Court's refusal last term to afford Leonel Torres Herrera an evidentiary hearing, despite his colorable showing of actual innocence, demonstrates just how far afield the Court has strayed from its statutorily and constitutionally imposed obligations. In *Herrera*, only a bare majority of this Court could bring itself to state forthrightly that the execution of an actually innocent person violates the Eighth Amendment. This concession was made only in the course of erecting nearly insurmountable barriers to a defendant's ability to get a hearing on a claim of actual innocence. Certainly there will be individuals who are actually innocent who will be unable to make a better showing than what was made by Herrera without the benefit of an evidentiary hearing. The Court is unmoved by this dilemma, however; it prefers "finality" in death sentences to reliable determinations of a capital defendant's guilt. Because I no longer can state with any confidence that this Court is able to reconcile the Eighth Amendment's competing constitutional commands, or that the federal judiciary will provide meaningful oversight to the state courts as they exercise their authority to inflict the penalty of death, I believe that the death penalty, as currently administered, is unconstitutional.

III

Perhaps one day this Court will develop procedural rules or verbal formulas that actually will provide consistency, fairness, and reliability in a capital-sentencing scheme. I am not optimistic that such a day will come. I am more optimistic, though, that this Court eventually will conclude that the effort to eliminate arbitrariness while preserving fairness "in the infliction of [death] is so plainly doomed to failure that it—and the death penalty—must be abandoned altogether." I may not live to see that day, but I have faith that eventually it will arrive. The path the Court has chosen lessens us all. I dissent.

SURGEON GENERAL ON SMOKING AND YOUNG PEOPLE
February 24, 1994

In releasing the first surgeon general's report on smoking and health devoted exclusively to smoking and young people on February 24, Dr. Jocelyn Elders called for a ban on tobacco advertising aimed at youngsters. She said the tobacco industry targeted young people with advertising and promotions designed to make them want to belong to a group she called the "Five S Club—They're slim, they're sexy, they're sociable, they're sophisticated and they're successful."

Elders dismissed claims by the tobacco industry that it did not target youngsters, noting that tobacco companies have to target children because they lose 2 million customers annually to death and people who give up tobacco. "Young people are the chief source of new customers," she said. "Each day 3,000 young people must be recruited to start smoking in order for the tobacco industry to continue at the same level of business."

Tobacco Firms Spent Billions on Promotion

According to Elders's report, in 1990 tobacco companies spent nearly $4 billion—between 10 and 12 percent of revenue—on promotion and advertising, making them the second largest advertisers in the United States after automobile manufacturers.

In the preface to the report, Elders commented on the debate about the effect of tobacco advertising on young people: "A misguided debate has arisen about whether tobacco promotion 'causes' young people to smoke—misguided because single-source causation is probably too simple an explanation for any social phenomenon. The more important issue is what effect tobacco promotion might have. Current research suggests that pervasive tobacco promotion has two effects: it creates the perception that more people smoke than actually do, and it provides a conduit between actual self-image and ideal self-image—in other words, smoking is made to look cool."

At her news conference, Elders said that while tobacco use was falling among adults, it was increasing among young people. Three million teen-agers smoked, Elders said, and another million used smokeless tobacco. "The tragedy is this: one-third to one-half of young people who try cigarettes go on to be daily smokers," Elders said.

R. J. Reynolds Co. Draws Criticism

In attacking tobacco advertising, Elders singled out for special criticism the R. J. Reynolds Co. for its use of the cartoon character Joe Camel in advertising and promotions. A female camel named Josephine had recently joined Joe, and Elders said the new character was aimed at getting girls to smoke. Elders said the Federal Trade Commission (FTC) should act on several pending petitions that sought to ban the ads. Dr. Antonia Novello, Elders's predecessor as surgeon general, joined her in calling for action from the FTC to stop the ads.

In a statement, R. J. Reynolds said that peer influence and parental example—not advertising—caused youngsters to start smoking. The company said that "if we believed Camel advertising caused youth to start smoking who otherwise would not, we would voluntarily pull the campaign without any outside urging."

The Joe Camel campaign suffered a blow in late November when the U.S. Supreme Court cleared the way for a suit challenging use of the character. The suit was filed by Janet Mangini, a San Francisco lawyer and antismoking activist who contended the Joe Camel character encouraged kids to take up smoking. The case, which was brought under a California law that bans unfair business practices, was one of a number of legal actions pending around the country against the Joe Camel campaign. Reynolds had sought to have the suit dismissed, contending that a federal law regulating tobacco advertising preempted the state action. The California Supreme Court said that despite the federal law, states had the right to prevent advertising that encourages youngsters to commit illegal acts, such as smoking. In papers filed with the U.S. Supreme Court, Mangini wrote: "This case is based on a rather unremarkable and universally accepted proposition: You cannot encourage someone to violate the law . . . California, like practically every other state, prohibits minors from purchasing or possessing tobacco products."

Study Looks at Effect of Beer Ads on Children

The effect of advertising on children was the focus of another study during 1994. In that study, titled "Television Beer Advertising and Drinking Knowledge, Beliefs, and Intentions Among Schoolchildren" and published in the February 1994 issue of the American Journal of Public Health, *researchers examined how beer commercials affected the attitudes of fifth- and sixth-grade schoolchildren toward drinking. They said the study suggested that alcohol advertising may predispose young people to drinking. "Children who were more aware of beer advertisements held more favorable beliefs about drinking, intended to drink more frequently as adults, and had more*

*knowledge of beer brands and slogans," the researchers wrote. They con-
cluded that the findings suggested "that attempts to prevent or delay drinking among young people should give attention to alcohol advertising. In particular, efforts should be made to reduce the extent to which it appeals to
children and to reduce their exposure to it."*

*The researchers suggested several ways to achieve that goal, including re-
stricting television alcohol advertising during prime viewing hours for children, limiting sponsorships by alcohol companies of concerts and other
events attended by children, working with alcohol advertisers to make their
commercials less appealing to children, and developing counter-advertising
about the hazards of drinking. They noted that two recent federal reports had
recommended limiting or banning alcohol advertising and requiring equal
time for public health messages about drinking.*

*Following are excerpts from the report titled "Preventing
Tobacco Use Among Young People: A Report of the Surgeon
General," which was released February 24, 1994:*

Research on the Effects of Cigarette Advertising and Promotional Activities on Young People

Introduction

A substantial and growing body of scientific literature has reported on
young people's awareness of, and attitudes about, cigarette advertising and
promotional activities. Research has also focused on the effects of these activities on psychosocial risk factors for beginning to smoke. Considered together, these studies offer a compelling argument for the mediated relationship of cigarette advertising and adolescent smoking. To date, however, no
longitudinal study of the direct relationship of cigarette advertising to smoking initiation has been reported in the literature. This lack of definitive literature does not imply that a causal relationship does not exist; rather, better
quantification of exposure, effect, and etiology is needed. Important data
from research conducted for the tobacco industry are not available; such information would add considerably to our knowledge. A definitive study, such
as a randomized control trial with young people exposed and not exposed to
cigarette advertising, is both practically and ethically impossible. What is possible and needed is research that is longitudinal and multivariate, that takes
advantage of recent statistical modeling methods, and that uses large samples
of children and young adolescents who have not tried smoking and who have
had relatively little exposure to cigarette advertising.

The issue of causality is addressed . . . by examining the effect of cigarette
advertising and promotional activities on the known psychosocial risk factors
for the initiation of smoking. If advertising and promotional activities consistently affect these factors—factors such as self-image, the functional mean-

ings of smoking, normative expectations, and intentions to smoke—then these activities may also affect smoking onset. This mechanism is especially plausible in the United States, where cigarette advertising and promotional activities are pervasive.

During an unusual historical period, July 1, 1967, through December 31, 1970, antismoking messages were widely aired on television and radio as part of the FTC's Fairness Doctrine. These messages were aired until a complete ban on prosmoking advertising on radio and television took effect on January 1, 1971. For those three and one-half years, the American public was exposed to both prosmoking and antismoking messages on radio and television. A carefully designed study of nearly 7,000 adolescents found that having both sets of messages on radio and television had the effect of reducing adolescent smoking rates; the impact was strongest during the first year of the antismoking messages. These study findings suggest that a nationwide, well-funded antismoking campaign could effectively counter the effects of cigarette advertising in its currently permitted media forms.

Young People's Exposure to Cigarette Advertising

Several research studies show that young people are aware of, and respond to, cigarette advertising. In a recent Gallup study, 87 percent of the 1,125 adolescents surveyed nationwide could recall recently seeing one or more tobacco company advertisements. Similarly, Pierce et al. found in their study of nearly 7,000 California adolescents that over 90 percent of the 12- and 13-year-olds could name a brand they had seen advertised. Half of the adolescents in the Gallup survey could identify the cigarette brand name associated with at least one of four cigarette slogans.

Chapman and Fitzgerald tried to determine the level of awareness of cigarette advertisements among 11- through 14-year-olds in Australia and the possibility of a relationship between awareness of advertisements and smoking behavior. Data were collected on smoking prevalence and preferred brands. Participants were asked to identify the cigarette brands advertised in photographs of eight print-media cigarette advertisements that had been edited to remove any identifying writing. The children were also asked to complete edited advertising slogans. Children who reported smoking in the last four weeks were almost two times more likely to correctly identify the advertisements and complete the slogans than were children who reported that they had not smoked during that period. Smokers' preferred brands generally corresponded with the advertisements and slogans most often correctly recognized. Of the 130 brands of cigarettes available on the market at the time of the study (1981), just four brands accounted for cigarettes smoked by nearly 80 percent of these adolescent smokers.

In the United Kingdom, Aitken, Leathar, and O'Hagan followed a procedure similar to that used by Chapman and Fitzgerald. They showed cigarette advertisements, interspersed among advertisements for other products, to groups of male and female schoolchildren (aged 6 through 16 years) from Glasgow's inner-city areas (most of whose residents were of lower socioeconomic status) and suburban areas (most of whose residents were of higher socioeconomic status). Chapman and Fitzgerald's findings that large proportions of children were aware of cigarette advertisements were supported in this study and were extended to include younger children. Among some of the 12-year-olds and most of the 14- and 16-year-olds in the Glasgow study, the advertising images elicited comments that indicated the young people's perceiving implicit, supposedly adult themes, such as independence, sex appeal, and success.

In a separate study, Aitken et al. showed nine color photographs of different cigarette advertisements. . . . When the young people were asked if they had seen any of the advertisements before, 83 percent of the 6- and 7-year-olds and 91 percent of the 16- and 17-year-olds recalled seeing the same ad. When asked to match the various ads to brief verbal descriptions of the ads, the study subjects in the three oldest age groups . . . succeeded at a level greater than chance.

Together, the results from these studies show that even relatively young children are aware of cigarette advertising and are able to recall particular advertisements. Older adolescents are moreover capable of interpreting the advertisements in imagistic terms related to attractive features of adult life.

Opinions on Cigarette Advertising and Smoking Behaviors

O'Connell et al. surveyed more than 6,000 students aged 10 through 12 who were drawn from a sample of 88 primary schools in New South Wales, Australia. Logistic regression was used to determine the relative importance of various personal and social environmental factors in relation to the proportion of children who reported smoking one or more times per week. The factors included friends' smoking, approval of tobacco advertising, siblings' smoking, the amount of money available to spend weekly, gender, age, and parents' smoking. As part of the same study, Alexander et al. identified factors associated with change in smoking status (both beginning and ceasing to smoke) over the 12 months between the baseline and follow-up surveys. Of the children who reported not smoking during the month preceding the baseline survey, significantly more of those who at baseline approved of cigarette advertising reported smoking during the month preceding the follow-up survey than did those who disapproved of cigarette advertising. Similar results were found for the children who reported smoking during the month preceding the baseline survey. The study thus found a positive relationship between approving of advertising and subsequently taking up smoking, and between disapproving of advertising and quitting smoking.

Armstrong et al. conducted a large randomized trial among seventh-grade students (13 years old) in Western Australia in which peer-led and teacher-led programs concerning social influences were evaluated. When the students were resurveyed one year and two years after the intervention, the results identified factors associated with beginning to smoke. Both boys and girls who at baseline reported that cigarette advertisements made them think they would like to smoke a cigarette were significantly more likely to have adopted smoking at the one-year and two-year follow-up surveys than those who did not report feeling this way.

Aitken and Eadie examined whether the awareness and appreciation of cigarette advertisements were independent of other predictors of adolescent smoking. In this study, 868 Glasgow adolescents between the ages of 11 and 14 years were selected at random and interviewed privately in their homes. Older adolescents, boys, and current smokers in the sample tended to approve of cigarette advertisements and were also more likely to correctly identify cigarette advertisements that carried no brand identification. In general, smokers were more successful than nonsmokers at identifying cigarette advertisements, were more likely to have siblings who smoked, tended to be more approving of cigarette advertisements, and were less likely to perceive that their parents strongly opposed smoking. These findings suggest that advertising may reinforce the habit of smoking, even among new, young smokers.

Young People's Responses to Different Types of Cigarette Advertisements

Huang et al. reported on the preferences of seventh- and eighth-grade children (average age 14) concerning three categories of cigarette advertisement: ads with cartoons, those picturing human models, and those with only the cigarette package and words (tombstone ads). The study was a cross-sectional survey conducted in April 1991 among 243 students in two junior high schools in Chicago. Seventy percent of the students were black, 22 percent white, 3 percent Hispanic, 2 percent Native American, 1 percent Asian, and 2 percent from other races. Analyses were limited to responses of the black and white subjects. The subjects first were asked to use five-point scales to rate how much they would like to embody the following 19 characteristics: athletic, good-looking, kind, slim, macho, smart, sexy, average, fun, special, independent, cool, afraid, overweight, underweight, tough, important, mature, and immature. They were then shown slides of 13 current cigarette ads representing nine brands taken from nine magazines obtained at a local supermarket newsstand. The students were asked to indicate how much they liked each ad and how likely they would be to buy the brand of cigarettes advertised. For each ad with either cartoon or human models, students were asked to rate the models on the same 19 characteristics used to describe their ideal self-image.

Students preferred advertisements with cartoons; ads with human models were the next most popular, and tombstone ads were liked least. Specifically, both black and white students ranked the two advertisements featuring Camel cigarettes' cartoon camel mascot Old Joe first and second; this preference was more marked among white students. Advertisements with black models were more appealing to black students than to whites, and ads featuring the Marlboro cowboy (who is white) were more appealing to white students than to blacks. Among students who smoked, the buying preferences for all brands closely paralleled the reported ad appeal.

A factor analysis based on the 19 rated attributes identified five groupings of the advertisements. Female models were seen as predominantly "slim" and "good-looking." Joe Camel was "cool" and "fun," as were the two black models in a Salem ad. The Marlboro man was perceived as "tough" and "macho." On the other hand, a Montclair model was ascribed no positive attributes, but was predominantly rated as "not sexy" and "not good-looking." All of the positive attributes reported for the cigarette ad images also were described as positive attributes for the students' ideal self-images.

Uutela et al. compared how children in Los Angeles and Helsinki perceived advertisements for cigarettes, beer, liquor, and cars. Although Finland does not permit advertising for either tobacco or liquor, the authors noted that Camel boot ads were allowed in the country, as were ads for the Philip Morris Company depicting the Marlboro cowboy. A total of 592 Los Angeles students and 660 Helsinki students between the ages of 8 and 17 years were asked the open-ended question, "What kinds of pictures come to your mind when you think of how a cigarette/beer/liquor/car ad might look?" Their responses were coded into 11 categories.

In Los Angeles, the dominant ad images reported for cigarettes, beer, and liquor all were images of "happy/fun/partying," whereas the ad images for cars were more likely to be in the "outdoors/sports" category. In Helsinki, however, the dominant ad images reported for cigarettes and for beer were "tough/macho"; for liquor, "rich/status/success"; and for cars, "glamorous/sexy/attractive." The authors concluded that young people in Helsinki perceived cigarette advertising as portraying themes that represent the "traditional man's role," whereas the perceived themes in Los Angeles were less gender specific. Finland is one of the few western countries where smoking continues to be significantly higher among boys than among girls.

Humor in Advertising

Nelson and While provided evidence for the role of humor in advertisements that appealed to youth in a study of 7,047 students aged 11 through 16 years old from 10 schools in the north, south, and midlands of England. Students first were asked two open-ended questions: "What is your favorite advertisement?" and "Why do you like it?" Ninety-one percent of the students reported a favorite ad; 53 percent of these students reported that humor was their main reason for liking their favorite advertisements. Boys (especially those 13 through 16 years old) were significantly more likely than girls to choose an ad because of its humor. Girls (especially those 15 and 16 years old) were more likely than boys to say they liked the personality appearing in their favorite ad. Children who chose ads for alcohol and tobacco products as their favorites were more likely than other respondents to cite humor as their reason for preferring these ads. Several research studies have demonstrated that adults, as well as children, prefer advertisements with humor. Nonetheless, cartoons with talking animals are generally considered to appeal more to children than to adults; Joe Camel and Willy Penguin (the cartoon mascot for Kool) would be highly atypical examples of advertising humor if the ads that feature them were meant only for an adult audience.

Responses to Advertisements for the Camel and Marlboro Brands

A few recent studies have compared the responses of children and adults to Camel cigarettes' Old Joe campaign. The subjects in the DiFranza et al. study were 1,055 high school students in grades 9 through 12 from five regions of the United States and 345 subjects 21 years of age and older from Massachusetts. The adult subjects were recruited from drivers renewing their licenses at the department of motor vehicles office. Seven different advertisements from Camel's Old Joe campaign were used as stimuli. In the first ad, clues to the product and brand were masked, and subjects were asked whether they had ever seen the ad and what product and brand were being advertised. They were then shown six other Joe ads, one at a time, and asked to rate the appeal of these ads.

The high school students were more likely than adults to recognize and correctly identify Old Joe (98 vs. 73 percent), to think the ads looked "cool" (58 vs. 40 percent), to think the ads were interesting (74 vs. 55 percent), to think that Old Joe is cool (43 vs. 26 percent), and to report that they would like to have Old Joe as a friend (35 vs. 14 percent). Data on brand preference collected from the high school students who smoked were compared with corresponding data from seven surveys completed before the kick-off of the Old Joe campaign early in 1988. The authors reported that in the three-year duration of the Old Joe campaign, the proportion of smokers under 18 years old who preferred Camel cigarettes over other brands rose from 0.5 percent to 33 percent.

Pierce et al. analyzed data from the California Tobacco Survey, a 1990 random-digit-dialed telephone survey of 24,296 adults aged 18 and over and 5,040 adolescents aged 12 through 17. Respondents were asked to "think back to the cigarette advertisements . . . recently seen on billboards or in magazines. What brand of cigarette was advertised the most?" Thirty-four percent of the adults named Marlboro as the most-advertised brand; 14 percent of the adults named Camel cigarettes. Among the adolescents, 42 percent identified Marlboro and 30 percent identified Camel as the most advertised brand. No more than 3 percent of either the adult or teenage respondents named any other single brand.

The percentage of respondents who named Marlboro increased with age among the adolescents, peaking at 48 percent among 16- and 17-year-olds before declining among adults. The percentage of respondents who named Camel was inversely related to age, ranging from 23 percent for 16- and 17-year-olds, to 20 percent for 18- through 24-year-olds, to 10 percent for respondents aged 45 years and older. Similar results were found by Pierce et al. and by a Gallup survey, although Camel advertisements were identified as the most pervasive ads according to McCan's analysis of the 1992 California Tobacco Survey. It is not surprising, given these results, that Marlboro and Camel cigarettes are used by up to 70 percent of adolescent smokers.

A study conducted by Fischer et al. suggested that even very young children were aware of the Joe Camel campaign. In this study, three- through six-year-old children were asked to match each of 22 brand logos on cards to one of 12 products pictured on a game board. Ten of the logos were from children's products, seven from adult products, and five from cigarette brands. The recognition rate for Old Joe ranged from 30 percent for three-year-olds to 91 percent for six-year-olds. By the age of six, the face of Old Joe and the silhouette of Mickey Mouse (the logo for the Disney Channel on cable television) were equally well recognized.

Young People's Self-Image and Implications for Tobacco Use

Intention to smoke is one of the strongest predictors of trying cigarettes and of becoming a smoker. Chassin et al. found that 9th- and 10th-grade students whose reported image of smokers correlated with their reported self-image, ideal-date image, and certain attributes of ideal self-image were likely to report that they intended to smoke. The attributes of ideal self-image that correlated with attributes of smokers' image were "tough," "foolish," "act big," "disobedient," and "interested in the opposite sex." A positive relationship of self-image and ideal-date image with smokers' image was also found to differentiate students who were already smokers from nonsmokers. Bowen et al. found that even among preadolescent, fifth-grade boys, reported images of smokers were more likely to match advertising images of smokers among those who had tried a cigarette than among those who had never tried cigarettes.

Barton et al. asked 6th- and 10th-grade students to evaluate slides of peer models posed with and without cigarettes. Children in both age groups rated smoking models as being less healthy, more foolish, tougher, poorer at schoolwork, more sociable, more ostentatious, and more disobedient than nonsmoking models. Grube et al. subsequently reported that both smokers and youth who intended to smoke were more likely than nonsmokers to have self-images like the images they attributed to smokers. McCarthy and Gritz found that among 6th-, 9th-, and 12th-grade boys and among 12th-grade girls, a correlation of ideal self-image to advertising images of smokers was associated with intentions to smoke.

Students in 11 seventh-grade classes in a working-class area of Pasadena participated in a study that investigated attributes of four categories of images: self, ideal self, smoker, and cigarette ad. A random sample of 122 students was asked to use a six-point scale to rate four attributes (healthy, wise, tough, and interested in the opposite sex) in responding to four questions: (1) "What sort of person are you?"; (2) "What sort of person would you like to be?"; (3) "What sort of person is a smoker?"; and (4) "In billboards, magazines and other advertisements, smokers are made out to be what?" Intention to smoke was assessed by the question, "Do you think you will ever smoke cigarettes in the future?" to which there were six possible responses.

Subjects who had small differences between their self-image and their image of smokers, and those who had large differences between their self-image and their ideal self-image, were found to have greater intentions to smoke.

These findings can bear closer scrutiny. Smokers' images received relatively low scores from all students, but to a lesser extent among students who had greater intentions to smoke. Since these students had also assigned themselves lower self-images than their peers, they were that much closer to the image scores they assigned to smokers. Also worth elaborating is the observed relationship between greater intention to smoke and greater disparity between self-image and ideal self-image: students intending to smoke assigned themselves lower scores for both images than did their peers. The authors conclude that youth with relatively low self-concepts who do not perceive themselves as being particularly healthy, wise, tough, or interested in the opposite sex may be drawn to smoking as a way of enhancing their low self-image, especially since smoking has been consistently associated with these attributes in advertising.

In a study conducted in 1991, 239 black and white seventh- and eighth-grade students in Chicago were asked to rate on a five-point scale their self-image and their ideal self-image according to 13 attributes. Some attributes (such as "special" and "important") were prominent in both scales; other attributes that were highly rated in one image scale were much lower in the other. The attributes that revealed the largest discrepancies between ideal self-image and self-image were "good-looking," "sexy," "tough," and "athletic." The same students were also asked to indicate on a three-point scale how much they would want to buy a given product. When responses to the two sets of questions were compared, having "sexy" as an ideal self-image attribute was associated with expressing an intention to purchase Camel cigarettes, and having "tough" as an ideal self-image attribute was associated with expressing an intention to purchase Marlboro cigarettes.

... The image attributions of adolescents described in this set of studies suggests a mechanism of smoking initiation. The visual images in advertisements may thus serve to shape the ideal self-image of this impressionable audience, since the ads may portray attributes that children and adolescents would like to have. The greater the discrepancy between their self-images and their ideal self-images, the more likely these young people are to try to make their self-images more like their ideal self-images (e.g., by "buying into" an improved self-image through responding with the purchase invited by the ads).

In commercial advertising theory, this notion informs imagery-advertising conceptualization, which presumes that the need for consistency or balance will motivate an individual to try to close the gap between self-image and ideal self-image. This conceptualization entails an active striving to make the self-image more like the ideal self-image, and not the other way around. Imagery-advertising conceptualization is most compatible with identification theories (e.g., role theories, reference-group theories, and self-presentation theories) that stress the need to expand identity by adopting distinctive thoughts, feelings, or actions. Thus, the teenaged girl who responds to a Virginia Slims advertisement that portrays independence is motivated to buy and use the product in order to enhance her sense of independence.

Young People's Misperceptions of Smoking Prevalence
and Implications for Tobacco Use

... [The] pervasiveness of cigarette ads leads youth to overestimate the prevalence of smoking and to consider smoking as normative. Studies have consistently reported that adolescents overestimate the prevalence of cigarette smoking; moreover, those who smoke overestimate smoking prevalence to a greater extent than do nonsmokers. Overestimating smoking prevalence has been found to be among the strongest predictors of smoking initiation and acquisition.

Burton et al. examined the relationships among cigarette advertising, estimates of smoking prevalence, and intentions to smoke. Children in Helsinki, Finland, where there has been a total tobacco advertising ban since 1978, were compared with children in Los Angeles, where tobacco is advertised in various print media and through promotional activities. Because the Finnish children may have been exposed to tobacco advertising through foreign magazines or through traveling to other countries, the study is characterized as comparing pervasive vs. occasional exposure to advertising. Classroom samples of 477 Helsinki students and 453 Los Angeles students—aged 8 through 14 years in both samples—whose lifetime cigarette use consisted of no more than a puff of a cigarette were asked how many of their peers and how many adults smoked. Respondents were also asked whether they had ever seen a cigarette ad and when an ad was last seen.

Los Angeles youth were more likely than Helsinki youth to overestimate the prevalence of peer smoking (a 417 percent overestimate vs. a 150 percent one) and of adult smoking (319 percent vs. 173 percent). Both between countries and within the Los Angeles respondents, reported cigarette advertising exposure was positively related to the amount of overestimation of both adult and peer smoking prevalence. Overestimates of smoking prevalence were found to be positively related to intentions to smoke. Interestingly, self-reported exposure to cigarette advertising and intentions to smoke had a direct relationship beyond that mediated by misperceptions of smoking prevalence.

In a recently published study of seventh- and eighth-graders, Botvin et al. found that exposure to cigarette advertising in periodicals and newspapers was predictive of current smoking status. Adolescents with high exposure to cigarette advertising were significantly more likely to be current, past-day, past-week, or past-month smokers than were those with low exposure to cigarette advertising. Significant associations were also found between exposure to cigarette advertising and students' estimates of smoking prevalence among their peers and among adults.

Studies have been equivocal concerning the relative importance of overestimates of peer smoking compared with overestimates of adult smoking. The general interpretation is that normative influences are operative in both cases; that is, smoking is more or less misperceived to be a usual and appropriate behavior. It also has been suggested that overestimates of adult smoking serve to increase the symbolism of smoking as a desired, adult behavior;

smoking therefore acquires greater meaning to an adolescent in transition to adulthood.

Discussion

Even though the tobacco industry asserts that the sole purpose of advertising and promotional activities is to maintain and potentially increase market shares of adult consumers, it appears that some young people are recruited to smoking by brand advertising. Two sources of epidemiologic data support this assertion. Adolescents consistently smoke the most advertised brands of cigarettes, both in the United States and elsewhere. Moreover, following the introduction of advertisements that appeal to young people, the prevalence of use of those brands—or even the prevalence of smoking altogether—increases. This association was seen among adolescent females after the 1968 introduction of the Virginia Slims brand; smoking prevalence among adolescent females nearly doubled between 1968 (8 percent) and 1974 (15 percent). A similar associated increase was seen for smokeless tobacco use among adolescent males after a major advertising and promotional campaign in the 1970s focused on "beginners." More recently, Camel's Old Joe advertising campaign appears to have substantially increased the brand's market share among persons less than 18 years old.

Advertising and promotional activities also appear to influence risk factors for adolescent tobacco use, even if this is not the intention of the tobacco industry. These psychosocial risk factors—having a low self-image, attributing positive meanings or benefits to smoking, and perceiving smoking as prevalent and normative—strongly predict smoking intentions and smoking onset.

In several countries, concern about the health consequences of smoking and the potential influence of advertising on consumption has prompted a nationwide ban on tobacco advertising. In 1975, Norway banned all tobacco advertising, sponsorship, and indirect tobacco advertising. In 1977, Finland banned all forms of tobacco advertising. Canada introduced a ban in 1989 on all tobacco advertising, sponsorship, and indirect advertising of Canadian origin. New Zealand introduced a ban in December 1990 on advertising in print media originating in New Zealand, on advertising in posters, and on sponsorship of sports. Although the bans in Canada and New Zealand have been relatively recent, the current evidence indicates that these actions have had a significant effect on consumption in each of the four countries. In each case, the banning of advertising was followed by a decrease in smoking rates that persisted even when controlled by changes in other factors, such as price. These studies focused on total cigarette consumption; although the bans appear to have influenced smoking rates among young people in Canada and Norway, more specific data concerning young people are forthcoming.

Conclusions

1. Young people continue to be a strategically important market for the tobacco industry.
2. Young people are currently exposed to cigarette messages through print

media (including outdoor billboards) and through promotional activities, such as sponsorship of sporting events and public entertainment, point-of-sale displays, and distribution of specialty items.

3. Cigarette advertising uses images rather than information to portray the attractiveness and function of smoking. Human models and cartoon characters in cigarette advertising convey independence, healthfulness, adventure-seeking, and youthful activities—themes correlated with psychosocial factors that appeal to young people.

4. Cigarette advertisements capitalize on the disparity between an ideal and actual self-image and imply that smoking may close the gap.

5. Cigarette advertising appears to affect young people's perceptions of the pervasiveness, image, and function of smoking. Since misperceptions in these areas constitute psychosocial risk factors for the initiation of smoking, cigarette advertising appears to increase young people's risk of smoking.

YELTSIN ADDRESS TO THE
NEW RUSSIAN PARLIAMENT
February 24, 1994

*In a speech to the new Russian parliament broadcast live to the nation
from the Kremlin February 24, President Boris N. Yeltsin reported that all
was not going well with the political and economic reforms he had pursued
for the past two years. He appealed to his political opponents to join him in
"new political style" to move Russia forward. The forty-minute speech appeared to reflect realities of an election the previous December when Russian
voters, in a backlash against the government's movement toward capitalism, had elected a parliament dominated by communists, ultranationalists,
and others who promised to slow the reform process.*

*The new parliament, formally known as the Federal Assembly, replaced
the old Congress of People's Deputies under terms of a new constitution that
Yeltsin himself advocated. In September 1993 Yeltsin dissolved the Congress, claiming it was an unacceptable barrier to reform. Many of its members and their allies defied his decree, setting off a violence-filled crisis lasting into October, when they surrendered to army troops loyal to Yeltsin. In
November, Yeltsin proposed a new constitution for Russian voters to accept
or reject on December 12, the same day they elected the new parliament. The
government's announcement of the constitution's approval by a bare majority was questioned by Yeltsin's political foes.* (Yeltsin on Crises in Russia,
Historic Documents of 1993, p. 769)

*Any hope that the new lawmakers would be less difficult for Yeltsin to
work with evaporated even before he addressed them. The previous day, over
Yeltsin's strong objections, the lower house of the parliament approved amnesty for the jailed leaders of the October crisis and for hard-line communists who tried to overthrow Mikhail S. Gorbachev in August 1991. Yeltsin's
heroics in thwarting the 1991 coup propelled him to the presidency that December when Gorbachev, unable to hold the Soviet Union together, was
forced to resign. Yeltsin quickly began to privatize state property, permit
Russians to engage in commerce, lift state price controls, and allow the ru-*

ble's value to be determined by international markets. (Failure of Soviet Coup Attempt; End of the Soviet Union and Gorbachev's Rule, Historic Documents of 1991, p. 515 and p. 785)

Yeltsin Eases Push for Reforms

In his speech, Yeltsin acknowledged that much had gone wrong with the economy, although he defended past decisions to remove state control so a free market could develop. He blamed crime, corruption, bureaucratic rigidity, and political obstruction for crippling the economic changes. Repeatedly, he appealed to the legislature to work with him in "constructive cooperation" under the new constitution.

In contrast to some of his earlier speeches, the president never lauded the democratic movement in Russia. "Yes, there is more freedom . . . but this is not enough," he said. "Our task is to make sure that Russia has more justice, more security, more confidence in the present day and in the future."

That Yeltsin spoke more softly for reform came as no surprise. Yegor Gaidar, a leading architect of a free-market economy, resigned his government post a week before the president's speech. Viktor S. Chernomyrdin, a conservative Soviet-era industrialist, became the prime minister in a new cabinet Yeltsin announced on January 20. Chernomyrdin promptly remarked: "The period of market romanticism is now over." Boris Fyodorov, a remaining pro-market spokesman, refused to continue as finance minister.

U.S. Government Reaction

All this appeared to embarrass President Bill Clinton, who on a visit to Russia in January said Yeltsin assured him that economic reforms had not been sidetracked. Of equal concern to American leaders were remarks Yeltsin made on foreign affairs, reflecting Russia's more conservative and nationalistic mood. Yeltsin struck a new note in his speech by asserting that his country must be the "guarantor of stability" throughout the former Soviet Union. In addition, he said the fate of ethnic Russians living in neighboring countries was "our national affair." Finally, he warned Eastern European countries not to join the North Atlantic Treaty Organization unless Russia also joined. "Russia has the right to act firmly and toughly when necessary to defend its national interests," he said.

Secretary of State Warren Christopher, testifying before the House Foreign Affairs Committee the day after Yeltsin spoke, said he found some "good signs" in the speech and sought to justify continued aid to Russia, which some Senate Republicans had begun to attack. Christopher said Yeltsin "came down in continuation of reform," but said the recent election had prompted the slowing of reform efforts.

Six weeks later, Secretary of Defense William J. Perry said the instability in Russia could lead to renewal of the Cold War. He made the remarks in a speech at George Washington University in Washington, D.C., two days before leaving for a visit to several former Soviet republics. Despite the instability, however, Perry argued for providing aid to the republics to dismantle their nuclear weapons and for continuing U.S. military cooperation with Russia.

> *Following are excerpts from President Boris N. Yeltsin's address to the Russian Federal Assembly on February 24, 1994, from an English translation provided by the Russian Embassy in Washington, D.C.:*

Distinguished Chairman of the Federation Council and State Duma!
Distinguished members of the Federation Council!
Distinguished deputies to the State Duma!

I have a special feeling ascending to this rostrum. Today's statement is a truly extraordinary event in my life and political career. It is for the first time that the new Russian parliament receives a presidential address. Russia begins to develop a new approach to policy planning.

. . . [M]y address contains an outline of the current situation and some ideas for the future you suggested during the election campaign and afterwards.

Unfortunately, many efforts were wasted in 1993 on sharp political confrontations. Extraordinary measures had to be taken, but we managed to prevent a civil war.

People were eventually convinced that there can be no winners in an irreconcilable struggle, which may only result in the devastation of Russia. Russia has already exhausted its feud limit.

The reform efforts have brought us both to success and sometimes to bitter disappointment. If you ask me today whether I was prepared to start these difficult transformations all over again, I would say a firm yes. I have always been convinced that we didn't have another option. In January 1992 we had to start doing what we couldn't ignore any longer.

We are drawing lessons from every month of our life. It is impossible to transform a country like Russia overnight. To do so, we need a flexible, long-term and preventive policy that would take into account both Russian national specificities, changing social interests and sentiments and the mindset of Russians that was evolving in a different direction for many years.

For the past months we have better understood that constructive cooperation is crucial for our success. This is a tremendous reserve we never used before. This is a top priority for all of us, those working in the parliament and elsewhere and responsible for the future of Russia.

We have to admit realistically that part of the opposition is seeking forceful revenge. Some people on both sides are blinded by the lust to take revenge on their ideological foes. Hatred and revenge may only aggravate the painful ailment of Russia, in fact.

I also want to say this. Social reconciliation shouldn't mean the forgiveness of all sins. It shall never run counter to law and morality.

There is a basis for social concord in Russia today, and it is a Constitution adopted by a popular vote. Is there any other equally solid foundation for it?

There is none.

No party, movement, group of intellectuals, individual politician or states-person has a support as large as enjoyed by the Constitution.

People of various convictions and orientations voted for the Constitution. Though generally disillusioned, people still came to the polls to cast their votes and give the state and state authorities a binding law.

Russia is currently living through a most difficult period in its history. How-ever, Russia existed before Peter the Great or the October 1917 revolution. Russia doesn't end with the disintegration of a communist superpower.

The empire that recently threatened mankind and suppressed Russians and other peoples exists no more. However, the Russian state has still failed to take its own place in the world community.

The state that used to be a stern jailer and merciless judge of its subjects is no more. However, Russia has failed to develop a fully fledged democratic and law-abiding state system so far, we have to admit.

Most people are permanently anxious over their future, the future of their children and retired parents. In the meanwhile, federal and local authorities prefer to give a blind eye to the rapid social stratification. We have to respon-sibly admit that we underestimate all threats that stratification harbours.

I am not appealing to come back to former notorious egalitarian practices, when all people were supposed to be equally poor and better-off people ripped off. However, this delicate and painful issue shall not be left until it solves by itself.

We are bitterly learning that the state-ruled self-consuming economy, in which ten people are busy with the work that can be reasonably done by one person, has no future.

We don't have a normal market economy so far. On the other hand, swin-dlers and rippers are feeling nice and easy. Honest and industrious people, who don't fear to be self-employed have enormous difficulties in getting on.

My heart is breaking to say this, but it is true. We have greater freedom in this country, yes. But this is not enough. Our strategic goal is to develop jus-tice, security and confidence in Russia.

We have been convinced that Russia cannot be recovered by fiat from any boss or political party or personality.

The time has come for a new political style based on confidence, construc-tive cooperation, mutual understanding and concerted efforts.

The time has come for a national effort that would pool all resources. That effort should be targeted at a stronger state identity of Russia.

We have to admit it finally, that a weak state system makes elementary order in the country unfeasible.

All citizens and nations of Russia are interested in a stable and strong insti-tutional system. No matter where people of different national identities are living, they need civil peace and don't want ethnic feuds. . . .

All political parties and movements, as well as all factions of the State Duma, should be interested in a stronger institutional framework, as they can expect the interests of their proponents to be realised only in a healthy and strong state system.

Our closest neighbours should also be interested to see a firm and strong Russian state, as it will reliably guarantee stability in the entire former Soviet Union.

The world community also needs a strong Russia, or it will become a permanent source of threat to its security.

A strong and active state is a major prerequisite for further transformations in this country. Otherwise, we won't have a healthy and civilised market and genuine democracy; the great Russian culture and morality will never get fully recovered.

A stronger state system is an obvious goal to attain, and this should unite all Russians in the current dramatic period.

A stronger state is our common goal that would enable the President, Federal Assembly, Government and members of the Federation to concentrate their efforts for the benefit of Russia.

We tackled that goal several times lately, but our efforts were sporadic, inconsistent and devoid of a legal pivot.

In its current shape, the state fails to perform its major functions, which includes in the first place the ensurance of public order, human rights and safety. The country is flooded by crime. Institutional structures are permeated by irresponsibility and arbitrariness.

Human life in our country is more and more ensnared by countless petty orders and limitations. The work of federal and local state authorities has been marked by muddle and great confusion. The army of bureaucrats has rapidly expanded.

At a time of extreme pressure on financial resources, the federal authorities expended with aplomb colossal amounts on their own living conditions.

Growing appetites are dealing greater blows to the state than any mistakes and miscalculations. Not to mention the damage to the taxpayer's pocket, whose money is being used to support each one of us.

All these factors bear witness to the new increasing alienation of power from the people and their daily needs. However, whereas in the past they were separated by bureaucracy and the nomenclature caste, today money has been added on. This shameful money now serves as the tool for solving many problems.

I am talking here about serious diseases affecting the young Russian state. And today it is the joint task of the President, Parliament and Government to stop their destructive activity. We do not need to think up some solution. We already have a single efficient cure—state consolidation on the basis of the Constitution. It will only yield results, if we are prepared to work together.

We need a general programme of state reforms in the Russian Federation. Here are its goals:

One. The state authorities should not work for themselves, but rather for Russia's interests and those of its citizens, which have been precisely revealed and formulated. This implies a transition from impulse responses to a strategy based on well-thought-out anticipatory steps.

Two. Power must be efficient. This implies a striving and ability to finish off what has been started and assess in the strictest possible manner the potential costs of decisions, which are to be taken. . . .

Three. We must bring an end to the bureaucracy's boundless nature, when any sensible decisions and initiatives are strangled by the deathly embrace of the bureaucracy. This goal can be achieved by well-known methods—a precise regulation of functions and responsibilities. Unfortunately, we lack this at present.

Four. Power must become open and understandable to the people. That means that we must develop a dialogue, contribute to the formation of a civic society. Power should not be screened off from the mass media, but rather aid and abet the latter and bring about the denationalization of the press.

However, this must be done in fair measure. The television channel, which preserves via the Orbita system the integrity of the Russian information space and encompasses ex-Soviet republics and European countries, should be state-owned.

A strong state is required above all to curb crime. This is the most important problem of the year. Here our collaboration is particularly essential. Citizens await from the Federal Assembly laws, which the state can rely on to ensure their safety and peace.

I believe that it would be correct here to combine two trends. On the one hand, continue drafting new criminal legislation. The existing criminal code is hopelessly outdated. The law enforcement agencies find it harder and harder to work within its limits to counteract crime. On the other hand, laws must be drafted, aiming to resolve urgent tasks and provide the law enforcement agencies with the requisite normative documents.

The swiftest drafting and adopting by Parliament of a law on urgent measures to suppress crime should constitute a first step in this direction. Russians will accept with understanding such a decision. A law enforcement system is ready to implement it. . . .

As well as long-term and wide-ranging measures, we must in the near future implement measures, capable of curbing street crime.

One specific topic concerns organised crime. Today it is trying to grab the country by the throat. Russia can only be defended by decisive and consistent actions. They were proposed a long time ago by specialists.

The legislative consolidation of corresponding measures will enable the law enforcement agencies to exploit the potential they have accumulated over the past few years to concentrate all strikes against organized crime and corruption.

For all Russian citizens the words "strengthening of the state" have yet another, deep meaning: The preservation of the country. We hold Russia too dear to even think about the possibility of its disintegration. Unity cannot be ensured by force or lies. It cannot be preserved by putting people against each other.

Russia can be really strengthened only via federalism. Its clear-cut contours have been drawn in the Constitution. However, this does not yet mean that we have already created the federation.

The delineation of powers and property between the federal authority and federation subjects proceeds extremely slowly. We must settle this question this year. . . .

The task of the year is to redress the injustice with the distribution of privileges between regions. We badly need common criteria for according privileges in federal taxes and credits. And the more clear these criteria, the fewer there will be abuses.

Ethnic conflicts, both in the country and close to its borders, present a real threat to stability in the Russian Federation. Any such conflict is a result of past injustices and mutual offences. But every day and hour of ethnic strife only multiply these injustices and offences. And the longer such conflict, the more difficult it is to find ways of settling it and healing now deep wounds.

Russia wants to settle ethnic conflict more than anyone else. It will not be content as long as it remains a frontline state.

Life proves that only Russia is prepared to shoulder the heavy burden of restoring peace in this part of the world. This makes its role even more important and responsible.

Time flies, and fifty years have already passed since one of the most barbarous crimes of Stalin's regime: persecution of whole nations. Deportations are shameful pages in the history of our country.

On behalf of the Russian Federation, as the legal successor of the Soviet Union, and as head of state I want to beg the forgiveness of all citizens of Russia and their families, who suffered from deportations.

It is our civic duty to eliminate all consequences of those horrible events. This difficult and delicate work must unite, not split, us. It must bring people together, not sow the seeds of new strife.

It is our duty to make 1994 a year of close attention to the people of Russian origin who live in neighbouring states. We have in our possession numerous acts, which indicate that our compatriots are discriminated against.

It is the duty of Russia to put an end of these practices in deed, not in word. If the legal rights of Russians are violated, this is not only their internal affair but also our state, national problem. I ask, no, I demand that all branches of the Russian state authority should consistently adhere to this principle.

A few words about our compatriots who are returning to Russia from the newly-emerged neighbouring states. They have not yet become Russia's children; they are its stepsons still. The flow of migrants and refugees does not ebb, which means that we must not tolerate the fact that their problems are not tackled in earnest and nobody is responsible for this.

This is an enormous problem. The social programme has been drafted and will be moved by the Government for the approval of the Federal Assembly. But it can be implemented only if we join our efforts and resources.

Dear members of the Federation Council,
Deputies of the State Duma,
We have seen from our own experience that without a strong, effective

state we will not overcome the economic crisis, create a true market economy, make the economic situation predictable or create conditions for economic growth.

I know that the people in Russia and abroad became worried over the economic policy of Russia after the December elections and reshuffles in the Government.

I want to dispel these worries. As long as I remain the President of Russia, I will protect and advocate the policy of economic reforms. In 1994 the continuation of the economic reforms will be a priority of Russia's internal policy.

In the past few years we have developed several major elements of market relations, such as economic freedom, the right of ownership, and working markets of goods and services. But it is too early yet to say that the Russian economy lives by market laws. What we have is a combination of new, still weak market mechanisms and old command bureaucratic levers.

The administrative distribution system has not disappeared without a trace; it changed. The bureaucrat who once drafted plans and distributed funds, has learned the doings of the market and distributes (and sometimes sells) central quotas and licenses. Lobby trends are developing, and the reform of the economic mechanism is proceeding very unstably.

We know the result: the crisis does not abate, the production slump slowly continues, and viable enterprises stop production. Inflation is wearing out the country. Social tensions remain very high.

The greatest mistake we can make today is offer society a false alternative: either the past state-directive economy, or the so-called pure market, absolutely independent of the state. Both alternatives would be fatal for Russia and its economy.

The task is to find a reasonable combination of the speed of reforms and their real social costs, use the powerful, but so far idling, reserves of the reforms, and find optimum ways of state participation in economic processes.

The past two years showed that not only the reforms entail social outlays. We suffer even great damage from the delays in long-overdue changes in the economic mechanism.

It is time to establish effective state regulation compatible with market mechanisms. This is a priority task of the current stage of the reforms.

The state should be the master of the state economic sector. Otherwise we will not overcome chaos and stop the squandering of the state sector by some economic managers.

We must continue to liberalise exports, and at the same time strengthen control over the export of strategic raw materials and energy carriers. . . .

The year 1994 must see the beginning of a restructuring of the Russian economy. Russia must produce only those goods which are needed by the public, state, and the world market. We must stop to produce goods not needed by anyone.

This is a very hard and expensive task to handle. It cannot be solved in a short time or by bans. However, this does not mean that we should again avoid doing this. Has the government not yet become convinced that without a restructuring policy we will have structural degradation?

Structural degradation is already here. We are gradually losing modern technological infrastructure and major sectors, high-tech products, in particular. We are beginning to lag behind not only of the best world achievements but also of ourselves.

The principle of "let survive those who can survive" is disastrous. In today's Russia the survivals are not those who make the best, quality goods. Or, at least, not only they alone. The survivals are people with the maximum of benefits and privileges, those who are patronised by authorities and who know how to squeeze money from the government.

If this trend goes on, Russia may become a market economy but this will be a primitive and inefficient economy. . . .

A painless economic reform does not exist. Its social costs are formidable. We must focus on poverty, the glaring inequality and unemployment. It is they that cause the greatest fears.

The President, the Federal Assembly and the Government must constantly remember the troubles of the workers of enterprises grinding to a halt who may tomorrow become unemployed; the poverty of many scientists and workers in higher education; the problems which make life unbearable for many young couples; the difficulties facing a significant part of the peasants.

Millions of people in our country live below the poverty line. It is inadmissible to accept for execution state programmes which would cause a further decline in the main standard-of-living indices, and there are such. . . .

One of the reserves for strengthening Russia, for continued transformation is Russian foreign policy. It is not only Russia that has changed beyond recognition over the recent period. The entire world has become different, more complex and unpredictable. The main task of our foreign policy now is the consistent advancement of Russian national interests.

The priority instrument of its fulfillment is openness and cooperation. But Russia has the right, if the protection of the lawful interests of the state calls for this, to act firmly and toughly when this is truly needed. . . .

We have clear-cut priorities in international policy. The most important among them is the prevention of a new global war, hot or cold. This is why we are explicitly for the strengthening of the regime of nonproliferation of mass destruction weapons and the latest military technologies. But we share this principle as binding on all, and not just on Russia, as some people imagine.

In 1994 we must end the erroneous practice of unilateral concessions. This concerns, in particular, the defence budget too. One should not forget that spending on defence is not quite the same thing as spending on war.

This money goes to finance a considerable part of our science. This money goes to build flats for homeless officers' families. This money goes for the upkeep of our children who serve in the Armed Forces.

We are for putting the international arms trade in order. And a major precondition for that will be the observance of the commercial interests of Russia. In the last few years they have suffered considerably.

We stand for a realistic approach to problems of European security. We favour partnership for peace open to all states of greater Europe without exception. But, respecting the sovereign rights of states and organizations, Russia is against NATO's expansion by admitting certain countries of the European continent without Russia. That's the road to new threats to Europe and peace. Russia is not a visitor in Europe; it is an equal member of the European community interested in its well-being. It is from this premise that we shall proceed. . . .

Russia favours the strengthening of the Commonwealth [of Independent States] above all along the lines of establishing an economic alliance, a common market of the Commonwealth, a collective security system and greater guarantees of human rights.

But there is a factor that should always be considered. Integration must not be detrimental to Russia itself, must not be effected through the over-exertion of our strength and resources, both material and financial. This will lead to only new disappointments and estrange our states, not bring them closer together. . . .

Russia is capable of starting out on a qualitatively new stage of its development. The period of total destructive processes of the former system is nearing its end. We are laying economic, legal and social foundations of a new Russian society. After receiving your proposals in response to the Address, I shall submit to you a concrete plan of my actions for its realization.

I know that among you are people who doubt whether or not we shall be able to cope with these tasks in conditions of the spiritual and ideological discord that is reigning in society and in our hearts now.

We will have to give a reply to that question all together. And certainly not by engaging in wearisome and fruitless debates, but in real cooperation. Only if we act jointly shall we be able to overcome mutual suspicion and regain trust in each other.

Only if we act jointly shall we be able, forever, to divert the threat of confrontation from Russia and go over to lasting civic accord.

Only if we act jointly shall we be able to break through the black veil of uncertainty, restore spiritual balance and find ourselves in the new conditions.

The citizens of Russia expect us to cooperate. And I am certain that they will support us. They will support us because they want to work normally and earn money. They will support us because they want to be safe in the streets and in their own homes. They will support us because they want peace and prosperity for Russia.

I hope that in a year's time we shall all together be able to look into our electors' eyes and say: "We had a hard time, but we have done our best and even more in that past year. We certainly have not wasted that time."

For my own part, I shall do all I can for it.

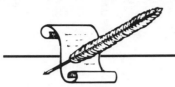

March

GAO TESTIMONY ON AMTRAK
March 23, 1994

The financial condition of Amtrak, the nation's passenger railroad, had rapidly deteriorated, a General Accounting Office official said March 23 in testimony before the House Subcommittee on Transportation and Hazardous Materials. Kenneth M. Mead, director of transportation at the GAO, said steps needed to be taken to improve Amtrak's financial picture if the railroad was to survive.

"Amtrak and the federal and state governments must decide whether Amtrak is to continue its present course, expand into areas such as high-speed rail service outside the Northeast Corridor, or limit its operations to those routes where losses can be minimized," Mead said. He said continued federal subsidies would be necessary because "only a few well-traveled routes may ever generate sufficient revenues to cover operating costs."

Congress created Amtrak in 1970 to revitalize the nation's passenger rail system. Previously, individual railroads had provided both passenger and freight service. The railroads had been losing huge amounts of money providing passenger service, so they were only too happy to turn this service over to Amtrak.

Since its creation, Amtrak—like all other modes of transportation—had required huge federal subsidies because its revenues from ticket sales were insufficient to cover its costs. In fiscal year 1994, Amtrak received more than $900 million in federal subsidies, or about $35 per passenger. The Amtrak subsidy was less than half the $2 billion in subsidies provided annually to general aviation, a figure that worked out to $65 per passenger. In fiscal year 1992, the federal government provided a total of about $3.7 billion in subsidies to mass transit, and state and local governments kicked in another $10 billion, Mead said.

For years, various federal officials had advocated eliminating all subsidies for Amtrak. However, Congress always provided enough money to keep the railroad running, although the amount was never sufficient to allow modernization of equipment, which ultimately would reduce the railroad's huge maintenance costs. Amtrak officials contended that the railroad would never become self-sufficient if it could not replace its aging passenger cars and locomotives with new equipment that cost less to maintain.

Financial Problems Worsen

Amtrak's financial condition had deteriorated since 1990, Mead said, because the railroad's operating expenses had been higher than expected while its revenues had been lower than expected. The federal subsidy had not bridged the gap. Mead said Amtrak officials blamed the recession for decreased revenues, but he added that increased competition from airlines and a decaying, unattractive Amtrak fleet also contributed to the railroad's woes.

In testimony before a separate congressional panel in March, Amtrak's new president said he agreed with the GAO's findings. "We are now, as America's railroad, promising a service we can't deliver," said Thomas M. Downs. "My fear is that this is the precise formula that thirty years ago led to the rapid decline and near demise of rail passenger service in the country."

Amtrak was not helped by publicity following four major accidents that occurred in 1993 and 1994, even though none of the wrecks were Amtrak's fault. The worst occurred in September 1993 when the Sunset Limited plunged off a bridge into a bayou near Mobile, Alabama, killing forty-seven people. Investigators determined that moments before the wreck, a barge had hit the bridge and pushed it slightly askew, causing the derailment.

Amtrak Board Slashes Service

In December, Amtrak's board of directors approved dramatic cutbacks in the railroad that eliminated some routes while reducing service on virtually all that remained. The Midwest was hardest hit by the cuts, with seven cities in Michigan and Missouri losing all passenger train service. The plan also eliminated 5,500 of the railroad's 25,000 jobs. Amtrak officials projected that the cuts, the first major service reductions since 1981, would save $295 million annually. The reductions were designed to close a $200 million deficit railroad officials projected for the fiscal year that began October 1, 1994.

In a press release announcing the cuts, Amtrak said its problems could be attributed to "the costs of an undercapitalized system being spread too thin, trying to provide more service than the corporation is capable of providing, and to brutal price competition from the airlines." At a press conference, Downs said he hoped the cuts would be enough to save the railroad. "There is no guarantee about our future," he said. "If this isn't enough, I haven't got any other answers."

The cuts, while severe, were likely not the last for Amtrak. Amtrak's board planned to meet in March 1995 to consider further service reductions. Railroad officials said they expected that by late 1995, trains on virtually all long-distance Amtrak routes would run less than once daily.

Following are excerpts from testimony on the financial condi-
tion of the Amtrak railroad system, given March 23, 1994, by
Kenneth M. Mead, director of transportation issues for the
General Accounting Office, before the House Subcommittee on
Transportation and Hazardous Materials:

We appreciate the opportunity to testify at Amtrak's reauthorization hearing. As you know, Amtrak was created in 1970 and charged with revitalizing
intercity rail passenger service. The inherited rail equipment was in a state of
disrepair, and most travelers had abandoned rail for air and auto travel. Today, Amtrak is at a crossroads, and we believe that important decisions need
to be made that will affect Amtrak in both the short and the long-run. The
House Committee on Energy and Commerce and four other Committees
asked us to comprehensively review Amtrak's operations. As agreed with the
Subcommittee, my statement today presents our preliminary findings on Amtrak's financial condition and the near-term challenges facing the corporation.
We will issue our final report later this year. Our overall points follow:

- Amtrak's financial condition has always been poor and has, in fact, deteriorated over the past three years. This should not come as a surprise,
  given the size of the task Amtrak has faced, the limited resources available, and the difficult economic and competitive environment in which it
  operates. Recognizing Amtrak's need for federal support, the Congress
  has provided both capital and operating assistance. In tight budget times,
  however, this support has not been adequate to provide high-quality, nationwide service. Moreover, Amtrak has been under pressure since the
  early 1980s to reduce its dependence on federal operating support. Since
  that time, Amtrak's revenues have covered a greater portion of its operating expenses. By 1993, Amtrak reported that its revenues covered about
  80 percent of its operations. This performance measure, however, can be
  misleading because it does not include all operating expenses. Moreover,
  this performance measure has masked a deteriorating financial condition
  and serious capital needs.
- Several indicators show that Amtrak's financial condition has deteriorated in recent years. Since 1990, Amtrak's federal subsidy has not covered the gap between operating expenses and revenues. During this period, total operating deficits have exceeded federal operating subsidies
  by $102 million in current year dollars ($110 million in 1994 dollars).
  This occurred because Amtrak's revenues have been less than projected
  while its expenses have been higher than expected. Furthermore, over
  the past 7 years, Amtrak has steadily reduced its working capital by $217
  million in current year dollars. In 1994 dollars, this amounts to a $252
  million reduction. If this deterioration continues, Amtrak may not be able
  to pay all its expenses and will not be able to provide quality nationwide
  service.

- Amtrak has dealt with the shortfall in passenger revenues by increasing other revenues and cutting back planned expenses. On the revenue side, for example, Amtrak has increased its commuter rail business and transport of U.S. mail. On the expense side, since 1991 Amtrak has lowered planned expenses by $120 million (in current year dollars) by reducing staff, maintenance, and service on some routes. These self-help initiatives, however, will not solve Amtrak's financial problems because they involve relatively few dollars. In fact, certain actions, such as reducing maintenance, will aggravate an already serious problem.
- Over the next few years, Amtrak will face difficult and costly challenges that must be met if it is to operate a viable nationwide network. These challenges include the need to (1) maintain its aging passenger cars; (2) modernize the Beech Grove, Indiana, repair facility, which services all equipment used outside the Northeast Corridor; (3) modernize its locomotive and passenger car fleet, acquire high-speed trains, and continue rail improvements in the Northeast Corridor; (4) negotiate, by 1996, new operating agreements with the freight railroads, which own about 97 percent of the track over which Amtrak operates; and (5) negotiate labor issues and work rules with Amtrak's union employees.

The President's proposed fiscal year 1995 budget for Amtrak of $987.6 million, which represents a nine percent increase over 1994, should help Amtrak address its growing operating deficit. However, it will not resolve the costly challenges facing Amtrak in both the near- and longer-term. For Amtrak to continue nationwide operations at the present level, enhance service quality and reliability, and improve its overall financial condition, requires substantial operating and capital funding. In European countries where competitive conditions are more conducive to rail travel, intercity passenger service has required substantial public funding. In the United States, only a few well-traveled routes may ever generate sufficient revenues to cover operating costs. Amtrak and the federal and state governments must decide whether Amtrak is to continue its present course, expand into areas such as high-speed rail service outside the Northeast Corridor, or limit its operations to those routes where losses can be minimized. Under any scenario, federal and state support will need to be commensurate with the assigned task.

Government Support for Passenger Rail

In 1970, the Congress created Amtrak to revitalize intercity passenger rail transportation. Before that time, individual railroads provided both passenger and freight rail service. Both passengers and the rail business suffered under this arrangement. Passengers lacked smooth connections between railroads, and the rail industry was losing money operating unprofitable passenger service. The combined losses of the railroads operating during 1970 totaled more than $1.7 billion in today's dollars. In comparison, Amtrak in 1993 received federal support totaling $891.5 million. In 1971, most railroads willingly gave up their passenger service and provided the personnel, equipment, and infrastructure that became Amtrak. Today, Amtrak operates about 25,000 route miles.

Recognizing the need for national passenger rail service, the Congress has provided significant funding for Amtrak since 1971. Amtrak receives federal funds through an operating and capital grant, the Northeast Corridor Improvement Project (NECIP) grant, and a mandatory payment by the Federal Railroad Administration (FRA) to the Railroad Retirement trust fund and for the Railroad Unemployment Repayment Tax. In fiscal year 1994, Amtrak will receive over $900 million in federal subsidies.

Operating and capital subsidies enable Amtrak to fund its operating deficits and make capital purchases and improvements. The NECIP grant is for improvements—such as bridge replacements, signal upgrades, station and yard repairs, and track electrification—to the railway between Washington, D.C., and Boston. Finally, the Federal Railroad Administration makes mandatory payments on Amtrak's behalf to the Railroad Retirement Trust Account. These payments are for amounts that Amtrak is required by law to contribute for benefits to retirees and for railroad unemployment insurance.

Federal operating and capital subsidies to Amtrak amount to about $35 per passenger or about $0.12 per passenger mile. In comparison, in the aviation area, the Essential Air Services Program provided $38.6 million in fiscal year 1993 for a subsidy of $50 per passenger and $0.40 per passenger mile. General aviation users also receive a larger federal subsidy than Amtrak riders—about $2.0 billion annually or about $65 per trip. Intercity bus service also receives federal assistance, but it amounts to less than $0.10 per passenger. Mass transit in fiscal year 1992 received about $3.7 billion from the federal government and about $10.0 billion from state and local governments. Together these subsidies amounted to $1.61 per trip or about $0.34 per passenger mile.

Amtrak's Financial Condition Has Deteriorated

Amtrak's financial condition has deteriorated in recent years. Since 1990, Amtrak's federal subsidy has not covered the gap between operating expenses and revenues because actual revenues have been lower than projected while expenses have been higher than projected. At the same time, the federal government has faced a very difficult budget environment.

Operating revenues have been lower than projected since 1991 because ridership and yield have not been as high as expected. This situation has been the result of, among other things: (1) the poor economy and recent recession; (2) increased price and service competition by airlines; and (3) old, unattractive, and poorly maintained facilities and equipment. In total, Amtrak overestimated its passenger revenues by $440 million for 1991 through 1993 in current year dollars ($468 million in 1994 dollars). For the first 4 months of fiscal year 1994, passenger revenues are 6 percent below the actual revenues for the same period last year and total revenues are 3 percent below the projections for fiscal year 1994.

According to Amtrak officials, the corporation's optimistic revenue projections resulted from underestimating the length and severity of the recent recession. Also, Amtrak was under increasing pressure to have a greater portion of its revenues cover operating expenses. As a result, Amtrak requested substantially less funding from the Congress than it needed to cover these expenses. This funding shortfall, in turn, has contributed to Amtrak's current financial condition. At the same time, the former Administration proposed much less funding for Amtrak. In addition, Amtrak has incurred additional expenses, including start-up costs for new services, such as extending the Sunset Limited route, and for wage increases.

Although Amtrak undertook activities to bring its expenses in line with projected revenues, its total operating deficits have exceeded federal operating subsidies by $102 million since 1990 in current year dollars ($110 million in 1994 dollars). In fiscal year 1993, Amtrak requested $58 million and received $45 million in additional grants. To cover the gap between its operating deficit and federal operating subsidies, Amtrak has drawn down its working capital from $113 million at the end of fiscal year 1987 to a negative $105 million by the end of fiscal year 1993. In 1994 dollars, this represents a draw down of $252 million.

If Amtrak's financial condition continues to deteriorate, it will be more difficult for Amtrak to cover future deficits and disasters—such as the effects of last year's flood in the Midwest—without additional federal funds. Not only would Amtrak have to cut routes, reduce the frequency of service, and cut amenities, but it would also be unable to restore services that were eliminated to deal with the recent operating deficits. . . .

Recent Activities by Amtrak
Have Helped in the Short Term

Amtrak's efforts to generate additional revenue and reduce operating costs have helped in the short term but will not be the answer to long-term financial problems. From fiscal years 1991 through 1994, Amtrak cut or intends to reduce planned operating expenses by $120 million (in current year dollars) by decreasing staff, marketing activities, and maintenance. In addition, Amtrak improved its cash position by reducing inventories, requiring advance payments from contractors, and stretching out payments on bills.

Amtrak has also increased revenues from commuter services, mail and baggage express, real estate development efforts, and other activities. Revenues from these activities have grown from $378 million in 1990 to $460 million in 1993 in current year dollars and now account for 33 percent of Amtrak's revenues. . . .

Amtrak Faces Increased Challenges
Over the Next Few Years

In the next few years, Amtrak will face difficult and costly challenges that must be met if it is to operate a viable intercity network. These challenges include the need to (1) maintain its passenger cars and locomotives; (2) modernize the Beech Grove, Indiana, overhaul facility, which services all equipment used outside the Northeast Corridor; (3) modernize its locomotive and passenger car fleet, acquire high-speed trains, and continue rail improvements in the Northeast Corridor; (4) renegotiate by 1996 its operating agreements with the freight railroads; and (5) renegotiate labor compensation and work rules with the various unions representing Amtrak's employees.

As Amtrak's Fleet Ages, It Will Be More
Costly to Operate and Maintain

Amtrak inherited much of its fleet of passenger and baggage cars from other railroads when it was formed. These "Heritage" cars are, on average, 34 years old (passenger cars alone are, on average, 40 years old) and comprise about 43 percent of Amtrak's 1,959-car fleet. The cars and their components are not standardized, and Amtrak must often manufacture parts to repair them—a very expensive requirement. Since it began operating its own equipment in 1976, Amtrak has maintained its cars through a program of periodic, preventive maintenance. In 1979, Amtrak established a policy of performing heavy overhauls on its cars every 3 to 4 years. These overhauls (during which a car is stripped bare and is completely rebuilt) can cost about $300,000 for each car. In comparison, a new car costs about $2 million. Except for 20 Superliners that have been delivered since July 1993, all cars require heavy overhauls.

To cope with its deteriorating financial condition, Amtrak cut back on maintenance, and starting in 1989 it began falling behind in overhauling its passenger cars. The overhaul backlog grew to nearly 40 percent of the fleet by the end of fiscal year 1993. At the same time, mandates were imposed on Amtrak to (1) replace refrigeration units in 168 food service cars to ensure food safety; (2) install by October 1996 retention-type toilets on 544 passenger cars, at a cost of $27,500 to $95,000 per car; and (3) fumigate cars more frequently for rodent control. Funds for these projects had to come from the Amtrak capital subsidy or from already stretched operating funds.

Amtrak's Chief Mechanical Officer recognized that the relatively few overhauled passenger cars were in pristine condition while a significant number, which were awaiting overhaul, were looking shabby and breaking down with increasing regularity. To address this situation, Amtrak adopted a new "progressive" maintenance and overhaul program in 1993. Under this program, cars will be inspected and will receive a limited overhaul each year. Basic safety components, such as brakes and wheel sets, will be serviced annually, while other components and furnishings will be replaced only as necessary. Every third year the overhaul will be more comprehensive. Under the new program, however, no cars will be upgraded to the condition resulting from the previous heavy overhaul procedures, but many more are expected to be maintained in better condition than cars now awaiting overhaul. . . .

Future Federal Capital Subsidies Have Already
Been Committed to Purchase New Equipment

Amtrak already commits a sizable portion of its federal capital subsidy to pay for previous purchases, mandated equipment modifications, and capital overhauls. As a result, Amtrak may have much less funding available for new purchases and capital improvements than the Congress may realize. From fiscal year 1991 to 1993, Amtrak made commitments to purchase 245 Superliner and Viewliner cars and 72 new locomotives. This equipment will give Amtrak added revenue-generating capacity and will be much easier to repair and overhaul than the so-called "Heritage" equipment that Amtrak inherited from its predecessors. Unlike the Heritage cars, for which replacement parts have to be specially manufactured, the new cars have standardized parts and modular components to allow for easier replacement. As these cars begin to replace Heritage cars—as Amtrak intends, although it has made no firm decisions yet about retiring the Heritage fleet—the need for manufacturing parts to supply the Heritage overhauls should diminish. Amtrak would then have more resources available to overhaul more cars. Amtrak has agreed to pay $924 million for both the cars and locomotives. Between 1994 and 2017, projected interest expense will amount to at least another $765 million. . . .

Contracts with Freight Railroads and Labor Unions Expire Over the Next 2 Years

Amtrak depends heavily on freight railroads in operating its passenger trains. Freight railroads own about 97 percent of the track over which Amtrak operates, and they provide essential services, such as dispatching trains, making emergency repairs to Amtrak trains, and maintaining stations. Some freight railroads also provide police and communications services and pay injury claims for Amtrak. When Amtrak was formed, it entered into 25-year agreements with freight railroads to compensate them for the incremental cost of providing Amtrak with these services. Under these agreements, Amtrak has paid freight railroads an average of about $80 million annually for the last five years. These agreements expire on April 30, 1996.

Freight railroad officials told us that compensation and liability are two key issues that will be negotiated when Amtrak's operating agreements with freight railroads expire. Freight railroads do not believe that they are adequately compensated for their services and may ask to change the methodology used to calculate costs. They may also seek higher payments from Amtrak for using their facilities and equipment—payments that more closely reflect commercial rates and consider the opportunity cost of property being used by Amtrak. For example, Amtrak pays as little as $1 per year to lease some stations owned by one freight railroad. Freight railroads are also concerned about their liability in settling high-cost claims from passenger train accidents occurring on their tracks and may seek to reduce their risk exposure and/or increase the amount of risk assumed by Amtrak.

In addition, Amtrak will be negotiating new agreements with 14 labor unions between 1994 and 1996. About 90 percent of Amtrak's approximately 25,520 employees are union members. Since labor costs represent a large portion—about 54 percent—of Amtrak's operating costs, these negotiations could lead to substantial changes in future operating costs. . . .

TESTIMONY ON THE ADDICTIVE NATURE OF TOBACCO
March 25 and April 14, 1994

In extraordinary hearings on Capitol Hill, one of the nation's top health officials charged that tobacco companies intentionally controlled nicotine levels in cigarettes to make them addictive, a claim that tobacco executives vehemently denied.

The issue was far from academic. If the Food and Drug Administration (FDA) could prove that tobacco companies adjusted nicotine levels in cigarettes, it might have the legal authority to regulate them. Before 1994, the FDA had never tried to regulate tobacco. "Some of today's cigarettes may, in fact, qualify as high technology nicotine delivery systems," said FDA Commissioner David A. Kessler in testimony March 25 before the House Subcommittee on Health and the Environment.

Kessler rejected contentions by the tobacco industry that smoking was a matter of personal choice. He said "accumulating evidence" suggested that cigarette manufacturers "may be controlling smokers' choice by controlling the levels of nicotine in their products in a manner that creates and sustains an addiction in the vast majority of smokers." As evidence, Kessler cited internal tobacco company memos and patent applications for technologies that adjusted nicotine levels in cigarettes. Kessler asked Congress for guidance about how his agency should proceed.

Less than a month later, the chief executives of the seven largest tobacco companies testified in a historic hearing before the same panel. They admitted that tobacco companies can control nicotine levels in cigarettes by adjusting tobacco blending, but said they did so only to improve cigarettes' flavor. They denied adjusting nicotine levels to make cigarettes addictive.

Smoking Ban Proposed

On the same day that Kessler testified before Congress, the Occupational Safety and Health Administration (OSHA) proposed a rule that would ban all smoking in the workplace. "OSHA has taken this action to prevent thousands of heart disease deaths, hundreds of lung cancer deaths, and the respiratory diseases and other ailments linked to these hazards," said Labor Secretary Robert B. Reich in announcing the proposed rule. Labor Department officials said it would affect more than six million workplaces, ranging from restaurants to factories.

The proposed OSHA regulation targeted secondhand smoke, which the U.S. Environmental Protection Agency blamed for 3,000 deaths annually in a 1993 report. In previous years, the U.S. Surgeon General, the National Research Council of the National Academy of Sciences, the World Health Organization, and the National Institute of Occupational Safety and Health all concluded that secondhand smoke causes lung cancer and other respiratory problems in nonsmokers. (EPA Report on the Effects of Secondhand Smoke, Historic Documents of 1993, p. 63)

The hearings and proposals to regulate tobacco were far from the only threats to the tobacco industry in 1994:

- *In January, Sears, Roebuck and Co. banned smoking at its nearly 800 stores and the Arby's fast-food chain did the same at its 257 corporate-owned restaurants.*
- *In February, the National Council of Chain Restaurants announced its support for a bill before Congress that would ban smoking in all public places. Previously, business groups had usually opposed smoking restrictions.*
- *Also in February, McDonald's banned smoking in its 1,400 corporate-owned restaurants.*
- *In March, Pentagon officials announced a ban on smoking in military workplaces around the world. The ban, which antismoking activists hailed as the most comprehensive ever adopted by a government agency or commercial firm, affected 2.6 million military and civilian personnel.*
- *Also in March, the editor of a major scientific journal said that in 1983 Philip Morris—a major tobacco company—had blocked publication of a paper by one of its own scientists showing that nicotine was addictive. In testimony at a congressional hearing, a top official at the National Institute on Drug Addiction said that withdrawal of the paper "set the field back six years at least before work like it could be accomplished by Canadian researchers."*
- *In April, the U.S. Environmental Protection Agency released a report that estimated that the benefits of imposing a smoking ban in all public places would outweigh the costs by at least $39 billion annually.*
- *Also in April, two former top researchers at Philip Morris during the early 1980s testified before a congressional panel that the company had abruptly fired them when their research indicated that nicotine was addictive. One of the researchers said his studies convinced him that the addictive nature of nicotine was "on a level comparable to cocaine." The*

researcher said Philip Morris officials had threatened him with legal action if he ever discussed his work.

- *In June, Kessler returned to Capitol Hill to charge that Brown & Williamson Tobacco Corporation, the nation's third-largest tobacco company, had secretly created a genetically engineered tobacco plant that contained double the usual amount of nicotine. Kessler said the company initially denied it had developed the plant, but later admitted it had at least three million pounds of the tobacco in U.S. warehouses after FDA officials unearthed U.S. Customs Service documents showing the tobacco had been imported from Brazil. Brown & Williamson said it stopped using the tobacco in cigarettes after the FDA expressed concern.*

- *In July, the federal Centers for Disease Control and Prevention reported that illnesses caused by smoking resulted in health care costs of at least $50 billion in 1993. That figure represented 7 percent of all health care costs in the United States.*

- *In August, the American Medical Association and the Robert Wood Johnson Foundation started a $10 million antismoking campaign in nineteen states. The campaign was aimed at persuading other states to adopt California's program of using money from tobacco taxes to pay for antismoking education.*

- *Also in August, the Minnesota attorney general joined with Blue Cross and Blue Shield of Minnesota in a suit accusing tobacco companies of conspiring to withhold information about the health hazards of smoking.*

- *In September, the National Academy of Sciences released a report that said that government regulation of tobacco and a $2-per-pack tax on cigarettes would be needed to help stop young people from taking up smoking.*

In some cases, tobacco companies struck back. For example, after several ABC News programs reported that tobacco companies added nicotine to cigarettes to hook smokers, in March Philip Morris sued the television network for libel. The suit sought $10 billion in damages.

In November, however, the tobacco companies' fortunes suddenly changed when Republicans won control of Congress. The Republican takeover meant that the Democrats no longer controlled the chairmanships of the congressional committees. Democrat Henry Waxman of California, who as chairman of the House Subcommittee on Health and the Environment had used his panel to attack the tobacco companies, was ousted. The incoming chairman of the House Commerce Committee, the parent of the subcommmitee that Waxman previously chaired, was Rep. Thomas J. Bliley, Jr. One of the tobacco industry's biggest friends in Congress, Bliley was a Virginia Republican whose district counted Philip Morris USA as its largest private employer. With Bliley as chairman, it seemed likely there would be no more hearings on tobacco and that Congress might try to block any efforts by the FDA to regulate tobacco.

Following are excerpts from testimony by David A. Kessler, commissioner of the Food and Drug Administration, before the House Subcommittee on Health and the Environment on March 25, 1994, as released by the FDA, and from testimony by William Campbell, president and chief executive of Philip Morris USA, before the same panel on April 14, 1994, as provided by Reuters:

KESSLER TESTIMONY

Mr. Chairman, the cigarette industry has attempted to frame the debate on smoking as the right of each American to choose. The question we must ask is whether smokers really have that choice.

Consider these facts:

- Two-thirds of adults who smoke say they wish they could quit.
- Seventeen million try to quit each year, but fewer than one out of ten succeed. For every smoker who quits, nine try and fail.
- Three out of four adult smokers say that they are addicted. By some estimates, as many as 74 to 90 percent are addicted.
- Eight out of ten smokers say they wish they had never started smoking.

Accumulating evidence suggests that cigarette manufacturers may intend this result—that they may be controlling smokers' choice by controlling the levels of nicotine in their products in a manner that creates and sustains an addiction in the vast majority of smokers.

That is the issue I am here to address: Whether it is a choice by cigarette companies to maintain addictive levels of nicotine in their cigarettes, rather than a choice by consumers to continue smoking, that in the end is driving the demand for cigarettes in this country.

Although FDA has long recognized that the nicotine in tobacco produces drug-like effects, we never stepped in to regulate most tobacco products as drugs. One of the obstacles has been a legal one. A product is subject to regulation as a drug based primarily on its intended use. Generally, there must be an intent that the product be used either in relation to a disease or to affect the structure or function of the body. With certain exceptions, we have not had sufficient evidence of such intent with regard to nicotine in tobacco products. Most people assume that the nicotine in cigarettes is present solely because it is a natural and unavoidable component of tobacco.

Mr. Chairman, we now have cause to reconsider this historical view. The question now before us all is whether nicotine-containing cigarettes should be regulated as drugs. We seek guidance from the Congress on the public health and social issues that arise once the question is posed. This question arises today because of an accumulation of information in recent months and years. In my testimony today, I will describe some of that information.

The first body of information concerns the highly addictive nature of nicotine. The second body of information I will be talking about—in some detail—concerns the apparent ability of cigarette companies to control nicotine levels in cigarettes. We have information strongly suggesting that the amount of nicotine in a cigarette is there by design. Cigarette companies must answer the question: what is the real intent of this design?

I. Nicotine Is a Highly Addictive Substance

Let me turn then to my first point about the addictive nature of nicotine.

The nicotine delivered by tobacco products is highly addictive. This was carefully documented in the 1988 Surgeon General's report. You can find nicotine's addictive properties described in numerous scientific papers. As with any addictive substance, some people can break their addiction to nicotine. But I doubt there is a person in this room who hasn't either gone to great pains to quit smoking, or watched a friend or relative struggle to extricate himself or herself from a dependence on cigarettes.

Remarkably, we see the grip of nicotine even among patients for whom the dangers of smoking could not be starker. After surgery for lung cancer, almost half of smokers resume smoking. Among smokers who suffer a heart attack, 38 percent resume smoking while they are still in the hospital. Even when a smoker has his or her larynx removed, 40 percent try smoking again.

When a smoker sleeps, blood levels of nicotine decrease significantly. But the smoker doesn't need to be an expert on the concept of nicotine blood levels to know full well what that means. More than one-third of smokers reach for their first cigarette within 10 minutes of awakening; nearly two-thirds smoke within the first half hour. Experts in the field tell us that smoking the first cigarette of the day within 30 minutes of waking is a meaningful measure of addiction.

I am struck especially by the statistics about our young people. A majority of adult smokers begin smoking as teenagers. Unfortunately, 70 percent of young people ages 12-18 who smoke say that they believe that they are already dependent on cigarettes. About 40 percent of high school seniors who smoke regularly have tried to quit and failed.

It is fair to argue that the decision to start smoking may be a matter of choice. But once they have started smoking regularly, most smokers are in effect deprived of the choice to stop smoking. Recall one of the statistics I recited earlier. Seventeen million Americans try to quit smoking each year. But more than 15,000,000 individuals are unable to exercise that choice because they cannot break their addiction to cigarettes. My concern is that the choice that they are making at a young age quickly becomes little or no choice at all and will be very difficult to undo for the rest of their lives.

Mr. Chairman, nicotine is recognized as an addictive substance by such major medical organizations as the Office of the U.S. Surgeon General, the World Health Organization, the American Medical Association, the American Psychiatric Association, the American Psychological Association, the American Society of Addiction Medicine, and the Medical Research Council in the United Kingdom. All of these organizations acknowledge tobacco use as a form of drug dependence or addiction with severe adverse health consequences.

Definitions of an addictive substance may vary slightly, but they all embody some key criteria: first, compulsive use, often despite knowing the substance is harmful; second, a psychoactive effect—that is, a direct chemical effect in the brain; third, what researchers call reinforcing behavior that conditions continued use. In addition, withdrawal symptoms occur with many drugs and occur in many cigarette smokers who try to quit. These are hallmarks of an addictive substance and nicotine meets them all.

When a smoker inhales, once absorbed in the bloodstream, nicotine is carried to the brain in only 7-9 seconds, setting off a biological chain reaction that is critical in establishing and reinforcing addiction.

Over the past few years, scientists have generated a tremendous amount of information on the similarities among different addictive substances. Some crucial information has come from the fact that, in a laboratory setting, animals will self-administer addictive substances. This self-administration may involve the animal pushing a lever or engaging in other actions to get repeated doses of the addictive substance. With very few exceptions, animals will self-administer those drugs that are considered highly addictive in humans, including morphine and cocaine, and will not self-administer those drugs that are not considered addictive.

Understanding that animals will self-administer addictive substances has fundamentally changed the way that scientists view addiction in humans. It has turned attention away from the concept of an "addictive personality" to a realization that addictive drugs share common chemical effects in the brain.

A number of top tobacco industry officials have stated that they do not believe that tobacco is addictive. They may tell you that smokers smoke for "pleasure," not to satisfy a nicotine craving. Experts tell us that their patients report that only a small minority of the cigarettes they smoke in a day are highly pleasurable. Experts believe that the remainder are smoked to primarily sustain nicotine blood levels and to avoid withdrawal symptoms.

The industry couches nicotine's effects in euphemisms such as "satisfaction" or "impact" or "strength." But these terms only sidestep the fact that the companies are marketing a powerfully addictive agent. Despite the buzzwords used by industry, what smokers are addicted to is not "rich aroma" or "pleasure" or "satisfaction." What they are addicted to is nicotine, pure and simple, because of its psychoactive effects and its drug dependence qualities.

To smokers who know that they are addicted, to those who have buried a loved one who was addicted, it is simply no longer credible to deny the highly addictive nature of nicotine.

II. Controlling the Level of Nicotine in Cigarettes

My second point today involves a growing body of information about the control of nicotine levels exercised by the tobacco industry. Mr. Chairman, I do not have all the facts or all the answers today. The picture is still incomplete. But from a number of pieces of information, from a number of sources, a picture of tobacco company practices is beginning to emerge.

The public thinks of cigarettes as simply blended tobacco rolled in paper. But they are much more than that. Some of today's cigarettes may, in fact, qualify as high technology nicotine delivery systems that deliver nicotine in precisely calculated quantities—quantities that are more than sufficient to create and to sustain addiction in the vast majority of individuals who smoke regularly.

But you don't have to take it from me. Consider how people in the tobacco industry itself view cigarettes.

Just take a moment to look at the excerpts from an internal memorandum written by a supervisor of research that circulated in the Philip Morris Company in 1972:

> Think of the cigarette pack as a storage container for a day's supply of nicotine. . . . Think of the cigarette as a dispenser for a dose unit of nicotine. . . . Think of a puff of smoke as the vehicle for nicotine. . . . Smoke is beyond question the most optimized vehicle of nicotine and the cigarette the most optimized dispenser of smoke.

"Dispensers of smoke . . . which is a vehicle for delivering nicotine." This quote is a revealing self-portrait.

Or listen to the words in one tobacco company patent:

> Medical research has established that nicotine is the active ingredient in tobacco. Small doses of nicotine provide the user with certain pleasurable effects resulting in the desire for additional doses.
>
> —patent no. 4,676,259 C1:21-24

The Design of Cigarettes

How does this industry design cigarettes?

The history of the tobacco industry is a story of how a product that may at one time have been a simple agricultural commodity appears to have become a nicotine delivery system.

Numerous patents illustrate how the industry has been working to sustain the psychoactive effects of nicotine in cigarettes. . . : eight patents to increase nicotine content by adding nicotine to the tobacco rod; five patents to increase nicotine content by adding nicotine to filters, wrappers and other parts of the cigarette; three patents that use advanced technology to manipulate the levels of nicotine in tobacco; eight patents on extraction of nicotine from tobacco; and nine patents to develop new chemical variants of nicotine.

Patents not only describe a specific invention. They also speak to the industry's capabilities, to its research, and provide insight into what it may be attempting to achieve with its products.

It is prudent to keep in mind that patents do not necessarily tell us what processes are currently being used in manufacturing cigarettes. Nevertheless, the number and pattern of these patents leaves little doubt that the cigarette industry has developed enormously sophisticated methods for manipulating nicotine levels in cigarettes. Today, a cigarette company can add or subtract nicotine from tobacco. It can set nicotine levels. In many cigarettes today, the amount of nicotine present is a result of choice, not chance.

All of this apparent technology for manipulating nicotine in tobacco products raises the question of how the industry determines how much nicotine should be in various products. More importantly, since the technology apparently exists to reduce nicotine in cigarettes to insignificant levels, why, one is led to ask, does the industry keep nicotine in cigarettes at all?

The tobacco industry would like you to believe that all it is doing is returning the nicotine that is removed during the process of producing reconstituted tobacco. It should be clear from what I have described thus far that the technology the industry may have available goes beyond such modest efforts.

Nicotine levels may be dictated in part by marketing strategies and demographics. A blatant example comes from information on the marketing of smokeless tobacco. There is evidence that smokeless tobacco products with lower amounts of nicotine are marketed as "starter" products for new users, and that advertising is used to encourage users to "graduate" to products with higher levels of nicotine. The evidence was developed in lawsuits brought against one manufacturer of smokeless tobacco.

The tobacco industry may tell you that nicotine is important in cigarettes solely for "flavor." There is a great deal of information that suggests otherwise. Some of the patents specifically distinguish nicotine from flavorants. An RJR book on flavoring tobacco, while listing around a thousand flavorants, fails to list nicotine as a flavoring agent. Even research scientists from the same company acknowledge that the nicotine in cigarettes provides pharmacological and psychological effects to smokers in addition to any mere sensory effects.

Similarities to the Pharmaceutical Industry

Mr. Chairman, this kind of sophistication in setting levels of a physiologically active substance suggests that what we are seeing in the cigarette industry more and more resembles the actions of a pharmaceutical manufacturer. Besides controlling the amount of a physiologically active ingredient, there are a number of other similarities.

One similarity between the cigarette industry and the pharmaceutical industry is the focus on bioavailability. Bioavailability is the rate and extent that pharmacologically active substances get into the bloodstream. For example, the pH of tobacco smoke affects the bioavailability of nicotine. The tobacco industry has conducted research on the pH of smoke and has undertaken to control the pH in tobacco smoke. In patent examples, chemicals have been added to tobacco to affect the pH of tobacco smoke. The industry has even performed bioavailability and pharmacokinetic studies on conventional and novel cigarettes.

The cigarette industry has undertaken research to look at the specific activity of added versus naturally occurring nicotine. Additional research looked at the differences between spiking, spraying and blending compounds into cigarettes.

Development of an "express" cigarette, a shorter, faster burning cigarette with the same amount of tar and nicotine, has been reported in the lay press recently. This is another example of how cigarette companies appear to be controlling the amounts of nicotine to deliver set levels.

The cigarette industry has also undertaken a significant amount of research looking at the potential "beneficial" effects of nicotine. It has studied the effects of nicotine on anxiety, heart rate, electroencephalographs (EEG's), and behavioral performance tasks. Such research on the physiological effects of an active ingredient is a common part of pharmaceutical drug development.

III. FDA Regulation of Nicotine in Cigarettes

The next task facing the FDA is to determine whether nicotine-containing cigarettes are "drugs" within the meaning of the Federal Food, Drug, and Cosmetic Act.

Our inquiry is necessarily shaped by the definition of "drug" in the Act. It is a definition that focuses on "vendor intent." More specifically, it focuses primarily on whether the vendor intends the product to "affect the structure or any function of the body."

Mr. Chairman, the evidence we have presented today suggests that cigarette manufacturers may intend that most smokers buy cigarettes to satisfy their nicotine addiction.

We do not yet have all the evidence necessary to establish cigarette manufacturers' intent. It should be clear, however, that in determining intent what cigarette manufacturers say can be less important than what they do. The fact that the technology may be available to reduce the nicotine to less than addictive levels is relevant in determining manufacturer intent.

It is important to note that the possibility of FDA exerting jurisdiction over cigarettes raises many broader public health and social issues for Congress to contemplate.

There is the possibility that regulation of the nicotine in cigarettes as drugs would result in the removal of nicotine-containing cigarettes from the market, limiting the amount of nicotine in cigarettes to levels that are not addictive, or otherwise restricting access to them, unless the industry could show that nicotine-containing cigarettes are safe and effective. If nicotine were removed, the nation would face a host of issues involving the withdrawal from addiction that would be experienced by millions of Americans who smoke.

There is, of course, the issue of black market cigarettes. With nicotine, as with other powerfully addicting substances, a black market could develop.

In these issues, we seek guidance from Congress.

The one thing that I think is certain is that it is time for all of us—for the FDA, for the Congress, for the American public—to learn more about the way cigarettes are designed today and the results of the tobacco industry's own research on the addictive properties of nicotine.

Thank you.

CAMPBELL TESTIMONY

Thank you, Mr. Chairman, distinguished members of the subcommittee. In recent weeks a number of charges have been leveled against the tobacco industry generally, and Philip Morris specifically. I sincerely hope that you and other members of the subcommittee are today interested in separating the facts from the rhetoric regarding issues raised a few weeks ago in Commissioner Kessler's presentation.

Be that as it may, our consumers are being misled and when that happens Philip Morris has and will continue to speak out loudly and clearly. Our consumers deserve to know the truth and I thank you for creating a forum that allows me the opportunity to set the record straight.

First of all, Philip Morris does not add nicotine to our cigarettes. Philip Morris does not manipulate nor independently control the level of nicotine in our products. There were a number of incorrect statements or assumptions in Commissioner Kessler's presentation. These issues are not new, many require a detailed rebuttal. The claim that cigarette smoking is addictive has been made for many years. The fact that tar and nicotine levels vary among our many products has been publicized for over 20 years. The process by which cigarettes are manufactured, and which at our invitation FDA representatives saw firsthand several weeks ago, has been publicly known for over 50 years. And the call for FDA to assert or be given jurisdiction over cigarettes has been made and rejected by the FDA and the courts on several occasions in the past.

To the extent possible in the time available today, my colleagues and I will try to answer the subcommittee's questions and will be happy to supplement the points we make in a detailed written submission.

Point one: Philip Morris does not add nicotine to our cigarettes. The claim that Philip Morris secretly adds nicotine during the manufacturing process to keep smokers addicted is false. The processes used to manufacture cigarettes have been a matter of public record for years in patent filing and in the public literature. The result of that processing, cigarettes with varying levels of tar and nicotine reflecting a wide variety of consumer preferences, has been closely monitored and reported by the Federal Trade Commission.

The manufacturers have published the deliveries in every advertisement for the past 25 years. The fact is that tar and nicotine levels have decreased dramatically over the past 40 years. Today the market is populated with a number of ultra-low brands which deliver less than five percent of the tar and nicotine levels of popular brands just 20 years ago. Philip Morris and other manufacturers have reduced nicotine deliveries in a number of ways.

The most important is through the use of increasingly efficient filters which substantially reduce main smoke components, including both tar and nicotine. Filtration alone reduces nicotine delivery by 35 to 45 percent, as compared to cigarettes made of simply tobacco and paper. Through a process called ventilation, which allows fresh air to be drawn through the cigarette, nicotine levels are reduced by a further 10 to 15 percent.

Through the use of expanded tobacco, a process developed by which Philip Morris puffed tobacco much like puffed rice cereal, tar and nicotine levels are reduced still further. A fourth manufacturing technique, the reconstituted tobacco process, also reduces the nicotine in cigarettes. This process, which has been thoroughly described in the literature for years, does not increase nicotine levels in tobacco or in cigarettes. Through this process, 20 to 25 percent of the nicotine in the tobacco used to make reconstituted leaf is lost and is not replaced.

These processes, when combined in the cigarettes Philip Morris sells today, reduce nicotine deliveries, for example, by 50 percent in the case of Marlboro and 90 percent in the case of Merit Ultima, again, compared to cigarettes made simply of tobacco and paper. Philip Morris has spent hundreds of millions of dollars to reduce tar and nicotine levels to provide the product that the marketplace demands. Why, if we were supposedly intent on adding nicotine to cigarettes, why would Philip Morris have spent over $300 million to develop a process to de-nicotinize tobacco and launch a near zero nicotine brand? I'll tell you why. Our public opinion research indicated smokers were interested in a no-nicotine cigarette. Our Maxwell House Coffee Company had pioneered processes for decaffination of coffee, and we used that technology as a spring board for de-nicotinization of tobacco.

The process worked, the resulting product did not. We gambled $300 million and lost. That's business. If Philip Morris does not drive constantly to meet consumer demands, we will fail in the American marketplace.

Point two, Philip Morris does not manipulate, nor independently control the level of nicotine in our product. We voluntarily opened our manufacturing operations to the FDA in a good faith effort to resolve the allegation that we add nicotine or control its level in our cigarettes.

As representatives of the FDA learned, nicotine levels in tobacco are measured at only two points in our manufacturing process—prior to the tobaccos being blended and then 18 months later when those leaves have been manufactured into finished cigarettes. Although Philip Morris maintains over 400 quality control checkpoints in the manufacturing process that measure things like moisture, weight, et cetera, none—not one—measure, report or analyze nicotine levels in tobacco.

Mr. Kessler indicated in his testimony that the nicotine-to-tar ratio increased as tar delivery decreased. The reason for the slight increase in the nicotine ratio in lowered tar and nicotine cigarettes is not the result of intentional manipulation, but the result of the difference between filtering tar and filtering nicotine. Simply put, filters are more efficient in removing tar than nicotine. As tar and nicotine levels fall, proportionally more tar is filtered out than nicotine. This does not mean that consumers of low tar cigarettes get more nicotine, quite the contrary.

On an absolute basis, far less nicotine is delivered per cigarette in lower tar and nicotine deliveries. Commissioner Kessler suggested that during the period 1982 to '91, tar delivery levels have remained flat, while nicotine delivery levels have increased. The fact is, after substantial decreases since the 1950s, tar and nicotine deliveries both have remained relatively flat during the past decade.

Fact three, Philip Morris has not used patented processes to increase or maintain nicotine levels. Commissioner Kessler spent a great deal of his testimony attempting to support the proposition that Philip Morris may be using secret, patented processes to increase or maintain nicotine delivery in our cigarettes. We have not; we are not.

Philip Morris, like every other corporation, applies for and obtains patents on virtually every innovation we pioneer. That is critical to ongoing research efforts. Philip Morris currently holds over 600 patents. Only about a quarter describe processes ever used. The processes described in the patent are no more secret than the regulations of the FDA. They are publicly disclosed upon issuance through the U.S. Patent Office. In his testimony, Commissioner Kessler said he had no evidence that Philip Morris or any of the other companies ever actually used any of these patents to increase or maintain nicotine levels.

As he correctly said, patents do not necessarily tell us what processes are currently being used in manufacturing cigarettes. To make myself perfectly clear, Philip Morris has never used any of the patents Commissioner Kessler cited, except those to reduce nicotine levels.

Fact four, cigarette smoking—point four, cigarette smoking is not addictive. During the March 25th hearing, Commissioner Kessler and members of the subcommittee contended that nicotine is an addictive drug, and therefore, smokers are drug addicts. I strenuously object to that premise; I strenuously object to that conclusion.

Cigarettes contain nicotine because it occurs naturally in tobacco. Nicotine contributes to the taste of cigarettes and the pleasures of smoking. The presence of nicotine, however, does not make cigarettes a drug or smoking addiction. Coffee, Mr. Chairman, contains caffeine and few people seem to enjoy coffee that does not. Does that make coffee a drug? Are coffee drinkers drug addicts? I think not. People can and do quit smoking. According to the 1988 Surgeon General's report, there are more than 40 million former smokers in the United States, and 90 percent of those who quit, did so on their own, without any outside help.

Smoking is not intoxicating; no one gets drunk from cigarettes and no one has said that smokers do not function normally. Smoking does not impair judgment. In short, no one is likely to be arrested for driving under the influence of cigarettes. Our consumers smoke for many reasons. Smokers are not drug users or drug addicts, and we do not appreciate or accept being characterized as such, because yes, Mr. Chairman, I am one of the 50 million smokers in this country.

Point five, Philip Morris research does not establish that smoking is addictive. At the March 25th hearing, Commissioner Kessler made the statement, supported by Dr. Henningfield, that in 1983, a company later identified as Philip Morris, suppressed research by one of its own scientists who allegedly concluded that nicotine was an addictive substance; that is false. In fact, that scientist published two full papers and five abstracts related to the working question, including one published in 1982, a year prior to the creation of the manuscript in question.

The manuscript subsequently provided to the committee by Commissioner Kessler, presented some evidence that rats will self-administer nicotine and that nicotine, therefore, is a weak reinforcing agent. The researcher later concluded that nicotine is a reinforcer in the class of non-addictive chemical compounds such as saccharin and water. In addition, and Commissioner Kessler failed to note this, the manuscript itself states, and I quote, "The termination of prolonged access to nicotine under conditions in which it functions as a positive reinforcer, does not result in physiological dependency." The manuscript did not conclude that nicotine is addictive and both Dr. Kessler and Dr. Henningfield know that.

More importantly, the committee should know that by the time the Philip Morris researcher was ready to publish his study in 1983, the positive reinforcing nature of nicotine had already been reported in other published literature. Indeed, the 1988 Surgeon General's report, to which Dr. Henningfield was a contributor, stated that such nicotine reinforcement was shown conclusively as early as 1981 based on government supported research. . . .

Point six, consumers are not misled by the published nicotine deliveries as measured by the FTC method. Contrary to the impression given by Commissioner Kessler that the FTC has somehow adopted a test procedure that can mislead the public as to the true levels of tar and nicotine they are inhaling, the routine analytical smoking methods derived from the FTC methods are nearly identical to those used throughout the world to measure tar and nicotine levels and accurately compare brand deliveries.

All of the tests are conducted on cigarettes obtained from the marketplace. They are therefore the same cigarettes smoked by consumers.

Commissioner Kessler suggested that the FTC figures were misleading because smokers might compensate for lower tar and lower nicotine brands by smoking those cigarettes differently. If Commissioner Kessler is also claiming that low-yield cigarette smokers smoke more cigarettes, he is simply wrong. The data shows smokers of low-yield brands smoke fewer cigarettes than smokers of high-yield brands.

Mr. Chairman, we at Philip Morris appreciate the opportunity to respond to some of the claims made against us. We will be pleased to answer any questions you may have about these matters and to provide a more detailed written submission should that be appropriate. Further, I extend to you and the other members of your subcommittee an invitation to come see our manufacturing process firsthand, as the FDA has already done. We're proud of our company, our products and the people at Philip Morris. Thank you, sir.

April

RESIGNATION OF
JAPANESE PRIME MINISTER
April 8, 1994

In a move that stunned Japan, Prime Minister Morihiro Hosokawa abruptly resigned April 8. Hosokawa's election by the Japanese Diet (parliament) only eight months earlier had ended nearly four decades of rule by the Liberal Democratic Party (LDP) and ushered in a short period of political reform. Hosokawa's resignation set off months of political uncertainty in the world's second-richest country.

President Bill Clinton said he was "very sorry" to see Hosokawa resign. Clinton said the prime minister had provided "amazing leadership" and had made the Japanese people "believe in the possibility of change."

Hosokawa resigned after the LDP renewed old charges of corruption involving financial dealings. Hosokawa was especially vulnerable to such charges because he entered office with a pledge to clean up political corruption. At a press conference where he announced his resignation, Hosokawa said that his "personal matter" had gotten "in the way of a smooth functioning of the Diet," although the issue had been "taken advantage of as a political tactic."

The primary allegation, which dated back to 1982, centered on a loan of 100 million yen, or about $400,000 at the time, which Hosokawa had received from the Sagawa Kyubil parcel delivery company. The company became notorious in the wake of financial scandals involving leading LDP members. Hosokawa was accused of using the loan to finance a political campaign, a charge he denied. He said he had used the money to rebuild one of his family's ancestral homes, and that he had repaid the loan. However, he admitted he had paid no interest.

The LDP also alleged that Hosokawa had evaded taxes in the purchase of shares in the Nippon Telephone and Telegraph Company. "Compared with the corruption that felled some LDP leaders, this was penny-ante stuff," Time *correspondent Bill Powell wrote in the April 18 issue. "But because of Hosokawa's Mr. Clean image, the charges stung."*

Hosokawa's Background

Only fifty-five when he became prime minister, Hosokawa was a telegenic member of Japan's nobility who began his career as a journalist on a daily newspaper. He had been a member of the ruling LDP for years and served in the upper house of the Diet before becoming governor of his home province.

He was elected prime minister on August 6, 1993, by the Diet, supported by a fragile coalition of seven parties, including the Japan New Party, which he had founded.

Events leading to Hosokawa's election had started three weeks earlier, when in general elections the LDP was denied a majority in the powerful lower house of the Diet. In the elections, the LDP—a conservative party despite its name—won only 223 seats in the 511-seat chamber, a sharp drop from its previous total of 275 seats. Kiichi Miyazawa, who was prime minister at the time, resigned four days after the election.

Hosokawa was Japan's most popular prime minster in many years. For most of his tenure, his public approval rating was well above 50 percent. A self-proclaimed reformer, Hosokawa launched a reform program that sought to clean up the corrupt political system, deregulate the nation's economy, and lower trade barriers. He also took steps to reduce the power of the bureaucracy, which resisted change.

American Reaction

Hosokawa's resignation deeply disappointed U.S. officials. "Here is a guy who offered a new Japan," Walter Mondale, the U.S. ambassador to Japan, told reporters. "He appealed to the young; he had a Kennedyesque appeal; he talked about political reform, administrative reform, opening Japan to the world, finally responding to the consumers. There was such hope. . . ."

Despite their inability to agree on trade policy at a meeting in Washington, D.C., a month before the resignation, President Bill Clinton and Hosokawa had forged a cordial relationship. In contrast to leaders of the LDP, a party that resisted change, Hosokawa was seen by U.S. officials as being willing to lower trade barriers and to take steps at home to increase consumer spending.

Successive U.S. administrations had pressed Japan to liberalize regulations governing foreign trade and to accept specified minimum quotas for foreign goods. However, in Washington Clinton and Hosokawa were unable to restart negotiations that had been abandoned only a few hours earlier by Mickey Kantor, the U.S. trade negotiator, and Japanese Foreign Minister Tsutomu Hata.

Ironically, Hata—a close adviser to Hosokawa who also was committed to political reform—was elected prime minister by the same seven-party coalition that earlier had elected Hosokawa. But on the day after he took office, Hata was confronted with a grave challenge. The Social Democratic Party of Japan (SDPJ) withdrew from the fragile coalition, leaving Hata without a majority in the lower house of the parliament.

Deprived of a majority in the Diet, Hata lasted only two months as prime minister. He resigned June 25, only hours before the lower house was to vote on an LDP motion of no confidence. With both the LDP and the SDPJ arrayed against him, Hata would have lost the vote.

The LDP Returns to Power

In a development called "surrealistic" by the New York Times, *the old guard politicians of the LDP returned to power in late June. They were able to patch together a bizarre coalition with their ideological enemies, the far-left SDPJ. The two parties, while disagreeing on nearly every issue, were unified in their opposition to political reform. Press reports said the Japanese people were shocked by the cynicism of the move.*

On June 29, the Diet elected Tomiichi Murayama, the head of the SDPJ, as prime minister. Murayama, 70, had never held a cabinet position. He was Japan's fourth prime minister in a year and the first Socialist to hold the office since 1948. With many observers believing the LDP-SDPJ coalition was inherently unstable, it was unclear how long he would last.

Following is the text of a statement by Japanese Prime Minister Morihiro Hosokawa announcing his resignation on April 8, 1994, as released by Japan's Foreign Press Center:

Only a moment ago, at the meeting of the leaders of the coalition parties, and also at the Extraordinary Session of the Cabinet, I officially expressed my intention to step down from the premiership.

Since I assumed office last August, I have continuously been tackling various issues, such as candidly expressing our feelings about the past, implementing political reform, completing the Uruguay Round, announcing a number of economic measures and measures on deregulation, and holding the Japan-United States summit talks. We have thus been able to achieve important reforms and accomplishments which had not been achieved during the LDP [Liberal Democratic Party] period, and we have been able to make headway in other important areas of reform. I am quite happy about our achievements, and for that I would like to express my sincere gratitude to the people of Japan.

What I regret, however, is that we have been unable to make full-fledged progress towards more important reforms in the area of education, the new approach of Japan toward disarmament—for example, the United Nations Arms Register system and Japan's efforts towards that end—and environmental issues, particularly the resolution of Minamata Disease, which is one of the important manifestations of the emerging environmental issue. We have been unable to tackle those important issues, which I very much regret.

In the past eight months, without rest, I have been busy working with important issues within and outside of Japan. As I mentioned earlier, I have now expressed my own determination as to my personal future. The reason why I made this important personal decision is that the deliberation on the budget, which has a very important bearing upon people's lives, has been suspended, and the Diet remains inoperative. With regard to my personal matter, although it has been taken advantage of as a political tactic, it is true that it has been in the way of smooth functioning in the Diet.

As for the truth, I have already frankly disclosed it, as I think I have a duty to expressly mention all the truth to the public. For example, with respect to my personal borrowing from Sagawa Express, as shown in the material presented to the Diet, we borrowed ¥100 million and we repaid the whole amount. That much is true. But as for the interest, through an agreement between my office and Sagawa Express, it became clear yesterday in a report from my office that it had been used for my political activities. I am sure that it was handled lawfully, according to the requirements of the law, and that due report was also made to the authorities. Concerning NTT [Nippon Telephone and Telegraph Company] shares, I have repeatedly mentioned that my father-in-law personally purchased them, that my former secretary was involved in that, and that the return on that service, at least part of it, was made to a coffer in the personal treasury of my father-in-law. I have made repeated efforts to further clarify that situation, and in that process, one problem has come to the surface which is a little bit different from what has been made known in the past. That is, from 1981 and for several years, my office let a certain person use the fund, and he gained personal profit from it. That person is an old personal friend of mine. He specifically requested that that money be entrusted to him, because he would manage it for profit. But there were some problems in the process of the management of that particular fund. The investigation of that particular situation has not yet been completed, and I cannot fully disclose the situation, but as I am the person supremely responsible for politics, I feel myself to be accountable, although this took place several years ago, and it was my office rather than myself which did the act. Even so, I consider myself accountable for that particular situation.

Because of this situation, and also because of the fact that the Diet has not been functioning, I have decided to take political responsibility for that and decided to step down from the premiership. The soonest deliberation should be made on the budget, and there are many other important issues facing us on which no further delay may be permitted.

This is indeed extremely regrettable for me, and I sincerely apologize to the people of Japan. But I sincerely hope that this particular act of mine will result in restoring the trust on the part of the public for the process of politics. That is what I sincerely wish for. As I have mentioned so far, I have decided to resign from the premiership. Many reforms are still underway and have not been completed, and my role will now be different. But I will continuously work towards the fruition of the pending reforms. At this point, I would like to express my sincere apology repeatedly to the Japanese people, and wish for your kind understanding.

SUPREME COURT ON
JURY SELECTION
April 19, 1994

Excluding potential jurors based on their sex violates the equal protection clause of the Fourteenth Amendment, the Supreme Court ruled April 19.

Women's rights groups hailed the decision, saying it would lead to more women serving on juries. Ironically, though, the case involved a man, James Bowman Sr., who claimed the jury selection process used in a paternity suit where he was the defendant violated his equal protection rights.

After some potential jurors were excused for cause, the jury pool for Bowman's trial included ten men and twenty-three women. The prosecutor and Bowman's lawyer questioned the potential jurors, and each attorney was allowed to make ten peremptory challenges. These challenges allowed the lawyers to remove people from the jury pool without giving a reason. The prosecutor used nine of his peremptory challenges to remove men, and Bowman's lawyer removed the remaining man. That left a jury of twelve women, which found that Bowman was the father of the child and owed the mother child support.

In appealing the verdict, Bowman contended that the prosecutor's deliberate removal of male jurors violated his right to equal protection. Writing for the 6-3 majority, Justice Harry A. Blackmun agreed. "Intentional discrimination on the basis of gender by state actors violates the Equal Protection Clause, particularly where, as here, the discrimination serves to ratify and perpetuate invidious, archaic, and overbroad stereotypes about the relative abilities of men and women," he wrote. Blackmun was joined in the majority by Justices John Paul Stevens, Sandra Day O'Connor, David H. Souter, Ruth Bader Ginsburg, and Anthony M. Kennedy, who wrote a separate concurring opinion.

Blackmun wrote that discrimination in jury selection, whether based on race or sex, harms the litigants, the community, and individual jurors who are excluded from participating in the judicial process: "The litigants are harmed by the risk that the prejudice which motivated the discriminatory selection of the jury will infect the entire proceedings . . . . The community is harmed by the State's participation in the perpetuation of invidious group stereotypes and the inevitable loss of confidence in our judicial system that state-sanctioned discrimination in the courtroom engenders."

In a mocking dissent, Justice Antonin Scalia blasted the Court majority for undermining lawyers' ability to remove potential jurors without giving a reason. "Today's opinion is an inspiring demonstration of how thoroughly up-to-date and right-thinking we Justices are in matters pertaining to the sexes (or as the Court would have it, the genders)," Scalia wrote, "and how sternly we disapprove the male chauvinist attitudes of our predecessors." Chief Justice William H. Rehnquist and Justice Clarence Thomas joined in Scalia's dissent.

Peremptory Challenges Date Back Centuries

Peremptory challenges have a long history in law. In theory, the challenges are designed to help obtain a fair and impartial jury. In practice, though, lawyers use them to remove potential jurors who they think will be unsympathetic to their case. In certain types of cases, sex had been one factor lawyers considered in deciding whether to challenge a particular juror. For example, in rape cases prosecutors frequently challenged men, believing that women would be more sympathetic to the alleged victim. In Bowman's case, the prosecutor presumably used nine of his ten challenges to remove men from the jury pool because he thought women would be more sympathetic to his client, who was seeking child support from Bowman.

The Court's opinion extended its 1986 decision in Batson v. Kentucky, *where the justices ruled that potential jurors could not be excluded based on race. Since the* Batson *decision, state and federal courts had split on whether its principles also applied to excluding potential jurors based on sex. (Historic Documents of 1986, p. 409)*

Most legal experts said the Court's ruling will result in more women serving on juries, since they are more often excluded from juries based on their sex than are men. Some, including Justice Sandra Day O'Connor, expressed fears that in many cases lawyers will be forced to prove that their challenges are not sex-based, further delaying trials. In a concurring opinion, O'Connor wrote that the majority's decision "is not costless" because it will increase the number of cases "in which jury selection—once a sideshow—will become part of the main event." Scalia agreed in his dissent, writing that the decision "will provide the basis for extensive collateral litigation" because "every case contains a potential sex-based claim." In her concurring opinion, O'Connor also said the Court's decision raises the possibility that biased people will end up on juries "because sometimes a lawyer will be unable to provide an acceptable gender-neutral explanation even though the lawyer is in fact correct that the juror is unsympathetic."

Although she joined in the majority opinion, O'Connor—the first woman appointed to the Supreme Court—appeared troubled by the fact that lawyers will no longer be able to use differences between men and women in challeng-

*ing jurors. She wrote that "one need not be a sexist to share the intuition that
in certain cases a person's gender and resulting life experience will be relevant to his or her view of the case. . . . Today's decision severely limits a
litigant's ability to act on this intuition, for the import of our holding is that
any correlation between a juror's gender and attitudes is irrelevant as a
matter of constitutional law. But to say that gender makes no difference as a
matter of law is not to say that gender makes no difference as a matter of
fact."*

*Following are excerpts from the majority, concurring, and
dissenting opinions in the Supreme Court's ruling April 19,
1994, in* J.E.B. v. Alabama, *in which it said that potential jurors cannot be excluded based on their sex:*

No. 92-1239

J. E. B., Petitioner *v.* Alabama ex rel. T. B.	On writ of certiorari to the Court of Civil Appeals of Alabama

[April 19, 1994]

JUSTICE BLACKMUN delivered the opinion of the Court.

In *Batson* v. *Kentucky* (1986), this Court held that the Equal Protection
Clause of the Fourteenth Amendment governs the exercise of peremptory
challenges by a prosecutor in a criminal trial. The Court explained that although a defendant has "no right to a 'petit jury composed in whole or in part
of persons of his own race,' " the "defendant does have the right to be tried by
a jury whose members are selected pursuant to nondiscriminatory criteria."
Since *Batson,* we have reaffirmed repeatedly our commitment to jury selection procedures that are fair and nondiscriminatory. We have recognized that
whether the trial is criminal or civil, potential jurors, as well as litigants, have
an equal protection right to jury selection procedures that are free from state-
sponsored group stereotypes rooted in, and reflective of, historical prejudice.
See *Powers* v. *Ohio* (1991); *Edmonson* v. *Leesville Concrete Co.* (1991); *Georgia* v. *McCollum* (1992).

Although premised on equal protection principles that apply equally to gender discrimination, all our recent cases defining the scope of *Batson* involved
alleged racial discrimination in the exercise of peremptory challenges. Today
we are faced with the question whether the Equal Protection Clause forbids
intentional discrimination on the basis of gender, just as it prohibits discrimination on the basis of race. We hold that gender, like race, is an unconstitutional proxy for juror competence and impartiality.

I

On behalf of relator T. B., the mother of a minor child, respondent State of Alabama filed a complaint for paternity and child support against petitioner J. E. B. in the District Court of Jackson County, Alabama. On October 21, 1991, the matter was called for trial and jury selection began. The trial court assembled a panel of 36 potential jurors, 12 males and 24 females. After the court excused three jurors for cause, only 10 of the remaining 33 jurors were male. The State then used 9 of its 10 peremptory strikes to remove male jurors; petitioner used all but one of his strikes to remove female jurors. As a result, all the selected jurors were female.

Before the jury was empaneled, petitioner objected to the State's peremptory challenges on the ground that they were exercised against male jurors solely on the basis of gender, in violation of the Equal Protection Clause of the Fourteenth Amendment. Petitioner argued that the logic and reasoning of *Batson* v. *Kentucky*, which prohibits peremptory strikes solely on the basis of race, similarly forbids intentional discrimination on the basis of gender. The court rejected petitioner's claim and empaneled the all-female jury. The jury found petitioner to be the father of the child and the court entered an order directing him to pay child support. On post-judgment motion, the court reaffirmed its ruling that *Batson* does not extend to gender-based peremptory challenges. The Alabama Court of Civil Appeals affirmed.... The Supreme Court of Alabama denied certiorari.

We granted certiorari to resolve a question that has created a conflict of authority—whether the Equal Protection Clause forbids peremptory challenges on the basis of gender as well as on the basis of race. Today we reaffirm what, by now, should be axiomatic: Intentional discrimination on the basis of gender by state actors violates the Equal Protection Clause, particularly where, as here, the discrimination serves to ratify and perpetuate invidious, archaic, and overbroad stereotypes about the relative abilities of men and women.

II

Discrimination on the basis of gender in the exercise of peremptory challenges is a relatively recent phenomenon. Gender-based peremptory strikes were hardly practicable for most of our country's existence, since, until the 19th century, women were completely excluded from jury service....

Many States continued to exclude women from jury service well into the present century, despite the fact that women attained suffrage upon ratification of the Nineteenth Amendment in 1920. States that did permit women to serve on juries often erected other barriers, such as registration requirements and automatic exemptions, designed to deter women from exercising their right to jury service....

This Court in *Ballard* v. *United States* (1946) first questioned the fundamental fairness of denying women the right to serve on juries. Relying on its supervisory powers over the federal courts, it held that women may not be excluded from the venire in federal trials in States where women were eligible for jury service under local law. . . .

Fifteen years later, however, the Court . . . found it reasonable, "despite the enlightened emancipation of women," to exempt women from mandatory jury service by statute, allowing women to serve on juries only if they volunteered to serve. The Court justified the differential exemption policy on the ground that women, unlike men, occupied a unique position "as the center of home and family life." [*Hoyt* v. *Florida* (1961).]

In 1975, the Court finally repudiated the reasoning of *Hoyt* and struck down, under the Sixth Amendment, an affirmative registration statute nearly identical to the one at issue in *Hoyt*. See *Taylor* v. *Louisiana* (1975). We explained: "Restricting jury service to only special groups or excluding identifiable segments playing major roles in the community cannot be squared with the constitutional concept of jury trial." The diverse and representative character of the jury must be maintained "partly as assurance of a diffused impartiality and partly because sharing in the administration of justice is a phase of civic responsibility.". . .

III

Taylor relied on Sixth Amendment principles, but the opinion's approach is consistent with the heightened equal protection scrutiny afforded gender-based classifications. Since *Reed* v. *Reed* (1971), this Court consistently has subjected gender-based classifications to heightened scrutiny in recognition of the real danger that government policies that professedly are based on reasonable considerations in fact may be reflective of "archaic and overbroad" generalizations about gender or based on "outdated misconceptions concerning the role of females in the home rather than in the 'marketplace and world of ideas.' ". . .

Despite the heightened scrutiny afforded distinctions based on gender, respondent argues that gender discrimination in the selection of the petit jury should be permitted, though discrimination on the basis of race is not. Respondent suggests that "gender discrimination in this country . . . has never reached the level of discrimination" against African-Americans, and therefore gender discrimination, unlike racial discrimination, is tolerable in the courtroom.

While the prejudicial attitudes toward women in this country have not been identical to those held toward racial minorities, the similarities between the experiences of racial minorities and women, in some contexts, "overpower those differences.". . .

. . . Under our equal protection jurisprudence, gender-based classifications require "an exceedingly persuasive justification" in order to survive constitutional scrutiny. Thus, the only question is whether discrimination on the basis of gender in jury selection substantially furthers the State's legitimate interest in achieving a fair and impartial trial. In making this assessment, we do not weigh the value of peremptory challenges as an institution against our asserted commitment to eradicate invidious discrimination from the courtroom.

Instead, we consider whether peremptory challenges based on gender stereo-types provide substantial aid to a litigant's effort to secure a fair and impartial jury.

Far from proffering an exceptionally persuasive justification for its gender-based peremptory challenges, respondent maintains that its decision to strike virtually all the males from the jury in this case "may reasonably have been based upon the perception, supported by history, that men otherwise totally qualified to serve upon a jury might be more sympathetic and receptive to the arguments of a man alleged in a paternity action to be the father of an out-of-wedlock child, while women equally qualified to serve upon a jury might be more sympathetic and receptive to the arguments of the complaining witness who bore the child."

We shall not accept as a defense to gender-based peremptory challenges "the very stereotype the law condemns." Respondent's rationale, not unlike those regularly expressed for gender-based strikes, is reminiscent of the argu-ments advanced to justify the total exclusion of women from juries. Respon-dent offers virtually no support for the conclusion that gender alone is an accurate predictor of juror's attitudes; yet it urges this Court to condone the same stereotypes that justified the wholesale exclusion of women from juries and the ballot box. Respondent seems to assume that gross generalizations that would be deemed impermissible if made on the basis of race are some-how permissible when made on the basis of gender.

Discrimination in jury selection, whether based on race or on gender, causes harm to the litigants, the community, and the individual jurors who are wrongfully excluded from participation in the judicial process. The litigants are harmed by the risk that the prejudice which motivated the discriminatory selection of the jury will infect the entire proceedings. . . . The community is harmed by the State's participation in the perpetuation of invidious group ste-reotypes and the inevitable loss of confidence in our judicial system that state-sanctioned discrimination in the courtroom engenders.

When state actors exercise peremptory challenges in reliance on gender stereotypes, they ratify and reinforce prejudicial views of the relative abilities of men and women. . . . Discriminatory use of peremptory challenges may cre-ate the impression that the judicial system has acquiesced in suppressing full participation by one gender or that the "deck has been stacked" in favor of one side. . . .

In recent cases we have emphasized that individual jurors themselves have a right to nondiscriminatory jury selection procedures. Contrary to respon-dent's suggestion, this right extends to both men and women. . . .

IV

Our conclusion that litigants may not strike potential jurors solely on the basis of gender does not imply the elimination of all peremptory challenges. Neither does it conflict with a State's legitimate interest in using such chal-lenges in its effort to secure a fair and impartial jury. Parties still may remove jurors whom they feel might be less acceptable than others on the panel; gender simply may not serve as a proxy for bias. Parties may also exercise their peremptory challenges to remove from the venire any group or class of individuals normally subject to "rational basis" review. Even strikes based on characteristics that are disproportionately associated with one gender could be appropriate, absent a showing of pretext. . . .

The experience in the many jurisdictions that have barred gender-based challenges belies the claim that litigants and trial courts are incapable of complying with a rule barring strikes based on gender. As with race-based *Batson* claims, a party alleging gender discrimination must make a prima facie showing of intentional discrimination before the party exercising the challenge is required to explain the basis for the strike. When an explanation is required, it need not rise to the level of a "for cause" challenge; rather, it merely must be based on a juror characteristic other than gender, and the proffered explanation may not be pretextual. . . .

V

Equal opportunity to participate in the fair administration of justice is fundamental to our democratic system. It not only furthers the goals of the jury system. It reaffirms the promise of equality under the law "that all citizens, regardless of race, ethnicity, or gender, have the chance to take part directly in our democracy. . . . When persons are excluded from participation in our democratic processes solely because of race or gender, this promise of equality dims, and the integrity of our judicial system is jeopardized.

In view of these concerns, the Equal Protection Clause prohibits discrimination in jury selection on the basis of gender, or on the assumption that an individual will be biased in a particular case for no reason other than the fact that the person happens to be a woman or happens to be a man. . . .

The judgment of the Court of Civil Appeals of Alabama is reversed and the case is remanded to that court for further proceedings not inconsistent with this opinion.

It is so ordered.

JUSTICE O'CONNOR, concurring.

I agree with the Court that the Equal Protection Clause prohibits the government from excluding a person from jury service on account of that person's gender. . . . I therefore join the Court's opinion in this case. But today's important blow against gender discrimination is not costless. I write separately to discuss some of these costs, and to express my belief that today's holding should be limited to the *government's* use of gender-based peremptory strikes.

Batson v. *Kentucky* (1986) itself was a significant intrusion into the jury selection process. *Batson* mini-hearings are now routine in state and federal trial courts, and *Batson* appeals have proliferated as well. Demographics indicate that today's holding may have an even greater impact than did *Batson* itself. In further constitutionalizing jury selection procedures, the Court increases the number of cases in which jury selection—once a sideshow—will become part of the main event.

For this same reason, today's decision further erodes the role of the peremptory challenge. . . . The principal value of the peremptory is that it helps produce fair and impartial juries. . . .

. . . [A]s we add, layer by layer, additional constitutional restraints on the use of the peremptory, we force lawyers to articulate what we know is often inarticulable.

In so doing we make the peremptory challenge less discretionary and more like a challenge for cause. We also increase the possibility that biased jurors will be allowed onto the jury, because sometimes a lawyer will be unable to provide an acceptable gender-neutral explanation even though the lawyer is in fact correct that the juror is unsympathetic. Similarly, in jurisdictions where lawyers exercise their strikes in open court, lawyers may be deterred from using their peremptories, out of the fear that if they are unable to justify the strike the court will seat a juror who knows that the striking party thought him unfit. Because I believe the peremptory remains an important litigator's tool and a fundamental part of the process of selecting impartial juries, our increasing limitation of it gives me pause.

Nor is the value of the peremptory challenge to the litigant diminished when the peremptory is exercised in a gender-based manner. We know that like race, gender matters. A plethora of studies make clear that in rape cases, for example, female jurors are somewhat more likely to vote to convict than male jurors. . . . Moreover, though there have been no similarly definitive studies regarding, for example, sexual harassment, child custody, or spousal or child abuse, one need not be a sexist to share the intuition that in certain cases a person's gender and resulting life experience will be relevant to his or her view of the case. . . .

Today's decision severely limits a litigant's ability to act on this intuition, for the import of our holding is that any correlation between a juror's gender and attitudes is irrelevant as a matter of constitutional law. But to say that gender makes no difference as a matter of law is not to say that gender makes no difference as a matter of fact. . . . Though we gain much from this statement, we cannot ignore what we lose. In extending *Batson* to gender we have added an additional burden to the state and federal trial process, taken a step closer to eliminating the peremptory challenge, and diminished the ability of litigants to act on sometimes accurate gender-based assumptions about juror attitudes.

These concerns reinforce my conviction that today's decision should be limited to a prohibition on the government's use of gender-based peremptory challenges. The Equal Protection Clause prohibits only discrimination by state actors. In *Edmonson*, we made the mistake of concluding that private civil litigants were state actors when they exercised peremptory challenges; in *Georgia* v. *McCollum*, we compounded the mistake by holding that criminal defendants were also state actors. Our commitment to eliminating discrimination from the legal process should not allow us to forget that not all that occurs in the courtroom is state action. Private civil litigants are just that—*private* litigants. . . .

Clearly, criminal defendants are not state actors. . . .

Accordingly, I adhere to my position that the Equal Protection Clause does not limit the exercise of peremptory challenges by private civil litigants and criminal defendants. This case itself presents no state action dilemma, for here the State of Alabama itself filed the paternity suit on behalf of petitioner. But what of the next case? Will we, in the name of fighting gender discrimination, hold that the battered wife—on trial for wounding her abusive husband—is a state actor? Will we preclude her from using her peremptory challenges to ensure that the jury of her peers contains as many women members as possible? I assume we will, but I hope we will not.

JUSTICE KENNEDY, concurring in the judgment.

I am in full agreement with the Court that the Equal Protection Clause prohibits gender discrimination in the exercise of peremptory challenges. . . .

. . . The only question is whether the Clause also prohibits peremptory challenges based on sex. The Court is correct to hold that it does. The Equal Protection Clause and our constitutional tradition are based on the theory that an individual possesses rights that are protected against lawless action by the government. . . . For purposes of the Equal Protection Clause, an individual denied jury service because of a peremptory challenge exercised against her on account of her sex is no less injured than the individual denied jury service because of a law banning members of her sex from serving as jurors. . . . The neutrality of the Fourteenth Amendment's guarantee is confirmed by the fact that the Court has no difficulty in finding a constitutional wrong in this case, which involves males excluded from jury service because of their gender.

The importance of individual rights to our analysis prompts a further observation concerning what I conceive to be the intended effect of today's decision. We do not prohibit racial and gender bias in jury selection only to encourage it in jury deliberations. Once seated, a juror should not give free rein to some racial or gender bias of his or her own. . . .

In this regard, it is important to recognize that a juror sits not as a representative of a racial or sexual group but as an individual citizen. . . . The jury pool must be representative of the community, but that is a structural mechanism for preventing bias, not enfranchising it. . . . Thus, the Constitution guarantees a right only to an impartial jury, not to a jury composed of members of a particular race or gender. . . .

CHIEF JUSTICE REHNQUIST, dissenting.

I agree with the dissent of JUSTICE SCALIA, which I have joined. I add these words in support of its conclusion. Accepting *Batson* v. *Kentucky* (1986) as correctly decided, there are sufficient differences between race and gender discrimination such that the principle of *Batson* should not be extended to peremptory challenges to potential jurors based on sex.

That race and sex discrimination are different is acknowledged by our equal protection jurisprudence, which accords different levels of protection to the two groups. Classifications based on race are inherently suspect, triggering "strict scrutiny," while gender-based classifications are judged under a heightened, but less searching standard of review. *Mississippi Univ. for Women* v. *Hogan* (1982). Racial groups comprise numerical minorities in our society, warranting in some situations a greater need for protection, whereas the population is divided almost equally between men and women. Furthermore, while substantial discrimination against both groups still lingers in our society, racial equality has proved a more challenging goal to achieve on many fronts than gender equality.

Batson, which involved a black defendant challenging the removal of black jurors, announced a sea-change in the jury selection process. In balancing the dictates of equal protection and the historical practice of peremptory challenges, long recognized as securing fairness in trials, the Court concluded that the command of the Equal Protection Clause was superior. . . .

Under the Equal Protection Clause, . . . the balance should tilt in favor of peremptory challenges when sex, not race, is the issue. Unlike the Court, I think the State has shown that jury strikes on the basis of gender "substantially further" the State's legitimate interest in achieving a fair and impartial trial through the venerable practice of peremptory challenges. . . . The two sexes differ, both biologically and, to a diminishing extent, in experience. It is not merely "stereotyping" to say that these differences may produce a difference in outlook which is brought to the jury room. Accordingly, use of peremptory challenges on the basis of sex is generally not the sort of derogatory and invidious act which peremptory challenges directed at black jurors may be.

JUSTICE O'CONNOR's concurrence recognizes several of the costs associated with extending *Batson* to gender-based peremptory challenges—lengthier trials, an increase in the number and complexity of appeals addressing jury selection, and a "diminished . . . ability of litigants to act on sometimes accurate gender-based assumptions about juror attitudes." These costs are, in my view, needlessly imposed by the Court's opinion, because the Constitution simply does not require the result which it reaches.

JUSTICE SCALIA, with whom THE CHIEF JUSTICE and JUSTICE THOMAS join, dissenting.

Today's opinion is an inspiring demonstration of how thoroughly up-to-date and right-thinking we Justices are in matters pertaining to the sexes (or as the Court would have it, the genders), and how sternly we disapprove the male chauvinist attitudes of our predecessors. The price to be paid for this display "a modest price, surely" is that most of the opinion is quite irrelevant to the case at hand. The hasty reader will be surprised to learn, for example, that this lawsuit involves a complaint about the use of peremptory challenges to exclude men from a petit jury. To be sure, petitioner, a man, used all but one of *his* peremptory strikes to remove *women* from the jury (he used his last challenge to strike the sole remaining male from the pool), but the validity of *his* strikes is not before us. Nonetheless, the Court treats itself to an extended discussion of the historic exclusion of women not only from jury service, but also from service at the bar (which is rather like jury service, in that it involves going to the courthouse a lot). All this, as I say, is irrelevant, since the case involves state action that allegedly discriminates against men. . . .

The Court also spends time establishing that the use of sex as a proxy for particular views or sympathies is unwise and perhaps irrational. The opinion stresses the lack of statistical evidence to support the widely held belief that, at least in certain types of cases, a juror's sex has some statistically significant predictive value as to how the juror will behave. . . . Personally, I am less inclined to demand statistics, and more inclined to credit the perceptions of experienced litigators who have had money on the line. But it does not matter. . . . Even if sex was a remarkably good predictor in certain cases, the Court would find its use in peremptories unconstitutional. . . .

The core of the Court's reasoning is that peremptory challenges on the basis of any group characteristic subject to heightened scrutiny are inconsistent with the guarantee of the Equal Protection Clause. That conclusion can be reached only by focusing unrealistically upon individual exercises of the peremptory challenge, and ignoring the totality of the practice. Since all groups are subject to the peremptory challenge (and will be made the object of it, depending upon the nature of the particular case) it is hard to see how any group is denied equal protection. That explains why peremptory challenges coexisted with the Equal Protection Clause for 120 years. This case is a perfect example of how the system as a whole is even-handed. While the only claim before the Court is petitioner's complaint that the prosecutor struck male jurors, for every man struck by the government petitioner's own lawyer struck a woman. To say that men were singled out for discriminatory treatment in this process is preposterous. . . .

Although the Court's legal reasoning in this case is largely obscured by anti-male-chauvinist oratory, to the extent such reasoning is discernible it invalidates much more than sex-based strikes. After identifying unequal treatment (by separating individual exercises of peremptory challenge from the process as a whole), the Court applies the "heightened scrutiny" mode of equal-protection analysis used for sex-based discrimination, and concludes that the strikes fail heightened scrutiny because they do not substantially further an important government interest. The Court says that the only important government interest that could be served by peremptory strikes is "securing a fair and impartial jury." It refuses to accept respondent's argument that these strikes further that interest by eliminating a group (men) which may be partial to male defendants, because it will not accept any argument based on " 'the very stereotype the law condemns.' " This analysis, entirely eliminating the only allowable argument, implies that sex-based strikes do not even rationally further a legitimate government interest, let alone pass heightened scrutiny. That places *all* peremptory strikes based on *any* group characteristic at risk, since they can all be denominated "stereotypes." . . .

Even if the line of our later cases guaranteed by today's decision limits the theoretically boundless *Batson* principle to race, sex, and perhaps other classifications subject to heightened scrutiny (which presumably would include religious belief), much damage has been done. It has been done, first and foremost, to the peremptory challenge system, which loses its whole character when (in order to defend against "impermissible stereotyping" claims) "reasons" for strikes must be given. . . . The loss of the real peremptory will be felt most keenly by the criminal defendant. . . . And make no mistake about it: there really is no substitute for the peremptory. Voir dire (though it can be expected to expand as a consequence of today's decision) cannot fill the gap. The biases that go along with group characteristics tend to be biases that the juror himself does not perceive, so that it is no use asking about them. It is fruitless to inquire of a male juror whether he harbors any subliminal prejudice in favor of unwed fathers.

And damage has been done, secondarily, to the entire justice system, which will bear the burden of the expanded quest for "reasoned peremptories" that the Court demands. The extension of *Batson* to sex, and almost certainly beyond, will provide the basis for extensive collateral litigation, which especially the criminal defendant (who litigates full-time and cost-free) can be expected to pursue. While demographic reality places some limit on the number of cases in which race-based challenges will be an issue, every case contains a potential sex-based claim. Another consequence, as I have mentioned, is a lengthening of the voir dire process that already burdens trial courts. . . .

In order, it seems to me, not to eliminate any real denial of equal protection, but simply to pay conspicuous obeisance to the equality of the sexes, the Court imperils a practice that has been considered an essential part of fair jury trial since the dawn of the common law. The Constitution of the United States neither requires nor permits this vandalizing of our people's traditions.

For these reasons, I dissent.

THE FUNERAL OF
RICHARD NIXON
April 27, 1994

At the funeral April 27 of the thirty-seventh president of the United States, who died April 22, the speakers tried to sum up the life of a man filled with contradictions. As a member of Congress, Richard Nixon had started his political career as a red-baiter, accusing respected political leaders of being communists or having communist sympathies; as president, Nixon opened the door to better relations with China and Russia, the world's two major communist countries. Nixon also won perhaps the most lopsided presidential election in American history, only to be forced to resign in disgrace over the Watergate scandal.

Besides being filled with contradictions, Nixon seemed to be the man for whom the word polarizing *was invented. People either loved him or hated him. To his supporters, Nixon was one of the great statesmen of the twentieth century, the man who made the early moves toward ending the Cold War and improving U.S. relations with the world's communist powers. To his detractors, Nixon was a paranoid liar and opportunist who came closer than any other president in history to plunging the nation into a constitutional crisis.*

No one could dispute that Nixon was one of the major figures in twentieth-century American politics. He entered public life in 1946, running for Congress in California. His campaign that year set the tone for all the others that followed: it was nasty, appealed to voters' fears, and included accusations from his opponent that Nixon's camp engaged in "dirty tricks." During the 1946 campaign Nixon claimed that his opponent, a respected Democrat who had served in Congress for ten years, was soft on communism and "communist-supported." Nixon won.

Upon reaching Washington, Nixon linked his career to the public's fear of communists, and he rose rapidly. He gained national prominence during investigations by the House Un-American Activities Committee into charges that State Department official Alger Hiss had given government secrets to the Soviet Union. In 1950 he ran for the Senate, facing Democrat Helen Gahagan Douglas. "My opponent is a woman," Nixon said at the time. "There will be no name-calling, no smears, no misrepresentations in this campaign." Despite the promises, the campaign turned ugly. Nixon called Douglas "the pink lady," implying she was soft on communism; she responded by labeling him "Tricky Dick." It was a moniker his opponents would use for the rest of his life. Again, Nixon won.

Two years later, in 1952, Dwight D. Eisenhower chose Nixon to be his running mate when he ran for president. The race had hardly begun before it was revealed that a group of California businessmen had given Nixon an $18,000 campaign fund. Some GOP leaders told Eisenhower he should drop Nixon from the ticket, and Eisenhower seemed unsure what to do. Nixon saved his candidacy by making a nationally televised speech, known as the "Checkers speech," in which he claimed that none of the money had gone for his personal use. He also contended that his critics were either communists or tools of communists.

Eisenhower and Nixon won the 1952 election, and at age thirty-nine Nixon became the second youngest vice president in the nation's history. Eisenhower and Nixon won again in 1956, and Nixon easily won the Republican nomination for president in 1960.

The 1960 presidential campaign pitted Nixon against John F. Kennedy, who prevailed with one of the closest presidential election victories in American history. Kennedy received 49.71 percent of the popular vote compared to Nixon's 49.55 percent, but Kennedy captured 303 of the 537 electoral college votes by winning just twenty-three of the forty-eight states.

Two years later, in 1962, Nixon ran for governor of California. This time he lost, apparently because voters felt he was more interested in running for president again than in running their state. The day after the election Nixon held a bitter press conference. "You won't have Richard Nixon to kick around anymore because, gentlemen, this is my last press conference," he told the assembled reporters. At that point, many political experts said he was finished.

He was not. He bounded back by grabbing the Republican nomination for president in 1968, a year that saw the assassinations of the Rev. Martin Luther King Jr. and Sen. Robert F. Kennedy, who was running for the Democratic nomination. It was also a year in which the nation was being ripped apart by disagreement over the war in Vietnam, race riots turned many American cities into blazing infernos, and President Lyndon Johnson announced he would not seek reelection.

Nixon beat Democratic candidate Hubert H. Humphrey, who had been Johnson's vice president, in a campaign in which he promised peace at both home and abroad.

But peace was not forthcoming. The Vietnam War dragged on, and with it the growing protests on American streets and college campuses. Yet Nixon had some remarkable triumphs. In 1972, after nearly three years of secret negotiations, Nixon visited China to reestablish diplomatic relations, which had been cut years before. Also in 1972, he traveled to Moscow to sign a major agreement aimed at limiting the nuclear arms race. On the domestic front, Nixon pushed to stop poverty, end job discrimination, tackle environmental problems, and provide national health insurance. The progressive nature of at least part of Nixon's domestic agenda placed him at odds with the Congress, which balked at some of his ideas.

Nixon's downfall started on June 17, 1972, with a bungled break-in at Democratic National Committee headquarters at the Watergate hotel. Both the press and the public largely ignored the break-in, which had been ordered by officials in Nixon's reelection campaign. It had little impact on that fall's presidential election, where Nixon overwhelmingly defeated Democratic candidate George McGovern to win a second term.

Eventually, dogged reporting by Carl Bernstein and Bob Woodward, two young reporters at the Washington Post, *revealed that Nixon and his top aides had committed a series of crimes in an effort to cover up the Watergate affair and to harass people they considered enemies. The final blow came when the Supreme Court ordered Nixon to turn over recordings of conversations he had secretly taped in the Oval Office. Those recordings proved without question that Nixon had ordered the coverup and had lied to the American people about his role in the affair. Three days after the Court's ruling, the House Judiciary Committee voted the first of three articles of impeachment, charging Nixon with high crimes and misdemeanors against the nation. The vote marked only the second time in U.S. history that a congressional committee had voted an article of impeachment against a president. The committee charged Nixon with obstruction of justice, abuse of presidential power, and contempt of Congress.*

Faced with virtually certain impeachment, Nixon resigned August 9, 1974. His vice president, Gerald R. Ford, became president and shortly thereafter caused an intense controversy by issuing Nixon a blanket pardon covering any crimes he may have committed. Without the pardon, Nixon might have ended up spending time in jail.

After leaving office Nixon wrote numerous books, some of which became bestsellers, and once again began rebuilding his image. He lobbied hard for additional aid to Russia after the collapse of the Soviet Union in 1991 and gradually acquired the stature of a senior statesman.

Even after his death, however, Nixon could not escape his past. Diaries kept by H. R. Haldeman, his White House chief of staff, were published one month after Nixon's death. They revealed that Nixon plotted political dirty tricks against his opponents, complained about the "total Jewish domination of the media," and believed that "the whole problem is really the blacks."

> *Following are the text of remarks by former secretary of state Henry Kissinger, Senate Minority Leader Bob Dole, and President Bill Clinton at the funeral for Richard Nixon, held April 27, 1994, at the Nixon Library in Yorba Linda, Calif., as released by the White House:*

KISSINGER'S REMARKS

During the final week of Richard Nixon's life, I often imagined how he would have reacted to the tide of concern, respect, admiration and affection evoked by his last great battle. His gruff pose of never paying attention to media comment would have been contradicted by a warm glow and the ever-so-subtle hint that another recital of the commentary would not be unwelcome. And without quite saying so, he would have conveyed that it would mean a lot to him if Julie and Tricia, David and Ed were told of his friends' pride in this culmination to an astonishing life.

When I learned the final news, by then so expected, yet so hard to accept, I felt a profound void. In the words of Shakespeare: "He was a man. Take him. For all in all, I shall not look upon his like again."

In the conduct of foreign policy, Richard Nixon was one of the seminal presidents. He came into office when the forces of history were moving America from a position of dominance to one of leadership. Dominance reflects strength. Leadership must be earned. And Richard Nixon earned that leadership role for his country with courage, dedication and skill.

When Richard Nixon took his oath of office, 550,000 Americans were engaged in combat in a place as far away from the United States as it was possible to be. America had no contact with China, the world's most populous nation. No negotiations with the Soviet Union, the other nuclear superpower. Most Moslem countries had broken diplomatic relations with the United States, and Middle East diplomacy was stalemated. All of this in the midst of the most anguishing domestic crisis since the Civil War.

When Richard Nixon left office, an agreement to end the war in Vietnam had been concluded, and the main lines of all subsequent policy were established: permanent dialogue with China; readiness without illusion to ease tensions with the Soviet Union; a peace process in the Middle East; the beginning, via the European Security Conference, of establishing human rights as an international issue; weakening Soviet hold on Eastern Europe.

Richard Nixon's foreign policy goals were long-range. And he pursued them without regard to domestic political consequences. When he considered our nation's interests at stake, he dared confrontations, despite the imminence of elections and also in the midst of the worst crisis of his life. And he bore, if with some pain, the disapproval of longtime friends and allies over relaxing tensions with China and the Soviet Union. He drew strength from a conviction. He often expressed to me the price for doing things halfway is no less than for doing it completely. So we might as well do them properly. That's Richard Nixon's greatest accomplishment. It was as much moral as it was political—to lead from strength at a moment of apparent weakness, to husband the nation's resilience and, thus, to lay the basis for victory in the Cold War.

Shy and withdrawn, Richard Nixon made himself succeed in the most gregarious of professions, and steeled himself to conspicuous acts of extraordinary courage. In the face of wrenching domestic controversy, he held fast to his basic theme that the greatest free nation in the world had a duty to lead, and no right to abdicate.

Richard Nixon would be so proud that President Clinton and all living former presidents of the United States are here, symbolizing that his long and sometimes bitter journey had concluded in reconciliation.

I wish that in his final hours I could have told him about Brian McDonald who, during the Cambodian crisis, had been fasting on a bench in Lafayette Park, across from the White House until, as he said, "President Nixon redeemed his pledge to withdraw American forces from their anguished country in two months"—a promise which was, in fact, kept.

Across the chasm of the decades, Brian called me the day Richard Nixon fell ill and left a message: "When you talk to President Nixon, tell him that I'm praying for him."

So let us now say goodbye to our gallant friend. He stood on pinnacles that dissolved in the precipice. He achieved greatly and he suffered deeply. But he never gave up. In his solitude, he envisaged a new international order that would reduce lingering enmities, strengthen historic friendships, and give new hope to mankind—a vision where dreams and possibilities conjoined.

Richard Nixon ended the war. And he advanced the vision of peace of his Quaker youth. He was devoted to his family. He loved his country. And he considered service his honor. It was a privilege to have been allowed to help him.

DOLE'S REMARKS

I believe the second half of the 20th century will be known as the age of Nixon. Why was he the most durable public figure of our time? Not because he gave the most eloquent speeches, but because he provided the most effective leadership. Not because he won every battle, but because he always embodied the deepest feelings of the people he led.

One of his biographers said that Richard Nixon was one of us. And so he was. He was a boy who heard the train whistle in the night and dreamed of all the distant places that lay at the end of the track. How American. He was a grocer's son who got ahead by working harder and longer than everyone else. How American.

He was a student who met expenses by doing research at the law library for 35 cents an hour while sharing a run-down farmhouse without water or electricity. How American. He was the husband and father who said that the best memorial to his wife was her children. How American.

To tens of millions of his countrymen, Richard Nixon was an American hero, a hero who shared and honored their belief in working hard, worshiping God, loving their families and saluting the flag. He called them the silent majority. Like him, they valued accomplishment more than ideology. They wanted their government to do the decent thing, but not to bankrupt them in the process.

They wanted his protection in a dangerous world, but they also wanted creative statesmanship in achieving a genuine peace with honor. These were the people from whom he had come and who have come to Yorba Linda these past few days by the tens of thousands—no longer silent in their grief. The American people love a fighter. And in Dick Nixon, they found a gallant one.

In a marvelous biography of her mother, Julie recalls an occasion where Pat Nixon expressed amazement at her husband's ability to persevere in the face of criticism, to which the President replied, "I just get up every morning to confound my enemies."

It was what Richard Nixon did after he got up every morning that not just confounded his enemies, but turned them into admirers.

It is true that no one knew the world better than Richard Nixon. And as a result, the man who was born in a house his father built would go on to become this century's greatest architect of peace.

But we should also not underestimate President Nixon's domestic achievements. For it was Richard Nixon who ended the draft, strengthened environmental and nutritional programs, and committed the government to a war on cancer. He leapfrogged the conventional wisdom to propose revolutionary solutions to health care and welfare reform, anticipating by a full generation the debates now raging on Capitol Hill.

I remember the last time I saw him—at a luncheon held at the Capitol honoring the 25th anniversary of his first inaugural. Without a note, President Nixon stood and delivered a compelling speech, capturing the global scene as only he could and sharing his vision of America's future. When it was over, he was surrounded by Democrats and Republicans alike, each wanting just one more word of Nixonian counsel, one more insight into world affairs.

Afterward, the President rested in my office before leaving the Capitol, only he got very little rest—for the office was filled with young Hill staffers, members of the Capitol police and many, many others, all hoping to shake his hand, get an autograph or simply convey their special feelings for a man who truly was one of us.

Today our grief is shared by millions of people the world over, but is also mingled with intense pride in a great patriot who never gave up and who never gave in. To know the secret of Richard Nixon's relationship with the American people, you need only to listen to his own words: "You must never be satisfied with success," he told us, "and you should never be discouraged by failure. Failure can be sad, but the greatest sadness is not to try and fail, but to fail to try. In the end, what matters is that you have always lived life to the hilt."

Strong, brave, unafraid of controversy, unyielding in his convictions, living every day of his life to the hilt, the largest figure of our time whose influence will be timeless—that was Richard Nixon. How American. May God bless Richard Nixon and may God bless the United States.

CLINTON'S REMARKS

President Nixon opened his memoirs with a simple sentence: "I was born in a house my father built." Today, we can look back at this little house and still imagine a young boy sitting by the window of the attic he shared with his three brothers, looking out to a world he could then himself only imagine. From those humble roots, as from so many humble beginnings in this country, grew the force of a driving dream—a dream that led to the remarkable journey that ends here today where it all began. Beside the same tiny home, mail-ordered from back East, near this towering oak tree which, back then, was a mere seedling.

President Nixon's journey across the American landscape mirrored that of his entire nation in this remarkable century. His life was bound up with the striving of our whole people, with our crises and our triumphs.

When he became president, he took on challenges here at home on matters from cancer research to environmental protection, putting the power of the federal government where Republicans and Democrats had neglected to put it in the past. He came to the presidency at a time in our history when Americans were tempted to say we had had enough of the world. Instead, he knew we had to reach out to old friends and old enemies alike. He would not allow America to quit the world.

Remarkably, he wrote nine of his ten books after he left the presidency, working his way back into the arena he so loved by writing and thinking, and engaging us in his dialogue.

For the past year, even in the final weeks of his life, he gave me his wise counsel, especially with regard to Russia. One thing in particular left a profound impression on me. Though this man was in his ninth decade, he had an incredibly sharp and vigorous and rigorous mind.

As a public man, he always seemed to believe the greatest sin was remaining passive in the face of challenges. And he never stopped living by that creed. He gave of himself with intelligence and energy and devotion to duty. And his entire country owes him a debt of gratitude for that service. Oh, yes, he knew great controversy amid defeat as well as victory. He made mistakes; and, they, like his accomplishments, are part of his life and record.

But the enduring lesson of Richard Nixon is that he never gave up being part of the action and passion of his times. He said many times that unless a person has a goal, a new mountain to climb, his spirit will die. Well, based on our last phone conversation and the letter he wrote me just a month ago, I can say that his spirit was very much alive to the very end. That is a great tribute to him, to his wonderful wife, Pat, to his children and to his grandchildren whose love he so depended on and whose love he returned in full measure.

Today is a day for his family, his friends and his nation to remember President Nixon's life in totality. To them, let us say, may the day of judging President Nixon on anything less than his entire life and career come to a close. May we heed his call to maintain the will and the wisdom to build on America's greatest gift—its freedom; to lead a world full of difficulty to the just and lasting peace he dreamed of.

As it is written in the words of a hymn I heard in my church last Sunday: "Grant that I may realize that the trifling of life creates differences, but that in the higher things, we are all one."

In the twilight of his life, President Nixon knew that lesson well. It is, I feel certain, a faith he would want us all to keep. And so, on behalf of all four former presidents who are here—President Ford, President Carter, President Reagan, President Bush—and on behalf of a grateful nation, we bid farewell to Richard Milhous Nixon.

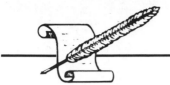

May

MANDELA'S INAUGURATION AS PRESIDENT OF SOUTH AFRICA
May 10, 1994

Four years after he was released from a twenty-seven-year stint in prison, African National Congress (ANC) leader Nelson Mandela was sworn in May 10 as South Africa's first democratically elected president. The jubilant celebration, attended by dignitaries from more than 150 countries, culminated a remarkable period in South African history that began when the nation's white president, F. W. de Klerk, released Mandela from prison February 11, 1990. The two went on to work together to create a new South African constitution in late 1993 and promote nonracial elections in April 1994. For their efforts to end the strict racial segregation known as apartheid, Mandela and de Klerk were jointly awarded the Nobel Peace Prize in October 1993. (De Klerk and Mandela on South African Changes, Historic Documents of 1990, p. 65; Statements on Awarding of Nobel Peace Prize, South African Constitution, Historic Documents of 1993, p. 877 and p. 1003)

The election was conducted over a three-day period in late April. Although there were fears that it would be chaotic, with the exception of a few terrorist incidents and logistical problems, the election took place without major problems. It ran smoothly largely due to the policies of de Klerk's interim government and the Independent Electoral Commission, which worked to assure the security and integrity of the process.

Late Agreement Clears Way for Election

A major breakthrough occurred a week before the election was to begin when Mangosuthu Buthelezi, president of the Zulu-based Inkatha Freedom Party, called off his threat to boycott the election. The Zulu president had expressed fears that the expected ANC-led government would undermine regional Zulu autonomy, but an agreement signed by Buthelezi, de Klerk, and Mandela assured the continuation of the Zulu monarchy, thereby ending months of failed negotiations and increasing political violence between the ANC and Inkatha loyalists.

"I am just over the moon," said Archbishop Desmond Tutu, a leading figure in ending apartheid. "This new dawn was going to be overcast, but now the sun is shining." U.S. president Bill Clinton also issued a statement welcoming the agreement.

During the election, voter turnout was heavy and orderly. Both South Africans and observers from other nations marveled at the sight of huge lines of people, black and white together, patiently waiting to cast their ballots. Nineteen parties were on the national ballot and twenty-six parties were on nine regional ballots, representing the diverse electorate of 23 million people who spoke a dozen different languages. Under South Africa's electoral system, a weighted system of proportional voting guaranteed runner-up parties a share of cabinet seats.

As expected, the ANC received about 64 percent of the vote, compared with 23 percent for de Klerk's National Party, and about 6 percent for the Inkatha Freedom Party. In conceding to Mandela May 2, de Klerk said, "Mr. Mandela has walked a long road, and now stands at the top of the hill. As he contemplates the next hill, I hold out my hand to Mr. Mandela in friendship and cooperation."

Speaking later before a crowd in a Johannesburg hotel ballroom, Mandela said, "I stand here before you filled with deep pride and joy." Acknowledging de Klerk's role in bringing about the historic change, the president-elect said, "I also want to congratulate him for the many days, weeks, and months and the four years that we have worked together, quarreled, addressed sensitive problems, and at the end of our heated exchanges were able to shake hands and to drink coffee."

Mandela Seeks Unity

The ANC won 252 of the 400 seats in the National Assembly, which on May 10 formally elected Mandela president without opposition. Delegates assembled in a chamber built in 1985 for joint sessions of a tricameral parliament, an apartheid system that excluded blacks but provided houses for representation of Indians and mixed-race people. Mandela entered a chamber filled with people of all races and dress with his arm around de Klerk.

Ninety minutes later, the new president appeared on a balcony at the old Cape Town City Hall. In a moving inaugural address before a cheering throng, Mandela pledged, "Never, never, and never again shall it be that this beautiful land will again experience the oppression of one by another and suffer the indignity of being the skunk of the world." He also promised that an amnesty would be announced for "various categories" of prisoners.

Later, attending a soccer match, Mandela chastised the largely black crowd, which balked at singing South Africa's two national anthems—the old one, "Die Stem" ("The Voice") and the new one, "Nkosi Sikelel iAfrika" ("God Bless Africa"). In short remarks about cultural inclusiveness, he urged everyone to learn Afrikaans, the language used by apartheid supporters, along with black languages.

De Klerk Named to Cabinet

By the day after his inauguration, Mandela had completed naming his twenty-seven-member cabinet. As had been previously agreed, de Klerk was named deputy president, as was Thabo Mbeki of the ANC. Buthelezi was named minister of home affairs. Roughly two-thirds of the cabinet members were from the ANC, with the rest divided between the National and Inkatha parties.

The new government faced a difficult road ahead. As a May 11 editorial in the Washington Post *noted, "South Africans must tackle a host of deep and abiding issues, ranging from double-digit unemployment and illiteracy rates to expectations of social change and improvement among the black majority—expectations that may be too high for any leader to achieve, let alone during a five-year term."*

In his first "state of the nation" speech before the new parliament on May 24, Mandela promised to avoid "permanent" new taxes, cut the government deficit, reduce inflation and interest rates, maintain a stable currency, and promote growth. "The realization of many of our objectives for a fair and equal treatment of all our people will not be possible unless we succeed in avoiding high inflation in the economy," Mandela said. He also outlined three modest social initiatives to be financed by cutting other government programs. They included providing free health care and nutritional programs for needy children, an electrification program, and a public works program to create jobs.

In a televised address to the nation and parliament three months later, Mandela said, "We have a government that is in control and whose programs are on course."

> *Following is the text of the speech by Nelson Mandela at his inauguration as president of the Democratic Republic of South Africa on May 10, 1994:*

Today, all of us do, by our presence here, and by our celebrations in other parts of our country and the world, confer glory and hope to newborn liberty. Out of the experience of an extraordinary human disaster that lasted too long, must be born a society of which all humanity will be proud. Our daily deeds as ordinary South Africans must produce an actual South African reality that will reinforce humanity's belief in justice, strengthen its confidence in the nobility of the human soul and sustain all our hopes for a glorious life for all.

All this we owe both to ourselves and to the peoples of the world who are so well represented here today. To my compatriots, I have no hesitation in saying that each one of us is as intimately attached to the soil of this beautiful country as are the famous jacaranda trees of Pretoria and the mimosa trees of the bushveld.

Each time one of us touches the soil of this land, we feel a sense of personal

249

renewal. The national mood changes as the seasons change. We are moved by a sense of joy and exhilaration when the grass turns green and the flowers bloom.

That spiritual and physical oneness we all share with this common homeland explains the depth of the pain we all carried in our hearts as we saw our country tear itself apart in a terrible conflict, and as we saw it spurned, outlawed and isolated by the peoples of the world, precisely because it has become the universal base of the pernicious ideology and practice of racism and racial oppression.

We, the people of South Africa, feel fulfilled that humanity has taken us back into its bosom, that we, who were outlaws not so long ago, have today been given the rare privilege to be host to the nations of the world on our own soil.

We thank all our distinguished international guests for having come to take possession with the people of our country of what is, after all, a common victory for justice, for peace, for human dignity. We trust that you will continue to stand by us as we tackle the challenges of building peace, prosperity, non-sexism, non-racialism and democracy.

We deeply appreciate the role that the masses of our people and their political mass democratic, religious, women, youth, business, traditional and other leaders have played to bring about this conclusion. Not least among them is my Second Deputy President, the Honorable F. W. de Klerk.

We would also like to pay tribute to our security forces, in all their ranks, for the distinguished role they have played in securing our first democratic elections and the transition to democracy, from blood-thirsty forces which still refuse to see the light.

The time for the healing of the wounds has come.

The moment to bridge the chasms that divide us has come.

The time to build is upon us.

We have, at last, achieved our political emancipation. We pledge ourselves to liberate all our people from the continuing bondage of poverty, deprivation, suffering, gender and other discrimination.

We succeeded to take our last steps to freedom in conditions of relative peace. We commit ourselves to the construction of a complete, just and lasting peace.

We have triumphed in the effort to implant hope in the breasts of the millions of our people. We enter into a covenant that we shall build the society in which all South Africans, both black and white, will be able to walk tall, without any fear in their hearts, assured of their inalienable right to human dignity—a rainbow nation at peace with itself and the world.

As a token of its commitment to the renewal of our country, the new Interim Government of National Unity will, as a matter of urgency, address the issue of amnesty for various categories of our people who are currently serving terms of imprisonment.

We dedicate this day to all the heroes and heroines in this country and the rest of the world, who sacrificed in many ways and surrendered their lives so that we could be free. Their dreams have become reality. Freedom is their reward.

We are both humbled and elevated by the honor and privilege that you, the people of South Africa, have bestowed on us, as the first President of a united, democratic, non-racial and non-sexist South Africa, to lead our country out of the valley of darkness.

We understand it still that there is no easy road to freedom. We know it well that none of us acting alone can achieve success. We must therefore act together as a united people, for national reconciliation, for nation building, for the birth of a new world.

Let there be justice for all.

Let there be peace for all.

Let there be work, bread, water and salt for all.

Let each know that for each the body, the mind and the soul have been freed to fulfill themselves.

Never, never and never again shall it be that this beautiful land will again experience the oppression of one by another and suffer the indignity of being the skunk of the world.

Let freedom reign.

The sun shall never set on so glorious a human achievement!

God bless Africa!

FEDERAL REPORT
ON HOMELESSNESS
May 17, 1994

The federal government should boost funding for programs aimed at help-ing homeless people and at preventing more people from ending up on the streets, according to a May 17 report by the Interagency Council on the Homeless. The council, a group representing seventeen federal agencies, also said homeless programs needed to be better coordinated.

"On our watch we'd like to reduce the number of homeless by a third," said Henry G. Cisneros, secretary of housing and urban development (HUD) and chairman of the council. Cisneros presented the report at a ceremony in Franklin Park, a gathering place for homeless people in Washington, D.C.

The report, written in response to an executive order signed by President Bill Clinton on May 19, 1993, set out a more ambitious plan than had been proposed by previous administrations to deal with a problem that many experts agreed had worsened during the 1980s. Under the plan, HUD's bud-get for homeless programs would double, from $823 million a year to $1.7 billion. Overall, federal funding for homeless programs would jump to an all-time high of $2.1 billion.

In its report, the council acknowledged that the problems that cause homelessness could not be solved quickly and that the country was not in the mood for expensive social programs. Adopting the Clinton administration theme of "reinventing government" to make it less cumbersome and costly, the council proposed consolidating the patchwork of homeless grant pro-grams authorized by the 1987 Stewart B. McKinney Homeless Assistance Act. Local governments would coordinate funding, leaving nonprofit insti-tutions such as churches free to build shelters, organize soup kitchens, and provide other services for the homeless.

Excessive Bureaucracy Criticized

Simplifying programs was the top priority of service providers, local offi-cials, and homeless people surveyed by the council in preparation for its report. Problems with one of the programs, which were publicized in a separate report by an advocacy group for the homeless, illustrated the challenges involved in translating government intentions into realities. Created by Congress in 1987, the program allowed nonprofit groups and local governments to convert vacant federal facilities such as military bases into housing for the homeless. However, according to the report issued by the National Law Center on Homelessness and Poverty on February 18, only about 800 of the 13,000 federal properties available had been put to use. The group blamed excessive bureaucracy, including an overly complex application process, for the lack of action.

Shelters alone were not enough to solve the problem of homelessness, the interagency council emphasized in its report. Instead, homeless people needed a "continuum of care" that included mental health services, job training, and other social supports as they moved toward self-sufficiency. "The challenge ahead of us is putting all the pieces together to create a comprehensive system of housing, services, and care," said Andrew M. Cuomo, assistant secretary at HUD and a key author of the report.

Advocates for the homeless and others praised the report not only because it called for spending more money, but also because of its characterization of homelessness. "It's remarkable, in contrast to the Reagan and Bush years, in its recognition of the scope and complexity of the homeless problem," said Martha Burt, an analyst with the Urban Institute, a think tank in Washington, D.C.

How Many Homeless Were There?

One of the most controversial aspects of the homeless problem was the issue of exactly how many people were homeless. Advocates claimed that the government had underestimated the number of homeless, thus shortchanging people in need. After attempting to count the homeless on one night in 1990, the Census Bureau announced in 1991 that its total of about 200,000 was low and did not represent a true count of the nation's homeless. By contrast, the council's report relied on two academic studies for its assertion that up to 600,000 people were homeless on any given night and that approximately 7 million Americans had been homeless at one point or another during the second half of the 1980s.

Attempting to downplay the dispute over numbers, the report contended that whatever the number of homeless at a given moment, many more people were "on the edge" of homelessness—waiting for public housing, living with friends or relatives, or paying rents that consumed too much of their incomes. "I don't think we'll ever know how many homeless there are," Cuomo said.

The report divided the homeless into two categories: poor people who temporarily became homeless and people with chronic disabilities such as mental illness, alcoholism, or drug addiction who tended to remain homeless over longer periods of time. Although the members of the second group were in the minority, they were more publicly visible. Many people believed that

*deinstitutionalization of the mentally ill had swelled the homeless popula-
tion during the 1980s, the report said, but in reality most of the mentally ill
homeless had never been in state mental hospitals.*

*Single men made up about three-fourths of the homeless population, ac-
cording to studies cited in the report. Most homeless families were headed by
women. About 40 percent of homeless people were African Americans and 30
percent to 45 percent of homeless men were veterans of the armed services.*

*The report emphasized that homelessness was caused not just by drug
abuse or mental illness but by a complex web of circumstances: a lack of
decent blue-collar jobs, increases in housing costs, reductions in the stock of
low-cost housing, cuts in welfare payments, and racial discrimination. Another report, issued February 2 by the Speaker's Task Force on
Homelessness, agreed that homelessness was a particularly visible aspect of
the larger problem of poverty. The task force recommendations were similar
to those made by the council, although the nine-member congressional panel
also endorsed increasing the minimum wage, an issue not discussed in the
council's report.*

*Although the various reports drew renewed attention to the problem of
homelessness, 1994 ended with Republicans preparing to take control of
both houses of Congress. During the fall campaign Republican candidates
had promised to slash spending for social programs, so it appeared unlikely
that homeless programs would receive the additional funding recommended
in the reports.*

> *Following are excerpts from "Priority: Home! The Federal
> Plan to Break the Cycle of Homelessness," a report released
> May 17, 1994, by the Interagency Council on the Homeless:*

The Face of Homelessness: No Longer a Poor Apart

A simple conviction lies at the heart of this document: it profits us nothing
as a nation to wall off homelessness as a novel social problem made up of a
distinctly "different" population. Nor is it something that requires separate
and distinctive mechanisms of redress, isolated from mainstream programs.
In fact, the more we understand about the root causes of homelessness, the
greater our sense of having been here before.

To put it plainly, homelessness in the 1990s reveals as much about the un-
solved social and economic problems of the 1970s as it does about more recent developments. This Plan reveals and documents that the crisis of
homelessness is greater than commonly known or previously acknowledged.
Researchers have found that as many as 600,000 people are homeless on any
given night. Recent research reveals the startling finding that about seven million Americans experienced being homeless at least once in the latter half of
the 1980s. Hence, its resolution will require tackling the enduring roots of
poverty, as well as complications introduced by psychiatric disability, sub-

stance abuse, and infectious disease. That task is rendered more difficult by today's economic realities and severe budget constraints.

By the middle of the 1980s, the number of homeless people had surpassed anything seen since the Great Depression. Disability, disease, and even death were becoming regular features of life on the streets and in shelters. For the first time, women and children were occupying quarters formerly "reserved" for skid-row men. Psychiatric hospitals continued to discharge people with little hope of finding, let alone managing, housing of their own. Crack cocaine emerged as a drug of choice for those on the margins of society. A new scourge—HIV/AIDS—joined an old one—tuberculosis—to become major afflictions of the homeless poor.

Yet for all that, there remained something disconcertingly familiar about this new homelessness. What America glimpsed on the streets and in the shelters in the 1980s was the usually hidden face of poverty, dislodged from its customary habitat.

Homelessness can be understood as including two broad, sometimes overlapping, categories of problems. The first category is experienced by people living in crisis poverty. Their homelessness tends to be a transient or episodic disruption in lives that are routinely marked by hardship. For such people, recourse to shelters or other makeshift accommodations is simply another way of bridging a temporary gap in resources. Their housing troubles may be coupled with other problems as well—dismal employment prospects because of poor schooling and obsolete job skills, domestic violence, or poor parenting or household management skills—all of which require attention if rehousing efforts are to be successful. But their persistent poverty is the decisive factor that turns unforeseen crises, or even minor setbacks, into bouts of homelessness.

For those individuals who fall in the second category—homeless men and women with chronic disabilities—homelessness can appear to be a way of life. Although a minority of those who become homeless over the course of a year, it is this group that is most visible and tends to dominate the public's image of homelessness. Alcohol and other drug abuse, severe mental illness, chronic health problems or long-standing family difficulties may compound whatever employment and housing problems they have. Lacking financial resources and having exhausted whatever family support they may have had, they resort to the street. Their homelessness is more likely to persist. Disability coupled with the toll of street-living make their situation more complex than that of those who are homeless because of crisis poverty. Those with chronic disabilities require not only economic assistance, but rehabilitation and ongoing support as well.

For the most part, homelessness relief efforts remain locked in an "emergency" register. Many existing outreach, drop-in, and shelter programs address the symptoms of homelessness and little else. Although of proven promise in dealing with the disabled homeless poor, supportive housing options remain in scarce supply. Increasingly, it has become clear that efforts to remedy homelessness cannot be fully effective if they are isolated from a broader community-based strategy designed to address the problems of extreme poverty and the inadequate supply of housing affordable by the very poor. Lasting solutions to homelessness will be found only if the issue is productively addressed in ongoing debates concerning welfare reform, health-care reform, housing, community and economic development, education, and employment policy. . . .

Characteristics of the Homeless Population

Findings from cross-sectional studies conducted during the past decade have added much to our understanding of characteristics of homeless populations. Although significant regional differences exist, it may be useful to offer a summary statistical sketch compiled from the studies that have been done.

Family Status

Single, unattached adults, unaccompanied by children, make up about three quarters of homeless persons. Men outnumber women by a factor of five. Families with children, more than 80 percent of whom are headed by a single mother, make up another fifth. The remainder are adults in couples or other groupings. In some communities, a substantial population of homeless young adults and adolescents may be discerned, though they are rarely included in standard studies. National estimates of this group range from 1.3 to 1.6 million homeless youth annually.

Age

The average age of unattached homeless adults is in the late 30s; that of mothers with children is in the early 30s.

Race and Ethnicity

Studies have repeatedly shown that minorities are disproportionately represented among the homeless population, especially among homeless families. African Americans, for example, form a larger fraction of both poor people (28%) and homeless persons (40%)—and have done so consistently throughout the 1980s—than their proportions of the general population.

Institutional History

Only one in four homeless men has no history of any institutional stay, whether hospitalization, jail or prison, or inpatient chemical dependency treatment.

Health Status

At least half of the adult homeless population has a current or past alcohol or drug use problem. Up to one-third of the adult homeless population have severe mental illness. Other health problems occur with uncommon frequency; most lethal among them are HIV/AIDS and resurgent tuberculosis.

Income and Employment

Homeless persons tend to be very poor. Average monthly household income among homeless people in Chicago was less than $174. In a national sample, average monthly household income among homeless persons was less than $200, regardless of household composition. The Urban Institute reported that over a third of the homeless persons enumerated in shelters in the 1990 Census had worked within the previous week. Only half of homeless men have completed high school.

Foster Care

For reasons still poorly understood, a disproportionate number of adult homeless persons—ranging from 9 to 39 percent, depending upon the study—spent some time in foster care as children. A New York study found that this was even more striking for unattached homeless women, who were twice as likely as their male counterparts to have had an institutional or foster-care placement as their principal living arrangement while growing up.

Homeless Children

Homeless children face significant barriers to receiving the same public education as their non-homeless peers. As many as one third of homeless children may not be attending school on a regular basis. Children who are homeless with their family members often suffer not only disruption in their education, but serious emotional and developmental problems that can persist long after their families find permanent housing. African-American children use shelters at the highest rate of any group.

Homeless Veterans

Approximately 30 to 45 percent of the entire adult male homeless population have served their country in the armed services. About 98 percent of homeless veterans are male, but the population of homeless female veterans is growing. In addition, approximately 40 percent of all homeless veterans are African American or Hispanic. Homeless veterans tend to be older and better educated than nonveteran homeless adults, but otherwise share the same characteristics as homeless nonveterans. One notable exception is that about 10 percent of homeless veterans also suffer from post-traumatic stress disorder (PTSD).

Causes of Homelessness

A decade of research and practical experience has confirmed that there are many varieties of contemporary homelessness. Manifold in its causes, duration, consequences, and co-existing disabilities, its steady growth in the early 1980s reflected the confluence of a number of factors.

In accounting for homelessness, it is useful to distinguish among a number of levels of causation. Understanding the structural causes of homelessness is especially important when considering preventive strategies. When fashioning measures to reach those who are currently on the street, personal problems that contribute to the prolongation of homelessness must be addressed.

If stable residence is the goal of policy, appreciating the role of risk factors is essential. Psychiatric disability, substance abuse, domestic violence and chronic illness not only add to the likelihood that someone will become homeless, but complicate the task of rehousing someone already on the street. Among generic risk factors, poverty is the common denominator, but other circumstances have also been identified that increase the likelihood of homelessness: prior episodes of homelessness; divorce or separation among men, and single parenthood among women; leaving home or "aging out" of foster care among unattached youth; a history of institutional confinement in jails, prisons, or psychiatric hospitals; and weak or overdrawn support networks of family and friends.

We must focus more attention on individual risk factors and the underlying structural causes potentiating these factors if the cycle of homelessness is to be broken.

Structural Causes

Poverty

In 1992, nearly 37 million Americans were officially classified as poor; this figure represented 14.5 percent of the population, up from 12.8 percent in 1989. Rates of poverty among African Americans are consistently three times higher than among whites (33 percent v. 11.6 percent in 1992); for Hispanic Americans, they are two and a half times higher. Female-headed households with children are particularly vulnerable to poverty; 48.3 percent of those living in these households were poor in 1992, a figure that rose to about 60 percent for African Americans and Hispanic Americans. Twenty-two percent of all children and 47 percent of African-American children lived below the poverty line in 1992. The percentage increase noted above translates into an increase of five million poor people between 1989 and 1992. During this period, the very poor (those whose incomes were less than 50 percent of the poverty threshold) increased by 3.0 million, adding greatly to the population highly vulnerable to homelessness.

Recent studies suggest that over the past twenty years, poverty has become both more concentrated and more segregated. From 1970 to 1990, the number of census tracts with 20 percent or more poverty in the 100 largest cities increased from 3,430 to 5,596. Overall, the percent of poor living in central cities increased dramatically, with African Americans having the highest concentration of poor in these areas.

Over the past quarter century, government assistance successfully reduced poverty among the elderly because public demands dictated that our elderly not be neglected. Government policies are likely to follow public dictates—and public opinion is often shaped by the perception of what is possible. Programs and policies such as Aid for Families with Dependent Children (AFDC) have not succeeded. By contrast, government efforts to improve the standard of living for elderly members of our society have succeeded.

Changes in Labor Market

The shift of the American economy from goods production to services over the past quarter century has substantially altered labor markets and the demand for workers, especially in cities of the Midwest and Northeast. Wage-based incomes have become more polarized; income differentials have widened. A host of developments have jeopardized the employment prospects of those who lack appropriate skills or adequate schooling. These include: plant relocations and closures, persistent racial discrimination, changes in industry that have increased demand for highly educated people, the decline in the real value of the minimum wage, and the globalization of the economy. This pernicious combination of factors that devastated America's cities and urban economies did not spare America's rural heartland. Rural communities, particularly those host to the farming sector, experienced severe economic shocks, losing jobs, homes, and indeed a way of life.

Young African-American men have been especially hard hit. This is reflected in both unemployment data and in changes in work force participation, which reflects the fact that there are many discouraged workers who have dropped out of the work force and are no longer counted in unemployment statistics. Work force participation (percent of those employed) was over 70 percent both for African-American and white men aged 16 to 24 in the early 1950s. By 1985, there was a large disparity between the two groups: less than 45 percent of African Americans were working in this age group compared to about 65 percent for whites. The relative odds ratio of being employed between the two groups increased from zero to over 2.4.

Prolonged periods of enforced idleness are hardly conducive to work habits, promotion of responsibility, or attachments to family or the labor force. In a culture that places a high premium on work, damage to self-esteem and the diminished respect of others surely follow. Not surprisingly, the lure of the "underground" economy as a source of income has grown.

The changing labor market also resulted in an increase in the number of workers who were working full time and still poor—particularly those whose schooling stopped with high school or earlier.

Income Assistance

Families on AFDC have seen the real value of their cash benefits steadily decline for the past twenty years. From 1970 to 1992, the median inflation-adjusted monthly State AFDC benefit in July for a family unit of four with no income dropped from $799 to $435 in 1992 dollars. In 1992, the combined value of AFDC and food stamp benefits for a family of four, on average, amounted to around two-thirds of the official poverty threshold of $14,335.

Changes in poverty have been influenced by government philosophy and priorities more than budgetary constraints. Over the past quarter century government assistance successfully reduced poverty among the elderly because public demands dictated that our elderly not be neglected. The percent of elderly that have been removed from poverty by cash transfer alone increased from 50 percent in 1967 to nearly 80 percent by 1985. By contrast, the percentage of female-headed families with children that have been removed from poverty dropped during this same period from around 17 percent to around 11 percent. Among the reasons is that cash benefits have been declining for this group in real dollars and non-cash benefits, such as food stamps, Medicaid, and housing assistance are not counted as income.

For single people, the picture was grimmer still: at the end of 1990, time-limited unemployment benefits reached a smaller proportion of the jobless than at any time in the previous twenty years. Never generous to begin with, state-administered "General Assistance" programs were severely cut and badly eroded by inflation during the 1980s. In 1991, reductions in benefits and culling of rolls affected over a third of General Assistance caseloads nationwide; similar cuts followed the next year, and more are contemplated.

Lack of Affordable Housing

Growing numbers of poor households find themselves competing for shrinking supplies of affordable housing. A comparison of the number of lowest-income renters to the units affordable at that income level illustrates the extent of this problem. In 1991, the poorest one-fourth of renters totaled nearly eight million households. But nationally, fewer than three million units were affordable to this group, i.e., rented for less than 30 percent of the highest income of those renters. (HUD's programs often require 30 percent of a household's adjusted income.) This "affordability gap" of five million in 1991 had widened by almost four million since 1970.

High real interest rates and increasing energy costs have contributed to the decline in the availability of housing affordable to very low income individuals by requiring landlords to charge higher rents to cover their capital and utility costs. Thus the cost of rental housing that meets minimal standards has risen out of the reach of many.

Losses of units with very low rents were particularly high among the marginal housing that once sheltered poor single adults, including old rooming houses and single room occupancy (SRO) hotels. Urban renewal and stronger housing code enforcement contributed to demolition or upgrading of this stock. Data on such units are imperfect, but huge numbers of inexpensive, unsubsidized units were lost. The number of people living in hotels and rooming houses with no other permanent address dropped from 640,000 in 1960 to 204,000 in 1980 and some 137,000 in 1990. Because most of these losses occurred during the 1960s and early 1970s, some analysts conclude that shortages in the 1980s were "created largely by rising demand and only secondarily by falling supply." It seems likely that many of those now homeless or in emergency shelters have incomes and needs similar to the former occupants of this vanished stock.

Shortages of housing were greatest for the very lowest income: special tabulations of 1990 census data for every state and locality show that on average the ratio of affordable rental housing to every renter household with incomes below 30 percent of median is only .79. While the overall national supply of housing appears adequate for very low income renters with incomes less than 50 percent of median, there were great regional disparities. Disparities by location were greatest for renters with incomes below 30 percent of median: in Western cities there were only .43 affordable units for each of these very poor households, while there were surpluses in non-metropolitan areas in all four census regions and in twenty states including North Dakota.

Widening gaps between numbers of very poor renters and of units they could afford translate into higher rent burdens. Between 1974 and 1989, the number of unassisted very low-income renter households paying more than one-half of their income for rent or living in substandard housing, or both, rose from 3.6 to 5.1 million, with all of the increase attributable to severe rent burdens.

Growth in these severe worst-case needs for housing assistance far outpaced increases in rental assistance during the 1980s, particularly among families with children. In 1990, nearly one-fifth (17.8 percent) of American renter households devoted more than half their income to meeting housing costs. Yet from 1981 to 1991, virtually alone among means-tested programs for the poor, budget authority for housing assistance actually declined.

As funding appropriated during the late 1970s produced housing during the 1977-1984 period, the number of additional households receiving assistance rose by an average of 219,000 each year. From 1985 to 1991, however, the average annual increase was only 61,285. Not surprisingly, then, in 1991 only 25 percent of eligible very low-income renters received rental assistance.

Rural poverty and housing affordability are also a problem. Nearly half of rural minority poor live in substandard housing. In 1990, there were 1.4 million rural occupied substandard housing units. Of the rural residents earning from $5,000 to $9,999 who are able to afford rent, 34 percent (770,000) must pay more than 30 percent of their income on rent. For those earning less than $5,000 who are able to afford rent, 28 percent (625,000) must pay 30 percent or more of their income on rent. In FY 1994, the FmHA section 515 rural rental housing program had $1.4 billion in applications and preapplication proposals, far exceeding the amount of funds available for assistance.

Changes in Family Structure

The rise in single-parent families is one of the most significant demographic shifts of the last quarter century. In 1970, single-parent families accounted for 14 percent of all families; by 1992, that figure had grown to 22 percent. (Among African Americans, the figure grew from 36 percent to 53 percent during the same period; for Hispanics, the figure grew from 22 percent to 32 percent from 1973 to 1992.) Female-headed households accounted for 39 percent of the officially poor population in 1991. Nearly half of all African-American children and over two-fifths of Hispanic-American children live in such households.

Single mothers with children constitute the largest percentage of AFDC recipients and make up 80 percent of homeless families as well. Chronically strapped for resources, such households are held hostage to the slightest change in fortune. Inexperienced in managing households of their own, many of these young single mothers are at a heightened risk of homelessness. These difficulties for families also profoundly affect their children, who frequently experience disruptions in their schooling. If members of minority groups, they often face the added burden of discrimination.

Families try to cope with poverty the way they always have, by resorting to traditional means of resource-pooling. In fact, during the 1970s, the prevalence of doubled-up households among poor people in cities increased substantially, especially among African Americans. However, the contributions of additional household members were less successful in raising these families above the poverty level than they had been a decade earlier.

Drugs, Disabilities, and Chronic Health Problems

The failure to address the treatment and rehabilitation needs of people with disabilities, chronic health problems, and mental health problems has contributed to a substantial increase in the number of people who are especially vulnerable to displacement and homelessness. Research studies throughout the 1980s consistently found that about half of the single homeless adult population suffers from substance abuse problems. Habitual heavy drinking and drug use also figure prominently among the precipitating causes of homelessness. Substance abuse eats away material resources (such as money otherwise available for rent) and can sorely test the supportive social relations that customarily allow people to ride out spells of hard times without resort to emergency shelters. The evidence is strong, in short, that substance abuse is an important factor in the "selection" of homeless people from among others who are also poor. At the same time, the experience of homelessness itself may trigger heavy drinking and drug use by people who have not had such problems in the past and may prompt renewed substance abuse by people whose earlier problems had been under control. Other chronic health problems, such as diabetes and HIV/AIDS, pose unmet treatment needs for some homeless people.

Why These Factors Translate into Homelessness

A number of analysts have suggested that the situation of households at risk of homelessness may be likened to a game of musical chairs. Too many people are competing for too few affordable housing units. In such a game, those troubled by severe mental illness, addiction, or potentially lethal infections, as well as those simply inexperienced in the delicate balancing act that running a household in hard times requires, are at a serious disadvantage.

Under such circumstances, the changes sketched above—in kinship, government support and work—greatly complicate the task of relocating people who have been displaced from their homes. Traditionally, as noted earlier, extended households were on hand as the recourse of last resort in difficult times. Those among the poor who were without family could make do in sections of central business districts where rooms were cheap and food could be had through the efforts of local charities. Even difficult behavioral problems could be accommodated: such people simply moved frequently, in effect spreading the burden throughout the marginal housing sector. For those still able, spot work opportunities provided a source of income.

But extended families are finding it difficult to make ends meet. The slack in cheap housing is gone. And studies suggest that what is left of the casual labor market prefers more compliant recruits.

Faced with these changes, Federal homelessness policy must be both preventive and remedial in scope. It must do more than merely relocate those who are currently homeless. It must also stabilize such housing placements once made, while securing the residences of those who are precariously housed. Government must seek, in effect, to do with deliberation and planning what the private market once accomplished: make housing work again. In today's environment, to make housing work will frequently require an infusion of fiscal resources and support services. Such services should be viewed, not as "add-on" frills, but as essential enabling ingredients—on a par with debt service, insurance or fire control measures—that are needed for some housing to be feasible at all.

SENATE REPORT ON
GULF WAR SYNDROME
May 25, 1994

The American people breathed a sigh of relief when the Gulf War ended in 1991 with relatively few casualties among the nearly 700,000 U.S. soldiers sent to liberate Kuwait after invasion by Iraq. The U.S. forces achieved their military objective quickly, with the loss of only 146 people in combat. The victory lost some of its sparkle in the months that followed the return of American troops, however, as a growing number of veterans reported an array of health problems that included skin rashes, fatigue, joint pain, headaches, and difficulty concentrating, among others. By 1994 this collection of symptoms, which became known as Gulf War or Persian Gulf syndrome, had been discussed at numerous hearings and was the subject of ongoing study.

Many theories were advanced—but no consensus reached—on what had caused it. One theory was that Gulf War soldiers had been exposed to chemical and biological agents such as nerve gas in levels too low to kill people but high enough to cause lingering health problems.

The Senate Committee on Banking, Housing and Urban Affairs first became interested in the veterans' medical complaints during a 1992 hearing on U.S. exports to Iraq before the Gulf War. The exports included "dual-use" items such as bacteria samples intended for medical purposes that the Iraqis may have used to develop some biological warfare capability. The result of the panel's investigation into the Gulf War syndrome was a 151-page staff report released May 25, 1994, with the endorsement of committee chairman Donald W. Riegle Jr. (D-Mich.) and ranking member Alfonse M. D'Amato (R-N.Y.).

The committee found substantial evidence that U.S. forces in the Persian Gulf were exposed to chemical and biological warfare agents, either from direct attacks or as a result of the bombing of Iraqi munitions dumps by the United States and its allies. This exposure, the report said, may have caused the symptoms of at least some of the veterans and their family members.

The Senate report said that "tens of thousands" of Persian Gulf War veterans were believed to be suffering from the symptoms labeled Gulf War syndrome, but no hard data existed on the number of people affected. By mid-1994, about 24,000 veterans had entered their names on a registry set up two years earlier by the Department of Veterans Affairs (VA). Any Gulf War veteran who signed the registry, whether ill or not, qualified for a free check-up at a VA hospital.

Defense Department Denies Exposure Claims

In a contentious hearing on the day the report was released, Defense Department officials said there was no evidence that chemical or biological weapons were used during the Gulf War. Riegle and other panel members expressed skepticism and challenged the officials to explain why so many veterans had fallen ill.

The Senate committee was no happier a month later when an eight-member scientific panel appointed by the Defense Department found no evidence of chemical or biological weapon exposure and no other evidence to explain Gulf War syndrome. Biologist and Nobel laureate Joshua Lederberg, who headed the panel, said on June 23 that although some veterans were ill, no theory accounting for a Gulf War syndrome "survived close scrutiny."

In an effort to curb rumors of a government cover-up, the Defense Department announced the same day that it would declassify most documents relating to the Gulf War. Deputy Secretary of Defense John Deutch contrasted the action with "past episodes" in which the government had delayed for years before releasing documents on exposure to hazardous chemicals. A prominent example of past delay involved Agent Orange, a defoliant blamed for causing illnesses among veterans of the Vietnam War.

Aside from chemical and biological exposure, other theories to explain Gulf War syndrome blamed psychological stress, parasitic infection, exposure to smoke from oil fires, and reactions to a drug given to Gulf War soldiers to block the effects of nerve gas. Some doctors connected the Gulf symptoms to chronic fatigue syndrome or to a condition called "multiple chemical sensitivity" in which exposure to toxic chemicals produces later reactions to common chemicals such as perfume and gasoline.

"It may turn out to be a single thing, though this seems unlikely," the Washington Post *concluded in an exhaustive three-part report on Gulf War syndrome published July 24-26. "It may turn out to be a few rare diseases, mixed in with many common ones. It may turn out to be many common diseases, and some normal conditions, that shared experience, media attention and cultural attitude have swept under a single heading."*

More Studies in Progress

By the end of 1994, a number of government-sponsored studies were underway or planned. The Department of Veterans Affairs had begun to collect data on the health of a random sample of 10,000 Gulf War veterans, to be compared to data from a comparable group of military personnel who had

*not served in the war. Another planned VA study was designed to determine
if a disproportionate number of Gulf War veterans had died after the war.*

*The Defense Department also was at work on a number of epidemiological
studies, including one on the question of whether children born to Gulf War
veterans exhibited unusual numbers of birth defects or other problems. This
possibility had been raised in the Senate panel's report. In other studies
intended to shed light on the mysterious health problems of the Gulf veterans, Defense Department scientists were using computer models to recreate
weather patterns and track the movements of U.S. troops throughout the
war.*

*While scientists and doctors worked to understand and treat the ailments
of Gulf War veterans, Congress and VA officials struggled with the issues of
whether and how the government should compensate them for a condition
that had not been defined or clearly linked to military service. Red tape, legal
concerns, and budget constraints contributed to frustration on the part of
the veterans and their advocates. "We want to pay compensation for a condition that we don't know exists," said Jesse Brown, secretary of veterans affairs. "This is precedent setting." After much debate, Congress in October
approved a bill authorizing—but not requiring—the government to compensate Gulf War veterans for their illnesses.*

> *Following are excerpts from a report of the Senate Committee
> on Banking, Housing and Urban Affairs titled "U.S. Chemical
> and Biological Warfare-Related Dual Use Exports to Iraq and
> Their Possible Impact on the Health Consequences of the Per-
> sian Gulf War," released May 25, 1994:*

Introduction

In October 1992, the Committee on Banking, Housing, and Urban Affairs,
which has Senate oversight responsibility for the Export Administration Act
(EAA), held an inquiry into the U.S. export policy to Iraq prior to the Persian
Gulf War. During that hearing it was learned that U.N. inspectors identified
many U.S.-manufactured items exported pursuant to licenses issued by the
U.S. Department of Commerce that were used to further Iraq's chemical and
nuclear weapons development and missile delivery system development programs.

On June 30, 1993, several veterans testified at a hearing of the Senate Committee on Armed Services. There, they related details of unexplained events
that took place during the Persian Gulf War which they believed to be chemical warfare agent attacks. After these unexplained events, many of the veterans present reported symptoms consistent with exposure to a mixed agent
attack. Then, on July 29, 1993, the Czech Minister of Defense announced that
a Czechoslovak chemical decontamination unit had detected the chemical
warfare agent Sarin in areas of northern Saudi Arabia during the early phases

of the Gulf War. They had attributed the detections to fallout from coalition bombing of Iraqi chemical warfare agent production facilities.

In August 1993, Senate Banking Committee Chairman Donald W. Riegle Jr. began to research the possibility that there may be a connection between the Iraqi chemical, biological, and radiological warfare research and development programs and a mysterious illness which was then being reported by thousands of returning Gulf War veterans. In September 1993, Senator Riegle released a staff report on this issue and introduced an amendment to the Fiscal Year 1994 National Defense Authorization Act that provided preliminary funding for research of the illnesses and investigation of reported exposures.

When this first staff report was released by Senator Riegle, the estimates of the number of veterans suffering from these unexplained illnesses varied from hundreds, according to the Department of Defense, to thousands, according to the Department of Veterans Affairs. It is now believed that tens of thousands of U.S. Gulf War veterans are suffering from a myriad of symptoms collectively labelled either Gulf War Syndrome, Persian Gulf Syndrome, or Desert War Syndrome. Hundreds and possibly thousands of servicemen and women still on active duty are reluctant to come forward for fear of losing their jobs and medical care. These Gulf War veterans are reporting muscle and joint pain, memory loss, intestinal and heart problems, fatigue, nasal congestion, urinary urgency, diarrhea, twitching, rashes, sores, and a number of other symptoms.

They began experiencing these multiple symptoms during and after—often many months after—their tour of duty in the Gulf. A number of the veterans who initially exhibited these symptoms have died since returning from the Gulf. Perhaps most disturbingly, members of veterans' families are now suffering these symptoms to a debilitating degree. The scope and urgency of this crisis demands an appropriate response.

This investigation into Gulf War Syndrome, which was initiated by the Banking Committee under the direction of Chairman Riegle, has uncovered a large body of evidence linking the symptoms of the syndrome to the exposure of Gulf War participants to chemical and biological warfare agents, chemical and biological warfare pre-treatment drugs, and other hazardous materials and substances. Since the release of the first staff report on September 9, 1993, this inquiry has continued. Thousands of government officials, scientists, and veterans have been interviewed or consulted, and additional evidence has been compiled. . . .

Since the Banking Committee began its inquiry, the position of the Department of Defense regarding the possible causes of Gulf War Syndrome has altered only when challenged with evidence that is difficult to dispute. Yet, despite the vast resources of the Department of Defense, several independent and congressional inquiries with limited resources continue to uncover additional evidence of hazardous exposures and suspicious events.

The Department of Defense, when first approached regarding this issue by Committee staff, contended that there was no evidence that U.S. forces were exposed to chemical warfare agents. However, during a telephone interview on September 7, 1993 with Walter Reed Army Medical Center commander Major General Ronald Blanck, Committee staff was informed that the issue of chemical and biological warfare agent exposure had not been explored because it was the position of "military intelligence" that such exposures never occurred.

Then, during a November 10, 1993 press briefing at the Pentagon, the Department of Defense acknowledged that the Czech government did detect chemical agents in the Southwest Asia theater of operations. After analyzing the results of the Czech report, the Department of Defense concluded that the detections were unrelated to the "mysterious health problems that have victimized some of our veterans." According to former Secretary of Defense Les Aspin, in some cases the wind was wrong and the distances too great to suggest a link. For instance, Seabees serving to the south and east of the detection site have complained of persistent health problems; but according to the Pentagon, the wind was blowing in the other direction at the time of the detections and the concentrations were too low to do harm over that kind of a distance.

The fact is, no one has ever suggested that there was a link between the Czech detections and what occurred during the early morning hours of January 19, 1991 near the Port of Jubayl. Former Defense Secretary Aspin said at the briefing that this incident could not have been from the Coalition bombings of the Iraqi chemical weapons facilities because the winds were blowing to the northwest. Yet according to available Soviet documents, the dispersal of chemical agents and other hazardous substances is controlled by other factors in addition to surface wind direction and velocity, such as topography, temperature, precipitation, vertical temperature gradient, and atmospheric humidity. These factors all contribute to the size and type of dispersal that will be observed. Unclassified visual and thermal satellite imagery confirms that the fallout from the bombings of Iraqi targets during the air and ground war moved to the southeast, with the weather patterns and upper atmospheric wind currents, towards Coalition force positions.

According to a knowledgeable source who has requested confidentiality, the Czechs believed that the detections were caused by the weather inversion which occurred that day (January 19, 1991) as the weather front moved southward. The Czechoslovak chemical detection unit reported this information to U.S. command officials immediately, but the responding units were unable to confirm their findings when they arrived, according to the Pentagon. Nonetheless, at the November 10, 1993 briefing, the Department of Defense admitted that the Czech detections were believed to be valid. The Department of Defense failed to disclose that the Czechoslovak chemical detection team also detected yperite (HD) that morning. The presence of both of these agents in such close proximity could only reasonably be the result of one of two possibilities: (1) direct Iraqi mixed agent attack, or (2) fallout from the Coalition bombings of Iraqi weapons facilities and storage bunkers.

Defense Department officials, having had possession of the Czech report for over a month, were at a loss to explain the chemical mustard agent detected by the Czechoslovak chemical detection team in the Saudi desert near King Khalid Military City on January 24, 1991. This despite the fact that both the Czechs and French claim that this detection was reported to U.S. command authorities during the Persian Gulf War. Additionally, during the Gulf War, the Czechs claimed that they detected chemical nerve agent *after a Scud missile attack.* These statements, heretofore only reported in the press, have been confirmed by a member of the U.S. 1st Cavalry Division and by an entire platoon of a U.S. Army chemical detection unit who trained with the Czechoslovak chemical detection unit near King Khalid Military City. These reports have not been addressed publicly by the Department of Defense. . . .

The contents of this report supports [*sic*] the conclusion that U.S. forces were exposed to some level of chemical and possibly biological warfare agents during their service in the Gulf War. Any review conducted by the Pentagon must extend far beyond the information being reported by the Czech Ministry of Defense. The Czech information, while important, represents just a small fraction of the evidence currently available. . . .

It is now the position of the Department of Defense that it has no other evidence that U.S. forces were exposed to chemical agents. Yet this report contains descriptions and direct eyewitness accounts that provide evidence which suggests that gas was detected, along with many other events which may have been actual attacks on U.S. forces.

This report supports the conclusion that U.S. forces were exposed to chemical agents. The assertion that the levels of nerve agent detected by the Czechs and others were not harmful is flawed. In subsequent requirements for chemical detection equipment, the Department of the Army acknowledges that the principal chemical agent detection alarm deployed during the war, the M8A1, was not sufficiently sensitive to detect sustained low levels of chemical agent and to monitor personnel for contamination. **Further, U.S. Army Material Safety Data Sheets (MSDS) indicate that chronic exposures to levels of over .0001 mg/m3 for Sarin (GB) is hazardous and requires the use of protective equipment. The *minimum* level of chemical agent required to activate the automatic chemical agent detection alarm M8A1, commonly in use during the war, exceeds this threshold by a factor of 1,000.** As the chemical agent alarms began to sound during the "air war," French, Czech, and many U.S. commanders confirmed that they were sounding from the fallout from the bombings. Over time, even at these levels, after repeatedly being told that there was no danger, many U.S. forces failed to take precautionary measures. Others report that the alarms were sounding so frequently that they were turned off. M8A1 alarms do not detect blister agents.

The findings of this report prepared at the request of Chairman Riegle detail many other events reported by U.S. servicemen and women that in some cases confirm the detection of chemical agents by U.S. forces. In other cases these reports indicate the need for further detailed investigation. But still the question remains: Is exposure to these and other chemical agents the cause of Gulf War Syndrome? We have received hundreds of reports that many of these symptoms are being experienced by family members. Numerous developments have taken place over the last several months which suggest that, while chemical agents and other environmental hazards may have contributed to the Gulf War illnesses, bacteriological, fungal, and possibly other biological illnesses may be the fundamental cause. This position is supported by the following:

First, Dr. Edward S. Hyman, a New Orleans bacteriologist, has treated a small number of the sick veterans and several of their wives for bacteriological infections, and has developed a protocol of treatment that has resulted in symptom abatement in many of his patients.

Second, during the November 10, 1993 unclassified briefing for Members of the U.S. Senate, in response to direct questioning, then Undersecretary of Defense John Deutch said that the Department of Defense was withholding classified information on the exposure of U.S. forces to biological materials. In a Department of Defense-sponsored conference on counter-proliferation, held at Los Alamos National Laboratory on 6-7 May, 1994, Dr. Deutch admitted that biological agent detection is a priority development area for the Department of Defense, since there currently is no biological agent detection system fielded with any U.S. forces anywhere in the world.

Third, the Department of Defense has named Dr. Joshua Lederberg to head its research team into the causes of Gulf War illnesses. Dr. Lederberg, among his other credits, is a Nobel Laureate and an expert in the fields of bacteriology, genetics, and biological warfare defenses.

Fourth, in detailed informational interviews conducted of 400 Gulf War veterans, it has been learned that over 3/4 of their spouses complain that they have begun to suffer from many of the same debilitating symptoms. . . .

This report includes a great number of first-hand accounts and other documentary evidence in addition to the anecdotal information that appeared in the print and electronic media during the Gulf War. It establishes convincingly that the Department of Defense assertions are inaccurate. We believe there is reliable evidence that U.S. forces were exposed to chemical and possibly biological agents. But regardless of whether U.S. forces were exposed or not, the entire official body of information, including all classified or heretofore unpublished information, available research data sets, case histories, and diagnostic breakdown information must be made available to independent civilian medical researchers in order to further the research into the causes of and treatments for these illnesses. *Absent a release of information by the Department of Defense of the science which forms the bases for their theories, the Department of Defense position must be viewed by qualified scientists as anecdotal and unsubstantiated.*

Given that there is also a growing body of evidence indicating that spouses and children of Gulf War veterans are vulnerable to similar illnesses, the Department of Defense must now share all of its information with civilian, nongovernmental researchers. These family members are civilians who may be at risk. This illness was first reported over three years ago.

On February 9, 1994, Chairman Riegle sent a letter to Secretary of Defense William Perry asking that he release all U.S. military personnel from any oath of secrecy they may have taken regarding classified information specifically pertaining to chemical or biological warfare agent exposure in the Persian Gulf theater. This request was based on a recommendation of the National Academy of Sciences, National Institute of Medicine in their 1993 publication *Veterans at Risk: The Health Effects of Mustard Gas and Lewisite*. On May 4, 1994, the Secretaries of Defense, Health and Human Services, and Veterans Affairs responded to the Chairman's letter stating that there was no classified information on chemical or biological detections or exposures. This directly contradicts the statement of Deputy Secretary Deutch in his November 10, 1993 unclassified briefing to Members and staff.

Why isn't the Department of Defense aggressively pursuing the answers to the questions surrounding the events which may have caused illnesses being suffered by many Gulf War veterans? One possible explanation lies in a 1982 article. Then Senate Armed Services Committee Chairman John Tower wrote, "Chemical training in the United States armed forces is, at best, perfunctory. It is rarely conducted in a simulated contaminated environment and stocks of individual protective equipment are too limited, and therefore too valuable, to risk them in the numbers necessary to allow troops to operate in them for realistic training. As a result, most U.S. personnel are relegated to a minimal and highly artificial exposure to the problems and hardships entailed in performing their respective combat missions should they have to 'button up'." As numerous U.S. General Accounting Office (GAO) reports have noted, the U.S. was not much better prepared prior to the Gulf War than it was when Senator Tower wrote his article.

According to Senator Tower, "Our greatest casualties will not be caused by direct exposure to chemical agents, but by the physical and mental disruption their use will cause our tactical planning and deployment. Certainly, physical on-the-ground contamination and casualties will exist, but their most decisive effect will be their mental intimidation and our unwillingness to operate in the chemical environment. This lack of confidence in our ability to operate in such conditions could be rapidly exploited by Soviet units having no such qualms." This lack of confidence could also have been exploited by the Soviet-trained Iraqi forces, who have an extensive history in the use of chemical and biological warfare.

If the Department of Defense intended to conceal these exposures during the Gulf War to avoid the physical and mental disruption their use would have had on our tactical planning and deployment, their actions would have been understandable. Hoping to avoid responsibility for the casualties of this conflict, however, is quite another matter. Our afflicted veterans are sick and suffering, and some have died. Others are now destitute, having spent tens of thousands of dollars, depleting their life savings, in an unsuccessful search for an explanation for their ailments. Our enemies surely know the extent of our vulnerabilities. They would not hesitate to exploit them, nor would they hesitate to reveal them to others. The veterans of the Gulf War have asked us for nothing more than the assistance they have earned. Our refusal to come to their immediate assistance can only lead others to question the integrity of the nation they serve.

The following is a summary of the findings and recommendations of this report:

Findings

1. Iraq had a highly-developed chemical warfare program with:
   - numerous large production facilities;
   - binary (precursor chemical/solvent) capabilities;
   - stockpiled agents and weapons;
   - multiple and varied delivery systems; and,
   - a documented history of chemical warfare agent use.

2. Iraq had an offensive biological weapons program with:
   - multiple research/production facilities;
   - evidence of weaponization experimentation; and,
   - a history of reported but unconfirmed use.

3. The United States provided the Government of Iraq with "dual use" licensed materials which assisted in the development of Iraqi chemical, biological, and missile-system programs, including:
   - chemical warfare agent precursors;
   - chemical warfare agent production facility plans and technical drawings (provided as pesticide production facility plans);
   - chemical warhead filling equipment;
   - biological warfare related materials;
   - missile fabrication equipment; and,
   - missile-system guidance equipment.

4. The United States military planned for the use of chemical and biological weapons by Iraq by:
   - discussing the chemical/biological threat in pre-war threat assessments;
   - designating chemical/biological production facilities priority bombing targets;
   - assigning a very high priority to SCUD missile units; and,
   - conferring with the U.S. national laboratories about the hazards associated with the bombings of the chemical, biological, nuclear weapons facilities.

5. The United States military made preparations for the expected use of chemical/biological weapons by Iraq, including:
   - acquiring German-made FOX NBC detection surveillance vehicles shortly before the war;
   - deploying as part of standard operating procedure, automatic chemical agent alarms, chemical agent detection equipment, chemical decontamination equipment, and chemical agent protection suits, gloves, boots, and masks;
   - administering anthrax vaccines, an experimental botulinum toxin

vaccine, and pyridostigmine bromide as a nerve agent pretreatment pill; and,

- preparing and using personnel medical questionnaires asking soldiers departing the theater about their health and whether or not they believed they were exposed to chemical or germ warfare.

U.S. General Accounting Office reports issued after the war noted deficiencies in U.S. military medical preparations for chemical/biological warfare, including potential shortages of vaccines, NBC equipment, and NBC capability.

6. United States and Coalition Forces did detect chemical warfare agents in conjunction with definable events, including:
    - multiple chemical alarms sounding repeatedly with the onset of the air war, and directly attributed by multiple official and unofficial sources to the fallout from the bombings of Iraqi chemical facilities;
    - multiple chemical agent alarm soundings and chemical detections after both missile attacks or otherwise unexplained explosions;
    - Czechoslovak, French, and British unit detections and reporting of chemical/biological agents in the air, in puddles on the ground, after SCUD attacks, and from artillery or chemical mine explosions;
    - U.S. units detected and/or reported chemical agents in the air, as a result of SCUD missile attacks, after artillery or mine explosions, and from Iraqi munitions bunkers;
    - multiple eyewitness reporting and corroboration of a number of direct attacks as well as ongoing alarms due to fallout from the Coalition bombings; and,
    - news reports during the war confirming that U.S. units made detections of chemical agents which they believed were the result of Coalition bombings.

7. U.S. and Coalition Forces were exposed to fallout from Coalition bombings of Iraqi chemical, biological, and nuclear facilities, as evidenced by:
    - pre-war concerns requiring consultations with the U.S. national laboratories regarding the fallout expected from the bombings;
    - post-war assessments of the degree of damage to these facilities and the quantities of agents which survived the Coalition attacks;
    - official weather documents showing a continual movement from Iraq of weather patterns down across Coalition troop emplacements throughout the air and ground wars;
    - chemical alarms that began sounding nearly contemporaneous with the initiation of the air war, and actual chemical detections confirming the reasons for the alarm soundings; and,
    - then Secretary of Defense Aspin's December 1993 comments that the U.S. needed to develop bombs that could target chemical and biological warfare facilities without releasing large amounts of agent into the air.

8. Wartime and post-war discoveries support the conclusion that Iraq had chemical and possibly biological weapons deployed with front line units and was prepared to use them, as evidenced by:
   - UNSCOM findings of large and well-financed chemical and biological warfare programs, including large stocks of missiles, artillery, aerial bombs, rockets, and mines;
   - U.S. military unit reports of finding chemical munitions in the forward area, including artillery, mines, and bulk agents;
   - captured Iraqi documents purportedly containing orders to use chemical weapons (documents currently being independently verified);
   - reported British intercepts of Iraqi communications giving orders to use chemical weapons at the onset of the ground war; and,
   - UNSCOM reports of the discovery and subsequent destruction of 28 Scuds with chemical agent warheads—obtained from the Soviet Union.

9. Use of biological weapons during the war can only be inferred at this time because:
   - no biological agent detectors are available for or fielded with any U.S. or Coalition forces;
   - no samples are known to have been collected in situ or from sick military personnel or animals for testing for the presence of biological agents; and,
   - current test results from sick veterans and contaminated equipment are not yet publicly available.

10. The symptomology of the Gulf War veterans is consistent with exposure to a chemical/biological exposure explanation, illustrated by:
    - large body of common symptoms; and,
    - distribution of illness that appears related to source of exposures, whether by proximity to an explosion, fallout, reaction to pills, contact with EPWs, contact with contaminated vehicles and equipment, or prolonged exposure to sick veterans.

Recommendations

1. All classified information regarding events before, during, and after the war relating to:
   - the nature of Iraqi chemical and biological warfare development programs,
   - the deployment of these materials, the location of Iraqi chemical/biological forces, equipment and weapons;
   - the intentional use of, inadvertent dispersal of, and destruction of Iraqi chemical and biological warfare agents; and,

- the detection or confirmation of chemical or biological agents should be immediately reviewed for declassification and released by the Department of Defense.

2. The massive amounts of testing data already collected by the Department of Defense and the Department of Veterans Affairs relating to the complaints of Persian Gulf War veterans should be made available to medical researchers and physicians treating these veterans and their family members.

3. A thorough and detailed epidemiological study involving all Gulf War veterans should be conducted by the Department of Defense to determine the origins and causes of the illnesses and the reported transmission of the symptoms to family members.

4. Independent testing of samples is needed from:
   - ground sites in Iraq and Kuwait;
   - sick veterans and affected family members; and,
   - contaminated equipment.

5. A post-conflict assessment of the impact of administration of cholinesterase inhibitors in a nerve agent pre-treatment program should be conducted. Particular attention should be focused on the potential synergistic or even potentiation effects administration of these drugs might produce when combined with other hazardous exposures.

6. Presumption of service-connection for the purposes of medical treatment and determining disability, compensation and vocational rehabilitation eligibility (until a diagnostic protocol can be established).

7. The Department of Veterans Affairs claims and appeals process must be streamlined.

8. Government financed health care (when no other medical insurance is available) for spouses and children determined to have contracted a service-connected illness from a Gulf War veteran.

9. Development of appropriate diagnostic and treatment protocols both on the battlefield and in identifying post-conflict casualties.

10. Greater efforts to develop NBC detectors, vaccines, personnel protective equipment, and decontamination equipment.

PAPAL LETTER REAFFIRMING BAN ON FEMALE PRIESTS
May 30, 1994

In an effort to remove "all doubt" regarding "a matter of great importance," Pope John Paul II wrote a letter to Catholic bishops reaffirming the church's position that women could not be ordained as priests. Church officials said the letter, which was dated May 22 and publicly released May 30, was designed to halt the debate over women becoming priests.

". . . I declare that the Church has no authority whatsoever to confer priestly ordination on women and that this judgment is to be definitively held by all the Church's faithful," the pope wrote. Some church officials said the letter's strong wording would make it difficult—and perhaps impossible—for a future pope to reverse the ban. The pope said he wrote the letter because, despite the church's longstanding position against female priests, "at the present time in some places it is nonetheless considered still open to debate."

The ban on female priests was not meant to discriminate against women, the pope said. "[T]he non-admission of women to priestly ordination cannot mean that women are of lesser dignity, nor can it be construed as discrimination against them," he wrote. "Rather, it is to be seen as the faithful observance of a plan to be ascribed to the wisdom of the Lord of the universe." He also wrote that while women could not become priests, their role in the "life and mission of the Church" remained "absolutely necessary and irreplaceable."

The church policy against ordaining women as priests is based on the fact that when Christ chose his apostles, he only selected men. Nuns and Catholic lay women who oppose the policy said Christ was simply adhering to cultural norms of his time, and that the church should update its policy so that men and women are treated equally.

In the United States, some church officials tried to smooth over any hard feelings that the pope's letter might have caused. Archbishop William H. Keeler of Baltimore, president of the National Conference of Catholic Bish-

ops, released a comment addressing "all those who might find this further affirmation of the church's authentic teaching difficult to accept." He asked them "to accept it lovingly" and to "pray for understanding."

Vatican Rejects Gender-Neutral Catechism

The letter became public only three days after the Vatican released the English translation of a new catechism. As submitted to the church, the catechism used gender-neutral language that, for example, referred to "humanity" instead of to "man." However, the gender-neutral language was removed before the Vatican released the document.

The letter and catechism were released at the same time that the pope and other church leaders were engaged in a fierce attack on the upcoming United Nations population conference in Cairo, Egypt. Church officials objected to proposals circulated before the conference that called for empowering women and for making abortion safe. In a meeting June 14 in Rome, the church's cardinals approved a measure stating that the proposals would legitimize "abortion on demand, sexual promiscuity and distorted notions of the family." At the Cairo conference, the Vatican was unable to muster strong support for its position. (UN Conference on World Population, p. 351)

At the same time the cardinals were meeting, the Pontifical Academy of Sciences—a lay panel associated with the church—released a report supporting efforts to halt population growth worldwide. The panel said there was an "unavoidable need to contain births globally." The document did not mention specific means of birth control, but the only method allowed by the church is sexual abstinence during ovulation. According to the New York Times, the report infuriated Pope John Paul II.

Synod Approves Greater Role for Nuns

In late October, a synod of Catholic bishops and others summoned to Rome by the pope announced that nuns would be given an increased role in running the church. However, the new policy gave no details about what role women would have, and it still appeared to block nuns from the highest positions in the church bureaucracy. American representatives were unhappy about the limited move, saying the synod was stacked against women because only 59 of the 348 participants were women. Some priests from Third World countries denounced any move to increase women's role in the church, attacking the idea as "cultural imperialism" originating in the United States. Only days before the decision was announced, four American nuns and their supporters staged a brief protest in St. Peter's Square. The nuns, who raised banners saying "They are talking about us without us" and "Women want to be a part, not apart," were quickly taken away by police, who released them after checking their identification.

American bishops who hoped to reach out to women suffered another blow in November when the Vatican rejected a gender-neutral Bible that the bishops had approved three years earlier. The new Bible had been translated by Catholic and Protestant scholars.

Following is the text of the letter from Pope John Paul II to Catholic bishops titled "Reserving Priestly Ordination to Men Alone," dated May 22, 1994, and released May 30, 1994:

Venerable Brothers in the Episcopate,

1. Priestly ordination, which hands on the office entrusted by Christ to his Apostles of teaching, sanctifying, and governing the faithful, has in the Catholic Church from the beginning always been reserved to men alone. This tradition has also been faithfully maintained by the Oriental Churches.

When the question of the ordination of women arose in the Anglican Communion, Pope Paul VI, out of fidelity to his office of safeguarding the Apostolic Tradition, and also with a view to removing a new obstacle placed in the way of Christian unity, reminded Anglicans of the position of the Catholic Church: "She holds that it is not admissible to ordain women to the priesthood, for very fundamental reasons. These reasons include: the example recorded in the Sacred Scriptures of Christ choosing his Apostles only from among men; the constant practice of the Church, which has imitated Christ in choosing only men; and her living teaching authority which has consistently held that the exclusion of women from the priesthood is in accordance with God's plan for his Church."

But since the question had also become the subject of debate among theologians and in certain Catholic circles, Paul VI directed the Congregation for the Doctrine of the Faith to set forth and expound the teaching of the Church on this matter. This was done through the Declaration *Inter Insigniores*, which the Supreme Pontiff approved and ordered to be published.

2. The Declaration recalls and explains the fundamental reasons for this teaching, reasons expounded by Paul VI, and concludes that the Church "does not consider herself authorized to admit women to priestly ordination." To these fundamental reasons the document adds other theological reasons which illustrate the appropriateness of the divine provision, and it also shows clearly that Christ's way of acting did not proceed from sociological or cultural motives peculiar to his time. As Paul VI later explained: "The real reason is that, in giving the Church her fundamental constitution, her theological anthropology—thereafter always followed by the Church's Tradition—Christ established things in this way."

In the Apostolic Letter *Mulieris Dignitatem*, I myself wrote in this regard: "In calling only men as his Apostles, Christ acted in a completely free and sovereign manner. In doing so, he exercised the same freedom with which, in all his behavior, he emphasized the dignity and the vocation of women, without conforming to the prevailing customs and to the traditions sanctioned by the legislation of the time."

In fact, the Gospels and the Acts of the Apostles attest that this call was made in accordance with God's eternal plan: Christ chose those whom he willed, and he did so in union with the Father, "through the Holy Spirit," after having spent the night in prayer. Therefore, in granting admission to the ministerial priesthood, the Church has always acknowledged as a perennial norm her Lord's way of acting in choosing the twelve men whom he made the foundation of his Church. These men did not in fact receive only a function which could thereafter be exercised by any member of the Church; rather they were specifically and intimately associated in the mission of the Incarnate Word himself. The Apostles did the same when they chose fellow workers who would succeed them in their ministry. Also included in this choice were those who, throughout the time of the Church, would carry on the Apostles' mission of representing Christ the Lord and Redeemer.

3. Furthermore, the fact that the Blessed Virgin Mary, Mother of God and Mother of the Church, received neither the mission proper to the Apostles nor the ministerial priesthood clearly shows that the non-admission of women to priestly ordination cannot mean that women are of lesser dignity, nor can it be construed as discrimination against them. Rather, it is to be seen as the faithful observance of a plan to be ascribed to the wisdom of the Lord of the universe.

The presence and the role of women in the life and mission of the Church, although not linked to the ministerial priesthood, remain absolutely necessary and irreplaceable. As the Declaration *Inter Insigniores* points out, "the Church desires that Christian women should become fully aware of the greatness of their mission: today their role is of capital importance both for the renewal and humanization of society and for the rediscovery by believers of the true face of the church." The New Testament and the whole history of the Church give ample evidence of the presence in the Church of women, true disciples, witnesses to Christ in the family and in society, as well as in total consecration to the service of God and of the Gospel. "By defending the dignity of women and their vocation, the Church has shown honor and gratitude for those women who—faithful to the Gospel—have shared in every age in the apostolic mission of the whole People of God. They are the holy martyrs, virgins, and the mothers of families, who bravely bore witness to their faith and passed on the Church's faith and tradition by bringing up their children in the spirit of the Gospel."

Moreover, it is to the holiness of the faithful that the hierarchical structure of the Church is totally ordered. For this reason, the Declaration *Inter Insigniores* recalls: "The only better gift, which can and must be desired, is love. The greatest in the Kingdom of Heaven are not the ministers but the saints."

4. Although the teaching that priestly ordination is to be reserved to men alone has been preserved by the constant and universal Tradition of the Church and firmly taught by the Magisterium in its more recent documents, at the present time in some places it is nonetheless considered still open to debate, or the Church's judgment that women are not to be admitted to ordination is considered to have a merely disciplinary force.

Wherefore, in order that all doubt may be removed regarding a matter of great importance, a matter which pertains to the Church's divine constitution itself, in virtue of my ministry of confirming the brethren I declare that the

Church has no authority whatsoever to confer priestly ordination on women and that this judgment is to be definitively held by all the Church's faithful.

Invoking an abundance of divine assistance upon you, venerable Brothers, and upon all the faithful, I impart my Apostolic Blessing.

From the Vatican, on 22 May, the Solemnity of Pentecost, in the year 1994, the sixteenth of my Pontificate.

John Paul II

INDICTMENT OF
REP. DAN ROSTENKOWSKI
May 31, 1994

On May 31, 1994, a federal grand jury indicted Rep. Dan Rostenkowski (D-Ill.), who as chairman of the House Ways and Means Committee was one of the most powerful men in Washington, D.C. Rostenkowski, who entered the House in 1958 and was a close ally of President Bill Clinton, was indicted on seventeen counts that alleged he had embezzled more than $500,000 from his expense accounts. He was charged with putting people on his government payroll who did little or no official work, stealing cash by disguising transactions at the House Post Office as stamp purchases, using taxpayer money to buy thousands of dollars in gifts for friends, buying personal vehicles with government money, and obstructing justice. The indictment charged that the crimes occurred over a period of more than twenty years.

"The allegations contained in today's indictment represent a betrayal of the public trust for personal gain," said U.S. Attorney Eric H. Holder Jr. at a press conference where the indictment was announced. Rostenkowski and his lawyers did not comment on the indictment. In a statement released several days earlier, the sixty-six-year-old lawmaker said he would fight any charges that might be filed against him. "Truth is on my side," he said.

Rostenkowski's legal fate remained up in the air as 1994 ended, but his political fate was sealed. In the November election the voters of his Chicago district ousted him from office in favor of a political unknown, an ignominious end for a man known in Washington as the master deal maker.

Investigation Started in 1991

A grand jury started examining Rostenkowski after federal prosecutors initiated a probe of possible illegal acts at the House of Representatives Post Office. The investigation, which started in 1991, initially focused on allegations of embezzlement and drug use by low-level employees. The probe later expanded after evidence was uncovered that members of Congress were stealing cash under the pretense of making official stamp purchases. In 1993, Robert V. Rota, the former House postmaster, pleaded guilty to embezzlement charges and said Rostenkowski was involved in the cash-for-stamps plot. The investigation of Rostenkowski later widened to examine numerous expenditures by the representative's office, the hiring of employees for his Chicago office, and his use of government cars.

In February 1994, Rostenkowski reimbursed the federal government $82,000 for office supplies purchased with taxpayer funds. In a letter released by his lawyer, Rostenkowski admitted using his official expense account to purchase unspecified items at the House stationery store for his personal use. House rules forbid such purchases. In his letter, Rostenkowski said the purchases occurred inadvertently. The reimbursement was made with checks drawn on Rostenkowski's personal and campaign accounts and covered purchases made during the previous six years.

Efforts at Plea Bargain Fail

By mid-May, attorneys for Rostenkowski had asked federal prosecutors about the possibility of negotiating a plea bargain that would allow Rostenkowski to keep his chairmanship of the House Ways and Means Committee. They wanted to avoid a felony indictment, which under House Democratic Caucus rules would force Rostenkowski to immediately give up his chairmanship.

Federal prosecutors, apparently comfortable with their case and wary of making a deal that might look like they were favoring the president's friend, would not comply. They reportedly wanted Rostenkowski to plead guilty to one or more felony counts, a move that almost certainly would result in him being imprisoned. Only days before the indictment, Rostenkowski rejected a plea agreement worked out by his attorney under which he would have served jail time.

No one was surprised by the indictment, but Rostenkowski's allies were shocked by the extent of the allegations against him. The charges were far more extensive and serious than had been previously believed.

The indictment was a serious blow for Clinton, who had expected that Rostenkowski would help him push health care and welfare reform plans through Congress. With the indictment, Rostenkowski lost his chairmanship and thus his platform for helping the president. The indictment also hurt Congress by feeding the cynical view of many Americans that members of Congress routinely abused their offices for personal gain.

In June, Rostenkowski entered a not guilty plea. After the court hearing, he vowed to fight the charges. "Talk is cheap," he said. "Allegations come easily. In court, they will be subjected to a higher standard. And when all is said and done, they will fail the test and I will be vindicated."

In the fall campaign, Rostenkowski hoped that his power and ability to deliver federal money to Chicago would get him quietly reelected. Most political observers thought he was a shoo-in. Thus, Chicago was shocked when thirty-two-year-old Michael Patrick Flanagan, a personal injury lawyer who ran virtually no campaign and received almost no help from national Republican organizations, easily defeated Rostenkowski.

As 1994 ended, Rostenkowski was reportedly looking for work so he could pay more than $500,000 in pending legal bills. In an interview with the Chicago Sun-Times, Rostenkowski said he had already used up a $1 million campaign fund and a $1 million legal defense fund. The New York Times reported earlier in the year that much of the money for the defense fund was contributed in 1993 by powerful interests that had business before the House Ways and Means Committee, which Rostenkowski chaired at the time.

Following is the text of a statement by U.S. Attorney Eric Holder Jr. on May 31, 1994, announcing the indictment of Rep. Dan Rostenkowski (D-Ill.), as reported by Reuters:

Earlier today a federal grand jury sitting here in Washington, D.C., indicted Congressman Daniel Rostenkowski on 17 felony counts, including embezzlement, mail and wire fraud, concealing material facts, conspiracy, and witness tampering. According to the indictment, Congressman Rostenkowski engaged in a pattern of corrupt activity for more than 20 years and embezzled hundreds of thousands of taxpayers' dollars from his congressional expense allowances in order to enrich himself, his family, and his friends.

Today's indictment represents a dramatic step forward in the investigation into criminal activity at the United States House of Representatives post office. The indictment alleges that Congressman Rostenkowski violated the law by abusing his congressional allowances in the following manner:

One. He regularly put people on his congressional payroll who did little or no official work but who instead performed a variety of personal services for him, his family, his family insurance businesses, and his campaign organizations. Government payments to these people exceeded one-half million dollars. He converted at least $50,000 in cash from the House post office by disguising transactions there as stamp purchases. He charged Congress, and ultimately the taxpayers, more than $40,000 for the purchase of valuable merchandise, including hand-painted chairs, crystal sculptures, and fine china, which he handed out as gifts to his friends. He caused Congress to pay over $70,000 for personal vehicles used by himself and his family. And finally, he obstructed justice by instructing a witness to withhold evidence from the grand jury that was investigating this matter.

I will now explain each part of the scheme in greater depth.

One, the congressional payroll. Today's indictment alleges that Congressman Rostenkowski violated the law by abusing his congressional payroll in a variety of ways. Between July of 1971 and July of 1992, the congressman placed at least—at least—14 people on his payroll who did little or no congressional work. Instead, most of these so-called employees performed personal services for him and his family or performed campaign-related activities.

For example, the indictment alleges that Rostenkowski put one person on the congressional payroll in exchange for that person's taking photographs at his daughters' weddings, at parties held at the family's residence in Wisconsin, and at political fundraisers. That person received approximately $20,000 in government salary payments. Another person, who later became the congressman's son-in-law, performed no work and was required to give a portion of the money he received back to Congressman Rostenkowski. A third person, who performed no congressional work, was paid $48,000 over a four-year period during the same time that that person's father had two of Rostenkowski's daughters on his payroll, where they were also paid a total of $48,000.

A fourth person was paid in congressional funds in exchange for renovating and remodeling Rostenkowski's home in Chicago. A fifth person received $61,000 over a 20-year period in which she kept the books for the Rostenkowski family insurance company. And a sixth person was paid with taxpayer money to mow the lawn at Rostenkowski's vacation home in Wisconsin.

Many of these people cashed the checks they received and were obligated to give this money to the manager of the congressman's office in Chicago. By putting these people and others on the congressional payroll and by falsely certifying that they had performed official duties, Congressman Rostenkowski misappropriated as much as $500,000 in United States taxpayer funds.

Two, the House Stationery Store. The indictment further alleges that Congressman Rostenkowski obtained from the House Stationery Store more than $40,000 worth of valuable merchandise, most of which he then handed out as gifts to personal friends and to associates. He charged the items to his official expense allowance, causing taxpayers to pay for them based on his false representation that the items were being purchased for official use.

In 1990 and '91, the congressman used his official expense allowance to obtain over 60 wooden armchairs, handpainted and inscribed with his name, and valued at over $23,000. In 1991 and '92, he similarly obtained over 60 crystal sculptures of the United States Capitol Building, totaling over $12,000. Between 1988 and 1992, he obtained over 250 pieces of fine china, costing over $5,000, and also charged it to his official account. In an 18-month period from April of 1990 to October of 1992, he charged over 26 pieces of luggage, costing over $2,200, to his official account.

Although none of these items were used for official congressional business, all were charged to Congressman Rostenkowski's official expense allowance.

Obstruction of justice, the third area. The indictment alleges that Congressman Rostenkowski obstructed justice by instructing a witness to withhold evidence from the grand jury. In 1991 Rostenkowski asked a House employee, whom he had placed on his congressional payroll earlier in the year, to engrave 50 brass plaques and to place them on the bases of 50 crystal sculptures of the United States Capitol.

The employee did the work as requested. In September of 1993, the engraver received a subpoena to testify before the federal grand jury sitting here in Washington, D.C., that was investigating possible criminal violations by Congressman Rostenkowski. The engraver went to see the congressman's administrative assistant in Washington, who had earlier told him that Rostenkowski's campaign committee was paying for lawyers for people who were called to testify before the grand jury.

After putting the engraver in contact with an attorney, the administrative assistant then told the engraver that Congressman Rostenkowski wished to speak to him. Over the telephone, the congressman instructed the engraver not to say anything to the grand jury about the crystal sculptures of the Capitol that he engraved for the congressman. In telling the engraver to withhold information from the grand jury, information about possible criminal conduct, the indictment alleges that Congressman Rostenkowski attempted to obstruct the grand jury's investigation.

Four, the House post office. To purchase postage stamps from the House post office, members of Congress are required to submit vouchers which must be signed by the member certifying that he or she has paid for or received the postage specified on the voucher. According to the indictment, on numerous occasions between 1978 and 1991, Congressman Rostenkowski instructed Robert Rota, the House postmaster, to give him cash in exchange for vouchers and for stamps. On some occasions Mr. Rostenkowski used his official expense allowance to buy large amounts of stamps but then later exchanged them for cash. On other occasions, he obtained cash from the House postmaster directly in exchange for postal vouchers. On each occasion, the congressman personally told the House postmaster how much cash he wanted and personally handled the vouchers for the stamps. During the two-year period from May of 1985 through May of 1987, Congressman Rostenkowski personally obtained $11,500 in House post office cash from the House postmaster.

In addition to using postage vouchers to steal cash from Congress, it is alleged that Mr. Rostenkowski cashed checks at the House post office which were written on the bank accounts of two political committees that he controlled. The congressman caused the checks he cashed to be reported to the Federal Election Commission as postage expenditures rather than as cash expenditures. By these means, Congressman Rostenkowski secretly and unlawfully obtained approximately $28,000 in cash.

Five, vehicle purchases. The indictment also alleges that between 1986 and 1992, Congressman Rostenkowski obtained seven vehicles with a value of over $100,000 from a suburban Chicago dealership. The congressman had a unique relationship with this dealership, enabling him to obtain immediate possession of and clear title to the vehicles without paying for them at the time of purchase. Instead Mr. Rostenkowski had a revolving credit account at the dealership permitting him to acquire the vehicles without making any down payment from his personal funds, without taking out a loan, without signing any promissory notes, without making regular payments, and without paying any interest on his outstanding debt.

Congressman Rostenkowski obtained these vehicles for the personal use of his friends—I'm sorry, of himself and for his family, and yet he only made a single personal payment to the car dealership of $5,294 from the bank account of one of his daughters. The remainder of the debt was paid from two sources—the House of Representatives and the congressman's campaign committee. Between 1987 and 1992, Congressman Rostenkowski caused the House of Representatives to pay $73,500 to the dealership, all of which was credited to his personal automobile account. The remainder of the $100,000 debt at the Ford dealership was paid by the congressman's political campaign committee. Mr. Rostenkowski caused that committee to pay over $28,000 to the dealership, which again was credited to his personal account.

The allegations contained in today's indictment represent a betrayal of the public trust for personal gain. In essence, this indictment alleges that Congressman Rostenkowski used his elective office to perpetrate an extensive fraud on the American people. The wrongful expenditure of taxpayer dollars by and at the behest of Congressman Rostenkowski rolls into the hundreds of thousands of dollars. This is not, as some have suggested, a petty matter, but in a larger sense, the true cost of such corruption by elected officials cannot be measured solely in dollar amounts, no matter how high this total. Rather the cost of such misconduct must also be measured in terms of the corrosive effect it has on our democratic system of government and on the trust our citizens have in their elected officials.

Let me be clear. Historically and presently, the vast majority of the members of Congress have been and are decent and honorable public officials who work incredibly hard and follow all of the rules. These women and men are as appalled by such acts of corruption as anyone else. But the criminal acts of a few feed the cynicism which increasingly haunts our political landscape. It causes too many of our citizens to assume that all persons in public life are motivated by greed and self-interest, and to succumb to the defeatist notion that we must resign ourselves to the fact that a certain level of political misconduct is a way of life. I reject that notion that there is an acceptable level of corruption. As a society, we must be committed to a policy of zero tolerance when it comes to official misconduct. Otherwise, its corrosive effect will undermine the very principles upon which this nation stands.

Therefore, today's indictment of Congressman Rostenkowski should stand as a firm and solemn reminder that the Department of Justice has an unwavering commitment to hold accountable all those who engage in corruption—regardless of their political position, regardless of their political party, and regardless of their political power.

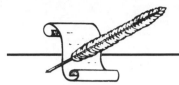

June

SUPREME COURT ON RESIDENTIAL SIGNS
June 13, 1994

In an important First Amendment decision, the Supreme Court ruled unanimously June 13 that cities cannot bar residents from putting up signs on their property.

The case began in December 1990 when Margaret P. Gilleo, who owned a home in the St. Louis, Missouri, suburb of Ladue, placed a sign in her front yard that said, "Say No to War in the Persian Gulf, Call Congress Now." At the time, U.S. intervention against Iraq was imminent. The first sign disappeared. After a replacement was knocked down, Gilleo called the police. They told her such signs were illegal in the city, and the City Council denied her petition for a variance. Gilleo then put an 8.5 × 11-inch sign in a window of her home that said, "For Peace in the Gulf," and filed suit against the city alleging that its sign ordinance violated her First Amendment right to free speech.

The sign ordinance in Ladue, a city described in press accounts as "wealthy," "elegant," and "pristine," barred residents from posting signs on their property other than "for sale" signs and small residential identification signs. Churches, other religious institutions, and schools were allowed to post signs, as were firms in the community's business district. The ordinance stated that the "proliferation of an unlimited number of signs . . . would create ugliness, visual blight and clutter," in addition to lowering property values, harming the community's privacy and "special ambience," and causing safety and traffic hazards.

Lower Courts Rule Against Ordinance

Two lower federal courts struck down the sign ordinance, ruling that it improperly gave preferential treatment to commercial signs over signs such as Gilleo's, which advocated a political view. The courts said the ordinance was unconstitutional because it discriminated based on the signs' messages. The city of Ladue then appealed to the Supreme Court.

The Supreme Court justices agreed with the lower courts' decisions but rejected their reasoning. The justices said the ordinance was unconstitutional because it prohibited too much speech that was protected by the First Amendment. This reasoning was much broader than that used by the lower courts.

Writing for the Court, Justice John Paul Stevens said that the lower courts' emphasis on content did not go far enough. Under the lower courts' reasoning, Stevens wrote, theoretically the city could simply change its ordinance to ban all signs. That would eliminate the discrimination based on content but would still leave Gilleo unable to post her sign, thus violating her First Amendment rights.

Court Cites Importance of Signs

Stevens wrote that the city's ordinance had "almost completely foreclosed a venerable means of communication that is both unique and important." He also rejected the city's contention that the sign ordinance simply regulated the "time, place, or manner" of speech because residents were still free to express themselves through hand-held signs, bumper stickers, letters, flyers, telephone calls, newspaper advertisements, speeches, and community meetings. Stevens wrote that no adequate substitutes existed for signs posted at a person's home. "Residential signs are an unusually cheap and convenient form of communication," he wrote. "Especially for persons of modest means or limited mobility, a yard or window sign may have no practical substitute. . . . Even for the affluent, the added costs in money or time of taking out a newspaper advertisement, handing out leaflets on the street, or standing in front of one's house with a hand-held sign may make the difference between participating and not participating in some public debate."

The decision still left Ladue and other cities free to regulate residential signs, Stevens wrote, as long as the regulations were not too broad. "We are confident that more temperate measures could in large part satisfy Ladue's stated regulatory needs without harm to the First Amendment rights of its citizens," Stevens wrote. He also noted that residents had strong personal incentives to avoid visual clutter so that their property values would not be harmed. "Residents' self-interest diminishes the danger of the 'unlimited' proliferation of residential signs that concerns the City of Ladue," he wrote.

Justice Sandra Day O'Connor wrote a separate concurring opinion. She said the Court should have used the analysis adopted by the two lower courts, which examined whether the ordinance discriminated based on the signs' messages.

In the case, municipal organizations including the National League of Cities and the U.S. Conference of Mayors backed Ladue's position. They said the city's ordinance was simply aimed at halting the proliferation of signs, not at blocking certain messages.

The Court's decision seemed in little doubt after oral arguments in the case in February. The justices repeatedly poked fun at the ordinance, with

Justice Antonin Scalia tangling with the city's lawyer, Jordan B. Cherrick, over a part of the ordinance that allowed residents to hang flags bearing messages of any kind—but only if the flags were rectangular. The ordinance did not allow triangular flags. "That's a pretty stupid judgment," Scalia said. "I don't understand the sense of it at all. Isn't that irrational?"

Following are excerpts from the Supreme Court's decision of June 13, 1994, in the case of City of Ladue v. Gilleo, *in which it struck down a city ordinance that had barred most residential signs:*

No. 92-1856

City of Ladue, et al., Petitioners v. Margaret P. Gilleo	On writ of certiorari to the United States Court of Appeals for the Eighth Circuit

[June 13, 1994]

JUSTICE STEVENS delivered the opinion of the Court.

An ordinance of the City of Ladue prohibits homeowners from displaying any signs on their property except "residence identification" signs, "for sale" signs, and signs warning of safety hazards. The ordinance permits commercial establishments, churches, and nonprofit organizations to erect certain signs that are not allowed at residences. The question presented is whether the ordinance violates a Ladue resident's right to free speech.

I

Respondent Margaret P. Gilleo owns one of the 57 single-family homes in the Willow Hill subdivision of Ladue. On December 8, 1990, she placed on her front lawn a 24- by 36-inch sign printed with the words "Say No to War in the Persian Gulf, Call Congress Now." After that sign disappeared, Gilleo put up another but it was knocked to the ground. When Gilleo reported these incidents to the police, they advised her that such signs were prohibited in Ladue. The City Council denied her petition for a variance. Gilleo then filed this action under 42 U. S. C. 1983 against the City, the Mayor, and members of the City Council, alleging that Ladue's sign ordinance violated her First Amendment right of free speech.

The District Court issued a preliminary injunction against enforcement of the ordinance. Gilleo then placed an 8.5- by 11-inch sign in the second story window of her home stating, "For Peace in the Gulf." The Ladue City Council responded to the injunction by repealing its ordinance and enacting a replacement. Like its predecessor, the new ordinance contains a general prohibition of "signs" and defines that term broadly. The ordinance prohibits all signs except those that fall within one of ten exemptions. Thus, "residential identification signs" no larger than one square foot are allowed, as are signs advertising "that the property is for sale, lease or exchange" and identifying the owner or agent. Also exempted are signs "for churches, religious institutions, and schools," "[c]ommercial signs in commercially or industrial zoned districts," and on-site signs advertising "gasoline filling stations." Unlike its predecessor, the new ordinance contains a lengthy "Declaration of Findings, Policies, Interests, and Purposes," part of which recites that the "proliferation of an unlimited number of signs in private, residential, commercial, industrial, and public areas of the City of Ladue would create ugliness, visual blight and clutter, tarnish the natural beauty of the landscape as well as the residential and commercial architecture, impair property values, substantially impinge upon the privacy and special ambience of the community, and may cause safety and traffic hazards to motorists, pedestrians, and children[.]"

Gilleo amended her complaint to challenge the new ordinance, which explicitly prohibits window signs like hers. The District Court held the ordinance unconstitutional, and the Court of Appeals affirmed. Relying on the plurality opinion in *Metromedia, Inc. v. San Diego* (1981), the Court of Appeals held the ordinance invalid as a "content based" regulation because the City treated commercial speech more favorably than noncommercial speech and favored some kinds of noncommercial speech over others. Acknowledging that "Ladue's interests in enacting its ordinance are substantial," the Court of Appeals nevertheless concluded that those interests were "not sufficiently 'compelling' to support a content-based restriction. . . ."

We granted the City of Ladue's petition for certiorari, and now affirm.

II

While signs are a form of expression protected by the Free Speech Clause, they pose distinctive problems that are subject to municipalities' police powers. Unlike oral speech, signs take up space and may obstruct views, distract motorists, displace alternative uses for land, and pose other problems that legitimately call for regulation. It is common ground that governments may regulate the physical characteristics of signs—just as they can, within reasonable bounds and absent censorial purpose, regulate audible expression in its capacity as noise. . . . However, because regulation of a medium inevitably affects communication itself, it is not surprising that we have had occasion to review the constitutionality of municipal ordinances prohibiting the display of certain outdoor signs.

In *Linmark Associates, Inc. v. Willingboro* (1977), we addressed an ordinance that sought to maintain stable, integrated neighborhoods by prohibiting homeowners from placing "For Sale" or "Sold" signs on their property. Although we recognized the importance of Willingboro's objective, we held that the First Amendment prevented the township from "achieving its goal by restricting the free flow of truthful information." In some respects *Linmark* is the mirror image of this case. For instead of prohibiting "For Sale" signs without banning any other signs, Ladue has exempted such signs from an otherwise virtually complete ban. Moreover, whereas in *Linmark* we noted that the ordinance was not concerned with the promotion of aesthetic values unrelated to the content of the prohibited speech, here Ladue relies squarely on that content-neutral justification for its ordinance.

In *Metromedia*, we reviewed an ordinance imposing substantial prohibitions on outdoor advertising displays within the City of San Diego in the interest of traffic safety and aesthetics. The ordinance generally banned all except those advertising "on-site" activities. The Court concluded that the City's interest in traffic safety and its aesthetic interest in preventing "visual clutter" could justify a prohibition of off-site commercial billboards even though similar on-site signs were allowed. Nevertheless, the Court's judgment in *Metromedia*, supported by two different lines of reasoning, invalidated the San Diego ordinance in its entirety. According to Justice White's plurality opinion, the ordinance impermissibly discriminated on the basis of content by permitting on-site commercial speech while broadly prohibiting noncommercial messages. On the other hand, Justice Brennan, joined by Justice Blackmun, concluded "that the practical effect of the San Diego ordinance [was] to eliminate the billboard as an effective medium of communication" for noncommercial messages, and that the city had failed to make the strong showing needed to justify such "content-neutral prohibitions of particular media of communication." The three dissenters also viewed San Diego's ordinance as tantamount to a blanket prohibition of billboards, but would have upheld it because they did not perceive "even a hint of bias or censorship in the city's actions" nor "any reason to believe that the overall communications market in San Diego is inadequate. . . ."

In *City Council of Los Angeles v. Taxpayers for Vincent* (1984), we upheld a Los Angeles ordinance that prohibited the posting of signs on public property. Noting the conclusion shared by seven Justices in *Metromedia* that San Diego's "interest in avoiding visual clutter" was sufficient to justify a prohibition of commercial billboards, in *Vincent* we upheld the Los Angeles ordinance, which was justified on the same grounds. We rejected the argument that the validity of the City's aesthetic interest had been compromised by failing to extend the ban to private property, reasoning that the "private citizen's interest in controlling the use of his own property justifies the disparate treatment." We also rejected as "misplaced" respondents' reliance on public forum principles, for they had "fail[ed] to demonstrate the existence of a traditional right of access respecting such items as utility poles . . . comparable to that recognized for public streets and parks."

These decisions identify two analytically distinct grounds for challenging the constitutionality of a municipal ordinance regulating the display of signs. One is that the measure in effect restricts too little speech because its exemptions discriminate on the basis of the signs' messages. . . . Alternatively, such provisions are subject to attack on the ground that they simply prohibit too much protected speech. . . . The City of Ladue contends, first, that the Court of Appeals' reliance on the former rationale was misplaced because the City's regulatory purposes are content-neutral, and, second, that those purposes justify the comprehensiveness of the sign prohibition. A comment on the former contention will help explain why we ultimately base our decision on a rejection of the latter.

III

While surprising at first glance, the notion that a regulation of speech may be impermissibly under-inclusive is firmly grounded in basic First Amendment principles. Thus, an exemption from an otherwise permissible regulation of speech may represent a governmental "attempt to give one side of a debatable public question an advantage in expressing its views to the people." Alternatively, through the combined operation of a general speech restriction and its exemptions, the government might seek to select the "permissible subjects for public debate—and thereby to control . . . the search for political truth."

The City argues that its sign ordinance implicates neither of these concerns, and that the Court of Appeals therefore erred in demanding a "compelling" justification for the exemptions. The mix of prohibitions and exemptions in the ordinance, Ladue maintains, reflects legitimate differences among the side effects of various kinds of signs. These differences are only adventitiously connected with content, and supply a sufficient justification, unrelated to the City's approval or disapproval of specific messages, for carving out the specified categories from the general ban. Thus, according to the Declaration of Findings, Policies, Interests, and Purposes supporting the ordinance, the permitted signs, unlike the prohibited signs, are unlikely to contribute to the dangers of "unlimited proliferation" associated with categories of signs that are not inherently limited in number. Because only a few residents will need to display "for sale" or "for rent" signs at any given time, permitting one such sign per marketed house does not threaten visual clutter. Because the City has only a few businesses, churches, and schools, the same rationale explains the exemption for on-site commercial and organizational signs. Moreover, some of the exempted categories (e.g., danger signs) respond to unique public needs to permit certain kinds of speech. Even if we assume the validity of these arguments, the exemptions in Ladue's ordinance nevertheless shed light on the separate question of whether the ordinance prohibits too much speech.

Exemptions from an otherwise legitimate regulation of a medium of speech may be noteworthy for a reason quite apart from the risks of viewpoint and content discrimination: they may diminish the credibility of the government's rationale for restricting speech in the first place. In this case, at the very least, the exemptions from Ladue's ordinance demonstrate that Ladue has concluded that the interest in allowing certain messages to be conveyed by means of residential signs outweighs the City's aesthetic interest in eliminating outdoor signs. Ladue has not imposed a flat ban on signs because it has determined that at least some of them are too vital to be banned.

Under the Court of Appeals' content discrimination rationale, the City might theoretically remove the defects in its ordinance by simply repealing all of the exemptions. If, however, the ordinance is also vulnerable because it prohibits too much speech, that solution would not save it. Moreover, if the prohibitions in Ladue's ordinance are impermissible, resting our decision on its exemptions would afford scant relief for respondent Gilleo. She is primarily concerned not with the scope of the exemptions available in other locations, such as commercial areas and on church property. She asserts a constitutional right to display an antiwar sign at her own home. Therefore, we first ask whether Ladue may properly prohibit Gilleo from displaying her sign, and then, only if necessary, consider the separate question whether it was improper for the City simultaneously to permit certain other signs. In examining the propriety of Ladue's near-total prohibition of residential signs, we will assume, arguendo, the validity of the City's submission that the various exemptions are free of impermissible content or viewpoint discrimination.

IV

In *Linmark* we held that the City's interest in maintaining a stable, racially integrated neighborhood was not sufficient to support a prohibition of residential "For Sale" signs. We recognized that even such a narrow sign prohibition would have a deleterious effect on residents' ability to convey important information because alternatives were "far from satisfactory." Ladue's sign ordinance is supported principally by the City's interest in minimizing the visual clutter associated with signs, an interest that is concededly valid but certainly no more compelling than the interests at stake in *Linmark*. Moreover, whereas the ordinance in *Linmark* applied only to a form of commercial speech, Ladue's ordinance covers even such absolutely pivotal speech as a sign protesting an imminent governmental decision to go to war.

The impact on free communication of Ladue's broad sign prohibition, moreover, is manifestly greater than in *Linmark*. Gilleo and other residents of Ladue are forbidden to display virtually any "sign" on their property. The ordinance defines that term sweepingly. A prohibition is not always invalid merely because it applies to a sizeable category of speech; the sign ban we upheld in *Vincent*, for example, was quite broad. But in *Vincent* we specifically noted that the category of speech in question—signs placed on public property— was not a "uniquely valuable or important mode of communication," and that there was no evidence that "appellees' ability to communicate effectively is threatened by ever-increasing restrictions on expression."

Here, in contrast, Ladue has almost completely foreclosed a venerable means of communication that is both unique and important. It has totally foreclosed that medium to political, religious, or personal messages. Signs that react to a local happening or express a view on a controversial issue both reflect and animate change in the life of a community. Often placed on lawns or in windows, residential signs play an important part in political campaigns, during which they are displayed to signal the resident's support for particular candidates, parties, or causes. They may not afford the same opportunities for conveying complex ideas as do other media, but residential signs have long been an important and distinct medium of expression.

Our prior decisions have voiced particular concern with laws that foreclose an entire medium of expression. Thus, we have held invalid ordinances that completely banned the distribution of pamphlets within the municipality, *Lovell v. Griffin* (1938); handbills on the public streets, *Jamison v. Texas* (1943); the door-to-door distribution of literature, *Martin v. Struthers* (1943); Schneider v. State (1939); and live entertainment, *Schad v. Mount Ephraim* (1981). . . . Although prohibitions foreclosing entire media may be completely free of content or viewpoint discrimination, the danger they pose to the freedom of speech is readily apparent—by eliminating a common means of speaking, such measures can suppress too much speech.

Ladue contends, however, that its ordinance is a mere regulation of the "time, place, or manner" of speech because residents remain free to convey their desired messages by other means, such as hand-held signs, "letters, handbills, flyers, telephone calls, newspaper advertisements, bumper stickers, speeches, and neighborhood or community meetings." However, even regulations that do not foreclose an entire medium of expression, but merely shift the time, place, or manner of its use, must "leave open ample alternative channels for communication." In this case, we are not persuaded that adequate substitutes exist for the important medium of speech that Ladue has closed off.

Displaying a sign from one's own residence often carries a message quite distinct from placing the same sign someplace else, or conveying the same text or picture by other means. Precisely because of their location, such signs provide information about the identity of the "speaker." As an early and eminent student of rhetoric observed, the identity of the speaker is an important component of many attempts to persuade. A sign advocating "Peace in the Gulf" in the front lawn of a retired general or decorated war veteran may provoke a different reaction than the same sign in a 10-year-old child's bedroom window or the same message on a bumper sticker of a passing automobile. An espousal of socialism may carry different implications when displayed on the grounds of a stately mansion than when pasted on a factory wall or an ambulatory sandwich board.

Residential signs are an unusually cheap and convenient form of communication. Especially for persons of modest means or limited mobility, a yard or window sign may have no practical substitute. . . . Even for the affluent, the added costs in money or time of taking out a newspaper advertisement, handing out leaflets on the street, or standing in front of one's house with a hand-held sign may make the difference between participating and not participating in some public debate. Furthermore, a person who puts up a sign at her residence often intends to reach neighbors, an audience that could not be reached nearly as well by other means.

A special respect for individual liberty in the home has long been part of our culture and our law; that principle has special resonance when the government seeks to constrain a person's ability to speak there. Most Americans would be understandably dismayed, given that tradition, to learn that it was illegal to display from their window an 8.5- by 11-inch sign expressing their political views. Whereas the government's need to mediate among various competing uses, including expressive ones, for public streets and facilities is constant and unavoidable, its need to regulate temperate speech from the home is surely much less pressing.

Our decision that Ladue's ban on almost all residential signs violates the First Amendment by no means leaves the City powerless to address the ills that may be associated with residential signs. It bears mentioning that individual residents themselves have strong incentives to keep their own property values up and to prevent "visual clutter" in their own yards and neighborhoods—incentives markedly different from those of persons who erect signs on others' land, in others' neighborhoods, or on public property. Residents' self-interest diminishes the danger of the "unlimited" proliferation of residential signs that concerns the City of Ladue. We are confident that more temperate measures could in large part satisfy Ladue's stated regulatory needs without harm to the First Amendment rights of its citizens. As currently framed, however, the ordinance abridges those rights.

Accordingly, the judgment of the Court of Appeals is

Affirmed.

SUPREME COURT ON
PRIVATE PROPERTY RIGHTS
June 24, 1994

In a major victory for property rights advocates, a 5-to-4 ruling by the Supreme Court June 24 made it harder for local governments to require that developers devote part of their land to public uses.

The case began when the owners of a plumbing and electric supply store in Tigard, Oregon, a suburb of Portland, sought a city permit to build a larger store on their property and to pave a parking lot. A portion of the property was part of a floodplain, and the property adjoined a creek.

The city, citing its land use plan, said it would grant a permit if the owner would grant an easement for two portions of the property for public use. The first was the portion of the property situated in the floodplain. The city said that the owner's plan to construct a larger building and a parking lot would increase the amount of impervious surfaces and the runoff into the adjoining creek. To combat the increased threat of flooding posed by the project, the city required an easement of the floodplain land for a greenway.

Second, the city said that the planned larger store—the new one was to be nearly double the size of the old one—would lead to increased traffic in an already congested downtown. It required that the property owner provide an easement for an additional fifteen-foot strip of land adjacent to the floodplain for the construction of a city pathway for pedestrians and bicyclists that was aimed at reducing auto congestion.

Altogether, the city required that about seven thousand square feet of land be dedicated to public use, or roughly 10 percent of the property. The property owner filed suit, contending that the easements were not related to the proposed project. The owner said the city's requirements amounted to a "taking" of the property in violation of the Fifth Amendment. The "Takings Clause" of the Fifth Amendment states that governments cannot take private property "for public use, without just compensation." The Oregon Supreme Court ruled for the city, finding that its requirements were reasonably related to the project.

Supreme Court Splits 5-4

On a 5-to-4 vote that split along ideological lines, the U.S. Supreme Court overturned the lower court. In the majority opinion, Chief Justice William H. Rehnquist wrote: "Cities have long engaged in the commendable task of land use planning, made necessary by increasing urbanization particularly in metropolitan areas such as Portland. The city's goals of reducing flooding hazards and traffic congestion, and providing for public greenways, are laudable, but there are outer limits to how this may be done." Rehnquist was joined in the opinion by Justices Sandra Day O'Connor, Anthony M. Kennedy, Antonin Scalia, and Clarence Thomas.

The Court established a new "rough proportionality" test to use in judging whether a government's requirements are reasonable. It said that requiring a public easement is constitutional only if the government can prove a rough proportionality between the requirement and the amount of damage caused by a development. "No precise mathematical calculation is required, but the city must make some sort of individualized determination that the required dedication is related both in nature and extent to the impact of the proposed development," Rehnquist wrote.

The city of Tigard had failed to meet the new test, the majority said. The city had not shown a reasonable relationship between the floodplain easement and the new building, the Court said, and also did not prove that creation of the bike path would actually lessen automobile congestion.

Besides establishing a new test, the majority decision shifted the burden in disputes over land use. Under previous Court rulings, a landowner challenging a land use restriction had to show that the requirement would destroy a property's economic value. But under the court's new test, when challenged the government had to justify its land use restriction.

Impact of the Decision Unclear

In a stinging dissent, Justice John Paul Stevens said the majority was wrong to shift the burden. "The Court has stumbled badly today," he wrote. It is impossible to predict the impact of new urban developments on the risks of floods, earthquakes, traffic congestion, or the environment, Stevens wrote. "When there is doubt concerning the magnitude of those impacts, the public interest in averting them must outweigh the private interest of the commercial entrepreneur," he said. "If the government can demonstrate that the conditions it has imposed in a land-use permit are rational, impartial and conducive to fulfilling the aims of a valid land-use plan, a strong presumption of validity should attach to those conditions. . . ." Stevens was joined in the dissent by Justices Harry A. Blackmun and Ruth Bader Ginsburg, and Justice David H. Souter filed a separate dissent.

The Supreme Court's decision did not end the dispute. Instead, the Court sent the case back to a lower court for hearings to see whether the city could meet the new test of "rough proportionality."

The full ramifications of the Court's decision were not immediately clear.

Some officials said local governments will have to conduct much more exten-
sive research than before about a project's impact, and will have to carefully
document their claims when requiring a developer to set aside land for pub-
lic use. Other officials predicted a relatively small impact from the ruling,
especially in jurisdictions where planners use a process known as condi-
tional zoning. Under this process, a developer voluntarily agrees to grant
easements, build a park, or otherwise devote land to public use in exchange
for approval of the project.

Following are excerpts from the majority and dissenting opin-
ions in the Supreme Court's ruling June 24, 1994, in Dolan v.
City of Tigard, *in which the Court said a "rough proportional-*
ity" test must be used when governments require developers to
dedicate a portion of their property to public use:

No. 93-518

Florence Dolan, Petitioner | On writ of certiorari to the Supreme
v. | Court of Oregon
City of Tigard |

[June 24, 1994]

CHIEF JUSTICE REHNQUIST delivered the opinion of the Court.

Petitioner challenges the decision of the Oregon Supreme Court which held that the city of Tigard could condition the approval of her building permit on the dedication of a portion of her property for flood control and traffic improvements. We granted certiorari to resolve a question left open by our decision in *Nollan* v. *California Coastal Comm'n* (1987) of what is the required degree of connection between the exactions imposed by the city and the projected impacts of the proposed development.

I

The State of Oregon enacted a comprehensive land use management program in 1973. . . . Pursuant to the State's requirements, the city of Tigard, a community of some 30,000 residents on the southwest edge of Portland, developed a comprehensive plan and codified it in its Community Development Code (CDC). The CDC requires property owners in the area zoned Central Business District to comply with a 15% open space and landscaping requirement, which limits total site coverage, including all structures and paved parking, to 85% of the parcel. After the completion of a transportation study that identified congestion in the Central Business District as a particular problem, the city adopted a plan for a pedestrian/bicycle pathway intended to encourage alternatives to automobile transportation for short trips. The CDC requires that new development facilitate this plan by dedicating land for pedestrian pathways where provided for in the pedestrian/bicycle pathway plan.

The city also adopted a Master Drainage Plan. The Drainage Plan noted that flooding occurred in several areas along Fanno Creek, including areas near petitioner's property. The Drainage Plan also established that the increase in impervious surfaces associated with continued urbanization would exacerbate these flooding problems. To combat these risks, the Drainage Plan suggested a series of improvements to the Fanno Creek Basin, including channel excavation in the area next to petitioner's property. Other recommendations included ensuring that the floodplain remains free of structures and that it be preserved as greenways to minimize flood damage to structures. The Drainage Plan concluded that the cost of these improvements should be shared based on both direct and indirect benefits, with property owners along the waterways paying more due to the direct benefit that they would receive.

Petitioner Florence Dolan owns a plumbing and electric supply store located on Main Street in the Central Business District of the city. The store covers approximately 9,700 square feet on the eastern side of a 1.67-acre parcel, which includes a gravel parking lot. Fanno Creek flows through the southwestern corner of the lot and along its western boundary. . . .

Petitioner applied to the city for a permit to redevelop the site. Her proposed plans called for nearly doubling the size of the store to 17,600 square feet, and paving a 39-space parking lot. . . . In the second phase of the project, petitioner proposed to build an additional structure on the northeast side of the site for complementary businesses, and to provide more parking. . . .

The City Planning Commission granted petitioner's permit application subject to conditions imposed by the city's CDC. . . . Thus, the Commission required that petitioner dedicate the portion of her property lying within the 100-year floodplain for improvement of a storm drainage system along Fanno Creek and that she dedicate an additional 15-foot strip of land adjacent to the floodplain as a pedestrian/bicycle pathway. The dedication required by that condition encompasses approximately 7,000 square feet, or roughly 10% of the property. . . .

Petitioner requested variances from the CDC standards. . . . Petitioner . . . argued that her proposed development would not conflict with the policies of the comprehensive plan. The Commission denied the request.

The Commission made a series of findings concerning the relationship between the dedicated conditions and the projected impacts of petitioner's project. First, the Commission noted that "[i]t is reasonable to assume that customers and employees of the future uses of this site could utilize a pedestrian/bicycle pathway adjacent to this development for their transportation and recreational needs.". . . In addition, the Commission found that creation of a convenient, safe pedestrian/bicycle pathway system as an alternative means of transportation "could offset some of the traffic demand on [nearby] streets and lessen the increase in traffic congestion."

The Commission went on to note that the required floodplain dedication would be reasonably related to petitioner's request to intensify the use of the site given the increase in the impervious surface. The Commission stated that the "anticipated increased storm water flow from the subject property to an already strained creek and drainage basin can only add to the public need to manage the stream channel and floodplain for drainage purposes.". . . The Tigard City Council approved the Commission's final order, subject to one minor modification. . . .

Petitioner appealed to the Land Use Board of Appeals (LUBA) on the ground that the city's dedication requirements were not related to the proposed development, and, therefore, those requirements constituted an uncompensated taking of their property under the Fifth Amendment. In evaluating the federal taking claim, LUBA assumed that the city's findings about the impacts of the proposed development were supported by substantial evidence. Given the undisputed fact that the proposed larger building and paved parking area would increase the amount of impervious surfaces and the runoff into Fanno Creek, LUBA concluded that "there is a 'reasonable relationship' between the proposed development and the requirement to dedicate land along Fanno Creek for a greenway." With respect to the pedestrian/bicycle pathway, LUBA noted the Commission's finding that a significantly larger retail sales building and parking lot would attract larger numbers of customers and employees and their vehicles. It again found a "reasonable relationship" between alleviating the impacts of increased traffic from the development and facilitating the provision of a pedestrian/bicycle pathway as an alternative means of transportation.

The Oregon Court of Appeals affirmed, rejecting petitioner's contention that in *Nollan* v. *California Coastal Comm'n* we had abandoned the "reasonable relationship" test in favor of a stricter "essential nexus" test. The Oregon Supreme Court affirmed. The court also disagreed with petitioner's contention that the *Nollan* Court abandoned the "reasonably related" test. Instead, the court read *Nollan* to mean that an "exaction is reasonably related to an impact if the exaction serves the same purpose that a denial of the permit would serve." The court decided that both the pedestrian/bicycle pathway condition and the storm drainage dedication had an essential nexus to the development of the proposed site. Therefore, the court found the conditions to be reasonably related to the impact of the expansion of petitioner's business. We granted certiorari (1993), because of an alleged conflict between the Oregon Supreme Court's decision and our decision in *Nollan*.

II

The Takings Clause of the Fifth Amendment of the United States Constitution, made applicable to the States through the Fourteenth Amendment, *Chicago, B. & Q. R. Co.* v. *Chicago* (1897), provides: "[N]or shall private property be taken for public use, without just compensation." One of the principal purposes of the Takings Clause is "to bar Government from forcing some people alone to bear public burdens which, in all fairness and justice, should be borne by the public as a whole." Without question, had the city simply required petitioner to dedicate a strip of land along Fanno Creek for public use, rather than conditioning the grant of her permit to redevelop her property on such a dedication, a taking would have occurred. . . .

On the other side of the ledger, the authority of state and local governments to engage in land use planning has been sustained against constitutional challenge as long ago as our decision in *Euclid* v. *Ambler Realty Co.* (1926). . . . A land use regulation does not effect a taking if it "substantially advance[s] legitimate state interests" and does not "den[y] an owner economically viable use of his land."

The sort of land use regulations discussed in the cases just cited, however, differ in two relevant particulars from the present case. First, they involved essentially legislative determinations classifying entire areas of the city, whereas here the city made an adjudicative decision to condition petitioner's application for a building permit on an individual parcel. Second, the conditions imposed were not simply a limitation on the use petitioner might make of her own parcel, but a requirement that she deed portions of the property to the city. In *Nollan*, we held that governmental authority to exact such a condition was circumscribed by the Fifth and Fourteenth Amendments. Under the well-settled doctrine of "unconstitutional conditions," the government may not require a person to give up a constitutional right—here the right to receive just compensation when property is taken for a public use—in exchange for a discretionary benefit conferred by the government where the property sought has little or no relationship to the benefit.

Petitioner contends that the city has forced her to choose between the building permit and her right under the Fifth Amendment to just compensation for the public easements. Petitioner does not quarrel with the city's authority to exact some forms of dedication as a condition for the grant of a building permit, but challenges the showing made by the city to justify these exactions. She argues that the city has identified "no special benefits" conferred on her, and has not identified any "special quantifiable burdens" created by her new store that would justify the particular dedications required from her which are not required from the public at large.

III

In evaluating petitioner's claim, we must first determine whether the "essential nexus" exists between the "legitimate state interest" and the permit condition exacted by the city. If we find that a nexus exists, we must then decide the required degree of connection between the exactions and the projected impact of the proposed development. . . .

A

. . . Undoubtedly, the prevention of flooding along Fanno Creek and the reduction of traffic congestion in the Central Business District qualify as the type of legitimate public purposes we have upheld. It seems equally obvious that a nexus exists between preventing flooding along Fanno Creek and limiting development within the creek's 100-year floodplain. . . .

The same may be said for the city's attempt to reduce traffic congestion by

providing for alternative means of transportation. In theory, a pedestrian/
bicycle pathway provides a useful alternative means of transportation for
workers and shoppers. . . .

B

The second part of our analysis requires us to determine whether the degree of the exactions demanded by the city's permit conditions bear the required relationship to the projected impact of petitioner's proposed development. . . .

The city required that petitioner dedicate "to the city as Greenway all portions of the site that fall within the existing 100-year floodplain [of Fanno
Creek] . . . and all property 15 feet above [the floodplain] boundary." In addition, the city demanded that the retail store be designed so as not to intrude
into the greenway area. The city relies on the Commission's rather tentative
findings that increased stormwater flow from petitioner's property "can only
add to the public need to manage the [floodplain] for drainage purposes" to
support its conclusion that the "requirement of dedication of the floodplain
area on the site is related to the applicant's plan to intensify development on
the site."

The city made the following specific findings relevant to the pedestrian/
bicycle pathway:

> "In addition, the proposed expanded use of this site is anticipated to generate
> additional vehicular traffic thereby increasing congestion on nearby collector and
> arterial streets. Creation of a convenient, safe pedestrian/bicycle pathway system
> as an alternative means of transportation could offset some of the traffic demand
> on these nearby streets and lessen the increase in traffic congestion."

The question for us is whether these findings are constitutionally sufficient
to justify the conditions imposed by the city on petitioner's building permit.
Since state courts have been dealing with this question a good deal longer
than we have, we turn to representative decisions made by them.

In some States, very generalized statements as to the necessary connection
between the required dedication and the proposed development seem to suffice. . . .

Other state courts require a very exacting correspondence, described as the
"specifi[c] and uniquely attributable" test. . . .

A number of state courts have taken an intermediate position, requiring the
municipality to show a "reasonable relationship" between the required dedication and the impact of the proposed development. . . .

We think the "reasonable relationship" test adopted by a majority of the
state courts is closer to the federal constitutional norm than either of those
previously discussed. But we do not adopt it as such, partly because the term
"reasonable relationship" seems confusingly similar to the term "rational basis" which describes the minimal level of scrutiny under the Equal Protection
Clause of the Fourteenth Amendment. We think a term such as "rough proportionality" best encapsulates what we hold to be the requirement of the

Fifth Amendment. No precise mathematical calculation is required, but the city must make some sort of individualized determination that the required dedication is related both in nature and extent to the impact of the proposed development. . . .

. . . We turn now to analysis of whether the findings relied upon by the city here, first with respect to the floodplain easement, and second with respect to the pedestrian/bicycle path, satisfied these requirements.

It is axiomatic that increasing the amount of impervious surface will increase the quantity and rate of stormwater flow from petitioner's property. Therefore, keeping the floodplain open and free from development would likely confine the pressures on Fanno Creek created by petitioner's development. In fact, because petitioner's property lies within the Central Business District, the Community Development Code already required that petitioner leave 15% of it as open space and the undeveloped floodplain would have nearly satisfied that requirement. But the city demanded more—it not only wanted petitioner not to build in the floodplain, but it also wanted petitioner's property along Fanno Creek for its Greenway system. The city has never said why a public greenway, as opposed to a private one, was required in the interest of flood control.

The difference to petitioner, of course, is the loss of her ability to exclude others. . . . It is difficult to see why recreational visitors trampling along petitioner's floodplain easement are sufficiently related to the city's legitimate interest in reducing flooding problems along Fanno Creek, and the city has not attempted to make any individualized determination to support this part of its request.

The city contends that recreational easement along the Greenway is only ancillary to the city's chief purpose in controlling flood hazards. It further asserts that unlike the residential property at issue in *Nollan*, petitioner's property is commercial in character and therefore, her right to exclude others is compromised. . . .

Admittedly, petitioner wants to build a bigger store to attract members of the public to her property. She also wants, however, to be able to control the time and manner in which they enter. . . . [T]he city wants to impose a permanent recreational easement upon petitioner's property that borders Fanno Creek. Petitioner would lose all rights to regulate the time in which the public entered onto the Greenway, regardless of any interference it might pose with her retail store. Her right to exclude would not be regulated, it would be eviscerated.

If petitioner's proposed development had somehow encroached on existing greenway space in the city, it would have been reasonable to require petitioner to provide some alternative greenway space for the public either on her property or elsewhere. . . . But that is not the case here. We conclude that the findings upon which the city relies do not show the required reasonable relationship between the floodplain easement and the petitioner's proposed new building.

With respect to the pedestrian/bicycle pathway, we have no doubt that the city was correct in finding that the larger retail sales facility proposed by petitioner will increase traffic on the streets of the Central Business District. . . . But on the record before us, the city has not met its burden of demonstrating that the additional number of vehicle and bicycle trips generated by the petitioner's development reasonably relate to the city's requirement for a dedication of the pedestrian/bicycle pathway easement. The city simply found that the creation of the pathway "could offset some of the traffic demand . . . and lessen the increase in traffic congestion.". . .

. . . No precise mathematical calculation is required, but the city must make some effort to quantify its findings in support of the dedication for the pedestrian/bicycle pathway beyond the conclusory statement that it could offset some of the traffic demand generated.

IV

Cities have long engaged in the commendable task of land use planning, made necessary by increasing urbanization particularly in metropolitan areas such as Portland. The city's goals of reducing flooding hazards and traffic congestion, and providing for public greenways, are laudable, but there are outer limits to how this may be done. . . .

The judgment of the Supreme Court of Oregon is reversed, and the case is remanded for further proceedings consistent with this opinion.

It is so ordered.

JUSTICE STEVENS, with whom JUSTICE BLACKMUN and JUSTICE GINSBURG join, dissenting.

. . . The Court is correct in concluding that the city may not attach arbitrary conditions to a building permit or to a variance even when it can rightfully deny the application outright. I also agree that state court decisions dealing with ordinances that govern municipal development plans provide useful guidance in a case of this kind. Yet the Court's description of the doctrinal underpinnings of its decision, the phrasing of its fledgling test of "rough proportionality," and the application of that test to this case run contrary to the traditional treatment of these cases and break considerable and unpropitious new ground.

I

Candidly acknowledging the lack of federal precedent for its exercise in rulemaking, the Court purports to find guidance in 12 "representative" state court decisions. To do so is certainly appropriate. The state cases the Court consults, however, either fail to support or decidedly undermine the Court's conclusions in key respects. . . .

Not one of the state cases cited by the Court announces anything akin to a "rough proportionality" requirement. For the most part, moreover, those cases that invalidated municipal ordinances did so on state law or unspecified grounds roughly equivalent to *Nollan*'s "essential nexus" requirement. . . . Thus, although these state cases do lend support to the Court's reaffirmance of *Nollan*'s reasonable nexus requirement, the role the Court accords them in the announcement of its newly minted second phase of the constitutional inquiry is remarkably inventive.

In addition, the Court ignores the state courts' willingness to consider what the property owner gains from the exchange in question. . . . In this case . . . Dolan's acceptance of the permit, with its attached conditions, would provide her with benefits that may well go beyond any advantage she gets from expanding her business. As the United States pointed out at oral argument, the improvement that the city's drainage plan contemplates would widen the channel and reinforce the slopes to increase the carrying capacity during serious floods, "confer[ring] considerable benefits on the property owners immediately adjacent to the creek."

The state court decisions also are enlightening in the extent to which they required that the entire parcel be given controlling importance. All but one of the cases involve challenges to provisions in municipal ordinances requiring developers to dedicate either a percentage of the entire parcel . . . or an equivalent value in cash . . . to help finance the construction of roads, utilities, schools, parks and playgrounds. In assessing the legality of the conditions, the courts gave no indication that the transfer of an interest in realty was any more objectionable than a cash payment. None of the decisions identified the surrender of the fee owner's "power to exclude" as having any special significance. Instead, the courts uniformly examined the character of the entire economic transaction.

II

It is not merely state cases, but our own cases as well, that require the analysis to focus on the impact of the city's action on the entire parcel of private property. . . .

The Court's narrow focus on one strand in the property owner's bundle of rights is particularly misguided in a case involving the development of commercial property. . . .

. . . The city of Tigard has demonstrated that its plan is rational and impartial and that the conditions at issue are "conducive to fulfillment of authorized planning objectives." Dolan, on the other hand, has offered no evidence that her burden of compliance has any impact at all on the value or profitability of her planned development. Following the teaching of the cases on which it purports to rely, the Court should not isolate the burden associated with the loss of the power to exclude from an evaluation of the benefit to be derived from the permit to enlarge the store and the parking lot.

The Court's assurances that its "rough proportionality" test leaves ample room for cities to pursue the "commendable task of land use planning"—even twice avowing that "[n]o precise mathematical calculation is required"—are wanting given the result that test compels here. Under the Court's approach, a city must not only "quantify its findings" and make "individualized determination[s]" with respect to the nature *and* the extent of the relationship between the conditions and the impact, but also demonstrate "proportionality." The correct inquiry should instead concentrate on whether the required nexus is present and venture beyond considerations of a condition's nature or germaneness only if the developer establishes that a concededly germane condition is so grossly disproportionate to the proposed development's adverse effects that it manifests motives other than land use regulation on the part of the city. The heightened requirement the Court imposes on cities is even more unjustified when all the tools needed to resolve the questions presented by this case can be garnered from our existing case law.

III

Applying its new standard, the Court finds two defects in the city's case. First, while the record would adequately support a requirement that Dolan maintain the portion of the floodplain on her property as undeveloped open space, it does not support the additional requirement that the floodplain be dedicated to the city. Second, while the city adequately established the traffic increase that the proposed development would generate, it failed to quantify the offsetting decrease in automobile traffic that the bike path will produce. Even under the Court's new rule, both defects are, at most, nothing more than harmless error.

In her objections to the floodplain condition, Dolan made no effort to demonstrate that the dedication of that portion of her property would be any more onerous than a simple prohibition against any development on that portion of her property. . . .

The Court's rejection of the bike path condition amounts to nothing more than a play on words. Everyone agrees that the bike path "could" offset some of the increased traffic flow that the larger store will generate, but the findings do not unequivocally state that it *will* do so, or tell us just how many cyclists will replace motorists. Predictions on such matters are inherently nothing more than estimates. Certainly the assumption that there will be an offsetting benefit here is entirely reasonable and should suffice whether it amounts to 100 percent, 35 percent, or only 5 percent of the increase in automobile traffic that would otherwise occur. . . .

IV

The Court has made a serious error by abandoning the traditional presumption of constitutionality and imposing a novel burden of proof on a city implementing an admittedly valid comprehensive land use plan. Even more consequential than its incorrect disposition of this case, however, is the Court's resurrection of a species of substantive due process analysis that it firmly rejected decades ago. . . .

This case inaugurates an even more recent judicial innovation than the regulatory takings doctrine: the application of the "unconstitutional conditions" label to a mutually beneficial transaction between a property owner and a city. The Court tells us that the city's refusal to grant Dolan a discretionary benefit infringes her right to receive just compensation for the property interests that she has refused to dedicate to the city "where the property sought has little or no relationship to the benefit." Although it is well settled that a government cannot deny a benefit on a basis that infringes constitutionally protected interests—"especially [one's] interest in freedom of speech," *Perry* v. *Sindermann* (1972)—the "unconstitutional conditions" doctrine provides an inadequate framework in which to analyze this case.

Dolan has no right to be compensated for a taking unless the city acquires the property interests that she has refused to surrender. Since no taking has yet occurred, there has not been any infringement of her constitutional right to compensation. . . .

Even if Dolan should accept the city's conditions in exchange for the benefit that she seeks, it would not necessarily follow that she had been denied "just compensation" since it would be appropriate to consider the receipt of that benefit in any calculation of "just compensation.". . . Particularly in the absence of any evidence on the point, we should not presume that the discretionary benefit the city has offered is less valuable than the property interests that Dolan can retain or surrender at her option. But even if that discretionary benefit were so trifling that it could not be considered just compensation when it has "little or no relationship" to the property, the Court fails to explain why the same value would suffice when the required nexus is present. In this respect, the Court's reliance on the "unconstitutional conditions" doctrine is assuredly novel, and arguably incoherent. The city's conditions are by no means immune from constitutional scrutiny. The level of scrutiny, however, does not approximate the kind of review that would apply if the city had insisted on a surrender of Dolan's First Amendment rights in exchange for a building permit. . . .

In our changing world one thing is certain: uncertainty will characterize predictions about the impact of new urban developments on the risks of floods, earthquakes, traffic congestion, or environmental harms. When there is doubt concerning the magnitude of those impacts, the public interest in averting them must outweigh the private interest of the commercial entrepreneur. If the government can demonstrate that the conditions it has imposed in a land-use permit are rational, impartial and conducive to fulfilling the aims of a valid land-use plan, a strong presumption of validity should attach to those conditions. The burden of demonstrating that those conditions have unreasonably impaired the economic value of the proposed improvement belongs squarely on the shoulders of the party challenging the state action's constitutionality. That allocation of burdens has served us well in the past. The Court has stumbled badly today by reversing it.

I respectfully dissent.

JUSTICE SOUTER, dissenting.

This case, like *Nollan* v. *California Coastal Comm'n* (1987), invites the Court to examine the relationship between conditions imposed by development permits, requiring landowners to dedicate portions of their land for use by the public, and governmental interests in mitigating the adverse effects of such development. *Nollan* declared the need for a nexus between the nature of an exaction of an interest in land (a beach easement) and the nature of governmental interests. The Court treats this case as raising a further question, not about the nature, but about the degree, of connection required between such an exaction and the adverse effects of development. The Court's opinion announces a test to address this question, but as I read the opinion, the Court does not apply that test to these facts, which do not raise the question the Court addresses.

First, as to the floodplain and Greenway, the Court acknowledges that an easement of this land for open space (and presumably including the five feet required for needed creek channel improvements) is reasonably related to flood control, but argues that the "permanent recreational easement" for the public on the Greenway is not so related. . . . It seems to me such incidental recreational use can stand or fall with the bicycle path, which the city justified by reference to traffic congestion. As to the relationship the Court examines, between the recreational easement and a purpose never put forth as a justification by the city, the Court unsurprisingly finds a recreation area to be unrelated to flood control.

Second, as to the bicycle path, the Court again acknowledges the "theor[etically]" reasonable relationship between "the city's attempt to reduce traffic congestion by providing [a bicycle path] for alternative means of transportation" and the "correct" finding of the city that "the larger retail sales facility proposed by the petitioner will increase traffic on the streets of the Central Business District." The Court only faults the city for saying that the bicycle path "could" rather than "would" offset the increased traffic from the store. . . .

I cannot agree that the application of *Nollan* is a sound one here, since it appears that the Court has placed the burden of producing evidence of relationship on the city, despite the usual rule in cases involving the police power that the government is presumed to have acted constitutionally. Having thus assigned the burden, the Court concludes that the city loses based on one word ("could" instead of "would"), and despite the fact that this record shows the connection the Court looks for. . . .

In any event, on my reading, the Court's conclusions about the city's vulnerability carry the Court no further than *Nollan* has gone already, and I do not view this case as a suitable vehicle for taking the law beyond that point. The right case for the enunciation of takings doctrine seems hard to spot.

SUPREME COURT ON
ABORTION CLINIC PROTESTS
June 30, 1994

By a 6-to-3 vote, the Supreme Court on June 30 upheld the creation of a buffer zone around an abortion clinic's entrances and driveway to stop protesters from blocking access to the clinic. The Court rejected claims by abortion opponents that the buffer zone violated their First Amendment right to free speech.

The case began in September 1992 when a state judge issued a permanent injunction barring members of the antiabortion group Operation Rescue and other individuals from blocking access to the Aware Woman Center for Choice in Melbourne, Florida, and ordering them not to physically abuse people who entered or left the clinic. Six months later the clinic's operators sought a broader order, saying the initial injunction was being violated. The judge agreed, finding that protesters were still blocking access to the clinic and also were engaging in a campaign of intimidation against clinic staff members and patients that included going to their homes, following them "in a stalking manner," and threatening them.

The judge broadened the injunction to bar members of Operation Rescue and others "acting in concert" with them from demonstrating closer than 36 feet from clinic property, picketing or demonstrating within 300 feet of the home of any clinic employee, physically approaching any person seeking services of the clinic in an area within 300 feet of the clinic unless the person indicated a desire to communicate, holding signs with slogans or pictures of fetuses that could be seen from inside the clinic, and making loud noises outside the clinic such as singing, shouting, and using bullhorns during morning hours when surgery was being performed, among other restrictions.

On appeal, the Florida Supreme Court upheld the judge's order, ruling that the protests had "placed in jeopardy the health, safety, and rights of Florida women." It said the lower court's order was constitutional "in light of the medical services provided at the clinic and Operation Rescue's past conduct." In a unanimous ruling, the court said: "While the First Amendment confers on each citizen a powerful right to express oneself, it gives the picketer no boon to jeopardize the health, safety, and rights of others."

The situation became murky, though, when in a separate appeal the 11th U.S. Circuit Court of Appeals ruled that the state judge's injunction violated the First Amendment's free speech guarantee. The case then went to the U.S. Supreme Court in an effort to resolve the judicial split.

Court Upholds Buffer Zone, Noise Restrictions

The Supreme Court upheld some provisions of the injunction, while overturning others. The majority opinion said the Court's job was to decide whether a provision of the injunction "burdens more speech than necessary to accomplish its goal." Using that test, the Court upheld the 36-foot buffer zone around clinic entrances and driveways and the prohibition on loud noises during times when surgery was being performed. The Court said the noise restrictions "burden no more speech than necessary to ensure the health and well-being of the patients at the clinic. The First Amendment does not demand that patients at a medical facility undertake Herculean efforts to escape the cacophony of political protests."

The Court overturned the provision that barred demonstrators from approaching people within 300 feet of the clinic, saying this restriction went too far and violated the First Amendment. The Court also struck down the ban on signs with slogans or pictures of fetuses, saying clinic employees could simply draw curtains to block out the signs. In addition, the Court overturned the 300-foot buffer zone around the homes of clinic employees, although it indicated that a smaller buffer zone with limits on the number of pickets and the time and duration of picketing would be upheld.

Significantly, the majority opinion was written by Chief Justice William H. Rehnquist, a strong opponent of abortion. He was joined by Justices Harry A. Blackmun, Sandra Day O'Connor, David H. Souter, and Ruth Bader Ginsburg, and Justice John Paul Stevens filed a concurring opinion.

In a strongly worded dissent, Justice Antonin Scalia said the Court's decision suppressed "normal and peaceful social protest." The protesters who were subject to the injunction had not violated any laws, wrote Scalia, who was joined in the dissent by Justices Clarence Thomas and Anthony M. Kennedy.

Scalia wrote that "the Court has left a powerful loaded weapon lying about today," implying that the decision could be used to suppress other types of protests in the future.

"What we have decided seems to be, and will be reported by the media as, an abortion case," he wrote. "But it will go down in the lawbooks, it will be cited, as a free-speech injunction case—and the damage its novel principles produce will be considerable." He concluded that the Court's ruling "ought to give all friends of liberty great concern."

President Signs Clinic Access Law

The Court's decision was especially important because only one month earlier, President Bill Clinton had signed a bill known as the Freedom of Access to Clinic Entrances Act. The law makes it a federal crime to obstruct the entrance of abortion clinics and to use force or threats to injure or interfere with clinic employees or patients. Persons who commit nonviolent offenses under the law can receive prison terms of up to eighteen months and fines of up to $25,000, while violent offenders can be sentenced to prison terms of up to ten years.

In signing the bill, Clinton said it was designed to eliminate violence and coercion. "We simply cannot—we must not—continue to allow the attacks, the incidence of arson, the campaigns of intimidation upon law-abiding citizens that have given rise to this law," he said. "No person seeking medical care, no physician providing that care, should have to endure harassments or threats or obstruction or intimidation or even murder from vigilantes who take the law into their own hands because they think they know what the law ought to be."

Passage of the Freedom of Access bill was a priority for abortion rights supporters, who said a federal law was needed because state and local laws were too weak to fight massive blockades and acts of violence directed against abortion clinics. Antiabortion groups attacked the law, saying it violated their First Amendment rights to free speech and religious freedom. Randall Terry, founder of Operation Rescue, said the law "shows the ever-growing anti-Christian persecution that is coming from our government."

Operation Rescue and a second antiabortion group, the American Life League, immediately filed separate lawsuits seeking to have the law over-turned. Legal observers said that based on the Supreme Court's decision in the Florida clinics case, the new law was likely to survive a constitutional challenge.

The Court's decision in the Florida case and passage of the clinic access bill were part of a series of defeats for the antiabortion movement in 1994. In January, the Supreme Court had ruled unanimously that abortion clinics could use the federal Racketeer Influenced and Corrupt Organizations (RICO) law to sue protesters who tried to shut them down. (Supreme Court on RICO and Abortion Protests, p. 26)

> *Following are excerpts from the majority and dissenting opinions in the Supreme Court's ruling June 30, 1994, in* Madsen v. Women's Health Center, *upholding the creation of buffer zones around abortion clinics:*

<u>No. 93-880</u>

Judy Madsen, et al., Petitioners	
v.	On writ of certiorari to the Supreme
Women's Health Center, Inc., et al.	Court of Florida

[June 30, 1994]

CHIEF JUSTICE REHNQUIST delivered the opinion of the Court.

Petitioners challenge the constitutionality of an injunction entered by a Florida state court which prohibits antiabortion protestors from demonstrating in certain places and in various ways outside of a health clinic that performs abortions. We hold that the establishment of a 36-foot buffer zone on a public street from which demonstrators are excluded passes muster under the First Amendment, but that several other provisions of the injunction do not.

I

Respondents operate abortion clinics throughout central Florida. Petitioners and other groups and individuals are engaged in activities near the site of one such clinic in Melbourne, Florida. They picketed and demonstrated where the public street gives access to the clinic. In September 1992, a Florida state court permanently enjoined petitioners from blocking or interfering with public access to the clinic, and from physically abusing persons entering or leaving the clinic. Six months later, respondents sought to broaden the injunction, complaining that access to the clinic was still impeded by petitioners' activities and that such activities had also discouraged some potential patients from entering the clinic, and had deleterious physical effects on others. The trial court thereupon issued a broader injunction, which is challenged here.

The court found that, despite the initial injunction, protesters continued to impede access to the clinic by congregating on the paved portion of the street—Dixie Way—leading up to the clinic, and by marching in front of the clinic's driveways. It found that as vehicles heading toward the clinic slowed to allow the protesters to move out of the way, "sidewalk counselors" would approach and attempt to give the vehicles' occupants antiabortion literature. The number of people congregating varied from a handful to 400, and the noise varied from singing and chanting to the use of loudspeakers and bullhorns.

The protests, the court found, took their toll on the clinic's patients. A clinic doctor testified that, as a result of having to run such a gauntlet to enter the clinic, the patients "manifested a higher level of anxiety and hypertension causing those patients to need a higher level of sedation to undergo the surgical procedures, thereby increasing the risk associated with such procedures."

The noise produced by the protestors could be heard within the clinic, causing stress in the patients both during surgical procedures and while recuperating in the recovery rooms. And those patients who turned away because of the crowd to return at a later date, the doctor testified, increased their health risks by reason of the delay.

Doctors and clinic workers, in turn, were not immune even in their homes. Petitioners picketed in front of clinic employees' residences; shouted at passersby; rang the doorbells of neighbors and provided literature identifying the particular clinic employee as a "baby killer." Occasionally, the protestors would confront minor children of clinic employees who were home alone.

This and similar testimony led the state court to conclude that its original injunction had proved insufficient "to protect the health, safety and rights of women in Brevard and Seminole County, Florida, and surrounding counties seeking access to [medical and counseling] services." The state court therefore amended its prior order, enjoining a broader array of activities. . . .

The Florida Supreme Court upheld the constitutionality of the trial court's amended injunction. That court recognized that the forum at issue, which consists of public streets, sidewalks, and rights-of-way, is a traditional public forum. It then determined that the restrictions are content neutral, and it accordingly refused to apply the heightened scrutiny dictated by *Perry Education Assn.* v. *Perry Local Educators' Assn.* (1983). . . . Instead, the court analyzed the injunction to determine whether the restrictions are "narrowly tailored to serve a significant government interest, and leave open ample alternative channels of communication." It concluded that they were.

Shortly before the Florida Supreme Court's opinion was announced, the United States Court of Appeals for the Eleventh Circuit heard a separate challenge to the same injunction. The Court of Appeals struck down the injunction, characterizing the dispute as a clash "between an actual prohibition of speech and a potential hinderance to the free exercise of abortion rights." It stated that the asserted interests in public safety and order were already protected by other applicable laws and that these interests could be protected adequately without infringing upon the First Amendment rights of others. The Court of Appeals found the injunction to be content based and neither necessary to serve a compelling state interest nor narrowly drawn to achieve that end. We granted certiorari (1994) to resolve the conflict between the Florida Supreme Court and the Court of Appeals over the constitutionality of the state court's injunction.

II

We begin by addressing petitioners' contention that the state court's order, because it is an injunction that restricts only the speech of antiabortion protestors, is necessarily content or viewpoint based. Accordingly, they argue, we should examine the entire injunction under the strictest standard of scrutiny. We disagree. To accept petitioners' claim would be to classify virtually every injunction as content or viewpoint based. An injunction, by its very nature, applies only to a particular group (or individuals) and regulates the activities, and perhaps the speech, of that group. It does so, however, because of the group's past actions in the context of a specific dispute between real parties. The parties seeking the injunction assert a violation of their rights; the court hearing the action is charged with fashioning a remedy for a specific deprivation, not with the drafting of a statute addressed to the general public. . . .

III

If this were a content-neutral, generally applicable statute, instead of an injunctive order, its constitutionality would be assessed under the standard set forth in *Ward* v. *Rock Against Racism* [1989], and similar cases. Given that the forum around the clinic is a traditional public forum, we would determine whether the time, place, and manner regulations were "narrowly tailored to serve a significant governmental interest."

There are obvious differences, however, between an injunction and a generally applicable ordinance. Ordinances represent a legislative choice regarding the promotion of particular societal interests. Injunctions, by contrast, are remedies imposed for violations (or threatened violations) of a legislative or judicial decree. . . .

We believe that these differences require a somewhat more stringent application of general First Amendment principles in this context. In past cases evaluating injunctions restricting speech, we have relied upon such general principles while also seeking to ensure that the injunction was no broader than necessary to achieve its desired goals. See *Carroll* v. *President and Comm'rs of Princess Anne* (1968); [*NAACP* v.] *Claiborne Hardware [Co.* (1982)]. Our close attention to the fit between the objectives of an injunction and the restrictions it imposes on speech is consistent with the general rule, quite apart from First Amendment considerations, "that injunctive relief should be no more burdensome to the defendants than necessary to provide complete relief to the plaintiffs." Accordingly, when evaluating a content-neutral injunction, we think that our standard time, place, and manner analysis is not sufficiently rigorous. We must ask instead whether the challenged provisions of the injunction burden no more speech than necessary to serve a significant government interest.

Both JUSTICE STEVENS and JUSTICE SCALIA disagree with the standard we announce, for policy reasons. JUSTICE STEVENS believes that "injunctive relief should be judged by a more lenient standard than legislation," "because injunctions are imposed on individuals or groups who have engaged in illegal activity." JUSTICE SCALIA, by contrast, believes that content-neutral injunctions are "*at least* as deserving of strict scrutiny as a statutory, content-based restriction." JUSTICE SCALIA bases his belief on the danger that injunctions, even though they might not "attack content *as content*," may be used to suppress particular ideas; that individual judges should not be trusted to impose injunctions in this context; and that an injunction is procedurally more difficult to challenge than a statute. We believe that consideration of *all* of the differences and similarities between statutes and injunctions supports, as a matter of policy, the standard we apply here.

JUSTICE SCALIA further contends that precedent compels the application of strict scrutiny in this case. Under that standard, we ask whether a restriction is "necessary to serve a compelling state interest and [is] narrowly drawn to achieve that end." JUSTICE SCALIA fails to cite a single case, and we are aware of none, in which we have applied this standard to a content-neutral injunction. . . .

JUSTICE SCALIA also relies on *Claiborne Hardware* and *Carroll* for support of his contention that our precedent requires the application of strict scrutiny in this context. In *Claiborne Hardware*, we stated simply that "precision of regulation" is demanded. JUSTICE SCALIA reads this case to require "surgical precision" of regulation, but that was not the adjective chosen by the author of the Court's opinion, JUSTICE STEVENS. We think a standard requiring that an injunction "burden no more speech than necessary" exemplifies "precision of regulation."

As for *Carroll*, JUSTICE SCALIA believes that the "standard" adopted in that case "is strict scrutiny," which "does not remotely resemble the Court's new proposal." Comparison of the language used in *Carroll* and the wording of the standard we adopt, however, belies JUSTICE SCALIA's exaggerated contention. . . .

The Florida Supreme Court concluded that numerous significant government interests are protected by the injunction. It noted that the State has a strong interest in protecting a woman's freedom to seek lawful medical or counseling services in connection with her pregnancy. See *Roe* v. *Wade* (1973). The State also has a strong interest in ensuring the public safety and order, in promoting the free flow of traffic on public streets and sidewalks, and in protecting the property rights of all its citizens. In addition, the court believed that the State's strong interest in residential privacy . . . applied by analogy to medical privacy. The court observed that while targeted picketing of the home threatens the psychological well-being of the "captive" resident, targeted picketing of a hospital or clinic threatens not only the psychological, but the physical well-being of the patient held "captive" by medical circumstance. We agree with the Supreme Court of Florida that the combination of these governmental interests is quite sufficient to justify an appropriately tailored injunction to protect them. We now examine each contested provision of the injunction to see if it burdens more speech than necessary to accomplish its goal.

A

1

We begin with the 36-foot buffer zone. . . . We examine each portion of the buffer zone separately.

We have noted a distinction between the type of focused picketing banned from the buffer zone and the type of generally disseminated communication that cannot be completely banned in public places, such as handbilling and solicitation. . . . Here the picketing is directed primarily at patients and staff of the clinic.

The 36-foot buffer zone protecting the entrances to the clinic and the parking lot is a means of protecting unfettered ingress to and egress from the clinic, and ensuring that petitioners do not block traffic on Dixie Way. The state court seems to have had few other options to protect access given the narrow confines around the clinic. . . .

The need for a complete buffer zone near the clinic entrances and driveway may be debatable, but some deference must be given to the state court's familiarity with the facts and the background of the dispute between the parties even under our heightened review. Moreover, one of petitioners' witnesses during the evidentiary hearing before the state court conceded that the buffer zone was narrow enough to place petitioners at a distance of no greater than 10 to 12 feet from cars approaching and leaving the clinic. Protesters standing across the narrow street from the clinic can still be seen and heard from the clinic parking lots. . . . On balance, we hold that the 36-foot buffer zone around the clinic entrances and driveway burdens no more speech than necessary to accomplish the governmental interest at stake.

JUSTICE SCALIA's dissent argues that a videotape made of demonstrations at the clinic represents "what one must presume to be the worst of the activity justifying the injunction." This seems to us a gratuitous assumption. The videotape was indeed introduced by respondents, presumably because they thought it supported their request for the second injunction. But witnesses also testified as to relevant facts in a 3-day evidentiary hearing, and the state court was therefore not limited to JUSTICE SCALIA's rendition of what he saw on the videotape to make its findings in support of the second injunction. Indeed, petitioners themselves studiously refrained from challenging the factual basis for the injunction both in the state courts and here. . . . We must therefore judge this case on the assumption that the evidence and testimony presented to the state court supported its findings that the presence of protestors standing, marching, and demonstrating near the clinic's entrance interfered with ingress to and egress from the clinic despite the issuance of the earlier injunction.

2

The inclusion of private property on the back and side of the clinic in the 36-foot buffer zone raises different concerns. The accepted purpose of the buffer zone is to protect access to the clinic and to facilitate the orderly flow of traffic on Dixie Way. Patients and staff wishing to reach the clinic do not have to cross the private property abutting the clinic property on the north and west, and nothing in the record indicates that petitioners' activities on the private property have obstructed access to the clinic. Nor was evidence presented that protestors located on the private property blocked vehicular traffic on Dixie Way. . . . We hold that on the record before us the 36-foot buffer zone as applied to the private property to the north and west of the clinic burdens more speech than necessary to protect access to the clinic.

B

In response to high noise levels outside the clinic, the state court restrained the petitioners from "singing, chanting, whistling, shouting, yelling, use of bullhorns, auto horns, sound amplification equipment or other sounds or images observable to or within earshot of the patients inside the [c]linic" during the hours of 7:30 a.m. through noon on Mondays through Saturdays. We must, of course, take account of the place to which the regulations apply in determining whether these restrictions burden more speech than necessary. We have upheld similar noise restrictions in the past. . . . Noise control is particularly important around hospitals and medical facilities during surgery and recovery periods. . . .

We hold that the limited noise restrictions imposed by the state court order burden no more speech than necessary to ensure the health and well-being of the patients at the clinic. The First Amendment does not demand that patients at a medical facility undertake Herculean efforts to escape the cacophony of political protests. "If overamplified loudspeakers assault the citizenry, government may turn them down." *Grayned* [v. *City of Rockford* (1972)]. That is what the state court did here, and we hold that its action was proper.

C

The same, however, cannot be said for the "images observable" provision of the state court's order. Clearly, threats to patients or their families, however communicated, are proscribable under the First Amendment.

But rather than prohibiting the display of signs that could be interpreted as threats or veiled threats, the state court issued a blanket ban on all "images observable.". . . This provision of the injunction violates the First Amendment.

D

The state court ordered that petitioners refrain from physically approaching any person seeking services of the clinic "unless such person indicates a desire to communicate" in an area within 300 feet of the clinic. The state court was attempting to prevent clinic patients and staff from being "stalked" or "shadowed" by the petitioners as they approached the clinic. . . .

But it is difficult, indeed, to justify a prohibition on *all* uninvited approaches of persons seeking the services of the clinic, regardless of how peaceful the contact may be, without burdening more speech than necessary to prevent intimidation and to ensure access to the clinic. . . . The "consent" requirement alone invalidates this provision; it burdens more speech than is necessary to prevent intimidation and to ensure access to the clinic.

E

The final substantive regulation challenged by petitioners relates to a prohibition against picketing, demonstrating, or using sound amplification equipment within 300 feet of the residences of clinic staff. . . . The same analysis applies to the use of sound amplification equipment here as that discussed above: the government may simply demand that petitioners turn down the volume if the protests overwhelm the neighborhood.

As for the picketing, our prior decision upholding a law banning targeted residential picketing remarked on the unique nature of the home, as "the last citadel of the tired, the weary, and the sick." *Frisby* [v. *Schultz* (1988)]. . . .

But the 300-foot zone around the residences in this case is much larger than the zone provided for in the ordinance which we approved in *Frisby*. . . . The record before us does not contain sufficient justification for this broad a ban on picketing; it appears that a limitation on the time, duration of picketing, and number of pickets outside a smaller zone could have accomplished the desired result.

IV

Petitioners also challenge the state court's order as being vague and overbroad. They object to the portion of the injunction making it applicable to those acting "in concert" with the named parties. But petitioners themselves are named parties in the order, and they therefore lack standing to challenge a portion of the order applying to persons who are not parties. Nor is that phrase subject, at the behest of petitioners, to a challenge for "overbreadth"; the phrase itself does not prohibit any conduct, but is simply directed at un-named parties who might later be found to be acting "in concert" with the named parties. . . .

Petitioners also contend that the "in concert" provision of the injunction impermissibly limits their freedom of association guaranteed by the First Amendment. . . . But petitioners are not enjoined from associating with others or from joining with them to express a particular viewpoint. The freedom of association protected by the First Amendment does not extend to joining with others for the purpose of depriving third parties of their lawful rights.

V

In sum, we uphold the noise restrictions and the 36-foot buffer zone around the clinic entrances and driveway because they burden no more speech than necessary to eliminate the unlawful conduct targeted by the state court's injunction. We strike down as unconstitutional the 36-foot buffer zone as applied to the private property to the north and west of the clinic, the "images observable" provision, the 300-foot no-approach zone around the clinic, and the 300-foot buffer zone around the residences, because these provisions sweep more broadly than necessary to accomplish the permissible goals of the injunction. Accordingly, the judgment of the Florida Supreme Court is

Affirmed in part, and reversed in part.

JUSTICE SOUTER, concurring.

I join the Court's opinion and write separately only to clarify two matters in the record. First, the trial judge made reasonably clear that the issue of who was acting "in concert" with the named defendants was a matter to be taken up in individual cases, and not to be decided on the basis of protesters' viewpoints. Second, petitioners themselves acknowledge that the governmental interests in protection of public safety and order, of the free flow of traffic, and of property rights are reflected in Florida law. . . .

JUSTICE STEVENS, concurring in part and dissenting in part.

The certiorari petition presented three questions, corresponding to petitioners' three major challenges to the trial court's injunction. The Court correctly and unequivocally rejects petitioners' argument that the injunction is a "content-based restriction on free speech," as well as their challenge to the injunction on the basis that it applies to persons acting "in concert" with them. I therefore join Parts II and IV of the Court's opinion, which properly dispose of the first and third questions presented. I part company with the Court, however, on its treatment of the second question presented, including its enunciation of the applicable standard of review.

I

I agree with the Court that a different standard governs First Amendment challenges to generally applicable legislation than the standard that measures such challenges to judicial remedies for proven wrongdoing. Unlike the Court, however, I believe that injunctive relief should be judged by a more lenient standard than legislation. As the Court notes, legislation is imposed on an entire community, regardless of individual culpability. By contrast, injunctions apply solely to an individual or a limited group of individuals who, by engaging in illegal conduct, have been judicially deprived of some liberty—the normal consequence of illegal activity. Given this distinction, a statute prohibiting demonstrations within 36 feet of an abortion clinic would probably violate the First Amendment, but an injunction directed at a limited group of persons who have engaged in unlawful conduct in a similar zone might well be constitutional. . . .

II

The second question presented by the certiorari petition asks whether the "consent requirement before speech is permitted" within a 300-foot buffer zone around the clinic unconstitutionally infringes on free speech. Petitioners contend that these restrictions create a "no speech" zone in which they cannot speak unless the listener indicates a positive interest in their speech. And, in Part III-D of its opinion, the Court seems to suggest that, even in a more narrowly defined zone, such a consent requirement is constitutionally impermissible. Petitioners' argument and the Court's conclusion, however, are based on a misreading of ¶ (5) of the injunction.

That paragraph does not purport to prohibit speech; it prohibits a species of conduct. Specifically, it prohibits petitioners "from physically approaching any person seeking the services of the Clinic unless such person indicates a desire to communicate by approaching or by inquiring" of petitioners. . . .

[III, IV omitted]

JUSTICE SCALIA, with whom JUSTICE KENNEDY and JUSTICE THOMAS join, concurring in the judgment in part and dissenting in part.

The judgment in today's case has an appearance of moderation and Solomonic wisdom, upholding as it does some portions of the injunction while disallowing others. That appearance is deceptive. . . .

Because I believe that the judicial creation of a 36-foot zone in which only a particular group, which had broken no law, cannot exercise its rights of speech, assembly, and association, and the judicial enactment of a noise prohibition, applicable to that group and that group alone, are profoundly at odds with our First Amendment precedents and traditions, I dissent.

I

The record of this case contains a videotape, with running caption of time and date, displaying what one must presume to be the worst of the activity justifying the injunction issued by Judge McGregor and partially approved today by this Court. . . .

Anyone seriously interested in what this case was about must view that tape. And anyone doing so who is familiar with run-of-the-mine labor picketing, not to mention some other social protests, will be aghast at what it shows we have today permitted an individual judge to do. . . .

The videotape and the rest of the record, including the trial court's findings, show that a great many forms of expression and conduct occurred in the vicinity of the clinic. . . . What the videotape, the rest of the record, and the trial court's findings do not contain is any suggestion of violence near the clinic, nor do they establish any attempt to prevent entry or exit.

II

A

Under this Court's jurisprudence, there is no question that this public sidewalk area is a "public forum," where citizens generally have a First Amendment right to speak. The parties to this case invited the Court to employ one or the other of the two well-established standards applied to restrictions upon this First Amendment right. Petitioners claimed the benefit of so-called "strict scrutiny," the standard applied to content-based restrictions: the restriction must be "necessary to serve a compelling state interest and . . . narrowly drawn to achieve that end." *Perry Education Assn.* v. *Perry Local Educators' Assn.* (1983). Respondents, on the other hand, contended for what has come to be known as "intermediate scrutiny". . . . That standard, applicable to so-called "time, place and manner regulations" of speech, provides that the regulations are permissible so long as they "are content-neutral, are narrowly tailored to serve a significant government interest, and leave open ample alternative channels of communication." The Court adopts neither of these, but creates, brand-new for this abortion-related case, an additional standard that is (supposedly) "somewhat more stringent" than intermediate scrutiny, yet not as "rigorous" as strict scrutiny. . . .

. . . The real question in this case is not whether intermediate scrutiny . . . should be supplemented because of the distinctive characteristics of injunctions; but rather whether those distinctive characteristics are not, for reasons of both policy and precedent, fully as good a reason as "content-basis" for demanding strict scrutiny. . . .

. . . And the central element of the answer is that a restriction upon speech imposed by injunction (whether nominally content-based or nominally content neutral) is *at least* as deserving of strict scrutiny as a statutory, content-based restriction. . . .

Finally, though I believe speech-restricting injunctions are dangerous enough to warrant strict scrutiny even when they are not technically content based, I think the injunction in the present case was content based (indeed, viewpoint based) to boot. The Court claims that it was directed, not at those who *spoke* certain things (anti-abortion sentiments), but at those who *did* certain things (violated the earlier injunction). If that were true, then the injunction's residual coverage of "all persons acting in concert or participation with [the named individuals and organizations], or on their behalf" would not include those who merely entertained the same beliefs and wished to express the same views as the named defendants. But the construction given to the injunction by the issuing judge . . . is to the contrary: all those who wish to express the same views as the named defendants are deemed to be "acting in concert or participation.". . .

B

I have discussed, in the prior subsection, the policy reasons for giving speech-restricting injunctions, even content-neutral ones, strict scrutiny. There are reasons of precedent as well, which are essentially ignored by the Court.

To begin with, an injunction against speech is the very prototype of the greatest threat to First Amendment values, the prior restraint. . . .

III

[A omitted]

B

I turn now to the Court's performance in the present case. I am content to evaluate it under the lax (intermediate-intermediate scrutiny) standard that the Court has adopted, because even by that distorted light it is inadequate.

The first step under the Court's standard would be, one should think, to identify the "significant government interest" that justifies the portions of the injunction it upheld, namely, the enjoining of speech in the 36-foot zone, and the making (during certain times) of "sounds . . . within earshot of the patients inside the [c]linic.". . .

Assuming then that the "significant interests" the Court mentioned must in fact be significant enough to be protected by state law (a concept that includes a prior court order), which law has been, or is about to be, violated, the question arises: what state law is involved here? The only one even mentioned is the original September 30, 1992, injunction, which had been issued (quite rightly, in my judgment) in response to threats by the originally named parties (including petitioners here) that they would " '[p]hysically close down abortion mills,' " "bloc[k] access to clinics," "ignore the law of the State," and "shut down a clinic.". . . According to the Court, the state court imposed the later injunction's "restrictions on petitioner[s'] . . . antiabortion message because they repeatedly violated the court's original order." Surprisingly, the Court accepts this reason as valid, without asking whether the court's findings of fact support it—whether, that is, the acts of which the petitioners stood convicted *were* violations of the original injunction.

The Court simply takes this on faith—even though violation of the original injunction is an essential part of the reasoning whereby it approves portions of the amended injunction, even though petitioners denied any violation of the original injunction, even though the utter lack of proper basis for the other challenged portions of the injunction hardly inspires confidence that the lower courts knew what they were doing, and even though close examination of the factual basis for essential conclusions is the usual practice in First Amendment cases. Let us proceed, then, to the inquiry the Court neglected. . . .

. . . There is no factual finding that petitioners engaged in *any* intentional or purposeful obstruction.

Now let us compare these activities with the earlier injunction, violation of which is the asserted justification for the speech-free zone. Walking the return leg of the picket line on the paved portion of Dixie Way (instead of on the sidewalk), and congregating on the unpaved portion of that street . . . assuredly did not violate the earlier injunction, which made no mention of such a prohibition. Causing the traffic along Dixie Way to slow down "in response to the congestion" is also irrelevant; the injunction said nothing about slowing down traffic on public rights of way. It prohibited the doing (or urging) of *only three things:* 1) "physically abusing persons entering, leaving, working or using any services" of the abortion clinic (there is no allegation of that); 2) "trespassing on [or] sitting in" the abortion clinic (there is no allegation of that); and 3) "blocking, impeding or obstructing ingress into or egress from" the abortion clinic.

Only the last of these has any conceivable application here, and it seems to me that it must reasonably be read to refer to *intentionally* blocking, impeding or obstructing, and not to such temporary obstruction as may be the normal and incidental consequence of other protest activity. That is obvious, first of all, from the context in which the original injunction was issued—as a response to the petitioners' threatened actions of trespass and blockade, *i.e.,* the physical shutting down of the local clinics. Secondly, if that narrow meaning of intentional blockade, impediment or obstruction was not intended, and if it covered everything up to and including the incidental and "momentary" stopping of entering vehicles by persons leafletting and picketing, the original injunction would have failed the axiomatic requirement that its terms be drawn with precision.... And finally, if the original injunction did not have that narrow meaning it would assuredly have been unconstitutional, since it would have prevented speech-related activities that were, insofar as this record shows, neither criminally or civilly unlawful nor inextricably intertwined with unlawful conduct....

If the original injunction is read as it must be, there is nothing in the trial court's findings to suggest that it was violated.... There was no sitting down, no linking of arms, no packing en masse in the driveway; the most that can be alleged (and the trial court did not even make this a finding) is that on one occasion protestors "took their time to get out of the way." If that is enough to support this one-man proscription of free speech, the First Amendment is in grave peril.

I almost forgot to address the facts showing prior violation of law (including judicial order) with respect to the other portion of the injunction the Court upholds: the no-noise-within-earshot-of-patients provision. That is perhaps because, amazingly, neither the Florida courts *nor this Court* makes the slightest attempt to link that provision to prior violations of law. The relevant portion of the Court's opinion, Part II-B, simply reasons that hospital patients should not have to be bothered with noise, from political protests or anything else (which is certainly true), and that therefore the noise restrictions could be imposed *by injunction* (which is certainly false). Since such a law is reasonable, in other words, it can be enacted by a single man to bind only a single class of social protesters. The pro-abortion demonstrators who were often making (if respondents' videotape is accurate) *more* noise than the petitioners, can continue to shout their chants at their opponents exiled across the street to their hearts' content....

... My point does not rely, as the Court's response suggests, upon my earlier description of the videotape. That was set forth just for context, to show the reader what suppression of normal and peaceful social protest is afoot here. Nor is it relevant to my point that "petitioners themselves studiously refrained from challenging the factual basis for the injunction." I accept the facts as the Florida court found them; I deny that those facts support its *conclusion* ... that the original injunction had been violated.... The earlier injunction did not, and could not, prohibit all "interference"—for example, the minor interference incidentally produced by lawful picketing and leafletting. What the Court needs, and cannot come up with, is a finding that the petitioners interfered *in a manner prohibited by the earlier injunction.* A conclusion that they "block[ed], imped[ed] or obstruct[ed] ingress ... or egress" (the terminology of the original injunction) within the only fair, and indeed the only permissible, meaning of that phrase cannot be supported by the facts found.

To sum up: The interests assertedly protected by the supplementary injunction did not include any interest whose impairment was a violation of Florida law or of a Florida-court injunction. Unless the Court intends today to overturn long-settled jurisprudence, that means that the interests cannot possibly qualify as "significant interests" under the Court's new standard.

C

Finally, I turn to the Court's application of the second part of its test: whether the provisions of the injunction "burden no more speech than necessary" to serve the significant interest protected.

This test seems to me amply and obviously satisfied with regard to the noise restriction that the Court approves: it is only such noise as would reach the patients in the abortion clinic that is forbidden—and not even at all times, but only during certain fixed hours and "during surgical procedures and recovery periods.". . . With regard to the 36-foot speech-free zone, however, it seems to me just as obvious that the test which the Court sets for itself has not been met. . . .

In his dissent in *Korematsu* v. *United States* (1944), the case in which this Court permitted the wartime military internment of Japanese-Americans, Justice Jackson wrote the following:

> "A military order, however unconstitutional, is not apt to last longer than the military emergency. . . . But once a judicial opinion . . . rationalizes the Constitution to show that the Constitution sanctions such an order, the Court for all time has validated the principle of racial discrimination in criminal procedure and of transplanting American citizens. The principle then lies about like a loaded weapon ready for the hand of any authority that can bring forward a plausible claim of an urgent need."

What was true of a misguided military order is true of a misguided trial-court injunction. And the Court has left a powerful loaded weapon lying about today.

What we have decided seems to be, and will be reported by the media as, an abortion case. But it will go down in the lawbooks, it will be cited, as a free-speech-injunction case—and the damage its novel principles produce will be considerable. The proposition that injunctions against speech are subject to a standard indistinguishable from (unless perhaps more lenient in its application than) the "intermediate scrutiny" standard we have used for "time, place, and manner" legislative restrictions; the notion that injunctions against speech need not be closely tied to any violation of law, but may simply implement sound social policy; and the practice of accepting trial-court conclusions permitting injunctions without considering whether those conclusions are supported by any findings of fact—these latest byproducts of our abortion jurisprudence ought to give all friends of liberty great concern.

For these reasons, I dissent from that portion of the judgment upholding parts of the injunction. . . .

July

ISRAEL AND JORDAN
END STATE OF WAR
July 25, 1994

As President Bill Clinton beamed, King Hussein of Jordan and Prime Minister Yitzhak Rabin of Israel on July 25 signed an eleven-page document that formally ended a forty-six-year state of war between the two nations. "Out of all the days of my life, I do not believe there is one such as this," Hussein said.

Despite the state of war, the two neighbors had peacefully coexisted for years. The Washington Declaration, which Hussein and Rabin signed at the White House, formalized the peace process and called for joint efforts to establish direct telephone links between the two nations, foster cooperation between police forces in the two countries to fight crime, develop a shared electricity grid, create new border crossings, and discourage economic boycotts.

In reaction to the move toward peace by Hussein and Rabin, militants stepped up terrorist attacks aimed at derailing the peace process. Militant Israelis opposed giving up any land, while some Palestinians were impatient with Israel's move to give them partial autonomy. Although most of the terrorist attacks occurred in the Middle East, some took place in other countries. On July 18, a week before the signing of the peace agreement, a car-bomb blast killed 96 people and wounded 200 others at a Jewish community center in Buenos Aires. On July 26, the day after the agreement was signed, a bomb exploded outside the Israeli Embassy in London, injuring 13.

Syria Becomes Last Holdout

It remained unclear whether the agreement would help prod Syria—the last major holdout in the Middle East—to sign a peace agreement with Israel. Talks between the two countries remained stalled on two issues: control of the Golan Heights and the establishment of diplomatic ties. Israel, which captured the Golan Heights from Syria in the 1967 war, had offered to gradually withdraw from them over eight years in exchange for normal rela-

tions. Syria had said the withdrawal must be completed before any discussion of future relations could occur. Syria remained on the U.S. State Department's list of nations that supported terrorism and the United States continued economic sanctions against the country.

The signing of the agreement came fifteen years after Egypt and Israel signed a peace treaty at the White House in March 1979. It came only one year after Israel and the Palestine Liberation Organization (PLO) signed a peace accord at the White House that ended three decades of hostilities. (Israeli-Palestinian Peace Accord, Historic Documents of 1993, p. 747)

In May 1994, Rabin and Yasir Arafat, the chairman of the PLO, followed up on the 1993 White House accord by signing an agreement that created the first areas of Palestinian rule in the West Bank and Gaza Strip. Israel had occupied the areas for twenty-seven years, but it started withdrawing troops within twenty-four hours of the signing.

Peace Treaty Signed

In October, Hussein and Rabin initialed and later signed the formal peace treaty that grew out of the Washington Declaration. Besides bringing peace, the treaty was expected to lead to some joint economic activities, increased tourism for both countries, and international investments to increase water supplies for both nations.

One key portion of the agreement concerned land that both countries claimed. In the agreement, Israel recognized that Jordan owned nearly all the contested land, but Jordan allowed Israel to lease much of it for twenty-five years. Some observers hoped a similar arrangement might work in negotiations with Syria. The treaty also provided for a formal exchange of ambassadors and a pledge not to allow any third party to use the disputed territory as a staging ground for attacks against either nation.

Yet even as many in the two countries celebrated the lessening of tensions, terrorists struck again. On October 19, two days after Hussein and Rabin initialed the treaty, a powerful bomb ripped through a bus during morning rush hour in the heart of Tel Aviv, killing twenty-two people and injuring forty-six others. It was one of the deadliest attacks in Israel's history. Responsibility for the attack, which was carried out by an apparent suicide bomber, was claimed by the militant Islamic group Hamas. In a television interview hours after the blast, Rabin suggested that some civil rights might be curtailed in an effort to halt the attacks.

Israeli officials vowed that they would not allow the Tel Aviv attack to halt the peace process. Foreign Minister Shimon Peres said Hamas wanted Israelis to "lose our heads and stop the peace process. No way on earth." However, the New York Times *quoted another person it identified only as being "close to the Prime Minister" as saying: "It's very clear that a couple of more events like this and there's no more peace process."*

On December 10, the Nobel Peace Prize was presented to Rabin and Peres of Israel and Arafat of the PLO in recognition of the Israel-PLO accord signed in Washington in 1993. It was the most controversial decision in the prize's ninety-three year history, with many Jews contending that Arafat was a terrorist who did not deserve a peace prize. One member of the five-person Nobel Committee resigned to protest the award to Arafat.

Following is the text of remarks by President Bill Clinton, Prime Minister Yitzhak Rabin of Israel, and King Hussein of Jordan on July 25, 1994, at the signing of the Washington Declaration in Washington, D.C., as released by the White House:

CLINTON'S REMARKS

Your Majesties, Prime Minister and Mrs. Rabin, distinguished guests:

Today we gather to bear witness to history. As this century draws to a close a new era of peace opens before us in ancient lands as brave men choose reconciliation over conflict. Today our faith is renewed.

As we write a new chapter in the march of hope over despair on these grounds and at this historic table, we remember the courage of Anwar Sadat and Menachem Begin, and the leadership of President Carter at Camp David 15 years ago; the efforts of President Bush to bring Israel and her neighbors together in Madrid two years ago; and that shining September day last year when Prime Minister Rabin and Chairman Arafat declared that their two peoples would fight no more.

Today, in that same spirit, King Hussein and Prime Minister Rabin will sign the Washington Declaration. After generations of hostility, blood and tears, the leaders of the Hashemite Kingdom of Jordan and the State of Israel will solemnly declare, with the world as their witness, that they have ended the state of belligerency between them. From this day forward, they pledge to settle their differences by peaceful means.

Both countries will refrain from actions that may adversely affect the security of the other, and will thwart all those who would use terrorism to threaten either side.

The Washington Declaration is the product of much hard work. Less than a year ago, Crown Prince Hassan of Jordan and Foreign Minister Peres of Israel met here publicly for the first time. Together, with the wise counsel and persistent energy of the Secretary of State, Warren Christopher, Israel and Jordan have pursued peace. And we are all in their debt.

It takes but a minute or two to cross the River Jordan, but for as long as most of us can remember, the distance has seemed immense. The awful power of ancient arguments and the raw wounds of recent wars have left generations of Israelis, Jordanians and Palestinians unable to imagine, much less build, a life of peace and security. Today, King Hussein and Prime Minister Rabin give their people a new currency of hope and the chance to prosper in a region of peace.

Under the Washington Declaration, Jordan and Israel have agreed to continue vigorous negotiations to produce a treaty of peace based on Security

Council Resolutions 242 and 338. King Hussein and Prime Minister Rabin will meet as often as necessary to shepherd and personally direct those negotiations. Their objective is a just, lasting and comprehensive peace between Israel and all its neighbors; a peace in which each acknowledges and respects the territorial integrity and political independence of all others, and their right to live in peace within secure and recognized boundaries.

In the meantime, Jordan and Israel have decided to take immediate steps to normalize relations and resolve disputes in areas of common concern. They have agreed to survey the international border based on the work of their boundary subcommission. They have resolved that negotiations on water resources should aim to establish the rightful allocation between the two sides of the waters of the Jordan and Yarmouk Rivers. They have determined that their police forces will cooperate in combatting crime, with a special emphasis on drug smuggling. They have set up as their joint purpose the abolition of all economic boycotts and the establishment of a bilateral economic cooperation.

And as of today, Jordan and Israel have agreed to take the first practical steps to draw their people together and to let the peoples of the world share in the wonders of their lands. They will establish direct telephone links; connect their two nations' electricity grids; open two border crossings between their nations, including one at Aqaba and Eilat and another in the north; accelerate the negotiations aimed at opening an international air corridor between the two countries; and give free access to third-country tourists traveling between their two nations. These are the building blocks of a modern peace in ancient holy lands.

Your Majesty, after our first meeting, you wrote me a heartfelt letter in which you referred to your revered grandfather, King Abdullah. You told me that his untimely assassination at the entrance to Jerusalem Al Aqsa Mosque had come at a time when he was intent on making peace with Israel. Had he completed his mission, you said to me, your region would have been spared four decades of war. Today, 43 years later, Abdullah's grandson has fulfilled his legacy.

And in the declaration you will sign, your role as guardian of Jerusalem's Muslim holy sites, Al Aqsa among them, has been preserved. And Israel has agreed to accord a high priority to Jordan's historic role regarding these holy sites in final status negotiations.

Prime Minister, when you first visited me in the White House, you spoke eloquently of your soldier's life, defending and guiding your nation through four bloody decades of struggling to survive. You told me your people had had enough bloodshed, that this was time to make peace. Ten months ago, you stood on this same lawn and shook the hand of Yasir Arafat, the leader of the Palestinian people.

Today you stand together with King Hussein, descendent of the Prophet Mohammed, to declare that Jordan and Israel have ended their conflict. In holding out to your people the hope of a normal, secure life, you, sir, have fulfilled the mission of your life and of all those who have fought by your side for so long.

Now as we go forward, we must guard against illusions. Dark forces of hatred and violence still stalk your lands. We must not let them succeed.

King Hussein, Prime Minister Rabin: As you and your people embark on this journey of peace, we know the road will not be easy. Just as we have supported you in coming this far, the United States will walk the final miles with you. We must all go on until we ensure that the peace you are seeking prevails in the Holy Land and extends to all Israel's Arab neighbors. Our common objective of a comprehensive peace must be achieved.

Now as we witness the signing of this declaration and applaud the bravery of these men, let us remember that peace is much more than a pledge to abide by words on a page. It is a bold attempt to write a new history. Guided by the blessings of God, let us now go forward and give life to this declaration. For if we follow its course, we will truly achieve a peace of the generations. Thank you very much.

HUSSEIN'S REMARKS

President Clinton, Prime Minister Yitzhak Rabin, ladies and gentlemen:

And so it is that on this day, at this house of the great American people, we have been able to take an historic step which we hope and pray will be to the benefit of our peoples within our entire region—Jordanians, Israelis, and others. This is the moment of a commitment and of a vision. Not all of what is possible is within the document we have just ratified, but a modest, determined beginning to bring to our region and our peoples the security from fear, which I must admit has prevailed over all the years of our lives; the uncertainty of every day as to how it might end; the suspicion, the bitterness, the lack of human contact. We are on our way now, truly, towards what is normal in relations between our peoples and ourselves, and what is worthy.

We will meet as often as we are able to and is required, with pleasure, to shepherd this process on in the times ahead.

At this moment, I would like to share with you all the pride I have in my people, the people of Jordan—in their maturity, in their courage, and what I have been blessed with, their trust and confidence, and I believe the commitment of the overwhelming majority to the cause of peace.

The term used in international documents as have affected us so far is "the state of belligerency" and the "end of the state of belligerency." I think both in Arabic and in Hebrew, our people do not have such a term. What we have accomplished and what we are committed to is the end of the state of war between Jordan and Israel.

Thank you so very much, indeed, Mr. President, for all your kindness. Thank you, Prime Minister. Thank you, all our dear friends. A warm thanks to the American people, our partners in the past, in the present and in the future. And bless you and bless our march for the future and towards the future of peace in our region.

RABIN'S REMARKS

The President of the United States, His Majesty King Hussein of the Kingdom of Jordan, friends, ladies and gentlemen:

I start with the Hebrew word, shalom.

A million of eyes all over the world are watching us now with great relief and great joy. Yet another nightmare of war may be over. At the same time a million eyes in the Middle East are looking at us now with great heartfelt hope that our children and grandchildren will know no more war.

Ladies and gentlemen, today we submit to our respective people a wonderful present. The declaration we have signed just now here in Washington is the closest thing to a treaty of peace. We have gone here a long way towards a full treaty of peace, and even though our work has not yet ended, it is my hope and belief that not long from today we shall return to sign a final and a permanent treaty of peace.

Mr. President, Your Majesty, it is dusk at our homes in the Middle East. Soon, darkness will prevail. But the citizens of Israel and Jordan will see a great light. We have today taken a major step on the road to peace. We and Jordan have chosen to speak to each other rather than to continue the state of war. From here, in the distance of thousands of miles from home, I would like to congratulate today the inhabitants of Israel and of Jordan, to remember the fallen in the wars on both sides, and to tell children on both sides of the border we hope and pray that your life will be different than ours.

I believe that we are a small country with a big heart. We are aware of world agonies and suffering of human beings anywhere. At this hour, when we are celebrating here in Washington, Israeli defense soldiers and medical units are trying to save the lives of thousands, if not more, of people on the verge of death in Rwanda. But at the very same time, Israeli soldiers, a rescue team in Buenos Aires, on the invitation of the Argentinean government, are endeavoring to rescue the lives or bodies of those who were attacked, killed and disappeared—bodies of their own brothers, as well as of the other human beings from buildings destroyed by vicious terrorists. This terrible crime was committed against Jews just because they were Jews.

The Israeli rescue soldiers in Rwanda, as well as those in Argentina, together with their comrades in arms defending us at home, are the same side of the same coin.

Mr. President, Your Majesty, there is much more in the Washington Declaration than parties were planning when they decided to prepare this declaration 10 days ago. It bears witness to our ability in Israel and Jordan to accelerate our efforts towards peace, to overcome obstacles, to achieve a breakthrough and to put an end to 46 years of hostility.

Mr. President, thank you—thank you for all you have done for us and for what you will do. We embark on a road which must still be completed. And I am appealing to the United States, the leader of peace efforts in the Middle East, to assist those countries, those peoples who demonstrate courage and who take risks—risks for peace—because it is a worthwhile goal.

The political achievements presented today to the public here in Washington are part of a whole agenda that must still be clarified in serious deliberations ahead of us—from the difficult subjects of boundaries and water, to trade and economic relations on which peace in our region will be based and, of course, security and diplomatic relations. Our duty, starting today, is to turn the articles written on the paper into a living reality.

This fine job could not have been completed without your leadership and determination in the Middle East peacemaking. You have already established your place in our history, an honorable place. And thank you.

Our heartfelt gratitude goes also to Secretary of State Warren Christopher and his peace team, who devotedly seek peace, and to generations of former U.S. administration members who have for years searched for a bridge between Israel, Jordan and the other Arab peoples.

Your Excellency, the President of the United States; Your Majesty, the King of Jordan; let me say a few words in Hebrew to the citizens of Israel who are watching us now: (Words spoken in Hebrew.)

Thank you very much.

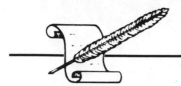
August

GAO REPORT ON CLEANUP OF NUCLEAR WEAPONS PLANTS
August 10, 1994

Despite spending $23 billion on environmental cleanup at the nation's nuclear weapons plants since 1989, the U.S. Department of Energy (DOE) had actually cleaned up little of the vast amount of radioactive and hazardous waste they generated. That was the conclusion of a report by the General Accounting Office (GAO), the investigative arm of Congress, dated August 10.

The report said that over a period of more than four decades the DOE and agencies that preceded it had disposed of more than 1 billion cubic feet of hazardous and/or radioactive waste at nuclear weapons plants around the country. Since at that time scientists knew little about the dangers posed by the waste, it was frequently stored in drums or cribs or poured directly into the ground. Many of the containers used to store waste had subsequently deteriorated, the report said, allowing the hazardous waste to seep through the soil and ultimately contaminate groundwater. More than 5,700 areas on DOE property had been contaminated.

The methods used to clean up contaminated sites were "often ineffective and extremely expensive," the report said, and added that the DOE had estimated that it would cost as much as $300 billion over a thirty-year period to clean up the sites. "Developing less costly and more effective cleanup technologies may be the only way the nation can afford to clean up the vast amounts of waste generated by the nation's nuclear weapons production complex," the report said. It added that many of the technologies currently employed produced only short-term results.

The DOE had spent at least $600 million since 1989 developing new technologies, according to the GAO. However, "little new technology finds its way into the agency's cleanup actions." The report blamed numerous factors: a lack of leadership and coordination at the DOE, local DOE officials' fear that they would miss deadlines if a new technology failed, conflicting priorities among various agencies involved in cleanups, a lack of *familiarity with new technologies by local officials, and DOE's reliance on recommendations from on-site contractors who might have financial investments in particular technologies.*

DOE officials did not dispute the report's overall conclusions. "We basically agree there are problems with getting innovative technology implemented due to a lot of different barriers, as pointed out in the report," said Gerald G. Boyd, deputy assistant energy secretary for technology development, in an interview with the Associated Press. However, both the report and Boyd said the DOE had taken steps aimed at solving the problems.

Uranium Leaks from Reactor

DOE officials had a more immediate problem in November, when it was revealed that 4.4 pounds of bomb-grade uranium had leaked from an old experimental reactor at the Oak Ridge National Laboratory in Tennessee. The uranium lodged in a pipe outside the reactor building, leading to fears that an uncontrollable nuclear chain reaction could occur. If it did, the material might explode and disperse radioactive contaminants over the area.

The leak perplexed DOE officials, who said they never expected it to occur. They pumped water out of the pipe, which they said stabilized the situation. The Oak Ridge Environmental Peace Alliance, which originally revealed the problem after obtaining DOE documents, disagreed. Alliance members said removing the water made it easier for the chemicals inside the pipe to attack it, possibly leading to a leak. DOE officials said that the actual removal of the uranium could take up to two years and would have to be done with remote-control technology. As a precaution, they evacuated an office building next to the reactor.

The plant, known as the Molten Salt Reactor Experiment, operated from 1965 to 1969. When the plant was shut down, the government had no long-term plan for dealing with the radioactive materials it contained or with the facility itself.

Report Warns of Hazards

The news only got worse in December. On December 6, the Energy Department released a massive report that revealed that 26 metric tons of plutonium were stored haphazardly at thirteen DOE sites around the country. The plutonium was left over when production of nuclear weapons stopped suddenly in the late 1980s. Since few people thought the shutdown was permanent, the plutonium was left in containers that could leak and in situations where nuclear chain reactions could occur. The report stated that "the department's inventory of plutonium presents significant hazards to workers, the public and environment, and little progress has been made to aggressively address the problem." The Energy Department released the document after part of it was leaked to the Rocky Mountain News *in Denver.*

On December 19, the General Accounting Office released a new report that found that the Hanford nuclear reservation in Washington had a backlog of approximately 1,500 repair projects on aging tanks filled with highly radio-

active waste. The backlog remained despite a cleanup effort that had cost $2 billion since 1991, the report said. Leaks had occurred in more than one-third of the 177 tanks, which were widely believed to be the largest environmental and safety threat at any DOE facility.

The GAO suggested that the backlog may have developed partly because of a misappropriation of staff at the Hanford site. The auditors reported that the 93 blue-collar workers who actually made the repairs were supervised by 146 managers, and that there also were 22 administrative staff members.

Also on December 19, the Clinton administration announced a sharp cutback in funding for the Energy Department, including a $4.4 billion reduction in cleanup funds for the weapons plants over five years. Although DOE officials said the cuts would primarily affect low-risk problems, environmentalists said the reductions would seriously hamper DOE cleanup efforts and would likely lead to a wave of lawsuits.

Following are excerpts from a report titled "Department of Energy: Management Changes Needed to Expand Use of Innovative Cleanup Technologies," released August 10, 1994, by the General Accounting Office:

The Department of Energy (DOE) faces the major challenge of cleaning up the waste generated by more than four decades of nuclear weapons production. The methods currently available to clean up contamination, however, are often ineffective and extremely expensive, as reflected by the agency's recent estimates that environmental cleanup could cost as much as $300 billion over a 30-year period. Developing less costly and more effective cleanup technologies may be the only way the nation can afford to clean up the vast amounts of waste generated by the nation's nuclear weapons production complex.

Our objective in this review was to evaluate the internal and external barriers that are inhibiting the use of new and innovative technologies in environmental cleanup. This report is one of a series of reports that we are issuing as part of our general management review of DOE.

Results in Brief

Although DOE has spent a substantial amount to develop waste cleanup technology, little new technology finds its way into the agency's cleanup actions. Even where new technology has been successfully demonstrated, agency officials are reluctant to try new approaches, tending instead to choose conventional techniques to clean up their facilities. As a result, opportunities for more effective cleanup solutions may be missed.

DOE's technology problems began by not having a well-coordinated and fully integrated technology development program. The agency's technology needs have neither been comprehensively identified to allow prudent research decisions, nor have various environmental program offices in headquarters and in the field worked together effectively to identify and evaluate all of the possible technology solutions available. Furthermore, internal decision-making processes have prevented a full discussion of the opportunities for new and promising technologies to find their way into cleanup actions.

DOE recognizes these obstacles to technology acceptance and is taking several actions. For example, a plan for restructuring technology development programs was approved in January 1994. This plan is currently being implemented at headquarters and the field. In addition, field officials have been instructed to more seriously consider new and improved technology. DOE is also working with regulators to achieve greater acceptance of new and innovative technology. While these are welcome changes, it remains to be seen whether the agency's strategy will ensure that all parties are involved in decisions affecting whether new technologies are used to clean up contaminated sites.

Background

DOE faces an enormous and expensive environmental challenge. Over the last 40 years, DOE and its predecessor agencies disposed of more than 1 billion cubic feet of hazardous and/or radioactive waste at weapons production facilities around the country. Since little was understood about the types of waste generated and their effect on the environment, the waste was often stored in drums or cribs or poured directly into the soil—techniques that would not be acceptable by today's standards. Over time, many of the original containers have deteriorated. At such disposal sites, liquid effluents can seep down into the soil and ultimately reach the groundwater. As a result of earlier disposal practices, soil and groundwater contamination is now widespread. Over 5,700 individual contaminated "plumes" have been identified on DOE lands.

To address technology issues, in 1989 DOE established the Office of Technology Development (OTD) within the Office of Environmental Restoration and Waste Management. OTD is responsible for managing a national program to support the technology needs of other environmental program offices. OTD accomplishes its mission by funding a variety of projects to demonstrate the potential of new and improved approaches to cleanup problems. OTD's goal is to ensure that the technology is developed to the stage where it can be commercialized and, thus, available in the private sector. OTD is charged with identifying technologies with DOE-wide potential and has demonstrations under way using such advanced technologies as ground-penetrating radar and bioremediation. For fiscal year 1993, OTD spent $380 million, and the office has spent about $600 million since its creation in 1989.

OTD supports the offices of Waste Management and Environmental Restoration within the Office of Environmental Management, which in turn work with DOE field offices, contractors, the states, and the Environmental Protection Agency (EPA) to identify and select the most appropriate technology to apply to a given situation. DOE has entered into enforceable agreements with EPA and the states, thereby committing the agency to milestones for completing cleanup work at each site. In support of the agreements, DOE evaluates a variety of cleanup technologies and recommends the preferred alternative to the regulator (EPA and/or the state). The regulator, in turn, is responsible for approving the technology that will be used to clean up the site. Whether a milestone can be achieved is often dependent on the technology selected for use at a particular site.

Innovative Technology Is Not Being Used to Clean Up Contaminated Sites

The need for improved technologies to clean up contaminated sites is widely recognized by DOE and its stakeholders, which include EPA, the states, and the public. Although OTD and others have conducted several demonstration projects to show the effectiveness of innovative cleanup approaches, new technologies are not being seriously considered or used to clean up DOE's contaminated sites.

DOE has received about $23 billion for environmental management since 1989, yet little cleanup has resulted. Experts agree that many cleanup technologies currently in use are extremely costly and offer only short-term solutions. For example, one of the most commonly used methods for treating contaminant plumes—pump-and-treat—does not remove the contamination source, thus failing as a permanent solution. Furthermore, current technologies to treat waste contaminated by both hazardous and radioactive material—mixed waste—need significant improvement. The vast majority of the agency's waste is mixed waste. DOE recently reported to the Congress that treatment technologies need to be modified for two-thirds of these identified mixed wastes.

DOE's own technology program summary states the technology challenge this way:

> . . . the development of new technology presents the best hope for ensuring a substantive reduction in risk to the environment and improved worker/public safety within realistic financial constraints.

Using cleanup technology that is faster, cheaper, and safer than conventional approaches is growing in importance. Over the next few years, agreements that DOE has signed require accelerated progress in cleaning up its vast number of contaminated sites. Given the leadtime from proposing solutions to applying them at a given site, DOE is entering a narrow "window" of time in which technical solutions for cleaning up sites must be evaluated and applied.

Many Barriers Limit Use of New and Innovative Technology

The process of choosing a technology for cleanup involves many decisionmakers, requires technical expertise, and is complicated by stakeholders' competing interests. The pressure to meet agreement milestones also influences the technology evaluation process at a given location—DOE is under pressure to work quickly toward solutions.

We found that new technologies are not being seriously considered or used to clean up DOE's contaminated sites. Senior headquarters environmental officials told us that new technologies have not been rigorously evaluated, much less employed by DOE. On the basis of our discussions with headquarters managers, local officials at two of DOE's largest contaminated sites (the Hanford Site near Richland, Washington, and the Savannah River Site in Aiken, South Carolina), and our analysis of studies, we found that the reluctance to consider newer technology has several basic causes.

- Local officials fear that using new technology may lead to missing milestones should the technology fail. DOE is under pressure to meet its scheduled milestones. DOE is already missing some of its milestones and anticipates more slippages in the future, as the pace of milestones due accelerates over the next few years.
- Conflicting priorities among stakeholders tend to prevent the approval of innovative approaches for site cleanup. For example, local governments may place a high priority on economic development and job creation and view faster cleanup as a threat to local economies. The public is primarily concerned about risks associated with the cleanup process. As a result, each stakeholder may view the value of an innovative approach differently. Accordingly, DOE must balance the interests of these diverse stakeholder groups, a difficult challenge.
- Field officials, as well as local stakeholders, may not be familiar with newer technologies that could apply to their locations, and thus may associate the newer technologies with an unacceptable level of risk.
- Field officials also often rely on recommendations from on-site contractors who may favor particular technologies on the basis of their own experiences and investments. DOE has long been criticized for its extensive reliance on contractors for technical decisions.

DOE's own studies, and those performed by other organizations, cite similar reasons why innovative technologies are not being applied at contaminated sites. For example, a spokesperson for the Western Governors' Association recently commented that effective and rapid cleanup of federal sites is hampered by a system that relies on traditional technologies selected by "risk averse" cleanup managers, who have no incentive to innovate. The official explained that there is a need to reduce the uncertainty surrounding the performance and cost of innovative technologies.

We previously reported similar barriers inhibiting the development and use of innovative technologies in EPA's technology program. Among other factors, we reported that the lack of reliable information on innovative technologies has led government officials, private contractors, and investors to avoid the possible risks associated with innovative technologies.

Our discussions with EPA regional staffs and state regulators indicate some hesitancy to approve innovative technologies. Regulators are sometimes reluctant to appear lenient with DOE, recognizing that their actions are closely watched by the public. Public frustration often results when regulators allow

DOE to miss cleanup milestones. However, regulators also note that their hesitancy is not as widespread as perceived by DOE field officials and point to several regulatory options that would allow the agency to use innovative technologies in combination with conventional techniques. For example, EPA published a technology innovation strategy in January 1994 designed to stimulate the adoption of new technologies by strengthening the incentives for innovation and reducing barriers within the regulatory framework.

Program Officers Not Working Together Effectively

DOE's internal program problems have also prevented the agency from maximizing its investments in technology development and implementation. Individual offices have not worked together as a well-coordinated and integrated unit to overcome the resistance to using improved technology, nor have offices worked together to develop a comprehensive assessment of technology needs.

Although OTD's mission is to manage a focused technology development program, other program offices within Environmental Management conduct their own projects, which often overlap and conflict with OTD's activities. For example, in 1993, in addition to the $380 million spent by OTD in 1993, the offices of Environmental Restoration and Waste Management spent almost $70 million and over $100 million, respectively, on technology development projects. When asked about these expenditures, headquarters managers explained that OTD develops technologies for problems that are common across the DOE complex, while program offices develop technologies that address problems that are specific to individual sites. However, our analysis of several hundred technology development activities throughout the environmental program offices revealed no clear distinctions between offices in the scope and objectives of projects. For example, descriptions of these activities that are funded because they apply to technology needs at a particular site frequently contain statements that the technologies being developed could be applied at other DOE sites. Thus, it is not at all clear that program offices are funding activities that OTD would not also fund.

DOE also does not have a comprehensive needs assessment from which technology development projects can be ranked and funded in the most effective way. Instead, the current technology-needs assessment process is highly fragmented. Program units have independently examined their technology development needs, and their studies are at various stages of completion. DOE field locations have also studied their own specific cleanup needs. For example:

- Although the Office of Environmental Restoration completed an initial description of its needs in 1991 (and updated it in Jan. 1993), OTD reported that these efforts do not provide the specificity needed to determine which technology needs are most pressing. We noted that the level of specific information on the problems at each site varied significantly. For example, the specific size, migration pattern, and contaminants within groundwater would be described in detail at one location, while the information provided at other locations would be described in very general terms such as "a source, a release mechanism, a receptor population, and toxic materials are present"—terms too broad to be useful to OTD.

- The Office of Waste Management has not provided OTD with a description of its needs. Waste Management officials told us that the early needs studies were too general to use. In response, Waste Management is currently conducting an in-depth, site-by-site examination of its current problems.
- DOE field locations are also studying their own specific cleanup needs at their particular sites. At both the Hanford and Savannah River sites, for example, field staff are using local laboratories to identify the kinds of technology that will be needed to clean up those sites.

OTD has also conducted its own needs assessment studies, in the absence of a comprehensive assessment from other program offices. As a result of not having an integrated assessment approach and strategy, OTD and program offices may not be developing the most appropriate technologies. In addition, DOE may be missing opportunities to maximize its funding choices to the areas of highest need or to identify problems that exist at several locations.

Flawed Decision-Making Process

Despite the crucial role technology plays in meeting the cleanup milestones specified in agreements, OTD's technical experts are not part of the decision-making process where technology choices for particular sites are made. For example, OTD does not have a role in negotiating agreements, the critical point in time when cleanup milestones are first established, although achieving these milestones is often dependent on the success of the particular technology used. In addition, OTD is not involved in decisions on potential technology options for the feasibility study phase of cleanup. Furthermore, OTD is not party to the final decision defining the technology that will be used to clean the site. In the absence of OTD's involvement at such key decision points, the full range of technology choices is not likely to be completely discussed or evaluated.

DOE Has Begun to Address Its Problems

The Office of Environmental Management began restructuring its technology development program in January 1994. Several changes being implemented, as a result of this restructuring, should address many issues discussed in this report. For example, the technology development program activities of the Offices of Waste Management, Environmental Restoration, and Technology Development would be centrally managed and coordinated under the direction of OTD. To help ensure that technology development activities are focused on the most pressing needs, five priority "focus" areas for technology development have been designated. They are:

- high-level waste tank remediation;
- characterization, treatment, and disposal of mixed waste;
- cleanup of contaminant plumes;
- stabilization of landfills; and
- decommission and final disposition of DOE facilities.

The Office of Environmental Management has established management "teams" at headquarters to manage technology development activities. The Office of Environmental Management is also in the process of establishing implementation teams for each of the five areas to facilitate the use of innovative and improved technologies. Management team members include officials from the headquarters program offices—the users of the technology—as well as selected regulators, among others.

The external peer review process for technology development is being modified around the five focus areas. DOE is also establishing performance measures to evaluate the actual use of innovative and improved technologies at the sites. At the field level, where technology decisions are made, site coordination teams have been established to oversee local technology development activities. However, Environmental Management has not clarified how regulators and other stakeholders will be included in these groups.

Recognizing that new and innovative technologies were not being evaluated, DOE's Office of Environmental Restoration directed its field staff in a July 1993 policy statement to consider new and innovative technologies early in the process of deciding what actions to take at cleanup sites. The goal of this policy was to provide the opportunity for new technologies—as well as conventional ones—to be given equal consideration.

DOE is also expanding research outreach to help ensure that technology development activities among agencies are closely coordinated to maximize benefits and reduce costs. These activities include working with EPA, the Departments of Defense and Interior, and others.

Conclusions

DOE and technology experts recognize that more advanced technologies are needed to meet DOE's significant and costly cleanup problems. DOE's inability to transfer demonstrated technologies to cleanup sites underscores the coordination flaws in DOE's cleanup program. Barriers restrict the wider use of new and promising technologies to clean up defense plant wastes.

Although DOE's new strategy should help correct coordination problems and eliminate duplication and overlap in its technology development program, insufficient emphasis is given to ensuring that all parties—at the level where decisions are made—are knowledgeable about the strengths of the technological innovations being studied. Specifically, DOE has not clarified the roles that stakeholders will play on site teams, yet these are the groups that must ultimately approve the technology to be used at a particular location. Reconciling the many different priorities among local regulators and other stakeholders is crucial to gaining agreement on the best cleanup technology. DOE's July 1993 policy, while a step forward, does not ensure that new technology will actually be selected. Obtaining agreement on an innovative approach is particularly difficult when officials are unfamiliar with innovative approaches and technology experts are not fully involved in the decision-making.

While DOE's new approach to technology development encourages cooperation among Environmental Management's program offices, it does not ensure that field decisionmakers include new technologies in agreements, preventing promising new techniques from being used to clean up sites—a stumbling block that places pressure on DOE to work more skillfully not only with its own staff, but also with federal and state regulators.

The strategy also does not directly link technology experts with field decisionmakers. OTD's technology staff are not formally involved in discussions of technological solutions to be used at the sites. OTD staff still do not have a role in negotiating/revising agreement milestones with regulators, although the ability to meet a milestone often depends on the technology being used.

Moreover, the strategy does not overcome contractors' resistance to recommending unfamiliar technology. DOE's strategy to commercialize technology results does not guarantee that new technologies are recognized or evaluated by a particular local staff or its on-site contractors.

Recommendations

To ensure that decisionmakers are aware of, and fully evaluate, innovative technologies to the maximum extent possible, we recommend that the Secretary of Energy direct the Assistant Secretary for Environmental Management to (1) fully involve regulators and other stakeholders in making decisions at the local level about the technology to be selected and (2) formally include OTD staff in the evaluation and selection of technologies to be used to clean up DOE sites. For example, OTD staff could be included in the feasibility study and discussions leading to the Record of Decision. . . .

September

UN CONFERENCE ON WORLD POPULATION
September 13, 1994

A United Nations conference on population and development, attended by delegates and high-level officials from more than 150 nations, on September 13 concluded a nine-day session in Cairo, Egypt, by adopting a twenty-year action plan aimed at stabilizing world population at about 7.27 billion people by the year 2015.

According to UN demographic projections, without active restraint world population could reach from 7.1 billion to 7.8 billion inhabitants in twenty years, a huge increase from the current 5.6 billion people. By the middle of the twenty-first century, the planet could have anywhere from 7.9 billion to 11.9 billion people. According to the projections, 90 percent of the growth would likely occur in the world's poorest countries.

Delegates worked under heavy guard after Islamic fundamentalists decried the conference as "morally wicked" and threatened violence. The conference also became the focal point of a Vatican-led attack on abortion that tied up work for several days.

The Cairo action plan focused on helping people in poor, developing countries gain access to birth control services and information. That objective was not new—it had been promoted in various forms by the two previous UN population conferences, in Bucharest in 1974 and Mexico City in 1984—but the strategy was different. The Cairo plan encouraged national governments to let women assume more control over their lives, assuming that if women were given a true choice they would opt to have fewer children.

Economic Improvement Emphasized

Falling birth rates in Europe and much of North America had not been matched in many other parts of the world. The poorest nations, which were concentrated in Asia, Africa, and Latin America, generally had the fastest population growth and were the least able to provide food, shelter, jobs, and needed services for the additional people. The Cairo plan noted that without a check on population, the affected countries would be condemned to perpetual poverty. That poverty, in turn, would continue to limit health care, including reproductive health care and family planning.

The document emphasized that economic improvement strategies had to be part of the global plan to limit population growth. The conference proposed several steps for individual governments and international development agencies to take, with eliminating barriers to women in the workplace receiving prominent mention.

The effort to empower women took the Cairo plan beyond the scope of the previous plans devised in Bucharest and Mexico City. At the conference, it was reported that the widespread distribution of condoms in Pakistan had not slowed population growth because in traditional Islamic families the women had no power to make the men use them. It was also reported that women in the nearby Indian state of Rajastan said the only means of birth control available to them was sterilization, which they feared because of the danger of infection and even death from operations performed in unsanitary settings.

The Fight Over Abortion

The Vatican, together with several Latin American and Islamic countries, objected that the document endorsed abortion. They specifically took offense to a paragraph stating that the practice "should be safe" in countries where abortion was legal. The Vatican's delegation argued that no abortion could be "safe" because it caused the death of the unborn child.

In a compromise aimed at keeping the paragraph intact, the delegates left the wording alone but switched the order of two sentences. As revised, the paragraph began: "In no case should abortion be promoted as a method of family planning." The Vatican delegation, unable to muster strong support for its position, welcomed the change. Its spokesman, Monsignor Joaquin Navarro-Valls, said the Vatican "did not wish to prolong the present discussion" and would formally append objections to the document upon its adoption. About twenty other predominantly Catholic or Islamic countries did likewise.

In its entirety, the compromise paragraph approved by the delegates read:

> *In no case should abortion be promoted as a method of family planning. All Governments and relevant intergovernmental and non-governmental organizations are urged to strengthen their commitment to women's health, to deal with the health impact of unsafe abortion as a major public health concern and to reduce the recourse to abortion through expanded and improved family planning services. Prevention of unwanted pregnancies must always be given the highest priority and all attempts should be made to eliminate the need for abortion. Women who have unwanted pregnancies should have ready access to reliable information and compassionate counselling. Any measures or changes related to abortion within the health system can only be determined at the national or local level according to the national legislative process. In circumstances in which abortion is not against the law, such abortion should be safe. In all cases women should have access to quality services for the management of complica-*

tions arising from abortion. Post-abortion counselling, education and family planning services should be offered promptly which will also help to avoid repeat abortions.

Following is the text of Chapter IV, titled "Gender Equality, Equity and Empowerment of Women," from the "Programme of Action of the United Nations International Conference on Population and Development," adopted at Cairo, Egypt, on September 13, 1994:

A. Empowerment and Status of Women

Basis for Action

The empowerment and autonomy of women and the improvement of their political, social, economic and health status is a highly important end in itself. In addition, it is essential for the achievement of sustainable development. The full participation and partnership of both women and men is required in productive and reproductive life, including shared responsibilities for the care and nurturing of children and maintenance of the household. In all parts of the world, women are facing threats to their lives, health and well-being as a result of being overburdened with work and of their lack of power and influence. In most regions of the world, women receive less formal education than men, and at the same time, women's own knowledge, abilities and coping mechanisms often go unrecognized. The power relations that impede women's attainment of healthy and fulfilling lives operate at many levels of society, from the most personal to the highly public. Achieving change requires policy and programme actions that will improve women's access to secure livelihoods and economic resources, alleviate their extreme responsibilities with regard to housework, remove legal impediments to their participation in public life, and raise social awareness through effective programmes of education and mass communication. In addition, improving the status of women also enhances their decision-making capacity at all levels in all spheres of life, especially in the area of sexuality and reproduction. This, in turn, is essential for the long-term success of population programmes. Experience shows that population and development programmes are most effective when steps have simultaneously been taken to improve the status of women.

Education is one of the most important means of empowering women with the knowledge, skills and self-confidence necessary to participate fully in the development process. More than 40 years ago, the Universal Declaration of Human Rights asserted that "everyone has the right to education." In 1990, Governments meeting at the World Conference on Education for All in Jomtien, Thailand, committed themselves to the goal of universal access to basic education. But despite notable efforts by countries around the globe that have appreciably expanded access to basic education, there are approximately 960 million illiterate adults in the world, of whom two thirds are women. More than one third of the world's adults, most of them women, have no access to printed knowledge, to new skills or to technologies that would improve the quality of their lives and help them shape and adapt to social and economic change. There are 130 million children who are not enrolled in primary school and 70 percent of them are girls.

Objectives

The objectives are:

(a) To achieve equality and equity based on harmonious partnership between men and women and enable women to realize their full potential;

(b) To ensure the enhancement of women's contributions to sustainable development through their full involvement in policy- and decision-making processes at all stages and participation in all aspects of production, employment, income-generating activities, education, health, science and technology, sports, culture and population-related activities and other areas, as active decision makers, participants and beneficiaries;

(c) To ensure that all women, as well as men, are provided with the education necessary for them to meet their basic human needs and to exercise their human rights.

Actions

Countries should act to empower women and should take steps to eliminate inequalities between men and women as soon as possible by:

(a) Establishing mechanisms for women's equal participation and equitable representation at all levels of the political process and public life in each community and society and enabling women to articulate their concerns and needs;

(b) Promoting the fulfillment of women's potential through education, skill development and employment, giving paramount importance to the elimination of poverty, illiteracy and ill health among women;

(c) Eliminating all practices that discriminate against women; assisting women to establish and realize their rights, including those that relate to reproductive and sexual health;

(d) Adopting appropriate measures to improve women's ability to earn income beyond traditional occupations, achieve economic self-reliance, and ensure women's equal access to the labour market and social security systems;

(e) Eliminating violence against women;

(f) Eliminating discriminatory practices by employers against women, such as those based on proof of contraceptive use or pregnancy status;

(g) Making it possible, through laws, regulations and other appropriate measures, for women to combine the roles of child-bearing, breast-feeding and child-rearing with participation in the workforce.

All countries should make greater efforts to promulgate, implement and enforce national laws and international conventions to which they are party, such as the Convention on the Elimination of All Forms of Discrimination against Women, that protect women from all types of economic discrimination and from sexual harassment, and to implement fully the Declaration on the Elimination of Violence against Women and the Vienna Declaration and Programme of Action adopted at the World Conference on Human Rights in 1993. Countries are urged to sign, ratify and implement all existing agreements that promote women's rights.

Governments at all levels should ensure that women can buy, hold and sell property and land equally with men, obtain credit and negotiate contracts in their own name and on their own behalf and exercise their legal rights to inheritance.

Governments and employers are urged to eliminate gender discrimination in hiring, wages, benefits, training and job security with a view to eliminating gender-based disparities in income.

Governments, international organizations and nongovernmental organizations should ensure that their personnel policies and practices comply with the principle of equitable representation of both sexes, especially at the managerial and policy-making levels, in all programmes, including population and development programmes. Specific procedures and indicators should be devised for gender-based analysis of development programmes and for assessing the impact of those programmes on women's social, economic and health status and access to resources.

Countries should take full measures to eliminate all forms of exploitation, abuse, harassment and violence against women, adolescents and children. This implies both preventive actions and rehabilitation of victims. Countries should prohibit degrading practices, such as trafficking in women, adolescents and children and exploitation through prostitution, and pay special attention to protecting the rights and safety of those who suffer from these crimes and those in potentially exploitable situations, such as migrant women, women in domestic service and schoolgirls. In this regard, international safeguards and mechanisms for cooperation should be put in place to ensure that these measures are implemented.

Countries are urged to identify and condemn the systematic practice of rape and other forms of inhuman and degrading treatment of women as a deliberate instrument of war and ethnic cleansing and take steps to assure that full assistance is provided to the victims of such abuse for their physical and mental rehabilitation.

The design of family health and other development interventions should take better account of the demands on women's time from the responsibilities of child-rearing, household work and income-generating activities. Male responsibilities should be emphasized with respect to child-rearing and housework. Greater investments should be made in appropriate measures to lessen the daily burden of domestic responsibilities, the greatest share of which falls on women. Greater attention should be paid to the ways in which environmental degradation and changes in land use adversely affect the allocation of women's time. Women's domestic working environments should not adversely affect their health.

Every effort should be made to encourage the expansion and strengthening of grass-roots, community-based and activist groups for women. Such groups should be the focus of national campaigns to foster women's awareness of the full range of their legal rights, including their rights within the family, and to help women organize to achieve those rights.

Countries are strongly urged to enact laws and to implement programmes and policies which will enable employees of both sexes to organize their family and work responsibilities through flexible work-hours, parental leave, day-care facilities, maternity leave, policies that enable working mothers to breast-feed their children, health insurance and other such measures. Similar rights should be ensured to those working in the informal sector.

Programmes to meet the needs of growing numbers of elderly people should fully take into account that women represent the larger proportion of the elderly and that elderly women generally have a lower socioeconomic status than elderly men.

B. The Girl Child

Basis for Action

Since in all societies discrimination on the basis of sex often starts at the earliest stages of life, greater equality for the girl child is a necessary first step in ensuring that women realize their full potential and become equal partners in development. In a number of countries, the practice of prenatal sex selection, higher rates of mortality among very young girls, and lower rates of school enrollment for girls as compared with boys, suggest that "son preference" is curtailing the access of girl children to food, education and health care. This is often compounded by the increasing use of technologies to determine foetal sex, resulting in abortion of female foetuses. Investments made in the girl child's health, nutrition and education, from infancy through adolescence, are critical.

Objectives

The objectives are:

(a) To eliminate all forms of discrimination against the girl child and the root causes of son preference, which results in harmful and unethical practices regarding female infanticide and prenatal sex selection;

(b) To increase public awareness of the value of the girl child, and concurrently, to strengthen the girl child's self-image, self-esteem and status;

(c) To improve the welfare of the girl child, especially in regard to health, nutrition and education.

Actions

Overall, the value of girl children to both their family and to society must be expanded beyond their definition as potential child-bearers and caretakers and reinforced through the adoption and implementation of educational and social policies that encourage their full participation in the development of the societies in which they live. Leaders at all levels of the society must speak out and act forcefully against patterns of gender discrimination within the family, based on preference for sons. One of the aims should be to eliminate excess mortality of girls, wherever such a pattern exists. Special education and public information efforts are needed to promote equal treatment of girls and boys with respect to nutrition, health care, education and social, economic and political activity, as well as equitable inheritance rights.

Beyond the achievement of the goal of universal primary education in all countries before the year 2015, all countries are urged to ensure the widest and earliest possible access by girls and women to secondary and higher levels of education, as well as vocational education and technical training, bearing in mind the need to improve the quality and relevance of that education.

Schools, the media and other social institutions should seek to eliminate stereotypes in all types of communication and educational materials that reinforce existing inequities between males and females and undermine girls' self-esteem. Countries must recognize that, in addition to expanding education for girls, teachers' attitudes and practices, school curricula and facilities must also change to reflect a commitment to eliminate all gender bias, while recognizing the specific needs of the girl child.

Countries should develop an integrated approach to the special nutritional, general and reproductive health, education and social needs of girls and young women, as such additional investments in adolescent girls can often compensate for earlier inadequacies in their nutrition and health care.

Governments should strictly enforce laws to ensure that marriage is entered into only with the free and full consent of the intending spouses. In addition, Governments should strictly enforce laws concerning the minimum legal age of consent and minimum age at marriage and should raise the minimum age at marriage where necessary. Governments and non-governmental organizations should generate social support for the enforcement of laws on minimum legal age at marriage, in particular by providing educational and employment opportunities.

Governments are urged to prohibit female genital mutilation wherever it exists and to give vigorous support to efforts among non-governmental and community organizations and religious institutions to eliminate such practices.

Governments are urged to take the necessary measures to prevent infanticide, prenatal sex selection, trafficking in girl children and use of girls in prostitution and pornography.

C. Male Responsibilities and Participation

Basis for Action

Changes in both men's and women's knowledge, attitudes and behaviour are necessary conditions for achieving the harmonious partnership of men and women. Men play a key role in bringing about gender equality since, in most societies, men exercise preponderant power in nearly every sphere of life, ranging from personal decisions regarding the size of families to the policy and programme decisions taken at all levels of Government. It is essential to improve communication between men and women on issues of sexuality and reproductive health, and the understanding of their joint responsibilities, so that men and women are equal partners in public and private life.

Objective

The objective is to promote gender equality in all spheres of life, including family and community life, and to encourage and enable men to take responsibility for their sexual and reproductive behaviour and their social and family roles.

Actions

The equal participation of women and men in all areas of family and household responsibilities, including family planning, child-rearing and housework, should be promoted and encouraged by Governments. This should be pursued by means of information, education, communication, employment legislation and by fostering an economically enabling environment, such as family leave for men and women so that they may have more choice regarding the balance of their domestic and public responsibilities.

Special efforts should be made to emphasize men's shared responsibility and promote their active involvement in responsible parenthood, sexual and reproductive behaviour, including family planning; prenatal, maternal and child health; prevention of sexually transmitted diseases, including HIV; prevention of unwanted and high-risk pregnancies; shared control and contribution to family income, children's education, health and nutrition; and recognition and promotion of the equal value of children of both sexes. Male responsibilities in family life must be included in the education of children from the earliest ages. Special emphasis should be placed on the prevention of violence against women and children.

Governments should take steps to ensure that children receive appropriate financial support from their parents by, among other measures, enforcing child-support laws. Governments should consider changes in law and policy to ensure men's responsibility to and financial support for their children and families. Such laws and policies should also encourage maintenance or reconstitution of the family unit. The safety of women in abusive relationships should be protected.

National and community leaders should promote the full involvement of men in family life and the full integration of women in community life. Parents and schools should ensure that attitudes that are respectful of women and girls as equals are instilled in boys from the earliest possible age, along with an understanding of their shared responsibilities in all aspects of a safe, secure and harmonious family life. Relevant programmes to reach boys before they become sexually active are urgently needed.

CANCELLATION OF THE
BASEBALL SEASON
September 14, 1994

On September 14, acting baseball commissioner Bud Selig canceled the remainder of the 1994 season, a season that had ended August 12 when baseball players went on strike. Besides interrupting a historic season, the strike wiped out the World Series, an event which had been held annually without interruption since 1904. Since 1994 ended with no settlement in sight, the strike also threatened the 1995 season.

Both sides bitterly blamed the other for the negotiating stalemate and the season's end. The strike centered on efforts by baseball owners to place a cap on players' salaries, although the cap was not the only issue. The owners said a cap was especially critical to teams in smaller markets, some of which claimed they were losing millions of dollars. The players, whose salaries had soared to an average of $1.2 million on the free market, vehemently opposed any cap. If small-market teams were losing money, the players said, then the large-market teams that were making lots of money should subsidize them.

Many baseball fans found it impossible to sympathize with either side. To them, the strike was all about greed on both sides, a battle by millionaires who had little respect or concern for the game or its fans. As columnist Thomas Boswell wrote in the Washington Post: *"Rich, vain men with special interests have bickered away the tradition of the World Series. That's unconscionable."*

Strike Costly in Many Ways

The strike, which was the eighth work stoppage in twenty-three years and the longest strike in baseball history, cost both sides dearly. In 1994, the strike reportedly cost players about $230 million and teams between $500 million and $600 million. Far harder hit were the stadium vendors, local businesses, and others whose livelihoods depended on baseball.

The strike also cost the players a chance at a historic season. Before the strike, 1994 was shaping up to be one of baseball's most exciting years in recent memory. Tony Gwynn of the San Diego Padres was trying to become the sport's first .400 hitter in more than five decades. Ted Williams last accomplished the feat in 1941, when he hit .406. Matt Williams of the San Francisco Giants, Ken Griffey Jr. of the Seattle Mariners, and Frank Thomas of the Chicago White Sox were all chasing the single-season home run record of sixty-one held by Roger Maris. Thomas and Albert Belle of Cleveland were both trying to win the Triple Crown by leading the league in home runs, runs batted in, and batting average when the season ended. The last man to accomplish that feat was Carl Yastrzemski in 1967. Even the lowly Cleveland Indians, the butt of baseball jokes for years, were enjoying their best season in forty years as they celebrated the opening of a new ballpark.

Other Sports Locked in Labor Disputes

Sports fans suffered another blow in the fall when the start of the 1994 National Hockey League (NHL) season was delayed when the club owners voted to lock out the players until labor negotiations were concluded. Like with the baseball strike, a salary cap was one of the major issues in the hockey dispute. The other major issues involved entry-level salaries, free agency, and salary arbitration. On December 29, commissioner Gary Bettman told officials of the NHL Players Association that if the season did not begin by January 16, 1995, it would be canceled.

The only good news for fans came in late October, when owners and players in the National Basketball Association (NBA) agreed to play the 1994-1995 season while labor negotiations continued. The agreement came only days before the owners were to vote on a lockout. Under the deal, owners agreed not to lock out players and the players agreed not to strike. The agreement guaranteed that the NBA, which like the National Football League already had a salary cap in place, would continue its history of never suffering a work stoppage. NBA players did not like the salary cap, but owners said it had saved the league from financial ruin when it was adopted in 1983.

Baseball Owners Impose Cap

On December 22, the owners of baseball teams declared an impasse in contract negotiations and imposed a salary cap, thereby setting back any hope that the strike would be settled soon. The owners' action provoked an angry response from government officials. Several senior members of Congress threatened to introduce legislation to revoke baseball's exemption from antitrust laws—an exemption established by the U.S. Supreme Court in 1922. Under the exemption, which was unique to baseball among major sports, the owners could block teams from moving and could unilaterally change the contract with players, and court challenges of their actions were very difficult. Sen. Orrin Hatch (R-Utah), the incoming chairman of the Senate Judiciary Committee, supported revoking the exemption. Previ-

ously, Hatch had opposed ending the exemption. "I am fast becoming convinced that the majority of the owners are trying to break the players' association," Hatch said in an interview with the New York Times. *"I do not want to become involved in collective bargaining negotiations, but I'm starting to believe, like many people, that these negotiations are not being done in good faith."*

As the year ended, the players were preparing to file an unfair labor practice charge over the salary cap with the National Labor Relations Board. Nearly all the owners were preparing to field replacement teams made up of major leaguers who would break ranks, minor leaguers, and others. For fans who loved baseball, it appeared that 1995 would be a very disappointing year.

> *Following is the text of a press release issued by the office of acting baseball commissioner Bud Selig on September 14, 1994, announcing the cancellation of the remainder of the baseball season:*

Due to the player strike that began on August 12, 1994, the Office of the Commissioner of Baseball, acting pursuant to a resolution of the major league clubs, reluctantly concluded today that the remainder of the 1994 season, the Division Series, the League Championship Series and the World Series will not be played.

"This is a sad day," said Allan H. (Bud) Selig, chairman of the Major League Executive Council. "Nobody wanted this to happen, but the continuing player strike leaves us no choice but to take this action. We have reached the point where it is no longer practical to complete the remainder of the season or to preserve the integrity of post-season play.

"On June 14, the clubs proposed a reasonable offer to the players' union which included a guarantee of $1 billion in salary and benefits for the players—the largest players' payroll ever. Since that time the clubs have asked the players to negotiate some reasonable division of revenues between players and clubs or some other method for controlling the growth in salaries and ensuring competitive balance.

"The union refused to bargain with us over costs and took a hard-line position that the clubs would fold as they had in past negotiations. That was a terrible mistake, one for which all of us must pay."

OTA REPORT ON NUCLEAR PROLIFERATION

September 23, 1994

The four republics in the former Soviet Union that possessed strategic nuclear weapons—Russia, Ukraine, Kazakhstan, and Belarus—were likely to adhere to international agreements aimed at preventing nuclear proliferation, the Office of Technology Assessment (OTA) concluded in a report issued September 23. However, the OTA warned that political and economic instabilities in the new nations had weakened government controls on the nuclear industry, thereby increasing opportunities for the unauthorized export and smuggling of materials.

The OTA, a nonpartisan congressional research agency, also warned that economic hardships had left thousands of skilled weapons scientists and engineers vulnerable to outside bids for their expertise. The United States should increase funding for programs to improve export controls and nuclear security systems in the former Soviet Union, the report said, as well as for programs aimed at improving economic conditions and creating new jobs for nuclear scientists, engineers, and security workers.

The OTA report, the fifth in a series on nuclear proliferation requested by the Senate committees on foreign relations and governmental affairs, came at a time of heightened international concern about the spread of nuclear weapons and materials.

Number of Nuclear Powers Grows

Before the Soviet Union dissolved in 1991, there were five acknowledged nuclear powers: the United States, the Soviet Union, France, the United Kingdom, and China. The number jumped to eight at least temporarily in 1991 with the addition of the new Soviet republics. Under the Nuclear Non-Proliferation Treaty (NPT), Russia was recognized as a nuclear state and successor to the Soviet Union, while the three other former Soviet republics were designated as nonnuclear states. The three at first showed some reluctance to relinquish their weapons, possibly because they hoped nuclear status would bring economic or political leverage, but Belarus and then Kazakhstan signed the NPT in 1993, and Ukraine followed in November 1994.

After President Leonid Kuchma of Ukraine finally convinced his parliament to sign the treaty, President Bill Clinton announced that the United States would provide $200 million in economic aid to the republic in addition to the $350 million already committed by the U.S. government to help dismantle Ukrainian warheads. Thus, Ukraine became the fourth largest recipient of U.S. foreign aid, with only Israel, Egypt, and Russia receiving larger sums.

Despite this apparent victory, treaties alone could no longer guarantee that nuclear weapons would remain in the hands of a few countries with an interest in not using them. Three nations—India, Pakistan, and Israel— had the ability to produce a bomb. A growing number of other countries were believed to have the nuclear materials necessary for developing weapons, among them Iran, Iraq, Egypt, South Africa, North Korea, and South Korea.

North Korea's announcement in March 1993 that it was withdrawing from the NPT and would not allow inspections of its nuclear sites touched off a period of worldwide anxiety over whether the small, isolated nation might be building a nuclear weapon using plutonium taken from commercial reactors. The crisis was resolved in October 1994 when North Korea agreed to a timetable for dismantling its nuclear development program in exchange for improved trade and diplomatic relations with the United States and aid in the construction of new commercial nuclear reactors.

Some observers questioned the wisdom of offering economic incentives to deter nuclear proliferation, fearing that the strategy might encourage rather than prevent weapons development. "Rewarding potential proliferators is problematic, to say the least," Doug Bandow of the Cato Institute wrote in the New York Times Magazine. *"But in some cases it may be the best of a bad set of options."*

Nuclear Smuggling Grows

As nuclear materials came into the hands of more and more countries, opportunities increased for terrorist or extremist groups to obtain them as well. The OTA report warned that economic and political instability in the former Soviet republics had increased the chances that uranium and plutonium, the key elements used to build nuclear weapons, could fall into the wrong hands.

Incidents in Germany during the spring and summer of 1994 dramatized the problem. The most serious occurred at the Munich airport on August 10, when police seized between 12 and 14 ounces of plutonium and arrested three people who were allegedly attempting to smuggle it out of Russia. The three, one Colombian and two Spaniards who arrived on a Lufthansa flight from Moscow, were said to be part of a larger smuggling plan to obtain four kilograms of plutonium. Three other arrests in Germany involved smaller amounts of plutonium and uranium.

Evidence of nuclear smuggling had been reported in other European countries and within the former Soviet Union, but the German incidents received the most publicity. After first denying that the nuclear materials could have come from Russia, the Russian government agreed to investigate the incidents and cooperate with the Germans in efforts to prevent any further smuggling.

The question of how much nuclear material was required to make a working nuclear bomb was raised in a report issued August 24 by the Natural Resources Defense Council, a Washington-based environmental group with expertise in nuclear issues. The International Atomic Energy Agency, a United Nations agency charged with enforcing nuclear safeguards, had long said a working bomb required a minimum of 8 kilograms, or just over 17 pounds, of plutonium or uranium. The environmental group argued that a workable atomic device could be constructed with as little as 1 kilogram, or 2.2 pounds, of plutonium—only about three times the amount of plutonium recovered in the Munich incident. The group urged tightening regulation of nuclear materials worldwide, including controls on "dual-use" materials exported for use in nonmilitary industries but capable of being used to build nuclear weapons.

The potential for nuclear proliferation as a result of the breakup of the Soviet Union became starkly clear in November when the U.S. government announced it had successfully concluded the secret transfer of a large quantity of highly enriched uranium from a poorly guarded warehouse in Kazakhstan to the nuclear complex at Oak Ridge, Tennessee. U.S. officials had feared that the uranium, enough to make at least twenty nuclear weapons, might end up in the possession of Iran, Iraq, or terrorists. The government of Kazakhstan agreed to the transfer and reportedly received a payment from the United States in return.

Following is an excerpt from the Executive Summary of "Proliferation and the Former Soviet Union," a report issued September 23, 1994, by the Office of Technology Assessment:

The collapse of the Soviet Union has led both to freedom and to the construction of democratic institutions for many of its former citizens. However, in many of the new republics that have emerged from the former Soviet Union (FSU), the collapse of the center has also led to economic deterioration and political chaos. In most, if not all of them, central political and administrative authority have markedly weakened. Part of this weakening is a devolution of power to democratic institutions on local and regional levels and could be considered a healthy development. But this reduction in central authority has also led to the build-up of local fiefdoms, as individuals and local authorities seek to assure their own futures. Other manifestations of this phenomenon have been increased disorder and crime, including corruption at all levels of government.

The outlook for many of these new nations is uncertain. Any instability in this large area of the world is regarded with apprehension, not only by neighbors, but also by nations that are continents and oceans removed. A major reason for this long-distance concern is the presence in the territory of the former Soviet Union of tens of thousands of nuclear weapons and hundreds of tons of nuclear material suitable for nuclear weapon manufacture. Another concern is the resident expertise in nuclear, chemical, and biological weapons and missile systems. Severe economic disruptions in the FSU and the decrease in central authority of many of the new governments increase the chances that weapons of mass destruction, their components, or related expertise could be transferred to foreign parties. **Such transfers would greatly aggravate the threat that proliferation of these capabilities already poses to U.S. interests and to international peace and security.**

This study examines the implications of the current situation in the FSU for the proliferation of weapons of mass destruction and their delivery systems. It **concentrates on the nuclear component of this broad issue,** which has thus far been foremost in the views of most western observers. However, it also addresses threats that the Soviet Union breakup has posed to the chemical and biological weapon nonproliferation regimes.

Findings and Policy Options

The following is a set of general findings and policy options regarding proliferation and the FSU. All points are discussed in detail in the body of the report. In addition, there are further findings and options specific to each of the four nuclear inheritor republics of the Soviet Union (e.g., those with strategic nuclear weapons on their territories when the Soviet Union ceased to exist) that may be found in the chapters on each of these nations (Belarus, Kazakhstan, Russia, and Ukraine).

The situation in the FSU has been fluid since the disintegration of the Soviet Union. **The analysis in this study, including findings and options, is current as of July 1994.** Major political or economic changes since that date could render some of the analysis obsolete. While this caveat holds in any analysis of current international politics, events in the former Soviet Union have moved particularly rapidly in the past three years and are likely to continue to do so.

Nonproliferation Policies and Agreements

Finding

From the perspective of adherence to international arms control agreements, the positions of the four nuclear inheritor states of the FSU have much improved since mid-1992. This shift constitutes a major success in strengthening the international nuclear non-proliferation regime.

In the first months following the end of the Soviet Union, Russia was the only one of the states with Soviet nuclear weapons on its territory that had agreed to ratify both the Nuclear Non-Proliferation Treaty (NPT) and the

START I arms reduction agreement. Its START ratification was (and still is) contingent on ratification of both agreements by the other three. Since then, due in part to major efforts by two U.S. administrations, all four inheritor states have ratified START I, and all but Ukraine have acceded to the NPT. Ukraine is believed likely to accede to the NPT shortly and, in any case, has agreed to return all strategic nuclear weapons on its territory to Russia within seven years. According to many statements from officials from both Russia and other FSU republics that are apparently accepted by the U.S. government, all tactical nuclear weapons had already been returned to Russia from the other republics of the FSU by mid-1992. These agreements and actions have removed a major threat to achievement of a long-term extension to the NPT at that treaty's Extension Conference in 1995, and are an important gain for the international nuclear nonproliferation regime.

Finding

The recent agreement by the United States and Russia to verify mutually their nuclear weapon dismantlement will strengthen the nuclear nonproliferation regime by instituting an international arrangement to protect and monitor the nuclear material from the weapons.

Under the so-called Nunn-Lugar program, the United States is providing assistance to the FSU for dismantling Soviet nuclear weapons and reducing the threat that these and other Soviet weapons of mass destruction pose to the United States and the rest of the world. In implementing this program, the United States must decide what degree of assurance it needs that such dismantlement is indeed being conducted. Monitoring nuclear weapon dismantlement could be carried out in several ways:

1. through bilateral inspections at the facilities where nuclear material from weapons is blended and stored;
2. through inspection by the International Atomic Energy Agency (IAEA) at blending and storage facilities;
3. through bilateral inspection at the dismantlement facilities themselves, in addition to the blending and storage facilities, and;
4. through inspection by the IAEA at blending, storage, and dismantlement facilities.

At present, the first of these options has been agreed to, and discussions are now underway regarding the second and third. In earlier informal discussions, Russian officials refused to consider verification of dismantlement in the absence of U.S. willingness to permit reciprocal verification of its own dismantlement activities. The United States government had previously resisted such verification for reasons of secrecy, but has recently become more flexible. As a result, the United States and Russia have agreed to institute mutual verification procedures at each other's facilities. The two countries have so far agreed only to permit monitoring of their storage areas, which in the United States include parts of the Pantex facility near Amarillo, Texas, where weapons are dismantled and nuclear components stored. However, it has not yet been settled whether there will be inspections at the actual buildings where dismantlement takes place. Even if only storage sites are inspected, procedures may still need to be implemented to protect classified weapon design information on each side.

Since only U.S. and Russian inspectors would be involved, there may be somewhat less concern about protecting weapon-related information than there would be if other nationals participated. Both the United States and Russia have sophisticated nuclear arsenals and would not likely gain significant advantage from whatever information on weapons might be revealed despite the confidentiality measures. Moreover, implementation agreements and inspection protocols should be easier to negotiate bilaterally than they would be if three or more parties were involved, which would be the case if the IAEA were to participate. The negative aspect of a bilateral arrangement between the United States and Russia is that it excludes the rest of the world. In particular, it excludes the three other declared weapon states—the United Kingdom, France, and China—that have direct interests in nuclear disarmament, and that may need to be involved in future nuclear arms reduction agreements.

Involving the IAEA in these inspections would give the world community an active role and stake in the disarmament process, setting an important precedent for future nuclear disarmament. Indeed, the U.S. government has committed itself unilaterally to submit to IAEA monitoring of nuclear material from weapons determined to be in "excess" of U.S. military requirements. The multilateral approach, however, has several disadvantages. First, inspectors from many countries, including possible would-be proliferants, would be routinely touring nuclear weapon facilities. Even basic weapon information would have to be protected during the process by which material inputs and outputs were to be quantitatively verified. This may be technically possible, but—even if the actual dismantlement process were not under international observation—IAEA involvement would probably cause ongoing concerns about the possible leakage of nuclear design information to non-nuclear-weapon states.

Blocking Access to Nuclear Weapons and Materials

Finding

All the nuclear inheritor states have difficulties in managing nuclear materials and nuclear weapon-related components on their territories.

These difficulties range from inadequate means of controlling, accounting for, and protecting the nuclear material on their territories (including a lack of international safeguards providing for external audits and technical verification of the national systems of accounting for the material) to inadequate border controls, customs, and export controls. These difficulties also extend to controls over dual-use items: objects having innocent, commercial applications but that also have uses related to nuclear weapons.

Finding

External aid is vital to bringing control over such materials and goods up to international standards in the shortest possible time.

Belarus, Kazakhstan, and Ukraine do not have adequate export control systems or national systems to control nuclear materials. Neither do they have nuclear safeguards agreements in place with the International Atomic Energy Agency (IAEA). For example, one or two years will be needed to put a national nuclear material accounting and control system in place in Kazakhstan and to implement a nuclear safeguards agreement with the IAEA, according to current estimates. Even in Russia, improvements in nuclear safeguards and export controls are essential. The sooner international safeguards are in place, the sooner one window for diversion will be closed.

Option

The United States could expedite its assistance for improving material control and accountancy and export control to all the nuclear inheritor states in an effort to close quickly any windows of opportunity that may now exist to divert nuclear material or information.

The process of dismantling thousands of nuclear weapons in the United States and in Russia, as outlined in the parallel initiatives of Presidents Gorbachev and Bush in 1991, is still in its early stages in both countries. In 1991, the United States also began a large-scale aid program referred to as the Nunn-Lugar or Cooperative Threat Reduction program. Through this program, four hundred million dollars have been provided in each of fiscal years 1992, 1993, and 1994 to assist Russia and the other nuclear inheritor states in the dismantlement of nuclear and chemical weapons and to fund related projects. In addition to weapon dismantlement, these funds may also be used to convert defense facilities to non-military use, as well as to help prevent proliferation of weapons of mass destruction through means such as developing export control systems, improving nuclear safeguards, and preventing the diffusion of related expertise from the FSU. **As of March 22, 1994, about $75 million have been proposed for obligations to improve nuclear safeguards and to develop export control systems. However, less than one million dollars have actually been obligated for these purposes and even less actually spent.**

The "Brain Drain"

Option

Any assistance that the United States and the West could provide to assure a minimal living standard for weapon scientists and custodians of nuclear weapons in the FSU would help protect those weapons and their nuclear material from unauthorized uses. Moreover, spending some U.S. Nunn-Lugar funds on contractors in Russia and the other inheritor states, as well as speeding implementation of U.S. assistance, could help dispel hostility to-

wards the United States and help dissuade weapon scientists and engineers from contributing to the development of weapons of mass destruction by other states.

More efficient delivery of U.S. and Western assistance could work to counter the impression, now prevalent among Russian scientists and politicians, that the U.S. program is mainly aimed at aiding U.S. industry and at disarming the Russian military. Such an impression, which has been strengthened by the slow progress made thus far in implementing the programs for U.S. assistance to the FSU, is not conducive to increased U.S.-Russian cooperation in nonproliferation and other areas. **Of the $1.2 billion authorized in fiscal years 1992-1994, only $117 million had been obligated as of March 22, 1994.** Indeed, Congress refused to roll over $208 million in fiscal year 1992 funds that had not been obligated by late 1993. In order to implement the projects planned for those funds, money was taken from the $400 million appropriated in fiscal year 1994.

Part of the delay in spending these funds had been due to difficulties in negotiating agreements with the FSU republics, but part of the problem was also the glacial rate at which the U.S. government approved projects and obligated and transferred funds. In addition to time-consuming review within the executive branch, Congress, represented by the Appropriations and Armed Services Committees in each house, must be notified by the Department of Defense (DOD) of the intent to obligate funds for each program. In practice, this means that individual programs may be blocked by objections from the Committees. Thus, in a sense, programs need to receive tacit approval from these committees before funds can be obligated.

The Defense Department has announced its intent to obligate an additional $420 million by the end of fiscal year 1994 and $430 million by the end of fiscal year 1995, having reached agreement with the receiver nations for over $900 million in future projects. These expenditures will come mostly from fiscal year 1993 and fiscal year 1994 funds. However, the successful expenditure of this amount by that time will require that Congress and the executive branch proceed more expeditiously on this matter than they have in the past.

In addition to providing specific help for weapon dismantlement, U.S. assistance could also help stabilize the economic situation in the Russian nuclear weapon complex. There are indications that housing and other conditions for officers in charge of manning and protecting strategic nuclear weapons in the FSU are poor, as it reportedly is among many elements of the Russian military. Improving the living conditions for personnel with control over nuclear weapons and nuclear materials could significantly improve their morale and substantially increase security over the nuclear arsenal.

Moreover, legislative restrictions on Nunn-Lugar spending that require the use of U.S. technology and experience "where feasible" could be relaxed, so that more than the current minimal level could be spent on local contractors in the FSU. Easing such restrictions could be done either in future legislation reauthorizing the Cooperative Threat Reduction Program, or by a less restrictive interpretation of the word "feasible" by the Department of Defense in the implementation of the program.

Another serious problem that Western assistance might ameliorate is the so-called "brain drain": the possibility that technical personnel with expertise in weapons of mass destruction might emigrate to would-be proliferant countries or otherwise provide relevant material, expertise, technology, or information to unauthorized parties outside the FSU. Severe economic stresses in Russia and other republics of the FSU could tempt such individuals to sell knowledge or material to which they have access. Aggravating this problem is the fact that funding for science in general, and for nuclear weapon institutions in particular, has become severely restricted in Russia. The two major nuclear weapon design laboratories, at Arzamas and Chelyabinsk, have had problems supplying their employees with minimal salaries, let alone the comfortable living standards that had been their due as honored and vital workers in the Soviet Union. As a result, scientific workers at these establishments have engaged in public demonstrations and protests. U.S. visitors to one of these sites report even a lack of basic medicines and anesthetics at hospitals. Although there is no evidence that deprivation has yet resulted in anyone emigrating beyond the FSU to perform weapon-related research, concern remains that such may occur if conditions continue to deteriorate.

The United States, along with allies in Western Europe and Japan, has set up an International Science and Technology Center (ISTC) in Russia for the FSU. A smaller, separate center (including Canadian participation as well) is planned for Ukraine. The goal of these centers is to provide non-military research opportunities for former Soviet scientists, in collaboration with colleagues from the West. These efforts have proceeded very slowly. The Ukraine Science and Technology Center is still blocked by political problems in Kiev. The ISTC, however, finally began operation in March 1994, broadening its original membership to include Kazakhstan, Belarus, Armenia, and Georgia.

Option

The United States could consider the establishment of independent science and technology centers in Belarus and Kazakhstan.

Both Belarus and Kazakhstan have acceded to the ISTC agreement, and the installation of ISTC branch offices in their respective capital cities is under review. However, no independent centers focused on weapon scientists in these two countries are now being considered. This somewhat offhand treatment might be viewed as making Belarus and Kazakhstan appear to be unimportant nations with whom the United States will deal only through the former imperial power, Russia. The lack of a separate center is of concern especially in Kazakhstan, which contains the original Soviet nuclear test facility and which has become the new home of a large number of its weapon scientists and technicians. Kazakhstan also has former Soviet chemical and biological weapon facilities on its territory.

Separate science and technology centers could be established either under the auspices of recently signed science and technology umbrella agreements with the two countries, or under the Nunn-Lugar program. Such arrangements would have the effect of providing research possibilities for weapon and civilian scientists, furnishing them with much desired contacts with Western colleagues. They would also assist these countries in the development of a scientific and technical base, essential to economic recovery in a time of difficult transition. Both results are important to preventing proliferation, since they would help in stabilizing economic conditions and promoting political calm.

Option

Expand the scope of the science and technology centers and laboratory-level collaborations and assure continuing funding for the Laboratory-Industry Partnership Program (LIPP). In addition, institute procedures to speed up operations and render the collaborations more efficient.

It is in the vital interests of the United States that former Soviet nuclear weapon scientists have some means other than selling nuclear secrets to provide minimal living standards for their families. The more effort expended on helping such scientists maintain both their professional activities—directed to peaceful research—and a decent standard of living, the better protected will be the information to which they have access. Furthermore, applying their skills to the production of commercially viable products could help stabilize the shaky economies of the FSU republics. Such stabilization, in turn, would improve the general prospects for an orderly society, vital for maintaining an effective nonproliferation regime in those nations. This last point argues for also involving scientists who are not weapon researchers in these assistance programs, as in fact is being done in the ISTC and other collaborative projects.

In addition to the ISTC, numerous laboratory-to-laboratory contacts and joint research projects have been organized between scientists at U.S. national laboratories and their colleagues in Russia and Ukraine. Some of these are aimed at basic research and others have the goal of developing commercially viable products, in collaboration with a third party: private industry in the United States. These activities, often initiated on a personal level, have resulted in a multimillion dollar effort that has provided support for a (still) relatively small number of former Soviet nuclear scientists and also provided them much desired contact with science and scientists in the West.

The Laboratory-Industrial Partnership Program (LIPP)—a formalized effort to fund industrial partnerships with scientists in the FSU—has been developed by the Department of Energy in cooperation with the Department of State. Funding at the level of $35 million is currently specifically earmarked in the Foreign Operations Appropriations Act for fiscal year 1994. However, no funding beyond fiscal year 1994 has yet been assured. A more regularized funding arrangement than the current one could be instituted. One possibility would be to include LIPP and, possibly, other laboratory-to-laboratory projects as a line item in the Department of Energy appropriations.

Finally, joint projects with FSU scientists have been impeded in the past by difficulties in obtaining multiple-entry visas for FSU scientists to visit the

United States and by frequent lack of timeliness by the Department of Energy in granting its scientists' travel requests to the FSU. Expediting these processes would contribute to the efficiency of collaborative efforts between the United States and republics of the FSU.

The China Connection

A further problem connected with limited employment opportunities among weapon scientists in Russia is the apparent increase in military research collaboration between Russia and China. Many Russian experts are reported to be working on Chinese military projects in the nuclear and missile areas. Although China already has advanced nuclear weapon and rocket technology, the transfer of additional capability is not in the interest of the United States for two reasons. First, China could thereby pose a greater military threat to other nations in the region and even to the United States itself. Second, China might sell some of its newly acquired technology to third parties that do not currently possess nuclear or long-range rocket capability, possibly threatening regional and even global stability. On the other hand, if the United States were to press this issue, Russia might expect the United States to increase its assistance to make up for any resources that would be forgone if this alleged collaboration with China were discontinued.

Option

The United States could make strong efforts to verify whether the reports of Russian/Chinese collaboration in nuclear weapon and missile research are true. If those reports are confirmed, the United States should consider taking up this issue in contacts with the Russian government, asking for assurances that nuclear weapon and rocket technology not be transferred to China.

Summary Finding

Russia and Ukraine are large countries with immense and complex problems. The United States and other external forces have only limited abilities to affect the course of events in those countries or in the rest of the FSU. Nevertheless, the United States can take some actions to counter the threat that the breakup of the Soviet Union poses to international nonproliferation regimes. Many such actions have been and are being assiduously pursued by the U.S. government. However, further steps can be taken. . . .

HOUSE REPUBLICAN
'CONTRACT WITH AMERICA'
September 27, 1994

In a ceremony September 27 on the steps of the U.S. Capitol in Washington, D.C., more than three hundred Republican candidates for the House of Representatives signed a document called the "Contract with America." By signing the document the candidates pledged that if elected, during the first one hundred days of the session beginning in January 1995 the House would vote on bills to reform congressional procedures, require a balanced federal budget, increase funding for prison construction and police officers, cut off welfare benefits to persons who had received them for two years, create an elderly dependent care tax credit, provide a $500-per-child tax credit, boost national defense, cut capital gains taxes, and set term limits for members of Congress, among other measures.

The contract was developed by House Republican leaders after they consulted extensively with pollsters to find out what Americans really wanted. It was the brainchild of Rep. Newt Gingrich (R-Ga.), who was in line to become the Speaker of the House if the Republicans managed to become the majority party. When the contract was signed, most observers expected that the Republicans would gain a substantial number of seats, but few believed they would become the majority party in the House, which the Democrats had controlled for forty years.

Before the election, some analysts believed the contract might become a political liability because it gave Democrats firm proposals to attack. Even on November 1, a week before the election, a New York Times *reporter wrote that the contract "may have been a political misstep."*

Democrats Predict Social Security Cuts

Democrats denounced the document, contending it would lead to massive cuts in federal programs, ranging from Medicare to student loans. In the week before the election, the Democratic National Committee stepped up the attack with television ads claiming that the contract would result in cuts in

Social Security benefits of nearly $2,000 annually per recipient. President Bill Clinton picked up the refrain in speeches throughout the country during the week before the election. Democrats said the Social Security cuts would be necessary if Republicans planned to balance the federal budget.

Republicans said they had no intention of cutting Social Security and that the contract's provisions would be financed by specific, relatively painless, spending cuts. Nonetheless, the contract did not provide specifics about how Republicans planned to make up the $700 billion federal deficit while at the same time providing huge tax cuts. The lack of specific proposals left the door open for Democrats to speculate that Republicans would cut Social Security.

An editorial in the New York Times *said the contract was "not only reckless but deceptive." The editorial was especially critical of the economic proposals. "The Republicans ought to admit that their programs would require cutting hundreds of billions out of about $1.5 trillion in Federal spending— thus slicing 20 percent or more out of every program from Social Security to the F.B.I.," the paper said. "Mr. Gingrich promised a positive vision. What voters got instead was duplicitous propaganda."*

Republicans Win Historic Victory

Instead of viewing the contract as propaganda, voters apparently saw it as a change in politics as usual. They gave Republicans a sweeping victory in the November election, and Republicans won control of both houses of Congress for the first time in two generations. (Clinton, Gingrich on Election Results, p. 513)

In the week after the election, Gingrich announced that hearings would be held around the country on a constitutional amendment to allow prayer in public schools—an issue not included in the Contract with America. Gingrich added that the House would vote on the measure by July 4. After the election, the Washington Post *reported that there had been a major fight within the Republican Party over whether to include the school prayer proposal in the contract.*

With expectations raised so high by the contract, Republicans had their work cut out for them. Some Republicans, seeking to lower expectations slightly, noted that in the contract they simply promised to bring bills to a vote within the first one hundred days—not necessarily to get them all passed. In trying to get the bills through the House, Republicans faced an institution resistant to change and one where a handful of members could easily disrupt the legislative process. It also remained unclear whether Senate Republicans, who had not embraced the contract, would go along with the House proposals.

The stakes were enormously high. If Republicans could produce, they might retain control of Congress and even bolster their position in the 1996 elections. Republican success on Capitol Hill also could improve the party's chances of winning back the White House in 1996. Voters were clearly tired of politicians who talked a good game but delivered nothing. If the Republi-

cans failed to fulfill the pledges made in the Contract with America, their control of Congress could end up being very short-lived.

> *Following is the text of the "Contract with America," signed in Washington, D.C., on September 27, 1994, by more than three hundred Republican candidates for the U.S. House of Representatives:*

As Republican Members of the House of Representatives and as citizens seeking to join that body we propose not just to change its policies, but even more important, to restore the bonds of trust between the people and their elected representatives.

That is why, in this era of official evasion and posturing, we offer instead a detailed agenda for national renewal, a written commitment with no fine print.

This year's election offers the chance, after four decades of one-party control, to bring to the House a new majority that will transform the way Congress works. That historic change would be the end of government that is too big, too intrusive, and too easy with the public's money. It can be the beginning of a Congress that respects the values and shares the faith of the American family.

Like Lincoln, our first Republican president, we intend to act "with firmness in the right, as God gives us to see the right." To restore accountability to Congress. To end its cycle of scandal and disgrace. To make us all proud again of the way free people govern themselves.

On the first day of the 104th Congress, the new Republican majority will immediately pass the following major reforms, aimed at restoring the faith and trust of the American people in their government:

> **FIRST,** require all laws that apply to the rest of the country also apply equally to the Congress;
>
> **SECOND,** select a major, independent auditing firm to conduct a comprehensive audit of Congress for waste, fraud or abuse;
>
> **THIRD,** cut the number of House committees, and cut committee staff by one-third;
>
> **FOURTH,** limit the terms of all committee chairs;
>
> **FIFTH,** ban the casting of proxy votes in committee;
>
> **SIXTH,** require committee meetings to be open to the public;
>
> **SEVENTH,** require a three-fifths majority vote to pass a tax increase;
>
> **EIGHTH,** guarantee an honest accounting of our Federal Budget by implementing zero base-line budgeting.

Thereafter, within the first 100 days of the 104th Congress, we shall bring to the House Floor the following bills, each to be given full and open debate, each to be given a clear and fair vote and each to be immediately available this day for public inspection and scrutiny.

1. THE FISCAL RESPONSIBILITY ACT

A balanced budget/tax limitation amendment and a legislative line-item veto to restore fiscal responsibility to an out-of-control Congress, requiring them to live under the same budget constraints as families and businesses.

2. THE TAKING BACK OUR STREETS ACT

An anti-crime package including stronger truth-in-sentencing, "good faith" exclusionary rule exemptions, effective death penalty provisions, and cuts in social spending from this summer's "crime" bill to fund prison construction and additional law enforcement to keep people secure in their neighborhoods and kids safe in their schools.

3. THE PERSONAL RESPONSIBILITY ACT

Discourage illegitimacy and teen pregnancy by prohibiting welfare to minor mothers and denying increased AFDC for additional children while on welfare, cut spending for welfare programs, and enact a tough two-years-and-out provision with work requirements to promote individual responsibility.

4. THE FAMILY REINFORCEMENT ACT

Child support enforcement, tax incentives for adoption, strengthening rights of parents in their children's education, stronger child pornography laws, and an elderly dependent care tax credit to reinforce the central role of families in American society.

5. THE AMERICAN DREAM RESTORATION ACT

A $500 per child tax credit, begin repeal of the marriage tax penalty, and creation of American Dream Savings Accounts to provide middle class tax relief.

6. THE NATIONAL SECURITY RESTORATION ACT

No U.S. troops under U.N. command and restoration of the essential parts of our national security funding to strengthen our national defense and maintain our credibility around the world.

7. THE SENIOR CITIZENS FAIRNESS ACT

Raise the Social Security earnings limit which currently forces seniors out of the work force, repeal the 1993 tax hikes on Social Security benefits and provide tax incentives for private long-term care insurance to let Older Americans keep more of what they have earned over the years.

8. THE JOB CREATION AND WAGE ENHANCEMENT ACT

Small business incentives, capital gains cut and indexation, neutral cost recovery, risk assessment/cost-benefit analysis, strengthening the Regulatory Flexibility Act and unfunded mandate reform to create jobs and raise worker wages.

9. THE COMMON SENSE LEGAL REFORM ACT

"Loser pays" laws, reasonable limits on punitive damages and reform of product liability laws to stem the endless tide of litigation.

10. THE CITIZEN LEGISLATURE ACT

A first-ever vote on term limits to replace career politicians with citizen legislators.

Further, we will instruct the House Budget Committee to report to the floor and we will work to enact additional budget savings, beyond the budget cuts specifically included in the legislation described above, to ensure that the Federal budget deficit will be less than it would have been without the enactment of these bills.

Respecting the judgment of our fellow citizens as we seek their mandate for reform, we hereby pledge our names to this Contract with America.

GAO TESTIMONY ON
UNSAFE CHEMICALS IN FOOD
September 28, 1994

The federal government's program for monitoring chemicals in the nation's food supply suffered from many weaknesses, according to testimony by a senior official at the General Accounting Office (GAO), the investigative arm of Congress. John W. Harman, director of food and agriculture issues for the GAO, testified September 28 at a hearing before the House Subcommittee on Human Resources and Intergovernmental Relations.

Harman noted that for twenty years, the GAO had recommended improvements in the nation's food safety system. He said the system continued to be fragmented, with primary responsibility resting with three separate agencies: the Food and Drug Administration (FDA), the U.S. Department of Agriculture (USDA), and the Environmental Protection Agency (EPA). The fragmentation led to inconsistencies in federal efforts to assess the risks posed by chemicals in food, Harman said. For example, the agencies assessed risks in different ways, meaning two agencies might assess the risk from a particular chemical differently. "This inconsistency raises questions about the reliability of agencies' decisions on which chemicals and what levels of chemicals may be found in food," said a GAO report titled "Food Safety: Fundamental Changes Needed to Improve Monitoring of Unsafe Chemicals in Food" that Harman released at the hearing.

The agencies also experienced coordination problems. Between 1989 and 1992, the USDA found 21,439 violations of chemical residue limits in meat and poultry products, Harman said. It then referred the cases to the FDA. Because of limited resources, the FDA could only investigate about 20 percent of the violations. Out of the original 21,439 cases, only one resulted in a prosecution.

Enforcement Authority Called Insufficient

The lack of prosecutions pointed to another problem, Harman said: the agencies lacked sufficient enforcement authority. For example, when the

*FDA—the primary enforcement agency—found food that violated govern-
ment regulations, it had no authority to detain the food and assess civil
penalties. Instead, it had to obtain a court order allowing it to seize the food.
The frequent result was that while FDA officials were going to court, the
unsafe food was shipped and sold to consumers.*

*Perhaps most importantly, Harman said the federal food safety system
was designed backwards. It relied on detecting chemical residues at the end
of the food production process, rather than on preventing them in the first
place. The benefits of identifying hazards early had been known for twenty
years, Harman said, but the federal government had "made little progress in
implementing such systems."*

*The problems were even worse with imported food, Harman noted, be-
cause American agencies had no control over the production of imported
foods. The FDA's inspection resources "cannot keep pace with the growing
volume of imported food," he said. In addition, some imported products
were not tested for chemicals that were used in exporting countries but not
approved for use in the United States.*

New Food Safety System Advocated

*The current food safety system was so bad it needed a complete restructur-
ing, Harman stated. He recommended that Congress pass laws to set uniform food safety standards for chemicals in food, give federal agencies
greater enforcement authority, change the system to place emphasis on preventing contamination rather than looking for it in finished products, and
require that all foods imported into the United States be produced under food
safety systems equivalent to those in the United States.*

*The report accompanying Harman's testimony also suggested that re-
sponsibility for food safety reside with one agency. It said that problems in
the current system "are primarily the result of the fragmented legal structure that divides responsibility among multiple federal agencies. This fragmentation has resulted in gaps and duplication in federal food monitoring
activities. GAO believes that a unified food safety system that allocates resources according to the greatest human health threats is needed."*

*The September hearing focused on unsafe chemical residues such as pesti-
cides, animal drugs, and food additives and environmental contaminants
such as lead and mercury that found their way into food. Earlier in the year,
the GAO released reports saying that major changes were also needed in the
food safety system to protect food from microbiological hazards such as
E. coli bacteria.*

> *Following is the text of testimony titled "Food Safety: Funda-
> mental Changes Needed to Improve Monitoring of Unsafe
> Chemicals in Food," presented by John W. Harman, director of
> food and agriculture issues for the General Accounting Office,
> at a hearing of the House Subcommittee on Human Resources
> and Intergovernmental Relations on September 28, 1994:*

Mr. Chairman and Members of the Subcommittee:

We are pleased to be here today to participate in this hearing on the need to improve the effectiveness of the federal food safety system. In previous reports and testimonies, we have stated that fundamental changes are needed to this system to better protect the nation's food supply from microbiological hazards. Today, we will discuss the federal government's system for ensuring that the food supply does not contain unsafe chemical residues and environmental contaminants. Our testimony is based on two reports requested by this Subcommittee, which are being released today—one analyzes the U.S. Department of Agriculture's National Residue Program (NRP) for monitoring chemical residues in meat and poultry, and the second examines the overall federal structure and systems for controlling chemicals in all foods.

In summary, our recent work demonstrates that there are improvements needed in the approach used to monitor chemicals in the food supply. Specifically we found the following:

- The NRP has weaknesses in testing and sampling, as well as in the support it receives from regulatory agencies. These weaknesses could be overcome if certain processes were strengthened. However, any improvements made would not address the basic problem with the program: reliance on detecting residues at the end of the production process to ensure safety rather than on preventing these problems from developing.
- We have identified five basic weaknesses in the structure and systems for monitoring chemicals in food. First, fragmentation of responsibility among multiple agencies results in inefficiencies and gaps in federal monitoring activities. Second, chemicals posing similar risks may be regulated differently under different laws. Third, federal agencies rely on programs to detect unsafe chemicals in food rather than preventing these problems from developing. Fourth, agencies lack strong enforcement authorities to adequately deter or penalize violators. Fifth, similar problems exist for imported foods, over which the United States has even less control.

Before we discuss the results of our work in more detail, some brief background information may be useful.

Background

Potentially unsafe chemicals can enter the food supply from chemicals used during food production as well as from the environment. Before they can be used legally in the United States, pesticides, animal drugs and chemical additives must be approved by the Environmental Protection Agency (EPA) and the Food and Drug Administration (FDA), respectively. If these chemicals leave residues, the cognizant agency is responsible for establishing a tolerance level—the amount of residues that can legally remain in or on raw and processed foods. Environmental contaminants, unlike chemical residues, are not intentionally used in food production but enter the food supply through their occurrence in the environment naturally or through air, water, and soil pollution.

Although chemical hazards are generally ranked as less important than microbiological hazards as a public health issue, the long-term and chronic effects of these hazards are an important public health concern. The U.S. Department of Agriculture (USDA) monitors chemical residues and environmental contaminants in meat, poultry, and some egg products, and FDA monitors them in all other food products.

USDA's Food Safety and Inspection Service (FSIS) uses the NRP to detect, measure, and reduce potentially harmful chemicals in meat and poultry products. Under the program, FSIS samples and analyzes domestic and imported meat and poultry for unsafe chemicals at the slaughterhouse. FSIS refers violations it identifies to EPA, FDA, and/or the states, as appropriate, for follow-up and regulatory action.

Problems with the National Residue Program

The NRP has basic flaws in the choice of chemicals tested and the methodology used to select samples for testing. In addition, the program suffers from limited support from EPA and FDA to identify potentially hazardous chemicals and to prosecute violations.

NRP's Test Results Are Not as Useful as They Should Be

The NRP's test results are not as useful as they should be in determining whether the meat and poultry supply does or does not contain potentially unsafe chemicals for the following reasons:

- FSIS cannot ensure that compounds presenting the greatest risk have been identified and are being tested for under the program. This occurs because (1) FSIS has ranked (prioritized) only about one-third of the 367 compounds it has identified as being of potential concern for meat and poultry and (2) test methods have not been developed for all compounds. Furthermore, only 24 of the 56 compounds tested in 1992 were high priority. Although FSIS plans to devote more resources to ranking additional compounds and developing more test methods, these tasks will take many years to complete.
- Flaws in the NRP's sampling methodology may bias the program's testing results. For example, we found that FSIS does not (1) consistently follow random sampling procedures, (2) adjust its sampling of some species to compensate for climatic/geographic and seasonal changes in slaughter rates and animal drug use, and (3) consistently sample different animal species and chemical compounds.
- Because the NRP's testing focuses on domestic compounds of concern, it is of limited value in determining whether imported meat and poultry contains animal drugs or pesticides not approved or banned for use in the United States. The potential for hazardous residues in imported products is a concern for two reasons: (1) Certain exporting countries have re-

ported finding high incidents of heavy metal residues in excess of their own domestic standards, and (2) some countries may use animal drugs or pesticides not approved or banned in the United States. However, FSIS does not adjust its testing of imports to reflect these concerns.

Other Agencies Provide Limited Support to the Program

EPA and FDA cannot always provide the support the NRP needs to be effective, as the following examples show:

- EPA and FDA may not be able to provide FSIS with the most current information on chemical risks and tolerances. EPA is in the process of reregistering pesticide products but may not complete this task until 2006, and FDA has not reevaluated all animal drugs approved in the past because of resource constraints.
- Because of limited resources, FDA investigated only about 20 percent of the 21,439 residue violations referred to it by FSIS from 1989 through 1992. Of those violations investigated, only about 9 percent resulted in regulatory action against violators, mostly in the form of warning letters that carry no penalty. Only one prosecution resulted from these investigations.

Fundamental Changes Needed in the Federal Food Safety System

The problems that we identified in the NRP are not unique. They exemplify problems GAO [General Accounting Office] and others have been describing for the past two decades for many federal programs that monitor chemicals in domestic and imported foods. For example, FDA faces many of the same problems when monitoring pesticides in fruits and vegetables or environmental contaminants in fish products. While the federal agencies have taken steps to address criticisms, we believe they cannot, by themselves, overcome five systemic and structural weaknesses that are responsible for the continuation of these problems. Because some of these weaknesses are the result of legislation and the design of the federal food safety system, successful corrective actions will depend on congressional initiatives.

Fragmentation of Responsibility Impedes the Identification of Chemical Risks

Under the current federal food safety system, responsibilities are fragmented across many agencies. As a result, the system is characterized by inefficiencies and gaps in monitoring. Nowhere is this more apparent than in agencies' efforts to assess chemical risks. To control unsafe chemicals effectively, agencies need a large amount of human exposure and residue data to first assess the risks posed by a chemical. However, because responsibility for collecting these data is split among FDA, EPA, and USDA, there is often little agreement on the data that should be collected, the methods for analyzing these data, and, ultimately, the results of the data analyzed. Consequently, the agencies may not reach the same conclusions on the level of risk posed by a particular chemical and the level of needed regulation.

Problems in the Legal and Regulatory Structure
Compromise Efforts to Reduce Risk

Even if agencies had reliable information to better control chemical risks, differences in the basic laws and regulations that govern chemicals in food do not support the agencies' efforts. For example, we found that federal food safety laws (1) have resulted in different standards for chemicals posing similar risks, (2) do not generally require the agencies to regularly reevaluate chemicals approved in the past against current scientific standards, and (3) do not specifically address the critical risk posed by environmental contaminants in food. In addition, as a result of federal regulation and policy that allow the use of unapproved pesticides and animal drugs to address emergency situations, the use of unapproved chemicals has become a routine practice.

Increased Focus on Prevention Is a Better Approach

The basic federal approach to ensuring food safety—end-product testing—is not only resource-intensive but ultimately ineffective in preventing contamination from occurring. This approach requires an ever-increasing amount of resources, both to keep pace with the commodity/chemical combinations of concern and to develop all the multiresidue tests needed to detect these residues. The problems in the NRP demonstrate the shortcomings of relying on end-product testing. Newer approaches to ensure food safety—such as the Hazard Analysis and Critical Control Point (HACCP) approach—recognize these difficulties and seek to build safeguards into food production. The HACCP approach generally integrates chemical prevention, detection, and control functions at critical points throughout the production process. Under this approach, end-product testing becomes a secondary rather than the primary method of ensuring that unsafe levels of chemical residues and environmental contaminants do not remain in food products. While the benefits of HACCP-based systems have been recognized for over 20 years, the federal government has made little progress in implementing such systems.

Limited Enforcement Authority Cannot
Effectively Deter or Penalize Violators

Federal enforcement efforts do not provide the backup that is necessary to ensure compliance with federal food safety standards when violations occur. FDA, the primary enforcing agency for food violations, does not always act on violations referred by other agencies, as demonstrated by the problems we found in the NRP, because of a lack of resources and other competing priorities. Moreover, FDA has inadequate enforcement authorities and cannot effectively prevent the distribution of violative products to consumers or prevent future violations from occurring. This happens because FDA lacks the authority to detain violative products and to assess civil penalties. When FDA finds a potentially violative product, it must obtain a court order to seize the products. However, while FDA is obtaining the court order, potentially unsafe food may be shipped and sold to consumers. Similarly, FDA must rely on the Justice Department to pursue criminal action against violators because FDA does not have the authority to assess civil penalties. However, the number of cases pursued under criminal law is minuscule because this is a resource- and time-intensive activity. For example, of the over 21,000 drug residue violations reported to FDA between 1989 and 1992, only 15 resulted in criminal action.

Similar Problems Exist with Imported Products

Finally, the problems we have identified in the domestic food safety system are also relevant for imported foods because federal agencies have even less control over the production of imported foods. U.S. agencies have no jurisdiction over food producers in exporting countries and therefore rely on the adequacy of exporting countries' food safety systems and/or U.S. inspecting and testing of imported products at the port of entry to ensure the safety of imported foods. However, not only are food safety systems in some exporting countries inadequate but also weaknesses in the U.S. system result in gaps in monitoring imported food for several reasons.

First, FDA's inspection resources cannot keep pace with the growing volume of imported food. Second, some imported products may not be tested for compounds that are used in exporting countries but are not approved for use in the United States because the agencies may have incomplete data on these chemicals, and/or because some of the testing focuses only on domestic compounds of concern. Third, as a result of weaknesses in its regulatory authorities, FDA, in some instances, has been unable to prevent the distribution of contaminated imported products to U.S. consumers. Although FDA has the authority to detain contaminated imports, it does not have the authority it needs to control and prevent the distribution of unsafe imports. For example, while meat and poultry can only be imported from countries that have food safety systems that have been reviewed and certified by USDA as being equivalent to the U.S. system, FDA must rely on voluntary agreements with foreign countries to ensure that imported products comply with U.S. standards. Similarly, as with domestic foods, FDA lacks civil penalty authority and must rely on another agency, in this case the Customs Service, to provide an economic deterrent to violators. However, because of poor coordination between the agencies, these damages are often not assessed.

In summary, Mr. Chairman, as we have continually reported over the past 20 years, the federal system designed to ensure that food is free from unsafe levels of chemicals needs significant improvement. We believe a restructuring of the federal monitoring system for chemical residues and environmental contaminants in food is needed. Our most recent reports suggest that the Congress should take the following steps:

- Enact a uniform set of food safety laws that include consistent standards for chemical residues and contaminants in food and provide federal agencies with the authorities needed to effectively carry out their oversight responsibilities.
- Revise the nature of the federal government's role for ensuring food safety by moving it away from end-product testing to preventing contamination from occurring. End-product testing would take a secondary role to monitor the effectiveness of the prevention system.
- Consider the feasibility of requiring that all food eligible for import to the United States—not just meat and poultry—be produced under equivalent food safety systems.

REPORT BY U.S. COMMISSION ON IMMIGRATION REFORM
September 30, 1994

To help curb illegal immigration, the federal government should create a computerized registry containing the names and Social Security numbers of every citizen and legal alien to allow employers to check the immigration status of people who apply for jobs. That recommendation, released September 30 in a report by the U.S. Commission on Immigration Reform, only added fuel to an already raging firestorm about what should be done to halt the flood of illegal immigrants entering the United States. It was estimated that the nation had at least four million illegal aliens, although no one knew the precise number.

Immigration reform was one of 1994's hottest and most emotional issues. There was widespread support for curbing illegal immigration, but there was little agreement about what specific actions the federal government should take. Many taxpayers were unhappy that the government was spending their money to provide food, health care, and housing subsidies to illegal immigrants. Yet in a nation that was built by immigrants, there also was strong sentiment to help those who sought a better life in the United States. To complicate matters further, groups that represented Hispanics and other minorities were quick to label as racist virtually any proposal to curb illegal immigration.

Congress created the U.S. Commission on Immigration Reform in 1990 and charged it with examining immigration policy and recommending improvements. The September report was an interim document, with a final report due in 1997.

Panel Also Backs Tighter Borders

Besides recommending the creation of a computer registry, the panel said the federal government should tighten control over borders, block illegal aliens from receiving any public services except in emergencies, promptly deport illegal aliens discovered in the country, develop a humane policy to deal with immigration emergencies such as the flight of Cubans to Florida, help improve economic conditions in other countries to reduce the allure of the United States, and improve the collection of data about the extent and impact of illegal immigration.

But the recommendation to create a computer registry for employment purposes caused the most controversy. Under the proposal, employers would have to check the registry before hiring to ensure that the potential worker was authorized to work in the United States. Federal law barred the employment of illegal immigrants. In its report, the panel said: "The Commission believes that reducing the employment magnet is the linchpin of a comprehensive strategy to reduce illegal immigration. The ineffectiveness of employer sanctions, prevalence of fraudulent documents, and continued high numbers of unauthorized workers, combined with confusion for employers and reported discrimination against employees, have challenged the credibility of current worksite enforcement efforts."

The computer registry proposal was attacked by a wide range of civil rights and minority organizations. The American Civil Liberties Union, Hispanic organizations, Jewish groups, and others said the registry would increase—not decrease—job discrimination against members of minority groups. They also expressed fears that the registry would lead to the issuance of a national identity card, although the commission said such fears were unfounded.

California Voters Approve Immigration Measure

The immigration issue came to a head in November, when California voters overwhelmingly approved Proposition 187, which would bar illegal aliens from receiving welfare, schooling, and most government-funded health care. It also would require educators and health workers to report suspected illegal aliens to immigration authorities. Civil rights and immigrant groups filed a flurry of lawsuits claiming the proposition was unconstitutional, and state and federal judges blocked the measure from taking effect pending further hearings.

The legal fight could take years, and most observers agreed the issue would eventually reach the U.S. Supreme Court. It was hard to predict how the Court might rule. In a 1982 Texas case, the Court ruled 5-4 that the state had to provide a free public education to children who were illegal immigrants. In the majority opinion, Justice William Brennan wrote: "It is difficult to understand precisely what the state hopes to achieve by promoting the creation and perpetuation of a sub-class of illiterates within our boundaries, surely adding to the problems and costs of unemployment, welfare and crime." But since that ruling the Court's composition had changed, making it more conservative and more deferential to state authority.

Immigration Movement Could Spread

Leaders of the California proposition movement said they would next seek to persuade Congress to approve stricter immigration laws. They also planned to seek approval of similar measures in other states with large numbers of illegal immigrants such as Arizona, Florida, and Texas.

California had more illegal aliens than any other state. State officials contended that providing services to them cost $3 billion annually. In April, the state of California sued the federal government to recover its costs for jailing illegal immigrants who committed crimes. The suit, like those filed in 1994 by Florida and Texas and considered by many other states, contended the federal government was responsible for expenses involving illegal aliens because it failed to properly control the nation's borders.

Immigration wasn't just an issue in the United States. On November 1, Canada announced that it would allow in fewer immigrants each year and would favor those who possessed marketable skills and who spoke English or French, the nation's two official languages. Previously, Canada's immigration policy had been one of the most open among major industrial nations. The new policy only affected legal immigrants, but illegal immigration was not a major problem in Canada.

> *Following are excerpts from the executive summary of a report by the U.S. Commission on Immigration Reform titled "U.S. Immigration Policy: Restoring Credibility," which was released September 30, 1994:*

Introduction

The U.S. Commission on Immigration Reform was created by Congress to assess U.S. immigration policy and make recommendations regarding its implementation and effects. Mandated in the Immigration Act of 1990 to submit an interim report in 1994 and a final report in 1997, the Commission has undertaken public hearings, fact-finding missions, and expert consultations to identify the major immigration-related issues facing the United States today.

This process has been a complex one. Distinguishing fact from fiction has been difficult, in some cases because of what has become a highly emotional debate on immigration. We have heard contradictory testimony, shaky statistics, and a great deal of honest confusion regarding the impacts of immigration. Nevertheless, we have tried throughout to engage in what we believe is a systematic, non-partisan effort to reach conclusions drawn from analysis of the best data available.

Underlying Principles

Certain basic principles underlie the Commission's work. The Commission decries hostility and discrimination against immigrants as antithetical to the traditions and interests of the country. At the same time, we disagree with those who would label efforts to control immigration as being inherently anti-immigrant. Rather, it is both a right and a responsibility of a democratic society to manage immigration so that it serves the national interest.

Challenges Ahead

The Commission believes that legal immigration has strengthened and can continue to strengthen this country. While we will be reporting at a later date on the impacts of our legal immigration system, and while there may even be disagreements among us as to the total number of immigrants that can be absorbed into the United States or the categories that should be given priority for admission, the Commission members agree that immigration presents many opportunities for this nation. Immigrants can contribute to the building of the country. In most cases, they have been actively sought by family members or businesses in the U.S. The tradition of welcoming newcomers has become an important element of how we define ourselves as a nation.

The Commission is mindful of the problems that also emanate from immigration. In particular, we believe that unlawful immigration is unacceptable. Enforcement efforts have not been effective in deterring unlawful immigration. This failure to develop effective strategies to control unlawful immigration has blurred the public perception of the distinction between legal and illegal immigrants.

For the Commission, the principal issue at present is how to manage immigration so that it will continue to be in the national interest.

- How do we ensure that immigration is based on and supports broad national economic, social, and humanitarian interests, rather than the interests of those who would abuse our laws?
- How do we gain effective control over our borders while still encouraging international trade, investment, and tourism?
- How do we maintain a civic culture based on shared values while accommodating the large and diverse population admitted through immigration policy?

The credibility of immigration policy can be measured by a simple yardstick: people who should get in, do get in; people who should not get in are kept out; and people who are judged deportable are required to leave.

During the decade from 1980 to 1990, three major pieces of legislation were adopted to govern immigration policy—the Refugee Act of 1980, the Immigration Reform and Control Act of 1986, and the Immigration Act of 1990. The Commission supports the broad framework for immigration policy that these laws represent: a legal immigration system that strives to serve the national interest in helping families to reunify and employers to obtain skills not available in the U.S. labor force; a refugee system that reflects both our humanitarian beliefs and international refugee law; and an enforcement system that seeks to deter unlawful immigration through employer sanctions and tighter border control.

The Commission has concluded, however, that more needs to be done to guarantee that the stated goals of our immigration policy are met. The immediate need is more effective prevention and deterrence of unlawful immigration. This report to Congress outlines the Commission's recommendations in this area.

In the long term, immigration policies for the 1990s and beyond should anticipate the challenges of the next century. These challenges will be substantially influenced by factors such as the restructuring of our own economy, the establishment of such new trade relationships as the North American Free Trade Agreement [NAFTA], and changing geopolitical relations. No less importantly, immigration policy must carefully take into account social concerns, demographic trends, and the impact of added population on the country's environment.

Finally, current immigration is the first to occur in what economists call a post-industrial economy, just as it is the first to occur after the appearance of the modem welfare state. The Commission's report to Congress in 1997 will cover these issues in assessing the impact of the Immigration Act of 1990. The present report reviews the progress of the beginning implementation of this legislation.

Recommendations

Serious problems undermine present immigration policies, their implementation, and their credibility: people who should get in find a cumbersome process that often impedes their entry; people who should not get in find it all too easy to enter; and people who are here without permission remain with impunity.

The Commission is convinced that unlawful immigration can be controlled consistent with our traditions, civil rights, and civil liberties. As a nation with a long history of immigration and commitment to the rule of law, this country must set limits on who can enter and then must credibly enforce our immigration law. Unfortunately, no quick and easy solutions are available. The United States can do a more effective job, but only with additional financial resources and the political will to take action. Our recommendations for a comprehensive, effective strategy follow.

Border Management

The Commission believes that significant progress has been made during the past several years in identifying and remedying some of the weaknesses in U.S. border management. Nevertheless, we believe that far more can and should be done to meet the twin goals of border management: preventing illegal entries while facilitating legal ones.

Land Borders

Credibility is a problem at U.S. land borders, given the ease of illegal entry and various obstacles to legal entry. These problems are particularly prevalent at the U.S.-Mexico border, as the Commission's visit to San Diego and El Paso demonstrated. The Commission believes that an underlying principle of border management is that prevention is far more effective and cost-efficient than the apprehension and removal of illegal aliens after entry. At the same time, the Commission believes that legal entry should be facilitated in order for the country to benefit from cross-border trade and tourism.

The Commission supports the strategy, now being tested as "Operation Hold the Line" in El Paso, that emphasizes prevention of illegal entry at the border, rather than apprehension following illegal entry. Prevention holds many advantages: it is more cost-effective than apprehension and removal; it eliminates the cycle of voluntary return and reentry that has characterized unlawful border crossings; and it reduces potentially violent confrontations on the border. The Commission recommends:

- Increased resources for prevention, including additional staff, such improved technology as sensors and infrared scopes, data systems that permit expeditious identification of repeat offenders, and such additional equipment as vehicles and radios.
- Increased training for border control officers to execute strategies that emphasize prevention of illegal entry.
- Formation of a mobile, rapid response team to improve Border Patrol anticipation of new smuggling sites and to augment their capacity at these locations. The Immigration and Naturalization Service [INS] must develop a capacity to respond quickly to changing patterns of unlawful immigration along the land border. Also, contingency plans should be developed to address increased boat arrivals that may arise from improved land border enforcement.
- Use of fences to reduce border violence and facilitate enforcement. However, the Commission does not support the erection of extraordinary physical barriers, such as unscalable walls, unless needed as a last resort to stop violence when other means have proved ineffective. Fences have been used effectively in San Diego to reduce border violence, deter illegal aliens from running across the interstate highway that leads from Mexico, and facilitate enforcement.
- Systematic evaluation of the effectiveness of any new border strategies by INS. The typical measurements of Border Patrol effectiveness—apprehension rates—have little meaning in assessing a prevention strategy. INS should develop new evaluation techniques that measure the effects of border management efforts in terms of the flow of unauthorized aliens and their impacts on U.S. communities.

The Commission supports efforts to reduce potentially violent confrontations between Border Patrol officers and those believed to be seeking illegal entry into the U.S. Such confrontations were reduced, for example, during "Operation Hold the Line," in terms of both reported human rights violations against suspected illegal aliens and attacks on Border Patrol officers.

The Commission supports efforts already underway to address complaints about human rights violations, including:

- Increased training and professionalism of Border Patrol officers to enable them to respond appropriately to potentially violent situations;

- Improved procedures for adjudicating complaints of Border Patrol abuses;
- Mechanisms to provide redress or relief to those subjected to improper actions; and
- More effective protection of Border Patrol officers from violence directed at them.

The Commission believes that port entry operations can be improved. Legal entry at the border should be facilitated as the United States benefits from trade, tourism, family visits and consumer spending. More specifically, the Commission supports:

- Additional resources for inspections at land border ports of entry.
- An expedited adjudication and issuance process for the Border Crossing Card [BCC]. Mexican nationals are required to have a visa (unlike Canadians). Because of the volume of BCC applications on the Mexican border, the Commission encourages negotiations between the U.S. and Mexico to amend the bilateral treaty to permit collection of fees to be used exclusively to expedite the issuance and adjudication of the card.
- Further steps to better ensure that the BCC is not misused by legal crossers who engage in unauthorized employment after entry. Each BCC should contain the legend indicating it is "not for work authorization," as currently appears on INS-issued cards.
- Development of a land border user fee to pay for needed improvements in the inspection of border crossers, with fees to be used exclusively to facilitate land border management.

The Commission supports increased coordination on border issues between the governments of the U.S. and Mexico. The Commission views favorably the discussions underway between the U.S. and Mexican governments. These discussions promote greater cooperation ... in solving problems of mutual concern. In particular, the Commission encourages:

- Continued cooperation in antismuggling efforts to reduce smuggling of people and goods across the U.S.-Mexico border.
- Bilateral discussions that take into account both U.S. entry and Mexican exit laws in devising a cooperative approach to regulating the movements of people across the U.S.-Mexican land border. Mexican law requires that Mexican nationals exit Mexico through official inspection stations. Thus, unauthorized migration into the United States generally violates not only U.S. law, but Mexican law as well.
- Cross border discussions and cooperative law enforcement efforts among federal, state, and local officials of both countries to develop cooperative approaches to combat violent crimes and auto and cargo theft along the border.
- Continued U.S. cooperation and support for Mexican efforts to address the problem of third-country nationals crossing Mexico to come to the United States.

Airports

Each year about 50 million citizens and aliens enter the country through airports.

The Commission supports a combined facilitation and enforcement strategy that would prevent the entry of unauthorized aliens while facilitating legal admissions at U.S. airports as efficiently as possible, including:

- The use of new technologies to expedite the inspections process and improve law enforcement, including more efficient processing of travelers with Machine Readable Documents.
- Programs that enhance the capacity of airline carriers to identify and refuse travel to aliens seeking to enter the U.S. on fraudulent documents, including the Carrier Consultant Program and other coordinated efforts to maintain complete, accurate, and reliable Advance Passenger Information System [APIS] data and improved lookout data systems.
- Continued government-airline industry discussions on improving inspections that have led to innovative proposals.
- Development of a system for mitigation of penalties or fines for those carriers that cooperate in screening and other programs and demonstrate success in reducing the number of unauthorized aliens they carry.
- Making INS, not the carrier, responsible for the actual physical custody of inadmissible air passengers.

Interagency Coordination

The Commission expresses its dissatisfaction with the past lack of coordination between the Customs Service and the INS at ports of entry. This has hampered effective border management by both agencies.

The Commission recommends implementation of initiatives to improve coordination between INS and Customs, as recommended by the General Accounting Office [GAO] and the National Performance Review. The Commission will monitor these efforts to improve coordination of border management, particularly as they relate to immigration matters.

If these efforts prove ineffective, the Commission will recommend more extensive action, such as creating a new immigration and customs agency or designating one agency as the lead agency on inspections.

Alien Smuggling

Organized smuggling operations undermine the credibility of U.S. enforcement efforts and pose dangers to the smuggled aliens.

The Commission recommends an effective prevention strategy that requires enhanced capacities to combat organized smuggling for commercial gain. Possible enhancements include:

- Expanded enforcement authorities, such as Racketeer Influenced and

Corrupt Organizations Act [RICO] provisions, wire-tap authority, and expanded asset forfeiture for smuggling aliens; and
- Enhanced intelligence gathering and diplomatic efforts to deter smuggling.

Worksite Enforcement

The Commission believes that reducing the employment magnet is the linchpin of a comprehensive strategy to reduce illegal immigration. The ineffectiveness of employer sanctions, prevalence of fraudulent documents, and continued high numbers of unauthorized workers, combined with confusion for employers and reported discrimination against employees, have challenged the credibility of current worksite enforcement efforts.

Verification

A better system for verifying work authorization is central to effective enforcement of employer sanctions.

The Commission recommends development and implementation of a simpler, more fraud-resistant system for verifying work authorization. The current system is doubly flawed: it is too susceptible to fraud, particularly through the counterfeiting of documents; and it can lead to increased discrimination against foreign-looking or foreign-sounding authorized workers.

In examining the options for improving verification, *the Commission believes that the most promising option for secure, non-discriminatory verification is a computerized registry* using data provided by the Social Security Administration [SSA] and the INS.

The key to this process is the social security number. For decades all workers have been required to provide employers with their social security number. The computer registry would add only one step to this existing requirement: an employer check that the social security number is valid and has been issued to someone authorized to work in the United States.

The Commission believes the computerized system is the most promising option because it holds great potential for accomplishing the following:

- Reduction in the potential for fraud. Using a computerized registry, rather than only an identification card, guards against counterfeiting of documents. It provides more reliable information about work authorization.
- Reduction in the potential for discrimination based on national origin and citizenship status, as well as inappropriate demands for specific or additional documents, given that employers will not be required to ascertain whether a worker is a citizen or an immigrant and will have no reason to reject documents they believe to be counterfeit. The only relevant question will be: "What is your social security number?"
- Reduction in the time, resources, and paperwork spent by employers in complying with the Immigration Reform and Control Act of 1986

[IRCA] and corresponding redirection of enforcement activities from paperwork violations to knowing hire of unauthorized workers.

The Commission recommends that the President immediately initiate and evaluate pilot programs using the proposed computerized verification system in the five states with the highest levels of illegal immigration as well as several less affected states. The President has the authority to do so under Section 274A(d)(4) of the Immigration and Nationality Act. A pilot program will: permit the testing of various approaches to using the proposed verification system; provide needed information about the advantages, disadvantages, and costs of the various approaches; develop and evaluate measures to protect civil rights and civil liberties; and ensure that any potential obstacles, such as the quality of the data used in the registry, are addressed prior to national implementation. Assuming the successful results of the pilot program, Congress should pass the necessary statutory authorities to support more effective verification. Pilot program features should include:

- A means by which employers will access the verification system to validate the accuracy of information given by workers. We have received conflicting testimony about the best way to check the applicant's identity. We have heard proposals for a more secure social security card, a counterfeit-resistant driver's license, and a telephone verification system that does not rely on any document. The pilot program presents an opportunity to determine the most cost-effective, fraud-resistant, and nondiscriminatory method available.

- Measures to ensure the accuracy of and access to the specific data needed to ensure that employers have timely and reliable information when seeking verification of work authorization. Improvements in the Social Security Administration and INS databases must be made to ensure that these data are available. Procedures must be developed to ensure timely and accurate entry, update, extraction, and correction of data. The Commission strongly urges INS and the Social Security Administration to cooperate in this endeavor, as the proposed registry would be built upon and—once implemented—would support the primary missions of those agencies.

- Measures to ensure against discrimination and disparate treatment of foreign-looking or -sounding persons. The Commission believes that the least discriminatory system would have the same requirements for citizens and aliens alike. To reduce the potential for discrimination and increase the security of the system, the Commission also believes that employers should not be required to ascertain immigration status in the process of verifying authorization for employment. Their only requirement should be to check the social security number presented by each employee against the registry and record an authorization number to prove that they have done so.

- Measures to protect civil liberties. It is essential that explicit protections be devised against use of the database—and any card or any other means used to gain access to it—for purposes other than those specified in law. The uses to be made of the verification system must be clearly specified. We believe the worksite verification system could be used, without damage to civil liberties, for verifying eligibility to receive public benefits. However, it should be stipulated that no one should be required to carry a card, if one is used, or to present it for routine identification purposes. There also should be penalties for inappropriate use of the verification process.

- Measures to protect the privacy of the information included in the database. The Commission is aware of the proliferation of databases and the potential for the invasion of privacy by both government and private agencies. There need to be explicit provisions for protecting privacy; the resultant system should incorporate appropriate safeguards regarding authorized users' access to individual information. In establishing privacy safeguards, it is important to take into account that, while access to any one piece of information may not be intrusive, in combination with other information such access may violate privacy.
- Estimates of the start-up time and financial and other costs of developing, implementing and maintaining a national system in such a manner that verification is reliable.
- Specification of the rights, responsibilities, and impact on individual workers and employers, for example: what individuals must do; how long it will take for newly authorized workers to get on the system and to correct inaccurate data; and what will be required of employers and at what expense. Provisions must also be developed to protect both workers from denial of employment and employers from penalties in cases where the information provided by the computer registry may be missing or inaccurate.
- A plan for phasing in of the system. The Commission recognizes that the proposed verification system will result in financial costs. The system should be phased in to lessen the immediate impact. The pilot programs should test various phase-in procedures. Given the required levels of accuracy, reliability, and convenience required, the evaluation should help measure the cost of phasing in the system nationally.

The Commission recommends evaluation of the pilot programs to assess the effectiveness of the verification system. The evaluation should include objective measures and procedures to determine whether current problems related to fraud, discrimination, and excessive paperwork requirements for employers are effectively overcome without imposing undue costs on the government, employers, or employees. The evaluation should pay particular attention to the effectiveness of the measures used to protect civil liberties and privacy.

The Commission supports INS efforts to improve its Telephone Verification System/SAVE [TVS/SAVE] database—but only as an interim measure. The improvements are essential for improving the data needed for the new, more effective verification process. The Commission is aware of the inadequacies of the current INS data that would be used in the proposed system. The Commission does not endorse the TVS/SAVE program as a long-term solution to the verification problem because use of TVS/SAVE requires the inadequate mechanism of self-attestation by workers as to their citizenship or alienage, thus making it easy for aliens to fraudulently claim U.S. citizenship. It also imposes requirements on legal immigrants that do not apply to citizens. Nevertheless, improvements in this database, as well as the Social Security Administration database, are essential to the development of a more secure, less potentially discriminatory verification system.

The Commission also recommends action that would reduce the fraudulent access to so-called "breeder documents," particularly birth certificates, that can be used to establish an identity in this country, including:

- Regulation of requests for birth certificates through standardized application forms;
- A system of interstate and intrastate matching of birth and death records;
- Making certified copies of birth certificates issued by states or state-controlled vital records offices the only forms accepted by federal agencies;
- Using a standard design and paperstock for all certified copies of birth certificates to reduce counterfeiting; and
- Encouraging states to computerize birth records repositories.

To address the abuse of fraudulent documents, the Commission recommends imposition of greater penalties on those producing or selling such documents. Document fraud and counterfeiting has become a lucrative and well-organized operation that may involve international networks that conspire to produce and sell the resulting fraudulent products. These documents are used in smuggling and terrorist operations, as well as for work authorization. RICO provisions designed to facilitate racketeering investigations should cover conspiracy to produce and sell fraudulent documents. Criminal penalties should also be increased for large-scale counterfeiting activities.

Antidiscrimination Strategies

The Commission is concerned about unfair immigration-related employment practices against both citizens and noncitizens that may occur under the current system of employer sanctions. A more reliable, simpler verification system holds great potential to reduce any such discrimination because employers will no longer have to make any determination as to immigration status. Nevertheless, mechanisms must effectively prevent and redress discrimination.

The Commission recommends that the Office of the Special Counsel [OSC] for Immigration-Related Unfair Employment Practices in the Department of Justice initiate more proactive strategies to identify and combat immigration-related discrimination at the workplace. OSC should target resources on independent investigations and on programs to assess the incidence and prevalence of unfair immigration-related employment practices.

The Commission also recommends a methodologically-sound study to document the nature and extent of unfair immigration-related employment practices that have occurred since GAO's 1990 report. The new study should measure the effects of immigration policy—as distinct from other factors—on discrimination at the worksite. As noted above, the pilot programs should be evaluated to determine if they substantially reduce immigration-related discrimination at the workplace.

Employer Sanctions and Labor Standards Enforcement

The Commission believes that enforcement of employer sanctions, wage/hour, child labor, and other labor standards can be an effective tool in reducing employment of unauthorized workers. The Commission finds, however, that current enforcement efforts are inadequate. In addition, the Commission expresses its concern that current coordination efforts between the Immigration and Naturalization Service and the Department of Labor are insufficient.

The Commission supports vigorous enforcement of labor standards and enforcement against knowing hire of unauthorized workers as an integral part of the strategy to reduce illegal immigration. Labor standards and employer sanctions should be seen as mutually reinforcing. Specifically, the Commission recommends:

- Allocation of increased staff and resources to the enforcement of labor standards to complement employer sanctions enforcement.
- Vigorous enforcement, increased staff and resources, and full use of current penalties against those who knowingly hire unauthorized workers. If the new verification system proposed by the Commission substantially reduces inadvertent hiring of unauthorized workers—as we believe will occur—Congress should discontinue paperwork penalties and evaluate the need for increased penalties against violators and businesses that knowingly hire or fail to verify work authorization for all employees.
- Targeting of investigations to industries that have a history of using illegal alien labor.
- Enhanced enforcement efforts targeted at farm labor and other contractors who hire unauthorized workers on behalf of agricultural growers and other businesses.
- Application of employer sanctions to the federal government. At a minimum, the President should issue an Executive Order requiring federal agencies to abide by the procedures required of other employers. Alternatively, legislation should stipulate that federal agencies follow the verification procedures required of other employers and be subject to penalties if they fail to verify work authorization.

The Commission urges the Attorney General and the Secretary of Labor to review the current division of responsibilities between the Departments of Justice and Labor in the enforcement of employer sanctions and labor standards. INS and the Department of Labor have signed a Memorandum of Understanding [MOU] that spells out each agency's responsibility for enforcing employer sanctions and labor standards. Preliminary evidence indicates that few warnings have been issued to employers under the MOU. The implementation of the MOU should be closely monitored over the next twelve months. Should the monitoring demonstrate that the joint efforts have not resulted in effective enforcement, it may be necessary to designate a single agency to enforce employer sanctions.

The Commission recommends enhanced coordination mechanisms to promote cooperation among all of the agencies responsible for worksite enforcement. Strategies to promote coordination at headquarters and in field operations include:

- Establishment of a taskforce in Washington, D.C., to review and set policy;
- Local taskforces of worksite investigators to coordinate field operations; and
- Continued joint training for worksite investigators from all applicable agencies.

Education

Thousands of new businesses begin operations each year. New workers enter the labor force each year as well.

The Commission recommends coordination and continuance of educational efforts by the Immigration and Naturalization Service, the Office of Special Counsel, and the Department of Labor regarding employer sanctions, antidiscrimination provisions, and labor standards. The Commission calls upon these agencies to develop and communicate a single message to all employers and employees. The Commission also recommends the development of new strategies, including the enhanced use of technology, to inform employers and workers of their rights and responsibilities under the law. . . .

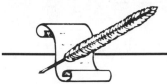
October

RESIGNATION OF
AGRICULTURE SECRETARY ESPY
October 3, 1994

Agriculture Secretary Mike Espy, the subject of a criminal investigation, resigned October 3 under intense pressure from the White House. His resignation followed the disclosure that a foundation run by Arkansas-based Tyson Foods Inc., the nation's largest poultry processor, had awarded a $1,200 scholarship to Espy's girlfriend, Patricia Dempsey. Despite Espy's request that she decline the scholarship, Dempsey initially accepted it before deciding to return the money.

The scholarship issue was the latest in a series of ethical problems for Espy, a former House member from Mississippi who went on to become the first black agriculture secretary. In September, a special prosecutor was appointed to conduct a criminal investigation of the secretary's activities. That investigation and a separate White House ethics inquiry focused largely on Espy's acceptance of free sports tickets, transportation, and lodging from Tyson Foods and other large agricultural companies; his partaking in personal travel to his home state of Mississippi at government expense; and his use of government vehicles for personal transportation. Federal law bars officials like Espy from accepting anything of value from companies regulated by the Agriculture Department. In his last few months as secretary, Espy reimbursed the Agriculture Department and commercial firms more than $7,500 for questionable expenses and gifts.

Questions about Espy's business dealings also focused on the influence exerted by Ronald Blackley, who had served as Espy's chief of staff at the Agriculture Department but was later demoted. Some department employees claimed that Blackley had ordered them to stop developing tougher poultry inspection standards, which were opposed by Tyson Foods. Questions also were raised about whether Blackley had intervened on behalf of clients from his former consulting business after he joined the Agriculture Department.

Espy Admits to Being 'Careless'

At a news conference, Espy said he resigned because the effort required to defend himself in investigations would distract him from the job of running the Agriculture Department. He admitted to being "careless in managing some of the details" of his personal business but said that he had not violated any laws or ethics rules. His resignation took effect December 31.

In a written statement, President Bill Clinton praised Espy's accomplishments while supporting his decision to resign. "Although Secretary Espy has said he has done nothing wrong, I am troubled by the appearance of some of these incidents and believe his decision to leave is appropriate," Clinton said. Espy's ethics problems—especially his acceptance of gifts from Tyson Foods—were an embarrassment to Clinton, who himself had strong political ties to Tyson dating back to his days as governor of Arkansas.

An editorial in the New York Times *said that whatever the truth of the charges against Espy, for many years the Agriculture Department had been too close to farmers and food companies. "Bill Clinton promised to end these snug relationships when he came to Washington, but Mr. Espy appears not to have heard him," the* Times *said. "Mr. Espy's behavior gave, at the very least, the appearance of conflict of interest. It was also colossally stupid."*

Espy was the second Clinton Cabinet member to resign. In December 1993 Defense Secretary Les Aspin quit after Clinton reportedly lost confidence in him.

Espy's Record Draws Praise, Criticism

Espy's short tenure included some significant accomplishments. Just hours before his resignation, the House of Representatives passed his bill to reorganize the Agriculture Department, a major item in the Clinton administration's plan to reinvent government. While the idea of reorganization originated with Sen. Richard G. Lugar (R-Ind.) and was first presented to Congress by Espy's predecessor, Edward R. Madigan, Espy was credited with pushing the bill through Congress. The measure called for dramatic cutbacks in the number of agencies within the department and the closing of more than 1,000 field offices. The reorganization was expected to cut 11,000 jobs from the Agriculture Department and save the government about $3.6 billion by 1999.

Consumer advocacy groups liked Espy because of his interest in food safety issues. During his first month as agriculture secretary, an outbreak of meat contamination caused four deaths and more than seven hundred illnesses. Espy responded by working to strengthen meat and poultry inspection policies. Just days after Espy's resignation, Michael R. Taylor, whom Espy appointed to head the department's inspection service, announced a ban on the sale of any raw ground beef contaminated with E. coli 0157:H7, the bacteria that caused the deaths and illnesses.

Ironically, many in the poultry industry—the industry to which Espy allegedly had close ties—were glad to see him go. Poultry processors were unhappy about his plans to improve meat and poultry inspections, claiming they were designed to improve his public image and were not based on scientific facts. They also complained that as his ethics problems worsened, Espy became almost totally inaccessible to them as he attempted to avoid the appearance of a conflict of interest. "Not only did we get no benefits, but we got tarred as if we were currying favor," said Gary Kushner, an attorney who represents poultry companies before the department, in an interview with the Washington Post. *"We weren't currying favor. If anything, the doors closed tighter."*

Slightly more than a week after Espy announced his resignation, the White House released its ethics report about his conduct. The review did not reach any conclusions about Espy's actions, nor did it recommend any actions against him. A senior White House official told the New York Times *that there was no point in taking action against Espy because he had already resigned and paid back the government for personal expenses.*

However, the criminal investigation of Espy heated up as 1994 ended. In December, Donald C. Smaltz, the independent counsel appointed to investigate Espy, told the Washington Post *that he had added investigators to his staff and broadened the investigation to look into possible "gratuity givers and gratuity takers" involved with the Agriculture Department. He also confirmed that he had subpoenaed documents from Tyson Foods.*

Following is the text of statements by Agriculture Secretary Mike Espy and his attorney, Reid Weingarten, at a press conference October 3, 1994, as reported by Reuters:

ESPY STATEMENT

Gosh, these are more folks than we've ever had here before. I appreciate the extreme interest in agriculture. I have a brief statement to make, and then I would like to take your questions. I also have my lawyer, Reid Weingarten, here, who will also make a statement and also he'll be pleased to answer questions as well.

Earlier today, I received word from the Capitol that the bill authorizing the secretary of agriculture to reorganize the USDA has passed the House of Representatives, and I am certainly confident that the Senate will act very shortly. The USDA will then be the first department of this government to succeed in answering the president's and the vice president's call to reinvent government. So I really do consider this a very important victory.

This is what it feels like to overcome huge obstacles and great resistance to doing something right for America. I send congratulations to President Clinton and to Vice President Gore. I send congratulations to the Congress and to the farmers and the consumers and all of the taxpayers who will have a better USDA, certainly a smaller USDA, and a more cost-efficient USDA. I congratulate the people of America who will have a better and a safer food supply, the farmers who will have a better chance of higher farm income, and the people of rural America who will have a real chance for a better life.

The Congress deserves credit for taking this historic step today. Reorganizing the USDA is a big step, and I certainly would be remiss if I didn't extend my personal thanks to Senators Leahy and Lugar, to Chairman Kika de la Garza and to Pat Roberts for seeing this thing through. If it can happen here in the most intransigent of departments, it can and will happen in the rest of the federal bureaucracy. I believe now that we can all hope that before 1996, Congress willing, this entire government will be leaner and will truly work better and cost less. Government is working and government is changing thanks to the firm leadership of President Bill Clinton.

Twenty-one months ago, I promised the then-president-elect that I would [do] at least 10 things on my now famous list, and at the top of that list was reinventing this department. Today I count some of these objectives accomplished and all of them started.

Today, as we stand at this new beginning for the USDA, I stand personally at a new beginning for myself as well. I must personally overcome the challenge to my good name that continues to distract me from my work at the United States Department of Agriculture. I have therefore decided to tender my resignation to the president effective December 31st of this year. The president deserves to have his agenda go forward with a minimum of distraction. I've talked to him about ten minutes ago and he has accepted my resignation with regret.

I have many people to thank, and I will thank them in the months ahead. I especially want to thank the Deputy Secretary Rich Rominger, and those under[secretaries] and assistant secretaries who have been on this team making history.

I thank the president once more for the opportunity to serve. I thank the people of American agriculture who have given me their support and encouragement as I worked very hard to bring about changes here at the Department of Agriculture. I now owe it to myself and my family to turn my full attention to the matter of a defense. I look forward to dedicating myself to vigorously answering all of the charges that are untrue and unfounded that have been made against me and to vigorously continue to support the goals of this administration and this president. In leaving, I believe that I have succeeded in serving the country and in fulfilling my oath of office. But inasmuch as I was indeed careless in managing some of the details of my personal activities, I have failed myself, and for that I apologize to the president and to the loyal people who have served so well.

Those of you who are familiar with this department know indeed that there are few secretaries who are able to stay on this bucking bronco for more than two years, and I am confident that the work we have done in these few short months will be reflected in higher farm income, stronger rural communities, greater opportunities in the global marketplace, better international markets for all of our commodities, whether food or non-food uses, and a more secure place for agriculture in our national economy for a long time to come.

As I lay down the mantle of my stewardship here, I really do look forward to spending more time with my children.

Finally, to the media, I must thank you, too. I really won't forget that a year ago, newspapers all across America had proclaimed that we were doing a pretty good job here. They were giving me high personal praise, and some complimented us effusively. Well, things have certainly changed, but I did not exclaim then and I won't complain now. I would only ask that you give me as much ink and air time on my exoneration as you certainly have on these charges.

So thank you. I'm going back to work. I'll be here for the next 90 days. I'm going to work hard, as assiduously as I can, because we, frankly, have a lot to accomplish in the next 90 days.

I'll be glad to answer a few questions now, but I will caution you that I cannot comment specifically on any of the charges before the independent counsel. That's why my lawyer, Reid Weingarten, is here. But I will certainly make a statement and answer questions after I leave.

WEINGARTEN STATEMENT

Good afternoon. My name is Reid Weingarten, and I have the high honor to be Secretary Espy's lawyer. As you all know, there is an independent counsel out there. As a legal matter, the independent counsel does not go out of business as a result of today's activities. It is our intention to do things the old-fashioned way. We intend to discuss all issues first with the independent counsel at an appropriate time. There will be no full discussion of the allegations today. I'm going to overrule my client: I am not going to take questions at the conclusion of this brief statement.

One issue, however, requires response because there have been so many misperceptions swirling around—surrounding this allegation, and that is Secretary Espy's relationship to Don Tyson, an Arkansas poultry man, and Don Tyson's businesses. The basic allegation that we've all heard so frequently is that Secretary Espy and a personal friend of his, Patricia Dempsey, received things of value from Mr. Tyson and/or Mr. Tyson's businesses. I would like to set the record straight.

First, the secretary never personally received anything of value from Mr. Tyson or his companies other than a football ticket, which has been paid back. Second, the oft-mentioned Russellville, Arkansas trip, 1993, was a routine appropriate matter, handled in the normal course of United States Department of Agriculture business. Third, earlier this year, the Tyson Foundation gave a $1,200 scholarship to Patricia Dempsey. This foundation has given scholarships for many years, and issues about 100 scholarships per year to worthy students. Ms. Dempsey used the money to resume her education at the University of Maryland. Secretary Espy did not seek, encourage nor approve of this scholarship. Patricia Dempsey is a mature, independent woman who has her own life and has her own relationship with the Tysons.

Most important, public policy has never been affected in any way at all by these issues. Let me make this point even clearer: There is not now and never will be a shred of credible evidence that Mr. Tyson or his businesses were benefited in any way at all as a result of these issues. I would like to add as a matter of legal prudence, Secretary Espy will not be personally involved in any Tyson issue or poultry inspection issue while he is secretary. The essence of prosecutorial power is prosecutorial discretion. If this independent counsel has a sense of justice, proportionality and fair play—and I believe and hope he does—he will take a quick and hard look at these issues, almost all of which are baseless, and a few of which involve insignificant instances of inattention, and then he will quickly and clearly exonerate this wonderful public servant and very fine man with a public declination.

PRIVATIZATION OF HARTFORD PUBLIC SCHOOLS
October 3, 1994

On October 3, Hartford, Connecticut, became the first city in the nation to turn over the operation of its public schools to a private company. The board of education hired Education Alternatives Inc. (EAI), a Minneapolis-based company, to run thirty-two schools serving 25,000 students.

The historic deal was sure to be watched by school districts nationwide, many of which were also looking at privatizing some or all of their schools. Privatization was an especially popular idea in large inner-city districts, where student test scores had plummeted while costs had kept rising.

Some backers of privatization saw it as a cure-all, a radical change that could turn around troubled schools. They said private firms could improve schools by employing innovative teaching methods and emphasizing technology, while also saving money through bulk purchases.

Detractors questioned whether a private firm that had to answer to its financial backers would always have students' best interests in mind. Teachers and administrators alike said they could improve schools if they could get some relief from the stifling, bloated bureaucracy that plagued many large districts.

Hartford, whose predominantly black and Hispanic student population comprised the largest school district in Connecticut, was clearly in trouble. It spent $8,450 annually to educate each student, well above the U.S. average of $5,920. Yet its students' scores on standardized tests were among the lowest in the state, and its dropout rate of 13.4 percent was higher than the national average of 11.4 percent.

Contract Approved by Split Vote

Despite the bitter opposition of the district's twelve unions, which represented teachers, teacher aides, principals, food-service workers, and others, on October 3 the board of education voted 6-3 to turn over the schools to EAI. "We basically are saying that the old model for delivering education wasn't working in Hartford and, frankly, it isn't working that well in any other urban school district either," board member Ted Carroll told the Washington Post. *"It is a structural problem. We have good people managing our schools, but they are not people who are necessarily trained as managers. They are well-intentioned and they are smart, but their only experience is with public schools which do not work. We want to team them up with people who have experience with organizations that have worked."*

Under the five-year deal, the district gave EAI its entire $171 million annual budget and the company agreed to spend $15 million of its own money to buy new computers, renovate schools, and improve training and curriculum. If the company spent more than the amount budgeted by the city, it would have to make up the difference itself. If it managed to spend less than the budgeted amount, it would receive half the savings. Since nearly $149 million of the district's $171 million budget went to salaries, and the contract required EAI to honor existing contracts, it was unclear where significant savings might be found.

EAI's Prior Operations Examined

Before it signed the Hartford contract, EAI operated a dozen schools around the country. Most were located in Baltimore, Maryland, where the company had operated nine schools for two years at the time of the Hartford contract. EAI's tenure in Baltimore had been controversial. The company aroused the ire of union officials when it replaced $13-an-hour unionized teachers' aides with $7-an-hour college students and hired nonunion custodians. It also was attacked for placing special education students in regular classrooms, a practice known as mainstreaming.

Perhaps most importantly, in October Baltimore officials announced that students' performance on standardized tests fell in several schools operated by EAI. Attendance at the EAI schools had improved, district officials said, but it had improved even more at other Baltimore schools.

Most observers agreed that EAI had done a great job of sprucing up the Baltimore schools it operated and cramming them full of technology. The company had invested $7.5 million of its own money to repair and improve the nine schools it managed, or nearly $1 million per facility. Detractors wondered whether EAI had pumped in lots of money to make its Baltimore schools look good to visitors from other districts, using them in effect as loss leaders as it sought larger contracts.

Baltimore officials said they would decide whether to continue the EAI contract after examining the results of a study of the EAI experiment being conducted by researchers from the University of Maryland. It was expected that the study would be completed in mid-1995.

Privatization Mulled in Other States

During 1994, officials in a number of other states and districts examined the possibility of privatizing public schools. In March, Massachusetts officials signed an agreement that allowed a total of thirteen different organiza-

tions to operate fifteen schools. Three of the schools were to be operated by the Edison Project, a private company founded in 1990 by Chris Whittle. Edison, which planned to start operating three elementary schools in August 1995, said it would use a school year running 210 days, much longer than the 180 days required by the state.

Also in March, Franklin L. Smith, superintendent of schools in Washington, D.C., dropped a plan to turn over 10 to 15 of the city's 165 schools to a private firm. The leading candidate to operate the schools had been EAI. Smith dropped the idea in the face of strong opposition. Ironically, the debate in Washington never really got to the issue of whether EAI could improve the city's schools. Instead, it focused largely on opposition to having white outsiders operate schools in a city that was overwhelmingly black.

Following are separate press releases concerning the operation of the Hartford, Connecticut, public schools by a private company, issued by the Hartford Board of Education and Education Alternatives Inc. on October 3, 1994:

BOARD OF EDUCATION STATEMENT

Schools That Work

A summary of the Public-Private Partnership Between the Hartford Board of Education and Education Alternatives Inc.

- By the authority given to the Hartford Board of Education through the Connecticut State statutes and the City Charter, the Board is entering into contract with Education Alternatives, Inc. to provide management of the entire Hartford public school system.
- Parties to the contract (the Hartford Board of Education and Education Alternatives) will work actively in partnership with the superintendent and Alliance members (Johnson Controls-Facility Management Services, KPMG Peat Marwick and Computer Curriculum Corporation) to manage the school system and implement the strategic plan.
- In the course of helping to implement the strategic plan, Education Alternatives and the Alliance will be accountable to the Board and will be expected to achieve the highest standards in a variety of areas essential for managing the school system effectively. Among the areas of accountability:

  - Facilities will be clean, safe and efficiently managed.
  - School governance teams will be established at every school. Each team will be responsible for determining how to reach the curriculum and standards set by the Board. Each team will have the opportunity to select for its school a research-based educational model previously qualified by the Board.

411

- Training for teachers and non-instructional staff, in-classroom resources, parental involvement and community involvement will increase.
- Education Alternatives will invest $1.6 million to repair and secure schools.
- Education Alternatives will identify and implement systems that eliminate waste and incorporate ongoing efficiencies.
- Within one year of the contract signing date, Education Alternatives will invest an estimated $14 million into technology for instruction and improved management of the system.
- The Board retains all legal authority under Connecticut law.
- The superintendent retains all authority provided by state statute and will serve as the chief executive officer of the school system.
- Terms of the contract: The Board anticipates a five-year partnership with Education Alternatives that can be cancelled with 90 days' notice without cause.
- All current union contracts will be honored.
- Education Alternatives will work cooperatively in collective bargaining.
- Education Alternatives will advance funds to cover all the school district's expenses except employee fringe benefits on a monthly basis. In turn, Education Alternatives will be paid back and compensated according to a formula in the contract that is in compliance with state statutes, up to the school board's authorized limits of expenditures (approximately $200 million this year). Any amount spent over that figure will be Education Alternatives' responsibility.
- The Board of Education and Education Alternatives will share savings equally to promote a spirit of partnership.
- Education Alternatives will establish the Tesseract Foundation for Hartford Children. Education Alternatives will match total annual donations to the foundation (from the city or any other party) up to five percent of its shared savings.
- The Board of Education and Education Alternatives commit to continue improving all special programs (such as special education, bilingual and Chapter 1) while administering each in accordance with all state and federal guidelines.
- Education Alternatives will have the authority to purchase supplies, materials and services directly from qualified vendors. Education Alternatives will exceed the city's standards and requirements for purchasing from small, minority and locally owned businesses.

EDUCATION ALTERNATIVES STATEMENT

The Hartford Board of Education and the *Alliance for Schools That Work* announced today a groundbreaking public-private partnership to improve education for more than 25,000 students.

The Hartford Board of Education voted 6 to 3 to approve the execution of a contract with Education Alternatives on Tuesday, October 4. Education Alternatives will manage the city's 32-school system in conjunction with other *Alliance* members KPMG Peat Marwick, Johnson Controls-Facility Management Services and Computer Curriculum Corporation. This public-private partnership, charged with the managerial oversight of the entire Hartford school district, is the first of its kind in the United States.

The Hartford Board of Education selected the *Alliance for Schools That Work* in a competitive bidding process in late July. Today the Hartford Board of Education voted to accept the terms of the contract. The *Alliance* will manage the 32 public schools in Hartford and oversee the school system's approximate $200 million per year school budget for five years.

Board member Kathy Evans said that the partnership will deliver results in the classroom, with the *Alliance* directly accountable to the board for meeting agreed-upon goals. "They will provide us with technology that we currently don't have, better teacher training and improved facilities," Evans said. "It is clearly a 'big win' for Hartford's children."

The *Alliance* will increase classroom resources to directly benefit students. New technology and capital improvements will be provided, including an investment of approximately $1.6 million to repair, secure and upgrade school buildings. In addition, the contract provides for an investment of about $14 million for classroom and office technology in the first year. Specific performance goals include greater parent and community involvement, improved technology in the classroom, expanded staff development for teachers and other school employees, and implementation of the school system's existing strategic plan for improving student performance.

"With declining student performance, high drop-out rates and escalating costs, the school board felt we needed to take a proactive step to implement a more responsive and more efficiently managed school system," said Stephanie Lightfoot, a member of the Hartford Board of Education.

The *Alliance* will work with school governance teams consisting of educators, parents and community leaders, to select an educational model for each school. For those schools that choose to implement it, Education Alternatives offers the Tesseract ® educational philosophy. The Tesseract approach is based on the belief that every child can learn effectively when the school climate and classroom practices are geared to the needs of each learner. KPMG Peat Marwick will identify cost savings from efficient financial management to help fund increased resources in the classrooms. Johnson Controls-Facility Management Services will ensure safe, well-maintained facilities for Hartford's children. Computer Curriculum Corporation will provide classroom technology to expand learning opportunities.

"This partnership is based on a shared vision for the children of Hartford. We see children thriving academically, socially and emotionally in a revitalized school system," said John T. Golle, chairman and chief executive officer of Education Alternatives. "Our goal is to generate cost savings within the

school system that will be directed back into the classroom. We plan to benefit Hartford's children first and investors over the course of the contract."

The *Alliance* provides management services to schools throughout the
United States to improve the quality of education for America's children.
Working in partnership with schools, parents, teachers and community leaders, the *Alliance* strives to nurture children academically and equip them with
tools they need to be successful in life. With the addition of the Hartford contract, the *Alliance* operates 44 schools in two states, bringing successful
teaching practices, technology, efficient facilities management and expanded
learning opportunities to more than 32,500 students.

HEALTH PROBLEMS IN
EASTERN EUROPE
October 6, 1994

A health crisis threatens the social stability and political and economic reforms in the countries of Eastern Europe, according to a report published October 6 by the United Nations Children's Fund. The report examined health conditions in Albania, Bulgaria, the Czech Republic, Slovakia, Hungary, Poland, Romania, Russia, and Ukraine.

"The mortality and health crisis burdening most Eastern European countries since 1989 is without precedent in the European peacetime history of this century," the report said. "It signals a societal crisis of unexpected proportions, unknown implications and uncertain solutions."

Health conditions were never good in the countries, the report noted. Yet between 1989 and 1993, the region experienced what the report termed "excess mortality" of more than 800,000 people. Surprisingly, those most affected were not children and the elderly, the two groups usually most susceptible to health problems. Instead, the highest increases in mortality were recorded for males between the ages of twenty and fifty-nine. "This surge is largely dependent on three broad, transition-related factors: widespread impoverishment, erosion of preventive health services, sanitary infrastructure and medical services, and social stress," the report said. Most of the extra deaths were caused by heart problems and sharp increases in the number of homicides and suicides. The report pointed out that in 1993 Russia's homicide rate was double that of the United States, a nation frequently cited as having a high homicide rate.

Much of the increase in mortality was caused by "an explosive rise in social stress," which the report tied to the difficult political and economic transitions occurring in the Eastern European nations. Other factors contributing to both illness and death included a crumbling health care infrastructure and severe environmental problems.

The death rates for infants, children, and adolescents were generally remaining stable, the report said, and in five of the nine countries the infant mortality rate was continuing to decline. However, children were sick more frequently and nutritional problems were increasing. In addition, the rise in the deaths of adults was increasing children's risk of living in poverty, being abandoned, or becoming orphans.

Health Crisis Could Block Reform

The report warned that the health crisis could have widespread consequences. "In parts of Eastern Europe, this health, nutrition and mortality crisis represents a clear threat to the political viability of the entire reform process," the report said. "Indeed, the whole transition could easily grind to a halt as mortality rises, health services worsen and consensus-building skills are slowly and painfully learned." The transition was complicated by the many problems inherited from former governments and by the "slow response of the West," the report added.

A second report, issued in the fall by the World Bank, was equally discouraging. It said that health problems were so bad in much of Eastern Europe that they were affecting the countries' ability to compete economically. Alexander S. Preker, who wrote the report, told the New York Times that the gap in the quality of health care between Western Europe and the former communist countries was "wide and growing."

Under communism, countries in Eastern Europe provided free health care to their citizens, although small bribes were often necessary. Health care was still free under the new system, but patients frequently complained they now had to pay hefty bribes. Even with bribes, the quality of care was almost uniformly poor. Medical equipment in many hospitals was so antiquated it could not be repaired when it broke. In some cases, families of hospital patients had to provide food and medical supplies so their loved ones could receive treatment.

Money Lacking for Health Care

The poor quality of care could be directly linked to the economic transition. Governments did not have money for hospitals, so health care was neglected. In some countries, doctors working at state-run hospitals made less money than bus drivers. The Czech Republic was the only nation that had created a system under which doctors could practice privately and receive insurance reimbursements.

Air and water pollution, which had been rampant under communism and were blamed for many health problems, continued unabated during the transition. A World Health Organization report said that most of the water used for drinking in Eastern Europe was contaminated and unfit for human consumption.

Government officials said that economic recovery had to take precedence over environmental concerns, at least for the time being. Yet some observers said that if the transition to a market economy did not include pollution controls, it might be impossible to impose them later.

Following are excerpts from the report titled "Crisis in Mortality, Health and Nutrition," which was released October 6, 1994, by the United Nations Children's Fund:

Overview

The mortality and health crisis burdening most Eastern European countries since 1989 is without precedent in the European peacetime history of this century. It signals a societal crisis of unexpected proportions, unknown implications and uncertain solutions.

In most of the region, this crisis has caused, and continues to cause, large numbers of avoidable deaths and threatens to erode social stability and indeed the entire transition process. In some of the nine countries monitored by this project, the 'excess mortality' accumulated between 1989-93 is far greater than that wrought by the 'Great Depression' of 1929-33 in North America. Leaving aside the Czech Republic and Slovakia (which did not experience any sizable increase in death rates) and Albania (affected by data problems), 'excess mortality' over the entire 1989-93 period amounts to approximately 800,000 people. . . .

In addition, recent changes in mortality, nuptiality and fertility parallel or even surpass those normally observed in wartime conditions. Information from other Eastern European countries in transition not covered by this project—the former East Germany, Latvia, Estonia, Lithuania, Belarus, Moldova and Slovenia—indicates that upsurges in mortality (and equally awesome falls in births and rises in poverty) are overwhelming practically the entire region.

Throughout Eastern Europe, the current crisis is also causing a sharp acceleration in the number of children, adolescents and adults suffering from various illnesses, invalidity, allergies and chronic diseases, or otherwise considered not to be in good health. Nutritional status and nutrition-related health problems have been influenced by three distinct but mutually reinforcing factors. Average calorie, protein and fat intake has declined significantly. For a growing number of very poor households, intake has fallen below the recommended dietary allowances. This is reflected in the increasing incidence of low birth weight babies in five of the nine countries monitored. Second, the substitution between expensive and cheap sources of nutrients triggered by the fall in incomes has protected energy intake but has aggravated dietary imbalances, thus further increasing the incidence of cardiovascular and chronic diseases. Third, large reductions in the consumption of milk, fresh fruit and vegetables have worsened micronutrient deficits already long prevailing in the region.

Contrary to most expectations, the health and mortality crisis afflicting the region during the last four years has not hit the traditionally most vulnerable groups, that is, children, adolescents, women and the elderly. Indeed, while most of the population has been affected to some degree, the highest increases in mortality have been recorded for male adults in the 20-59 age group. This surge is largely dependent on three broad, transition-related factors: widespread impoverishment, erosion of preventive health services, sanitary infrastructure and medical services, and social stress. While the entire population has felt the effects of the first two factors, cultural, biological and behavioural reasons have meant that stress has hit young and middle-aged men particularly hard.

Fortunately, infants, children and young adolescents in most countries have not been greatly affected in a direct manner by the current mortality crisis. In five of the nine countries monitored in this study, the infant mortality rate has continued to decline during this period, and even in the others the upswing in mortality among infants has been substantially less dramatic than among adults and the elderly. Furthermore, with the exception of the Czech Republic, death rates for children in the 1-4 and 5-14 age brackets fell in all countries, including those affected by large rises in the overall number of deaths. However, in more indirect ways the situation of children has been severely threatened: more frequent sickness and greater nutritional imbalances are being recorded and the upturn in adult deaths is leading to a considerably heightened risk of poverty, abandonment, or orphanhood. In other areas too, child welfare has suffered, as is well illustrated by the deterioration in child care and education services and an unstoppable increase in youth crime rates.

A preponderant proportion of the excess deaths (reaching 80 per cent of the total in some countries) is explained by a true epidemic of heart and circulatory diseases. While the incidence of these ailments has traditionally been high in Eastern Europe, a variety of transition-related stress, dietary, hygienic and curative factors are behind this unprecedented 'social adaptation crisis'. Though homicide and suicide rates have edged upwards everywhere, violent causes explain a sizeable part of the increase in mortality only in Russia, Ukraine and, to a lesser degree, Hungary. In these countries, up to two thirds of additional mortality among adults in the 35-45 age bracket is explained by alcohol poisoning and psychosis, murder, suicide and various types of accidents including drowning, falls, suffocation, fire, and car and work-related accidents. This bleak picture underlines the depth of the current social crisis, the extent of the collapse of most institutions of the state and civil society, the breakdown of law and order and basic health services as well as the spread of criminal behaviour in large parts of the region.

In the countries of South-Eastern and Eastern Europe, there is also evidence that infectious and parasitic diseases have contributed to higher mortality and morbidity among both children and the rest of the population. Tuberculosis incidence rose in all countries with a one-year lag following the surge in poverty rates. Furthermore, Russia and Ukraine were hit by a deadly epidemic of diphtheria due to low and diminishing vaccination coverage among infants, lack of immunity among adults and loss of potency of vaccines. In addition, several countries experienced outbreaks of hepatitis, bacillary dysentery and salmonellosis, sexually-transmitted diseases (including, increasingly, among children) and greater incidence of parasitic and skin diseases.

The crisis has not affected all Eastern European countries with the same intensity. Four and a half years from the inception of the reform, clearly diverging welfare trends have emerged in the region. A rising variation in performance may be seen not only in mortality and other welfare indicators but also in economic growth and political stability. The crisis is without doubt most pronounced in Eastern and South-Eastern Europe. Of the nine countries covered by this report, only the Czech Republic and Slovakia have been spared an increase in mortality. Since 1993, Poland also appears to have almost entirely reabsorbed the surge in death rates recorded in the earlier phases of the transition.

Most of the additional mortality due to heart problems, suicide, homicide, alcohol psychosis and cirrhosis of the liver appears to be related to an explosive rise in social stress, a condition which arises when individuals have difficulty responding to new and unexpected situations. Greater poverty, unemployment, migration, divorce, separation, loss of relatives, lack of hope, loss of self-esteem, insecurity about and fear of the future, increase in criminal offences, conflicts at work and in the family are the main sources of stress.

This 'social adaptation crisis' has been exacerbated by the collapse of the political, social and economic organizations which framed people's lives for 50 or more years—a collapse entailing loss of national pride, a widespread sensation of meaninglessness and loss of purpose. Indeed, this institutional collapse has carried social costs in addition to those caused by economic factors and psychosocial stress. They include a rapid decay of health infrastructure, a drop in the quality and range of public services, unclear administrative rules, massive surges in crime rates and in social chaos. While in many instances economic hardship and greater psychosocial stress have created the conditions for violent, irrational or illegal reactions, rises in 'external mortality' as large as those described in this report could not have taken place without a major collapse of the regulatory, inspection and police apparatuses of the state.

In parts of Eastern Europe, this health, nutrition and mortality crisis represents a clear threat to the political viability of the entire reform process. Indeed, the whole transition could easily grind to a halt as mortality rises, health services worsen and consensus-building skills are slowly and painfully learned. Increasing tensions are the many problems inherited from former regimes and the slow response of the West. To be sure, market reforms are highly desirable, necessary and—in view of the failure of communism—inescapable. Efforts to reform the ailing economy, poor social services and sclerotic political systems, while preserving the positive achievements of the past in education, child care and social security, must continue. Yet, the many problems encountered so far need to be recognized, clearly documented and—most of all—tackled in a way that ensures an equitable distribution of sacrifices and benefits.

If even more devastating developments are to be avoided, this social adaptation crisis needs to be addressed with greater urgency and more vigorous resolve than has been the case to date. Without an adequate response, more than the political stability of any single government stands to be lost. Faced with increasingly severe hardships and social chaos, many may question the viability of reforms—or even the viability of democracy itself—in creating firm foundations for a new order. Recent political shifts point to a very real danger of derailment of the reform process. The stakes are high. Unless more successful economic and social policies are introduced and more favourable external conditions can be achieved, and unless these policies generate perceptible improvements over the short term, this danger may become a harsh reality.

Update on Four Hard Years of Transition

As the difficulties of the transition in Eastern Europe endure, analysis of poverty and social deprivation is receiving far greater attention than in the past, or even as recently as two or three years ago. Indeed, in the countries most affected, the persistence or further deepening of the current crisis represents a major threat to the overall transition process. In some countries health and food intake has severely suffered with the crisis and this has become a crucial topic in political debate. Thus, analysis of poverty and social deprivation not only serves the purpose of documenting the extent of the problem and the groups most affected, but is also increasingly used to assess the impact of various policies and to design adequate social responses. In this chapter, the main changes which have occurred in various aspects of human welfare are reviewed, with particular attention given to the situation of children.

1. A Rapid and Lasting Surge in Poverty and Extreme Poverty

The last four years have witnessed an unprecedented rise in the number of people whose income per capita has fallen below a conventional poverty line, i.e. an income which would ensure the satisfaction of essential needs and a broader, though still basic, socialization. People whose incomes have dropped below this threshold are often no longer able to enrol their children in kindergartens, summer camps and higher education because of the mounting costs of fees and educational materials. They are also increasingly unable to spare any resources for leisure or adequate clothing and have tended to reduce their intake of good-quality food, though serious problems of undernutrition may not have surfaced yet.

Living standards, health and nutritional status have also fallen much more sharply for a smaller number of households now living below an extreme poverty line, i.e. an income permitting only the satisfaction—assuming rational economic behaviour—of the essentials needed for survival. People whose income per capita falls below this threshold (referred to as the *extremely poor*) are likely to suffer considerable health and mortality risks, inadequate food intake, stress and acute social deprivation. . . .

There is no doubt that reporting, measurement and interpretation problems are clouding the picture. Yet, in spite of the above limitations there is ample evidence that the proportion of the poor and, particularly, of the *extremely poor* increased significantly in the entire region over the 1989-93 period. However, the initial year, intensity and duration of such increases vary considerably among the countries. The steepest increases in the proportion of people living in extreme poverty have occurred in Bulgaria, Poland, Romania, the urban sector of Albania, Russia and, very likely, Ukraine (for which data problems do not allow clear conclusions, though most analyses point to a sharp increase in the number of the poor).

In these countries, between 15 and 26 per cent of the population could be considered as extremely poor in 1992-3, while an additional 28 to 38 per cent was affected by less acute, but nonetheless debilitating, low income levels and poverty. Overall, the incidence of extreme poverty almost tripled in Poland between 1989 and 1990, in parallel with drops in net income per capita of almost 30 per cent. It has broadly stagnated since then, in spite of some recovery of output in 1992 and 1993, as a result of the continuous increase in income inequality. In Russia, the number of people living in extreme poverty increased from 2.5 per cent to 23.2 per cent between 1991 and 1992. This massive rise followed a much larger than expected increase in inflation and a subsequent large drop in incomes. Though estimates of recent poverty trends cannot be presented here due to methodological problems, available information indicates that the percentage of people in extreme poverty declined from the end of 1992. However, despite the stabilization of the economy at a low level, the number of people in poverty remained broadly constant because of rapidly widening income differentials among various groups of the population.

Following the overthrow of the Ceaucescu regime in Romania, a series of unsustainable policy measures involving general increases in real wages and transfer payments, the lowering of prices of key items as well as the artificial creation of half a million new jobs temporarily reduced the proportion of the extremely poor. However, this unrealistic situation changed with the drastic drop in real wages, inadequate social transfers and the surge in income inequality which started in November 1991, and led to a rapid rise in the number of the extremely poor. The proportion of the population living in extreme poverty spiralled to 19 per cent in 1992 and there are signs that the situation might have marginally worsened or, at best, stagnated in 1993.

With regard to Bulgaria, the proportion of people living in extreme poverty is estimated to have increased sharply between 1990 and 1991. This was provoked by the introduction of price and trade liberalization policies as well as the enormous shock caused by the break-up of Comecon and the subsequent huge rise in the cost of imported oil. The number of people living in extreme poverty continued to rise sharply in 1992, and then more moderately in 1993. The thirtyfold increase between 1990 and 1992 in the number of social assistance recipients confirms that destitution is now affecting a significant share of the population.

In Albania real agricultural incomes increased by 30 per cent between 1991 and 1993, at a time when real incomes and transfers in the public sector declined by more than 30 per cent. The number of people in cities earning below subsistence incomes (after emigrant remittances) is estimated to have increased from 85,000 to 475,000 between the first half of 1991 and the second half of 1993, while in the countryside it fell from 31,000 to zero. Poverty levels were much less drastic than would have been the case had a social safety net not been in place. The population was buffered from part of the effect of the breakdown in production by the introduction of compensatory payments for food price increases, the adjustment of benefits in line with inflation and the system of 80 per cent payments to idle public enterprise workers from July 1991 to July 1992 and of unemployment insurance thereafter.

In contrast, the spread of extreme poverty in the Czech Republic, Slovakia and Hungary was contained to less than 4 per cent. In these countries, inflationary explosions were avoided, drops in real wages were more limited, the extensive safety nets created in the past were broadly maintained and changes in income inequality were relatively small, all of which meant that the number of the poor was also kept down to more tolerable dimensions. In addition, while in 1992 and 1993 both poverty indicators adopted in this study were still edging upward in the Eastern and South-Eastern European countries, they experienced a small decline in the Czech Republic and broadly stabilized in the other two European countries. In Hungary, it is possible that poverty has risen further over the last two years, particularly as the situation regarding real wages and unemployment worsened until the end of 1993. However, this cannot be confirmed as the most recent poverty data refer to 1991.

These data on the incidence of poverty and extreme poverty need some qualification. Firstly, the intensity of poverty—measured by the 'poverty gap', i.e. the average amount of money required to raise family income to the poverty line—has increased by far less than the poverty rates. In Bulgaria, for instance, the percentage of people living in extreme poverty rose almost 13 times between 1990 and 1993, i.e. from 2.0 to a shocking 26.2 per cent. However, the poverty gap only increased 1.2 times. Thus, it appears that many of the new extreme poor have fallen only a short way below the extreme poverty threshold and that a moderate broad-based recovery would reduce their number rapidly. The poverty and extreme poverty rates appear very sensitive to the poverty threshold chosen, indicating that there is considerable potential for many of the new poor and extremely poor to rise above the line. . . .

2. Deterioration in Human Welfare over 1989-93: A Bird's Eye View

In spite of the great hopes placed on a rapid transition to political democracy and a market economy, four and a half years after the launch of the Balczerowicz Plan—which symbolizes the beginning of the transition—it is now evident that the reforms have met with large, unexpected and, at times, unmanageable obstacles. The reforms have also provoked a deterioration of unparalleled proportions in human welfare throughout most of the region and particularly in Albania, Bulgaria, Romania, Russia and Ukraine. . . .

A. A Large Overall Deterioration Affects the Entire Region

To begin with, for about 72 per cent of the variables for which information is available, the 1993 (or most recent) level indicates a deterioration, often a serious one, in relation to its 1989 level. Of the 29 indicators considered, only two (maternal mortality and 1-4 year death rate) show convincing improvements. In addition, in 56 per cent of the cases (mostly in the hard-hit countries of Eastern and Southern Europe), the deterioration exceeds 10 per cent, a level normally indicating acute deterioration. Only in 28 per cent of the cases are there signs of possible improvements in human welfare, though some of these may be somewhat misleading. Indeed, the present analysis focuses only on a 'point-to-point' comparison and on improvements or deteriorations that have occurred during the intermediary period. As this approach does not pick up negative changes of briefer duration, i.e. which had been reabsorbed by 1993 (as occurred for several mortality indicators for the Czech Republic and, more recently, Poland) the extent of the crisis as measured by these indicators is to a certain extent understated.

B. Income-based and Demographic Indicators Show the Most Frequent and Sharpest Deteriorations

The most frequent deteriorations have been recorded for the income-based and demographic indicators. *Incomes per capita* declined and *poverty rates* shot up in all countries monitored, including the better-off Central European region, and children were more than proportionately affected. Only in the Czech Republic has some recovery occurred. A rise in the *food share* in all countries, except the Czech Republic and Poland, confirms the substantial drop in welfare levels in the region. This is further verified by the falls in average per capita daily *calorie consumption*, with no known exceptions, by between 100-600 calories (or by 290 calories on average). While this drop may not seem dangerous in itself, given the high intake prior to 1989, closer examination reveals that pre-existing serious nutritional imbalances and nutrition-related health problems have been aggravated by recent changes.

Changing nuptiality and fertility patterns are perhaps the most revealing indicators of individual perceptions of the crisis. With rising youth unemployment, skyrocketing costs for housing and overall uncertainty about the future, *crude marriage rates* have dropped in all nine countries by between 4 per cent in Albania and 34 per cent in Bulgaria. *Remarriage rates* have fallen in all countries and even more rapidly, by 28 per cent on average and up to 50 per cent in Bulgaria, the most extreme case. Only Albania and Ukraine show signs of some recovery for marriage rates. However, as *crude birth rates* plummeted further in 1993 in these two countries, the improvement in marriage rates more likely reflects abandoned expectations than a return to normality. Furthermore, the birth rate has fallen by more than 20 per cent in Albania, Bulgaria and Ukraine and by a shocking 34 and 32 per cent in Russia and Romania respectively. A more favourable outcome may be seen in the drop in *crude divorce rates* in all countries, except Slovakia, Russia and Ukraine. It is worth noting, however, that while the preservation of existing marriages is a rational response to growing economic hardship and uncertainty, it does not necessarily imply stable family life.

C. The Social Fabric Is Being Rapidly Eroded in All Countries

The magnitude of the crisis is also underscored by a high number of indicators showing that social cohesion and personal safety are under serious threat in practically all the countries of the region. *Crime and homicide rates* of precipitous proportions in all countries are signs of a weakening social fabric and widespread perceptions of growing income and wealth differentials, higher unemployment and greater alcohol consumption. Despite an increasing share of unreported and undetected crimes (which are presumably behind the decline of cases in Bulgaria and the Czech Republic), the number of *youth sentenced* has risen dramatically in most countries.

The only exception in this set of indicators is the rise in the number of *adoptions* recorded in Slovakia, Russia and Ukraine. Interestingly, the increase in adoption rates in these countries might also be a positive sign of growing social cohesion and solidarity. However, given that these are the same countries which recorded increased divorce rates, a more pessimistic interpretation of this development may be called for. Furthermore, there is a steadily increasing proportion of *births to women of very young ages* in all nine countries, indicating that a greater share of children might be suffering the risk of abandonment and inadequate family support. At present, every fifth and fourth newborn in Ukraine and Bulgaria respectively has a mother below age 20.

D. Health and Education Are Also Affected in Most Countries

Health and education conditions have also shown a high frequency of deterioration (though to a slightly lesser extent than for those indicators discussed in the two previous paragraphs). A surge in *new tuberculosis cases* was witnessed in all countries, confirming again that poverty is on the rise. Similarly, *low birth weight* incidence has steadily escalated, except in Albania where food aid has been very important, and Hungary where it rose only temporarily in 1990-91. In contrast, some positive changes were recorded for the number of *abortions per 100 live births,* an indicator which gives important information on maternal health. It showed extremely high values in the past, with the notable exception of Poland, and also Albania and Romania where extreme pro-natalist policies prevailed. After jumping significantly during the first phase of the transition (due to the drop in birth rates and the legalization of abortion in Romania), the abortion rate started to decline slowly in most countries in 1993. Only Albania has maintained an upward trend, while Poland has displayed a stronger decline in line with strict legislation introduced in 1993. In all countries, however, a further decline in the number of abortions is still hindered by a lack of health education, inadequate access to modern contraceptives and prohibitive costs.

In many areas of the region, the care and education of children suffered between 1989 and 1993. *Creche enrolment rates* dropped, despite shrinking child cohorts in all countries. Romania, where the fall in fertility has been very large, is the only exception to this trend. *Parental leave* provisions were not able to compensate for this drop, as its coverage rate has also declined (with the notable exception of Hungary). *Pre-primary enrolment rates* fell by 6-16 percentage points, with severe consequences for child care and early child development. Again, Hungary is the only exception. Some recovery was also registered in 1992 in Bulgaria, Slovakia and Romania, but levels remained well below those of 1989. Only Russian and Hungarian data are available so far for 1993, and these reinforce the earlier negative trend in Russia and the positive trend in Hungary. Worsening *primary education rates* have been reported for four countries (Albania, Bulgaria, Poland and Romania). In Albania, Bulgaria and Romania, the child population not covered by primary education has substantially grown, reaching 15, 11 and 6 per cent respectively, according to the latest available official figures. Most of the countries reported deteriorations in *secondary enrolment rates* between 1989 and 1992. Only Slovakia exhibited a perceivable improvement, though this trend was reversed in 1993.

E. Deterioration in Mortality Mostly Affects Adult Men

While the transition has witnessed a steep increase in overall mortality, the young child (1-4 years) death rate has improved in all countries. So too, *maternal mortality* has exhibited a steady decline almost everywhere, and particularly in Romania and Albania following more liberal approaches to abortion. Only in Poland and Russia was a surge recorded. As a drop in maternal deaths is an expectable outcome of falling fertility rates, the increase recorded in these two countries reflects the alarming state of their health sectors.

Infant mortality rates, in turn, deteriorated in four countries out of nine between 1989 and 1993. In Albania, Russia and Ukraine, IMR is still rising, while in Bulgaria the trend turned in 1992. For most other age groups, however, there has been a far more pronounced worsening in rates. *Adolescent mortality rates* have only improved in Hungary, Poland and Romania, with again a transient, though less dramatic, regression occurring after 1989. Mortality data point to a health crisis of near epidemic proportions for *adults* (and men in particular) in most countries.

Life expectancy at birth, the most comprehensive health indicator, has deteriorated in the majority of countries since the onset of the transition. For men, life expectancy increased only in the Czech Republic and in Poland (in 1993) and for women it has risen in the Czech Republic, Poland and Romania between 1989 and the most recent period for which data are available. However, in the first one to two years of large-scale economic and political transformation, an increase in the number of deaths proved unavoidable everywhere.

F. A High Coincidence Between Changes in Income-based Welfare Indicators and Those Focusing on Human Capabilities and Demographic Behaviour

The singularity of the Eastern European situation is in many ways underscored by the massive and unexpected deterioration in human welfare precisely at a time when large welfare improvements were expected. This singularity is underlined even more dramatically by the very considerable coincidence observed between the changes registered in income-based indicators, human capabilities indicators and demographic variables. This presents an important and firm confirmation of the fact that high adjustment costs are being borne by large sections of the Eastern European population. This coincidence exists both in terms of intensity and direction, though it is clear that in the Central European countries the relationships between different types of indicators are weaker and at times statistically non-significative. In South-Eastern Europe, in contrast, large income falls and poverty rate increases have been paralleled by dismaying regressions in mortality, morbidity and education.

G. South-Eastern and Eastern Europe Are Most Affected

While on a sector-wide basis the most acute deteriorations were observed in the fields of income per capita, poverty rates, demography and social cohesion, regionwide it may clearly be seen that the crisis has assumed a very different pattern. A first group of countries—Russia, Ukraine, Bulgaria, Albania and Romania—shows more frequent, lasting and pronounced retrogressions than the second group of Central European countries—Hungary, Czech and Slovak Republics and Poland. While negative outcomes are recorded for 80-90 per cent of the indicators for the first group of countries, this figure drops to 60 per cent of cases for the second. Of the nine countries monitored, Russia presents the worst performance and Poland and the Czech Republic the least negative. . . .

3. How Children in Eastern Europe Are Affected by the Transition

The above discussion . . . illustrate[s] that the recent mortality crisis has first and foremost affected males in the central age groups and that—fortunately—children have not always been hit the hardest in a direct manner. Yet, both directly and perhaps even more so indirectly, the last four years have aggravated the situation of children and particularly adolescents, at least in some countries. The following discussion examines how this has happened.

A. Increasing Numbers of Poor Children

As mentioned in the first part of this chapter, child poverty rates have generally risen much faster than for any other group because of the rapid spread of unemployment and low-paying jobs, together with the less than proportional indexation of child allowances. These allowances formerly constituted a large proportion of families' income, especially for families with more than one child and for low-income or single-parent families. The trend toward a greater relative impoverishment among children may have intensified in 1993 in Hungary, Romania and Slovakia, in parallel with the sharp upswing in unemployment and the proliferation of low-paying jobs.

Simultaneously, child allowances have lost a considerable part of their purchasing power, most of all in Romania and Russia. However, several proposals have been made for targeting child and family allowances to poor families, and the Czech and Slovak Republics have taken some steps in this direction. In some cases such benefits have been extended to the children of the registered unemployed.

B. Nutrition and Health of Children Affected

Children's food intake has deteriorated during the transition. It is still unclear whether and to what extent the general decline in food consumption—as well as the greater dietary imbalances experienced by a growing proportion of the population—have affected the health status of children in the short term. Nevertheless, lower real incomes and less favourable relative prices have generally aggravated long-standing dietary imbalances typical of the countries of this region. The shift in dietary composition to less expensive and more filling foods has compounded the problem of a diet too rich in animal fats and starch, and too poor in minerals, vitamins and other micronutrients essential to proper growth and development. While the short-term impact on nutrition may not be too serious, that on long-term health conditions is likely to be more severe. Furthermore, the decline in food intake and the deterioration in hygiene, sanitary and housing conditions have caused an increase in the pathologies (such as tuberculosis and rickets) traditionally associated with poverty. Worsening nutritional conditions are also evidenced by an increase in the incidence of low birth weight (LBW) babies in all countries but Hungary and Albania.

In contrast, the crisis may have had a positive impact on the incidence and duration of breastfeeding. Growing unemployment and inactivity among women, together with the tendency to assign women a more 'traditional role' in the family, should have led to a greater incidence of breastfeeding and, by implication, improvement in the health status of very young children. It is unclear, however, whether the 'social values' surrounding breastfeeding have facilitated a move in this direction, though in some countries there is evidence that the proportion of young infants being breastfed is on the rise.

Death rates for infants, children and youth are also increasing, though less frequently and at a much slower pace than for middle-aged people in Albania, Bulgaria, Russia and Ukraine, where social costs have been particularly marked. The increased mortality was largely due to perinatal causes, but in those countries where vaccination coverage dropped it was also due to infectious diseases, particularly tuberculosis, measles and diphtheria. In Bulgaria—where the steepest IMR rise was recorded between 1989 and 1991—most of the increase in IMR occurred in the perinatal period. This rise has been associated with the greater incidence of low birth weight, an increase in the share of births to young and poorly educated mothers and to the worsening medical infrastructure. While mortality for children in the 1-4 age group has declined in all countries, that for youth shows a more general though moderate increase due to accidents, poisonings, violence, and especially to suicide.

These unfavourable trends are partly due to budgetary restrictions, which have led to an extreme shortage of financial and material resources. This has affected the functioning of both preventive health services and of hospitals and clinics. Recent labour force trends have exacerbated this situation. In almost all countries, there has been a drop in the number of parents taking leave from work to care for sick children. In Russia, for example, the situation has reached a critical point. According to recent estimates, the number of cases of leave taken accounts for only half the number of disease cases among children, and just a fraction of the number of cases of chronic diseases. As a result, even in the case of absolute need, many children are without the care of their parents. This often leads to more acute illnesses in many children or to the development of chronic conditions.

C. Some Negative Effects of 'The Demographic Adjustment'

The drastic 'demographic adjustment' observed over the 1989-93 period carries some clear and generally adverse medium- and long-term implications for the welfare of children. An absolute decline of the population, particularly when driven by a contraction of births, leads to an aging of the population and to possible deteriorations of the dependency ratios. As has been evidenced in many Western countries, and already in some Central and Eastern European countries, this can result in a shift in public resources away from children towards the elderly—who hold a more direct sway over the political process.

There is evidence that the decline in the number of births in the countries where fertility has contracted sharply has generally come about through an *increase in the total number of abortions* and not through other birth control methods (although sterilization is becoming more common). Not only does this lead to an increase in health risks for mothers, but it also has long-term detrimental effects on fertility. The contraction in fertility has resulted in an increase in the number of childless and one-child families. In view of the generalized decline in the coverage of pre-school education, a growing proportion of children, particularly from younger couples, risks *ceteris paribus* facing a 'peer socialization gap'. At the same time, the increase in the proportion of births to under-age and/or unmarried mothers raises the share and number of 'children at risk' of abandonment, institutionalization, poverty and psychological maladjustment. Such risks, as well as the risk of orphanhood, are obviously exacerbated by rapidly growing mortality rates among men in the 30-49 age bracket.

The social and emotional development of children has also been affected by sharp rises in mortality among men aged 40-59 and, to a lesser extent, those aged 20-39. This is of considerable concern, not only because of the growing number of premature deaths recorded, but also because of their negative impact on children. Many more children are now growing up as orphans, and therefore face higher dangers of poverty and social maladjustment. Orphanhood, it should be remembered, has traditionally been a main risk factor of child poverty, abandonment and disrupted educational achievement.

D. Widespread Decline in School Enrolment

One of the most pronounced, generalized and consistent changes observed in the post-reform years has been the slump in the proportion of children attending kindergarten, with the single exception of Hungary. The decline in enrolment is certainly cause for acute concern, particularly in relation to children in the 5-6 age group. This may cause considerable damage to child socialization, peer interaction and preparation for school—all areas in which 'family substitutes' can be only of limited relevance, particularly in the growing number of one-child families and problematic families. Confronted with a mounting financial crisis, local authorities have introduced or raised fees for tuition, school meals, uniforms, heating and bus services. However, the liberalization of prices for food, fuel and other items has meant that the fees introduced now represent a substantial proportion of the average wage and thus put kindergartens out of reach for many parents.

The gravity of the current crisis is also underscored by the decline in both *primary and secondary enrolment rates* observed in Bulgaria, Poland and Romania (out of the six countries for which complete information is available). The fall in secondary enrolment rates between 1989 and 1992 was more pronounced, reaching 20 percentage points in Romania, 7 in Bulgaria and 5 in Russia. Even where secondary enrolment rates have not drifted downward, budgetary restrictions and the significant size of adolescent cohorts in the relevant age bracket have resulted in fewer facilities, lower subsidies, higher fees for non-basic activities (books, meals and learning materials) and a likely deterioration in the quality of education. Declines in the number of student stipends granted and in the number of places available in student hostels, as well as rising costs of meals in school canteens are typical examples of changes jeopardizing the educational prospects of many students, particularly.

E. An Increasingly Difficult Socialization and Growing Crime Rates Among Youth

The rising problems faced by those 'institutions' entrusted with the socialization of children, adolescents and young adults (i.e., the family, school, work and youth associations) and the weakening of administrative and police controls that have accompanied the transition to the market economy have brought about a pernicious institutional and cultural vacuum. Problems mushrooming in the school system (overcrowding, loss of relevance and greater private costs) and the subsequent decline in enrolment rates and rise in drop-out rates have certainly contributed to an increasing number of adolescents, particularly in urban areas, being pushed 'onto the street'. Even for those young people able to complete their professional training, the difficulties faced in finding their way into a protected work environment have mounted. In addition, many of the institutions established to provide recreational and cultural activities have folded, or have had their services severely cut back. Public libraries and subsidized art centres have been closed, the 'pioneers' have been disbanded or have lost government support and summer camp attendance has declined considerably.

The number of reported crime cases motivated by financial gains has risen sharply and steadily in all countries of the region. One of the most alarming features of the recent 'crime wave' is the growing share of young offenders in the total. In Slovakia, for instance, the proportion of crimes committed by youngsters rose from 14 per cent in 1989 to 28 per cent in the first half of 1993. In Hungary, the share of traced indictable young offenders (including young adults) rose from an already high 37.7 per cent in 1989 to an even higher 41.7 per cent in 1992. Similar trends have been observed in Romania, Russia and other countries of the region.

CLINTON STATEMENT ON IRAQI TROOP BUILDUP
October 10, 1994

Faced with Iraqi troop movements that threatened Kuwait, President Bill Clinton vowed during a televised speech October 10 to halt any Iraqi aggression. In the days before his speech, Clinton ordered a rapid military buildup in the Persian Gulf region, dispatching thousands of Army troops to Kuwait, two Patriot antimissile batteries to Saudi Arabia, and an aircraft carrier battle group and 350 Air Force planes to the area.

Clinton's speech and troop orders came in response to a buildup of Iraqi troops on the border with Kuwait. Iraqi President Saddam Hussein had moved 14,000 of his elite Republican Guard troops into positions along the border, giving him 64,000 troops in the region. Some of the troops, who were supported by 700 tanks and 900 troop carriers, were within twelve miles of the border with Kuwait. American officials said the Iraqi troop movements resembled those that preceded the 1990-1991 Gulf War, when Iraq invaded Kuwait before being driven back by an international force led by American troops.

No one could predict the Iraqi leader's intentions. On October 8, the United Nations Security Council warned Hussein not to attack Kuwait. The next day, Clinton, Secretary of State Warren Christopher, and Defense Secretary William J. Perry did likewise. The American officials wished to avoid a repeat of 1990, when Hussein apparently believed that weak messages from the Bush administration gave him the green light to attack Kuwait. This time, the American officials wanted to ensure that Hussein knew he would pay a heavy price if he attacked.

Movements Tied to Deal on Sanctions

While most observers did not expect Iraq to invade Kuwait, they could not explain the reason for the troop movements. The movements came only days before the United Nations Security Council was to review economic sanctions imposed after the Gulf War that had crippled Iraq. Some Iraqi diplo-

mats suggested the movements were aimed at cutting a deal: Iraq would leave Kuwait alone if the UN would lift the sanctions.

The UN had imposed economic sanctions August 6, 1990, four days after Iraq invaded Kuwait. Initially, the sanctions—which the UN imposed for only the third time in its history—were aimed at pressuring Iraq to obey UN directives to immediately withdraw from Kuwait. (UN Action Against Iraq with U.S.-Soviet Cooperation, Historic Documents of 1990, p. 545)

As part of the peace agreement that concluded the war, the UN also ordered Iraq to pay billions of dollars in damages for its invasion; to accept Kuwait's borders; to destroy and agree not to rebuild its weapons of mass destruction, such as chemical and nuclear weapons; and to halt terrorist activities. Altogether, the Security Council passed more than two dozen resolutions the Iraqis had to comply with before the sanctions would be lifted. (UN Peace Terms; Iraq's Acceptance, Historic Documents of 1991, p. 191)

The sanctions barred all foreign trade by Iraq except for food and medicine. Most importantly, they stopped Iraq from exporting its huge reserves of oil. Iraq had the second-largest oil reserves in the world, after Saudi Arabia, and had exported three million barrels of oil a day before the sanctions were imposed. A month before Iraq again threatened Kuwait's border, the sanctions had forced the Iraqi government to cut in half the rations of flour, rice, and cooking oil that it supplied to citizens. Even before the cut, the rations did not meet minimal nutritional requirements. American officials said the UN had authorized Iraq to export $1.6 billion of oil to buy food and medicine, but Iraq had refused to do so because it claimed restrictions on its exports constituted foreign interference in its internal affairs.

If Hussein intended by moving his troops to coerce the UN into lifting the sanctions, his action seriously backfired. The troop buildup only gave more ammunition to those who argued that the sanctions should remain as a check on Iraq's renegade behavior.

Ironically, Iraq had been making diplomatic gains in the weeks before the troop movements. Iraq had been cooperating with UN inspectors who were overseeing the destruction of its nuclear, biological, and chemical weapons systems. Based on that cooperation, some countries appeared willing to lift the sanctions. The troop movements set back all diplomatic efforts and even isolated Iraq from its Arab neighbors, some of whom had supported its 1990 invasion of Kuwait.

Iraq Withdraws Troops

On October 10, the same day that Clinton made his televised address, Iraq announced the withdrawal of its troops from the border region. Nonetheless, the American military buildup continued as officials watched to make sure Iraq was really withdrawing.

The new threat to Kuwait was possible because in 1991 President George Bush and his advisers had halted the war against Iraq after one hundred hours. American troops had been poised to destroy Iraq's army, but Bush's order to end the war let many of Iraq's best troops escape.

As the 1994 crisis ended with the Iraqi withdrawal, the overriding question was how to keep Hussein from repeatedly threatening Kuwait. In late October, the United States and Britain demanded that Hussein keep the elite Republican Guard troops at least 150 miles away from the Kuwaiti border. To back up the demand, the United States nearly doubled the number of warplanes that were deployed indefinitely in the Persian Gulf. Eventually, there would be about 130 American aircraft stationed in the region, including A-10 "Warthog" attack jets that can be used to destroy tanks. The United States also increased the amount of equipment prepositioned in the Persian Gulf region so American troops could respond quickly to any new threats.

Iraq Recognizes Kuwait

On November 10, Iraq finally agreed to recognize Kuwait's sovereignty, one of the major conditions imposed by the UN before it would lift the economic sanctions. Four days later, the UN Security Council decided to continue the sanctions. However, France and Russia were pushing hard to get the sanctions lifted if Iraq continued complying with UN orders. Both had enormous financial stakes in the issue. Russia had just signed a $10 billion economic cooperation agreement that would take effect immediately when the sanctions ended, and France had been working on oil contracts with Iraq.

Some diplomats, both from Iraq and other countries, questioned the real intent of the sanctions. They charged that the United States would keep the sanctions in place indefinitely because it hoped to starve the Iraqi people into revolting against their government. U.S. officials denied the charge, saying the sanctions would be lifted when there was proof that Iraq intended to be a peaceful member of the international community.

Following is the text of a televised speech by President Bill Clinton on October 10, 1994, concerning the Iraqi troop buildup, as released by the White House:

Good evening. Tonight I want to speak with you about the actions we are taking to preserve stability in the Persian Gulf in the face of Saddam Hussein's provocative actions. But first, let me take just a minute to report to you on today's events in Haiti.

Three weeks ago today our troops entered Haiti. They went there to keep America's and the world community's commitment to restore the democratically-elected government to power by October 15th. Today, Lt. General Cedras and Brigadier General Biamby, the two remaining coup leaders, have resigned. They have said they will leave Haiti shortly. I am pleased to announce that President Aristide will return home to resume his rightful place this Saturday, October 15th.

I want to express again my pride in what our men and women in uniform have done in Haiti, and how well they have measured up to their difficult mission. In just three weeks the level of violence is down, the Parliament is back, refugees are returning from Guantanamo. And now the military leaders are leaving.

But I also want to caution again, the job in Haiti remains difficult and dangerous. We still have a lot of work ahead of us. But our troops are keeping America's commitment to restore democracy. They are performing their mission very, very well with firmness and fairness, and all Americans are proud of them.

The strength of America's foreign policy stands on the steadfastness of our commitments. The United States and the international community have given their word that Iraq must respect the borders of its neighbors. And tonight, as in Haiti, American troops with our coalition partners are the guarantors of that commitment, the power behind our diplomacy.

Three and a half years ago, the men and women of our armed forces, under the strong leadership of President Bush, General Powell and General Schwarzkopf, fought to expel Iraq from Kuwait and to protect our interests in that vital region. Today we remain committed to defending the integrity of that nation and to protecting the stability of the Gulf region.

Saddam Hussein has shown the world before, with his acts of aggression and his weapons of mass destruction, that he cannot be trusted. Iraq's troop movements and threatening statements in recent days are more proof of this. In 1990, Saddam Hussein assembled a force on the border of Kuwait and then invaded. Last week, he moved another force toward the same border. Because of what happened in 1990, this provocation requires a strong response from the United States and the international community.

Over the weekend, I ordered the George Washington carrier battle group, cruise missile ships, a marine expeditionary brigade and an army mechanized task force to the Gulf. And today, I have ordered the additional deployment of more than 350 Air Force aircraft to the region. We will not allow Saddam Hussein to defy the will of the United States and the international community.

Iraq announced today that it will pull back its troops from the Kuwait border. But we're interested in facts, not promises; in deeds, not words, and we have not yet seen evidence that Iraq's troops are, in fact, pulling back. We'll be watching very closely to see that they do so.

Our policy is clear: We will not allow Iraq to threaten its neighbors or to intimidate the United Nations as it ensures that Iraq never again possesses weapons of mass destruction. Moreover, the sanctions will be maintained until Iraq complies with all relevant U.N. resolutions. That is the answer to Iraq's sanctions problems—full compliance, not reckless provocation.

I'm very proud of our troops who tonight are the backbone of our commitment to Kuwait's freedom and the security of the Gulf. I'm also proud of the planners and the commanders who are getting them there so very quickly, and in such force. They all are proof that we are maintaining and must continue to maintain the readiness and strength of the finest military in the world.

That is what we owe to the men and women of America who are putting their lives on the line today to make the world a safer place. And it is what we owe to the proud families who stand with them. They are protecting our security as we work for a post-Cold War world of democracy and prosperity.

Within the last two weeks, America hosted two champions of post-Cold War democracy. South African President Nelson Mandela came to thank the United States for our support of South Africa's remarkable democratic revolution, and to seek a partnership for the future. And Russian President Boris Yeltsin came to further the partnership between our two nations so well expressed by the fact that now Russian and U.S. missiles are no longer pointed at each other's people, and we are working to reduce the nuclear threat even more.

In short, we are making progress in building a world of greater security, peace and democracy. But our work is not done. There are difficulties and dangers ahead, as we see in Iraq and in Haiti. But we can meet these challenges and keep our commitments. Our objectives are clear. Our forces are strong and our cause is right.

Thank you and God bless America.

ARISTIDE'S RETURN TO HAITI
October 15, 1994

Urging the Haitian people to remain calm and not to seek retribution against those who had oppressed them, Father Jean-Bertrand Aristide, the exiled president who regained power backed by thousands of American soldiers, celebrated his return to Haiti October 15 with a speech on the steps of the National Palace. "Let us live in peace," Aristide said. "All the guns must be silent."

Aristide became the first democratically elected president in Haiti's history when he took office in February 1991, but only seven months later he was forced into exile following a bloody coup by the military. Backed by the police and wealthy businessmen, the military then unleashed a reign of terror aimed at solidifying its hold on power. Aristide supporters were tortured and killed, women were raped, and children were kidnapped.

Thousands of Haitians left their country in open boats to attempt the perilous 600-mile journey to the United States. Some were fleeing for their lives, while others simply sought to leave Haiti, which was the poorest country in the Western Hemisphere, for greater economic opportunities in the United States.

U.S. Coast Guard Intercepts Haitians

On May 24, 1992, President George Bush issued a controversial executive order authorizing the U.S. Coast Guard to intercept U.S.-bound Haitians at sea and turn them back to their homeland without a hearing to determine if they were political refugees who qualified for asylum. In justifying the policy, Bush administration officials estimated that 200,000 to 500,000 Haitians might attempt to reach the United States if the gates were left open. (Bush and Court on Return of Haitian Refugees, Historic Documents of 1992, p. 453)

Human rights groups challenged the decision in court, contending that people returned to Haiti were subject to retaliation. On June 21, 1993, the

U.S. Supreme Court upheld the president's authority to issue the order.
(Court on Return of Haitian Refugees, Historic Documents of 1993, p. 413)

Efforts to Restore Aristide to Power

In an effort to drive the coup leaders from power, in June 1993 the United Nations Security Council imposed an oil and arms embargo on Haiti. The embargo had little impact because of massive smuggling across Haiti's border with the Dominican Republic. The next month, Aristide and Lt. Gen. Raoul Cédras, the coup leader, signed a UN-brokered agreement that called for Cédras to leave power and Aristide to return to Haiti by October 30. That deadline came and went, and a new deadline of January 15, 1994, was imposed for Aristide to return to power. It also came and went with no action, emboldening Haiti's leaders to step up their repression because it appeared the international community would do nothing to stop them.

By April, there was a growing chorus in Congress and among human rights groups demanding action to restore Aristide. On April 21, Aristide— who was living in exile in the United States—bitterly attacked the Clinton administration, saying its policy of repatriating refugees was racist and was contributing to a holocaust in his country. On May 6, the UN voted to tighten its embargo by barring all commerce with Haiti except food, medicine, and cooking oil.

In the two-month period between May 8 and July 6, American policy regarding Haitian refugees changed twice. In May, President Bill Clinton— who had attacked Bush's interdiction policy as a presidential candidate but continued it after he was elected—said Haitians detained at sea would receive political asylum hearings and those granted asylum could enter the United States. That change led to a new flood of refugees, so Clinton changed course on July 6 and said those who qualified for asylum would not be brought to the United States. Instead, they would be taken to another Caribbean nation until the political situation in Haiti stabilized.

Military Invasion Was Unpopular

While some were pressuring the United States to invade Haiti to topple the military dictators, most Americans opposed military action. In a September 2 editorial, the New York Times *acknowledged that Haiti's leaders had looted the country and brazenly murdered civilians. "But as morally and legally reprehensible as their actions have been, the United States has no calling to invade countries in the absence of any clear threat to vital American interests or to international peace," the newspaper said.*

On September 15, as American warships sailed toward Haiti, Clinton made a televised address in which he told the Haitian dictators they must step down or face removal by force. The next day, he dispatched former president Jimmy Carter, Gen. Colin Powell, and Sen. Sam Nunn (D-Ga.) to Haiti for a last-ditch attempt at a negotiated departure for the junta leaders. On September 18, after American planes had already taken off from Pope Air Force Base in North Carolina to start the invasion, Haiti's military leaders agreed to step down and to restore Aristide to power. The planes turned around.

The next day, more than 2,000 American troops landed in Haiti to pave the way for Aristide's return and to provide security. Although the troops assumed combat positions as they arrived on land, they met no opposition. Eventually, the military force grew to more than 20,000. On October 10, Cédras resigned as commander in chief of Haiti's military, and promised to leave Haiti within days. His departure removed the last major hurdle for Aristide's return, which occurred October 15.

Aristide Faced Huge Task

Aristide faced a formidable job of rebuilding a nation that had been devastated by military terror, economic chaos, and corruption. All services in the country, ranging from schools to roads, had collapsed. Haiti's infant mortality rate was the highest in the hemisphere, and half of Haiti's children under age five were malnourished. The nation's per capita income was only $250 per year, only a quarter of the adult population was literate, and unemployment in the cities was 70 percent.

Aristide's overwhelming task was to create democratic institutions and rebuild the economy simultaneously, while also working to keep his supporters from taking revenge on the people who had terrorized them. And he had to do everything quickly, both because the expectations of the Haitian people were enormously high and because his term ended in sixteen months and Haitian law barred him from running again.

With the arrival of Aristide, the international community pledged $550 million in the first year to rebuild the nation, with $195 million coming from the United States. Over five years, Haiti expected to receive $1.2 billion in foreign aid. Yet there was a very real question about whether Haiti's economy could really absorb and use all the aid. Some Haitians worried that all the American economists, diplomats, and other experts who traveled to Haiti to help with the transition would end up dominating the country.

> *Following are excerpts from a speech by President Jean-Bertrand Aristide upon his return to Haiti on October 15, 1994, as translated by an interpreter and reported by Reuters:*

Mr. Prime Minister Robert Malval, Mr. Secretary of State of the United States of America Warren Christopher, Mr. Minister of Foreign Affairs of Canada Andre Ouellet, Mr. Minister of Foreign Affairs of Argentina Guido Di Tella, Mr. Minister of Foreign Affairs of Suriname Charles Mungra, Madame Counselor of the Helvetica Federation Ruth Dreifuss, Mr. Vice Minister of Foreign Affairs of Jamaica Benjamin Clarke, Mr. Special Counselor of President Bill Clinton for Haiti William Gray, ladies and gentlemen, distinguished officials and friends of the international community, ladies and gentlemen, ministers of the constitutional government, Mr. President of the chamber of the Senate and the Deputies, honorable senators and deputies of the Republic of Haiti, honorable members of the United States Congress, members of the Argentinian Congress, Mr. Commander-in-Chief, officers, enlisted members of the Haitian armed forces, dear friends, Haitian people: Honor, respect! Honor, respect!

Under the hat of the honor of the Haitian people, respecting one another, I open my heart and my arms to salute you. . . .

Welcome. Feel at home. You are home. We are at home. Home is home. Home is home. We are happy to show a bouquet of flowers to the international community. The perfume of this thanks go directly to President Clinton, and with reason. The mayor of Port-au-Prince has taken the key of the city, has given it to me, and I offer it to all of you friends of the Haitian people which is happy to come here and feast with us for this party of reconciliation.

Since September 1994, thanks to the Operation Restoration Democracy, we are more rested, less anxious, more happy, less anxious. It is in this same vein of thanks that we will get some flowers for Secretary of State Warren Christopher, who is a very knowledgeable man. When you don't talk, we know that your head is working. Thank you for your presence among us.

Many thanks to the United States, Canada, France, Venezuela, Argentina, and all the other countries which have rallied around the Resolution 940 of the United Nations, beginning with CARICOM [Caribbean Community and Common Market]. We reserve many medals of honor to many defenders of the Haitian people, especially our brother William Gray. . . .

To all the foreign countries which have sent their sons and daughters which culminated in Resolution 940, to bring about this great moment of change in Haiti, we say thank you.

While the light of vigilance guides us, we take advantage to thank the Lord for his manifestation of the readiness of the people, in the fidelity of the priests, especially Father Jean-Marie Vincent. Father Jean-Marie Vincent died honorably. My brother, Jean, you died for the honor of Haiti. Honor and respect for you.

Honor and respect for all the victims, Minister Guy Malary, our brother Antoine Izmery, as well as the other innocent victims which have died. You are all heroes who will shine like the stars. My deepest regrets to your parents and your friends, and in honor and respect we will walk together with all the pastors, priests, monsignors, Catholics, Protestants, all of you who pray—all of you who pray. May our prayers be answered.

They come, they go, that they are. It is today the 15th of October, 1994. It is that day, the 15th of October, 1994. That day—this day is a day on which the sun of democracy has arisen to never set. Today is the day of national reconciliation, for reconciliation to always grow. Today is the day for the door of justice to open and never close. Today is the day for personal security to be widespread in the morning and at night. In the morning—security. At midday—security. And at night—security for all.

Security promotes peace. This peace is the oxygen for our political parties to develop, to multiply, to work freely. This peace is the oxygen for the senators, the deputies, the mayors, and all other constitutionally elected people, just the way it is prescribed in the constitution. This peace is the oxygen for all social professional organizations, present organizations, popular organizations, syndicates, and people platforms for all. The closer elections come, the more we need this oxygen.

Elections for senators and deputies are not far away, probably December. Presidential elections will be here very shortly as well. We must have peace for all this to be done correctly. To have peace, there must be tolerance. Tolerance is very important. Tolerance means one respecting the rights of others. It is the undoing of respect that brought about all the tribulations here. During these three years, we had a lot of problems, but we finally brought about this day of respect one for the other. What a beautiful day this day is.

They come, they go, this day—ah! It is today, the 15th of October, 1994. Today, hand in hand between us, hand in hand with the international community, we are celebrating a day of delivering, a day without violence, a day of no violence. During three years we have waited, but we have not become beans. Better be late and bring good results.

Has my return brought about democracy? [Crowd: "Yes!"]

Has my return brought about peace for people? [Crowd: "Yes."]

Has my return brought about reconciliation and hope? [Crowd: "Yes."]

Hope brings life, and my return gives me a feeling for life. . . . Never, never, never, never, never will blood be shed in this country. Never again must one more drop of blood flow. We are all thirsty for peace. Let us all live in peace. . . .

To all those who question their dreams, remember October 15th. To all those who are discouraged in the pursuit of their dreams, remember October 15th. October 15th affirms the strength of solidarity, the fortitude of conviction, the power of dreams. The individual efforts of all world citizens committed to democracy share the responsibility for the great hope for the future that today symbolizes.

You who traveled with us home to Haiti demonstrate that your journey with the people of Haiti continues. Your words, your energy, your enthusiasm, your spirit are rewarded by this momentous first step towards lasting peace. With you, Secretary of State Christopher, again and again we will continue to say no to violence, no to vengeance, yes to reconciliation.

Today we embark on a new beginning, ready to share peace, reconciliation and respect among all our citizens. The success of this mission on this small corner of the universe will reflect the kind of new world order that we can recreate. . . . To our neighbors in the CARICOM and in Latin America, how great it is to be participating in a process that will strengthen the historic bonds that tie us and to promote together the cause of democracy. . . .

Let me renew the oath I had taken before the national assembly in February 1991. I swear before God and before the nation to observe the laws of the constitution, to observe and to ensure the observation of the rights of the Haitian people, to maintain national independence and the integrity of the territory. . . .

Today we have come to spread the coffee of reconciliation in such a way that there is no violence, no vengeance. . . . With this coffee of reconciliation, we will find the strength to combat misery even though life is difficult. We can bring about momentous change in Haiti because many hands make a heavy load lighter.

One finger cannot ensure the consumption of okra. This way the light of democracy must be lit 24 hours a day. How can this happen? Firstly, put the gas of justice and soon it will light. Light will spread, hope will spread, and Haiti will smile. At that time, when we have the light of reconciliation spread all over. When things don't go properly, you lose hope. We will work to bring order and discipline, order above, order below, yes; order and discipline all the time, everywhere, yes; in respect of one for the other, yes, it can happen.

You may relax. Just relax. We will spread the syrup of relaxation. . . . Watch above, watch below, look before you, look after you, and dance on the cadence of democracy, sweetly, calmly, coolly. Dance to the cadence coolly. Spread peace among us, peace in our country, peace everywhere. If a military attaché comes toward you and you apprehend him, turn him over to the proper authorities. Every day walk hand in hand with Haitian militaries who want peace, with American military members who are here to provide security for everyone, and as well as with the international peace monitors.

Officers, enlisted members, soldiers, I have come to bring peace to you all. I have come here to bring peace to you, hand in hand with us. Together we will rebuild our country in the good wind of reconciliation. The entire world is looking at us. Among the peoples which have championed doing the right things, we are prime example. Violence, no. Vengeance, no. Reconciliation, yes. Justice and peace, yes.

I'd like to hear your voices, to hear your response. Violence? [Crowd: No!]
Vengeance? [Crowd: "No!"]
Reconciliation? [Crowd: "Yes!"]
Justice and peace? [Crowd: "That's what we want."]

Let me hear your response. Let the entire world hear your response, and let the words spread throughout the entire world. Let them hear your voice as a grand people which want peace and reconciliation. Violence? [Crowd: "No!"]
Vengeance? [Crowd: "No!"]
Reconciliation? [Crowd: "Yes!"]
Justice and reconciliation? [Crowd: "That's what we want."]

Look at us. We are great people. We are grand people. Don't be surprised if I'm in love with you. Don't be surprised if many people embrace you and with you work to rebuild Haiti, for Haiti to flourish, and for everyone to smile. I take my hat off to Haiti and to its youth. To all the youth in the nine departments of Haiti, I wish you much love and I send you many kisses. The youth of Haiti, where are you? [Crowd: "We're here."]
Youth of Haiti, where you are? [Crowd: "We're here."]
Children of Haiti, where are you? [Crowd: "We're here."]
Haitian people, where are you? [Crowd: "We're here."]
You're here and I'm here.

We are here together. We are walking together. We will change the country together and ensure its progress together. Do you love to walk with the soldiers who are here? [Crowd: "Yes."]

Are you happy to walk hand in hand with the soldiers of foreign countries? [Crowd: "Yes."]

Have the foreign troops provided security for us all? [Crowd: "Yes."]

Security in the morning, during the day, security for all. On your behalf, I sent them a bouquet of flowers and my many thanks to all the countries which have consented to send us sons and daughters to work with us to change this country.

Let me pick up all this warmth of this love to say to you again, I love you all. I love you all. The youth of Haiti, I give you my compliments for your show of solidarity which I hope you will continue to show. Strong women of Haiti, where are you? You strong women of Haiti, which have never stopped working, you strong women of Haiti, of the nine departments of Haiti and of the diaspora, let me tell you that I take off my hat for your strength and your courage. Yes, ladies of Haiti, as for having what you have, you have quite a lot of it.

Today the men of Haiti, which know their role with women, especially at this time when the entire world is watching us, you must sing a beautiful poetic song for them. In 1992, when President Clinton was being inaugurated, there was a woman there to say a poem. Today, in 1994, I say to you that women have strength, great souls, women of power, women of Haiti are real women. When they are suffering, they are resilient. . . .

Given all tribulations of life, the women of Haiti are always there, always there. Women of Haiti are not sugar cane, for the syrup of sugar cane brings about ants. The life of democracy runs strongly in Haiti. If women and men of Haiti do not work together, we're going nowhere. Men and women of Haiti are one strong crowd working for peace, for national reconciliation and for what's good for the country.

The rich, the poor, civilians, military people, let us all smile one at another, hand in hand. Let us smile at one another hand in hand. Just look at the person next to you and look at that person and how that person looks at you and smile at him or at her. And take his or her hand and smile back. And when you smile, you can notice how happy that person is. And that is the way that we must go forth and spread the coffee of reconciliation in such a way that there is no vengeance, no violence. We are feeble alone, strong when we are together. Together we are Lavalas.

DECISION ON SAFETY OF
GENERAL MOTORS TRUCKS
October 17, 1994

In a press conference October 17, Secretary of Transportation Federico Peña charged that older General Motors (GM) trucks posed a safety risk that company officials knew about for years but did nothing to correct. "GM management in place at that time appears to have made a decision favoring sales over safety," he said.

Peña's finding that all full-sized GM pickups manufactured between 1973 and 1987 had a design flaw that increased the risk of fire when they were hit in the side was the first step in forcing GM to recall the trucks. The trucks, which included the GMC Sierra and the Chevrolet C/K 1500 and 2500 series, each had two 20-gallon fuel tanks mounted outside the trucks' protective frame. GM manufactured 9 million of the trucks, and between 5 million and 6 million were still on the road. Starting with 1988 models, GM redesigned the trucks to place a single 34-gallon tank inside the frame.

Peña said 150 people had died in fires resulting from crashes that otherwise were survivable, and that other people had been badly burned. Based on accident statistics, another 32 people would die in crash fires before all the trucks were off the road, Peña said. Consumer advocates said Peña's figures were too conservative. Approximately 600 people had actually died in crash fires, said Joan Claybrook, president of the consumer group Public Citizen, which was one of two groups that started the department's investigation two years earlier by asking for a recall of the trucks. Claybrook had been administrator of the National Highway Traffic Safety Administration from 1977 to 1981.

GM officials vehemently defended the safety of their trucks. In a press release, GM said Peña's initial finding was "totally unjustified." GM said there was no legal or scientific basis for recalling the trucks and that it would fight a recall in court. The company also denounced Peña's suggestion that GM put sales ahead of safety, saying the claim was "outrageous and wrong."

Trucks Met Safety Standards

Both sides agreed that the trucks met federal safety standards. The dispute centered on an interpretation of the National Traffic and Motor Vehicle Safety Act, which Congress passed in 1966. Transportation Department officials said that under the act, besides meeting safety standards the trucks also had to actually be safe to drive on the streets. GM officials disputed that interpretation, contending that the trucks simply had to meet federal safety standards.

Peña's press conference came just over a year after the Transportation Department asked General Motors to voluntarily recall the trucks. GM refused. GM had not publicly estimated how much it would cost to repair the trucks, but analysts quoted by the New York Times *estimated the tab could be $1 billion.*

For GM, the stakes were much higher than the repair cost of the trucks. The company faced several dozen lawsuits across the country arising from truck fires. Any recall by the federal government would give plaintiffs strong ammunition in their suits. The federal investigation promised to be a public relations nightmare for GM, since the Transportation Department scheduled a public hearing on the recall for December 6. At that hearing, burn victims and the families of people killed in truck fires were expected to testify.

Based on that hearing, Transportation Department officials would decide whether to close the investigation or order a recall. Any recall was certain to lead to a court battle that could last for years. Even if the Transportation Department won, it could only order GM to recall trucks made during the previous eight years.

Only days after Peña's press conference, the federal investigation suffered a setback when it was revealed that safety and technical advisers at the National Highway Transportation Safety Administration had recommended that the investigation be closed. They said the GM trucks posed a safety risk, but that risks posed by other vehicles were just as high if not higher. Peña had overruled them to continue the investigation. The dispute raised the very real possibility that in any legal proceeding, GM would call federal safety advisers to testify against the government.

GM Files Suit

On November 17, GM sued the Transportation Department. GM contended that because the trucks complied with federal safety standards, the government had no right to pursue a recall. The day after GM filed the suit, settlement talks began between the company and the federal government.

On December 2—only four days before the public hearing was to occur—Peña announced that GM and the government had reached an unprecedented agreement that would close the investigation. Under the agreement, GM did not admit to any safety problems with the trucks but agreed to contribute $51.3 million to safety programs. The programs bought thousands of *child safety seats for low-income families, studied the prevention of auto fires, and provided education about drunk driving and using seat belts.*

The settlement was widely viewed as a huge victory for GM. Peña justified the settlement by saying the safety programs would save more people than the trucks would kill. He said the department had two bad alternatives: "to close the case with no public benefit or to proceed with a forced recall, which would have involved years of litigation, an uncertain outcome, and prevented few, if any, deaths."

Sen. Howard Metzenbaum (D-Ohio) attacked the settlement, contending it "smells like a political deal." Some consumer advocates also expressed dismay. "A multibillion-dollar conglomerate has essentially bought the government's silence for a pittance," said Claybrook. Some other consumer advocates said that based on the uncertain legal case, the settlement was probably the best that the government would get.

Following is the text of a statement by Secretary of Transportation Federico Peña at a press conference October 17, 1994, as reported by Reuters, and of a press release issued by General Motors Corporation the same day:

PENA STATEMENT

Today I am announcing the department's initial decision that a safety defect exists in General Motors CK pickup trucks with fuel tanks outside the frame rails.

As in any decision that involves the safety of the traveling public, we have faced many difficult issues in this case. This is a case that is virtually unprecedented, extremely complex, and highly charged. Before going further, I want to commend the professionalism and the expertise of the staff at NHTSA for their work on this matter.

Since this investigation began in December of 1992, NHTSA has received and reviewed well over 100,000 pages of documents, conducted crash tests, and completed statistical and other analyses related to the alleged defect. It is that extensive investigation that has led me to this decision.

Today we are distributing the engineering analysis report that details the major points of this investigation. I believe that this report speaks for itself, and I encourage you to read it very carefully.

I want to take a few minutes to discuss the major findings that served as the basis for this initial decision. I will then outline the process that the department will follow over the next several weeks.

As respects the findings, first, NHTSA found that, since these GM pickups were first introduced in 1973, approximately 150 people have died as a result of side impact fires in these trucks in crashes that were otherwise survivable. Many others suffered serious burn injuries in such crashes.

Second, based on past trends, NHTSA projects that 32 more lives will be lost over the remaining use of the vehicles, compared to what would have occurred if these trucks had the same impact fire performance as comparable Ford pickups do.

Third, NHTSA attributes this vulnerability to fatal side impact fires to GM's design and placement of the fuel tanks outside of the frame rails of these trucks. This design was selected for marketing reasons, including a desire to increase fuel capacity and driving range—a feature GM believed appealed to certain drivers. But because the tanks are outside the frame rails, they do not have the protection offered by the frame rails.

Fourth, NHTSA's review of police accident reports of side impact fatal crashes with fires in these GM trucks demonstrates that they occurred at speeds less than those required to cause side impact fires in comparable Ford pickups.

Fifth, and of critical importance in this matter, is the evidence that GM was aware, possibly as early as the mid 1970s, but certainly by the early 1980s, that this design made these trucks more vulnerable and that fatalities from side impact fires were occurring.

However, GM chose not to alter the design for 15 years.

It is important to note that the National Traffic and Motor Safety Act places manufacturers under two broad statutory mandates: first, to meet applicable safety standards in producing vehicles; and second, to produce vehicles that operate safely in real-world conditions. Meeting a safety standard does not absolve a manufacturer of its responsibility to produce safe vehicles.

This investigation opened in December of 1992, in response to a petition submitted by the Center for Auto Safety and Public Citizen in August of that year. I first became involved in this matter in April of 1993, when there was no senior appointee at NHTSA. The Safety Act assigns a responsibility for carrying out these investigations to the secretary. In general, these responsibilities have been delegated to senior officials at NHTSA. However, due to the complexity of the case and the degree of public concern over the alleged defect, those officials brought this issue to me. At that point, I assumed the role of decision maker in this process and will continue to do so.

Since he joined NHTSA, Deputy Administrator Chris Hart has provided some factual analysis. But I made the judgment call in this case. Dr. Ricardo Martinez, the new administrator, recused himself from this matter and has played no role.

Under the Safety Act, manufacturers must conduct a recall campaign if their vehicles contain a defect that relates to motor vehicle safety. Consistent with the law, the analysis of whether a defect exists in this case has focused on two primary questions: first, is there an increased risk associated with the alleged defects, and if so, is that risk unreasonable.

The investigation to date has demonstrated that the answer to both questions is yes. The record clearly shows that there is an increased risk associated with these GM pickups, and leads me to conclude at this point that that risk is unreasonable. This initial conclusion is supported by these key factors: Unlike many of the investigations that NHTSA conducts, this case involves not only serious injury but a significant number of fatalities in crashes that were otherwise avoidable. There is evidence that GM was aware of the increased risk associated with this design at the time that the vehicle was introduced but did not take steps to provide adequate protection. In addition, despite mounting evidence of a safety risk over the intervening years, GM did not move the tanks inside the frame rails until model year 1988. An alternative design, similar to that used by its competitors, was available and could have addressed the problem for little or no cost.

Instead, GM management in place at that time appears to have made a decision favoring sales over safety. As secretary of transportation, charged with overseeing the safety of our highways and all other modes of transportation, I believe that auto manufacturers can and should do better than that, especially when safer and viable alternatives exist. As required under the law, the next step for the department is to conduct a public proceeding to allow all interested parties to provide additional information and arguments on the issues raised by this investigation. This proceeding will be chaired by NHTSA Deputy Administrator Chris Hart and will be held in Washington beginning on Tuesday, December 6th. I want to ensure that this process is open and fair to everyone and that we have as much relevant information as possible before moving on to the next decision.

I also recognize that consumers may continue to be confused over the status of these trucks. It is my intention to bring this work to a conclusion as quickly as possible after the public meeting. I again want to note that this case has been a very difficult and a very complex one. There has been a great deal of discussion and various views about it in many quarters, but based on NHTSA's technical analysis, this was my decision to make.

In closing let me say that this morning I spoke to Jack Smith at General Motors. I pointed out to him my view that he heads a new management team at General Motors which was not in place at the time that these decisions were made. It's a new generation of leadership that has generated its commitment to new ways of thinking and acting. I sincerely hope that they'll work with us to address this problem.

GENERAL MOTORS PRESS RELEASE

The initial decision of the Secretary is totally unjustified. These trucks are recognized even by the National Highway Traffic Safety Administration to have fully met the applicable safety standards for fuel system integrity in collision. They outperform many newer vehicles in terms of both fuel system crash worthiness and occupant protection. General Motors stands fully behind these trucks, their safety record and the engineers who designed them.

Reliable reports appearing in the press indicate to us that Secretary Pena's decision is contrary to the objective appraisal of these trucks by others in government who advised the Secretary that a recall is not justified under the law. The unusual personal intervention of the Secretary in this matter after nearly two years of deliberation and indecision constitutes an unfortunate politicization of the regulatory process and renders suspect any subsequent action which may be taken by the Department. The suggestion that GM put sales ahead of safety is outrageous and wrong.

There is simply no legal or scientific basis on which to seek a recall of these trucks under the Vehicle Safety Act. If necessary, we will defend their safety in court.

BRITISH PRIME MINISTER MAJOR ON NORTHERN IRELAND
October 21, 1994

In a speech to businessmen in Belfast, Northern Ireland, British Prime Minister John Major promised October 21 to open exploratory talks with Sinn Féin, the political arm of the Irish Republican Army (IRA), if the IRA's seven-week-old ceasefire continued. He also announced that Britain would ease controls on the border between Northern Ireland and the Republic of Ireland and would lift a twelve-year ban on visits to Britain by Gerry Adams and Martin McGuiness, two top Sinn Féin leaders. Major's speech was a major step forward in the effort to end the sectarian violence that had ripped apart Northern Ireland over the last twenty-five years.

More than 3,100 people had died in that violence, which had its roots in ancient quarrels dating back hundreds of years. The quarrels started in the seventeenth century when the English monarchy defeated a rebellion by Catholics in Northern Ireland. The victors then encouraged British subjects in Scotland—who were Protestant—to move to Northern Ireland and take the land of the defeated Catholics. The two sides had been fighting ever since.

The most recent round of "troubles," as they were called, had started in 1969 when British troops entered Northern Ireland to stop rioting by Catholic civil rights marchers. Eventually, 18,000 British troops helped local police keep order. In 1972, Britain assumed direct rule of Northern Ireland, which was a British province.

British rule was just fine with most of the province's 950,000 Protestants, but it did not sit well with most of its 650,000 Catholics. The Catholics were committed to the goal of ending British rule and uniting Northern Ireland with the Republic of Ireland to the south.

In the late 1960s, paramilitary groups sprang up on both sides. What had been largely a war of words became a war punctuated by blasts from plastic explosives and automatic weapons. On the Catholic side, the Irish Republican Army sought to drive the British from Northern Ireland. On the Protes-

tant side, the Ulster Freedom Fighters and similar groups sought to retain control, which oftentimes took the form of random acts of violence and terror in the Catholic neighborhoods.

Prime Ministers Seek End to Violence

The latest peace efforts began in October 1993, when Major and Irish Prime Minister Albert Reynolds issued a joint statement promising that "new doors could open" toward peace if the IRA stopped its campaign of violence. The next month, the British government issued an extraordinary statement admitting that secret talks had occurred between emissaries of Major and the IRA, despite Major's denials of such meetings. (Statements on British-Irish Efforts to Find Peace, Historic Documents of 1993, p. 923)

In December 1993, the British and Irish governments issued the "Downing Street Declaration." In it, they promised that if the IRA permanently renounced violence, Sinn Féin would be included in any negotiations about the future of Northern Ireland. The governments also affirmed that any proposed change in Northern Ireland's government would be put to a referendum.

The next step came in August 1994, when the IRA declared that an unconditional ceasefire would take effect September 1. In a five-paragraph statement, the secret IRA leadership said it was time for political solutions— rather than force—to resolve the problems of Northern Ireland. "We believe we are entering a new situation, a new opportunity," the statement said.

Some observers believed the IRA sought peace because its campaign against the British had reached a stalemate. No matter how many troops Britain stationed in Northern Ireland, it could never wipe out the IRA's guerillas and their thousands of supporters. At the same time, the IRA could never kill enough British soldiers to persuade Britain to withdraw its troops and let Northern Ireland join the Republic of Ireland.

Two days after the announcement of the IRA ceasefire, members of the Protestant militia murdered a Catholic man in North Belfast. There had been fears that the Protestants would step up their attacks in an effort to goad the IRA into violating its ceasefire, but the IRA did not retaliate.

Clinton Lifts Ban on Sinn Féin Contacts

On October 3, President Bill Clinton lifted a twenty-year ban on contacts between the United States and Sinn Féin. The IRA remained on the State Department's list of terrorist organizations, but lifting the ban on Sinn Féin was seen as a way of rewarding the IRA's political arm for seeking peace.

Ten days later, the Protestant paramilitary organizations announced their own ceasefire, pledging not to fight as long as the IRA ceasefire continued. "Let us firmly resolve to respect our differing views of freedom, culture and aspiration and never again permit our political circumstances to degenerate into bloody warfare," said a statement issued by the Combined Loyalist Military Command, an umbrella group for the Protestant forces.

On November 1, less than one month after lifting the ban on contacts with

Sinn Féin, Clinton announced that the United States would boost its economic aid to Northern Ireland in 1995 to $30 million, well above the previously planned level of $20 million. The increased aid was aimed at helping reduce high unemployment levels in Northern Ireland, one of the factors that contributed to the ongoing violence. Clinton also announced that a conference would be held in Philadelphia in April 1995 to examine ways to increase American trade with Northern Ireland and the Republic of Ireland.

On December 10, representatives of the British government and Sinn Féin met in Belfast for historic talks. These were simply exploratory talks, but they represented the first time the two sides had ever talked together in public.

Full-scale peace talks involving all parties in Northern Ireland were not expected to begin before the summer of 1995. While the ceasefires and preliminary talks were encouraging, the overwhelming task remained of trying to craft a plan that would suit everyone. With one faction wanting to keep Northern Ireland aligned with Britain and the other wishing to join it with the Irish Republic, there were no simple solutions. Yet as long as the talking continued, the guns were silent and the people of Northern Ireland could live in peace.

Following is the text of a speech by British Prime Minister John Major on October 21, 1994, at a meeting in Belfast, Northern Ireland, of a business group known as the Institute of Directors, as released by the British Embassy in Washington, D.C.:

Mr. Chairman,

From the moment I stepped into Downing Street, I believed that the overwhelming majority of the people of Northern Ireland wanted peace.

Over the years they have demonstrated this in countless ways—the remarkable peace movement of the 1970s, the many groups and individuals who have worked so hard to heal community divisions.

It was this conviction that gave birth to the Downing Street Declaration. An opportunity for peace existed and the Taoiseach [prime minister]—Albert Reynolds—and I both wished to take it.

The Downing Street Declaration recognised the rights of both main traditions in Northern Ireland, but threatened the interests of neither. It showed that violence had no justification—and it offered a route into legitimate politics for those who abandoned violence.

When I spoke to you in March, many people had lost hope that the Downing Street Declaration could lead to peace. I mention this only to remind everyone that we should not accept setbacks. There may be more. And, if there are, we should persist and overcome them.

I expressed hope against the prevailing wind. Today there is a chance—a chance not a certainty—that hope will become reality.

Seven months after I last spoke to you, seven weeks after the IRA [Irish Republican Army] ceasefire, seven days after the Loyalist paramilitary ceasefire, Northern Ireland is at peace. There is a different atmosphere.

Fear has been lifted from daily life.

People have begun to take the bars off their windows.

Trade in the High Street has gone up by 6 percent in one month.

Even sceptical commentators—with years of history to support their scepticism—are beginning to wonder whether, perhaps, a corner has been turned.

As to that, we shall see. But there has been a very encouraging beginning.

Now we have to move on. Towards a full return to democratic life. Towards a time when violence will be no more than a bad memory. Towards a just and lasting peace.

We have practical obstacles to overcome. Some of them will be difficult. We also have history to overcome and that will be even harder. Old enmities, old suspicions, old fears still swirl around and obscure opportunities that may lie ahead.

We are right to be cautious. But there is no entirely risk-free approach. With care and with calculation we must judge the art of the possible and deliver it.

I cannot guarantee success. But I do believe the chances of success are better than for generations.

Let me set out, therefore, the next steps I propose to take.

Our task is to make sure that the violence is over for good. We must aim to make a return to violence unthinkable.

Throughout these seven weeks, Sinn Fein and the IRA have sought to convey the impression that the ceasefire is permanent, but they have not stated this unambiguously. Because they left scope for doubt, I resisted pressure to set an early date for exploratory talks.

Instead, we have reviewed their *actions*. These have been more compelling than their words.

As a result, I am now prepared to make a working assumption that the ceasefire is intended to be permanent. This means we can move carefully towards the beginning of dialogue between Sinn Fein and the Government.

The basis for this dialogue is unchanged. There must be a genuine commitment by Sinn Fein to use and support only peaceful methods in a democratic political arena. We shall expect to see continuing practical evidence of this commitment. We shall not be able to proceed if it is called into question.

If we continue reasonably to assume that Sinn Fein is establishing a commitment to exclusively peaceful methods; if the IRA continues to show that it has ended its terrorism; then we shall be ready to convene exploratory talks before this year is out.

This preliminary dialogue between representatives of the Government and of Sinn Fein will be crucial.

It will explore how Sinn Fein can make a transition to normal political life. How it would be able to play the same part as the existing constitutional parties. How it could enter the political talks process.

And we shall discuss the practical consequences of ending violence—most obviously how illegal weapons and explosives are going to be removed from life in Northern Ireland. Peace cannot be assured finally until the paramilitaries on both sides hand in their weapons. This is a difficult issue but it cannot be ducked. We must consider therefore how guns and explosives can best be deposited and decommissioned. These weapons are both North and South of the border. So we shall be consulting the Irish Government on a coordinated approach.

It is through the political talks process that we wish to secure a lasting settlement. And I repeat today the promise I have given before: When these talks between the constitutional parties and the two Governments are over, we shall seek the approval of the people of Northern Ireland for the outcome as a whole in a referendum. Their consent is essential.

As you know, the British and Irish Governments are working on a *Joint Framework Document*. I shall be discussing it with the Taoiseach on Monday.

I know there is concern about the document. Let me repeat: it will *not* be a blueprint. It is intended to help further discussion and negotiation and it will represent our joint understanding of what is most likely to secure widespread acceptance.

When the document is finished, we shall publish it, for all to see. It will not be kept a secret with the danger that it will cause suspicions. As with the Downing Street Declaration, everyone will be able to get a copy, to see exactly what it says and what it does not say.

This way it should not be misunderstood or misinterpreted.

I am determined the people of Northern Ireland will have the chance to give their views. I want them to see that it is faithful to the Downing Street Declaration and to our unshakeable constitutional guarantee that *their* future lies in *their* hands.

The Joint Framework Document concentrates on relations between the two Governments, and between Northern Ireland and the Republic.

But, as part of an overall settlement, the British Government is also concerned with new arrangements for government *within* Northern Ireland. This is a matter for discussion between the British Government and the Northern Ireland parties.

We therefore intend to publish simultaneously our own proposals on a possible way forward within Northern Ireland. These, too, like the Joint Framework Document, will be a guide for discussions and negotiations aimed at widespread acceptance.

In this way the people of Northern Ireland will be able to see the full shape of a possible settlement. It is the overall shape of the whole package which must secure consent if it is to succeed.

We want to restore local accountability. We shall therefore include proposals for an assembly—drawing, without attribution, on the work done in the 1992 Talks and the lessons of Michael Anoram's exchanges with the parties. Again, we will be seeking a basis for broad agreement. Neither a purely internal solution, nor a return to domination of one side by the other, would achieve this. Local democracy requires support across the community.

Mr. Chairman, the loyalist ceasefire is very welcome. There are no circumstances which could justify a resumption of *their* violence.

The route to democratic politics is open to all who renounce violence, and we of course want Loyalists to be able to express their views democratically.

Therefore, once they have sufficiently demonstrated their commitment to exclusively peaceful methods, they can take part in public life. At the appropriate time, the Government will enter into contact with them.

We will be looking for ways of taking their views into account in the talks process. We want to hear the concerns, not least the social concerns, of the communities from which they come.

Mr. Chairman, in matters of security we shall not take risks. We shall not make concessions to those who defy the law. We shall not lower our guard prematurely. But of course we want Northern Ireland to return to a more relaxed and normal way of life.

The ceasefire has already allowed the security forces to respond to a diminished threat. Today, on their advice, the Secretary of State has rescinded *all the remaining* closer orders on border *crossings*. This will allow freer movement, although the security forces will continue to patrol the border for the time being.

Exclusion Orders have been another constraint required to counter terrorism. We hope that the day is approaching when they will no longer be needed. The numbers are already lower than they were when Parliament renewed the Prevention of Terrorism Act in March.

Now that we are moving towards preliminary dialogue, I can announce that the Home Secretary has today lifted the Orders which excluded Mr. Gerry Adams and Mr. Martin McGuiness from Great Britain. They are free to travel anywhere within the United Kingdom, provided they remain committed to the democratic process.

Other Exclusion Orders will remain in place for the time being, but the Home Secretary and the Secretary of State for Northern Ireland will keep the need for them under review.

Let me turn now to the policing of the streets and of the countryside.

We had to deploy additional troops in Northern Ireland from 1969 in support of the police because of the level of violence. And the Army has done an outstanding job here.

While Northern Ireland remains part of the United Kingdom, there will always be a peacetime role for some members of the Armed Forces, just as there is in other parts of the United Kingdom. We shall keep as many policemen and troops as we need, for as long as we need to protect the population. But the need for soldiers to patrol the streets will continue to be reviewed in relation to the threat, and it is our firm objective to return to exclusively civilian policing.

Terrorism has prevented the Royal Ulster Constabulary from operating in the same way as police forces in the rest of the United Kingdom. Its officers have shown extraordinary courage and tenacity. They have made many sacrifices. They have every reason to look forward to lasting peace, and to the prospect of leading more normal lives.

They know that an end to the threat of violence will bring new challenges. They know they need to police by consent, and they will have our full support in seeking to achieve that. But let me make clear here and now: no groups can—or will—be allowed to take the law into their own hands. All sections of the community must have confidence in the police and must enjoy equal protection from crime. In Northern Ireland the role and duty of enforcing the law must rest with the police alone.

Mr. Chairman, peace will give a massive boost to Northern Ireland's economy. Equally, the chance of more prosperity, more jobs, better security for families, must be the most powerful incentive for peace.

I know that the business community is already preparing for new opportunities. So is the Government, in partnership with you.

I can now announce that we shall be convening a large investment conference here in Belfast in December.

I hope that many of you will take part. We shall be asking the Institute of Directors and the CBI at national level to encourage their members to look at investment opportunities here. We shall invite senior figures from the City of London. And we shall also invite potential investors and business leaders from overseas—from Europe, the United States, and the Far East.

We are of course already in close touch with the European Commission. The President of the European Commission has established a special task force to look at a new European Community programme for Northern Ireland. This initiative aims to fund new projects to regenerate the inner cities. It will focus on action to cut long term unemployment, attract inward investment and stimulate tourism.

The details of the European Commission's initiative are still being worked out, in consultation with us and with others. From my latest contacts with Jacques Delors, I am confident that this initiative will result in a substantial package of new measures and new money.

I say *new* money. The European Union's programme will be *in addition to* the British Government's own expenditure plans for Northern Ireland. These, as you know, have long been supported by the EU's structural funds. The European Union has also increased its contribution to the International Fund for Ireland.

Let me make two further points on economic and social support.

First, we have long recognised the particular needs of Northern Ireland. We have set public spending at a level above the UK average, and provided a subvention of over £3 billion last year to finance this.

The people of Northern Ireland will get our continued support in the future. We understand that they face exceptional economic and social difficulties. Some will result, indeed, from the transition to peace—such as the consequences for employment of an end to terrorism.

I can assure you that the Government will take full account of Northern Ireland's special needs in setting future levels of public spending for the Province. We want to help the Province to enjoy higher levels of economic growth and much greater prosperity throughout the community in the future.

Second, we need *your* ideas, the ideas of people throughout Northern Ireland on the projects we and the European Union should back and the support we can most usefully give. So the Government will now start consultations with business and financial interests in the Province. We shall also consult the leaders and chief executives of the local councils in Northern Ireland. They are in day to day touch with people. So I intend shortly to issue invitations to them to meet me at Downing Street. I believe they can play a significant role in carrying forward our plans for a better future.

Mr. Chairman, from this moment we are in a new phase of the peace process. A transitional phase which will lead to exploratory talks.

For twenty-five years violence has been the enemy of progress in Northern Ireland.

Think what opportunities have been lost, what could have been done to advance all areas of life here, were it not for the burden of terrorism.

Local democracy has been held back. A generation of politicians has been denied full responsibility.

In the community, walls have been going up where we should have spent the past twenty-five years breaking them down.

In the economy, for every million pounds of investment you have attracted, there should have been many millions. For every tourist there should have been thirty. For every hotel, factory or shop repaired after a bomb, we could have built a new one.

We cannot make up twenty-five lost years overnight. We shall have to make Herculean efforts. That is the purpose of the initiatives I have announced today. To begin to improve the lives of *everyone* in Northern Ireland as quickly as we can.

Above all, we must make the price of breaking the peace so high that there would be no shred of sympathy, no glimmer of support for anyone who contemplated using violence again.

Every day without violence shows more clearly the benefits of peace.

Mr. Chairman, the future of Northern Ireland lies in the hands of its own people. Not just of those leaders—the leaders of political parties, of the churches, of the business community—who have always stood by peaceful methods. But of *all* the people.

I *know* that they want peace. And *they* know that peace has not been brought through any secret deals or promises.

They know of our commitment to the balanced and even-handed principles of the Downing Street Declaration, including consent and the search for agreement among all the people living in Ireland.

They will be invited to comment on the Joint Framework Document, and on our proposals for local accountability.

They will be asked to vote on the outcome of the three-stranded talks.

They must establish a just basis for living together in the future, giving parity of esteems and equity of treatment to both main traditions and enabling all law abiding citizens to live free from the threat of violence.

Let me speak directly to each and every person in Northern Ireland. If you want peace, say so now. Loudly. Don't sit back. Join the crusade for the future. Go to your friends. Go to your neighbours. Go to anyone you know who has ever supported violence.

You have not had this chance in years and you cannot afford to miss it. Let your voices be heard.

Ultimately you, and you alone, can ensure that Northern Ireland never goes backwards. And the benefits will be yours.

HUBBLE FINDINGS ON AGE OF THE UNIVERSE
October 26, 1994

New measurements from the Hubble Space Telescope indicated that the universe might be only 8 billion to 12 billion years old, much younger than scientists had previously believed. Earlier research had determined that some stars were 15 billion to 18 billion years old, ages that would not be possible if the new measurements were confirmed. The new findings were released at a press conference October 26 and in an article in the October 27 issue of the journal Nature.

An international team of astronomers used the Hubble, which is far more reliable than ground-based telescopes, to measure the distance to a galaxy in the Virgo Cluster known as M100. They calculated that M100 is 56 million light-years from Earth. Being able to measure across the vast reaches of space helps astronomers calculate the expansion rate of the universe, called the Hubble Constant. Knowing that expansion rate is one of the key factors in determining the universe's age and size. If scientists can determine the universe's expansion rate, they can then backtrack to determine how long it has been expanding—and thus determine when the universe was born.

"This is the first big step," said John P. Huchra of Harvard University and the Smithsonian Astrophysical Observatory at the press conference. He said the results were "a factor of ten better than other previous data," yet cautioned that there were still "a lot of pitfalls along the way."

Other researchers praised the new measurements. Robert Kirchner of Harvard University, the director of another team that obtained similar results using another method, told the Washington Post *that the data "are really good. . . . It moves the debate from the realm of speculation and mythology to the status of experimental science."*

Additional Research Required

The new measurements, while an important step in determining the universe's age, were not the final word on the subject. Research involving the

Hubble and ground-based telescopes was expected to provide data over the next few years that would help buttress—or deflate—the new findings.

The $1.5 billion telescope, the largest and most complex scientific instrument ever put into orbit, was released from the space shuttle Discovery *on April 24, 1990. Almost immediately, it was discovered that one of the telescope's mirrors was critically flawed. (*Hubble Telescope Flaws, NASA's Future Direction, Historic Documents of 1990, *p. 753)*

The Hubble Space Telescope was made fully functional following a spectacular repair mission in December 1993. Astronauts from the space shuttle Endeavor *grabbed the telescope in space, repaired the mirror and other components, and placed it back into orbit.*

The telescope was named for astronomer Edwin P. Hubble, who in the 1920s advanced the idea that the universe contained at least a hundred billion other galaxies that were rushing away from Earth. Hubble's work supported the Big Bang theory, which holds that the universe started as a hot, infinitely dense point of matter that exploded.

Universe Is Still Expanding

The new measurements found that the M100 galaxy is moving away from Earth at a rate of 3 million miles per hour. The researchers said this number implies that the universe is still rapidly expanding and that the drag of gravity has not yet slowed the process. The measurements were made by using the Hubble to locate twenty Cepheid stars in the M100 galaxy. Cepheids are pulsating stars with very regular light variations used in determining distances across space. The brightness of the stars changes over a period of days or weeks according to a rhythm that can be measured. By measuring the brightness, astronomers can calculate how far the stars are from Earth.

Despite the new findings, not everyone in the scientific community was convinced of the universe's youthful age. "There is enough uncertainty associated with the current measurement that it does not exclude" a universe that is much older, said Abhijit Saha in an interview with the Washington Post. *Saha is a member of another team that is using the Hubble. The team is led by Alan Sandage, a proponent of theories favoring an older universe.*

While there was some dispute about the new findings, astronomers agreed that it would be only a matter of a few years before the Hubble Space Telescope helped them unlock some mysteries of the universe that had tantalized them for generations. In a Nature *article that accompanied the report about the new measurements, George H. Jacoby of the National Optical Astronomy Observatories in Arizona wrote: "We live in a special time: after millennia of not knowing the size and age of our universe, we soon will."*

> *Following is the text of a NASA press release dated October 26, 1994, concerning measurements taken by the Hubble Space Telescope, titled "Important Step Taken to Determine Age, Size of Universe":*

Astronomers using NASA's Hubble Space Telescope (HST) have taken an important step toward determining the age and size of the universe.

They announced today that they have been able to calculate with considerable precision the distance to a remote galaxy, M100, in the Virgo cluster of galaxies.

The ability to make accurate distance measurements over vast reaches of space will help provide a precise calculation of the expansion rate of the universe, called the Hubble Constant, which is crucial to determine the age and size of the universe.

"Although this is only the first step in a major systematic program to measure accurately the scale, size, and age of the universe," noted Dr. Wendy L. Freedman, of the Observatories of the Carnegie Institution of Washington, "a firm distance to the Virgo cluster is a critical milestone for the extragalactic distance scale, and it has major implications for the Hubble Constant."

HST's detection of Cepheid variable stars in the spiral galaxy M100, a member of the Virgo cluster, establishes the distance to the cluster as 56 million light-years (with an uncertainty of +/– 6 million light-years). M100 is now the most distant galaxy in which Cepheid variables have been measured accurately.

The precise measurement of this distance allows astronomers to calculate that the universe is expanding at the rate of 80 km/sec per megaparsec (+/– 17 km/sec). For example, a galaxy one million light-years away will appear to be moving away from us at approximately 60,000 miles per hour. If it is twice that distance, it will be seen to be moving at twice the speed, and so on. This rate of expansion is the Hubble Constant.

These results are being published in the Oct. 27 issue of the journal "Nature." The team of astronomers is jointly led by Freedman, Dr. Robert Kennicutt (Steward Observatory, University of Arizona), and Dr. Jeremy Mould (Mount Stromlo and Siding Spring Observatories, Australian National University).

Dr. Mould noted, "Those who pioneered the development of the Hubble Space Telescope in the 1960s and 1970s recognized its unique potential for finding the value of the Hubble Constant. Their foresight has been rewarded by the marvelous data that we have obtained for M100."

Using Hubble's Wide-Field and Planetary Camera (WFPC2), the team of astronomers repeatedly imaged a field where much star formation recently had taken place, and was, therefore, expected to be rich in Cepheids—a class of pulsating stars used for determining distances. Twelve one-hour exposures, strategically placed in a two-month observing window, resulted in the discovery of 20 Cepheids. About 40,000 stars were measured in the search for these rare, but bright, variables. Once the periods and intrinsic brightness of these stars were established from the careful measurement of their pulsation rates, the researchers calculated a distance of 56 million light-years to the galaxy. (The team allowed for the dimming effects of distance as well as that due to dust and gas between Earth and M100.)

Many complementary projects are currently being carried out from the ground with the goal of also providing values for the Hubble Constant. However, they are subject to many uncertainties which HST was designed and built to circumvent. For example, a team of astronomers using the Canada-France-Hawaii telescope at Mauna Kea recently has arrived at a distance to another galaxy in Virgo that is similar to that found for M100 using HST—but their result is tentative because it is based on only three Cepheids in crowded star fields.

"Only Space Telescope can make these types of observations routinely," Freedman explained. "Typically, Cepheids are too faint and the resolution too poor, as seen from ground-based telescopes, to detect Cepheids clearly in a crowded region of a distant galaxy."

Although M100 is now the most distant galaxy in which Cepheid variables have been discovered, the Hubble team emphasized that the HST project must look into even more distant galaxies before a definitive number can be agreed on for the age and size of the universe. This is because the galaxies around the Virgo Cluster are perturbed by the large mass concentration of galaxies near the cluster. This influences their rate of expansion.

Refining the Hubble Constant

These first HST results are a critical step in converging on the true value of the Hubble Constant, first developed by the American astronomer Edwin Hubble in 1929. Hubble found that the farther away a galaxy is, the faster it is receding away from us. This "uniform expansion" effect is strong evidence the universe began in an event called the "Big Bang" and that the universe has been expanding ever since.

To calculate accurately the Hubble Constant, astronomers must have two key numbers: the recession velocities of galaxies and their distances as estimated by one or more cosmic "mileposts," such as Cepheids. The age of the universe can be estimated from the value of the Hubble Constant, but it is only as reliable as the accuracy of the distance measurements.

The Hubble Constant is only one of several key numbers needed to estimate the universe's age. For example, the age also depends on the average density of matter in the universe, though to a lesser extent.

A simple interpretation of the large value of the Hubble Constant, as calculated from HST observations, implies an age of about 12 billion years for a low-density universe, and 8 billion years for a high-density universe. However, either value highlights a long-standing dilemma. These age estimates for the universe are shorter than the estimated ages of some of the oldest stars found in the Milky Way and in globular star clusters orbiting our Milky Way. Furthermore, small age values pose problems for current theories about the formation and development of the observed large-scale structure of the universe.

Cosmic Mileposts

Cepheid variable stars rhythmically change in brightness over intervals of days (the prototype is the fourth brightest star in the circumpolar constellation Cepheus). For more than half a century, from the early work of astronomers Edwin Hubble, Henrietta Leavitt, Allan Sandage, and Walter Baade, it has been known that there is a direct link between a Cepheid's pulsation rate and its intrinsic brightness. Once a star's true brightness is known, its distance is a relatively straightforward calculation because the apparent intensity of light drops off at a geometrically predictable rate with distance. Although Cepheids are rare, once found, they provide a very reliable "standard candle" for estimating intergalactic distances, according to astronomers.

Besides being an ideal hunting ground for the Cepheids, M100 also contains other distance indicators that can in turn be calibrated with the Cepheid result. This face-on, spiral galaxy has been host to several supernovae, which are also excellent distance indicators. Individual supernovae (called Type II, massive exploding stars) can be seen to great distances, and can be used to extend the cosmic distance scale well beyond Virgo.

As a crosscheck on the HST results, the distance to M100 has been estimated using the Tully-Fisher relation (a means of estimating distances to spiral galaxies using the maximum rate of rotation to predict the intrinsic brightness) and this independent measurement also agrees with both the Cepheid and supernova "yardsticks."

HST Key Projects are scientific programs that have been widely recognized as being of the highest priority for the HST and have been designated to receive a substantial amount of observing time on the telescope. The Extragalactic Distance Scale Key Project involves discovering Cepheids in a variety of important calibrating galaxies to determine their individual distances. These distances then will be used to establish an accurate value of the Hubble Constant.

The Key Project Team on the Extragalactic Distance Scale consists of Sandra Faber, Garth Illingworth and Dan Kelson (Univ. of California, Santa Cruz); Laura Ferrarese and Holland Ford (Space Telescope Science Institute); Wendy Freedman, John Graham, Robert Hill and Randy Phelps (Carnegie Institution of Washington); James Gunn (Princeton University); John Hoessel and Mingsheng Han (University of Wisconsin); John Huchra (Harvard-Smithsonian Center for Astrophysics); Shaun Hughes (Royal Greenwich Observatory); Robert Kennicutt, Paul Harding, Anne Turner and Fabio Bresolin (Univ. of Arizona); Barry Madore and Nancy Silbermann (JPL, Caltech); Jeremy Mould (Mt. Stromlo, Australian National University); Abhijit Saha (Space Telescope Science Institute); and Peter Stetson (Dominion Astrophysical Observatory).

The Space Telescope Science Institute is operated by the Association of Universities for Research in Astronomy, Inc., for NASA, under contract with the Goddard Space Flight Center, Greenbelt, MD. The HST is a project of international cooperation between NASA and the European Space Agency.

The Wide Field and Planetary Camera 2 was developed by NASA's Jet Propulsion Laboratory, Pasadena, CA, and is managed by the Goddard Space Flight Center for NASA's Office of Space Science, Washington, DC.

CENSUS BUREAU REPORT
ON HEALTH INSURANCE
October 30, 1994

According to the latest government figures released October 30, approximately 25 percent of Americans lacked health insurance for part or all of the period from 1990 to 1992. Some 9 million people—approximately 3.5 percent of all Americans—did not have health insurance for the entire thirty-two-month period studied in the Census Bureau report titled "Dynamics of Economic Well-Being: Health Insurance 1990 to 1992."

A second survey, conducted by the Gallup Organization for the American Medical Association, found that the percentage of Americans with health insurance had seriously declined between 1991 and 1994. In 1994, 83 percent of Americans had health insurance, a 5-percentage-point decrease from 1991.

Despite the surveys finding that large numbers of Americans lacked health insurance, President Bill Clinton's plan to provide coverage for all Americans died in the 103rd Congress. The struggle over health care reform was the biggest political fight of 1994, but one that ultimately accomplished little other than to reinforce images shared by many Americans of an ineffective president, a gridlocked Congress, and a political system dominated by special interests.

The president's plan, which he outlined in a speech to a joint session of Congress on September 22, 1993, had two goals: to provide health insurance coverage for all Americans and to control skyrocketing health care costs. To provide universal coverage, the plan called for virtually all businesses to provide insurance to their workers and to pay 80 percent of the premium cost. To control costs, the plan called for creating about two hundred regional health alliances that would serve, in effect, as large health insurance purchasing cooperatives that would seek the lowest possible health insurance rates. (Clinton's Health Care Plan, Historic Documents of 1993, p. 781)

Special Interests Attack Plan

The president's 1,364-page bill never really made it out of the gate in Congress. Part of the reason was that special interest groups representing everyone from doctors to business owners to insurance companies fiercely attacked the measure. Three different studies documented special interests' influence:

- *During 1993 and 1994, hundreds of special interests spent a total of more than $100 million to influence the health care debate, according to a July report by the Center for Public Integrity, a Washington research group that studied lobbying. "Health care reform has become the most heavily lobbied legislative initiative in United States history," the report said.*
- *Citizen Action, a public interest group, reported that during the seventeen-month period that ended in May 1994, political action committees for health and insurance interests had contributed $26 million to congressional campaigns. Over the previous fourteen years, those interests had given more than $150 million to congressional campaigns, the report stated.*
- *The Annenberg School for Communication at the University of Pennsylvania predicted that by October 1994 lobbyists in the health care debate would spend $60 million on television advertising alone. Nearly all the money was spent to defeat Clinton's plan. The $60 million spent on television advertising surpassed the $50 million spent on advertising in the 1992 presidential campaign.*

Competing Bills Introduced

With the president's bill already in deep trouble when it reached Capitol Hill, members of Congress fashioned a multitude of other bills aimed at improving the nation's health care system. While the competing bills generated tremendous debate and contributed to the lobbying frenzy, they never settled on a common ground. On August 25, Senate Majority Leader George J. Mitchell (D-Maine) announced that the Senate would recess without voting on any major health care reform legislation. His announcement represented the death of health care reform in the 103rd Congress.

The demise of health care reform led to lots of finger pointing, but there was more than enough blame to go around. Most observers blamed Clinton for introducing a bill that was too complex and that prompted fears of a huge new federal bureaucracy. Supporters of reform were faulted for failing to respond quickly and efficiently to attacks. Republicans were blamed for engaging in partisan bickering, while Democrats in Congress were criticized for splitting into numerous camps instead of working together. Special interests came under attack for spending whatever it took to kill any effort at reform.

Clinton's health care bill was one of the factors that cost Democrats control of Congress in the November election, according to Democratic Party poll-

sters. The bill tagged Clinton and the Democrats as the party of big govern-ment, according to a poll by Stan Greenberg for the Democratic Leadership Council.

For his part, Clinton promised that health care reform would be a major issue once again in 1995. While some in the new Congress also wanted to pursue reform, virtually everyone agreed that any changes in the current system would be modest.

Following are excerpts from a Census Bureau report titled "Dynamics of Economic Well-Being: Health Insurance, 1990 to 1992," which was released October 30, 1994:

Introduction

This report uses data from the Survey of Income and Program Participation (SIPP) to examine issues related to health insurance coverage. It focuses pri-marily on the extent to which people are covered by health insurance over a 32-month period beginning in early 1990. The source of this information is the 1990 panel of the SIPP, which contains records for each survey person for whom a reasonably complete set of data for a 32-month period was obtained. Efforts were made during the life of the panel to follow persons that moved to ensure that the sample remained representative of the noninstitutional popu-lation of the United States. . . .

Health insurance in this report refers to the following types of coverage: 1) employer- or union-provided insurance, 2) other privately purchased health insurance, 3) Medicare, 4) military health care, and 5) Medicaid. . . .

Highlights

- Estimates for both the 1990 and 1991 calendar years show that about 17 million persons were uninsured for each 12-month period. Nine million were uninsured for the full 32-month period from early 1990 to mid-1992.
- Over calendar year 1990, 80 percent of all persons had continuous health insurance coverage over the year; thus, 20 percent, or 47 million persons, lacked insurance for at least 1 month. This percentage was slightly lower than the 21 percent who experienced a lapse in coverage over calendar year 1987.
- Over a 32-month period, 75 percent of all persons had continuous health insurance coverage; 25 percent, or 60 million persons, lacked insurance for at least 1 month.
- Young adults (those between the ages of 18 and 24 years old) were the most likely of any age group to lack insurance for at least 1 month. Less than one-half, or 47 percent of the persons of this age group, were cov-ered by insurance for the entire 32-month period.
- Work experience has a significant effect on health insurance coverage. Eighty-eight percent of persons who worked full-time for the entire pe-

riod were covered continuously by health insurance, compared with 78 percent for full-period, part-time workers, and 62 percent for workers with one or more job interruptions.

- Of those who participated in a major public assistance program at some point over the 32-month period, 47 percent spent 1 or more months without health insurance. The comparable proportion for those who did not participate in any of these programs was 21 percent. However, as a result of their increased likelihood of Medicaid coverage, persons with 32 months of assistance participation were about as likely to have continuous health insurance as those who did not participate at all in a major assistance program.

- The relationship between lack of health insurance coverage and months with low income is not a linear one. Sixty-eight percent of those persons with 13 to 24 low income months experienced 1 or more months without health insurance coverage, which was significantly higher than any other group.

- Of all observed spells without health insurance (experienced by 25 percent of persons), half of them lasted for 6.0 months or longer. This estimate was significantly longer than the 4.2 months of non-coverage for the earlier 1987 panel, which covered a shorter survey time period of 28 months.

Estimates of Health Insurance Coverage

Health insurance coverage is commonly associated with other life circumstances, such as employment, retirement, and program participation. As a result, there exists a strong likelihood that for some segments of the population health insurance status will change over time. Through the use of longitudinal estimates, it is possible to examine the dynamics of health insurance coverage, and the extent to which persons experience a lapse in coverage during a given time period.

The 1990 SIPP panel file was used to examine the number of months persons were covered by health insurance over time up to a 32-month period. Interviews from this panel were conducted between February 1990 and September 1992, allowing examination of health insurance coverage for two full calendar years, 1990 and 1991. During the 1990 calendar year, 80 percent of all persons had health insurance coverage for the entire year; 20 percent, or 47 million persons, lacked coverage for at least 1 month. Seven percent, or 17 million persons, were never covered in 1990. The 1991 calendar year estimates were similar, showing 81 percent, 19 percent, and 7 percent, respectively.

Between 1990 and 1992, 75 percent of all persons had continuous health insurance coverage over the entire 32-month period; 25 percent lacked health insurance for at least 1 month. Six percent of all persons (or one-fourth of those who lacked health insurance for at least 1 month) were covered by insurance for 6 months or less (4 percent of all persons lacked coverage for the entire period, and another 2 percent were covered for 1 to 6 months). Eighty-six percent of those with continuous coverage over the 32-month period were covered by private health insurance; 6 percent were covered by Medicaid.

Comparisons

The proportion of persons with lapses in coverage tends to fluctuate when measured over different time periods. For example, 81 percent were continuously covered over the 12-month period from January to December 1990, but only 75 percent had coverage for the entire 32 months of the survey.

An earlier report which examined patterns of health insurance coverage between 1987 and 1989 reported gaps in coverage over a 28-month period. Since percentages vary with the time period over which they are measured, the appropriate comparison is a 28-month period beginning in 1990. Comparisons of estimates over a 28-month period from the 1990 panel with those from the 1987 panel reveal different patterns of health insurance coverage between the 1987-1989 period and the 1990-1992 period. A slightly higher proportion of persons had continuous coverage in the later period—the percent covered for the entire 28-month period rose from 74 percent in the 1987-1989 period to 76 percent from 1990-1992. This increase was primarily due to an increase in continuous private health insurance coverage, which rose from 64 to 66 percent.

Results from comparing 1990 calendar year estimates with previous 1987 calendar year estimates show a slight decline in the proportion of persons with a lapse in coverage for 1990 (20 percent versus 21 percent). The remainder of this report will focus primarily on the 32-month period from February 1990 to September 1992.

Sex, Race, and Hispanic Origin

Over the 32-month period beginning in February 1990, women were more likely than men to have continuous health insurance coverage. Twenty-seven percent of all men lacked health insurance for at least 1 month; the comparable figure for women was 24 percent. The difference between the percentages of men and women with continuous private health insurance coverage was not significant. The difference between men and women in overall health insurance coverage is partially attributable to differences in economic status. Women are more likely than men to live in families with incomes below poverty, and are more likely to participate in means-tested assistance programs. Thus, women were more likely than men to take part in Medicaid, both in terms of continuous coverage (6 percent) and coverage for at least 1 month (15 percent). The comparable figures for men were 3 percent and 10 percent, respectively.

A second factor contributing to the difference in health insurance coverage between men and women is age. More women than men are 65 years old and over, and virtually everyone in that age group is covered by Medicare.

The relationship between race or Hispanic origin and health insurance was a strong one. The percentages of persons who spent at least 1 month without health insurance were 21 percent for Whites (not of Hispanic origin), 36 percent for Blacks, and 48 percent for persons of Hispanic origin. Whites were also much more likely than Blacks or those of Hispanic origin to be covered by private health insurance. Ninety-two percent of all Whites (not of Hispanic origin) were covered by private health insurance for at least 1 month. The comparable figures for Blacks and persons of Hispanic origin were about 75 percent and 72 percent, respectively.

Blacks were more likely to be covered by Medicaid than Whites or those of Hispanic origin. The percentages of Whites (not of Hispanic origin), Blacks, and Hispanic-origin persons with at least 1 month of Medicaid coverage were 8 percent, 31 percent, and 28 percent, respectively. Fifteen percent of all Black persons had continuous Medicaid coverage over the time period covered by the panel. The comparable percentages for Whites (not of Hispanic origin) and Hispanic-origin persons were 2 percent and 11 percent, respectively.

Age

Young adults (those between the ages of 18 and 24) were the most likely of any age group to spend at least 1 month without health insurance coverage. Almost one-half (47 percent) of all persons between the ages of 18 and 24 lacked health insurance for at least 1 month; 11 percent were covered for less than 7 months.

Generally, for persons 18 years old and over, there was a positive relationship between age and continuous health insurance coverage. Continuous health insurance coverage rates for persons by age group from 18 to 24 to 65 years old and over monotonically increased from 53 percent to 99 percent, respectively.

Young children (those under 6 years old) were the most likely to have been covered by Medicaid at some time during the period covered by the 1990 panel. Twenty-nine percent of all young children were covered by Medicaid for at least 1 month. The least likely persons to be covered by Medicaid were those who were 35 to 44 years old. Persons 65 years old and over who were covered by Medicaid were much more likely to have been covered for the entire 32-month period than non-elderly adults (18 to 64 years old) with Medicaid coverage. Nearly three-fifths (59 percent) of all persons 65 years old and over with at least 1 month of Medicaid coverage were covered for the entire 32-month period. The comparable percentage for persons under 18 years old was 34 percent. . . .

Months with Low Income

One way to examine differences in economic status between individuals over time is to characterize those persons by the number of months in which the person or family income was below their monthly poverty threshold. As would be expected, persons living above the poverty line (no low-income months) were much more likely to have continuous health insurance coverage than persons who experienced 1 or more low-income months. Only 13 percent of those above the poverty line spent 1 or more months without health insurance, compared with over one-half (52 percent) of those with 1 or more low-income months.

However, the relationship between lack of health insurance coverage and months with low income is not a linear one. Those with 13 to 24 low-income months were more likely to experience 1 or more months without health insurance coverage (68 percent) than any other group, and persons with 32 low-income months were less likely to lack health insurance for at least 1 month (31 percent) than those with 1 to 6 low-income months (48 percent). The higher health insurance coverage rates of those with more low-income months is attributable to their level of Medicaid coverage. Seventy-eight percent of those with 32 low-income months were covered by Medicaid for at least 1 month; 56 percent were covered every month. The comparable figures for those with 25 to 31 low-income months were 58 and 25 percent, respectively.

Income-to-Poverty Ratios

Income-to-poverty ratios represent another way of characterizing individuals by their relative economic status. These ratios are computed by summing the person or family income over the entire 32-month period, and dividing this total by the summed monthly poverty thresholds. Thus, a ratio of under 1.0 indicates that an individual's family income over the 32-month period was less than the sum of that family's poverty threshold over that time. In the 32-month period covered here, 9 percent of persons had an income-to poverty ratio less than 1.0. About one-half (49 percent) of these persons lacked continuous health insurance, and 11 percent were not covered at all during the 32-month period, compared to 23 and 3 percent, respectively, for all others.

Those with lower income-to-poverty ratios were slightly more likely to be covered by Medicaid. Seventy-seven percent of all persons with ratios less than 0.5 were covered by Medicaid for at least 1 month. The comparable proportion for those with income-to-poverty ratios between 0.5 and 0.99 was 60 percent.

As would be expected, there is a strong correlation between income-to-poverty ratios and the likelihood of continuous health insurance. The percentage of persons with health insurance for the entire 32 months rose from about 53 percent for those with ratios under 2.0 to 93 percent for those with ratios of 6.0 and over. Differences in continuous private health insurance coverage by income-to-poverty ratio are even more dramatic, from 8 percent for persons with ratios under 1.0 to 91 percent for those with ratios of 6.0 or more.

Type of Family

Persons who were members of married-couple families the entire 32-month period were less likely to spend 1 or more months without health insurance than persons who did not spend any time in this type of family. However, persons spending part (but not all) of the 32-month period in a married-couple family were more likely to lack insurance coverage for 1 or more months than those who spent no time in a married-couple family or those who spent all 32 months in such a family. The proportions of persons without continuous health insurance coverage were 20 percent for those who spent the entire period in a married-couple family, 31 percent for those who spent no time in a married-couple family, and 44 percent for those who spent some (but not all) months in this type of family.

The reliance on Medicaid of families with a female householder, no husband present, with related children, is evident. Forty-one percent of persons who spent the entire 32 months in this type of family were covered by Medicaid for at least 1 month; 24 percent were covered for the entire period. In contrast, only 7 percent of those that spent none of the period in this type of family were covered by Medicaid for at least 1 month.

Only 65 percent of persons that spent the entire period in a family with a female householder, no husband present, with related children, were covered by private health insurance for at least 1 month, compared with 92 percent for those that spent none of the 32-month period in this type of family. For those who spent all 32 months in a married-couple family, private health insurance coverage for at least 1 month was 93 percent.

Employment Status

The relationship between health insurance coverage and employment is an important one, given the fact that such a large proportion of total health insurance is derived through an employer (either as a primary policyholder or as a dependent). In order to examine the relationship between health insurance coverage and employment status, wage and salary workers 18 to 64 years old were separated into three groups: 1) those who worked full-time for the entire period, 2) those who worked part-time for the entire period, and 3) those with one or more job interruptions. Workers were characterized by their private or government health coverage, their private coverage, and their own employer-provided coverage. This latter type of coverage is a subset of private health insurance coverage.

Eighty-eight percent of all full-period, full-time workers were covered by health insurance for the entire period and 67 percent were covered through their own employer-provided plans. There was no difference between the proportion of male and female full-period, full-time workers who were continuously covered by health insurance. However, there was a significant difference in the continuous health insurance coverage rates of White and Black full-period, full-time workers. Hispanic-origin workers in this category were less likely than Whites (not of Hispanic origin) or Blacks to have continuous coverage; the comparable rates for these groups are 70, 90, and 78 percent, respectively.

Full-period, part-time workers were less likely than their full-time counterparts to have continuous health insurance coverage. Twenty-two percent of these workers lacked continuous coverage, compared with 13 percent of full-period, full-time workers.

There was a major difference between full- and part-time workers in their levels of own employer-provided coverage. Of part-time workers with continuous coverage, only 19 percent were covered through their own employer-provided plans. The comparable figure for full-time workers was 67 percent. The difference between the private and employer-provided health insurance rates for this group implies that many of these workers are covered as dependents (78 percent of full-period, part-time workers were women).

Less than one-half (38 percent) of workers with one or more job interruptions experienced 1 or more months without health insurance coverage. Men in this category were more likely than women to lack health coverage for at least 1 month (46 to 33 percent), and men in this category were more likely than women to be covered continuously by their own employer-provided plan (22 to 11 percent).

Younger full-period, full-time workers were less likely than their older counterparts to have been covered by health insurance continuously. Forty-two percent of full-period, full-time workers 18 to 21 years old spent 1 or more months without health insurance. For workers 22 years old and over, comparable percentages ranged from 10 percent (workers 35 to 44 years old) to 23 percent (workers 22 to 24 years old).

Fifty-three percent of younger workers (those 18 to 24 years old) with job interruptions spent 1 or more months without health insurance coverage. For workers 25 years old and over, comparable percentages ranged from 24 percent (workers 45 to 64 years old) to 45 percent (workers 25 to 34 years old). . . .

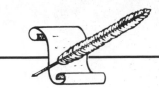

November

SENATE REPORT ON
AMES ESPIONAGE CASE
November 1, 1994

Espionage committed by Aldrich H. Ames, a highly placed career officer for the Central Intelligence Agency (CIA), amounted to "a disaster of unprecedented proportions," according to a report released November 1 by the Senate Select Committee on Intelligence. The report detailed how a series of investigative debacles allowed Ames to supply the Soviet Union with sensitive military secrets for nine years, until his arrest in February 1994. It concluded that "there was gross negligence—both individually and institutionally—in creating and perpetuating the environment in which Ames was able to carry out his espionage activities for nine years without detection."

According to the 116-page report—the product of eight months of hearings, briefings, and interviews—the CIA neglected for seven years to give the Federal Bureau of Investigation (FBI) critical information about the case. The CIA's reluctance to examine its own agents "led to the loss of virtually all of CIA's intelligence assets targeted at the Soviet Union at the height of the cold war," the panel said.

Espionage Results in Executions

Ames spent most of his thirty-one-year CIA career in the Directorate of Operations, which is responsible for conducting CIA covert operations abroad. He was promoted in 1983 to the position of counterintelligence chief for the agency's Soviet division.

On April 16, 1985, Ames entered the Soviet embassy in Washington, D.C., and offered his services to the KGB, the Soviet security services, in exchange for money. Ames's subsequent espionage had devastating repercussions for U.S. intelligence, according to a press release the Senate panel issued with its report. "This relationship, which continued until his arrest on February 21, 1994, resulted in the execution of 10 Soviet sources, the imprisonment of many others, the compromise of over 100 intelligence operations against the Soviet Union, and the passing of several thousand classified documents (contained in his office and home computer) to the KGB," the panel said. The CIA had not investigated Ames, despite the fact that he exhibited "a serious alcohol problem, numerous security lapses, and chronic performance deficiencies," besides engaging in extramarital affairs. He continued to be promoted and given key assignments.

Ames and his wife, Rosario, pleaded guilty to espionage activities on April 28. During their sentencing, Ames acknowledged that he had been paid more than $1.8 million by the KGB, much of which went to support the couple's lavish lifestyle. Ames was sentenced to life without parole, and his wife was subsequently sentenced to just over five years in prison.

Ames Downplays His Actions

Speaking before a full courtroom at his sentencing, Ames admitted that he had "betrayed a serious trust," but said that his role as a double agent was "a sideshow" that had "no real impact on our significant security interests over the years." Ames said he had worried more about being detected by Soviet defectors than by the CIA or FBI.

In his statement, Ames gave two reasons for betraying his country. "First, I had come to dissent from the decades-long shift to the extreme right in our political spectrum and from our national security and foreign policies," he said.

"Second, I had come to believe that the espionage business, as carried out by the CIA and a few other American agencies, was and is a self-serving sham, carried out by careerist bureaucrats who have managed to deceive several generations of American policy makers and the public about both the necessity and the value of their work."

In its report, the Senate committee said its investigation "found a bureaucracy which was excessively tolerant of serious personal and professional misconduct among its employees, where security was lax and ineffective. And we found a system and a culture unwilling and unable to face, assess and investigate the catastrophic blow Ames had dealt to the core of its operations." The committee criticized three former CIA directors who served in the 1980s for their "incomprehensible failure" to undertake a serious investigation of the case.

The report also faulted the disciplinary action taken by James Woolsey, the current CIA director. The CIA's inspector general had recommended that twenty-three current and former employees be held accountable for the agency's failure to detect and prevent Ames's espionage activities. However, Woolsey had chosen only to issue letters of reprimand to seven retired and four current employees. That response, the committee said, was "seriously inadequate and disproportionate to the magnitude of the problems identified in the Inspector General's report."

CIA Faces Hard Questions

The fallout from the Ames affair on the CIA was considerable, both on Capitol Hill and among members of the public. "The Committee's report on the Ames case paints a picture which will come as a shock to most Americans," said Senate committee chairman Dennis DeConcini (D-Ariz.), on releasing the report. "While Aldrich Ames certainly cannot be viewed as typical of CIA employees, how the Agency dealt with him, personally, professionally, and once he came under suspicion, speaks volumes about the attitudes, competence, and judgment of many of his colleagues and supervisors . . . [T]he case suggests the need for a fundamental change in the culture of the CIA."

The Ames case also exacerbated already strained relations between the CIA and FBI. In the aftermath of the case, Woolsey said he was beginning a broad internal review of the agency's procedures for collecting and analyzing intelligence. The director's announcement apparently did not satisfy members of Congress, who decided in late September to establish an independent commission to review the role of the CIA and the eleven other U.S. military and civilian intelligence agencies. Leading CIA officials strongly opposed creation of the commission.

On November 30, less than a month after the Senate panel released its report, the House Permanent Select Committee on Intelligence released the findings of its own investigation. In most respects, its findings mirrored those issued by the Senate panel. Like the Senate report, the House report was sharply critical of both the CIA and FBI. It also asserted that there had been "a pattern of lack of candor by senior CIA officials in answering questions by committee members" between 1988 and 1992 about the loss of U.S.-paid agents in the Soviet Union. If the officials had been more forthcoming, the committee said, it might have pursued a more vigorous investigation that would have revealed Ames's activities sooner. Rep. Larry Combest (R-Texas), the ranking Republican who later assumed the committee chairmanship when the GOP gained control of the House in 1995, said the Ames affair would "be a prime subject of hearings."

On December 28, the Ames case claimed another victim when Woolsey resigned as CIA director. While other factors also contributed to the resignation, Woolsey's mild punishment of CIA employees involved in the Ames case seriously damaged his reputation with Congress, making it increasingly difficult for him to run the agency.

> *Following are excerpts from the Conclusions and Recommendations from the report titled "An Assessment of the Aldrich H. Ames Espionage Case and Its Implications for U.S. Intelligence," released November 1, 1994, by the Senate Select Committee on Intelligence:*

Over the months since his arrest, it has become clear that Aldrich Hazen Ames caused more damage to the national security of the United States than any spy in the history of the CIA. Ten Soviet sources of the CIA and the FBI were executed as a result of Ames' treachery and others were imprisoned.

Ames has admitted to compromising over 100 intelligence operations of the CIA, FBI, military departments, and allied governments, and there are likely others he does not specifically recall. Literally thousands of classified documents—on subjects ranging from U.S. defense capabilities to international narcotics trafficking—were turned over by Ames to his KGB handlers. Although the formal assessment of the damage caused by Ames has yet to be completed, his betrayal stands as the most egregious in American history.

Obviously, something went terribly wrong. For a CIA officer to carry on espionage activities without detection for almost nine years indicates, on its face, a failure of the system. As the Committee began to look into this failure, we found a bureaucracy which was excessively tolerant of serious personal and professional misconduct among its employees, where security was lax and ineffective. And we found a system and a culture unwilling and unable—particularly in the early years of Ames' betrayal—to face, assess, and investigate the catastrophic blow Ames had dealt to the core of its operations.

The system which permitted Ames' prolonged betrayal must be changed. The country cannot afford such calamities in the future, and the CIA cannot afford further erosion of the public's confidence. In the wake of the Cold War, the CIA still has an important mission to perform—a mission that is vital to the national security of the United States. Like all government agencies, the CIA ultimately depends upon the support of the American people and the Congress to carry out its unique functions and maintain its unique capabilities. To restore that confidence, the CIA must deal effectively with the serious deficiencies highlighted by the Ames case.

In the discussion which follows, the Committee sets forth where we believe the system failed and what we believe should be done to correct it. In its action on the Intelligence Authorization Act for Fiscal Year 1995 (P.L. 103-359), the Committee undertook legislative remedies for many of these shortcomings by requiring coordination of counterintelligence matters with the FBI and by providing authorized investigative agencies with new authority to obtain access to financial information and travel records of federal employees who have access to classified information. While these legislative initiatives are an important beginning, far more is needed to correct the deficiencies evident in the Ames case than legislation alone can achieve.

In the end, regardless of what the Committee may recommend or what Congress may enact, fundamental change will come only if the Director of Central Intelligence [DCI], supervisors at all levels, and the employees of the CIA bring it about. The Committee intends to monitor the Agency's progress in this regard, but the leadership must come from within.

The Committee undertook its inquiry not for the purpose of assessing individual blame—which is the exclusive responsibility of the Executive branch—but rather to learn what had gone wrong and to evaluate the institutional lessons to be learned from the Ames case. Nevertheless, the Committee believes that the recent actions taken by the Director of Central Intelligence, R. James Woolsey, against past and current CIA officials implicated in the Ames case warrant comment.

On March 10 of this year, Director Woolsey appeared before the Committee in closed session to outline his interim responses to the Ames case. One area for reform which was cited by the Director was "management accountability." According to the Director: "[T]o my mind, this is very much at the heart of the entire matter." The Committee strongly shares this view.

Despite the CIA Inspector General's recommendation that 23 current and former CIA officials be held accountable for the Agency's failure to prevent and detect Ames' espionage activities, Director Woolsey chose only to issue letters of reprimand to 11 individuals—7 retired and 4 current Agency employees. None of the individuals cited by the Inspector General was fired, demoted, suspended or even reassigned as a result of this case. In response to what was arguably the greatest managerial breakdown in the CIA's history, the disciplinary actions taken by the Director do not, in the collective experience and judgment of the Committee, constitute adequate "management accountability."

All Committee Members believe that the Director's disciplinary actions in this case are seriously inadequate and disproportionate to the magnitude of the problems identified in the Inspector General's report. It is clear, given the immense national security interests at stake, that there was "gross negligence"—both individually and institutionally—in creating and perpetuating the environment in which Ames was able to carry out his espionage activities for nine years without detection.

The Committee is concerned about the message that Director Woolsey's mild disciplinary actions will send to the overwhelming majority of CIA employees who are dedicated, conscientious, patriotic, and hard-working professionals, many of whom are exposed daily to risk and hardship. For the current employees who were faulted by the Inspector General for their role in the Ames case to remain in their grades and positions falls far short of the level of accountability expected by the Committee. Indeed, in the wake of the Director's decision, many professionals within the Intelligence Community have contacted the Committee to register the same sentiment.

As this report documents, the failures evident in the Ames case were numerous and egregious. While it might be argued that the majority of individuals cited by the Inspector General were guilty of acts of omission rather than commission, the seriousness of these omissions cannot be overstated. The failures of the individuals cited by the Inspector General led to the loss of virtually all of CIA's intelligence assets targeted against the Soviet Union at the height of the Cold War. Ten of these agents were executed. The inability of the CIA to get to the bottom of these losses in a timely way was itself a significant management failure.

If there is not a higher standard of accountability established by DCIs, then a repeat of the Ames tragedy becomes all the more likely. Management accountability within the Intelligence Community should be no less than the highest levels found elsewhere in the Executive branch. Director Woolsey's actions do not meet this standard.

Having noted in strong terms the magnitude of CIA's failures, the Committee would be remiss not to point out what went right. A traitor, responsible for heinous acts of espionage, was identified and convicted. He has been imprisoned for life. In the end, this was accomplished by the work of a small group of CIA and FBI personnel who took part in what became a long and arduous inquiry—for some, lasting almost nine years. At least one member of this group appears to have pushed from the very beginning to get to the bottom of the 1985 compromises. It was his impetus that eventually put the investigation back on track in 1991. Over time, the scope and pace of the investigation had taken many twists and turns, some caused by the KGB and some by internal factors beyond the control of the investigators themselves. The commentary which follows is not intended to diminish in any way what was ultimately accomplished by this dedicated group of investigators and analysts.

Finally, the Committee notes that its recommendations are based upon the situation that pertained through early 1994. Director Woolsey has promulgated some new policies since then and has announced his intention to institute still others. While the Committee believes in general that stronger measures are needed, it is too early to pass judgment on the Director's recent actions.

The Failure to "Fix" Past Counterintelligence Problems

The counterintelligence function at the CIA is weak and inherently flawed. Despite repeated internal and external reports which have recognized a long-standing cultural problem with the counterintelligence function, CIA managers have, judging from the Ames case, failed to fix it.

In particular, the Committee was struck by the number of internal and external studies undertaken after 1985—which became known as the "Year of the Spy" following the exposure of spies John Walker, Ronald Pelton, Edward Lee Howard, and Jonathan Pollard—which pointed out the systemic and deeply-rooted problems in the CIA's conduct of counterintelligence.

As summarized by the recent report of the CIA Inspector General, these internal and external reports over the years focused on common themes:

- that a counterintelligence career was held in low esteem at the CIA and did not attract high caliber officers. This was, in part, because officers gained promotions by agent recruitments, not by analyzing problems in recruitment operations;
- that there was an ambiguous division of responsibility for counterintelligence among CIA offices;
- that counterintelligence information was not being shared properly among CIA components; and
- that CIA was reluctant to share counterintelligence information fully and in a timely manner with the FBI. (IG Report, pp. 16-22)

The poor state of counterintelligence at the CIA in the mid-1980s can be explained in part by the reaction to the so-called "Angleton era." James Angleton had been the head of the Counterintelligence Staff of the CIA from

1954 until 1974 (when he was involuntarily retired by DCI William Colby). He became convinced that the KGB had penetrated the CIA. Accordingly, Angleton was suspicious of virtually every Soviet agent who was recruited by the CIA and suspicious of every CIA officer responsible for such recruitment. On occasion, his suspicions led to CIA officers being fired without adequate justification.

While several of the officers who had been unjustly fired were later compensated, the counterintelligence function was effectively undermined by the negative reaction to Angleton's relentless pursuit of spies, particularly within the Soviet-East European (SE) Division of the Directorate of Operations, which had the principal responsibility for recruiting Soviet agents for the CIA.

In addition, there appears to have been an excessive focus within the Directorate on the recruitment of intelligence sources to the exclusion of counterintelligence concerns. Few officers wanted to go into counterintelligence because promotions and recognition came from successful recruitments, not from questioning, or identifying problems with, ongoing operations. Further, there was an image of a "corporate elite" constructed among these officers which led them to dismiss too readily the possibility of a spy among them.

By all accounts, these attitudes were prevalent within the Directorate of Operations at the time Ames sabotaged the Agency's Soviet operations in the summer of 1985, and they greatly contributed to management's failure to focus upon the CIA employees who had had access to the compromised cases (as explained in detail below).

The CIA made some efforts to address these shortcomings after "the Year of the Spy." In 1988, the head of the counterintelligence staff was made an "Associate Deputy Director" in the Directorate of Operations, and was double-hatted as the head of a new Counterintelligence Center (CIC). The CIA and FBI also signed a new Memorandum of Understanding (MOU) in 1988, which provided, at least on paper, for improved sharing of information in counterintelligence cases.

But these new bureaucratic "trappings" for the counterintelligence function did not overcome the fundamental problems which continued to be cited in reports issued in the 1990s. Despite the formation of a "lead office" for counterintelligence and the 1988 MOU with the FBI, the sharing of counterintelligence information between CIA components and with the FBI continued to be a serious problem, as was clearly evident in the Ames case.

In conclusion, the Committee finds that, despite repeated internal and external reports which recognized a longstanding cultural problem in the counterintelligence function, the CIA failed to implement adequate solutions. Indeed, the Committee believes the fundamental problems persist.

Recommendation #1

The Director of Central Intelligence should revise the CIA's strategy for carrying out the counterintelligence function. The Director should institute measures to improve the effectiveness of counterintelligence to include (1) establishing as a requirement for promotion among officers of the Directorate of Operations, service in a counterintelligence or counterintelligence-related position during their careers; (2) establishing incentives for service in a counterintelligence position; (3) instituting effective and comprehensive counterintelligence training for all officers of the Directorate of Operations and for appropriate officers assigned elsewhere in the CIA; and (4) ensuring adequate access to ongoing foreign intelligence operations by those charged with the counterintelligence function. The Committee will make this a "special interest area" for purposes of oversight until it is satisfied the weaknesses noted above have been adequately addressed.

The Failure to Deal with Suitability Problems

As the Ames case all too clearly demonstrates, the CIA Directorate of Operations is too willing to dismiss, deny, or ignore suitability problems demonstrated by its officers.

From the outset of his career at the CIA, Ames demonstrated serious suitability problems which, over the years, should have led his supervisors to reassess his continued employment. These problems included drunkenness, disregard for security regulations, and sloppiness towards administrative requirements. In the years immediately before he began to commit espionage and during the rest of his career, his supervisors were aware of his personal and professional deficiencies, but did not make his problems part of his official record, nor act effectively to correct them. Despite his recognized unsuitability, there is little evidence that his assignments, activities, or access to sensitive information were in any way limited as a result.

Prior to Ames' assignment to the counterintelligence staff of the SE Division in 1983, his supervisor in Mexico City sent a message to CIA headquarters recommending that Ames be counseled for alcohol abuse when he returned. While Ames' supervisor recognized a chronic problem, the message to headquarters apparently stemmed from an incident which occurred at an official reception at the U.S. Embassy where Ames was drunk and became involved in a loud argument with a Cuban official. On another occasion, Ames was involved in a traffic accident in Mexico City and was so drunk he could not answer police questions nor recognize the U.S. Embassy officer sent to help him. In fact, based upon recent interviews with his colleagues, Ames was notorious for long, alcoholic lunches, often slurring his speech when he returned to the office. None of this behavior prompted any serious effort to correct the problem while Ames was overseas, or when he later returned to CIA headquarters.

In April 1983, when CIA headquarters asked Ames' supervisors in Mexico City whether Ames qualified for a staff position in another Latin American country, they recommended against it, citing his alcohol problem, his failure to do financial accountings, and his generally poor performance. Nevertheless, six months later, when a former supervisor of Ames requested him to fill a position in the SE Division at headquarters—the most sensitive element of the Directorate of Operations—there is no indication that Ames' alcohol problem or poor performance were ever noted. Indeed, Ames was placed in a position which provided him access to the identities of virtually all of the Soviet intelligence officers by the CIA without his new supervisors being aware of the problems he had had in Mexico City.

The alcohol abuse counseling that Ames ultimately did receive upon his return to headquarters amounted to one conversation with a counselor, who, according to Ames, told him that his case was not a serious one when compared to many others in the Directorate of Operations.

In 1983, during the assignment in Mexico City, Ames also began an extramarital relationship with a Colombian national, Rosario Casas Dupuy (hereinafter "Rosario"), herself a recruited asset of the CIA. Over time, the seriousness of their relationship became apparent to several of Ames' colleagues, but this never led to any action by Ames' supervisors, despite the fact that CIA regulations prohibit sexual relationships with recruited assets and require that reports of "close and continuing" relationships with foreign nationals be submitted by employees. Despite the security implications of this relationship, the violation of Agency regulations was ignored.

In fact, Ames did not file an official report concerning his relationship with Rosario until April 1984, four months after she came to the United States to live with him. Indeed, it appears that until their marriage in August 1985, Ames (still married to his first wife) and Rosario continued to live together, without any perceptible concern being registered by the CIA. While the counterintelligence staff recommended in February 1985, that in view of the anticipated marriage, Ames be moved to a less sensitive position, nothing changed. Ames continued in the same position.

While his alcohol problem abated during this assignment to the SE Division—at least as a matter of attracting official attention—it resurfaced during his assignment in Rome. He was known among colleagues for his long, alcoholic lunches, for sleeping at his desk, for often slurred speech, and generally as a marginal performer. On one occasion, after an Embassy reception, he was so drunk that he passed out on a street and awakened in a hospital. While his supervisor was unhappy, this incident did not become part of Ames' record, nor does it appear that this episode led to counseling or any serious reevaluation of Ames' fitness for continued service. Indeed, the same supervisor extended Ames' tour in Rome for a third year.

Over his career, Ames repeatedly demonstrated carelessness and disdain for security requirements. In 1975, while on his way to meet a CIA source in New York, Ames left a briefcase of classified materials identifying the source on a subway train. Although the briefcase was ultimately recovered, it might well have compromised the source's relationship with the CIA. In the fall of 1984, he brought Rosario to CIA housing where CIA undercover officers were staying, in violation of security regulations. In August 1985, he took her to the safe house where the Soviet defector Yurchenko was being debriefed, again in violation of security procedures. In Rome, he was known to prepare classified reports at home. During his assignments at CIA headquarters between 1989 and 1994, he was occasionally found in other CIA offices where he had no reason to be, and with materials he had no reason to have.

He was equally negligent throughout his career in complying with the administrative requirements imposed on officers of the Directorate of Operations, such as submitting financial accountings for the cases he was handling.

Despite these and other incidents, Ames never received a single official reprimand during his 31-year career at the CIA. Indeed, most of the incidents and shortcomings which have come to light since Ames was arrested were never made a matter of official record. Once on board, his fitness to serve in the Directorate of Operations was never reevaluated.

The Committee appreciates that intelligence officers of the Directorate of Operations are often placed in jobs and situations with stresses and strains that far exceed those of the average government employee. But these positions also demand self-control and personal discipline. Particularly in overseas assignments, it may be impossible to separate an intelligence officer's private life from his or her public, official one. A single misstep can prove his undoing or that of other officers.

It is the Committee's perception, which the Ames case confirms, that the Directorate of Operations has been far too willing to dismiss or ignore flagrant examples of personal misconduct among its officers. Excessive drinking and extramarital relationships with sources have all too often been seen as part of the job, rather than as indicators of problems. Security concerns are too often dismissed as the bureaucratic whining of small-minded administrators. All too often an officer who has been through training, gone through the polygraph examination, and had an overseas assignment, is accepted as a "member of the club," whose fitness for assignments, promotions, and continued service becomes immune from challenge.

Director Woolsey, in a recent speech, said that the "culture" of the directorate must be changed. The Committee shares that view. Such change will not come solely by changing regulations or personnel. It will come only when supervisors at every level of the directorate take seriously their responsibilities as managers. Personal misconduct should be documented. Officers who do not meet acceptable standards of personal behavior should not be assigned to sensitive positions nor qualify for supervisory positions. Personal shortcomings should be factored into consideration of promotions and bonus awards. While officers with personal problems should be given an opportunity, as well as appropriate assistance, to rehabilitate themselves, failing that, their employment with the directorate, if not with the Agency itself, should be terminated.

Recommendation #2

The Director of Central Intelligence should ensure that where evidence of suitability problems comes to the attention of supervisors, it is made a matter of official record and factored into the consideration of assignments, promotions, and bonus awards; that efforts are made to counsel and provide assistance to the employee where indicated; and, if the problem persists over time, the employment of the individual is terminated. The Committee will make this a "special interest area" for purposes of oversight until it is satisfied these policies have been instituted and are being observed within the Directorate of Operations.

Recommendation #3

The Director of Central Intelligence should, in particular, take prompt and effective action to deal with what appears to be a widespread problem of alcohol abuse by ensuring that CIA employees experiencing such problems are identified and are put into effective counseling and/or treatment. During this period, these employees should be suspended from their duties until they have demonstrated to a qualified professional their fitness to return to service. Should their problems continue, their employment should be terminated.

Recommendation #4

The Director of Central Intelligence should institute, consistent with existing legal authority, an "up or out" policy for employees of the CIA, similar to that of the Foreign Service, without waiting for the report required by section 305 of the Intelligence Authorization Act for Fiscal Year 1995, pertaining to the Intelligence Community as a whole. Chronically poor performance should be grounds for dismissal from the Agency. If the Director decides not to institute such a policy and does not provide a persuasive rationale to the Committee for his decision, the Congress should enact legislation requiring such a policy during the next Congress.

Recommendation #5

The Director of Central Intelligence should review and revise the performance appraisal reporting system of the CIA, to include a review of the factors upon which employees are rated and the grading system which now exists, to institute a system which reflects more accurately job performance. Where supervisors are concerned, their rating should include an assessment of how well they have supervised the performance and development of their subordinates.

The Failure to Coordinate Employees' Operational Activities

The Ames case provides a striking example of CIA supervisors failing to critically evaluate the contacts of an operations officer—with known personal shortcomings and in an extremely sensitive position—with Soviet officials in 1984 and 1985. Further, the fact that Ames virtually ceased submitting reports of such contacts, in violation of standard Agency procedures, never became known to his SE Division supervisors or made part of his official record.

In 1984, while occupying a position within the SE Division which gave him access to the identities of Soviet agents working for the CIA and FBI, Ames, with the approval of his immediate supervisor, began making contacts with Soviet Embassy officials in Washington, D.C. According to testimony received by the Committee, it was not infrequent that Director-ate of Operations officers at CIA headquarters were asked to "help out" other CIA elements that had responsibility for establishing relationships and maintaining contacts with foreign individuals located in the Washington area.

The Committee has been advised that Ames' senior supervisors in the SE Division were unaware that he was having these meetings and would have disallowed them had they known.

In any event, to permit a person in Ames' position, and someone with the personal and professional shortcomings already noted, to meet alone with Soviet Embassy officials substantially increased the risk of the di-saster that eventually occurred. It provided Ames with an opportunity that he otherwise may not have had, or may have had difficulty in contriving on his own.

After June 1985, after his espionage activities had begun, Ames repeatedly failed to submit reports of his contacts with Soviet officials. While his failure prompted complaints from the FBI, the CIA element that Ames was support-ing failed to bring this to the attention of his supervisors in the SE Division, nor was it reflected in his official record. Again, had Ames' SE Division super-visors been aware of his failure to file these reports, it may have alerted them to a possible problem. Since the advancement of Directorate of Operations officers depends upon their official reporting, the failure to file such reports should have suggested something was amiss.

A similar failure occurred during his assignment in Rome. While his super-visor was aware that he was meeting alone with Soviet officials in Rome (one of whom was Ames' KGB contact), Ames explained his failure to file reports of such meetings on the basis that he had obtained little worthwhile informa-tion. This apparently was enough to satisfy the supervisor.

Recommendation #6

The Director of Central Intelligence should revise the policies and pro-cedures governing the operational activities of CIA officers to ensure that these activities are better supervised, controlled, coordinated, and documented.

The Failure to Apply a Structured Methodology to the Investigation of Intelligence Compromises

The most puzzling deficiency in the Ames case was the failure, in the wake of the 1985-86 compromises, to aggressively investigate the possibility that CIA had been penetrated by a KGB spy.

Certainly by the fall of 1986, the CIA was aware that it had suffered a disas-ter of unprecedented proportions which was not explained by the defection of Edward Lee Howard. Within a matter of months, virtually, its entire stable of Soviet agents had been imprisoned or executed. In the days of the Cold War, Soviet operations represented the Agency's principal *raison d'etre*. There were no operations which had greater importance to its mission. The CIA was left virtually to start from scratch, uncertain whether new operations would meet the same fate as its old ones.

To be sure, these compromises involved extremely sensitive agents. There was a need for discretion in terms of how the matter was handled. But this does not explain or excuse the Agency's tentative, tepid response. Initially, some CIA officers could not believe that the KGB would "roll up" all of CIA's sources at once if the KGB had a source in the CIA who was still in place. Taking some comfort that new operations appeared to be surviving, some believed the problem had gone away. But this in no way explains the seeming lack of urgency to get to the bottom of what had gone so drastically wrong.

The obvious place to begin would have been with the CIA employees who had had access to the information which had been compromised. At least one official in the SE Division made a strong plea to his supervisors at the time that they needed to "investigate it, not study it." But this did not happen. The CIA task force created in October 1986, undertook what was largely an analytical review of the compromised cases. The task force did oversee an Office of Security review of personnel who had served in Moscow, but no broader examination was made of all CIA officers who had had access to the compromised cases. No systematic effort was made to identify and investigate problem employees and their activities, as was eventually done in 1991-92.

Later, the CIA came to suspect that the KGB was running ploys against them, purposely suggesting reasons for the compromises other than a penetration of the CIA itself. Even then, however, any sense of urgency was lacking. CIA analysts waited for things to happen, for more information to surface. They continued to analyze and conjecture. There was no clear sense of purpose, no clear methodology, and no clear sense of what was required to get to the bottom of the compromises.

In a related counterintelligence investigation of a report suggesting that the KGB may have recruited a source in a particular office in the CIA, a CIA investigator conducted a systematic investigation of over 90 employees who were assigned to that office. The inquiry took more than a year. But investigators did not conduct the same type of inquiry of the CIA employees who had had access to the information that was actually compromised in 1985 until 1991-1992.

The FBI was officially brought into the case in October 1986, when the CIA learned that two sources recruited by the FBI had been compromised. But the two agencies worked their investigations separately, despite the likelihood that the compromises were caused by the same source (whether it be human or technical). While the FBI and CIA task forces regularly exchanged information on the compromises and on the progress of their respective analyses, they never performed a systematic assessment, together, of the CIA employees who had had access to the compromised information, until mid-1991.

Why CIA management during the 1986-1991 period did not attach more importance or urgency to getting to the bottom of the 1985 compromises is incomprehensible to the Committee. While CIA Director William Casey and

Deputy Director for Operations (DDO) Clair George, who were in office at the time the compromises occurred, reportedly regarded them as "a huge problem," the Agency's response was to create a 4-person team to analyze the problem. No one believed there was a basis for bringing in investigators from the FBI at this juncture, apparently because CIA was unable to pin responsibility on a particular CIA employee.

While Casey and George became deeply enmeshed in the Iran-contra scandal in the fall of 1986 and spring of 1987, this circumstance does not explain, in the view of the Committee, why a problem so close to the heart of the CIA's mission was not given more attention by senior management. Indeed, once Casey and George departed the scene, it does not appear that their successors—either as DCI or as DDO—gave the inquiry any particular emphasis or priority. DCI William Webster, his deputy Robert M. Gates, and the new DDO Richard Stolz were briefed on the compromises in 1988, but did not delve deeply into either the nature of the problem (which was now several years old) or what the Agency was doing to resolve it. . . .

The Committee believes that those in charge of the CIA during the 1986-1991 period—Director William Casey, Acting Director and later Deputy Director Robert Gates, Director William Webster, and Deputy Director and later Acting Director Richard Kerr—must ultimately bear the responsibility for the lack of an adequate investigative response to the 1985 compromises. Whatever they may have personally understood the situation to be, they were in charge. It was their responsibility to find out what was being done to resolve the 1985 compromises. Based upon the information available to the Committee, they failed to do so.

Their failure is especially disheartening when one realizes that the information developed in August 1992, which finally focused the investigation on Ames—correlating his bank deposits in 1985 and 1986 with his meetings with Soviet officials—was available to investigators since 1986. Unfortunately, no one asked for it even when alerted to Ames' unexplained affluence in October 1989.

Although the 1985-86 compromises represented a unique situation for the CIA, the Ames case demonstrates the lack of a clear *modus operandi* for dealing with situations where intelligence sources are known to have been compromised.

Recommendation #7

The Director of Central Intelligence should establish procedures for dealing with intelligence compromises. At a minimum, these procedures should entail a systematic analysis of all employees with access to the relevant information and, if suspects are identified, provide an investigative methodology, to determine whether there is evidence of unexplained affluence, unreported travel, unreported contacts, or other indicators of possible espionage. This type of systematic analysis should begin when a known compromise occurs, not after CIA has eliminated the possibility of a technical penetration, or after CIA has narrowed the range of possible suspects to one or two employees. Analysis and investigation should be undertaken on the basis of access and opportunity, and should not be delayed waiting for evidence of culpability.

Recommendation #8

Pursuant to section 811 of the Intelligence Authorization Act for Fiscal Year 1995, the FBI should be notified immediately of any case where it is learned that an intelligence source has been compromised to a foreign government, regardless of whether the CIA believes at the time that there is a basis for an FBI counterintelligence or criminal investigation of a particular employee or employees. The CIA should also coordinate with the FBI subsequent investigative actions involving employees potentially involved in the case in order not to prejudice later criminal or counterintelligence activities of the FBI and in order to benefit from the investigative assistance and expertise of the FBI.

Recommendation #9

The Director of Central Intelligence should require that all employees assigned as counterintelligence investigators have appropriate training, experience, and supervision which ensures, at a minimum, such investigators will be familiar with, and know how to utilize, the investigative authorities available to the CIA and the FBI.

Recommendation #10

CIA management must ensure that adequate analytical and investigative resources are assigned to counterintelligence cases, and that other kinds of staff assistance (e.g., legal support, administrative support) are made available. In turn, those involved in these cases must ensure that their needs are communicated to their supervisors. The Inspector General of the CIA should periodically assess the counterintelligence cases of the CIA to ensure that adequate resources are being afforded to particular cases.

Recommendation #11

The status of significant counterintelligence investigations must be regularly briefed to senior Agency officials, including the Director of Central Intelligence. Such briefings should include an explanation of the resources and expertise being brought to bear upon a particular case.

The Failure to Expedite the Inquiry After 1991

The period after the CIA and FBI decided to join forces in June 1991—compared with the period between 1985 and 1991—was relatively intense and focused. For the first time, investigators conducted a systematic review of the CIA employees who had had access to the compromised information, and there was an intensive, productive effort to link Ames and other priority suspects to the compromises.

Yet even during this phase, the investigation took an inordinate amount of time and was plagued by past inefficiencies. The joint investigative unit still had only four people (two from each agency); and there was still a lone CIA investigator working with them. While members of the joint investigative unit did obtain support from the CIA Office of Security and the FBI Washington Metropolitan Field Office, they were still but a few people carrying an extraordinarily demanding workload.

In August 1991, the joint investigative unit developed a list of 29 CIA employees for priority scrutiny. Ames was at the top of the list.

Yet the first letters to go out to financial institutions requesting access to Ames' financial records did not go out until June 1992, almost 10 months later.

In August 1992, when investigators correlated the records of Ames' bank deposits with what was known about Ames' 1985 meetings at the Soviet Embassy, the joint investigative unit suspected they had their man. When they learned in October of Ames' Swiss bank accounts, their suspicions were confirmed.

But according to the Inspector General's report, this crucial information was not presented to FBI headquarters until January 1993. It was explained to the Committee that the joint investigative unit was looking at possible suspects in addition to Ames. But this still does not explain why significant information pertaining to Ames was not passed contemporaneously to the FBI, particularly given the presence of two FBI agents on the joint investigative unit.

On the basis of the work of the joint investigative unit—which culminated in the March 1993 SKYLIGHT/PLAYACTOR report—the FBI assembled an investigative team and asked the team members to acquaint themselves with the facts. The FBI began an intensive investigation of Ames shortly thereafter. The Committee was advised in the course of its investigation that FBI Headquarters had determined that the earlier information developed on Ames by the joint investigative unit did not meet the standards for an intensive FBI investigation. The Committee believes, however, that there was ample evidence by October 1992 to reasonably suggest that Ames was acting in 1985 (and thereafter) as an agent of the Soviet Union. The FBI's hesitation resulted in a six-month delay before the FBI began to apply the full array of its investigative capabilities against Ames. Once applied, they produced impressive results. Indeed, the FBI investigative team from the Washington Metropolitan Field Office, together with the CIA, did a superb job in bringing the investigation to a successful conclusion.

Recommendation #12

The Director of the FBI should ensure that adequate resources are applied to counterintelligence cases involving the CIA and other federal agencies, and that FBI headquarters is apprised immediately of significant case developments which could form the basis for the FBI's opening an intensive counterintelligence investigation.

Recommendation #13

The Attorney General and the Director of the FBI should review the FBI's guidelines for the conduct of counterintelligence investigations to determine whether clearer guidance is needed in determining whether a subject of a counterintelligence inquiry is acting as an agent of a foreign power.

Failure to Restrict the Assignments and Access of Suspects in Counterintelligence Cases

The Ames case reveals glaring weaknesses in the CIA's procedures for dealing with the career assignments of employees who are under suspicion for compromising intelligence operations. The CIA failed to restrict Ames' assignments and access even after information surfaced in 1989 which indicated Ames was a possible counterintelligence problem. . . .

In April 1991, while Ames was assigned to the CIC, the Office of Security carried out an updated background investigation of Ames. The results of this investigation were evaluated and shared with the investigator assigned to the special task force. Reflecting interviews with his co-workers in Rome and his Arlington, Virginia neighbors, the investigation produced information that Ames had frequent contacts in Rome with Soviet and East European officials not fully explained by his work requirements, frequently violated security regulations by leaving his safe open and doing classified work at home, and lived far beyond his CIA salary in both Rome and Arlington. (One of those interviewed went so far as to say that he would not be surprised if Ames were a spy.)

Inexplicably, the CIA security officer who reviewed the investigative report evaluated it as "raising no CIA concerns," and the task force investigator assigned to the case did not regard the report as providing any new information. Ames retained his security clearance and his job in the Counterintelligence Center, and no further action was taken to follow-up on the information developed in this report. Indeed, the special task force members viewed the investigative report, together with the favorable results of the April 1991 polygraph, as giving Ames "a clean bill of health."

In September 1991, despite having been "booted out" of the SE Division a year earlier, and despite the special task force inquiry then underway, Ames was allowed to return to the SE Division to conduct a special study of the KGB. While the study itself did not call for particularly sensitive access, Ames once again was given access to the personnel and records of the SE Division.

In December 1991, he was assigned to the Counternarcotics Center (CNC) where he remained until his arrest in 1994. This apparently was the first assignment made on the basis of the security concerns about Ames. But due to the sensitivity of the investigation into the 1985-86 compromises, CNC senior managers were not told of the investigation or the suspicions about Ames until the beginning of the FBI's intensive investigation in 1993. Even then, there was little or no effort made to evaluate and control the extent of Ames' access to classified information. Indeed, investigators later learned that Ames had computer access to a vast range of classified information that did not pertain to counternarcotics. Moreover, when a computer upgrade was installed in November 1993, it provided Ames with the capability to "download" vast quantities of information onto computer discs which he could take out of the building. Fortunately, Ames was arrested before he was able to pass these discs to his KGB handlers. But the fact that he was provided this capability at all at a time when his arrest was imminent is indicative of the CIA's lack of attention to this security problem.

Recommendation #14

The Director of Central Intelligence should establish procedures to inform current and prospective supervisors about employees under suspicion in counterintelligence cases. While the need to protect the secrecy of the investigation is essential, as well as the need to protect the employees themselves from unfair personnel actions, the assignment of employees under suspicion without frank consultations at the supervisory level increases the likelihood of serious compromises and leads to conflict between CIA elements.

Recommendation #15

The Director of Central Intelligence should issue procedures to require, in any case in which an employee is under suspicion for espionage or related activities, that a systematic evaluation be made of the employee's access to classified information, and that appropriate and timely actions be taken to limit such access. While care must obviously be taken to ensure that such actions do not tip off the employee that he or she is under suspicion, the failure to evaluate the access of an employee in these circumstances may eventually result in damage that might have been prevented.

Recommendation #16

The Director of Central Intelligence should establish more stringent criteria for CIA employees serving on promotion and assignment boards, which, among other things, prevent the appointment to such panels of employees with poor performance records or records of suitability problems.

Deficiencies in Security Procedures

The Ames case demonstrated numerous deficiencies in the CIA's use of the polygraph, its control over classified documents and materials, and its coordination of security and counterintelligence functions.

The Polygraph

Ames was able to pass polygraph examinations in 1986 and 1991 with relative ease. Although deeply involved in espionage activities, he was able to answer questions such as whether he worked for a foreign intelligence service, or had contacts with foreign nationals which he failed to report, without showing signs of deception.

The CIA Inspector General's report faults the 1986 examination, finding that the examiner was "too chummy" with Ames. When Ames showed a slight reaction to a question asking whether he had ever been "pitched," i.e., asked to work for a foreign intelligence service, the examiner appeared to readily accept his explanation that he was concerned about being "pitched" in his upcoming assignment in Rome.

The 1991 polygraph examination, according to the Inspector General's report, was deficient in that the examiners ... were not sufficiently familiar with the existing information on Ames' unexplained affluence, or with the information developed in the April 1991 background investigation of Ames. The examination was also deficient in that the investigator assigned to the special task force had not participated directly in the examination process, and there had been no prior planning in terms of how CIA would handle the situation if Ames suddenly made damaging admissions.

According to Ames' debriefings, he did not take drugs or use any particular technique to pass the polygraph examinations. Acting on the advice of the KGB, he tried only to be cooperative and stay as calm as he could. Since he was acquainted with how polygraph examinations were conducted, he also was able to manipulate the process to prevent a "problem" from arising.

If Ames' account is true, it seems to indicate problems beyond those cited by the Inspector General's report, i.e. that examiners should be better informed and prepared. Indeed, it suggests that the CIA's reliance on the results of polygraph examinations needs to be far more circumspect than in the past.

Recommendation #17

The Director of Central Intelligence should tighten polygraph procedures to make the polygraph more useful. Such procedures should include random examinations instead of exams at regular intervals, with little or no prior notice, and variations in the polygraph technique. These procedures should also ensure that polygraph examinations involving employees under suspicion are carefully planned and constructed, and that appropriate prior notification is made to the Federal Bureau of Investigation if such cases have potential criminal implications. In addition, the Director should review the policies applicable to the training, supervision, and performance appraisal of polygraph examiners to ensure that polygraph examinations are conducted in a professional manner and produce optimum results.

Recommendation #18

The Director of Central Intelligence should institute a fundamental reevaluation of the polygraph as a part of CIA's security program. As the Ames case demonstrates, the polygraph cannot be relied upon with certainty to detect deception. This necessarily puts far more reliance on other aspects of the security process, e.g., background investigations, supervisory reporting, psychological testing, financial reporting, etc. The DCI's review should also include a reevaluation of the use of inconclusive polygraph test results. Even where the polygraph does indicate deception, such information is often useless unless damaging admissions are also obtained from the subject. The Committee believes that if an employee with access to particularly sensitive information does not make such admissions but continues to show deception to relevant questions after adequate testing, there should be additional investigation of the issues in question to attempt to resolve them. Should such investigation fail to do so, the CIA should have the latitude, without prejudice to the employee, to reassign him or her to less sensitive duties.

Control of Classified Documents and Materials

The Ames case also demonstrated gaps in the control of sensitive classified information. Ames was able—without detection—to walk out of CIA headquarters and the U.S. Embassy in Rome with bags and envelopes stuffed with classified documents and materials. Many of the classified documents he passed to his KGB handlers were copies of documents that were not under any system of accountability. Ames did not even have to make copies of them. In his last job in the Counternarcotics Center at the CIA, Ames was able to "download" a variety of classified documents onto computer discs and then simply remove them to his home. When he attended a conference in Turkey in 1993, he brought a lap-top computer to do work in his hotel room. This apparently raised no security concern among those familiar with the incident. He was also able to visit offices he had no reason to be in, and gain access to information he had no business seeing.

In the late 1970s, the CIA instituted a policy calling for random and unannounced spot-checks of personnel leaving Agency compounds. But the policy was discontinued soon thereafter due to the inconvenience caused to those subject to such searches.

Ames recounted later that his KGB handlers were amazed at his ability to gain access to sensitive operations and take large bundles of classified information out of CIA offices without arousing suspicion, a sad commentary on the laxness of security at the CIA.

Recommendation #19

The Director of Central Intelligence should reinstate the policy making persons leaving CIA facilities subject to random searches of their person and possessions, and require that such searches be conducted unannounced and periodically at selected locations. Such searches should be conducted frequently enough to serve as a deterrent without unduly hampering the operation of the facilities involved.

Recommendation #20

The Director of Central Intelligence should institute computer security measures to prevent employees from being able to "download" classified information onto computer diskettes and removing them from CIA facilities. In addition, existing policies for the introduction, accountability, dissemination, removal, and destruction of all forms of electronic media should be reevaluated. The ability of the CIA's security managers to "audit" specific computer-related functions in order to detect and monitor the actions of suspected offenders should be upgraded.

Recommendation #21

The Director of Central Intelligence should institute a policy requiring employees to report to their supervisor any instance in which a CIA employee attempts to obtain classified information which the CIA employee has no apparent reason to know. In turn, supervisors should be required to report to the CIA Counterintelligence Center any such case where a plausible explanation for such a request cannot be ascertained by the supervisor.

Recommendation #22

The Director of Central Intelligence should institute new policies to improve the control of classified documents and materials within the CIA. In particular, the Directorate of Operations should undertake an immediate and comprehensive review of its practices and procedures for compartmenting information relating to clandestine operations to ensure that only those officers who absolutely need access can obtain such information. Further, the Directorate should establish and maintain a detailed, automated record of the access granted to each of its employees.

Coordination of Security and Counterintelligence

The Ames case demonstrated a serious division between security and counterintelligence activities in the CIA. Even though an investigator from the Office of Security (OS) participated in the investigation of the 1985-86 compromises under the auspices of the Counterintelligence Center (CIC), he failed to coordinate properly with OS with respect to Ames' 1991 polygraph examination. OS had initiated a background investigation of Ames in March 1991, but went ahead with the polygraph in April without the benefit of the background investigation. As it turned out, the background investigation provided significant information about Ames that was largely ignored by the investigator assigned to the CIC in light of Ames' passing the polygraph examination.

Citing senior security officials, the Inspector General's report noted there had always been a "fault line" in communications between the CIC and its predecessors, and the OS. The CIC had not always shared information regarding its counterintelligence investigations and had failed to make use of OS's investigative expertise. Indeed, the search to find the cause of the 1985 compromises might have moved more quickly from analysis to investigation if there had been better coordination between security and counterintelligence.

The Inspector General's report also found "a gradual degradation" of the resources and authority given the security function since 1985, concluding that "this degradation has adversely affected the Agency's ability to prevent and deter activities such as those engaged in by Ames. . . ." The Committee shares the view that this decline has been too great and too precipitous. The Committee had recommended an increase in personnel security funding for the CIA and other agencies for Fiscal Year 1995, but was unable to sustain its initiative due to the lack of interest shown by the agencies involved. . . .

Recommendation #23

The Director of Central Intelligence should reexamine the decision to combine the Office of Security with the other elements of the CIA's new personnel center, and should ensure sufficient funding is provided to the personnel security function in Fiscal Year 1995 and in future years. The Director should also clarify the relationship between security and counterintelligence, specifying their respective functions and providing for effective coordination and cooperation between them.

Failure to Advise the Oversight Committees

The CIA failed to notify the congressional oversight committees in any meaningful way of the compromises of 1985-1986, as required by applicable law.

Indeed, in the hearings held annually on counterintelligence matters and in numerous staff briefings on the subject from 1985 until 1994, the massive compromises of 1985-86 were never once mentioned by representatives of the CIA or the FBI.

Based upon the recollections of individuals, there were two occasions when the 1985-86 compromises were alluded to in discussions with Members or staff of the Senate Select Committee on Intelligence (SSCI). The first mention came during a staff visit to Moscow in December 1988. The second occurred in 1992 during a visit to Moscow by two Members of the Committee. But on each occasion, the information provided was fragmentary and anecdotal and did not specifically address what was being done by the CIA about the problem. Informal staff efforts to follow-up on each of these conversations were put off by the CIA.

The Committee strongly believes that both the CIA and the FBI had an obligation to advise the oversight committees at the time of the 1985-86 compromises. Section 502 of the National Security Act of 1947 specifically requires intelligence agencies to report to the oversight committees "any significant intelligence failure." The compromises of 1985-86 resulted in a virtual collapse of CIA's Soviet operations at the height of the Cold War. According to the SE Division officer's memorandum of November 1986, the evidence was at that point "overwhelming" and clearly indicated a problem of disastrous proportions. The oversight committees were responsible for funding the activities of the Directorate of Operations. They should have been formally notified pursuant to section 502 of the National Security Act of 1947.

The Need for Continued Follow-up

Many of the problems identified by the Committee are deep-seated and pervasive and will not be solved easily or quickly. Yet these problems are too important and too integral to the functioning of an agency with important national security responsibilities not to merit continuing and intensive scrutiny by both CIA managers and the congressional oversight committees.

While the Committee intends to make the CIA's response to this report an area of "special oversight interest" in the years ahead, the Committee also directs the Inspector General of the CIA to provide the Committee, through the Director of Central Intelligence, with a report no later than September 1, 1995, and annually thereafter, on the CIA's progress in responding to the recommendations contained in this report and to the continuing counterintelligence and security challenges that the CIA faces.

REAGAN LETTER ANNOUNCING HE HAS ALZHEIMER'S DISEASE
November 5, 1994

In a handwritten letter addressed to "my fellow Americans," former president Ronald Reagan announced November 5 that at age eighty-three he was suffering the early stages of Alzheimer's disease, a brain disease for which there is no cure. Reagan said that by writing the letter, he hoped to increase public awareness about the devastating illness.

A statement by five of his doctors that accompanied Reagan's letter said his condition was discovered during an annual medical examination. The doctors said that Reagan's health was "otherwise good," although they expected "that as the years go on, it will begin to deteriorate."

The symptoms of Alzheimer's disease, a progressive, irreversible neurological disorder, can include memory loss, disorientation, coordination problems, restlessness, incontinence, and sharp personality changes. People suffering from advanced stages of the disease often do not recognize their own family members and can even attack them.

In his letter, Reagan acknowledged that Alzheimer's disease is rough on the patient's family. "Unfortunately, as Alzheimer's Disease progresses, the family often bears a heavy burden," Reagan wrote. He also expressed the wish that there was some way he could spare his wife, Nancy, "from this painful experience."

Alzheimer's is difficult to diagnose because the first symptom is usually a subtle loss of short-term memory. Such memory loss seems to occur normally as people age, so it is difficult for doctors to determine whether it is normal or whether it signals the beginning of Alzheimer's. In examining a patient who they suspect may have the disease, neurologists and psychiatrists review the patient's medical history and perform neurological and blood tests, gradually eliminating other possible causes of the problem. Doctors are able to diagnose the disease accurately in 80 to 90 percent of cases before death, but the only way to confirm the diagnosis is to remove brain tissue. That is usually only done during an autopsy.

Even an early diagnosis is not very useful, however, because there is no effective treatment for the disease. The primary drug used in treating Alzheimer's patients, tacrine, has little effect.

Impact of Alzheimer's Is Growing

It is believed that about 4 million Americans have Alzheimer's, although firm numbers are not available. The disease is becoming a major public health problem because people are living longer. Of those aged sixty-five, only about 5 percent have Alzheimer's; of those aged eighty-five, about one-third suffer from Alzheimer's.

The progression of Alzheimer's varies greatly from person to person. Some people with the disease deteriorate rapidly and die within a year, while others in whom the disease progresses more slowly can live for a decade or even longer and sometimes die from something other than Alzheimer's. Experts said the sketchy details released by Reagan's doctors about his condition made it impossible to determine how far the disease had progressed in his case.

Reagan was elected president in 1980 when he was nearly seventy years old, making him the oldest elected president. He always showed remarkable vigor in public and was often shown chopping wood and riding horses at his ranch. He overcame a series of medical problems, including a severe wounding in a 1981 assassination attempt, colon cancer, skin cancer, and an operation to remove a pool of blood from his brain after a horse threw him.

Experts said it was unlikely that Reagan suffered from Alzheimer's before he left office in January 1989. They noted that as president he received thorough examinations at least annually that included checks for any mental deterioration.

Close family friends said that in the months before Reagan's announcement he had appeared to be in declining health. They also noted that he had been conspicuously absent from recent events, including a conference at the Reagan Library in California the month before his announcement.

In his letter, Reagan said he still felt fine and planned to "live the remainder of the years God gives me on this earth doing the things I have always done." Reagan said he planned to spend time with his family, enjoy the outdoors, and stay in touch with his friends and supporters.

Characteristically for the man dubbed the "great communicator," Reagan ended his letter on an upbeat note. "I now begin the journey that will lead me into the sunset of my life," he wrote. "I know that for America there will always be a bright dawn ahead."

New Diagnostic Test Reported

Less than a week after Reagan's announcement, researchers at Harvard Medical School reported that a new, simple test using eye drops was successful in diagnosing Alzheimer's. Writing in the November 11 issue of the journal Science, *the researchers said the test involves measuring the speed at which pupils dilate when special eye drops are added.*

499

With no cure or even good treatment for Alzheimer's yet available, some questioned the usefulness of the new test. Supporters of the test said that people who tested negative would be relieved that their symptoms were not caused by Alzheimer's and that those who tested positive would have time to get their affairs in order before their inevitable deterioration began. Detractors said a positive test could devastate people. They also noted that the test is not infallible and that those incorrectly diagnosed as having Alzheimer's could suffer terrible anguish.

Following is the text of the letter released November 5, 1994, in which former president Ronald Reagan announced he had been diagnosed as being in the early stages of Alzheimer's disease:

My Fellow Americans,

I have recently been told that I am one of the millions of Americans who will be afflicted with Alzheimer's Disease.

Upon learning this news, Nancy and I had to decide whether as private citizens we would keep this a private matter or whether we would make this news known in a public way.

In the past Nancy suffered from breast cancer and I had my cancer surgeries. We found through our open disclosure we were able to raise public awareness. We were happy that as a result many more people underwent testing.

They were treated in early stages and able to return to normal, healthy lives.

So now, we feel it is important to share it with you. In opening our hearts, we hope this might promote greater awareness of this condition. Perhaps it will encourage a clearer understanding of the individuals and families who are affected by it.

At the moment I feel just fine. I intend to live the remainder of the years God gives me on this earth doing the things I have always done. I will continue to share life's journey with my beloved Nancy and my family. I plan to enjoy the great outdoors and stay in touch with my friends and supporters.

Unfortunately, as Alzheimer's Disease progresses, the family often bears a heavy burden. I only wish there was some way I could spare Nancy from this painful experience. When the time comes I am confident that with your help she will face it with faith and courage.

In closing let me thank you, the American people, for giving me the great honor of allowing me to serve as your President. When the Lord calls me home, whenever that may be, I will leave with the greatest love for this country of ours and eternal optimism for its future.

I now begin the journey that will lead me into the sunset of my life. I know that for America there will always be a bright dawn ahead.

Thank you, my friends. May God always bless you.

Sincerely,
Ronald Reagan

OREGON BALLOT MEASURE ON PHYSICIAN-ASSISTED SUICIDE
November 8, 1994

By a narrow margin of 52 percent to 48 percent, Oregon voters approved a measure on the November 8 ballot that allows doctors to prescribe lethal drugs for terminally ill patients who request them. The Oregon law, which has strict rules doctors must follow before writing such prescriptions, leaves the final step of actually taking the drugs up to the patient. Approval of the "Death with Dignity Act" made Oregon the only state in the nation that allows doctors to help patients commit suicide.

Under the Oregon law, doctors can only write lethal prescriptions for patients who have six months or less to live, and their diagnosis must be confirmed by a second doctor. Both doctors must ensure that the patient has rejected all other alternatives. The law also requires that the patient request the prescription three times—once in writing—before the doctor can write it.

Supporters of the measure said it would allow people who were in great pain to end their suffering and die with dignity. Opponents, which included the Catholic Church, the American Medical Association (AMA), and both Oregon gubernatorial candidates, argued that the measure was subject to abuse and would start Oregon down a "slippery slope" that would eventually lead to mercy killing and extermination of unwanted people. The Vatican called approval of the initiative "a day of mourning for all humanity."

AMA Opposes Physician-Assisted Suicide

The medical community was sharply split about the propriety of physician-assisted suicide. In 1992, the AMA's Council on Ethical and Judicial Affairs issued a report reaffirming its opposition to the practice. "In certain carefully defined circumstances, it would be humane to recognize that death is certain and suffering is great," the council said. "However, the societal risks of involving physicians in medical interventions to cause patients' deaths is too great in this culture to condone euthanasia or physician-assisted suicide at this time."

A survey of Wisconsin physicians published in the March 14, 1994, issue of the Archives of Internal Medicine *found that 28 percent of doctors would be willing to perform euthanasia if it were legalized, 61 percent were not, and 11 percent were unsure. The survey of 740 physicians also found that 357 had been asked to perform euthanasia by patients and that 16 had actually done so despite laws barring the practice.*

The American public seemed increasingly willing to support physician-assisted suicide. In 1982, only 53 percent of people responding to a Louis Harris poll said doctors should be allowed to help a dying patient end his or her life. By November 1993, that percentage had grown to 73 percent.

In 1991 and 1992 voters in Washington and California defeated ballot measures that would have legalized physician-assisted suicide. The two measures differed from the 1994 Oregon initiative in that they would have allowed doctors to administer lethal drugs, rather than leaving the final act to patients as did the Oregon initiative.

Kevorkian Acquitted

In 1994, the issue of physician-assisted suicide attracted growing public attention because of the ongoing legal troubles of Dr. Jack Kevorkian, a sixty-six-year-old retired pathologist in Michigan who between June 1990 and November 1993 had helped twenty people commit suicide. On May 2, a Michigan jury found Kevorkian not guilty of violating Michigan's law banning assisted suicide. In the case, Kevorkian had helped a thirty-year-old man who suffered from Lou Gehrig's disease, a degenerative nerve disease, to end his life. Kevorkian had placed a mask over the man's face and connected it to a tank of carbon monoxide. The patient then yanked a string that made the gas flow and died within twenty minutes.

Two days after Kevorkian's acquittal, U.S. District Judge Barbara Rothstein of Seattle struck down a 140-year-old Washington State law that banned assisted suicide. Her decision, which tied the right to assisted suicide to the right to abortion, said Washington's law violated the Fourteenth Amendment because it allowed the state to infringe upon individual liberty. "There is no more profoundly personal decision, nor one which is closer to the heart of personal liberty, than the choice which a terminally ill person makes to end his or her suffering and hasten an inevitable death," the judge wrote. Her ruling, which was a watershed decision for the right-to-die movement, was appealed.

On November 26, only hours after Michigan's law banning assisted suicide expired, Kevorkian helped a seventy-two-year-old woman commit suicide using the carbon monoxide method. The woman suffered from severe rheumatoid arthritis, advanced osteoporosis, and other health problems that had led to amputation of both legs and the removal of one eye. Kevorkian attacked the Oregon ballot measure during interviews with reporters following the suicide. He said it was impossible to determine how long a person might live and that the overriding issue should be the patient's quality of life.

Two weeks later Kevorkian suffered another legal setback when the Michigan Supreme Court overruled lower courts and upheld the state's ban on assisted suicide. The ruling came in four combined cases, three of them involving charges against Kevorkian. His lawyer said he would appeal the decision to the U.S. Supreme Court, and the doctor vowed to keep fighting for what he termed "a fundamental human right—the right not to suffer—that cannot be taken away by any law."

As 1994 ended, based on the court's ruling Michigan prosecutors were studying whether to file criminal charges against Kevorkian in numerous cases.

Following is the text of the Oregon Death with Dignity Act, along with explanatory information provided to voters by the State of Oregon, as approved November 8, 1994:

Ballot Title 16 Allows Terminally Ill Adults to Obtain Prescription for Lethal Drugs

Question: Shall law allow terminally ill adult patients voluntary informed choice to obtain physician's prescription for drugs to end life?

Summary: Adopts law. Allows terminally ill adult Oregon residents voluntary informed choice to obtain physician's prescription for drugs to end life. Removes criminal penalties for qualifying physician-assisted suicide. Applies when physicians predict patient's death within 6 months. Requires:

15-day waiting period;
2 oral, 1 written request;
second physician's opinion;
counseling if either physician believes patient has mental disorder, impaired judgment from depression.

Person has choice whether to notify next of kin. Health care providers immune from civil, criminal liability for good faith compliance.

Estimate of Financial Impact: No financial effect on state or local government expenditures or revenues.

The Oregon Death with Dignity Act

Section 1: General Provisions

1.01 Definitions

The following words and phrases, whenever used in this Act, shall have the following meanings:

(1) "Adult" means an individual who is 18 years of age or older.

(2) "Attending physician" means the physician who has primary responsibility for the care of the patient and treatment of the patient's terminal disease.

(3) "Consulting physician" means a physician who is qualified by specialty or experience to make a professional diagnosis and prognosis regarding the patient's disease.

(4) "Counseling" means a consultation between a state licensed psychiatrist or psychologist and a patient for the purpose of determining whether the patient is suffering from a psychiatric or psychological disorder, or depression causing impaired judgment.

(5) "Health care provider" means a person licensed, certified, or otherwise authorized or permitted by the law of this State to administer health care in the ordinary course of business or practice of a profession, and includes a health care facility.

(6) "Incapable" means that in the opinion of a court or in the opinion of the patient's attending physician or consulting physician, a patient lacks the ability to make and communicate health care decisions to health care providers, including communication through persons familiar with the patient's manner of communicating if those persons are available. Capable means not incapable.

(7) "Informed decision" means a decision by a qualified patient, to request and obtain a prescription to end his or her life in a humane and dignified manner, that is based on an appreciation of the relevant facts and after being fully informed by the attending physician of:
(a) his or her medical diagnosis;
(b) his or her prognosis;
(c) the potential risks associated with taking the medication to be prescribed;
(d) the probable result of taking the medication to be prescribed;
(e) the feasible alternatives, including, but not limited to, comfort care, hospice care and pain control.

(8) "Medically confirmed" means the medical opinion of the attending physician has been confirmed by a consulting physician who has examined the patient and the patient's relevant medical records.

(9) "Patient" means a person who is under the care of a physician.

(10) "Physician" means a doctor of medicine or osteopathy licensed to practice medicine by the Board of Medical Examiners for the State of Oregon.

(11) "Qualified patient" means a capable adult who is a resident of Oregon and has satisfied the requirements of this Act in order to obtain a prescription for medication to end his or her life in a humane and dignified manner.

(12) "Terminal disease" means an incurable and irreversible disease that has been medically confirmed and will, within reasonable medical judgment, produce death within six (6) months.

Section 2: Written Request for Medication to
End One's Life in a Humane and Dignified Manner

2.01 Who May Initiate a Written Request for Medication

An adult who is capable, is a resident of Oregon, and has been determined by the attending physician and consulting physician to be suffering from a terminal disease, and who has voluntarily expressed his or her wish to die, may make a written request for medication for the purpose of ending his or her life in a humane and dignified manner in accordance with this Act.

2.02 Form of the Written Request

(1) A valid request for medication under this Act shall be in substantially the form described in Section 6 of this Act, signed and dated by the patient and witnessed by at least two individuals who, in the presence of the patient, attest that to the best of their knowledge and belief the patient is capable, acting voluntarily, and is not being coerced to sign the request.

(2) One of the witnesses shall be a person who is not:
   (a) A relative of the patient by blood, marriage or adoption;
   (b) A person who at the time the request is signed would be entitled to any portion of the estate of the qualified patient upon death under any will or by operation of law; or
   (c) An owner, operator or employee of a health care facility where the qualified patient is receiving medical treatment or is a resident.

(3) The patient's attending physician at the time the request is signed shall not be a witness.

(4) If the patient is a patient in a long term care facility at the time the written request is made, one of the witnesses shall be an individual designated by the facility and having the qualifications specified by the Department of Human Resources by rule.

Section 3: Safeguards

3.01 Attending Physician Responsibilities

The attending physician shall:

(1) Make the initial determination of whether a patient has a terminal disease, is capable, and has made the request voluntarily;

(2) Inform the patient of:
   (a) his or her medical diagnosis;
   (b) his or her prognosis;
   (c) the potential risks associated with taking the medication to be prescribed;
   (d) the probable result of taking the medication to be prescribed;
   (e) the feasible alternatives, including, but not limited to, comfort care, hospice care and pain control.

(3) Refer the patient to a consulting physician for medical confirmation of the diagnosis, and for a determination that the patient is capable and acting voluntarily;

(4) Refer the patient for counseling if appropriate pursuant to Section 3.03;

(5) Request that the patient notify next of kin;

(6) Inform the patient that he or she has an opportunity to rescind the request at any time and in any manner, and offer the patient an opportunity to rescind at the end of the 15 day waiting period pursuant to Section 3.06;

(7) Verify, immediately prior to writing the prescription for medication under this Act, that the patient is making an informed decision;

(8) Fulfill the medical record documentation requirements of Section 3.09;

(9) Ensure that all appropriate steps are carried out in accordance with this Act prior to writing a prescription for medication to enable a qualified patient to end his or her life in a humane and dignified manner.

3.02 Consulting Physician Confirmation

Before a patient is qualified under this Act, a consulting physician shall examine the patient and his or her relevant medical records and confirm, in writing, the attending physician's diagnosis that the patient is suffering from a terminal disease, and verify that the patient is capable, is acting voluntarily and has made an informed decision.

3.03 Counseling Referral

If in the opinion of the attending physician or the consulting physician a patient may be suffering from a psychiatric or psychological disorder, or depression causing impaired judgment, either physician shall refer the patient for counseling. No medication to end a patient's life in a humane and dignified manner shall be prescribed until the person performing the counseling determines that the patient is not suffering from a psychiatric or psychological disorder, or depression causing impaired judgment.

3.04 Informed Decision

No person shall receive a prescription for medication to end his or her life in a humane and dignified manner unless he or she has made an informed decision as defined in Section 1.01(7). Immediately prior to writing a prescription for medication under this Act, the attending physician shall verify that the patient is making an informed decision.

3.05 Family Notification

The attending physician shall ask the patient to notify next of kin of his or her request for medication pursuant to this Act. A patient who declines or is unable to notify next of kin shall not have his or her request denied for that reason.

3.06 Written and Oral Requests

In order to receive a prescription for medication to end his or her life in a humane and dignified manner, a qualified patient shall have made an oral request and a written request, and reiterate the oral request to his or her attending physician no less than fifteen (15) days after making the initial oral request. At the time the qualified patient makes his or her second oral request, the attending physician shall offer the patient an opportunity to rescind the request.

3.07 Right to Rescind Request

A patient may rescind his or her request at any time and in any manner without regard to his or her mental state. No prescription for medication under this Act may be written without the attending physician offering the qualified patient an opportunity to rescind the request.

3.08 Waiting Periods

No less than fifteen (15) days shall elapse between the patient's initial oral request and the writing of a prescription under this Act. No less than 48 hours shall elapse between the patient's written request and the writing of a prescription under this Act.

3.09 Medical Record Documentation Requirements

The following shall be documented or filed in the patient's medical record:

(1) All oral requests by a patient for medication to end his or her life in a humane and dignified manner;
(2) All written requests by a patient for medication to end his or her life in a humane and dignified manner;
(3) The attending physician's diagnosis and prognosis, determination that the patient is capable, acting voluntarily and has made an informed decision;
(4) The consulting physician's diagnosis and prognosis, and verification that the patient is capable, acting voluntarily and has made an informed decision;
(5) A report of the outcome and determinations made during counseling, if performed;
(6) The attending physician's offer to the patient to rescind his or her request at the time of the patient's second oral request pursuant to Section 3.06; and
(7) A note by the attending physician indicating that all requirements under this Act have been met and indicating the steps taken to carry out the request, including a notation of the medication prescribed.

3.10 Residency Requirement

Only requests made by Oregon residents, under this Act, shall be granted.

3.11 Reporting Requirements

(1) The Health Division shall annually review a sample of records maintained pursuant to this Act.

(2) The Health Division shall make rules to facilitate the collection of information regarding compliance with this Act. The information collected shall not be a public record and may not be made available for inspection by the public.

(3) The Health Division shall generate and make available to the public an annual statistical report of information collected under Section 3.11(2) of this Act.

3.12 Effect on Construction of Wills, Contracts and Statutes

(1) No provision in a contract, will or other agreement, whether written or oral, to the extent the provision would affect whether a person may make or rescind a request for medication to end his or her life in a humane and dignified manner, shall be valid.

(2) No obligation owing under any currently existing contract shall be conditioned or affected by the making or rescinding of a request, by a person, for medication to end his or her life in a humane and dignified manner.

3.13 Insurance or Annuity Policies

The sale, procurement, or issuance of any life, health, or accident insurance or annuity policy or the rate charged for any policy shall not be conditioned upon or affected by the making or rescinding of a request, by a person, for medication to end his or her life in a humane and dignified manner. Neither shall a qualified patient's act of ingesting medication to end his or her life in a humane and dignified manner have an effect upon a life, health, or accident insurance or annuity policy.

3.14 Construction of Act

Nothing in this Act shall be construed to authorize a physician or any other person to end a patient's life by lethal injection, mercy killing or active euthanasia. Actions taken in accordance with this Act shall not, for any purpose, constitute suicide, assisted suicide, mercy killing or homicide, under the law.

Section 4: Immunities and Liabilities

4.01 Immunities

Except as provided in Section 4.02:

(1) No person shall be subject to civil or criminal liability or professional disciplinary action for participating in good faith compliance with this Act. This includes being present when a qualified patient takes the prescribed medication to end his or her life in a humane and dignified manner.

(2) No professional organization or association, or health care provider, may subject a person to censure, discipline, suspension, loss of license, loss of privileges, loss of membership or other penalty for participating or refusing to participate in good faith compliance with this Act.

(3) No request by a patient for or provision by an attending physician of medication in good faith compliance with the provisions of this Act shall constitute neglect for any purpose of law or provide the sole basis for the appointment of a guardian or conservator.

(4) No health care provider shall be under any duty, whether by contract, by statute or by any other legal requirement to participate in the provision to a qualified patient of medication to end his or her life in a humane and dignified manner. If a health care provider is unable or unwilling to carry out a patient's request under this Act, and the patient transfers his or her care to a new health care provider, the prior health care provider shall transfer, upon request, a copy of the patient's relevant medical records to the new health care provider.

4.02 Liabilities

(1) A person who without authorization of the patient willfully alters or forges a request for medication or conceals or destroys a rescission of that request with the intent or effect of causing the patient's death shall be guilty of a Class A felony.

(2) A person who coerces or exerts undue influence on a patient to request medication for the purpose of ending the patient's life, or to destroy a rescission of such a request, shall be guilty of a Class A felony.

(3) Nothing in this Act limits further liability for civil damages resulting from other negligent conduct or intentional misconduct by any person.

(4) The penalties in this Act do not preclude criminal penalties applicable under other law for conduct which is inconsistent with the provisions of this Act.

Section 5: Severability

5.01 Severability

Any section of this Act being held invalid as to any person or circumstance shall not affect the application of any other section of this Act which can be given full effect without the invalid section or application.

Section 6: Form of the Request

6.01 Form of the Request

A request for a medication as authorized by this act shall be in substantially the following form:

Request for Medication to End My Life in a Humane and Dignified Manner

I, _____, am an adult of sound mind. I am suffering from _____, which my attending physician has determined is a terminal disease and which has been medically confirmed by a consulting physician. I have been fully informed of my diagnosis, prognosis, the nature of medication to be prescribed and potential associated risks, the expected result, and the feasible alternatives, including comfort care, hospice care and pain control. I request that my attending physician prescribe medication that will end my life in a humane and dignified manner.

Initial One:

_____ I have informed my family of my decision and taken their opinions into consideration

_____ I have decided not to inform my family of my decision.

_____ I have no family to inform of my decision.

I understand that I have the right to rescind this request at any time.

I understand the full import of this request and I expect to die when I take the medication to be prescribed.

I make this request voluntarily and without reservation, and I accept full moral responsibility for my actions.

Signed: _____

Dated: _____

Declaration of Witnesses

We declare that the person signing this request:

(a) Is personally known to us or has provided proof of identity;
(b) Signed this request in our presence;
(c) Appears to be of sound mind and not under duress, fraud or undue influence;
(d) Is not a patient for whom either of us is attending physician.

_____ Witness 1/Date

_____ Witness 2/Date

Note: One witness shall not be a relative (by blood, marriage or adoption) of the person signing this request, shall not be entitled to any portion of the person's estate upon death and shall not own, operate or be employed at a health care facility where the person is a patient or resident. If the patient is an inpatient at a health care facility, one of the witnesses shall be an individual designated by the facility.

Explanatory Statement

This measure would allow an informed and capable adult resident of Oregon, who is terminally ill and within six months of death, to voluntarily request a prescription for medication to take his or her life. The measure allows a physician to prescribe a lethal dose of medication when conditions of the measure are met. The physician and others may be present if the medication is taken.

The process begins when the patient makes the request of his or her physician, who shall:

- Determine if the patient is terminally ill, is capable of making health care decisions, and has made the request voluntarily.
- Inform the patient of his or her diagnosis and prognosis; the risks and results of taking the medication; and alternatives, including comfort care, hospice care, and pain control.
- Ask that the patient notify next of kin, but not deny the request if the patient declines or is unable to notify next of kin.
- Inform the patient that he or she has an opportunity to rescind the request at any time, in any manner.
- Refer the patient for counseling, if appropriate.
- Refer the patient to a consulting physician.

A consulting physician, who is qualified by specialty or experience, must confirm the diagnosis and determine that the patient is capable and acting voluntarily.

If either physician believes that the patient might be suffering from a psychiatric or psychological disorder, or from depression causing impaired judgment, the physician must refer the patient to a licensed psychiatrist or psychologist for counseling. The psychiatrist or psychologist must determine that the patient does not suffer from such a disorder before medication may be prescribed.

The measure requires two oral and one written requests. The written request requires two witnesses attesting that the patient is acting voluntarily. At least one witness must not be a relative or heir of the patient.

At least fifteen days must pass from the time of the initial oral request and 48 hours must pass from the time of the written request before the prescription may be written.

Before writing the prescription, the attending physician must again verify the patient is making a voluntary and informed request, and offer the patient the opportunity to rescind the request.

Additional provisions of the measure are:

- Participating physicians must be licensed in Oregon.
- The physician must document in the patient's medical record that all requirements have been met. The State Health Division must review samples of those records and make statistical reports available to the public.

- Those who comply with the requirements of the measure are protected from prosecution and professional discipline.
- Any physician or health care provider may decline to participate.

This measure does not authorize lethal injection, mercy killing or active euthanasia. Actions taken in accordance with this measure shall not constitute suicide, assisted suicide, mercy killing or homicide, under the law.

Anyone coercing or exerting undue influence on a patient to request medication, or altering or forging a request for medication, is guilty of a Class A felony.

CLINTON, GINGRICH ON ELECTION RESULTS
November 9 and 11, 1994

In an election that Newsweek *called "one of the most profound electoral routs in American history," on November 8 Republicans won control of Congress for the first time in forty years. The election also swelled Republican ranks in statehouses and in lesser offices across the country. It was the largest Republican victory since 1946. Not a single Republican incumbent was defeated in the Senate, House, or state governor races.*

In a press conference the day after the election, President Bill Clinton— whom the New York Times *described as appearing "wobbly and shell-shocked"—accepted some of the blame for the defeat. "With the Democrats in control of both the White House and the Congress, we were held accountable yesterday," Clinton said. "And I accept my share of the responsibility in the result of the election." The public still did not like what it saw in Washington, the president said, although he added that many people also did not realize all the positive things that had been accomplished.*

Two days later, a buoyant Rep. Newt Gingrich (R-Ga.), the incoming Speaker of the House and a key architect of the Republican victory, said in a speech to a business group that "what is ultimately at stake in our current environment is the future of American civilization." In his first speech since the election, Gingrich vowed not to compromise with the White House. "I am prepared to cooperate with the Clinton administration," he said. "I am not prepared to compromise. The two words are very different."

Voters Increasingly Alienated

While some observers portrayed the election results as a repudiation of Clinton, exit polls did not bear them out. Voters reported they were as unhappy with Democratic and Republican members of Congress as they were with Clinton.

The sweeping Republican victory seemed to be the result of an increasing alienation with the political system. Shortly before the election, a New York

Times/CBS News poll found that voters felt more cynical than at any time since 1979. "Voters are profoundly alienated from their elected representatives and from the political process and confess to a deepening powerlessness and pessimism over the future of the nation," said a Times *story about the poll. Three of every four people disapproved of the job Congress was doing.*

Much of the Republican support came from the most alienated voters, according to exit polls. One in three voters told pollsters the government could not solve the nation's problems, and these people voted for Republicans by a 3-to-1 margin. Another major factor in the Republican victory was that many voters pegged Democrats as the party of big government and higher taxes, a party whose solution for every problem was to create a new, expensive government program. Whether or not that image was true, voters clearly wanted a smaller government.

The much-ballyhooed "Contract with America," in which Republican House candidates laid out their legislative agenda if they won power, apparently had little impact on the election. Exit polls found that most voters had not heard of the contract. In September, more than three hundred Republican House candidates had signed the document, in which they promised within one hundred days of assuming power to vote on bills to reform congressional procedures, require a balanced federal budget, increase funding for prison construction, cut off welfare benefits to persons who had received them for two years, boost national defense, and set term limits for members of Congress, among other measures. (House Republican 'Contract with America,' p. 374)

The Republican victory toppled many of the biggest stars in the Democratic party. In Washington state, Steve Stockman defeated House Speaker Tom Foley, marking the first time in 134 years that a House Speaker had been defeated in a reelection bid. In New York, George Pataki beat Gov. Mario Cuomo, who had served for twelve years. In Texas, George W. Bush, the son of the former president, defeated Gov. Ann Richards. In Chicago, Michael Flanagan, an attorney who had never run for public office, defeated Rep. Dan Rostenkowski, the powerful chairman of the House Ways and Means Committee who had been indicted on seventeen counts that alleged he had embezzled more than $500,000 from his expense accounts. (Indictment of Rep. Dan Rostenkowski, p. 281)

Did the Election Represent a Political Shift?

One overriding question arose from the election results: Did they represent a long-term switch to the Republican party, or did they simply represent the whim of a volatile electorate that might turn on Republicans in two years? While no one knew the answer, pollsters on both sides of the political spectrum warned Republicans not to read too much into the results. They pointed out that in 1992 voters turned against many Republicans and in 1994 turned against many Democrats. This suggested that voters might keep pursuing change until they got a government they liked.

Some observers also pointed to the lessons of history. In 1946, the last time Republicans gained control of Congress in a midterm election, Democrat Harry Truman was an unpopular president who helped cost the Democrats fifty-six seats in the House. However, over the next two years Republicans squandered their new-found power, and Truman blasted a "do-nothing" Congress. In the 1948 election, Democrats gained seventy-five seats in Congress—more than making up for their losses just two years earlier.

Whether or not this was a long-term shift in the American political landscape, the election results led to other questions:

- *Could Republicans, who in the 103rd Congress had spent much of their time obstructing Democratic initiatives, carry forward a program of their own?*
- *Could Republicans heal the deep differences in the party between religious conservatives and more moderate members so they could present a unified agenda?*
- *Faced with a hostile Congress, would Clinton be able to direct policy or would he be reduced to following the lead of Congress?*
- *Would Clinton, who favored an activist government, pull back because he had fewer supporters in Congress or would he engage in an all-out battle with Congress?*

The ultimate question was whether Clinton and Congress could work together to move the country forward, or whether they would just engage in partisan bickering that would lead to gridlock and further alienate voters. If the two major parties could not govern effectively, some predicted the rise of a third party by 1996. The stakes for the two parties—and more importantly, for the country—were enormous.

> *Following are excerpts from a press conference by President Bill Clinton at the White House on November 9, 1994, as released by the White House, and from a speech by Rep. Newt Gingrich (R-Ga.) at a symposium held by the Washington Research Group on November 11, 1994, as reported by Reuters:*

CLINTON PRESS CONFERENCE

Ladies and gentlemen, last night and again this morning I spoke with both Republicans and Democrats to congratulate those who won and console those who lost their elections. I also called the leaders of the next Congress, Senator [Bob] Dole and Congressman [Newt] Gingrich, to tell them after this hard-fought campaign that we are ready to work together to serve all the American people in a nonpartisan manner.

The American people sent us here to rebuild the American Dream, to change the way Washington does business, and to make our country work for ordinary citizens again. We've made a good start by cutting the deficit, by reducing the size of the federal government, by reinventing much of our government to do more with less. We have increased our investment in education and expanded trade, and our economy has created more than five million jobs.

We've also made a serious start in the fight against the terrible plague of crime and violence in this country. I remain committed to completing the work we have done. Still, in the course of this work, there has been too much politics as usual in Washington; too much partisan conflict; too little reform of Congress and the political process. And though we have made progress, not enough people have felt more prosperous and more secure, or believe we were meeting their desires for fundamental change in the role of government in their lives.

With the Democrats in control of both the White House and the Congress, we were held accountable yesterday. And I accept my share of the responsibility in the result of the elections.

When the Republican Party assumes leadership in the House and in the Senate, they will also have a larger responsibility for acting in the best interest of the American people. I reach out to them today, and I ask them to join me in this center of the public debate where the best ideas for the next generation of American progress must come.

Democrats and Republicans have often joined together when it was clearly in the national interest. For example, they have often chosen to put international affairs above politics. I urge them to do so again by passing the GATT [General Agreement on Tariffs and Trade] agreement this year. Our prosperity depends upon it, and there can be no compromise when the national interest and the livelihood of American households are at stake.

Last night the voters not only voted for sweeping changes, they demanded that a more equally divided Congress work more closely together with the president for the interest of all the American people. So I hope that we can do that on GATT, and that by doing so, we will pave the way for further cooperation on welfare reform and on health care reform, on a continued investment in our people's educational opportunities, and the continued strength of our economy.

We must also take more steps to restore the people's faith in our political institutions, and agree that, further, in the best tradition of our own foreign policy, that politics will continue to stop at the water's edge.

To those who believe we must keep moving forward, I want to say again, I will do everything in my power to reach out to the leaders and the members of this new Congress. It must be possible to make it a more effective, more functioning institution. It must be possible for us to give our people a government that is smaller, that is more effective, that reflects both our interests and our values.

But to those who would use this election to turn us back, let me say this: I will do all in my power to keep anyone from jeopardizing this economic recovery, by taking us back to the policies that failed us before. I will still work for those things that make America strong—strong families, better education, safer streets, more high-paying jobs, a more prosperous and peaceful world.

There is too much at stake for our children and our future to do anything else. Well, a lot has changed since yesterday. But what hasn't changed is the reason I was sent here and the reason the members of the Congress will be sent here—to restore the American Dream and to make this country work, this government work, this city work for the interest of ordinary Americans again. That is what the American people expect of us.

Last night, they said they were not satisfied with the progress we had made. They said the Democrats had been in control of the White House and the Congress. They said they were going to make a change, and they did make a change. But they still want the same goal. I pledge today to work with all the members of the Congress, and especially the new Republican leadership, to achieve that goal. If they will work with me, and they have pledged to do so today, then we can make great progress for this country. We should be optimistic and we should work to make that optimism real.

Question: Yesterday not a single Republican incumbent lost in any race for governor, House or Senate while the Democratic Party, your party, suffered its worst losses for decades. Do you view this as a repudiation of you, or is there another common denominator in this election that we're missing?

Clinton: Well, I think that I have some responsibility for it. I'm the President. I am the leader of the efforts that we have made in the last two years. And to whatever extent that we didn't do what the people wanted us to do, or they were not aware of what we had done, I must certainly bear my share of responsibility, and I accept that.

You know, a lot of us haven't had a lot of sleep, and we're going to need a few days to digest all these results. There will be a lot of you doing exit surveys, asking the American people what they meant and said. But what I think they said is, they still don't like what they see when they watch us working here. They still haven't felt the positive results of things that have been done here that they agree with when they hear about them, but they don't feel them. They're still not sure that we understand what they expect the role of government to be.

I think they want a smaller government that gives them better value for their dollar, that reflects both their interest and their values, that is not a burden to them, but empowers them. That's what I have tried to do, but I don't think they believe we're there yet—by a long shot. They want us to do more.

I went back today and read my announcement speech for President, and I said in that speech that the job of government was to create opportunity and then to expect citizens to assume the responsibility to make the most of that opportunity. I think that's about where the American people are. They don't think we've done that yet.

And the only thing I think they knew to do yesterday was to try to make a change in the people who were in control and who had been. I regret that some of the people who lost are people who made this a lot better country and who will always, when the history books are written, get the credit they deserve, with hindsight, for helping to make the American people more secure.

I don't believe the American people were saying we're sorry the deficit has been reduced; we're sorry the size of government has been reduced; and we're sorry you've taken the tough stand on crime; we're sorry you're expanding trade. I don't believe that. I don't think they were disagreeing with a lot of the specifics. I do think they still just don't like it when they watch what we do up here, and they haven't felt the positive impact of what has been done. And since I'm the President, I have to take some responsibility for that.

Question: Would you have survived if you had been on the ballot yesterday?

Clinton: Well, some Democrats did. I like to think I would have because I believe that I would have been a ferocious defender of what we have done, and I hope that I could have characterized what the choices were. But I don't know that, and neither does anybody else.

I think it's important to say that yesterday's election, like every election, was fundamentally about the American people. And they looked at us and they said, we want some more changes, and we're going to try this and see if this works. There is a lot of evidence—I've read it in a lot of your reporting—that the American people believe, a majority of them, and have believed for decades now that divided government may work better than united government. As you know, I disagree with that—why I did my best to make it work the other way.

But they didn't agree, and they're in charge. We all work for them, every one of us. And their will, their voice was heard. We got the message. And now we have to think about it, analyze it, rest up and move on. But this country is facing its problems. And what I think they told us was, look, two years ago we made one change; now we made another change. We want you to keep on moving this country forward, and we want you to accelerate the pace of change in the areas that I mentioned.

I do not believe they voted for reversals of economic policy or the positions on crime. I don't think they voted for a reversal of the Brady Bill or the military assault weapons ban. I don't believe that. So—but I do think they sent us a message, and I tried to hear it. And we're going to work together and do the best we can. . . .

Question: Mr. President, did you mean to say here, sir, that the message the voters sent yesterday was basically an extension of the demand for change they made when you were elected in '92, and that you've been going in the right direction, but perhaps made to go farther and faster with the sense of the same agenda?

Clinton: Well, I think they were saying two things to me—or maybe three . . .

I think they were saying, look, we just don't like what we see when we watch Washington—and you haven't done much about that. You know, we haven't changed the lobbying reform laws. Congress is still not required to live under the same laws that it imposes on private employers. There's still no line item veto. There's still not campaign finance reform. We don't like it when we look at it. It's too partisan, too interest group oriented—things don't get done, too many people up there playing politics. Democrats are in charge; we're holding you accountable. And we hope you hear this, Mr. President. I think they said that.

The second thing I think they said is, look, you may have done all these things, although we haven't heard much of it — we're not sure we believe it. But even if the deficit is down, the government is smaller, more is being invested in education, the crime bill passed, and the economy is growing—we still feel insecure. We don't feel that our incomes are going up, that our jobs are more stable, that our neighborhoods are safer, that the fabric of American life is growing more civilized and more law-abiding.

Then I think the third thing they were saying—and this maybe gets to the point of your question—is there are things we expect government to do, but we don't think government can solve all the problems. And we don't want the Democrats telling us from Washington that they know what is right about everything. We want the government to be smaller. We want it to be more efficient. We want it to create opportunity, to empower us. And we want it to demand responsibility of people who aren't behaving responsibly.

In short, we want it to reflect our interests and our values. And I think what they were saying is that the Republicans did a good job of defining us as the party of government, and that's not a good place to be. I think that was a clear message that they were sending in the election. . . .

GINGRICH'S REMARKS

Well, I apologize for breaking in on what is normally a pretty relaxed lunch as I remember from a couple of years ago. (Laughter.) When Gary Andrews asked me if I would come and do this I remembered that we had had a very lively exchange and a lot of interesting ideas and I said, sure, I don't think I'll be all that busy on the Friday after the election. (Laughter.) And Marianne and I were planning on driving back up yesterday anyway and it seemed after a while a little more busy than we planned it to be. . . .

Let me say first of all that in a way that is peculiarly fitting, 76 years ago today the armistice was declared at the 11th hour of the 11th day of the 11th month in what was then called the Great War. In an indirect way that had an enormous impact on my life because it was while my dad was stationed with the Army in Europe and I was a 14-year-old freshman in high school that we went to the battlefield in Verdun, which was the largest battlefield in the Western front of that war, and spent a weekend with a friend of his who had been on a death march in the Philippines and served three years in a Japanese prison camp. The Great War was both an example of what happens when leadership fails and societies collide and it was an example in its aftermath of what happens when people lie to themselves about the objective realities of the human condition because instead of leading to world peace as Woodrow Wilson had so devoutly hoped, it, in fact, ultimately led to the second world war. And instead of leading to greater freedom for all human beings, as Woodrow Wilson's 14 points had hoped, it led to Nazism and the Soviet empire, the Gulag and Auschwitz.

And so it is both good for us today to remember the cost paid by those who believe enough in freedom to have died for it and useful to remind ourselves that that price has to be paid every year and every week and that it is better by far to pay that price in peacetime by being vigilant and by trying to do that which is right than it is to allow your society to decay or to have inadequate leadership and drift into a cataclysm comparable to the first and second world wars.

And that's not just a foreign policy or national defense battle cry. I think it's important to recognize that what is ultimately at stake in our current environment is literally the future of American civilization as it has existed for the last several hundred years. I'm a history teacher by background, and I would assert and defend on any campus in this country that it is impossible to maintain civilization with 12-year-olds having babies, with 15-year-olds killing each other, with 17-year-olds dying of AIDS, and with 18-year-olds ending up with diplomas they can't even read. And that what is at issue is literally not Republican or Democrat or liberal or conservative, but the question of whether or not our civilization will survive. . . .

Now, there's been an enormous effort in the Washington elite to avoid the reality that this lesson was actually about some fairly big ideas—Which direction do you want to go in?—and that those who argued for counter-culture values, bigger government, redistributionist economics and bureaucracies deciding how you should spend your money were on the losing end in virtually every part of the country. . . .

So the first point I would argue is this was clearly a historic election which clearly had a mandate. And that's outside the Washington elite's view, and they don't want to believe that because it's not the mandate they wanted.

Second, I want to draw a distinction between two words, because we're going to get into a lot of confusion at the vision level about these two words. I am very prepared to cooperate with the Clinton administration. I am not prepared to compromise. The two words are very different. On everything on which we can find agreement, I will cooperate.

On those things that are at the core of our contract, those things which are at the core of our philosophy, and on those things where we believe we represent the vast majority of Americans, there will be no compromise. So let me draw the distinction: Cooperation, yes; compromise, no.

Third, the—this happened by pure happenstance two days ago, and it worked, so I'll share it with you. People have been trying to figure out how to put me in a box, and it's very hard because I don't fit boxes very well. . . . The best description of me is that I'm a conservative futurist. Marianne and I have for a long time been friends with Alvin and Heidi Toffler, the authors of "Future Shock" and "The Third Wave." We really believe it's useful to think about the 21st century. On the other hand, I believe the most powerful single doctrine for the leadership of human beings and for their opportunity to pursue happiness is the *Federalist Papers*, de Toqueville's travels in "Democracy in America," the Declaration of Independence, and the Constitution. . . .

There are five large changes we have to go through. . . . I want to just describe the five changes very briefly to give you a taste of what they are because I think they're central to everything that will be organizing our activities over the next two years.

First, we have to accelerate the transition from a second wave mechanical, bureaucratic society to a third wave information society, to use Alvin Toffler's model. Two simple examples: One, imagine the speed and ease with which you use a bank teller card anywhere on the planet and electronically verify your account and get money and then call the federal government about a case. (Laughter.) There's no objective reason that institutions of government have to be two or three generations behind the curve in information systems and management, but they are. And that means, for example, if we're really serious about distance medicine and about distance learning and about distance work, we could revolutionize the quality of life in rural America and create the greatest explosion of new opportunity for rural America ever in history. And yet, we're currently moving in the opposite direction so that at a time when the IRS [Internal Revenue Service] should be making it easier to have a home office, they make it harder. Now that's foolish. It's exactly the wrong direction.

Second—the second example I'll give you is we will change the rules of the House to require that all documents and all conference reports and all committee reports be filed electronically as well as in writing and that they cannot be filed until they are available to any citizen who wants to pull them up simultaneously so that information is available to every citizen in the country at the same moment that it is available to the highest paid Washington lobbyist. That will change over time the entire flow of information and the entire quality of knowledge in the country and it will change the way people will try to play games in the legislative process.

The second big change is to recognize the objective reality of the world market, to realize that we create American jobs through world sales and to make a conscious national decision that we want to have the highest value added jobs on the planet with greatest productivity so we can have the highest take-home pay and the greatest range of choices in lifestyles. In order to do that we have to literally rethink the assumptions that grew up in a self-indulgent national economy and they have to recognize that litigation, taxation, regulation, welfare, education, the very structure of government, the structure of health—all those things have to be reexamined from the standpoint of what will make us the most competitive society on the planet, the most desirable place to invest to create jobs and the place with the best trained and most entrepreneurial work force, most committed to Deming's concepts of quality.

Now that's a big challenge. One step, frankly, has to be that every child in America should be required to do at least two hours of homework a night or they're being cheated for the rest of their lives in their ability to compete with the Germans and the Japanese and the Chinese. . . .

Third, we have to replace the welfare state with an opportunity society. Let me be very explicit. It is impossible to take the Great Society structure of bureaucracy, the redistributionist model of how wealth is acquired, and the counter-culture value system that now permeates the way we deal with the poor, and have any hope of fixing them. They are a disaster. They ruin the poor, they create a culture of poverty and a culture of violence which is destructive of this civilization, and they have to be replaced thoroughly from the ground up.

Now, that should be done in cooperation with the poor. The people who have the most to gain from eliminating the culture of poverty and replacing it with a culture of productivity are the people currently trapped in a nightmare, living in public housing projects with no one going to work, living in neighborhoods with no physical safety, their children forced to walk into buildings where there will be no learning, and living in a community where taxes and red tape and regulation destroy their hope of creating new entrepreneurial small businesses and doing what every other generation of poor Americans have done, which is to leave poverty behind by acquiring productivity. . . .

Fourth, we have to recognize that American exceptionalism—to use Everett Carl Ladd's phrase—is real; that this has been the most successful civilization in the history of the human race at liberating people to pursue happiness. I think that's an objective fact. There is no other society in history where as many people from as many cultures speaking as many languages could come together and become a nation, and where they could then be liberated to go off and be who they wanted to be. This is a country where Colin Powell and John Shalikashvili can both be chairman of the Joint Chiefs and nobody even thinks about the remarkable difference in ethnicity because they're Americans, and that's the way it should be.

And that means we have to say to the counter-culture: Nice try, you failed, you're wrong. And we have to simply, calmly, methodically reassert American civilization and reestablish the conditions, which I believe starts with the work ethic. You cannot study 300 years of American civilization without coming to the conclusion that working and being expected to work and being involved—and work may be for money or it may be at home, it may be a hobby that you pursue, but the sense of energy, the pursuit of happiness, which is not—it's an active verb—not happiness stamps, not a department of happiness, not therapy for happiness. Pursuit. (Laughter.) This is also a muscular society and we've been kidding ourselves about it. The New Hampshire slogan is, "Live free or die." It is not "Live free or whine." (Laughter.) And so we have to think through what are the deeper underlying cultural meanings of being American and how do we reassert them.

Lastly, and this is one where I, frankly, became more radical all fall. I realized as I would talk to audiences—I was in 127 districts in the last two years— and I realized as I would talk to audiences that there was an enormous danger that they were going to say, "Terrific speech, let's elect Gingrich speaker, let's elect our local candidate to the House, they'll do the job."

And let me tell all of you flatly, the long experiment in professional politicians and professional government is over, and it failed. You cannot hire a teacher to teach your child, and walk off and then blame the teacher. You cannot hire a policeman to protect your neighborhood and then walk off and blame the police. You cannot hire a public health service to protect your health and then walk off and blame the public health service.

We have to reestablish—and I particularly want to thank Gordon Wood, who will probably get in a lot of trouble at Brown University for my using his name, but Gordon Wood's understanding of the origins of the American Revolution and his understanding of the core intent of Jeffersonian politics was for me a liberating moment because it's his argument that what Jefferson understood was that you had to have limited but effective government precisely in order to liberate people to engage in civic responsibility, and that the larger government grew, the more you would crowd out civic responsibility, and that in the end, you could never replace civic responsibility with professional government.

Now, this means that my challenge to the American people is real simple. You really want to dramatically reduce power in Washington? You have to be willing to take more responsibility back home. You really want to reduce the bureaucracy of the welfare state? You have to accept greater responsibility back home. . . .

Let me say one last thing. If this just degenerates after an historic election back into the usual baloney of politics in Washington and pettiness in Washington, then the American people I believe will move towards a third party in a massive way. I think they are fed up with this city, they are fed up with its games, they are fed up with petty partisanship. I don't think they mind grand partisanship, and there's a big difference. To have a profound disagreement over the direction of your country or over the principles by which your economy works, or over the manner in which your government should structure resources, that is legitimate and the American people believe in that level of debate and relish it. . . .

And so we have an enormous amount of work to do. All I can promise you on the side of the House Republicans is that we're going to be open to working with everyone, that we will cooperate with anyone, and we will compromise with no one, and that's the base of where we're going and that's what we believe this election is all about.

EXECUTIVE ORDER ON GOVERNMENT SECRETS
November 10, 1994

On November 10, President Bill Clinton signed an executive order declassifying nearly 44 million pages of government records, some dating as far back as the beginning of World War I. All the documents had been classified on national security grounds. Despite the order, hundreds of millions or even billions of federal government documents—no one was sure exactly how many—remained classified.

The newly declassified documents included 21 million items from World War II and nearly 6 million pages from the Vietnam War. White House press secretary Dee Dee Myers said the order covered nearly all classified documents dating from World War II and earlier. Among the World War II items declassified were hundreds of thousands of index cards from the files of the Office of Strategic Services, some 1.7 million pages about bombing runs by planes, and 9.5 million pages of documents about operations in Europe and the Mediterranean area.

While the declassification order covered an enormous number of documents, it appeared that officials had removed from the group being considered for declassification any documents dealing with such sensitive subjects as atomic weapons, intelligence tools, and negotiations with foreign governments. The New York Times *reported that nearly 5 million pages were not released after military and intelligence officials objected. Historians said the selective removal of the documents diminished the usefulness of Clinton's order.*

During the 1992 presidential campaign, Clinton had pledged to increase government openness and to make more federal documents available to the public. But in his first year in office, Clinton's staff actually classified documents at a higher rate than did the administration of George Bush during its final year in office. Clinton appointees also were slower than Bush appointees in declassifying documents, leading to a net growth of millions of pages of classified documents during Clinton's first year as president.

Thousands Employed Keeping Secrets

In May, the New York Times *reported that a survey by the Office of Management and Budget (OMB) found that more than 32,400 people were employed keeping government secrets. The newspaper also said that industry estimates and the OMB report suggested the federal government may spend more than $16 billion annually to safeguard government secrets. The vast bulk of the cost—$13.8 billion—came from defense contractor bills to the government for classification expenses. Ironically, OMB did not make its report about government secrets public.*

Two months earlier, the chairmen of the Senate and House Intelligence Committees had introduced bills that would cut the number of classified documents and shorten the time they could remain secret. While the bills offered by Sen. Dennis DeConcini (D-Ariz.) and Rep. Dan Glickman (D-Kan.) differed in their particulars, both sought to reduce the number of documents being classified and to shorten the waiting period before documents were reviewed for possible declassification. Under current federal law, most documents were not reviewed for thirty years after being classified.

DeConcini called the current system "nonsensical," and said it had to be changed. "I, for one, have a hard time believing that it is vital to national security to keep this much information from the American people," he said. Glickman agreed. "Too much information is kept secret, for too long, at too high a level of classification and at too great an expense," he said. Both of their bills died in committee.

Commission Backs Automatic Release of Documents

In March, the same month DeConcini and Glickman introduced their bills, a joint Pentagon-Central Intelligence Agency (CIA) commission presented a report to the Senate Intelligence Committee that concluded that "the classification system, largely unchanged since the Eisenhower Administration, has grown out of control." It said that classified documents were "stored in locked containers inside locked strong rooms within secure buildings in fenced facilities patrolled by armed guards—overkill even at the height of the cold war, much less in today's security environment." The commission recommended that many secret documents be automatically released after ten years and that most others be released after twenty-five years.

Also in March, the Clinton administration released a draft executive order that was aimed at declassifying over a four-year period millions of documents from the 1950s and 1960s. The proposal, which was developed by National Security Council staff and distributed to senior agency officials in the government, also would reverse the balancing act used in deciding whether a document should be secret.

Under a 1981 executive order issued by Ronald Reagan, officials presumed that documents should be secret. Under the new draft executive order, officials would instead presume that documents should be public unless there was a good reason for making them secret. The order would also require that secret documents be automatically declassified after twenty-five years unless an agency head, such as the secretary of defense, ordered a document withheld.

The draft order ran into a storm of opposition throughout the government. Many officials, particularly in the defense and intelligence communities, said it would lead to too much openness and could damage national security. "We must guard against the release of documents that have passed the scheduled declassification date but contain information that still merits protection," said Elizabeth Rindskopf, general counsel for the CIA, at a congressional hearing.

Some officials also complained that they had inadequate resources to quickly review for declassification all the documents included under the draft order. Some historians held out hope that the draft order would survive and someday be signed, but that day did not appear likely to dawn anytime soon.

Following are the text of the executive order signed by President Bill Clinton on November 10, 1994, declassifying nearly 44 million pages of documents, and the White House press release that accompanied the order:

THE EXECUTIVE ORDER

By the authority vested in me as President by the Constitution and the laws of the United States of America, it is hereby ordered:

Section 1. The records in the National Archives of the United States referenced in the list accompanying this order are hereby declassified.

Sec. 2. The Archivist of the United States shall take such actions as are necessary to make such records available for public research no later than 30 days from the date of this Order, except to the extent that the head of an affected agency and the Archivist have determined that specific information within such records must be protected from disclosure pursuant to an authorized exemption to the Freedom of Information Act, 5 U.S.C. 552, other than the exemption that pertains to national security information.

Sec. 3. Nothing contained in this order shall create any right or benefit, substantive or procedural, enforceable by any party against the United States, its agencies or instrumentalities, its officers or employees, or any other person.

WILLIAM J. CLINTON
THE WHITE HOUSE, November 10, 1994.

THE PRESS RELEASE

In an important step towards creating a more open and accountable government for all Americans, President Clinton signed today an Executive Order authorizing the National Archives to declassify a selected group of records amounting to 43.9 million pages. This bulk declassification represents approximately 14 percent of the National Archives' holdings of classified material.

The documents represent almost all the classified holdings dating from World War II and before. In addition, nearly 23 million pages of documents relating to the Vietnam War, Naval Operating Forces, and the records of the Headquarters, U.S. Air Force also have been declassified by this Order.

The declassified documents offer a wealth of insight into some of the most important military events of our recent history, and will be of great value to military historians, researchers, veterans, and ordinary citizens alike.

The Executive Order underscores the President's commitment to address the backlog of some 325 million pages of records now stored at the National Archives and hundreds of millions more held in agencies throughout the Executive branch.

LETTERS QUESTIONING MILITARY READINESS
November 14 and 15, 1994

In an exchange of letters with congressional leaders on November 14 and 15, Defense Secretary William J. Perry admitted that one-fourth of the Army's divisions were not fully ready for combat. Pentagon officials said it was the first time in twelve years that any defense forces were not fully combat ready.

The letter exchange began November 14 when Rep. Floyd D. Spence (R-S.C.), the ranking member of the House Armed Services Committee who would take over the chairmanship when the new Republican majority took office in January 1995, wrote to John Deutch, deputy secretary of defense. In the letter, Spence challenged Deutch's claim at a Defense Department press briefing on October 13 that all U.S. military units were fully combat ready. At the press conference, Deutch said U.S. forces were "more ready and capable than they've ever been."

Spence said that Deutch's claim "sharply conflicts with the reality of the reduced readiness condition facing operational units across all services and commands." He added that evidence from the field showed that U.S. military units were caught "in the early stages of a downward readiness spiral" that showed no signs of ending soon. "Wholesale categories of combat units are in a reduced state of readiness and those that are not are managing to preserve short-term readiness only through engaging in a desperate 'shell game' with dwindling resources—a practice that eats away at sustainability stocks, maintenance of equipment and other readiness resources," Spence wrote.

The next day, Perry wrote a letter to Spence and other congressional leaders admitting that three of the Army's twelve divisions were not ready to undertake all the missions for which they were designed. He said the Defense Department had cash flow problems because near the end of the fiscal year U.S. forces had been deployed in or around Rwanda, Cuba, Haiti, and Kuwait "in rapid succession." Those operations cost $1.7 billion more than *had been budgeted, forcing Pentagon officials to make cuts in "readiness-related activities" such as training and maintenance for some units that were not on the front lines. Most of the units recovered quickly once Congress passed a supplemental appropriations bill for the Defense Department and new cash flowed in with the beginning of fiscal year 1995, Perry said, but the three Army units whose readiness ratings had been downgraded were not expected to recover until the second quarter of fiscal year 1995.*

To avoid such problems in the future, Perry said the Defense Department needed to be given more money for operations and maintenance. In addition, Congress had to act faster when the Pentagon requested supplemental appropriations to fund unforeseen operations overseas.

Readiness Issue Could Affect Haiti Operation

Spence was not satisfied with Perry's letter, contending that the Pentagon was "still minimizing the magnitude of the readiness problem." He directed his staff on the Armed Services Committee to conduct a series of field visits to determine the actual state of military readiness of U.S. forces. Other Republican members of Congress were expected to bring up the readiness issue as they sought to bring U.S. forces home from Haiti, where they had been deployed to restore President Jean-Bertrand Aristide to power. The administration of President Bill Clinton had estimated that the Haiti operation would cost about $500 million, but Republican senators said the real figure was at least $1.5 billion and growing every day. Some Republicans also were expected to use the readiness issue in arguing for increases in the Pentagon's budget.

Perry's letter admitting that U.S. forces were not up to par was an embarrassment to the Clinton administration. Some analysts said the readiness problem occurred because the Clinton administration was using military forces for nontraditional missions such as helping refugees in Rwanda and restoring Aristide to power in Haiti. Paying for those operations took money away from other units that would constitute the second wave of U.S. forces in any conventional fight.

Clinton Called Unfit to Serve as Commander in Chief

Only days after the exchange of letters about military readiness, during a television interview Sen. Jesse Helms (R-N.C.), the incoming chairman of the Senate Foreign Relations Committee, again stirred up the issue of Clinton's fitness to serve the nation as commander in chief. During the 1992 presidential campaign, it was revealed that in 1969, after it became clear that Clinton was safe from the Vietnam draft, he had revoked an earlier pledge to join a Reserve Officers Training Corps (ROTC) program. Critics contended that Clinton had simply used the ROTC pledge to dodge the draft, and that he was unfit to lead the nation's armed forces. (Clinton Letter on Draft, Historic Documents of 1992, p. 155)

Asked if he thought Clinton was "up to the job" of commander in chief, Helms replied: "No, I do not. And neither do the people in the armed forces." His remarks stirred up a tempest, even among his fellow conserva-tives. Helms made things worse in a second interview where he said that Clinton was extremely unpopular on North Carolina military bases and "better watch out if he comes down here. He'd better have a bodyguard." Helms's remarks were widely criticized, and some Democrats called for Re-publicans to block his appointment as chairman of the Senate Foreign Rela-tions Committee, but Helms assumed that role at the start of the 104th Congress.

Russian Readiness Also in Doubt

The U.S. Army was not the only superpower military force facing readi-ness problems. Only days after readiness became a major issue in the United States, Russia's defense minister told the parliament that the nation's army was in terrible shape.

"Not a single army in the world is in such a catastrophic state," Gen. Pavel S. Grachev told the Russian parliament. "I ask you to take this as a warning." He said that Russia's military forces did not have enough money or equipment and were losing their ability to defend Russia. If the military did not get more money, Grachev said, "the irreversible process of losing our capability will occur, and the armed forces will then collapse."

> *Following is the text of two letters about defense readiness, the first sent on November 14, 1994, by Rep. Floyd D. Spence (R-S.C.) to John Deutch, deputy secretary of defense, and the second sent on November 15, 1994, by Secretary of Defense William J. Perry to Rep. Ronald V. Dellums (D-Calif.) and other congressional leaders:*

SPENCE LETTER

Dear Mr. Secretary:

The dramatically increased pace of the defense drawdown over the past two years has brought much needed focus to the state of readiness of our military forces. I am encouraged by the attention recently extended to this issue and I look forward to reviewing a Fiscal Year 1996 defense budget re-quest that will hopefully reflect a meaningful commitment to protecting mili-tary readiness.

However, I was surprised by your widely-reported comments of October 13, 1994, during a Department of Defense press briefing. Your statement as-sessing the readiness picture has been reported as follows:

> I think that the record shows that the readiness of the forces as [sic] high as they have ever been—higher, in my judgment, than they were in 1991 when we were— 1990, when we were worrying about Iraq the first time. . . So I would say to you that the practical measures of seeing what our troops are doing on the ground

argues that these forces are ready, and more ready and capable than they've ever been.

Mr. Secretary, if this indeed represents your judgment on the current state of U.S. military readiness, it sharply conflicts with the reality of the reduced readiness condition facing operational units across all services and commands. While the recent "Vigilant Warrior" deployment in response to Iraq's aggression validated the previous Administration's decision to preposition equipment in the region, it hardly represented a valid test of how ready U.S. forces are to execute a major regional contingency (MRC) such as Desert Storm, not to mention two nearly simultaneous MRC's as required by the Administration's current national military strategy.

The volume of evidence from the field is as clear as it is unavoidable—U.S. military units are caught in the early stages of a downward readiness spiral that shows no prospect of easing in the foreseeable future. Wholesale categories of combat units are in a reduced state of readiness and those that are not are managing to preserve short-term readiness only through engaging in a desperate "shell game" with dwindling resources—a practice that eats away at sustainability stock, maintenance of equipment and other readiness resources.

The anecdotal evidence of a serious readiness problem is overwhelming and empirical indicators have also recently begun to confirm that readiness is on a decidedly downward trend. A brief sampling:

- Two of the six Army contingency Corps units normally resourced to be the readiest in the force are now reporting a reduced readiness rating with little prospect for improvement in FY [Fiscal Year] 95 and beyond. One of these units suffering reduced readiness was slated to serve as a significant component of the enhanced ground deployment to the Persian Gulf had Iraq persisted in its recent saber rattling against Kuwait.
- Every forward deployed army division reports below par readiness ratings and the CONUS-based follow-on divisions report an even lower readiness status.
- USAFE air crews are so overextended in supporting peacekeeping and humanitarian operations that training for their primary combat mission has been seriously impacted. For instance, as of June, 1994, 100% of F-15E and 64% of F-15C crews in Europe needed waivers from training requirements in order to keep flying. This means that should a contingency arise in the near term, we would not be able to deploy a single F-15E crew out of Europe that had not suffered recent training deficiencies.
- For the 12 month period ending this past July, seven types of aircraft in the Air Force Air Combat Command (ACC) inventory were deployed in excess of the 120 days TDY per air crew maximum, and three aircraft types were deployed in excess of 150 days.
- Navy surface combatants are similarly committed beyond what a reduced force structure and budget can reasonably support. According to the Navy's Atlantic Command, as of September, 1994, CINCLANTFLEET had

61 surface ships available yet required 68 in order to meet its peacetime requirement in a manner that did not violate personnel deployment standards. This requirement increased to 73 ships when on-going counter-drug, Cuban and Haiti operations are considered. The result is that the available 61 ships and crews are overextended as they are called upon to do the job of 73 ships.

• Due to depleted Operations and Maintenance funding, 28 Marine Corps and Navy tactical aviation *squadrons* had to ground over 50% of their aircraft for the entire month of September, 1994. Eight East Coast Marine Corps aviation squadrons were completely grounded for the month of September, 1994.

As you are undoubtedly aware, the above represents only a small sampling of available indicators that paint an increasingly dire readiness picture. I believe that these accounts are more than temporary "snapshots" or superficial anecdotes and indicate a disturbing trend that calls into direct question the adequacy of the current state of readiness of our forces. Further, this long list of readiness problems certainly appears to challenge your conclusion that the readiness of the forces is "as [*sic*] high as they have ever been" and more specifically, that it is "higher . . . than they were in 1990."

I have long understood that people can and will disagree on any given topic, but I am seriously concerned that the department's public posturing on the readiness question suggests a disturbing misinterpretation of the gravity of the readiness problem facing U.S. military forces. Therefore, I request your assistance in reconciling the apparent discrepancy between your October 13 statement and the reality of what I am seeing and learning in the field by providing me with a more precise rationale and basis on which your public assessment was made. I trust an expeditious response will clarify your thinking on this important matter.

Sincerely,
Floyd D. Spence
Ranking Republican, House Armed Services Committee

PERRY LETTER

Dear Chairman Dellums:

On 4 August of this year, when I testified on behalf of an emergency supplemental and the Department's reprogramming request, I expressed concern about the impact of our operations on readiness. I noted that, if we were not reimbursed for the expenses of these operations, the Defense operation and maintenance accounts of the defense budget would pay for it, and this would have a direct and predictable negative impact on readiness. At that time, I promised to keep you advised of the effect of these and other actions resulting from readiness cash flow problems.

I have recently reviewed the readiness performance of our forces this year. Based on this review, I conclude that our force is, overall, ready to carry out the nation's tasks. It has performed magnificently in recent deployments to Rwanda, Haiti and Kuwait.

As anticipated, however, we have seen some readiness concerns that I would like to bring to your attention. As you know from my testimony before your committee, FY 1994 funding levels for operations and maintenance had little safety margin built into them. On top of this, our forces engaged in a variety of unforeseen operations that forced us to expend $1.7 billion more than we planned in our enacted budget. Thankfully, as a result of Congressional leadership, relief was provided through supplemental appropriations.

Nevertheless, the Department did suffer some difficult readiness cash flow shortages, particularly in the fourth quarter of FY 1994. In part, these were triggered by high year-end demands on our forces—Rwanda, Cuba, Haiti, and Kuwait in rapid succession. In part, these shortages were exacerbated by the second increment of supplemental funds being made available only after FY 1994 ended. It is critical that we receive FY 1995 supplemental funds by the March/April time frame to preclude repetition of our FY 1994 experience.

The Department took aggressive measures to minimize the effects of these temporary cash flow shortages. Examples include withdrawing rapidly forces once their missions were accomplished, using financial management measures to ensure our engaged troops could carry out their missions, and freeing operating funds by reductions in the training, maintenance, and supply of selected units.

Notwithstanding these measures, each of the Services had to selectively cut back on readiness-related activities. In most cases, the readiness of units affected is recovering quickly with the influx of funds in FY 1995. A notable exception, however, involves three later deploying heavy reinforcing divisions in the Army. The readiness of these units fell late in FY 1994 to a point where they were capable of undertaking most, but not all, portions of the missions for which they were designed. Thus, they were rated as "C-3" under our readiness reporting system.

The Army is carrying out a readiness recovery plan to put these divisions on a sounder readiness footing in the second quarter of FY 1995. Nevertheless, I am not satisfied with the current readiness of these divisions and am determined to work with you and others to avoid a repetition of these circumstances in the future. The success of their recovery is directly dependent on additional funding in FY 1995.

In this regard, please permit me to suggest two areas for our cooperation in the coming year. First, we must ensure adequate funding of operations and maintenance for core readiness. As you know, my judgment is that FY 1994 funding was cut too fine for readiness, so I proposed, with the concurrence of the President and the Congress, that we increase operations and maintenance funding for FY 1995. My intention is similarly to request operations and maintenance funds for FY 1996 that will be sufficient to keep our forces ready.

Second, we must work together to provide timely supplemental appropriations. When we do not have rapid approval of these appropriations, we put our readiness at risk. We must avoid last fiscal year's experience where there was a lag of several months between submission and approval of our reprogramming requests and our second supplemental request. For the coming legislative year, my intention is to submit early, for your consideration, a request for supplemental appropriations to cover added FY 1995 costs of ongoing operations, as well as costs we have not recouped for engagements in FY 1994.

Given your steadfast commitment to keeping our forces ready and to supporting the men and women who operate them, I know I can count on your leadership to gain congressional support for these readiness funding initiatives.

Sincerely,
William J. Perry

NTSB RECOMMENDATIONS ON COMMUTER AIRLINE SAFETY
November 15, 1994

In a draft report approved November 15, the National Transportation Safety Board (NTSB) recommended that commuter planes that seat twenty or more people should have to follow the same safety rules as large passenger aircraft, and those that seat ten to nineteen people should have to follow those rules "wherever possible." At the time, the safety rules for commuter planes were less stringent than for larger planes. "We need to make sure the paying passenger gets the same level of safety regardless of which type of service he's on," said James E. Hall, chairman of the NTSB.

The board said that regulations governing commuter airlines had not kept pace with changes in the industry. According to the NTSB, commuter airlines transported 53 million passengers in 1993, up from just 15 million in 1980. It noted that commuter airlines were flying larger, more complicated airplanes and that many were entering into marketing agreements with major carriers.

The NTSB recommendations, which followed a nine-month investigation by the board's staff, particularly focused on improving crew performance. The NTSB said that under current regulations, commuter pilots did not get enough rest, did not have enough time between flights to perform their jobs properly, and were not properly trained. Those findings came in the wake of two commuter plane crashes that were blamed at least partly on pilot errors. The first was a crash near Hibbing, Minnesota, in December 1993 in which eighteen people died; the second was a January 1994 crash near Columbus, Ohio, that killed five.

Board Criticizes FAA Inspections

The NTSB also sharply criticized inspections of commuter airlines by the Federal Aviation Administration (FAA), the agency charged with guaranteeing airline safety. "Federal Aviation Administration surveillance of commuter airlines is often conducted by inspectors who have neither ex-

perience in air carrier operations nor familiarity with the specific aircraft types operated by the air carriers they oversee," the report said. It noted that in a survey of sixteen commuter airlines, fifteen claimed that the FAA was not consistent in interpreting and enforcing regulations.

The NTSB's recommendations came just one day after the International Airline Passengers Association, a consumer organization, told its 110,000 members they should avoid flying on commuter planes with fewer than thirty-one seats. The association said smaller commuter planes had a disproportionately high number of accidents.

The passenger group's recommendation angered NTSB members, who called it irresponsible. NTSB members also criticized recent media reports about the safety of commuter aircraft, noting that with the exception of the very smallest aircraft, commuter airlines were just as safe to fly as the major airlines and had similar accident rates.

The NTSB is limited to making recommendations, with the FAA being responsible for developing and enforcing rules. FAA officials said they agreed with the NTSB's recommendations and would incorporate them into rules. In a statement, FAA Administrator David R. Hinson said the FAA was developing a proposal that would require pilots of planes with thirty or fewer seats to receive the same training as those flying larger aircraft. However, critics accused the FAA of moving too slowly, noting that it had promised for at least two years to make safety rules equal between different types of airlines.

In another major recommendation, the NTSB said that people buying airline tickets should know whether they were flying a major carrier or a commuter line. Under current rules, the NTSB said, a person could buy a ticket from a major carrier only to find upon arriving at the airport that transportation was being provided by a smaller commuter airline that might not be controlled or inspected by the larger carrier. The NTSB said larger carriers participating in this "code-sharing" should oversee their smaller partners.

"A major airline participating in a code-sharing arrangement with a commuter airline is perceived by the traveling public to be owner of the commuter airline and accountable for the safety of its operations," the NTSB said. "The major airline should participate in oversight of its commuter partner that includes a program of regular safety audits of flight operations, training programs, maintenance, and inspection."

NTSB Recommends Grounding Planes

A week before the report was issued, the NTSB issued other recommendations involving commuter aircraft following the crash of an Avions de Transport Regional ATR-72 in an Indiana soybean field. All sixty-eight people aboard were killed. The NTSB said that type of plane and a related plane, the ATR-42, should be barred from flying when icy conditions were predicted. Preliminary investigations pointed to icing on the wings as being the likely cause of the crash. Commuter airlines in the United States had a total of 41 ATR-72 and 109 ATR-42 planes in their fleets.

Initially, the FAA did not go as far as the NTSB recommended. Instead, it barred pilots of the affected planes from using the autopilot during icy conditions. The plane that crashed had been on autopilot when it went down. Federal safety officials said that if the pilot had been flying manually, he might have noticed an ice buildup in time to avoid an accident.

On December 9, the FAA went further and banned flying the ATR-72 and ATR-42 in conditions where ice was likely to develop on the wings. It was the first time the FAA had issued such an order. Airlines that owned the planes scrambled to move them to warmer parts of the country where icing conditions were less likely to occur.

Following are excerpts from draft recommendations issued November 15, 1994, by the National Transportation Safety Board on improving commuter airline safety:

Summary of NTSB Conclusions

The Federal regulations that govern the safety of flight represent the minimum acceptable standard of safety by which all airlines must operate. The [National Transportation] Safety Board believes that the standards for safety should be based on the characteristics of the flight operations, not the seating capacity of the aircraft, and that passengers on commuter airlines should be afforded the same regulatory safety protections granted to passengers flying on Part 121 airlines. In this regard, the Board believes that the regulations contained in 14 CFR Part 135 have not kept pace with changes in the commuter airline industry. The commuter airline segment of commercial aviation can no longer be viewed as primarily an industry comprising small air carriers that operate small, 10-seat airplanes to provide essential air service to remote communities. Many commuter airlines today operate extensive route systems, and use highly sophisticated transport category aircraft, the safe operation of which depends upon crewmembers who should be qualified and trained to the same standards as are required of crewmembers who fly Part 121 operations. Further, the proliferation of code-sharing arrangements has given rise to coordinated air service between commuter airlines and major air carriers that should be governed by a single regulatory standard, wherever possible.

However, the Safety Board recognizes that the commuter airline industry is diverse, and that some requirements necessary to improve the standard of safety in one aspect of the industry, may be impractical in other aspects. The Board believes that scheduled Part 135 air service that uses high performance, transport category aircraft should be operated under the same regulatory standards as govern the Part 121 air carriers that also operate these aircraft. Consequently, the Safety Board believes that the FAA [Federal Aviation Administration] should revise the Federal Aviation Regulations such that all scheduled passenger service conducted in aircraft with 20 or more passenger seats be conducted according to the provisions of 14 CFR Part 121, or its functional equivalent, wherever possible. The Board believes that these regulatory changes, in combination with the FAA's anticipated revisions to the flight crew training requirements that will create a single training for flightcrews, will enhance the safety of commuter airline operations to a level that is equivalent to Part 121 standards.

Findings

1. The commuter air carrier industry has experienced major growth in passenger traffic and changes in its operating characteristics since 1980. There has been a trend toward operating larger, more sophisticated aircraft, and many carriers have established code-sharing arrangements with major airlines. The regulations in Part 135 have not kept pace with many of the changes in the industry.

2. Part 135 regulations on flight time and crew rest allow air carriers to establish schedules that result in reduced rest, and many commuter airlines routinely take advantage of these reduced rest provisions for scheduling flightcrews rather than using the provisions for the intended purpose of accommodating unforeseen circumstances.

3. Self reports from most pilots who were surveyed (87 percent) indicated that they have flown while fatigued. The most common reasons given for flying while fatigued were length of duty days, early shift duty followed by late shift duty, and inadequate rest periods.

4. The practice of scheduling Part 135 pilots for training, check flights, or other nonrevenue flights at the end of a full day of scheduled revenue flying reduces the value of the training and increases the potential for fatigue-related accidents.

5. Pressures on Part 135 pilots to accomplish several tasks between flights in shorter periods of time increase the risk of critical mistakes that could jeopardize the safety of flight.

6. Results of the commuter airline survey suggest that many commuter airlines still do not provide formal crew resource management (CRM) training to their flightcrews, and other airlines fail to provide comprehensive training that includes recurrent practice and feedback on the use of CRM skills.

7. About 30 percent of pilots who were surveyed indicated that they did not believe that newly-trained pilots are adequately trained for their duties. These pilots reported that CRM training and initial operating experience (for first officers) would be beneficial.

8. The use of flight simulators enables air carriers to train pilots more effectively on hazardous maneuvers and emergency procedures such as wind shear recovery and low-altitude stall recovery; however, new aircraft continue to be certificated by the Federal Aviation Administration and introduced into revenue service before a training simulator for the aircraft is designed and manufactured.

9. Although the Federal Aviation Administration encourages the use of

simulators in flight crew training through Appendix H to Part 121, there is no counterpart for Part 135. A Part 135 operator is allowed to conduct pilot training in a simulator only if the operator is granted an exemption from applicable Part 135 regulations.

10. Most commuter airlines that were surveyed have a company policy that addresses the pairing of inexperienced crewmembers. The most common policy is a requirement that at least one pilot have a minimum of 100 hours in the aircraft type.

11. Hands-on emergency drills are a necessary part of the flight attendant training curriculum, and substituting visual information and documentation for actual practice can lead to degraded flight attendant performance during actual emergencies.

12. Many community airports served by commuter airlines are not certificated in accordance with the airport certification and operations standards in 14 CFR Part 139; consequently, passengers flying into and out of those airports may not be provided adequate airport safety or emergency response resources.

13. Results of the commuter airline survey and discussion at the public forum on commuter airline safety suggest that substantial improvements have been made that address many of the maintenance problems identified in the Safety Board's 1980 study of commuter airline safety.

14. Results of the commuter airline survey indicate that, consistent with past Safety Board recommendations, Federal Aviation Administration inspections of commuter airline maintenance operations are being accomplished frequently, are often unannounced, and occur during night shifts when maintenance activity is greatest.

15. A mandatory airline safety program would enhance a commuter air carrier's ability to identify and correct safety problems before they lead to an accident. Federal Aviation Administration Advisory Circular 120-59, "Air Carrier Internal Evaluation Programs," provides a comprehensive framework that includes necessary elements for an effective safety program.

16. A major airline participating in a code-sharing arrangement with a commuter airline is perceived by the traveling public to be owner of the commuter airline and accountable for the safety of its operations. The major airline should participate in oversight of its commuter partner that includes a program of regular safety audits of flight operations, training programs, maintenance, and inspection.

17. The Federal Aviation Administration (FAA) is not perceived as being consistent in the interpretation and enforcement of regulations across FAA inspectors, offices, and regions by 15 out of 16 airlines in the commuter airline survey (94 percent).

18. Federal Aviation Administration surveillance of commuter airlines is often conducted by inspectors who have neither experience in air carrier operations nor familiarity with the specific aircraft types operated by the air carriers they oversee.

19. Self-policing initiatives such as Air Carrier Internal Evaluation Programs and Air Carrier Voluntary Self-Disclosure Reporting Procedures are positive steps toward improving surveillance. To be fully effective, Internal Evaluation Programs should be mandatory for all air carriers, and the Federal Aviation Administration should systematically track the use of Internal Evaluation Programs and the information they generate to enhance the efficiency of its air carrier surveillance.

UN REPORT ON SECURITY IN RWANDAN REFUGEE CAMPS

November 18, 1994

The United Nations should send several thousand troops to Zaire to create secure conditions for 1.2 million Rwandan refugees living in camps and to help persuade them to return home, UN Secretary General Boutros Boutros-Ghali recommended in a November 18 report to the Security Council. However, this report—like his earlier pleas for the international community to send troops to Rwanda—got only a lukewarm reception.

By the time of the report, an estimated half million Rwandans had been killed in a campaign of genocide carried out by militant members of the Hutu tribe against members of the Tutsi tribe and moderate Hutus. Hutus made up 85 percent of the population in Rwanda, a tiny Central African country of 7.7 million people. Hatred between the two tribes dated back centuries, and they had periodically clashed ever since Rwanda gained its independence from Belgium in 1962.

The latest violence started on April 6, when a plane carrying President Juvenal Habyarimana of Rwanda and President Cyprien Ntaryamira of Burundi was apparently shot down outside of the Rwandan capital of Kigali. The two Hutu leaders, who were returning from a regional summit in Tanzania aimed at ending the civil wars that had plagued their countries for decades, both died in the crash. The Rwandan government blamed rebel forces of the Tutsi-led Rwandan Patriotic Front for the attack, but Belgian officials who later investigated the crash believed that extremist Hutus shot down the plane because Habyarimana had made efforts to include Tutsis in a coalition government. Those efforts had been part of a peace agreement that the government and rebels had signed in August 1993 to end a three-year civil war.

Widespread Slaughter of Tutsis

As soon as the plane crashed, Hutu soldiers, militiamen, and civilians started systematically slaughtering Tutsis in Kigali. They abducted and killed Prime Minister Agathe Uwilingiyimana, a Tutsi who Habyarimana had appointed in July 1993 as a peace gesture, and killed many other cabinet ministers. The Hutus also killed ten Belgian soldiers who were part of a 2,500-member UN peacekeeping force. The peacekeepers were under orders not to intervene in the violence and sat helplessly in their bunkers as the slaughter went on about them. In response to the killings by Hutus, Tutsi-led rebels launched an offensive of their own and marched into the capital's suburbs.

On April 21, just two weeks after the plane crash, the International Committee of the Red Cross estimated that 100,000 Rwandans had died in the tribal slaughter, which it called a "human tragedy on a scale we have rarely witnessed." The same day, the UN Security Council voted to sharply reduce the number of peacekeeping troops in Rwanda. Human rights groups attacked the move, saying it would lead to the slaughter of people who had sought UN protection. The UN had tried to negotiate a ceasefire, but neither side was interested.

A week later, Boutros-Ghali asked the Security Council to reconsider its decision to reduce the peacekeeping force. He said the force actually should be expanded so that the massacres, which he said had killed up to 200,000 people, could be halted. In a report, the secretary general said he was "convinced that the scale of human suffering in Rwanda and its implications for the stability of neighboring countries leave the Security Council with no alternative but to examine this possibility." Western members of the Security Council were not eager to send troops, remembering that the troops they had sent to Somalia a year earlier to stop tribal warfare had suffered casualties while largely failing in their mission. If UN troops intervened in Rwanda, they were virtually certain to suffer casualties and there were no assurances that they would be any more successful than the troops in Somalia.

At the end of April, Boutros-Ghali wrote to the heads of African nations asking them to contribute troops to a peacekeeping force. Not a single African country made a firm offer. On May 25, Boutros-Ghali blasted the international community for doing nothing to stop the bloodshed. "More than 200,000 people have been killed and the international community is still discussing what ought to be done," he said.

In a commencement address the next day at the U.S. Naval Academy, President Bill Clinton said: "We cannot solve every such outburst of civil strife or militant nationalism simply by sending in our forces." Shortly thereafter, administration spokesmen were instructed not to say that "genocide" was occurring in Rwanda. Instead, they were told to say that "acts of genocide may have occurred."

France Sends Troops

After getting approval from the UN Security Council, France announced on June 22 that it was sending 2,500 troops to Rwanda. French officials said the troops would help protect civilians. The action was complicated by the fact that for at least several years France had quietly aided the Hutu government in its battles with the Tutsi rebels.

By mid-July, the rebels had defeated the remainder of the Rwandan army, and in a four-day period an estimated 1.2 million Rwandans fled across the border into eastern Zaire. Most were Hutus who were fleeing the fighting and who feared that the Tutsis might engage in reprisals. The mass of refugees overwhelmed relief officials. On July 22 Clinton ordered the Pentagon to undertake a massive airlift to deliver supplies to the refugees. The most urgent priority was to build water purification and distribution systems because cholera was sweeping through the camps. Clinton said the situation might be "the world's worst humanitarian crisis in a generation." The same day, the European Union promised an additional $183 million in aid.

Even with the aid, the camps remained "overcrowded, chaotic and increasingly insecure," according to a November UN report. Beyond the issue of simply keeping the refugees alive was the broader issue of how to get them to return home. On November 17, a team of officials from the UN and the Zairean government concluded that the only way to get the refugees to leave was to bring in thousands of foreign troops to remove former government soldiers, militiamen, and government officials from the camps. Those forces were running the camps and threatening anyone who tried to leave. There also were fears that the remaining elements of the Rwandan army and militias were regrouping for a new war.

As before, there was little support for sending a large international force to Rwanda or Zaire. The job of disarming the camps was seen as too risky, and there still had not been any firm commitments of troops for an international force. The year ended with the Rwandan refugees waiting for an elusive peace that would allow them to return home.

Following are excerpts from a report, dated November 18, 1994, by United Nations Secretary General Boutros Boutros-Ghali about security in the Rwandan refugee camps:

I. Introduction

1. The present report is submitted in pursuance of the statement of the President of the Security Council dated 14 October 1994, which noted the Council's concern at the plight of the millions of Rwandese refugees and displaced persons, reiterated the view that their return to their homes was essential for the normalization of the situation in Rwanda and deplored the continuing acts of intimidation and violence within the refugee camps, which were designed to prevent the refugee population there from returning home.

2. In my report on the situation in Rwanda dated 6 October, I indicated that, as a result of his visit to Zaire from 12 to 14 September, my Special Representative for Rwanda, Mr. Shaharyar Khan, concluded that the most effective way of ensuring the safety of the refugees and their freedom to return to Rwanda

would be the separation of political leaders, former Rwandese government forces and militia from the rest of the refugee population. I also noted, however, that that would be a difficult and complex undertaking, especially as those to be separated would be likely to resist, and incite others to resist, any attempt to relocate them. In order to address more fully the problems associated with separating the former Rwandese government forces' political leaders, military and militia from the refugees, and to evaluate the logistic and other requirements involved, a joint Zairian/United Nations working group was established, composed of officials of the Government of Zaire, the United Nations High Commissioner for Refugees (UNHCR) and the United Nations Development Programme (UNDP). A technical team from the United Nations Assistance Mission for Rwanda (UNAMIR) was sent to Zaire to join the working group. In my report . . . I also indicated that my Special Representative had recommended that attention be focused, as a matter of priority, on the camps in Zaire, where the problems were significantly more acute than in those established in the United Republic of Tanzania. Accordingly, the present report addresses mainly the issue of security in the camps located in Zaire. . . .

4. Following consultations between the Secretariat and UNHCR on possible options for addressing the security situation in the camps, I convened a high-level meeting at Geneva on 8 November, which focused on various aspects of the crisis in Rwanda and most importantly on the situation in the refugee camps. The meeting was attended by the United Nations High Commissioner for Refugees and the United Nations High Commissioner for Human Rights, the Executive Director of the World Food Programme, the Under-Secretaries-General for Political Affairs and for Humanitarian Affairs, the Legal Counsel, one of my special advisers, my Special Representatives for Rwanda and Burundi, my Special Humanitarian Envoy for Rwanda and Burundi, the Military Adviser in the Department of Peace-keeping Operations and a representative of the United Nations Children's Fund (UNICEF).

5. The meeting concluded that the most urgent problems were the security in the camps and the Government's need for support to enable it to carry out its functions. It was agreed that those problems must be addressed under an overall strategy leading to the repatriation and reintegration of refugees and internally displaced persons. The meeting also concluded that longer-term efforts, including efforts on a regional basis, towards national reconciliation, rehabilitation and reconstruction of the country should contribute to the resolution of the more urgent problems related to the safe return of refugees and internally displaced persons.

II. Present Situation in the Rwandese Refugee Camps in Zaire

A. Conditions in the camps

6. An estimated 1.2 million people fled Rwanda over a four-day period in mid-July to the Kivu region of Zaire, in one of the largest and most sudden

movements of refugees in modern history. UNHCR estimates that there are 850,000 refugees in north Kivu, in the Goma areas of Mugunga, Kibumba and Katale, and about 370,000 in south Kivu, in the Bukavu and Uvira areas. The camps, which sprawl over miles, are overcrowded, chaotic and increasingly insecure. The refugees live in makeshift huts and are completely dependent on United Nations and relief agencies for basic needs assistance.

7. The former Rwandese political leaders, Rwandese government forces, soldiers and militia control the camps, though the degree of control varies from area to area. They are determined to ensure by force, if necessary, that the refugees do not repatriate to Rwanda. They also make it difficult for relief agencies to carry out their work in safety, because they attempt to control the agencies' activities in the camps and prevent relief supplies from reaching those in need. It is believed that these elements may be preparing for an armed invasion of Rwanda and that they may be stockpiling and selling food distributed by relief agencies in preparation for such an invasion. There have already been some cross border incursions. Security is further undermined by general lawlessness, extortion, banditry and gang warfare between groups fighting for control of the camps. As a result of these threats to security, non-governmental organizations responsible for the distribution of relief supplies in the camps have begun to withdraw.

8. There are approximately 230 Rwandese political leaders in Zaire, including former ministers, senior civilian and military officials, members of parliament and other political personalities, many of whom live in good conditions in hotels and houses outside the refugee camps. With their dependants, they amount to about 1,200 persons. These leaders exert a hold on the refugees through intimidation and the support of military personnel and militia members in the camps.

9. Estimates of the number of former Rwandese government forces personnel in Zaire differ but they probably amount to about 50,000 persons, including dependants. In south Kivu, they are located in two separate military camps. In north Kivu, on the other hand, they are living among the refugees and are often indistinguishable from them, since many no longer wear uniforms. It seems to be their intention to regain power in Rwanda and there are reports of continuing military activity by them along the Zairian/Rwandese border in Kanganiro and Kamanyola. However, they have not so far been as significant a factor for insecurity in the camps as have the militia.

10. The militia have a significant presence in the camps in the Goma area, where they control access into and out of the camps and resort openly to intimidation and force to stop refugees who are inclined to return to Rwanda. Like the Rwandese government forces personnel, they possess firearms, as the Zairian authorities were unable to disarm all the Rwandese government forces and militia personnel when they sought refuge in Zaire in July 1994. They also possess vehicles and communication equipment. It is difficult to determine their exact number as they neither wear uniform nor carry any insignia that would distinguish them from the rest of the refugee

population. However, an estimate of their number can be made by reference to the militia's pre-war organization. Each of the 147 communes in Rwanda had between 100 and 150 organized militia, which would represent a total of between 14,700 and 22,050 personnel. Allowing for war attrition, this number may have fallen as low as 10,000 when the refugee camps were established but, in view of the political activity in the camps, it could have risen since that time.

11. There is little information available on the former Presidential Guard, which is estimated to consist of 800 men located in both Goma and Bukavu. There are reports that it may be housed in clandestine camps.

B. Factors impeding repatriation

12. In August and early September, an estimated 200,000 refugees returned to Rwanda. This movement, however, was interrupted by the activity of militia and political leaders opposed to voluntary repatriation. Since September, the number of refugees returning home has fallen drastically, although small numbers of refugees continue to trickle back to Rwanda in spite of threats by the militia and dissuasion by political leaders. During the same period, some 400,000 refugees of mainly Tutsi origin, many of whom had been in exile in Uganda and Burundi for decades, have returned to Rwanda and, in many cases, settled on land belonging to those who have fled most recently, thus creating another problem relating to property rights. The Government has set up a land commission to resolve that problem but it is unable to provide alternative solutions for those refugees, because of a lack of funds.

13. The refugees' fear of reprisals by the Government for atrocities committed against Tutsis and moderate Hutus seems to be another main reason for their hesitancy about returning to Rwanda. While this fear has been exacerbated by efforts on the part of political leaders, Rwandese government forces elements and militia to dissuade the refugees from returning home, it also appears to be rooted in the history of the relationship between Hutus and Tutsis in Rwanda. In expressing their distrust of the Government, refugees have also indicated a desire for their security to be guaranteed by a neutral body or for their own leaders to participate in the new Government.

14. In the light of the above, the UNAMIR technical team sought the views of the political and military leaders in the camps on conditions that would enable them to allow refugees the freedom of choice to return to Rwanda. These conditions included negotiations with the new Government; involvement of the exiled leadership in all negotiation processes; involvement of the United Nations in facilitating negotiations between the Government and the leadership in exile; revival of acceptable elements of the Arusha Accord; power-sharing; setting up of an international tribunal that would address not only the atrocities and acts of genocide committed after the events of 6 April 1994, but also alleged massacres committed by forces of the Rwandese Patriotic Front (RPF) since 1990; organization of early elections; security guarantees, especially for the safe return of all refugees; and guarantees for the repossession by the refugees of their property.

III. Measures for the Establishment of Secure Conditions in the Camps

A. Initial measures

15. In response to a request from the Government of Zaire, consideration has been given, in consultation with UNHCR, to measures aimed at providing immediate, but temporary, assistance to the Zairian security forces in protecting humanitarian operations in the camps. These measures would promote bilateral arrangements between the Government of Zaire and other Governments for the deployment of security experts to train and monitor the local security forces. . . .

17. Efforts to improve security in the camps should also be supported by a public information campaign that would provide factual information on the situation both in the camps and in Rwanda. To this end, as indicated in my report of 6 October, UNAMIR is building a broadcasting capacity that can reach the camps. However, the Government of Rwanda has yet to grant the necessary authorizations for UNAMIR to begin broadcasting and for a frequency allocation. It is important that these authorizations should be forthcoming soon.

B. Deployment of a United Nations peace-keeping operation

18. In order to improve security, one option would be to deploy a United Nations peace-keeping force to the camps in Zaire, with the consent of the Government of Zaire, as is the established practice for such operations. The task of such a force would be to provide security for international relief workers, protection for the storage and delivery of humanitarian assistance and safe passage to the Rwandese border for those refugees who wish to return. From the border, UNAMIR troops would then provide assistance in returning the refugees to their home communities. Such a force would have a mandate separate from that of UNAMIR but would be under the operational control of, and supported logistically by, UNAMIR.

1. First phase

19. In the first phase, two well-trained and well-equipped mechanized battalions would spearhead the operation in the camps north of Lake Kivu. Each battalion would establish secure areas within large camp sites, providing safe conditions for the refugees in those areas. The force would establish screening procedures to keep weapons out of the secure areas. Humanitarian assistance operations would be intensified within these secure areas. The aim during this first phase would be to create conditions conducive to the voluntary repatriation to Rwanda of as many refugees as possible from each secure area. This, of course, would depend on the establishment within Rwanda of conditions under which the refugees could return to their homes in safety and dignity.

20. Within each secure area, local security units would be formed and

trained to take over the security functions being performed by the peace-keeping force when reasonably secure conditions were deemed to have been created. At that time, the United Nations contingents would move forward to create similar secure areas in other locations. . . .

2. Second phase

22. In the second phase, lightly equipped motorized units would be deployed in the areas rendered secure during the first phase. Their main task would be to escort refugees to the Rwandese border and, in the meantime, to ensure that these areas continued to enjoy secure conditions. . . .

23. Under this option, it is estimated that a force of 3,000 all ranks would be required. A parallel operation, launched simultaneously in the area south of Lake Kivu, where conditions are marginally better, could have a stabilizing effect on Burundi where the situation is still very fragile. To conduct such an operation, an additional 2,000 troops would be required. . . .

25. The incremental approach to establishing security proposed under this option is unavoidable as the dimensions of the problem are such as to make it impossible to address all refugee camps at the same time. Depending on the situation in the camps and the rate of repatriation, it is estimated that, given a force strength of 3,000 all ranks, it would take 24 to 30 months to complete the operation. However, with the additional 2,000 troops mentioned in paragraph 23, it is estimated that the duration of the operation could be reduced by about 10 months.

C. Action under Chapter VII of the Charter

26. The option outlined above does not provide for the separation of the political leaders, former Rwandese government forces troops and militia from the rest of the camp population, which, as indicated in my report of 6 October, is considered to be the most effective way of ensuring the safety of refugees and their freedom to exercise their right to return to Rwanda. That report also noted that the Government of Zaire had expressed its commitment to addressing the refugee crisis and to improving security in the camps. To this end, it has indicated that the military and militia elements could be moved to new camps at a distance from the present refugee camps. It has also indicated that it would prefer the political leadership of the former Government of Rwanda to be located in third countries, although they could stay in Kinshasa while awaiting relocation.

27. The political leaders, the military hierarchy of the Rwandese government forces and the militia have made evident their opposition to either their removal from Goma and Bukavu or their separation from the refugee population prior to an overall settlement of the conflict. It is difficult to determine how far these groups would resist attempts to relocate them. Given their expressed opposition, however, and their proven propensity for violence, it can be assumed that they would not move voluntarily and would be likely to use force to resist being moved.

28. Should it be decided to undertake the separation of former political

leaders, military and militia, the operation would also be undertaken in phases. In the first phase, while the new camps were being prepared, a strong, well-trained and well-equipped force would be deployed inside the existing refugee camps with the initial mandate of ensuring the security of international relief workers and the delivery of humanitarian assistance. During the second phase, once the new camps were established, the former political leaders, Rwandese government forces personnel and militia would be moved to the new sites, on a voluntary basis if possible, with force being used only where voluntary separation was resisted. . . .

IV. Concluding Observations

32. In considering the above options, it is important to bear in mind that any operation conducted without parallel efforts towards national reconciliation in Rwanda will be futile. Indeed, it might merely have the effect of intensifying extremist activities in the refugee camps in Zaire and also those in other countries bordering Rwanda. It is evident that national reconciliation will require both a political understanding between the former leadership of the country and the present Government and the establishment of conditions in the camps, and in Rwanda itself, conducive to the return of the refugees. Neither is imminent. Any operation that encouraged the repatriation of refugees who were then not able to return to their home communities would merely add to the 1.5 to 2 million persons who are already internally displaced persons inside Rwanda and should therefore be avoided. . . .

35. The Government must assume its responsibilities for establishing the conditions necessary for the return of refugees to Rwanda in safety and dignity. However, in the wake of the cataclysm that has overtaken Rwanda, it finds itself without even the minimal resources to run an administration, much less reconstruct a shattered country and nation. The Government has indicated its commitment to creating conditions for the safe repatriation of refugees and has requested assistance from the international community for this purpose. This will require the rehabilitation of the basic economic and social infrastructure. Measures to be taken inside Rwanda must include the establishment of a fair and effective judicial system and the issue of property rights. As mentioned above, large numbers of longer-term refugees are returning to Rwanda and, in some cases, are occupying the land of those who have recently fled. The Government needs immediate and major financial and technical assistance from the international community to reintegrate the earlier refugees who are now returning and to ensure that those who recently left the country are able to reclaim their properties upon their return. . . .

UN SECURITY COUNCIL RESOLUTION ON BOSNIA
November 19, 1994

On November 19, the United Nations Security Council adopted Resolution 959—yet another resolution condemning aggression by Serbs in the Republic of Bosnia and Herzegovina. Within a week, forces of the North Atlantic Treaty Organization (NATO) backed up the UN's words with a series of airstrikes against Serb positions.

The conflict in Bosnia dated to the period between June 1991 and April 1992, when four of the six former republics in the Yugoslav federation—Croatia, Slovenia, Bosnia and Herzegovina, and Macedonia—declared their independence. The two remaining republics, Serbia and Montenegro, combined to form the new Federal Republic of Yugoslavia. (Independence of Yugoslav Republics, Historic Documents of 1991, p. 367)

In 1992, Serbs living in Bosnia said they did not want to be a minority under Bosnia's Muslim-led government and started a war aimed at seceding and taking a large block of Bosnian territory with them. Serbs living in Croatia started a similar war. In May 1992 the United Nations imposed economic sanctions on the Federal Republic of Yugoslavia because the Serb-led government was supporting Serb aggression in Bosnia and Croatia. In August 1992 the Senate Foreign Relations Committee released a report stating that Serb militias were engaging in wholesale murder and brutality in Bosnia aimed at slaughtering or driving from the land all Croat and Muslim inhabitants. A month later, the UN General Assembly revoked the membership of the Federal Republic of Yugoslavia, only the second time in the UN's forty-seven-year history that it in effect expelled a member nation. (Senate Staff Report on Yugoslav 'Ethnic Cleansing,' United Nations on Yugoslavia's Membership, Historic Documents of 1992, p. 771 and p. 875)

In 1993, four State Department officials resigned over their frustration with U.S. inaction regarding Bosnia. Also in 1993, a report by Amnesty International further documented Serb atrocities in Bosnia. (Amnesty International Report on Human Rights, Historic Documents of 1993, p. 559)

By 1994, tens of thousands of people—many of them civilians—had died in the Bosnian fighting, the bloodiest European conflict since the end of World War II. Thirteen thousand UN "peacekeeping" troops were in Bosnia, but they concentrated on delivering food, medicine, and other humanitarian supplies to the civilian population rather than intervening in the war. Serb militias often blocked UN aid convoys; the UN troops responded by simply turning around and returning to their bases to try again another day.

Sarajevo Attack Kills Dozens

World attention focused on Bosnia on February 5 when a mortar shell landed in a crowded market in Sarajevo, Bosnia's capital, killing 68 and wounding more than 200. Sarajevo had been under siege by Bosnian Serbs since April 1992, and civilians had been frequent targets of Serb shells and snipers. Bosnia's government blamed Serbs for the market attack, but the Serbs claimed that Bosnian soldiers had launched the mortar against their own people in an effort to force NATO to make threatened airstrikes against Serb positions. No evidence supported the Serb claims.

Despite the attention drawn by the Sarajevo attack, the international community could not figure out how to stop the fighting. Airstrikes against Serb positions were risky, since they could result in Serb retaliation against the lightly armed UN troops in Bosnia. There also were fears that airstrikes could lead to a full-scale war between the NATO forces and the Bosnian Serbs—a war that Serbia, which was the chief supplier for the Bosnian Serbs, might openly join. Sending in UN troops to stop the war was even riskier, since it would require placing more than 100,000 soldiers in the middle of an intense war that could drag on for years.

On February 9, in response to the Sarajevo attack, NATO leaders gave the Bosnian Serbs ten days to remove their heavy weaponry and mortars from around Sarajevo. The Serbs were ordered to pull the weapons back at least twelve miles from the city or face airstrikes. The Serbs complied, at least for the time being, primarily by hauling their weapons to other cities for new assaults. In August, NATO planes attacked Serbian heavy weapons that were violating the exclusionary zone around Sarajevo.

A month earlier, the Serbs rejected a peace plan drawn up by the United States, Britain, France, Germany, and Russia. Under the plan, a Muslim-Croat federation would get 51 percent of Bosnia's land and the Serbs would get 49 percent. The plan would have required the Serbs to give up about one-third of the land they had won militarily.

U.S., Allies Split on Strategy

As the war dragged on, tensions mounted between the United States and its European allies. One of the biggest sources of tension was the arms embargo that the UN had imposed in 1991 against all the former Yugoslav republics. The United States wanted the embargo lifted against Bosnia but kept in place for the other republics. The European nations strongly opposed the idea, saying that lifting the embargo would lead to an escalation of the

*war. On November 3, the UN General Assembly approved a resolution intro-
duced by the United States that urged the Security Council to lift the arms
embargo against Bosnia. The vote was 97-0, with 61 abstentions.*

*A week later, in a major split with the NATO allies, President Bill Clinton
ordered the U.S. military to stop helping to enforce the arms embargo
against Bosnia. Under Clinton's order, U.S. Navy ships stopped diverting
ships carrying weapons to Bosnia or Croatia and U.S. intelligence agencies
stopped sharing information about such shipments with other nations that
continued enforcing the embargo. Clinton's move greatly upset the European allies, who said it threatened NATO's solidarity and could set back
peace efforts.*

*Late in the month, NATO launched two airstrikes against Serb positions.
On November 21, NATO planes bombed an air base in Croatia that the Serbs
had used to launch planes carrying napalm and cluster bombs in raids on
the Bihac area in Bosnia, which the UN had declared was a safe zone. The
NATO strike, which involved a total of thirty-nine planes from the United
States, Britain, France, and the Netherlands, was the largest military action
undertaken by NATO since its creation in 1949. Two days later, NATO
planes struck Serbian missile sites in northwestern Bosnia.*

U.S. Switches Policy

*In an effort to heal relations with the other NATO members, the Clinton
administration on November 28 switched positions and dropped its efforts
to convince the allies that extensive airstrikes and other military measures
should be employed against the Serbs. The move was the latest in a series of
abrupt policy changes dating back to the administration of George Bush.*

*On December 20, former president Jimmy Carter, who went to Bosnia on
an unofficial peace mission, announced that the warring factions had
agreed to a ceasefire that would last at least four months. More than thirty
other ceasefires had been announced since the war began in 1992, and each
had quickly collapsed. It was unclear how long the newest ceasefire would
last, but for the embattled Bosnian civilians any relief from the fighting was
welcome.*

*Following is the text of Resolution 959, adopted November 19,
1994, by the United Nations Security Council, which condemns the conflict in the Republic of Bosnia and Herzegovina:*

Resolution 959 (1994)

Adopted by the Security Council at its 3462nd meeting, on 19 November
1994

The Security Council,

Recalling all its previous relevant resolutions on the conflict in the Republic of Bosnia and Herzegovina and in particular its resolutions 824 (1993) and 836 (1993),

Reaffirming the need for a lasting peace settlement to be signed by all the Bosnian parties, and implemented in good faith by them, and condemning the decision by the Bosnian Serb party to refuse to accept the proposed territorial settlement (S/1994/1081),

Reaffirming also the independence, sovereignty and territorial integrity of the Republic of Bosnia and Herzegovina,

Expressing special concern about the escalation in recent fighting in the Bihac pocket, including those in, from and around the safe areas, and the flow of refugees and displaced persons resulting from it,

Bearing in mind the importance of facilitating the return of refugees and displaced persons to their homes,

Taking note of the reports of the Secretary-General of 10 March 1994 (S/1994/291) and 16 March 1994 (S/1994/300) and of his recommendations concerning the definition and implementation of the concept of safe areas in his report of 9 May 1994 (S/1994/555),

Recalling the statements by the President of the Security Council of 6 April 1994 (S/PRST/1994/14), 30 June 1994 (S/PRST/1994/31), 13 November 1994 (S/PRST/1994/66) and 18 November 1994 (S/PRST/1994/69),

Reaffirming its previous calls on all parties and others concerned to refrain from any hostile action that could cause further escalation in the fighting, and to achieve urgently a cease-fire in the Bihac area,

Reiterating the importance of maintaining Sarajevo, the capital of the Republic of Bosnia and Herzegovina, as a united city and a multicultural, multi-ethnic and pluri-religious centre, and noting in this context the positive contribution that agreement between the parties on the demilitarization of Sarajevo could make to this end, to the restoration of normal life in Sarajevo, and to achieving an overall settlement, consistent with the Contact Group peace plan,

Taking note of the communique on Bosnia and Herzegovina issued on 30 July 1994 by the Troika of the European Union and the Foreign Ministers of the Russian Federation, the United Kingdom of Great Britain and Northern Ireland and the United States of America (S/1994/916) and, in particular, of their commitment to strengthen the regime of safe areas,

1. Expresses its grave concern over the recent hostilities in Bosnia and Herzegovina;
2. Condemns any violation of the international border between the Republic of Croatia and the Republic of Bosnia and Herzegovina and demands that all parties and others concerned, and in particular the so-called Krajina Serb forces, fully respect the border and refrain from hostile acts across it;
3. Expresses its full support for the efforts by the United Nations Protection Force (UNPROFOR), to ensure implementation of the Security Council resolutions on safe areas;

4. Calls upon all the Bosnian parties to respect fully the status and functions of UNPROFOR and to cooperate with it in its efforts to ensure implementation of the Security Council resolutions on safe areas and demands that all parties and others concerned show maximum restraint and put an end to all hostile actions in and around the safe areas in order to ensure that UNPROFOR can carry out its mandate in this regard effectively and safely;

5. Requests the Secretary-General to update his recommendations on modalities of the implementation of the concept of safe areas and to encourage UNPROFOR, in cooperation with the Bosnian parties, to continue their efforts to achieve agreements on strengthening the regimes of safe areas taking into account the specific situation in each case, and recalls its request to the Secretary-General in the statement by the President of the Security Council of 13 November 1994 to report as soon as possible on any further measures to stabilize the situation in and around the safe area of Bihac;

6. Further requests the Secretary-General and UNPROFOR to intensify efforts aimed at reaching agreement with the Bosnian parties on the modalities of demilitarization of Sarajevo, bearing in mind the need for the restoration of normal life to the city and for free access to and from the city by land and air and the free and unimpeded movement of people, goods and services in and around the city in line with its Resolution 900 (1994), particularly operative paragraph 2;

7. Requests the Secretary-General to report on the implementation of the present resolution by 1 December 1994;

8. Decides to remain seized of the matter.

CLINTON'S REMARKS ON GATT
November 28, 1994

At a White House event held November 28 to rally support for the General Agreement on Tariffs and Trade (GATT), President Bill Clinton said the pact would add $1,700 to the average family's income and create hundreds of thousands of high-wage jobs. Only days earlier Clinton had cut a deal with Senate Minority Leader Bob Dole (R-Kan.) that saved GATT from an almost certain defeat in the Senate. Both the House and the Senate ultimately approved GATT by wide margins.

GATT, the largest free trade agreement in decades, was actually the eighth expansion of a pact that had originally been approved in 1947. The latest expansion resulted from a dozen years of negotiating among 124 countries. China, which had extensive trade barriers, was the only major country that did not participate.

GATT's purpose was to strike down barriers that blocked free trade between countries. Trade delegates had finished hammering out the pact's details in late 1993. In a message to Congress asking it to approve the measure, President Bill Clinton had said that GATT would produce expanded trade and "add as much as $100 billion to $200 billion per year to our economy once it is fully phased in." (Clinton Letter to Congress on Renewal of Trade Agreement, Historic Documents of 1993, p. 997)

Some of GATT's major provisions will:

- *Reduce tariffs on imported goods by an average of one-third. Tariffs are taxes added to low-cost imported goods to raise their price so that goods made in the importing country are competitive.*
- *Eliminate quotas, which countries use to ban or limit the import of certain products. Countries can replace quotas with tariffs, although the tariffs must be gradually reduced.*
- *Require all countries to protect intellectual property rights such as patents, copyrights, and trademarks. This provision was aimed at stop-*

ping the production of pirated copies of everything from books to pre-
scription drugs.

- *Ban countries from requiring that high levels of "local content" be used*
  in such products as cars.

Critics Fear Loss of U.S. Sovereignty

GATT's most controversial provision creates a new World Trade Orga-
nization (WTO), which will handle trade disputes that arise among coun-
tries. When a trade dispute occurs, the WTO will appoint a three-member
panel of trade experts who will hear the case in secret. If the United States
lost a case, it would have three options:

- *Congress could change the law that was found to violate GATT rules.*
- *The United States could negotiate a settlement with the nation that filed*
  the complaint.
- *The United States could ignore the ruling, but then the complaining na-*
  tion could retaliate by raising tariffs on American goods.

GATT's critics, who included everyone from consumer advocate Ralph
Nader to conservative Sen. Jesse Helms (R-N.C.), contended that creation of
the WTO would lead to a loss of U.S. sovereignty. They said other nations
could attack U.S. laws that protect consumers, workers, and the environ-
ment, claiming they were actually barriers to free trade. The United States
would have no choice but to change its laws, the critics said, because it could
not risk higher tariffs on American goods.

As an example, critics pointed to a 1991 case that arose when GATT had
weak enforcement powers. In that case, the United States had banned im-
ports of tuna from Mexico because Mexican fishermen used nets that could
also trap dolphins. Mexico protested the ban, and a GATT panel ruled that
the United States could not impose its environmental rules on other coun-
tries. Otherwise, the panel said, the United States could use its rules as a
"back door" method of blocking foreign imports.

GATT's supporters—including the White House, most large businesses,
and many members of Congress—said concerns about the WTO were over-
blown. They said other countries needed access to American markets, so they
were likely to negotiate any disputes rather than ending up in a trade war
with the United States.

Deal Saves GATT from Defeat

When Congress convened in a lame-duck session after the November elec-
tion to consider GATT, it appeared that the WTO issue would lead to defeat of
the pact in the Senate. But on November 23 Clinton and Dole reached a deal
that rescued GATT. Under the deal, a U.S. commission consisting of five
federal appellate judges will examine all WTO rulings that go against the
United States to determine if they are fair. If over a five-year period the
commission finds that three decisions are unfair, Congress can start pro-
ceedings to withdraw the United States from the agreement. Previously, it

had been assumed that any decision to drop out of the agreement was up to the president.

Besides attacking the WTO, critics also argued that dropping tariffs would lead to the importing of cheap foreign goods, and thus a loss of American jobs, especially in industries such as textiles. Supporters, while agreeing there would be some job loss, said there would actually be a net gain in jobs because the opening of foreign markets would lead to greater exports of high-tech American goods. They also said American consumers would benefit because they would have more access to inexpensive goods produced in foreign countries.

With the Clinton-Dole deal in place, GATT sailed through Congress despite misgivings by some conservatives that the deal was insufficient. On November 29, the House approved the measure on a 288-146 bipartisan vote, which Clinton called a "historic vote for American workers, farmers and families." On December 1, the Senate approved GATT 76-24.

GATT was the second major free trade pact to be adopted since 1993. In November 1993 Congress approved the North American Free Trade Agreement (NAFTA), which linked the United States with Canada and Mexico in a free trade area with a population of 370 million and a gross national product of $6 trillion. (Clinton Remarks on House Passage of NAFTA, Historic Documents of 1993, p. 953)

> *Following is the text of remarks by President Bill Clinton at a White House event held November 28, 1994, to rally support for the General Agreement on Tariffs and Trade, as released by the White House:*

Thank you very much, Mr. Vice President.

Jim Miller and Jim Baker, thank you for your moving and compelling remarks. Mr. Speaker, Leader Michel, members of the Congress, members of the Cabinet, and to all of you who have come here from previous administrations and from different walks of life, proving that this GATT [General Agreement on Tariffs and Trade] agreement not only tears down trade barriers, it also bulldozes differences of party, philosophy and ideology: I thank you all for being here.

We have certainly demonstrated today that there is no partisan pride of ownership in the GATT agreement. It is not a Republican agreement or a Democratic one, it is an American agreement, designed to benefit all the American people in every region of our country from every walk of life.

Jim Baker spoke so eloquently about how this represents yet another historic choice for the United States in the 20th century. When we walked away from our leadership and engagement responsibilities, as we did after the first world war, the world has paid a terrible price. When we have attempted to lead, as we did after the second world war, it has not only helped the world, it has helped the people of the United States. We saw the greatest expansion of the middle class in our country, and prosperity for working families in our country in the years after we tried to put together a system that would preserve peace and security and promote prosperity after World War II.

We have done as much as we could here at home to try to deal with the difficult and daunting economic challenges we face—to bring the deficit down, to shrink the size of the government, to simultaneously increase our investment in education and technology and defense conversion. But we know that without the capacity to expand trade and to generate more economic opportunities we will, first of all, not be able to fulfill our global responsibilities, and secondly, not be able to fulfill our responsibilities to the American people.

I'd like to address a third argument, if I might, just from my heart. It's been raised against this agreement and raised against NAFTA [North American Free Trade Agreement]. Jim Miller adequately disposed of the arguments that this is a budget buster and that this somehow impinges on our sovereignty. That isn't true. And he did a very compelling job of that. But let me say there is another big argument against this trade agreement that no one has advanced today but that is underlying all of this. And I saw it in an article the other day written by a columnist generally sympathetic to me. He said, there he goes again with one of his crazy, self-defeating economic ideas, pushing this GATT agreement, which is one more prescription for the demise of the lower-wage working people in America, which is the reason the Democratic Party's in the trouble it's in today, doing things like this that just kill working people.

That is a wrong argument. But that is really the undercurrent against this GATT. The idea is that since we live in a global economy and there are people other places who can work for wages we can't live on, if we open our markets to them, they will displace our workers and they will aggravate the most troubling trend in modern American life, which is that the wages of noncollege-educated male workers in the United States have declined by 12 percent after you take account of inflation in the last 10 years.

Now, that has great superficial appeal. Why is it wrong? It's wrong because, number one, if we don't do anything, we'll have some displacement from foreign competition. But if we move and lead, we will open other markets to our products. And our nation has gone through a wrenching period over the last several years of improving its productivity, its ability to compete. We can now sell and compete anywhere.

When we did NAFTA, they made the same argument. What's happened? A hundred thousand new jobs this year. What's happened? A 500-percent increase in exports of American automobiles to Mexico. What's the biggest complaint in Detroit now? The autoworkers have too much overtime they have to do. If you think about where we were 10 years ago, that's what, at home, we call a high-class problem.

Now, that is the problem we face in America. And the resentments of people who keep working harder and falling further behind, and feel like they've played by the rules and they've gotten the shaft—they will play themselves out, these resentments, in election after election after election in different and unpredictable ways, just like they did in 1992 and 1994. But our responsibility is to do what is right for those people over the long run. That is our responsibility. And the only way to do that is to open other markets to American products and services even as we open our markets to them.

Yes, we have to improve the level of lifetime training and education for the American work force. Yes, we have to deal with some of the serious, particular problems of the American economy. But in the end, the private sector in this country and the working people of this country will do their jobs if they have half a shot at the high-growth areas of the world. And what are the highest-growth areas of the world? Not the wealthy advanced economies, but Latin America, Asia and other places.

GATT, along with NAFTA and what we're trying to do with the Asian Pacific countries, and what we're going to try to do at the Summit of the Americas— this keeps America leading the world in ways that permits us to do both things we have to do at the end of the Cold War—to continue to be engaged, to continue to lead, to work toward a more peaceful and secure and prosperous world; and at the same time, to deal with the terrible, nagging difficulties that so many millions of American families face today.

There is no other way to deal with this. There is no easy way out. There is no slogan that makes the problems go away. This will help to solve the underlying anxiety that millions and millions of Americans face, and I might add, millions of Europeans and millions of Japanese and others in advanced economies all around the world, and at the same time, make the world a better place and the future more secure for our children. And we have to do it now. We can't wait until next year. We don't want to litter it up like a Christmas tree and run the risk of losing it.

Every time I talked to a world leader in the last six months, they have asked me the same thing: When is the United States going to act on GATT? The rest of the world is looking at us.

So we have a golden opportunity here to add $1,700 in income to the average family's income in this country over the next few years, to create hundreds of thousands of high-wage jobs, to have the biggest global tax cut in history, and to fulfill our two responsibilities—our responsibility to lead and remain engaged in the world, and our responsibility to try to help the people here at home get ahead.

We need to get on with it and do it now. Thank you very much.

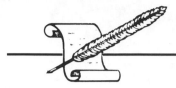

December

INAUGURAL ADDRESS OF ERNESTO ZEDILLO
December 1, 1994

In his inaugural address December 1, newly elected Mexican president Ernesto Zedillo promised to step up investigations into the assassinations during 1994 of two of Mexico's major political figures. Such investigations could prove embarrassing, since there was evidence that top officials in Zedillo's own party, the Institutional Revolutionary Party, were involved in the killings. The party, commonly known by its Spanish initials PRI, had ruled Mexican politics for sixty-five years. The two slain men were PRI members.

"The brutal assassinations of two of Mexico's most outstanding public figures have deeply hurt our citizens, sown seeds of concern and doubt regarding some institutions, and divided the people of Mexico," Zedillo said. "Thus far, the investigations have not been to the entire satisfaction of society."

That was an understatement. The investigations had been so badly bungled and had involved so much infighting among federal, state, and local authorities that most Mexicans suspected a government cover-up. Many believed that the investigations were being manipulated for political reasons.

The first assassination occurred March 23, when forty-four-year-old Luis Donaldo Colosio was gunned down while campaigning in Tijuana. Colosio was the PRI presidential candidate and, as the hand-picked successor to President Carlos Salinas De Gortari, was a virtual shoo-in. A gunman, who was captured, shot Colosio at point-blank range as he mingled in a crowd of thousands of supporters.

Party Officials Suspected in Killing

Almost immediately, some observers wondered whether PRI officials might be involved, since a battle was underway in the party. Hard-line forces had been known to use electoral fraud and control of everything from the judicial system to the news media to retain power and, frequently, to amass huge personal fortunes. Reformers, such as Salinas and Colosio, pressed for economic reforms and to make Mexico a real democracy. Experts estimated that tens of billions of dollars were at stake in the fight. To make matters even more complicated, many old-line PRI leaders were associated with drug traffickers, who also did not want reform.

The assassination of Colosio caused Mexico's worst political crisis since 1928, when the PRI took power after Mexico's last military strongman was killed. The biggest concern was that Salinas's success in attracting billions of dollars in foreign investment by liberalizing the economy and portraying Mexico as a stable country might be jeopardized. The assassination and subsequent bungled investigation also caused many Mexicans to doubt their government.

A month after Colosio's death, files about suspects in the killing disappeared from the office of Tijuana police chief Jose Federico Benitez, who had conducted a secret investigation of the case. Thirty-six hours after the theft was discovered, Benitez and his bodyguard were shot and killed by unidentified gunmen. Although there was no clear connection with Colosio's assassination, the slaying of Benitez added to the mystery surrounding the case.

Investigations by Benitez and federal special prosecutor Miguel Montes focused on the forty-five-member security detail that had been put together by local PRI officials for Colosio's appearance. Montes claimed that members of the detail had helped the gunman by blocking Colosio's path and preventing the candidate's own bodyguards from reaching him. Benitez reportedly had evidence that many members of the security detail were former policemen who had been fired for corruption, including torture.

In early June, Montes abruptly changed course and announced that the gunman had acted alone. He closed the case a month later, saying the gunman was a disturbed individual who murdered Colosio because he hated the PRI. Montes then resigned. His actions only heightened speculation about a cover-up.

Zedillo Elected President

On August 21, Ernesto Zedillo Ponce de Leon, the PRI's replacement for Colosio, was elected president of Mexico. Zedillo was a forty-two-year-old American-trained economist who had been closely associated with Salinas's efforts to modernize Mexico and increase its economic ties with the United States. Zedillo, who was known for his integrity, was part of the reform wing of the PRI.

A month later, Jose Francisco Ruiz Massieu, who was to have been the PRI's legislative leader for Zedillo's reform program, was gunned down on a Mexico City street. The assassin, who was caught at the scene, said others had ordered the killing. Government officials believed the assassination was ordered by factions of the party that opposed reform. A hit list also surfaced that named other reform politicians.

Deputy Attorney General Mario Ruiz Massieu, the brother of the slain politician, claimed November 17 that the PRI was hindering the investigation into his brother's death. Party leaders said the prosecutor was on a witch hunt and denied the charge. Less than a week later Massieu resigned. He charged that his brother's killing had been ordered by a leading group in the PRI and that party leaders and Mexico's attorney general were blocking him from proving it.

The assassinations were only one of many problems Zedillo faced as he took office. He also had to contend with a peasant uprising that had erupted in January in the southern Mexican state of Chiapas. The rebels demanded improved treatment of Indians, reform of Mexico's political system, and economic help for Mexico's poorest citizens.

Trying to improve economic conditions for Mexico's poor was perhaps Zedillo's biggest challenge. The nation suffered huge income disparities, with nearly half the people living at or below the poverty level. The poorest people had yet to reap the benefits of Mexico's expanded international trade through such agreements as the North American Free Trade Agreement. In his inaugural address, Zedillo promised to improve conditions for the poor. "Many millions of Mexicans lack the bare essentials," he said. "Many have not benefited from the fruits of progress. Many live in a state of poverty that is a source of indignation to the nation."

> *Following is the text of a speech by Ernesto Zedillo upon his inauguration as president of Mexico on December 1, 1994, as released by the Mexican Embassy in Washington, D.C.:*

Honorable Congress of the Union; Mexicans:

I assume the Presidency of the Republic to serve the people of Mexico with all my strength.

I shall exercise the authority set forth in the Constitution with rectitude, open to the Nation and attentive to the criticism of citizens. My conscience dictates that it be so. The lofty example set by those who forged our country demands that it be so. The Mexico of today demands that it be so.

I succeed a President who governed with vision, who conceived major transformations with intelligence and patriotism, and who implemented them with determination. I extend my respect and appreciation to him. I am sure that Carlos Salinas de Gortari will always enjoy the gratitude and affection of the Mexican people.

Today, with profound sadness, I invoke the memory of our friend, colleague and leader, Luis Donaldo Colosio. I shall honor the example he set with his love of and service to Mexico.

My first responsibility as Head of State will be to safeguard national sovereignty. I hereby take over the Supreme Command of the Armed Forces, who will continue to serve Mexico patriotically, loyally and effectively. I will exercise this responsibility with honor.

Mexico is respected worldwide, as evidenced by the distinguished presence of leaders and representatives of peoples with whom we share close ties. We extend our gratitude and friendship to them.

The self-determination of all peoples, the peaceful settlement of conflicts, the equality of States and equity in exchanges between countries are the principles that have guided our foreign policy and accord us moral authority in the world.

I shall continue to apply those principles in order to preserve our national sovereignty and promote Mexico's legitimate interests in a world of keen competition for resources and markets. I shall do so by practicing an active, open nationalism with full respect for all nations.

I shall take special care to defend, lawfully and decisively, the dignity and human rights of Mexicans living beyond our borders. We are aware that the best defense lies in securing dignified living standards and opportunities for employment and self-improvement within Mexico. I shall devote my efforts to that end.

We Mexicans want to build a better country for our children. This task demands that we recognize what we have achieved. It also means facing up to the injustices that continue to exist, the deficiencies that plague us and the magnitude of the problems that we face.

Society and government together will tackle these injustices, deficiencies and problems. I have every confidence that united we shall overcome them; today, as always, if Mexico is united, it will raise above them.

We are inspired by the example of our parents and their parents before them. Starting with the profound social transformation brought about by the Revolution of 1910, each generation has made a contribution to Mexico.

During the past 75 years, education, health care, employment, communications and services have improved for millions of Mexicans, although the population has increased from 14 to 90 million.

Mexico has certainly prospered. Our parents and grandparents realized major achievements. But they are not enough; we cannot feel fully satisfied.

Many millions of Mexicans lack the bare essentials. Many have not benefited from the fruits of progress. Many live in a state of poverty that is a source of indignation to the nation.

That is why our generation must do more, work harder, make greater efforts. Because Mexico is all of us, I appeal to each and every Mexican today to embark on a renewed endeavor. The challenge is great; it calls for everyone to work together in order for success to be shared by everyone.

Our most important challenge is to provide dignified living conditions for every Mexican family. Economic progress only makes sense if it reaches every Mexican household.

The aim of economic policy must be to attain increasing levels of well-being for all persons and their families. That well-being is based on dignified, stable, well-paid jobs. Mexico needs many more such jobs and our commitment is to create them.

In order to create those jobs, the economy must grow in a sustained manner, at a far greater rate than that of the population. For jobs to be increasingly well-paid, there must be a sustained increase in productivity.

We now have an unprecedented opportunity to achieve the economic growth our population needs. In addition to an expanding domestic market, we now have access to enormous foreign markets as a result of trade negotiations with other countries.

Mexicans will be able to take advantage of the trade agreements reached to help generate the jobs we need and raise living standards.

A necessary condition for promoting economic growth is to ensure that each year we make sufficient investments in our infrastructure. We shall build and upgrade the highways, ports, telecommunications and other public works that Mexico needs in rural areas and cities alike.

We shall continue to fight inflation so as to achieve sustained economic growth which will benefit all. We want jobs and real wages to increase, not prices. Price stability is essential if permanent, well-paid jobs are to multiply. We shall not destroy the stability that we have achieved with so many sacrifices on the part of our people. We shall therefore maintain strict discipline in public finances.

Sustained growth calls for a framework of economic and financial stability to ensure certainty and confidence for saving, planning, investing and working productively. It calls for clear rules and fair treatment for all.

Fair treatment means legal certainty in contractual relations, something that will ensure workers' rights and promote business efficiency.

Fair treatment means fighting monopolistic practices, abuses and privileges. It means precise, simple regulations to prevent corruption and promote economic activity.

Fair treatment means a simple, transparent and equitable tax system, and the capacity to defend oneself against possible abuses on the part of authorities.

Fair treatment means reciprocity and support when competing abroad, and also incentives to adopt and create new forms of technology to strengthen productivity.

Fair treatment means strengthening Mexico's agrarian sector by ensuring that production conditions and support are similar to those of our competitors.

Fair treatment means expanding opportunities by providing better training for our labor force.

My administration will support agricultural producers, workers, business people and merchants. We shall provide support for small and medium-sized companies as never before, because they are the most important source of employment. We shall give a new impetus to Mexico's agrarian sector by strengthening investment, increasing productivity and encouraging producers' organizations.

We shall implement an economic policy committed to people, aimed at improving family well-being while respecting the environment. We shall maintain a responsible approach to public finances, to consolidate price stability and achieve a growth economy. We shall aim for a more vigorous, more equitable economy, focusing more on preserving an ecological balance.

Throughout our history, education has been the most important means of achieving self-improvement and social justice. For decades, the efforts of teachers, parents and the authorities have made education accessible to many people. It is time for it to be available to all. It is time for us to advance decisively in the quality of education. As such, education will be an unquestionable priority of my administration.

We shall undertake a national crusade for Mexicans to receive a quality education inspired by Article Three of the Constitution and directed toward freedom and justice, toward work and well-being.

My administration will spearhead an exceptional effort to implement the constitutional mandate that makes primary and secondary education obligatory.

We shall make an exceptional effort to radically reduce illiteracy and broaden education among the adult population.

We shall also pay great attention to other levels of education, including job training, technological education, higher education and research in the humanities and sciences. Education will be a sure means of overcoming poverty.

As President of the Republic, my highest duty and my strongest commitment is the fight against the poverty in which millions of Mexicans live. Poverty is the most painful burden in our history. Every day we are confronted with all that remains to be done in this area.

Our greatest commitment, therefore, must be to those who have the least. Now that we are able to build a more prosperous Mexico, we must—and we can—make it a more just Mexico.

We have made progress in the fight against poverty, but it persists throughout the nation and it is becoming more acute in regions and groups that face major obstacles in surmounting it.

Over the years, Mexico's agrarian sector has felt the effects of severe crises. In low-income neighborhoods there are major deficiencies and unemployment. Indigenous communities suffer grave deprivations, injustices and lack of opportunities, which have made poverty their history and destiny. That is unacceptable.

We have a historical duty, a mandate from the people and an ethical commitment to fight poverty.

We shall all unite against poverty: government, society and the affected communities, for defeating it would benefit Mexico as a whole.

We shall fight poverty by working with the sectors in greatest need to improve nutrition, health and housing conditions and other essential services.

We shall fight poverty by promoting education and job training, particularly in the states and regions with severe shortcomings.

We shall fight poverty by making justice accessible to the people who most need it. That is, to the indigenous groups and all those with the most pressing needs.

Let us break the vicious circle of illness, ignorance, unemployment and poverty in which many Mexicans are trapped.

Mexico should be and needs to be a united nation. Our unity is the measure of our strength. To strengthen our unity, we shall recover justice and peace. To secure justice and peace, we shall address the roots of violence and desperation.

This year, Mexicans' spirits have been saddened by the events in Chiapas, by the violence and, even more so, by conditions of deep-rooted injustice; by the conditions of extreme poverty and neglect that fueled that violence.

I am convinced that it is possible to achieve a new negotiation in Chiapas, that will lead us to a just, honorable and definitive peace. There will be no violence by the government and I am confident that neither will there be by those who dissent. The Mexican Army will maintain its unilateral ceasefire. We will seek by all possible means to reach an arrangement grounded in harmony, democracy and opportunities for development.

We want a homeland of peace, a nation of equity, a Mexico of justice for all. Progress and social peace are lasting only under a rule of law in which the exercise of individual rights goes hand in hand with respect for the rights of others. The law applies equally to all. No one can be above the law.

Every violation of the law undermines the fundamental principles of our coexistence, harms our respect as a civilized people and sets a sad example for our children.

In the last few years, particularly in recent months, we have lived in a climate of growing anxiety and insecurity. We have suffered major public crimes that have not been altogether clarified; we have suffered from violence on a daily basis and from a deficient performance by the institutions in charge of public safety and law enforcement.

It makes us indignant to know that women suffer aggressions on the streets, that children and adolescents are the victims of abuses outside their schools, that workers lose their wages in street muggings and that the owners of small businesses lose their payrolls in violent robberies. It makes us indignant to hear of impunity resulting from the abuse of authority, venality and corruption.

Armed robberies in homes and public meeting places, the murder of men and women defending their property and the kidnappings that have proliferated in this country are intolerable. Our indignation is far greater when the illegal acts are committed by those who should enforce the law. The impunity of drug trafficking is intolerable. Drug trafficking is the greatest threat to national security, the gravest risk to the health of society and the bloodiest source of violence.

Today more than ever, Mexico must be a country of laws. That is what everyone, everywhere, is calling for. And that task will demand effort, discipline, firmness and perseverance. Solutions will take time. We must therefore begin working on them right now.

It is essential that the Constitution, and the legal order stemming from it, are fully observed. The authorities must act in line with the regulations, individual rights must be recognized and discrepancies must be settled in accordance with the law.

All the efforts of several generations; all the work of our own generation;

the whole of our children's future could be lost if we do not succeed in consolidating ourselves as a country of laws.

We cannot invest all our expectations in the certainty of the law but live in the uncertainty of its enforcement. We Mexicans need, want and demand an effective system of justice; we want the law to be the true measure of our coexistence.

Thus, in order to tackle the rampant crime, the frequent violations of civil and human rights, and the grave public insecurity, we will launch an in-depth and genuine reform of the institutions in charge of the procurement of justice.

It is in there where incompetence, corruption and institutional breakdowns are most common and most damaging to public security.

The brutal assassinations of two of Mexico's most outstanding public figures have deeply hurt our citizens, sown seeds of concern and doubt regarding some institutions, and divided the people of Mexico. Thus far, the investigations have not been to the entire satisfaction of society. We, the people of Mexico, want to be sure that we know the truth.

At this moment, I am specifically directing the Attorney General of the Republic to significantly intensify the investigations and inform the public of the progress made until the investigations come to an end. We will not rest until justice has been served.

Fortunately, at the core of the judicial branch, we have the Supreme Court of Justice of the Nation, which has diligently gained the respect of Mexican society as a result of its ethical and professional performance. In recent years, emphasis has been placed on its responsibility to oversee the constitutionality of the actions of public authorities. Today we must strengthen that capacity.

A judicial branch with renewed strength will be consolidated as a factor in the democratic balance between the powers of the Union, and will permeate the entire justice system with the highest values of the Mexican legal tradition.

In the short term, I will submit to the consideration of this sovereign nation a bill for an amendment to the Constitution which, if approved, will be the first step toward a profound transformation to our justice system. I respectfully invite the Honorable Congress of the Union to examine, and where need be, enhance this initiative in order to attain a more independent and stronger Judicial Branch, that is better equipped to fulfill its obligations.

I am determined to head the creation of a nation where the Rule of Law prevails, as all Mexicans deserve, and I will do so by presiding over a government of laws within a framework of strengthened democracy which will renew the life of the Republic, ensure participation, encourage respect and acknowledge plurality.

We, the people of Mexico, seek a life of democracy that will rise to the heights of our history, to the heights of our diversity.

Nevertheless, we must acknowledge the fact that the progress we have made in terms of democracy is still insufficient.

The time has come to join efforts without sacrificing our differences. The time has come to join in the creation of a new democracy encompassing an improved relationship between citizens and government, between states and the Federal Government; a new code of ethics for political contenders and a definitive electoral reform. The time has come for democracy to encompass all spheres of social coexistence.

I ratify my invitation to all parties, to all political organizations and citizens' groups to participate with an open and determined spirit in the integral democratization of our life, of our Nation.

Concrete actions will allow us to create a presidential regime better balanced by the other powers of the State. I will hold a permanent dialogue with all political forces and I will be open to the scrutiny and criticism of the citizenry.

The time has come to do away with centralism and promote the forces of the different regions that provide Mexico's identity, energy and plurality.

In keeping with the demands of the Mexican people, we will progress toward a new federalism in which the states and municipal governments will be stronger, in which the decisions will always be shared to the benefit of local communities.

The time has come for a new federalism where local governments will have the resources and decision-making power to better serve their citizens.

The basis of the relations between the Executive and Legislative branches is the strict respect of their autonomy. The plural composition of the Congress of the Union represents a fundamental element for its political independence.

Thus, I propose to work respectfully and in concerted action with Congress. Thus, I will back, among other measures, increased monitoring by the Chamber of Deputies of how the government spends the people's money and to ensure responsible, honest and efficient conduct by civil servants.

To a great extent, the progress of democracy depends on the strength of our party system. It depends on the capacity of all Mexicans to favor consensus over differences, cohesive objectives over discrepancies, unity over confrontation.

As President of the Republic, I will seek treatment based on dialogue, respect and truth with all political parties equally. That will be the basis of my relations with party leaders and elected representatives. I will strictly adhere to the law by governing for all, without distinctions or favoritism of any sort.

I emphatically repeat that, as President of the Republic, I will not intervene under any circumstances in the processes or decisions pertaining to my party.

Mexico demands a reform which, based on the broadest political consensus, will eradicate suspicion, recrimination and distrust that mar the electoral process.

All the political forces, all the party leaders, all the social organizations may, and should, help in leaving behind, once and for all, the doubt and controversy regarding electoral legality.

In order to carry out this definitive reform, we must all be willing to address all relevant issues, including of course party funding, ceilings for campaign expenditures, access to the media and the autonomy of the electoral authorities.

Electoral democracy can no longer be at the core of the political debate or the cause of dispute and division. We must resolve, in keeping with the most advanced practices worldwide, each and every one of the issues still causing dissatisfaction in terms of democracy.

Although this national reform will be put into practice for the first time in the 1997 federal elections, we must make an effort to implement it as soon as the necessary consensus allows. Our common goal must be for the 1997 elections to be indisputable, so that we are all content with the process, regardless of the results.

I will assume my responsibility to create a more equitable electoral system and I am sure that all political parties will understand that democratic competition is a decisive element for representing the Mexican people.

Mexico wants a government that encourages democracy and responds to the demands of change inspired by justice, liberty and peace. A change toward well-being; a change with room and opportunity for all; a change effected out of consensus and ruled by democracy.

Mexico wants a government for change with stability,

That is the government that, as of today, I will head.

Honorable Congress of the Union:

I call today upon all Mexicans to unite so that we each play our part. So that no one looks upon another Mexican as an enemy. So that no one puts personal interests above the interests of the nation. Let us at all times unite our efforts, our determination and our hopes.

Let us move forward in the strength of our unity. Rather than doubts, let us sow confidence. Rather than hesitation, let us share well-founded hopes. Rather than malice, let us cultivate truth. Rather than discord, let us share a common purpose. But above all, let us increase our faith in our work, our faith in Mexico.

I shall fulfill the mandate vested in me by the people of Mexico to gain their trust every day. I shall fulfill each of the commitments that I have made to Mexicans throughout the length and breadth of the country.

Mexico does not want a government estranged from society. I shall therefore head a government for all, without prejudices or privileges. A government that will inform citizens periodically and truthfully on every matter of importance for the well-being of families and the national interest. I come to the Presidency of the Republic with no other commitment than to serve the people.

I have invited honest, capable, decent women and men who are ready to work untiringly for Mexico to collaborate in my administration. Each and every one of them has my trust and I know they will fulfill their responsibilities.

Let me reiterate to all Cabinet Secretaries, to all who participate in my administration, that their duty is to work honestly and unstintingly, to the best of their ability, giving a clear accounting of their acts to the people and their representatives.

They have been called upon to serve, to respect the will of the people and the public interest; not to further their own success or advancement. The government is not a place for amassing wealth. He who has such aspirations should do so outside my administration and in accordance with the law. I shall govern by serving and I shall demand that my colleagues devote themselves to service.

I would like to remind all those who serve in my administration of the words of President Juárez:

> "Public officials must not use public finances irresponsibly. They must not act in accordance with their whims, but in accordance with the law. They must not contrive to make fortunes, nor sink into idleness and dissipation, but devote themselves assiduously to their work, living in the honest moderation derived from the remuneration provided for by the law."

Today I assume the Presidency of the Republic to represent Mexico with pride; to work with enthusiasm for Mexico; to serve all Mexicans with dedication.

We have before us a great task that demands the united will of all Mexicans. Ahead of us lies a long road of work and hope; a lofty project for our country; the firm determination that Mexico's well-being be the well-being of Mexicans; that Mexico's progress be the progress of Mexicans; that Mexico's greatness be the greatness of Mexicans.

At this historic moment, let no one shirk his responsibilities, let no one spare his efforts, let no one fall into the temptation of letting his spirits flag.

The just, prosperous Mexico that we dream of is within our reach. Let it be said of us that we dared to have lofty dreams and that we were able to make those dreams a reality. This is our opportunity, this is our obligation and this will be our reward.

Let each play his part, honestly and courageously. I pledge to do my part.

I shall work with an unbreakable spirit and nationalist conviction. My efforts will be multiplied by those of all Mexicans. I shall work, like all Mexicans, with honesty, hope and passion.

I shall work for the Mexico which our forefathers bequeathed to us.

For the Mexico which today unites our will.

For the Mexico that we owe to our children.

Long live Mexico!

FBI REPORT ON VIOLENT CRIME
December 4, 1994

A report released December 4 by the Federal Bureau of Investigation (FBI) entitled "Crime in the United States 1993" stated that violent crime actually declined slightly in 1993. However, the report, which was based on data from Uniform Crime Reports, also pointed out that the homicide rate—perhaps the most dramatic piece of the crime picture—increased by about 3 percent.

The FBI also reported that murder victims and suspected killers had become younger, killers were using guns more often, and killers knew their victims less often than in previous years. "Every American now has a realistic chance of murder victimization in view of the random nature the crime has assumed," the report said.

"Crime problems are so grave that few Americans will find much comfort in a small reduction in the overall amount of reported crime," FBI Director Louis J. Freeh said in May upon the release of preliminary crime figures. Other experts predicted that crime would escalate in coming years. "This may be the last good report that we see in a long time," said Jack Levin, a criminology professor at Northeastern University, in an interview with the Associated Press. Levin predicted that the murder rate would climb again when the large group of young teenagers with access to guns reached the eighteen- to twenty-four-year-old age group that usually commits the most murders.

A number of other reports and surveys were not encouraging:

- *Crime surpassed economic issues as the country's "most important" problem, according to a New York Times/CBS News Poll conducted in April 1994. "It's no wonder crime is America's No. 1 concern," Rep. Charles E. Schumer (D-N.Y.), chairman of a House subcommittee on crime, told the Associated Press. "We've become a society of victims or people afraid of becoming victims."*

- *Carjackings, in which criminals forced drivers from their vehicles, became as common as deaths caused by auto accidents, according to a Justice Department study released April 2. Carjackings epitomized the increasingly random and violent nature of crime that left people everywhere feeling vulnerable. Although the victims usually escaped uninjured, the study said, at least 60 percent of carjackings involved handguns. The data on carjackings was part of the National Crime Victimization Survey, which unlike the FBI's Uniform Crime Reports included crimes not reported to the police. Nine of ten successful carjackings were reflected in the FBI's statistics, while only six in ten failed carjackings ever reached police blotters. Overall results of the victimization survey, announced October 30, showed a marked increase in violent crimes other than murder in 1993.*
- *The homicide rate among teenage males had reached epidemic levels, the Centers for Disease Control and Prevention warned in a study released October 13. Homicide deaths for men aged fifteen to nineteen increased by 154 percent from 1985 to 1991, while murder arrests for that group rose by 127 percent. The number of murder victims and arrests dropped during the same period for older men. The increase in teenage homicide affected all racial groups, although the rate for young African American males was higher than for whites. Almost all the increased teenage homicides were the result of gun use, the study said.*
- *More than 1 million people were imprisoned in the United States in 1994, the highest number in the nation's history, according to a Justice Department report released October 27. The prison population had tripled since 1980, the report said, with a rise in drug-related arrests and longer sentences for drug offenders contributing to the increase. In 1994, the incarceration rate in the United States was higher than for any other country except Russia. Despite increased spending in many states on prison construction, overcrowding remained a pressing problem.*
- *Children were not even safe in schools, according to a report issued November 1 by the National League of Cities. "Reports of attacks, shootings, searches for weapons, gang activity and other incidents have created fear, anxiety and uncertainty about what's happening when kids go to school each day," the league said.*

Congress Passes Crime Bill

Public concern about crime encouraged state legislatures to pass new anticrime measures in 1994. Although most criminal cases were handled at the state or local levels, Congress in late August approved a major piece of federal anticrime legislation advocated by President Bill Clinton. The crime bill, the first significant crime legislation passed by Congress in six years, authorized $30.2 billion to hire more police, build more prisons, and support prevention programs such as job training. The measure also created dozens of new federal capital crimes, required life in prison for three-time *violent offenders, and banned nineteen types of semiautomatic assault weapons.*

A group of moderate Republicans helped Democrats pass the measure, but only after months of debate and parliamentary maneuvering. The National Rifle Association, a powerful lobbying group opposed to gun control, fought to defeat the bill because of the assault weapons ban. The final bill represented a compromise between liberals who favored prevention programs and conservatives who wanted tougher punishment of criminals.

Clinton predicted that the new law would "make every neighborhood in America safer." Others, including bill supporters, sought to keep expectations modest. "This is not the sole solution to crime," said Jack Brooks (D-Texas), a key House sponsor. "This is a step in the right direction."

Supporters predicted that the legislation would result in the hiring of 100,000 more police officers nationwide. Critics argued that local governments, already stretched financially, would not be able to come up with the matching funds necessary to accomplish such an ambitious goal.

Uncertainty remained about how much the federal government could or should do about a problem that was handled primarily at the state and local levels. According to one observer, law professor Frank Zimring of the University of California, the crime bill's real importance was not in what it could do to fight crime but "as a symbolic denunciation and expression of concern."

Following are excerpts from "Crime in the United States 1993," a report released December 4, 1994, by the Federal Bureau of Investigation:

Crime Index Offenses Reported

. . . The total number of murders in the United States during 1993 was estimated at 24,526. Monthly figures show that more persons were murdered in the month of December in 1993, while the fewest were killed in February.

When viewing the regions of the Nation, the Southern States, the most populous region, accounted for 41 percent of the murders. The Western States reported 23 percent; the Midwestern States, 19 percent; and the Northeastern States, 17 percent. Among the regions, the Northeast experienced a 5-percent increase; the South and West each recorded 4-percent increases; and the Midwest registered a less than 1-percent increase.

The murder volume was up 3 percent nationwide in 1993 over 1992. In the Nation's cities overall, murder increased 4 percent, with the greatest increase—10 percent—registered in cities with populations of 100,000 to 249,999. The greatest decrease—6 percent—was recorded in cities with populations of 10,000 to 24,999. The suburban counties recorded a 2-percent rise in the murder volume and the rural counties, a 3-percent increase for the 2-year period. . . .

The 10-year trend showed the 1993 total 31 percent above the 1984 level.

Rate

Up 2 percent over the 1992 rate, the national murder rate in 1993 was 10 per 100,000 inhabitants. Five- and 10-year trends showed the 1993 rate was 9 percent higher than in 1989 and 20 percent above the 1984 rate.

On a regional basis, the South averaged 11 murders per 100,000 people; the West, 10 per 100,000; and the Midwest and Northeast, 8 per 100,000. Compared to 1992, murder rates in 1993 increased in three of the four geographic regions. The Midwest experienced no change.

The Nation's metropolitan areas reported a 1993 murder rate of 11 victims per 100,000 inhabitants. In the rural counties and in cities outside metropolitan areas, the rate was 5 per 100,000.

Nature

Supplemental data provided by contributing agencies recorded information for 23,271 of the estimated 24,526 murders in 1993. Submitted monthly, the data consist of the age, sex, and race of both victims and offenders; the types of weapons used; the relationships of victims to the offenders; and the circumstances surrounding the murders.

Based on this information, 77 percent of the murder victims in 1993 were males; and 87 percent were persons 18 years of age or older. Forty-eight percent were aged 20 through 34 years. Considering victims for whom race was known, an average of 51 of every 100 were black, 46 were white, and the remainder were persons of other races.

Supplemental data were also reported for 26,239 murder offenders in 1993. Of those for whom sex and age were reported, 91 percent were males, and 85 percent were persons 18 years of age or older. Seventy-seven percent were aged 15 through 34 years. Of offenders for whom race was known, 56 percent were black, 42 percent were white, and the remainder were persons of other races.

Data based on incidents involving one victim and one offender showed that in 1993, 94 percent of the black murder victims were slain by black offenders, and 84 percent of the white murder victims were killed by white offenders. Likewise, males were most often slain by males (88 percent in single victim/single offender situations). These same data showed, however, that 9 of every 10 female victims were murdered by males.

As in previous years, firearms were the weapons used in approximately 7 of every 10 murders committed in the United States. Of those murders for which weapons were reported, 57 percent were by handguns, 5 percent by shotguns, and 3 percent by rifles. Other or unknown types of firearms accounted for another 5 percent of the total murders. Among the remaining weapons, cutting or stabbing instruments were employed in 13 percent of the murders; blunt objects (clubs, hammers, etc.) in 4 percent; personal weapons (hands, fists, feet, etc.) in 5 percent; and other dangerous weapons, such as poison, explosives, etc., in the remainder.

Past years' statistics on relationships of victims to offenders showed that over half of murder victims knew their killers. However, in the last few years (1990 through 1993) the relationship percentages have shifted. In 1993, 47 percent of murder victims were either related to (12 percent) or acquainted with (35 percent) their assailants. Fourteen percent of the victims were murdered by strangers, while the relationships among victims and offenders were unknown for 39 percent of the murders. Among all female murder victims in 1993, 29 percent were slain by husbands or boyfriends. Three percent of the male victims were killed by wives or girlfriends.

Arguments resulted in 29 percent of the murders during the year. Nineteen percent occurred as a result of felonious activities such as robbery, arson, etc., while another 1 percent were suspected to have been the result of some type of felonious activity. Three percent of the murders were committed during brawls while offenders were under the influence of alcohol or narcotics.

Law Enforcement Response

The clearance rate for murder continued to be higher than for any other Crime Index offense. Law enforcement agencies nationwide recorded a 66-percent clearance rate for 1993. Eighty percent of murders in rural counties and 65 percent of those in suburban counties and in the Nation's cities were cleared. Of the city population groups, those with populations under 10,000 reported the most successful clearance rate, 76 percent.

Geographically, the South, the most populous region, registered the highest murder clearance rate, 71 percent. Following were the Northeastern States with 66 percent, the Midwestern States with 61 percent, and the Western States with 59 percent.

Persons under 18 years of age accounted for 9 percent of the willful killings cleared by law enforcement nationally. Only persons in this young age group accounted for 10 percent of clearances in the Nation's cities, 8 percent of those in the suburban counties, and 7 percent of the rural county clearances. This proportion of juvenile involvement was lower than for any other Index offense.

An estimated 23,400 arrests for murder were made in 1993. Fifty-seven percent of the arrestees in 1993 were under 25 years of age. The 18- to 24-year age group accounted for 41 percent of the total.

Ninety-one percent of those arrested were males and 9 percent, females. Blacks comprised 58 percent of the total arrestees for murder in 1993. Whites made up 41 percent, and the remainder were of other races.

Compared to the 1992 level, the 1993 murder arrest total increased 4 percent. Arrests of persons aged 18 and over increased 2 percent, and those of younger persons were up 14 percent. During the same 2-year period, female arrests increased 1 percent and male arrests rose by 4 percent.

Long-term trends indicate the 1993 murder arrest total was 11 percent above the 1989 level and 25 percent higher than the 1984 figure. . . .

Homicide Patterns: Past and Present

Murder has always been regarded as the most serious of all crimes. Today, the prevailing public perception is that homicides, in general, are more vicious and senseless than ever before. In an effort to address this issue, the following study examines the changing nature of murder from 1965 to 1992.

While the Nation's homicide rate per 100,000 residents was 9.3 in 1992, the historical high actually occurred 13 years prior (10.2 in 1980). What, then, has spurred the current national debate on how to curtail murders and violent crime? Ostensibly, something has changed in the constitution of murder to bring about the unparalleled level of concern and fear confronting the Nation.

A historical review of the U.S. murder rate trend reveals that after a rapid escalation from 5.1 in 1965 to 9.4 in 1973, the rate stabilized in subsequent years, ranging from 8.0 to 10.2. This study focuses on significant changes in the types of victims, arrestees, related circumstances, and weapons usage as possible contributing factors for the current trepidation associated with homicides.

Victim Profile

The most striking change in murder victimization since the 1980s is the youthfulness of the victims. Of particular note are the increases in the number of murder victims in the age groups "under 1" and "10 to 14." The number of victims in these two age groups, while remaining relatively small overall, increased 46 percent and 64 percent, respectively, from 1975 to 1992. Further, the number of victims in the "15 to 24" age group, the most murder prone, increased nearly 50 percent. These three age groups were primarily responsible for the 16-percent increase in total homicides nationwide between 1975 and 1992. The same held true for the 25-percent increase in homicides from 1985-1992.

Conversely, the number of murder victims aged 50 and over decreased 32 percent between 1975 and 1992. As this population segment is among the Nation's fastest growing, an increase in the number of victims contained in it was expected. The decline confirms a definitive trend toward more youthful murder victims.

Victim data by race and age reveal that blacks aged 24 or younger constituted 41 percent of black murder victims during 1992, up from 29 percent in 1975. The 1992 statistic is in concert with the finding of the U.S. Department of Health and Human Services that homicide is now the leading cause of death for young black males. The corresponding percentage for whites rose only slightly from 28 percent to 31 percent, 1975 versus 1992. These data indicate that black victims are, on average, more youthful than white victims.

The gender distribution for murder victims has remained virtually unchanged from 1975 to 1992. Homicide victims are predominantly male.

Circumstances/Relationships

Nationally, the circumstances/relationships associated with homicides have changed significantly since the 1960s. Historically, the vast majority of murders have been between people with some type of relationship or acquaintance. During the 1990s, however, there is evidence that this is no longer the case. For example, in 1965, only 5 percent of murder circumstances were unknown, while in 1992, this figure rose to 28 percent. When addressing victim/offender relationships, murders by strangers and unknown persons represented 53 percent of the murders in the Nation during 1992. This percentage represents a historical high.

The prevalence of murder among family members as a percentage of all murders also experienced a prominent shift. In 1965, nearly 1 out of 3 (31 percent) murder victims was killed by a person or persons within his or her family. In 1992, however, the figure fell to only 12 percent, supporting the trend of murders becoming less family-oriented. The Nation's drug trade is widely considered to be a major contributing factor to the rise in murders whose circumstances are unknown.

From a longitudinal perspective, after peaking in the mid-1970s, felony murders and suspected felony murders have been relatively stable in spite of some minor variations. This trend also holds true when considering the percentage of the total these murders represent. It should be cautioned, however, that from 1985 to 1992, known felony-related murders increased 47 percent. This increase was primarily driven by a 147-percent rise in narcotics felony-related homicides.

While murder has traditionally been called a crime of passion resulting from romantic triangles and lovers' quarrels, recent statistics reveal that these types of murders have been declining as a percentage of total homicides. In fact, the number of murder victims killed under these circumstances declined 22 percent from 1975 to 1992.

The fastest growing murder circumstance is juvenile gang killings. It should be noted that in a juvenile gang killing the perpetrator is associated with a juvenile gang but may be of any age, i.e., an adult gang leader. The victim, whether juvenile or adult, is not necessarily associated with a gang. Prior to 1980, the number of murders in this category was well below 200 per year. From 1980 to 1992, juvenile gang killings increased 371 percent. Further, 95 percent of victims of juvenile gang killings in 1992 were slain with firearms. When considering the race of the victims, 68 percent were white and 27 percent were black. Sixty-nine percent of the victims killed by juvenile gangs were age 18 and older.

Homicide is one of the most intraracial crimes when considering victims and offenders. This dimension of murder has been constant throughout time. A review of homicide incidents during 1992 which involved one victim and one offender showed that 94 percent of black murder victims were killed by black offenders, and 83 percent of white murder victims were killed by white offenders.

Weapons Usage

The Nation experienced an increase in the percentage of homicides committed with guns during the period 1985 to 1992. Conversely, the percentage of knives/cutting instruments used in murders has declined since 1965. The use of other types of weapons, e.g., blunt objects, poison, explosives, has been relatively stable.

An examination of weapons used against victims of various ages showed the leading weapon used against those under the age of 5 from 1975 through 1992 was personal weapons (hands, fists, and feet). The gun category was the leading weapon type for all remaining age groups, especially the "15 to 19" age group. In 1975, 66 percent of the murders of persons in this group were attributable to guns, while in 1992 the figure rose to 85 percent. This increase supports the theory that today's high school-aged youths are exposed to an environment that includes guns. . . .

Profile of Arrestees

As with other aspects of homicide, the profile of the murder arrestee has changed somewhat since 1970. The most notable difference relates to white murder arrestees. The number of whites arrested for homicide rose 67 percent from 1970 to 1992, accounting for most of the overall increase in the national murder arrest total. Moreover, the number of white juvenile murder arrestees increased 204 percent and the number of white adult murder arrestees was up 56 percent for the 23-year period. The increase in the number of white juvenile arrestees was the largest among all racial groups by age classification (adult and juvenile).

When considering black murder arrestees, there have been significant increases for both adults and juveniles, but not at the rate experienced by their white counterparts. It should be mentioned, however, that after falling to less than 50 percent of homicide arrests in 1980, blacks constituted 55 percent of the murder arrest total in 1992.

In conjunction with the youthfulness of murder victims, as earlier discussed, the average age of murder arrestees has fallen significantly since 1965 as well. The decline from 1985 to 1992 is particularly noteworthy. This latter decline tends to indicate that the surge in the number of youthful murder offenders commenced during the latter part of the 1980s.

Although the total number of murder arrests has risen substantially over time, this increase does not reflect the movement of the Nation's murder clearance rate. Specifically, the percent of murders cleared by arrest has fallen from 91 percent in 1965 to an all-time low of 65 percent in 1992. The primary reason for this trend may be that circumstances and victim/offender relationships composing today's murders are more likely to be unknown.

Conclusions

The typical assumptions associated with homicides throughout this century must be reevaluated in view of the unprecedented shift in national homicide patterns as evidenced during the 1990s. Every American now has a realistic chance of murder victimization in view of the random nature the crime has assumed. This notion is somewhat supported by the fact that a majority of the Nation's murder victims are now killed by strangers or unknown persons. The advent of this trend has generated a profound fear of murder victimization in that the circumstances surrounding homicides are perceived to be more irrational. In the past, the accepted normality was based upon clearly defined circumstances such as felonies, passion, and arguments among family members or acquaintances. The concern about homicide is further perpetuated by youthfulness of both victims and offenders, as illustrated by the rise in juvenile gang killings during the past decade. The reasons for these changes in homicide patterns are multidimensional. Some suggested causal factors are related to the illicit drug trade, the disintegration of the family unit, and weapon proliferation.

CLINTON, YELTSIN AT
EUROPEAN SECURITY SUMMIT
December 5, 1994

Delegates to a summit in Budapest, Hungary, aimed at improving security in Europe after the Cold War heard rhetoric from Russian president Boris Yeltsin indicating that the suspicions and distrust that were hallmarks of that conflict had not faded away.

Yeltsin made the remarks December 5 at a summit of the Conference on Security and Cooperation in Europe (CSCE), a group created in the early 1970s to improve communications between East and West. It is comprised of fifty-three members, including all the countries of Europe, the United States, and Canada. It has no army but attempts to prevent conflicts through negotiations. In recent years, it helped the United Nations enforce sanctions against the former republics of Yugoslavia and tried to help resolve conflicts in Ukraine, Tajikistan, Georgia, Moldova, and Macedonia.

In a speech to the delegates, Yeltsin expressed particular unhappiness over a plan by the North Atlantic Treaty Organization (NATO) to allow former members of the communist Warsaw Pact to join. Both NATO and the Warsaw Pact were organizations where members agreed to defend each other in the event of an attack. A week before the summit, NATO had announced plans that would eventually allow such countries as Poland, Hungary, and the Czech Republic to join the organization.

Yeltsin blasted the plan, suggesting that the United States was attempting to split Europe. "Why sow the seeds of distrust?" he asked. "After all, we are no longer adversaries, we are partners." Such a plan threatened to plunge Europe "into a cold peace," Yeltsin said.

Russia Fears Isolation

Russian officials felt isolated by the move and were concerned that an expanded NATO could become a threat to Russia's western border. They also believed the expansion signified that the West had given up on democracy in Russia. If it had not, they argued, why expand a security organization?

In a pointed barb at Washington, Yeltsin also cautioned leaders at the summit not to let one country dominate the world. "History proves that it is a dangerous illusion to believe that the destinies of continents and the world community as a whole can somehow be managed from one single capital," he said.

Yeltsin's hard-line rhetoric caught American officials by surprise. They had sought to develop a U.S.-Russian partnership to help keep Europe from dividing again. However, the two countries took opposing sides on many international issues. For example, Moscow and Washington sharply differed over how to stop the war in Bosnia, with Moscow backing the Serbs and Washington favoring the Muslims. Moscow wanted to lift economic sanctions imposed against Iraq during the Gulf War, while Washington wanted to continue them. The issue of NATO expansion also split the two countries. To complicate matters further, nationalist sentiment was once again growing in Russia, prompting Russian officials to take a harder stand toward the West.

Bosnian President Attacks West

At the summit, Western nations also were blasted in a speech by President Alija Izetbegovic of the Republic of Bosnia and Herzegovina. Using vitriolic language not commonly heard in diplomatic circles, Izetbegovic criticized Western leaders for not coming to his nation's aid in its war against the Serbs. "What shall be the result of the war in Bosnia, which is now being prolonged due to a mixture of incapability, hesitation and sometimes even ill will of the West?" he asked. "The result shall be a discredited United Nations, a ruined NATO, Europeans demoralized by a feeling of inability to respond to the first crisis after the Cold War." He said the West's failure to act had created "a worse world in which the relations between Europe and the U.S.A., the West and Russia, and the West and the Muslim world shall never again be the same." By the time of his speech, tens of thousands of people had been killed in the war, which pitted the Muslim-led government against Serbs who were fighting to secede. (UN Security Council Resolution on Bosnia, p. 550)

The summit accomplished little toward trying to defuse the old ethnic and religious conflicts that ignited in Eastern Europe with the collapse of communism. The delegates approved sending a 3,000-member international peacekeeping force to Nagorno-Karabach, a section of the former Soviet republic of Azerbaijan that Armenia and Azerbaijan were fighting over. However, the troops were not to be sent until a formal ceasefire was declared, and it remained unclear what countries would contribute troops to the force.

The summit ended in frustration with the failure of a resolution that condemned Serb forces for fighting in the Bosnian area of Bihac, which was only several hundred miles from the conference site. Russia, which backed the Serb forces, blocked the resolution, saying it would interfere with peace efforts in Bosnia.

> *Following is the text of speeches at the Conference on Security and Cooperation in Europe in Budapest, Hungary, on December 5, 1994, by United States president Bill Clinton, as released by the White House, and by Russian president Boris Yeltsin, as released by the Russian Embassy in Washington, D.C.:*

CLINTON'S SPEECH

Thank you, President [Thomas] Klestil [Austria], President [Arpád] Goncz [Hungary]. I am delighted to be here in this great city in Central Europe at this historic meeting.

The United States is committed to building a united, free and secure Europe. We believe that goal requires a determined effort to continue to reduce the nuclear threat; a strong NATO adapting to new challenges; a strong CSCE [Conference on Security and Cooperation in Europe], working among other things to lead efforts to head off future Bosnias; and a strong effort at cooperating with the United Nations; and an effort by all the nations of Europe to work together in harmony on common problems and opportunities.

In the 20th century, conflict and distrust have ruled Europe. The steps we are taking today will help to ensure that in the 21st century, peace and prosperity rein.

The forces that tore Europe apart have been defeated. But neither peace nor democracy's triumph is assured. The end of the Cold War presents us with the opportunity to fulfill the promise of democracy and freedom. And it is our responsibility working together to seize it, to build a new security framework for the era ahead. We must not allow the Iron Curtain to be replaced by a veil of indifference. We must not consign new democracies to a gray zone.

Instead we seek to increase the security of all; to erase the old lines without drawing arbitrary new ones; to bolster emerging democracies; and to integrate the nations of Europe into a continent where democracy and free markets know no borders, but where every nation's borders are secure.

We are making progress on the issues that matter for the future. Today, here, five of this organization's member states—Belarus, Kazakhstan, Russia, Ukraine and the United States—will bring the START I [Strategic Arms Reduction Talks] treaty into force and reduce the nuclear threat that has hung over our heads for nearly a half century.

START I will eliminate strategic bombers and missile launchers that carried over 9,000 warheads. And it opens the door to prompt ratification of START II, which will retire another 5,000 warheads. These actions will cut the arsenals of the United States and the former Soviet Union more than 60 percent from their Cold War peak. The world will be a safer place as a result.

But even as we celebrate this landmark gain for peace, the terrible conflict in Bosnia rages not 300 miles from this city. After three years of conflict, the combatants remain locked in a terrible war no one can win. Now each faces the same choice: They can perpetuate the military standoff, or they can stop spilling blood and start making peace.

The government of Bosnia-Herzegovina has made the right choice by accepting the international peace plan and agreeing to recent calls for a cease-fire. So I say again to the Bosnian Serbs: End the aggression, agree to the cease-fire and renewed negotiations on the basis of the Contact Group plan. Settle your differences at the negotiating table, not the battlefield.

We mustn't let our frustration over that war cause us to give up our efforts to end it. And the United States will not do so. If we have learned anything from the agony of Bosnia, it is clearly that we must act on its lessons. In other parts of Europe, ethnic disputes and forces of hatred and despair, demagogues who would take advantage of them threaten to reverse the new wave of freedom that has swept the continent.

So as we strive to end the war in Bosnia, we must work to prevent future Bosnias. And we must build the structures that will help newly-free nations to complete their transformation successfully to free market democracies and preserve their own freedom.

We know this is not something that will happen overnight, but over time, NATO, the CSCE, other European and transatlantic institutions, working in close cooperation with the United Nations can support and extend the democracy, stability and prosperity that Western Europe and North America have enjoyed for 50 years. That is the future we are working to build.

NATO remains the bedrock of security in Europe, but its role is changing as the continent changes. Last January NATO opened the door to new members and launched the Partnership for Peace. Since then 23 nations have joined that partnership to train together, conduct joint military exercises and forge closer political links.

Last week we took further steps to prepare for expansion by starting work on the requirements for membership. New members will join country by country gradually and openly. Each must be committed to democracy and free markets and be able to contribute to Europe's security. NATO will not automatically exclude any nation from joining. At the same time, no country outside will be allowed a veto expansion—to veto expansion.

As NATO does expand, so will security for all European states, for it is not an aggressive, but a defensive organization. NATO's new members, old members and nonmembers alike will be more secure.

As NATO continues its mission, other institutions can and should share the security burden and take on special responsibilities. A strong and vibrant Conference on Security and Cooperation in Europe is vital.

For more than a decade the CSCE was the focal point for courageous men and women who at great personal risk confronted tyranny to win the human rights set out in the Helsinki Accords. Now, the CSCE can help to build anew an integrated continent. It has unique tools for this task.

The CSCE is the only regional forum to which nearly every nation in Europe and North America belongs. It has pioneered ways to peacefully resolve conflicts, from shuttle diplomacy to longstanding missions in tense areas. Now that freedom has been won in Europe, the CSCE can play an expanding role in making sure it is never lost again.

Indeed, its proposed new name, the Organization for Security and Cooperation in Europe, symbolizes the new and important mission we believe it must undertake. The CSCE should be our first flexible line of defense against ethnic and regional conflicts. Its rules can guard against the assertion of hegemony or spheres of influence. It can help nations come together to build prosperity. And it can promote Europe's integration piece by piece.

By focusing on human rights, conflict prevention, dispute resolution, the CSCE can help prevent future Bosnias. We are taking important steps at this meeting for that crucial goal by strengthening the High Commissioner for National Minorities, establishing a code of conduct to provide for democratic civilian control of the military, reinforcing principles to halt the proliferation of weapons of mass destruction, and preparing to send CSCE monitors and peacekeepers to potential trouble spots outside Bosnia. These actions will not make triumph and headlines, but they may help to prevent tragic ones.

The principles adopted in Rome made clear that any peacekeeping mission must aim for a freely negotiated settlement by the parties themselves, not a solution imposed from the outside. And they hold that no country can use a regional conflict, however threatening, to strengthen its security at the expense of others.

I am very encouraged that with the support and involvement of the Russian Federation we are on the verge of an agreement that the CSCE will lead a multinational peacekeeping force in Nagorno-Karabakh. The United States appreciates the willingness of many nations to contribute troops and material for this mission.

The continuing tragedy in Nagorno-Karabakh demands that we redouble our efforts to promote a lasting cease-fire and a fair settlement. The United States strongly supports this effort and calls upon all CSCE members to contribute toward it.

The CSCE also has an important role to play in promoting economic growth while protecting Europe's resources and environment. We should strengthen its efforts to increase regional and cross-border cooperation. Such efforts can bring people together to build new highways, bridges and communication networks—the infrastructure of democracy.

Since 1975, when the countries of Europe expressed the desire to form a community founded on common values and founded the CSCE, more progress has occurred than even dreamers might have hoped. We know the change is possible. We know that former enemies can reconcile. We know the eloquent intentions about democracy and human rights can promote peace when transformed from words into actions.

Now, almost 20 years later, our challenge is to help the freedoms we secured spread and endure. The task will require energy and strength. Old regimes have crumbled, but new legacies and mistrust remain. Nations have been liberated, but ethnic hatred threatens peace and tolerance. Democracy and free markets are emerging, but change everywhere is causing fear and insecurity.

Three times before in this century, our nations have summoned the strength to defeat history's dark forces. They have left us still with a great responsibility and an extraordinary opportunity. Our mission now is to build a new world for our children—a world more democratic, more prosperous and more secure. The CSCE has a vital role to play.

Thank you very much, Mr. Chairman.

YELTSIN'S SPEECH

Mr. Chairman, President Goncz, Colleagues,

First of all, I wish to thank the Hungarian leadership for the excellent preparation of this meeting and for your hospitality. The fact that the summit is taking place in Budapest is a recognition of the growing role of the Central European countries in European politics.

Two years ago in Helsinki we reaffirmed our strategic goal of creating a common space of security and cooperation among democratic states. The Helsinki principles have stood the test of time. Today, they guarantee inviolability of borders in Europe and constitute the basis for coordinated actions in the interests of security and democracy.

However, let us honestly admit that our deeds are often at variance with adopted declarations. Having just rid itself of the Cold War legacy, Europe risks to immerse itself into a "cold peace." How to avoid this is a question that we must put to ourselves.

History proves that it is a dangerous illusion to believe that the destinies of continents and the world community as a whole can somehow be managed from one single capital. Blocs and coalitions will not provide true security guarantees either.

Establishment of a full-fledged all-European organization with a solid legal basis has become a vital necessity for Europe. Russia believes that the basis for its activity should be the jointly developed "Program for Europe approaching the 21st century." In essence, it involves the creation of an all-European comprehensive security system.

Present in this room are the leaders of 50 countries of the world. In terms of its scope and the potential of the participating States the CSCE is a unique structure. It should become a strong and effective instrument of peace, stability and democracy.

This path is not an easy one, yet it may not be too long. It would be appropriate if two years later, when we meet again, we discuss and approve a security model for the future Europe.

Now, how does Russia envision this model, as a country destined to be the Eastern pillar of security and stability?

The basis of an all-European security system could be a strong fabric of bilateral agreements on good-neighborship and cooperation in all areas among the participating States. There is also a need for mutual guarantees to individual States or groups of States. Russia is prepared to discuss guarantee issues on a bilateral or multilateral basis.

This is a foundation upon which all-European institutions could be created. Their goal would be settlement and early prevention and resolution of conflicts.

The decisions we make today provide a good start for our joint work in the name of a stable and democratic Europe. I am referring, first and foremost, to the political-military dimension.

For the first time, we are laying the foundation for a unified space of confidence-building in the military area, which encompasses a significant portion of three continents and the world ocean.

For the first time we are adopting a Code of Conduct of States in the political-military area. It affirms an important principle of a law-governed State, that of democratic political control over the armed forces and their use.

We who gathered today here in this room are very different, but we share common values and are committed to the same principles. Respecting the interests and positions of all States, Russia expects that her interests too will be respected.

In our country we are asking a question: how, for example, will the process of changes in the CSCE relate to the transformation of the existing security structures? We are concerned over the ongoing changes in NATO. What will this mean for Russia?

NATO was created in the Cold War times. Today, it is trying not without difficulty to find its place in Europe. It is important that this search would not create new divisions, but promote European unity.

We believe that the plans of expanding NATO are contrary to this logic. Why sow the seeds of distrust? After all, we are no longer adversaries, we are partners.

Some explanations that we hear imply that this is "expansion of stability," just in case developments in Russia go the undesirable way.

If this is the reason why some want to move the NATO area of responsibility closer to the Russian borders, let me say this: it is too early to give up on democracy in Russia!

Let us not repeat mistakes of the past. No major country will live under the laws of isolation and will not play such a game.

Mr. Chairman,

Our best intentions to build a unified Europe will crumble unless they are translated into real actions.

Now, what should be the primary objective for the CSCE to aim at?

First, and foremost, at ensuring human rights, the rights of minorities, at curbing aggressive nationalism. At present, these efforts are clearly inadequate. This is acutely felt by millions of Russians in certain CIS countries and in the Baltics.

Infringement on their rights is manifesting itself in increasingly diverse forms. Thus, lately there have been increasing instances of restrictions placed upon the Orthodox Church in the Baltics, particularly in Estonia.

It is necessary that all CSCE countries abide by the spirit of the UN Declaration on the rights of persons belonging to national, ethnic, religious and language minorities and the CSCE Declaration on aggressive nationalism, racism, chauvinism, xenophobia and anti-Semitism.

The Council of Europe is playing an important role in ensuring human rights on the continent. The CSCE agenda contains the goal of making it truly all-European, Russia's early joining the Council will contribute to reaching this goal. An urgent task is to provide the CSCE with effective peace-keeping potential. We feel this need perhaps more than anyone else in Europe.

While carrying out peace-keeping duty, Russia is interested in sharing political and economic responsibility for peace-keeping operations with its UN and CSCE partners, be that in Karabakh, Tajikistan, Georgia, or Moldova. But of course this should not be a detriment to the effectiveness of the operations.

The CSCE ought to have an important say in matters concerning strengthening of the borders and territorial integrity of the participating States. Attempts to revise the fundamental Helsinki principles can cost very dearly to our continent.

Europe will truly become unified when it creates a common all-European economic space. We are moving in this direction. The membership of the European Union is expanding. Russia and the European Union have recently made a step toward each other by concluding the Agreement on Partnership and Cooperation. It would be in our common interest to make it truly effective.

It is time to involve Mediterranean countries in all-European cooperation. Progress made in the Middle East settlement opens up new possibilities for this.

Reliability of the CSCE will depend on an interaction pursued in common interests between all European organizations and forums—the CIS, NATO, WEU, EU, the Council of Europe and others.

The Commonwealth of Independent States is playing an increasing role in the life of Europe. We have no intention of creating a new bloc within the CIS, which would be in confrontation to anyone. As Chairman of the Council of the CIS Heads of State I declare that the CSCE principles underlie the CIS Charter. All matters relating to integration within the CIS are in strict compliance with them. The Commonwealth will continue to strengthen. This is what our people want. This is the primary condition of stability not only in the East of Europe, but on the entire European continent.

Mr. Chairman, Esteemed Leaders of the CSCE participating States,

The year of 1995 will mark the 50th anniversary of the end of World War II. Now, after half a century, we are becoming increasingly aware of the true meaning of the Great Victory—the need for historic reconciliation of Europe. There must never be enemies, the victors or the vanquished on the continent.

For the first time in its history our continent has a real chance to achieve unity. To miss that chance means to forget the lessons of the past and to question the future.

The memory of the dead and the life of succeeding generations require utmost responsibility from us. Let us measure up to our duty.

RESIGNATION OF
SURGEON GENERAL ELDERS
December 9, 1994

After learning of remarks made by Surgeon General Joycelyn Elders regarding teaching children about masturbation, on December 9 President Bill Clinton demanded and received the resignation of the controversial doctor.

Elders made the remarks December 1 in response to a question after her speech at an event sponsored by the United Nations to mark World AIDS Day. The questioner asked Elders about the prospects for "a more explicit discussion and promotion of masturbation" as a method for slowing the spread of AIDS. In her response, Elders noted that she strongly advocated teaching sex education in schools starting at an early age. "As per your specific question in regard to masturbation," Elders said, "I think that is something that is a part of human sexuality and it's a part of something that perhaps should be taught. But we've not even taught our children the very basics."

In a subsequent interview with the Associated Press, Elders said she had not advocated teaching children about masturbation. "That's not what I was trying to say," she stated. "You can't teach people how to do that, just like you can't teach them how to have sex." But she did not back down from the remarks. "I don't regret what I said," she told the wire service. "I could have said it better."

Elders Is Lightning Rod for Conservatives

As surgeon general, Elders championed children's health issues. She campaigned against smoking, against teenage pregnancy, and in favor of sex education programs. Her blunt statements had made her controversial ever since her days as head of the Arkansas Department of Health while Clinton was governor. Her outspoken views about drugs, abortion, and sexuality also made her a lightning rod for conservative critics. Elders backed studying the legalization of drugs, saying legalization would "markedly reduce our crime rate." After her son was arrested for selling cocaine and was sentenced to ten years in prison, she said, "I don't feel that was a crime." She also had told antiabortion activists to "get over your love affair with the fetus." Elders advocated sex education for children starting at age five and was in favor of distributing contraceptives in schools. Her views had led to an active campaign by conservative Republicans and even some moderate Democrats to get her fired.

Before Elders's comment about masturbation, senior administration officials had repeatedly warned her to be more discreet in her public remarks. The comment on masturbation was the last straw. As soon as the White House learned about it, Clinton demanded her resignation. In a written statement, Clinton said that Elders's public statements "reflecting differences with administration policy and my own convictions have made it necessary for her to tender her resignation." At a White House press conference, Chief of Staff Leon Panetta said the president did not support Elders's comment. "The president feels that's wrong, feels that it's not what schools are for, and it is not what the surgeon general should say," Panetta stated.

Usually, administration officials who resigned were allowed to do so gracefully in an exchange of letters with the president. In this case, administration officials went to great lengths to let it be known that Elders had been forced out. At the White House press conference, Panetta said Elders would have been fired if she had not resigned.

Politics Seen Behind Decision

While conservative lawmakers and antiabortion groups applauded Clinton's decision to get rid of Elders, his action was criticized by gay rights groups, some abortion rights organizations, and liberals. Many saw the firing, which came only a month after the Republicans won control of Congress in a landslide election, as part of an effort by Clinton to move to the center politically. In an editorial, the New York Times *said Clinton "made a sensible and probably necessary political call." On ABC television's* Nightline, *Elders said she believed there was "a political component" in her firing, although she continued to express her admiration and support for Clinton.*

In a New York Times *op-ed piece that appeared eleven days after her resignation, Elders wrote that the discussion of sexual practices was best left to consenting adults behind closed doors. "But sex becomes a proper subject for government when sexual behavior endangers public health, as is clearly the case with AIDS and other diseases," she wrote, "or when it leads to increased poverty, ignorance and enslavement, as is the case with unplanned, unwanted children."*

Following her resignation, the sixty-one-year-old Elders returned to her position as a teacher and medical researcher at the University of Arkansas for Medical Sciences. She had been a professor of pediatrics at the school for twenty-six years before taking an unpaid leave of absence to become director of the Arkansas health department in 1987.

Following is the text of a statement by President Bill Clinton about the resignation of Surgeon General Joycelyn Elders, as released by the White House December 9, 1994:

Dr. Joycelyn Elders is a physician of outstanding ability, energy and commitment. As a pediatrician, she dedicated her life to improving the health of children. As Surgeon General, she worked tirelessly to reduce teen pregnancy and AIDS, and to improve the health of all Americans, especially our children.

Dr. Elders' public statements reflecting differences with administration policy and my own convictions have made it necessary for her to tender her resignation.

Those statements in no way diminish her devotion to her work and the enormous positive impact she has had on the problems she tackled and the people she served.

I will always be grateful for her service.

SUMMIT OF THE AMERICAS DECLARATION OF PRINCIPLES
December 11, 1994

The leaders of thirty-four Western Hemisphere nations pledged at the Summit of the Americas to negotiate a free trade agreement by the year 2005. The agreement would remove barriers to trade and investment, making the Western Hemisphere the world's largest free trade zone.

"When our work is done, the free trade area of the Americas will stretch from Alaska to Argentina," said President Bill Clinton, who hosted the summit, held December 9-11 in Miami, Florida. "In less than a decade, if current trends continue, this hemisphere will be the world's largest market."

While leaders of all the nations attending the summit praised the plan to negotiate a free trade agreement by 2005, some wanted to move faster. "It would be a tragic mistake to engage in a prolonged process where struggling nations with fragile democracies must wait 10, 15, maybe 20 years in economic purgatory," said Bolivian President Gonzalo Sanchez de Lozada. "The cost could be nothing less than the democratic foundations of our countries."

Other leaders said much time was needed for the enormous task of figuring out how to integrate the economies of all the nations, which included major industrialized nations like the United States and Canada; underdeveloped countries such as Mexico and Brazil, which had the potential to become major industrial powers; and tiny Caribbean nations.

U.S. Eagerly Eyes Latin American Markets

For the United States, Latin America's growing economies were prime markets for American goods, and administration officials said that increasing exports would lead to job growth. In the decade before the summit, American exports to Latin America had doubled and direct investment had quadrupled. For their part, the Latin American countries were eager to compete in U.S. markets and in the markets of other Latin American nations.

The major dissenting voice about lowering American trade barriers came from organized labor, which worried that American jobs would be lost to low-cost imports.

Before the summit, some Latin American leaders were frustrated by what they perceived as Washington's slowness at reducing trade barriers. In recent years, many Latin American countries had severely reduced such trade barriers as tariffs, allowing American products to flood into their markets. Those lowered barriers allowed Latin America to become the fastest growing market for American goods in the world and the only region in the world where the United States had a trade surplus.

Latin American leaders complained that the United States was slow at lowering its own trade barriers, and that many of their products were still kept out of American markets. In an interview with the New York Times just before the summit, Sebastian Edwards, the World Banks' chief economist for Latin America, said: "The Latin leaders feel in a way that they have been double-crossed. The trade liberalization has been the most traumatic in history. But these guys opened up in exchange for nothing." American officials rejected such charges, arguing that the United States had the lowest trade barriers of any nation in the hemisphere. Clinton administration officials also pointed to their efforts to lower barriers further through the North American Free Trade Agreement (NAFTA) and expansion of the General Agreement on Tariffs and Trade (GATT).

Latin Nations Open Markets

Many Latin American nations had not waited for a hemisphere-wide trade accord to open markets, but had negotiated smaller trade deals on their own. On January 1, 1995, three major trade agreements were to take effect:

1. Brazil, Argentina, Uruguay, and Paraguay were to remove duties on 90 percent of commerce among their countries.

2. Venezuela, Colombia, Ecuador, Peru, and Bolivia were to equalize their tariffs on imported goods.

3. Mexico, Colombia, and Venezuela were to start the process of eliminating all tariffs and quotas on goods sold among their countries.

The Miami summit was the first such meeting of Western Hemisphere nations since April 1967, when President Lyndon B. Johnson and the leaders of seventeen Latin American nations met in Uruguay. At the 1967 meeting, leaders approved a plan to create a hemispheric common market by 1985, but nothing ever transpired. Most experts believed the new agreement would have a much better chance, at least partially because so much had changed since 1967. Back then, many of the nations of Central and South America were ruled by dictators and had economies dominated by state-run enterprises. By 1994, all the Western Hemisphere nations attending the Miami summit had elected, civilian governments. The only nation not at the meeting was Cuba, which was not invited because Communist Fidel Castro was still in power. By 1994, too, many of the Latin American nations were actively fighting their tough economic problems and seeking to improve living standards for their people.

The summit's second major accomplishment was an invitation that the United States, Canada, and Mexico extended to Chile to start negotiations to make Chile a member of the North American Free Trade Agreement. In recent years, Chile had privatized many of its state-owned businesses, cut tariffs, liberalized its markets, and worked hard to attract foreign investment, leading to strong economic growth and increased wages. Eventually, Clinton administration officials wanted other nations, such as Brazil and Argentina, to join NAFTA as well.

NAFTA was only one of three major trade deals concluded by the United States in 1993. The others were the General Agreement on Tariffs and Trade and an agreement to develop a free-trade zone with seventeen Pacific Basin countries. (Clinton Remarks on House Passage of NAFTA, Historic Documents of 1993, p. 953; Clinton Remarks on GATT, p. 555)

Following is the text of the Declaration of Principles adopted December 11, 1994, at the Summit of the Americas in Miami, Florida:

Partnership for Development and Prosperity: Democracy, Free Trade and Sustainable Development in the Americas

The elected Heads of State and Government of the Americas are committed to advance the prosperity, democratic values and institutions, and security of our Hemisphere. For the first time in history, the Americas are a community of democratic societies. Although faced with differing development challenges, the Americas are united in pursuing prosperity through open markets, hemispheric integration, and sustainable development. We are determined to consolidate and advance closer bonds of cooperation and to transform our aspirations into concrete realities.

We reiterate our firm adherence to the principles of international law and the purposes and principles enshrined in the United Nations Charter and in the Charter of the Organization of American States (OAS), including the principles of the sovereign equality of states, non-intervention, self-determination, and the peaceful resolution of disputes. We recognize the heterogeneity and diversity of our resources and cultures, just as we are convinced that we can advance our shared interests and values by building strong partnerships.

To Preserve and Strengthen the Community of Democracies of the Americas

The Charter of the OAS establishes that representative democracy is indispensable for the stability, peace and development of the region. It is the sole political system which guarantees respect for human rights and the rule of law; it safeguards cultural diversity, pluralism, respect for the rights of minorities, and peace within and among nations. Democracy is based, among other fundamentals, on free and transparent elections and includes the right of all citizens to participate in government. Democracy and development reinforce one another.

We reaffirm our commitment to preserve and strengthen our democratic systems for the benefit of all people of the Hemisphere. We will work through the appropriate bodies of the OAS to strengthen democratic institutions and promote and defend constitutional democratic rule, in accordance with the OAS Charter. We endorse OAS efforts to enhance peace and the democratic, social, and economic stability of the region.

We recognize that our people earnestly seek greater responsiveness and efficiency from our respective governments. Democracy is strengthened by the modernization of the state, including reforms that streamline operations, reduce and simplify government rules and procedures, and make democratic institutions more transparent and accountable. Deeming it essential that justice should be accessible in an efficient and expeditious way to all sectors of society, we affirm that an independent judiciary is a critical element of an effective legal system and lasting democracy. Our ultimate goal is to better meet the needs of the population, especially the needs of women and the most vulnerable groups, including indigenous people, the disabled, children, the aged, and minorities.

Effective democracy requires a comprehensive attack on corruption as a factor of social disintegration and distortion of the economic system that undermines the legitimacy of political institutions.

Recognizing the pernicious effects of organized crime and illegal narcotics on our economies, ethical values, public health, and the social fabric, we will join the battle against the consumption, production, trafficking and distribution of illegal drugs, as well as against money laundering and the illicit trafficking in arms and chemical precursors. We will also cooperate to create viable alternative development strategies in those countries in which illicit crops are grown. Cooperation should be extended to international and national programs aimed at curbing the production, use and trafficking of illicit drugs and the rehabilitation of addicts.

We condemn terrorism in all its forms, and we will, using all legal means, combat terrorist acts anywhere in the Americas with unity and vigor.

Recognizing the important contribution of individuals and associations in effective democratic government and in the enhancement of cooperation among the people of the Hemisphere, we will facilitate fuller participation of our people in political, economic and social activity, in accordance with national legislation.

To Promote Prosperity Through Economic Integration and Free Trade

Our continued economic progress depends on sound economic policies, sustainable development, and dynamic private sectors. A key to prosperity is trade without barriers, without subsidies, without unfair practices, and with an increasing stream of productive investments. Eliminating impediments to market access for goods and services among our countries will foster our economic growth. A growing world economy will also enhance our domestic prosperity. Free trade and increased economic integration are key factors for raising standards of living, improving the working conditions of people in the Americas and better protecting the environment.

We, therefore, resolve to begin immediately to construct the "Free Trade Area of the Americas" (FTAA), in which barriers to trade and investment will be progressively eliminated. We further resolve to conclude the negotiation of the "Free Trade Area of the Americas" no later than 2005, and agree that concrete progress toward the attainment of this objective will be made by the end of this century. We recognize the progress that already has been realized through the unilateral undertakings of each of our nations and the subregional trade arrangements in our Hemisphere. We will build on existing subregional and bilateral arrangements in order to broaden and deepen hemispheric economic integration and to bring the agreements together.

Aware that investment is the main engine for growth in the Hemisphere, we will encourage such investment by cooperating to build more open, transparent and integrated markets. In this regard, we are committed to create strengthened mechanisms that promote and protect the flow of productive investment in the Hemisphere, and to promote the development and progressive integration of capital markets.

To advance economic integration and free trade, we will work, with cooperation and financing from the private sector and international financial institutions, to create a hemispheric infrastructure. This process requires a cooperative effort in fields such as telecommunications, energy and transportation, which will permit the efficient movement of the goods, services, capital, information and technology that are the foundations of prosperity.

We recognize that despite the substantial progress in dealing with debt problems in the Hemisphere, high foreign debt burdens still hinder the development of some of our countries.

We recognize that economic integration and the creation of a free trade area will be complex endeavors, particularly in view of the wide differences in the levels of development and size of economies existing in our Hemisphere. We will remain cognizant of these differences as we work toward economic integration in the Hemisphere. We look to our own resources, ingenuity, and individual capacities as well as to the international community to help us achieve our goals.

To Eradicate Poverty and Discrimination in Our Hemisphere

It is politically intolerable and morally unacceptable that some segments of our populations are marginalized and do not share fully in the benefits of growth. With an aim of attaining greater social justice for all our people, we pledge to work individually and collectively to improve access to quality education and primary health care and to eradicate extreme poverty and illiter-

599

acy. The fruits of democratic stability and economic growth must be accessible to all, without discrimination by race, gender, national origin or religious affiliation.

In observance of the International Decade of the World's Indigenous People, we will focus our energies on improving the exercise of democratic rights and the access to social services by indigenous people and their communities.

Aware that widely shared prosperity contributes to hemispheric stability, lasting peace and democracy, we acknowledge our common interest in creating employment opportunities that improve the incomes, wages and working conditions of all our people. We will invest in people so that individuals throughout the Hemisphere have the opportunity to realize their full potential.

Strengthening the role of women in all aspects of political, social and economic life in our countries is essential to reduce poverty and social inequalities and to enhance democracy and sustainable development.

To Guarantee Sustainable Development and Conserve Our Natural Environment for Future Generations

Social progress and economic prosperity can be sustained only if our people live in a healthy environment and our ecosystems and natural resources are managed carefully and responsibly. To advance and implement the commitments made at the 1992 United Nations Conference on Environment and Development, held in Rio de Janeiro, and the 1994 Global Conference on the Sustainable Development of Small Island Developing States, held in Barbados, we will create cooperative partnerships to strengthen our capacity to prevent and control pollution, to protect ecosystems and use our biological resources on a sustainable basis, and to encourage clean, efficient and sustainable energy production and use. To benefit future generations through environmental conservation, including the rational use of our ecosystems, natural resources and biological heritage, we will continue to pursue technological, financial and other forms of cooperation.

We will advance our social well-being and economic prosperity in ways that are fully cognizant of our impact on the environment. We agree to support the Central American Alliance for Sustainable Development, which seeks to strengthen those democracies by promoting regional economic and social prosperity and sound environmental management. In this context, we support the convening of other regional meetings on sustainable development.

Our Declaration constitutes a comprehensive and mutually reinforcing set of commitments for concrete results. In accord with the appended Plan of Action, and recognizing our different national capabilities and our different legal systems, we pledge to implement them without delay.

We call upon the OAS and the Inter-American Development Bank to assist countries in implementing our pledges, drawing significantly upon the Pan American Health Organization and the United Nations Economic Commission for Latin America and the Caribbean as well as sub-regional organizations for integration.

To give continuity to efforts fostering national political involvement, we will convene specific high-level meetings to address, among others, topics such as trade and commerce, capital markets, labor, energy, education, transportation, telecommunications, counter-narcotics and other anti-crime initiatives, sustainable development, health, and science and technology.

To assure public engagement and commitment, we invite the cooperation and participation of the private sector, labor, political parties, academic institutions and other non-governmental actors and organizations in both our national and regional efforts, thus strengthening the partnership between governments and society.

Our thirty-four nations share a fervent commitment to democratic practices, economic integration, and social justice. Our people are better able than ever to express their aspirations and to learn from one another. The conditions for hemispheric cooperation are propitious. Therefore, on behalf of all our people, in whose name we affix our signatures to this Declaration, we seize this historic opportunity to create a Partnership for Development and Prosperity in the Americas.

NORTH KOREAN
NUCLEAR AGREEMENT
December 12, 1994

With an agreement signed October 21 in Geneva, Switzerland, the United States and North Korea stepped back from the brink of war over the communist nation's efforts to develop nuclear weapons. Under the agreement, North Korea promised to halt its efforts to build nuclear weapons in exchange for billions of dollars in aid. On December 12, Ambassador-at-Large Robert L. Gallucci, the chief U.S. negotiator in Geneva, discussed the agreement in a speech at the U.S. State Department.

The crisis started in 1993, when North Korea announced it was withdrawing from the Nuclear Nonproliferation Treaty, which it had signed in 1985. Under the treaty, countries that do not have nuclear weapons agree not to develop them and must allow international inspectors to check their nuclear power facilities to ensure that no nuclear materials are being diverted from civilian to military use. North Korea said it would not allow any further inspections of its nuclear power program, which the Central Intelligence Agency believed had produced enough plutonium for one or two nuclear weapons. Concerns also were heightened because since the beginning of 1993, North Korea had been building up its conventional military forces and concentrating them near its border with South Korea.

North Korea Warns of War

As 1994 began, tensions were very high on the Korean peninsula as the United States tried using diplomacy to convince North Korea to abide by the nuclear treaty. U.S. officials warned that if diplomatic efforts failed, they would seek economic sanctions against North Korea through the United Nations. North Korea responded that such a move could lead to war.

On February 15, less than a week before the UN Security Council was expected to consider economic sanctions, North Korea agreed to let inspectors from the International Atomic Energy Agency (IAEA) check seven sites that were believed to be part of a nuclear weapons program. Weeks later, tensions rose again when North Korea barred inspectors from taking samples at a plutonium reprocessing plant. On March 21, the United States started the push for UN economic sanctions, and President Bill Clinton dispatched Patriot antimissile batteries to South Korea to be deployed at airports and ports where American troops might land in a military crisis. In early April, American officials said March inspections had revealed that North Korea had nearly doubled its capacity to produce plutonium for nuclear weapons.

The crisis hit a new high point May 14, when North Korea announced it was removing spent fuel from a nuclear reactor without having international inspectors present. Previously, Washington had said that such an action could lead to economic sanctions. Officials of the IAEA wanted to watch the fuel removal to make sure none of the spent fuel was diverted for use in nuclear weapons. The Central Intelligence Agency said that with reprocessing, North Korea might be able to extract enough plutonium from the spent fuel for four to five nuclear weapons.

The problem with economic sanctions was there was no certainty they would work. North Korea had one of the most closed societies in the world, and experts estimated it imported only 10 percent of the goods it consumed. The nation also was desperately poor, so its citizens were accustomed to deprivation. Another option, some sort of military action, was considered extremely dangerous. Any airstrikes on North Korea's nuclear facilities would likely lead to full-scale war on the Korean peninsula, possibly resulting in tens of thousands of casualties. If North Korea really did have a nuclear bomb, there was always the chance the country might use it.

North Korean Leader Dies

On June 18, in a deal brokered by former U.S. president Jimmy Carter, the presidents of North Korea and South Korea agreed to have a summit meeting for the first time since Korea was divided nearly five decades earlier. The two leaders were to discuss how to defuse the nuclear crisis. The meeting was put on hold when North Korean president Kim Il Sung, who had ruled since 1948, died July 9. Sung's death raised concerns that North Korea could become unstable during the transfer of power to his son, Kim Jong Il, but the transfer ultimately appeared to go smoothly.

A breakthrough finally came August 13 in negotiations in Geneva between North Korea and the United States. Under the agreement, which the two sides signed October 21, North Korea agreed to close all its nuclear facilities and eventually dismantle them. In exchange, the United States put together an international consortium headed by South Korea and Japan that would give North Korea two light-water nuclear reactors worth $4 billion. Those reactors produced less plutonium than the graphite-moderated reactors North Korea had and was building. As part of the complex deal, the United States also arranged for North Korea to receive vast quantities of oil to make up for the energy lost through the closing of its nuclear reactors, agreed to ease trade restrictions against North Korea, and agreed to open a diplomatic liaison office in North Korea, among other steps.

Agreement Arouses Controversy

One of the pact's most controversial provisions allowed North Korea to keep for at least five years thousands of spent fuel rods laden with plutonium. North Korea agreed to send the rods to another country once the first new nuclear plant started operating. U.S. negotiators and IAEA officials wanted the rods removed immediately, but North Korea refused.

In another controversial part of the pact, North Korea got a lengthy delay in the first international inspection of two sites the United States believed contained nuclear waste. The IAEA said that an inspection of the sites could reveal how much plutonium had previously been diverted into bombs. Under the agreement, inspections would not occur at the secret sites until substantial progress had been made in building the first reactor, a process that could take years.

Critics, especially Republicans in Congress, said the United States had capitulated to nuclear blackmail. They were particularly concerned that North Korea would retain for years the ability to drop out of the agreement and quickly resume development of nuclear weapons. Administration officials responded that the agreement contained a whole series of reciprocal steps, giving the United States leverage if North Korea balked at any point.

Critics also said the deal set a precedent for other nations to seek economic and political concessions in exchange for scrapping their nuclear programs. Some Republican senators initially vowed to block the agreement, but eventually backed down after apparently deciding that reneging on the deal could lead to renewed tensions on the Korean peninsula that would be blamed on Republicans.

An unidentified U.S. official quoted by the Washington Post *said no one was happy about giving North Korea special treatment, but "it's a question of whether this is better than war." Other senior U.S. officials told the newspaper that no deal would have been possible without concessions. The only alternatives were increasing the military stakes, a move that had potentially disastrous consequences, or allowing North Korea to continue its nuclear program, which U.S. officials said could have produced dozens of nuclear weapons by the decade's end and destabilized the entire region.*

> *Following are excerpts from the text of a speech by U.S. Ambassador-at-Large Robert L. Gallucci at the Secretary's Open Forum, which was held at the U.S. Department of State in Washington, D.C., on December 12, 1994, as reported by Reuters:*

. . . What I'd like to do in the period in which I talk at you before you talk at me is, of course, talk about the agreed framework that we negotiated and that I signed on the 21st of October. But before doing that, I wanted to make some comments about the setting and the backdrop for this agreed framework. . . . I have become aware as people have evaluated the framework that it has seemed to me that very often the context is missing in the evaluation, that the character of the threat, the nature of the regime is put aside and there's a rather sterile, antiseptic approach which I don't think captures the reality that the president has had to deal with in concluding the agreement with the DPRK [Democratic People's Republic of Korea, or North Korea].

I begin at the obvious point in talking about North Korea and that is that this is a country with whom we engaged in a rather bloody war 40 years ago, that that war produced for us over 50,000 lost lives; it produced hundreds of thousands of casualties on both North and South; and it is a war that was then followed by roughly 40 years of an uneasy truce called an armistice. That's the beginning of the setting.

Through the '60s, '70s and '80s there were intermittent points in which the threat of hostilities breaking out were with us.

Incidents in the '60s include the shooting down of the EC-121, the U.S. naval vessel the *Pueblo* being taken, the attack on the Blue House in the '60s. In the '70s there were more hostilities. We recall the attack, the AX attack on the DMZ, the tunneling, the terrorist attacks in the '80s, the attack on the South Korean cabinet in Rangoon in '83, and the blowing up of the South Korean airliner in 1987. There's a fair amount of history here of bad relations between not only North and South but between the North and everybody else.

The North Korean regime under Kim Il Sung has been isolated and has been insulated and, some believe with some cause, it has been paranoid in its approach to the international scene. The philosophy of North Korea is known as *juche*, and I've been told that that translates into a sort of aggressive self-reliance or independence. This is a very unusual regime and one that has marked its history with violence.

Through the '80s and '90s against this overall setting, '80s and early '90s, the United States, South Korea and Japan—and indeed the rest of the world— watched North Korea develop weapons of mass destruction and delivery systems. We observed the construction of a 5-megawatt gas graphite moderated reactor that would produce about a bomb's worth of plutonium each year. We observed the construction of another reactor that was ten times the size of that and a third that was four times the size of that, 50 and 200-megawatt reactors. We observed the construction of fuel fabrication so that *juche* could be applied to the nuclear program—that is to say, they could be completely independent—and the construction of a chemical separation reprocessing facility so the plutonium produced could be separated for nuclear weapons.

We also observed a ballistic missile program of some significance, not only extended range Scud missiles but also the development of Nodong and then follow-on to Nodong missiles, with ranges first in the thousand and then in the several thousand kilometer range, not deployed yet but being developed. These missiles had . . . a lot longer range than what was necessary to cover the entire Korean peninsula—obviously for other purposes. The accuracy was poor, suggesting that the delivery vehicle would be for weapons of mass destruction, and nuclear weapons being the weapons of choice.

Against this background of nuclear weapons and ballistic missiles, we have over the years, particularly the last 10 years, a building of conventional forces by the North Koreans and a forward deployment of those forces.

Sixty percent of the million man army is forward deployed. They are supported by a significant artillery and multiple launch rocket system, deployment forward. Many of the systems can range on Seoul. . . .

We would be looking at a country that had the potential for instability, for volatility it had demonstrated already, a country that I think in the current language you could call economically challenged, a country that was failing economically with an enormous plutonium production coming online, in the order of 175 kilograms of plutonium a year, or roughly 35 nuclear weapons a year. That's enough not only for a substantial strategic nuclear program that would be of interest to all of Northeast Asia, but also for export of plutonium and nuclear weapons around the world. A ballistic missile program not only that threatened Japan and other neighbors in Asia, but also for export, and North Korea is the only country in the world exporting ballistic missiles and components these days.

So the idea of exporting ballistic missiles of extended range and nuclear materials or weapons to the Middle East is something that we could not ignore. . . . It is against this background that we negotiated and dealt with the nuclear issue. The issue came to us in part because the North Koreans decided to adhere to the Non-Proliferation Treaty [NPT] in 1985, and although it took seven years, ultimately accepted the international safeguards under that treaty.

Unfortunately, in the first year of implementing the safeguards regime—the inspections—the North Koreans found that they could not abide by the safeguards obligations of that treaty and when the inspectors found what they call, in their terminology, an anomaly, and sought to resolve the anomaly, the North Koreans refused. What happened in very simple terms is that they did an inspection in North Korea and the inspection turned up a difference between the amount of plutonium that it appeared the North Koreans would likely have separated and the amount of plutonium the North Koreans declared as having separated, and this showed up in the isotopics of the samples that were taken in one of the facilities.

And so the IAEA asked to conduct two special inspections at radioactive waste sites which might shed more light on how much plutonium the North Koreans actually had, and the North Koreans refused. When they refused, the IAEA took the matter to the [United Nations] Security Council, the Security Council passed some resolutions and thus authorized the bilateral talks between the North Koreans and the United States that began in the early summer or late spring of last year in New York. At that time, the North Koreans also announced their intention to withdraw from the Non-Proliferation Treaty.

We began those negotiations with the North Koreans with two rather straightforward objectives, but only really two. One was to get the North Koreans back into the treaty and accept full-scope safeguards; the other was to get them to implement the North-South declaration on denuclearization, which among other things would have required the North Koreans to give up any reprocessing capability they had. These discussions went from round one in New York to round two in Geneva the next month, in July of 1993—the first time the North Koreans suggested that they might be willing to give up their whole gas-graphite nuclear weapons program in exchange for light-water reactors.

The talks did not resume after that session in Geneva, not for actually a full year. . . . Ultimately the logjam was broken, in part by the South Koreans who agreed to remove—actually it was at their initiative—to remove the requirement or the prerequisite that there be an exchange of envoys before a meeting between the United States and the DPRK could occur.

We were about then to meet in June of this year when the North Koreans did something that we had warned them not to do, and that was not to discharge fuel from their five-megawatt reactor in a way that would make it impossible for the IAEA to use analysis of the fuel to determine the reactor operating history. That was one way for the IAEA to get at the history question—how much plutonium the North Koreans really had. When they did that, we announced that there was no basis for our dialogue to continue, we were now going to go to the U.N. Security Council, attempt to build the necessary coalition and impose sanctions on North Korea. We proceeded then in June along that course, and it is my personal judgment that we're doing quite well. . . .

In addition to doing this, though, and this is a key point, the United States had been proceeding with a very deliberate program along with the Republic of Korea to improve the readiness of our forces on the Korean peninsula. This included the replacement of Cobra helicopters with Apaches, the delivery of additional Bradley fighting vehicles, the delivery of counter-battery radars—very important to deal with that artillery threat from the North Koreans—and the delivery of the Patriot missile system to defend against the Scud missiles from the North.

In addition, as we are moving in the direction of sanctions, the president of the United States was prepared to take other steps to improve the readiness and capability of U.S. forces in the Northeast Asian region in order to deal with what was assessed to be an increased risk of hostilities as a result of the sanctions resolution. . . .

At that time, you will remember, former President Carter went to North Korea. We believe he went to North Korea at a time when Kim Il Sung well recognized that he was on the verge of losing the opportunity of negotiating with the United States, losing the possibility of gaining the light-water reactors, which by then he had been quite clear he genuinely wished to have, increasing his isolation and therefore the economic problems for his regime, and possibly confronting a military situation with the Republic of Korea and the United States and its allies. That was the backdrop. President Carter reported from Pyongyang the proposal of a freeze as a basis for the resumption of discussions between the United States and the DPRK. President Clinton responded by defining the freeze in such a way that it was extended and provided a better basis for resumption of talks. The freeze would include the freeze on a 5-megawatt reactor so it would not start, that the IAEA inspectors would be in continuous presence, there would be no reprocessing, and the continuity of IAEA safeguards would be maintained.

That's the basis upon which we resumed talks, went to what some would call "round three" of talks with the North Koreans. They lasted intermittently from August through October when we concluded with the agreed framework of the 21st. As we look at the agreed framework and how we got from the initial stages to the language of that framework, I would say that we evolved in our own objectives in the agreed framework and broadened them substantially and focused them particularly on the real threats to our national security and to regional stability. We shifted to an emphasis on . . . North Korean access to plutonium. With that emphasis, the prioritization of objectives informed us as negotiators as we went off to deal with the DPRK negotiators.

I would say that with respect to our nuclear elements of the agreed framework that all our objectives were achieved. We first wanted to be sure that the spent fuel that the North Koreans discharged into the pond that we assessed had between 25 and 30 kilograms, enough for four or five nuclear weapons, the spent fuel that was in the pond would not be taken out of the pond. That was a primary objective.

Secondly, over the longer term our objective was to get that fuel entirely out of North Korea so that it would not be available for later reprocessing to the North Koreans. That was achieved. Under the terms of the agreement, we stabilize the fuel in the pond with the North Koreans and it is ultimately shipped out of the country. First objective. Second, we wanted the reprocessing plant never to operate again. Under the terms of the agreed framework it is sealed now. It is under IAEA inspection and it is ultimately dismantled.

The third objective: We wanted to make sure that five-megawatt reactor was not restarted so we didn't start getting production of more plutonium. Under the agreed framework, the fuel for the reloading of the reactor has been moved away from the reactor, and the five-megawatt reactor is not to be restarted and it is ultimately to be dismantled. The 50-megawatt reactor and the 200-megawatt reactors, those reactors, together with the five-megawatt reactor, could produce, as I said to you, 175 kilograms of plutonium a year. Our objective was to make sure these reactors were never finished. Under the terms of the agreed framework, the construction of those reactors is frozen and they are ultimately dismantled.

With respect to special inspections, our objective was that they be conducted and the question of the past be finally and fully resolved and they come into full compliance with the NPT and full-scope safeguards. Under the agreed framework, all that happens. They agree in principle to the special inspections, and ultimately special inspections are conducted. With respect to the Non-Proliferation Treaty, we wanted them not to withdraw. They remain in the treaty. I would say all objectives achieved.

In exchange, the North Koreans achieve what they have wanted, which is the acquisition of two light-water reactors, 1,000-megawatt reactors, and for that they give up their gas-graphite reactor program. They get interim energy, that is to say heavy fuel oil for running their oil-fueled plant in an amount comparable to the energy that would have been produced by the reactors that they do not complete—so 255 megawatts of electrical generating capacity translated into heavy fuel oil.

Third, they get improved relations with the United States, including a liaison office, and ultimately full diplomatic relations at the ambassador level if other issues are resolved, and those other issues . . . include that ballistic missile program, they include the conventional force deployment.

The structure of the agreed framework is very simple and very important. It goes far beyond the Non-Proliferation Treaty and safeguards. All that dismantlement is not required by the NPT and safeguards. All the access to plutonium that we wanted to limit could not be achieved if we merely got IAEA safeguards and the NPT. That's only achieved by getting rid of the gas graphite program, that's only achieved by exchanging that for light-water reactors.

Second, the structure of the agreement is parallel steps. They go first; they freeze their program. It is now frozen. We then step; we provide the first tranche of heavy fuel oil. We expect to do that within the next month. Then an international consortium delivers the non-nuclear components for the first light-water reactor. Then they go; they conduct the special inspections and begin to ship out the spent fuel. Then this international consortium that will be formed that we're calling KEDO—the Korean Energy Development Organization—does deliver the nuclear components for the first reactor, light-water reactor, and at that point the North Koreans simultaneously begin to ship out the spent fuel. When the first light-water reactor is complete, all the fuel must be gone with that plutonium and the dismantlement begins. By the time the second reactor is complete, all the dismantlement must be completed.

It is a parallel process of steps. I would argue to you that it is easily verifiable by the IAEA, recently confirmed in their discussions. I argue to you furthermore that the United States and its allies are better off with this agreement; moreover, that if the North Koreans do not comply we are still better off no matter when they start non-compliance. I would argue to you that financially it is a good deal for everyone. The South Koreans are quite prepared to bear the central burden of constructing and financing these reactors. The international consortium will help with both the oil and the reactors. The U.S. bill in all this will not be insignificant, but it will be relatively small, we estimate in the tens of millions of dollars annually. . . .

In sum, the agreement is in our national security interest. The Republic of Korea and Japan are satisfied with the agreement. . . . I think we've done very well and we feel fully supported. I do believe the IAEA safeguards regime and the Non-Proliferation Treaty is better off with the position the United States has taken, not walking away from the material safeguards violation, supporting these regimes. I also believe that we negotiated in Geneva from strength and that's why we got the agreement that we did. The opportunities exist for us now to engage the North Koreans on their ballistic missile program, to engage them on their conventional force deployment and other issues that will arise over the coming years. . . .

CLINTON'S 'MIDDLE-CLASS BILL OF RIGHTS'
December 12, 1994

In a move to regain the initiative and halt his slide toward playing second fiddle to a Republican-dominated Congress, President Bill Clinton made a nationally televised speech December 12 in which he promised a "middle-class bill of rights" that would include $60 billion in tax cuts over five years. The speech came one month after Republicans won control of Congress for the first time in forty years in an overwhelming victory. (Clinton, Gingrich on Election Results, p. 513)

Clinton never directly mentioned the election in his address, but the aim of the speech was clearly to regain the public arena that the Republicans had dominated ever since their landslide victory. The weeks since the election had not been pleasant for Clinton. At a December 7 meeting of the centrist Democratic Leadership Council (DLC), a group that Clinton had helped found and once directed, party leaders blamed Clinton for the Republican victory. In a speech at the meeting, Clinton was portrayed as a "transitional figure" by Rep. Dave McCurdy (D-Okla.), the current DLC president and an old friend of Clinton's. "While Bill Clinton has the mind of a new Democrat, he retains the heart of an old Democrat," McCurdy said. "The result is an administration that has pursued elements of a moderate and liberal agenda at the same time, to the great confusion of the American people." McCurdy, who had lost a bid for the Senate, blamed anti-Clinton sentiment for his defeat.

Clinton Promises Return to Centrist Principles

Clinton, who addressed the DLC meeting only hours after McCurdy, was "unbowed and unapologetic," according to a report in the Washington Post. *Clinton said Democrats lost because voters were angry about their struggles to improve their lives and believed Republicans would help them more than Democrats. Nonetheless, Clinton also vowed to return to the centrist principles upon which he had campaigned two years earlier.*

The day after the DLC speeches, a poll found that two of three Democratic voters believed Clinton should be challenged for the party's nomination in 1996. The poll, conducted by the Times-Mirror Center for the People and the Press, also found that only 41 percent of the public approved of Clinton's performance in office, while 47 percent disapproved. The same day the poll results were reported, a front-page headline in the New York Times *read: "A Crippled President Strives Not to Become a Lame Duck."*

In his televised address to the American public, Clinton abandoned his past emphasis on reducing the deficit as the best way to improve the nation's economic position. Instead, he embraced tax cuts, which Republicans had advocated for years. Clinton's package included four major proposals:

1. *Make tuition for college or technical schools tax deductible for families with incomes of up to $120,000.*
2. *Provide a tax cut of up to $500 for every child up to age thirteen in families with incomes below $75,000.*
3. *Allow families with incomes of less than $100,000 to place $2,000 a year in a tax-deferred Individual Retirement Account. People could withdraw the money without a tax penalty to pay for college, a first home, a major illness, or the care of an elderly parent.*
4. *Eliminate sixty different federal job retraining programs and instead give people who qualified vouchers for $2,000 to $3,000 each to use at private facilities.*

Five Departments Face Cuts

Clinton said he would pay for the tax cuts by reducing government spending. A week after his televised address, Clinton unveiled a plan to consolidate or eliminate programs in the General Services Administration, the Office of Personnel Management, and the departments of Energy, Transportation, and Housing and Urban Development. Clinton said the cuts would save $24 billion over five years.

Most economists said the president's tax cut plan would accomplish little, describing it as a political gesture that would not provide the economic growth needed to really improve the lives of average Americans. Most economists estimated the plan would give the average family only a few extra dollars a week and warned that tax cuts could lead to higher interest rates unless they were offset by cuts in government spending.

Political analysts generally agreed that the president's tax plan was dead in the water as soon as it reached Capitol Hill. Republicans had already proposed broader cuts and were expected to pursue them rather than the president's ideas.

Near the end of his speech, Clinton appealed for a lessening of the savage rhetoric that had characterized the fall campaign and much of the subsequent political discussion. "We need less hot rhetoric and more open conversation; less malice, and more charity," the president said. "We need to put aside the politics of personal destruction and demonization that have

dominated too much of our debate." Yet as the Democratic president and the
new Republican-controlled Congress prepared to do battle, there seemed little
chance the tone of the political debate would become any more civil.

Following is the text of a nationally televised address by
President Bill Clinton on December 15, 1994, as released by
the White House, and of the Republican response by senator-
elect Fred Thompson (R-Tenn.), as reported by Reuters:

CLINTON'S SPEECH

Good evening. My fellow Americans, ours is a great country with a lot to be proud of. But at this holiday season, everybody knows that all is not well with America; that millions of Americans are hurting, frustrated, disappointed, even angry.

In this time of enormous change, our challenge is both political and personal. It involves government, all right, but it goes way beyond government, to the very core of what matters most to us. The question is, what are we going to do about it?

Let's start with the economic situation. I ran for President to restore the American Dream and to prepare the American people to compete and win in the new American economy. For too long, too many Americans have worked longer for stagnant wages and less security. For two years, we pursued an economic strategy that has helped to produce over five million new jobs. But even though the economic statistics are moving up, most of our living standards aren't. It's almost as if some Americans are being punished for their productivity in this new economy. We've got to change that. More jobs aren't enough. We have to raise incomes.

Fifty years ago, an American president proposed the G.I. Bill of Rights, to help returning veterans from World War II go to college, buy a home, and raise their children. That built this country. Tonight, I propose a Middle Class Bill of Rights.

There are four central ideas in this Bill of Rights: First, college tuition should be tax deductible. Just as we make mortgage interest tax deductible because we want people to own their own homes, we should make college tuition deductible because we want people to go to college.

Specifically, I propose that all tuition for college, community college, graduate school, professional school, vocational education or worker retraining after high school be fully deductible, phased up to $10,000 a year for families making up to $120,000 a year. Education, after all, has a bigger impact on earnings and job security than ever before. So let's invest the fruits of today's recovery into tomorrow's opportunity.

Second, bringing up a child is a tough job in this economy. So we should help middle-class families raise their children. We made a good start last year by passing the Family Leave Law, making college loans more affordable, and by giving 15 million American families with incomes of $25,000 a year or less an average tax cut of more than $1,000 a year.

Now, I want to cut taxes for each child under 13, phased up to $500 per child. This tax cut would be available to any family whose income is less than $75,000.

Third, we should help middle-income people save money by allowing every American family earning under $100,000 to put $2,000 a year tax-free in an IRA, an Individual Retirement Account. But I want you to be able to use the money to live on, not just retire on. You'll be able to withdraw from this fund, tax-free—money for education, medical expenses, the purchases of a first home, the care of an elderly parent.

Fourth, since every American needs the skills necessary to prosper in the new economy—and most of you will change jobs from time to time—we should take the billions of dollars the government now spends on dozens of different training programs and give it directly to you, to pay for training if you lose your job or want a better one.

We can pay for this Middle Class Bill of Rights by continuing to reduce government spending, including subsidies to powerful interests based more on influence than need. We can sell off entire operations the government no longer needs to run, and turn dozens of programs over to states and communities that know best how to solve their own problems.

My plan will save billions of dollars from the Energy Department, cut down the Transportation Department, and shrink 60 programs into four at the Department of Housing and Urban Development. Our reinventing government initiative, led by Vice President Gore, already has helped to shrink bureaucracy and free up money to pay down the deficit and invest in our people. Already, we've passed budgets to reduce the federal government to its smallest size in 30 years, and to cut the deficit by $700 billion. That's over $10,000 for every American family.

In the next few days, we'll unveil more of our proposals. And I've instructed the Vice President to review every single government department program for further reductions.

We've worked hard to get control of this deficit after the government debt increased four times over in the 12 years before I took office. That's a big burden on you. About five percent of your income tax goes to pay for welfare and foreign aid, but 28 percent of it goes to pay for interest on the debt run up between 1981 and the day I was inaugurated president. I challenge the new Congress to work with me to enact a Middle Class Bill of Rights without adding to the deficit and without any new cuts in Social Security or Medicare.

I know some people just want to cut the government blindly, and I know that's popular now. But I won't do it. I want a leaner, not a meaner government, that's back on the side of hard-working Americans; a new government for the new economy—creative, flexible, high quality, low cost, service oriented—just like our most innovative private companies.

I'll work with the new Republican majority and my fellow Democrats in Congress to build a new American economy and to restore the American

Dream. It won't be easy. Believe you me, the special interests have not gone into hiding just because there was an election in November. As a matter of fact, they're up here stronger than ever. And that's why, more than ever, we need lobby reform, campaign finance reform and reform to make Congress live by the laws it puts on other people.

Together, we can pass welfare reform and health care reform that work. I'll say more about what I'll do to work with the new Congress in the State of the Union address in January.

But here's what I won't do. I won't support ideas that sound good, but aren't paid for—ideas that weaken the progress we've made in the previous two years for working families; ideas that hurt poor people who are doing their dead-level best to raise their kids and work their way into the middle class; ideas that undermine our fight against crime, or for a clean environment, or for better schools, or for the strength and well-being of our Armed Forces in foreign policy. In other words, we must be straight with the American people about the real consequences of all budgetary decisions.

My test will be: Does an idea expand middle class incomes and opportunities? Does it promote values like family, work, responsibility and community? Does it contribute to strengthening the new economy? If it does, I'll be for it, no matter who proposes it. And I hope Congress will treat my ideas the same way. Let's worry about making progress, not taking credit.

But our work in Washington won't be enough. And that's where you come in. This all starts with you. Oh, we can cut taxes and expand opportunities, but governments can't raise your children, go to school for you, give your employees who have earned it a raise, or solve problems in your neighborhood that require your personal commitment. In short, government can't exercise your citizenship. It works the other way around.

The problems of this new world are complicated, and we've all got a lot to learn. That means citizens have to listen as well as talk. We need less hot rhetoric and more open conversation; less malice, and more charity. We need to put aside the politics of personal destruction and demonization that have dominated too much of our debate. Most of us are good people trying to do better. And if we all treated each other that way, we would do better. We have got to be a community again.

Yes, some people do take advantage of the rest of us—by breaking the law, abusing the welfare system, and flaunting [sic] our immigration laws. That's wrong, and I'm working to stop it. But the truth is that most people in this country, without regard to their race, their religion, their income, their position on divisive issues, most Americans get up every day, go to work, obey the law, pay their taxes and raise their kids the best they can. And most of us share the same real challenges in this new economy. We'll do a lot better job of meeting those challenges if we work together and find unity and strength in our diversity.

We do have more in common, more uniting us than dividing us. And if we start acting like it, we can face the future with confidence. I still believe deeply that there is nothing wrong with America that can't be fixed by what's right with America. This is not about politics as usual. As I've said for years, it's not about moving left or right, but moving forward; not about government being bad or good, but about what kind of government will best enable us to fulfill our God-given potential. And it's not about the next election, either. That's in your hands.

Meanwhile, I'm going to do what I think is right. My rule for the next two years will be: Country first and politics as usual dead last. I hope the new Congress will follow the same rule. And I hope you will, too.

This country works best when it works together. For decades after World War II, we gave more and more Americans a chance to live out their dreams. I know—I'm blessed to be one of them. I was born to a widowed mother at a time when my state's income was barely half the national average; the first person in my family to finish college, thanks to money my parents couldn't really afford—scholarships, loans, and a half a dozen jobs. It breaks my heart to see people with their own dreams for themselves and their children shattered. And I'm going to do all I can to turn it around. But I need your help. We can do it.

With all of our problems, this is still the greatest country in the world—standing not at the twilight, but at the dawn of our greatest days. We still have a lot to be thankful for. Let's all remember that.

Happy holidays, and God bless America.

THOMPSON'S RESPONSE

Hello, I am Fred Thompson.

On November 8, the voters of Tennessee elected me to represent them in the United States Senate, and tonight I have been asked to speak to you on behalf of the new Republican majority in Congress and Republican elected officials in your state and community.

The first thing I want to do is thank you for the support and confidence you placed in Republicans on Election Day. You elected a record number of Republican governors, state legislators and mayors all around the country. And for the first time in 40 years Republicans will be in the majority in both the House and the Senate. Our government, especially in Washington, needed that big change.

Those of us who just came to town don't claim to have all the answers. I am still just unpacking my boxes. But one thing we do know, we know why you sent us here, to cut big government down to size, to turn Congress around, and to set our country in a new direction.

We campaigned on these principles and now we're going to do something that has become all too unusual in American politics. We're going to do exactly what we said. In fact, the change is already taking place.

First, Congress is getting its own house in order. Republicans are cutting the number of committees and we're cutting staff. One of the first bills we pass in January says that Congress has to live under the same laws that Congress imposes on everybody else. Maybe Congress won't pass so many laws when it actually starts having to live under a few of them.

We are also working with Republican governors. We're going to stop the Washington-knows-best crowd from mandating that your state and local governments do all kinds of things that end up costing you higher taxes. And we're going to pass a balanced budget amendment to the Constitution to control government spending. That's what we'll do in January.

Other changes will take more time, but we will continue to move straight ahead, to term limits, and to reducing the tax burden on families and working people. And we're going to tackle a welfare system that pays people more not to work than to work.

One of our most important efforts will be to cut back the executive branch of government and the faceless bureaucracies which more and more run our lives. This week the Republican congressional leadership asked the president to immediately stop federal agencies from issuing new regulations until we've had a chance to cut some of the old ones.

On some of these issues we need the support of the president and the Democrats in Congress, and we want to work together with them. But over the past two years the president and the Democrat-controlled Congress have opposed the balanced budget amendment, proposed more big government spending, and tried to put a bunch of new government bureaucrats in charge of your health care. Until a few weeks ago they were even saying, "We didn't even need a tax cut." Yet, from what we heard tonight, the president's vision for the future now looks a lot like what Republicans just campaigned for, at least until we start looking at the details.

Your vote this election apparently got the president's attention. If the president's new position tonight represents a real change of heart we say, "Welcome aboard." If we can actually cut Washington down to size and put the savings back into the pockets of the people who earned it, we won't need to argue over who gets the credit, or who thought of the idea first. If, however, the president's words are based more upon public opinion polls than real conviction, if we're just talking about politics here instead of a fundamental change in direction, then we're going to be very much at cross purposes. We must do more than reshuffle agencies and take money from one place just to add it somewhere else.

We welcome the president to help us lead America in a new direction. But if he will not, we will welcome the president to follow because we're moving ahead. We know it's time to change a system where Americans who work hard, raise their families and obey the law are taxed, regulated and ignored while their government becomes bigger and more arrogant every day.

Republicans have come together to reverse that trend and set America back on the right road. That's what you hired us for. It's your government and your continued support can change it because whatever Americans can dream, we can do.

Thanks for listening and may you and your family have a happy and healthy holiday season.

CUMULATIVE INDEX, 1990-1994

A

Abbas, Mahmoud
Israeli-Palestinian Peace Accord, 747,
751, 761, 765 (1993)
Abbas, Maldom Bada
Human Rights Report, 560 (1993)
Abortion. *See also* Birth control
Democratic Party Platform, 696-697
(1992)
Eastern Europe, 428 (1994)
Irish Case, 249-254 (1992)
Parental Consent for Teenage Abortions,
387-407 (1990)
Pope's Encyclical on Moral Theology,
843-850 (1993)
Quayle's Murphy Brown Speech, 444-445
(1992)
Republican Party Platform on, 799-800,
817 (1992)
Souter Confirmation Hearing, 624-627
(1990)
State Restrictions
Florida Bill Defeated, 217 (1990)
Idaho Bill Vetoed, 215-219 (1990)
Supreme Court Decisions, 162-163
(1994)
Abortion Advice from Family Clinics,
257-273 (1991)
Abortion Clinic Protests, 311-326
(1994)
Abortion Rights Upheld, 589-613
(1992)
Clinic Blockades, 93-112 (1993)
Parental Consent Cases, 387-407
(1990)
RICO and Abortion Protests, 26-33,
313 (1994)
Thomas Confirmation Hearings, 551,
559-561, 563-565, 570-571 (1991)
UN Population Conference, 352-353
(1994)

Vice Presidential Debate on, 991-994
(1992)
Abrams, Elliott
Iran-Contra Affair, 430-431, 619 (1991);
13, 18 (1994)
Abrams, Floyd, 336 (1992)
Abrams, Kathryn, 941 (1993)
**Acquired immune deficiency syndrome
(AIDS)**
Arthur Ashe's AIDS Announcement,
335-338 (1992)
CDC Report on Unsafe Sex Risks of High
School Students, 339-343 (1992)
Democratic Party Platform on, 694
(1992)
Elder's Resignation, 592-593 (1994)
Glaser Speech at Democratic Conven-
tion, 669, 783 (1992)
Haitian Refugees, 371-383 (1993)
HIV-Positive Speakers at Political
Conventions, 709-715, 783 (1992)
Homeless Report, 255-256, 262
Homosexual March on Washington,
320-331 (1993)
Magic Johnson's Resignation from AIDS
Commission, 710-711, 891-893 (1992)
Magic Johnson's Retirement from
Basketball, 747-749 (1991); 335, 340 (1992)
National Commission on AIDS Final
Report, 447-457 (1993)
Presidential Debates on, 924-926 (1992)
Rape in America Report, 391-393 (1992)
Republican Party Platform on, 811-812
(1992)
Tuberculosis Report, 1010-1011 (1992);
857-858, 860 (1993)
Women, 654 (1993)
Adams, Gerry
Northern Ireland Peace Efforts, 925
(1993)
British Travel Ban Lifted, 449, 454 (1994)
Administrative Procedure Act, 381-383
(1993)

C

F

S